Presented to the

Library, Westmar College

by Wayne K. Detloff, M. D.

Class 1942

BOLLINGEN SERIES XX

THE COLLECTED WORKS

OF

C. G. JUNG

VOLUME 18

EDITORS

† SIR HERBERT READ

MICHAEL FORDHAM, F.R.C.PSYCH., HON. F.B.PS.S.

GERHARD ADLER, PH.D.

WILLIAM MCGUIRE, *executive editor*

THE SYMBOLIC LIFE

LIFE

MISCELLANEOUS
WRITINGS

C. G. JUNG

TRANSLATED BY R. F. C. HULL

BOLLINGEN SERIES XX

PRINCETON UNIVERSITY PRESS

EDITORIAL NOTE

When these Collected Works were planned, during the late 1940's, in consultation with Professor Jung, the Editors set aside a brief final volume for "reviews, short articles, etc., of the psychoanalytic period, later introductions, etc., Bibliography of Jung's Writings, and General Index of the Collected Works." Now arriving at publication soon after Jung's centenary year, this collection of miscellany has become the most ample volume in the edition—and no longer includes the Bibliography and General Index, which have been assigned to volumes 19 and 20 respectively.

Volume 18 now contains more than one hundred and thirty items, ranging in time from 1901, when Jung at 26 had just accepted his first professional appointment as an assistant at the Burghölzli, to 1961, shortly before his death. The collection, touching upon virtually every aspect of Jung's professional and intellectual interest during a long life devoted to the exegesis of the symbol, justifies its title, taken from a characteristic work of Jung's middle years, the seminar given to the Guild of Pastoral Psychology in London, 1939.

This profusion of material is the consequence of three factors. After Jung retired from his active medical practice, in the early 1950's, until his death in June 1961, he devoted most of his time to writing: not only the longer works for which a place was made in the original scheme of the edition, but an unexpectedly large number of forewords to books by pupils and colleagues, replies to journalistic questionnaires, encyclopaedia articles, occasional addresses, and letters (some of which, because of their technical character, or because they were published elsewhere, are included in Volume 18 rather than in the *Letters* volumes). Of works in this class, Jung wrote some fifty after 1950.

Secondly, research for the later volumes of the Collected Works, for the *Letters* (including *The Freud/Jung Letters*), and for the General Bibliography has brought to light many reviews, short articles, reports, etc., from the earlier years of Jung's career. A considerable run of psychiatric reviews from the years 1906–1910 was discovered by Professor Henri F. Ellenberger and turned over to the Editors, who wish to record their gratitude to him.

Finally, the Jung archives at Küsnacht have yielded several manuscripts in a finished or virtually finished state, the earliest being a 1901 report on Freud's *On Dreams*. A related category of material embraces abstracts of lectures, evidently unwritten, the transcripts of which were not read and approved by Jung. The abstracts themselves have been deemed worthy of inclusion in this volume.

"The Tavistock Lectures" and "The Symbolic Life" are examples of oral material to whose transcription Jung *had* given his approval. The former work has become well known as *Analytical Psychology: Its Theory and Practice,* under which title the present version was published in 1968.

Around 1960, the Editors conceived the idea of adding to Volume 15, *The Spirit in Man, Art, and Literature,* some of the forewords that Jung had written for books by other persons, on the ground that these statements were an expression of the archetype of the spirit. Jung was invited to make the choice, and his list comprised fifteen forewords, to books by the following authors: Lily Abegg, John Custance, Linda Fierz-David, Michael Fordham, M. Esther Harding (two books), Aniela Jaffé, Olga von Koenig-Fachsenfeld, Rose Mehlich, Fanny Moser, John Weir Perry, Carl Ludwig Schleich, Gustav Schmaltz, Hans Schmid-Guisan, and Oscar A. H. Schmitz. Subsequently, as the plan for a comprehensive volume of miscellany took form, these forewords were retained in Volume 18.

The contents of the present volume—following after the three longer and more general works in Parts I, II, and III—are arranged as Parts IV through XVI, in the sequence of the volumes of the Collected Works to which they are related by subject, and chronologically within each Part. The result is sometimes arbitrary, as certain items could be assigned to more than one volume. Some miscellanea were published in later editions or printings of the previous volumes, e.g., "The Realities of Practical Psychotherapy," now an appendix in Volume 16, 2nd edition; the prefatory note to the English edition of *Psychology and Alchemy,* now in the 2nd edition of Volume 12; and the author's note to the first American/English edition of *Psychology of the Unconscious* (1916), now in Volume 5, 2nd edition, 1974 printing.

The death of the translator, R.F.C. Hull, in December 1974, after a prolonged illness, was a heavy loss to the entire enterprise. He had, however, translated by far most of the contents of Volume 18. The contributions of other translators are indicated by their initials in a footnote at the beginning of the translated item: A.S.B. Glover, Ruth Horine, Hildegard Nagel, Jane D. Pratt, Lisa Ress, and Wolfgang Sauerlander. To them the Editors are deeply grateful. Mr. Glover, up until his death in 1966, also played an important part in the compilation and editing of the papers. Special acknowledgement must be made to two co-workers at the source, as it were, who contributed greatly by searching out material and helping to identify and annotate the texts: Marianne Niehus-Jung (d. 1965), who was a co-editor of the Swiss edition of her father's collected works, and Aniela Jaffé, who had been Jung's secretary and collaborator with him in the writing of his memoirs.

Acknowledgement is made also to the following, who gave valued assistance with research and advice with various editorial problems: Mrs. Doris Albrecht, Dr. E. A. Bennet, Professor Ernst Benz, Jonathan Dodd, Dr. Martin Ebon, Mrs. Antoinette Fierz, C.H.A. Fleurent (*British Medical Journal*) Dr. M.-L. von Franz, Dr. W. H. Gillespie, Michael Hamburger (also for permission to quote his translation of a poem of Hölderlin), J. Havet (Unesco), Dr. Joseph Henderson, Mrs. Aniela Jaffé, Mrs. Ernest Jones, Mrs. Jean Jones (American Psychiatric Association), Mr. and Mrs. Franz Jung, Dr. James Kirsch, Pamela Long, Professor Dr. C. A. Meier, Professor W. G. Moulton, Professor Henry A. Murray, Mrs. Julie Neumann, Jacob Rabi (*Al Hamishmar*), Lisa Ress, Professor Paul Roazen, Professor D. W. Robertson, Jr., Wolfgang Sauerlander, G. Spencer-Brown, Gerald Sykes, Professor Kurt Weinberg, and Mrs. Shirley White (BBC).

TABLE OF CONTENTS

xi

III

THE SYMBOLIC LIFE (1939)

IV

ON OCCULTISM (C.W., vol. 1)*

V

THE PSYCHOGENESIS OF MENTAL DISEASE
(C.W., vol. 3)

* The contents of each part are related to volumes of the Collected Works as
indicated. Dates are of first publication or, when known, of writing.

VI

FREUD AND PSYCHOANALYSIS (C.W., vol. 4)

VII

ON SYMBOLISM (C.W., vol. 5)

VIII

TWO ESSAYS ON ANALYTICAL PSYCHOLOGY
(C.W., vol. 7)

IX

THE STRUCTURE AND DYNAMICS OF THE PSYCHE
(C.W., vol. 8)

X

THE ARCHETYPES AND THE
COLLECTIVE UNCONSCIOUS (C.W., vol. 9)

XI

CIVILIZATION IN TRANSITION
(C.W., vol. 10)

XII

PSYCHOLOGY AND RELIGION
(C.W., vol. 11)

XIII

ALCHEMICAL STUDIES
(C.W., vols. 12, 13, 14)

XIV

THE SPIRIT IN MAN, ART, AND LITERATURE
(C.W., vol. 15)

XV

THE PRACTICE OF PSYCHOTHERAPY
(C.W., vol. 16)

XVI

THE DEVELOPMENT OF PERSONALITY
(C.W., vol. 17)

I

THE TAVISTOCK LECTURES
On the Theory and Practice of
Analytical Psychology

EDITORIAL NOTE

C. G. Jung was invited by the Institute of Medical Psychology (Tavistock Clinic), Malet Place, London, at the instigation of Dr. J. A. Hadfield, to give a series of five lectures, which he delivered September 30 to October 4, 1935. According to the 1935 report of the Institute, the Lectures when announced were not titled. The audience, of some two hundred, consisted chiefly of members of the medical profession. A stenographic record was taken of the lectures and the subsequent discussions; the transcript was edited by Mary Barker and Margaret Game, passed by Professor Jung, and printed by mimeograph for private distribution by the Analytical Psychology Club of London, in 1936, under the title "Fundamental Psychological Conceptions: A Report of Five Lectures by C. G. Jung . . ." The work has become widely known as "The Tavistock Lectures" or "The London Seminars."

Passages from the Lectures were published in a French translation by Dr. Roland Cahen in his edition of Jung's *L'Homme à la découverte de son âme* (Geneva, 1944; cf. infra, pars. 1357ff.), where the editor inserted them in a transcript of a series of seminars that Jung gave to the Société de Psychologie of Basel in 1934. Jung included much of the same material in both the London and Basel series as well as in lectures given in 1934 and 1935 at the Eidgenössische Technische Hochschule, Zurich.

The present text underwent stylistic revision by R.F.C. Hull, under the supervision of the Editors of the Collected Works, and the footnotes inserted by the original editors were augmented (in square brackets). The text was published in 1968 under the title *Analytical Psychology: Its Theory and Practice; The Tavistock Lectures* (New York: Pantheon Books, and London: Routledge & Kegan Paul), with the addition of a foreword, by E. A. Bennet, and an appendix giving biographical details of the participants in the discussion (both now omitted).

Grateful acknowledgment is made to Mrs. Barker and Mrs. Game, for their co-operation; to those living among the participants in the discussions who gave permission to reproduce their remarks; to Dr. Roland Cahen; and to Mr. Sidney Gray, present secretary of the Tavistock Institute of Medical Psychology, for his assistance. For advice in the preparation of the notes, the Editors are obliged to Joseph Campbell, J. Desmond Clark, Etienne Gilson, Norbert Guterman, Mrs. Lilly Jung, E. Dale Saunders, and Mrs. Ruth Spiegel.

PREFATORY NOTE TO THE
ORIGINAL EDITION

This report of Professor Jung's Lectures to the Institute of Medical Psychology is edited under the auspices of the Analytical Psychology Club, London.

On the whole the report is verbatim, though it has been considered advisable to alter the construction of certain sentences with a view to avoiding any ambiguity of meaning. The editors can only hope that in making these minor changes they have not destroyed the very individual flavour of the Lectures.

In a few cases it was found impossible to ascertain the names of those taking part in the discussions, nor was it practicable to submit proofs of their questions to each of the speakers. For this deficiency and for any possible errors in the reporting of questions we offer our apology.

The stencils of the charts, diagrams, and drawings have been cut with Professor Jung's permission from the originals in his possession.[1]

Our thanks are due to the Institute of Medical Psychology not only for giving the Analytical Psychology Club permission to report the Lectures but also for facilitating the work in every way. To Miss Toni Wolff we would express our special gratitude for helping us with our task. Finally, and above all, we wish to thank Professor Jung for answering questions about difficult points and for passing the report in its final form.

Mary Barker
Margaret Game

London, October 1935

---

[1] [The charts and diagrams have been re-executed, and photographs of the drawings (actually water-colours) have kindly been furnished by Dr. E. A. Bennet.]

LECTURE I

The Chairman (Dr. H. Crichton-Miller):

1   Ladies and Gentlemen, I am here to express your welcome
to Professor Jung, and it gives me great pleasure to do so. We
have looked forward, Professor Jung, to your coming for several
months with happy anticipation. Many of us no doubt have
looked forward to these seminars hoping for new light. Most of
us, I trust, are looking forward to them hoping for new light
upon ourselves. Many have come here because they look upon
you as the man who has saved modern psychology from a dangerous isolation in the range of human knowledge and science
into which it was drifting. Some of us have come here because
we respect and admire that breadth of vision with which you
have boldly made the alliance between philosophy and psychology which has been so condemned in certain other quarters. You
have restored for us the idea of value, the concept of human
freedom in psychological thought; you have given us certain
new ideas that to many of us have been very precious, and above
all things you have not relinquished the study of the human
psyche at the point where all science ends. For this and many
other benefits which are known to each of us independently and
individually we are grateful to you, and we anticipate with the
highest expectations these meetings.

Professor Jung:

2   Ladies and Gentlemen: First of all I should like to point out
that my mother tongue is not English; thus if my English is not
too good I must ask your forgiveness for any error I may commit.

3   As you know, my purpose is to give you a short outline of
certain fundamental conceptions of psychology. If my demonstration is chiefly concerned with my own principles or my own

5

point of view, it is not that I overlook the value of the great contributions of other workers in this field. I do not want to push myself unduly into the foreground, but I can surely expect my audience to be as much aware of Freud's and Adler's merits as I am.

4   Now as to our procedure, I should like to give you first a short idea of my programme. We have two main topics to deal with, namely, on the one side the concepts concerning the *structure of the unconscious mind* and its *contents;* on the other, the *methods* used in the *investigation* of contents originating in the unconscious psychic processes. The second topic falls into three parts, first, the word-association method; second, the method of dream-analysis; and third, the method of active imagination.

5   I know, of course, that I am unable to give you a full account of all there is to say about such difficult topics as, for instance, the philosophical, religious, ehical, and social problems peculiar to the collective consciousness of our time, or the processes of the collective unconscious and the comparative mythological and historical researches necessary for their elucidation. These topics, although apparently remote, are yet the most potent factors in making, regulating, and disturbing the personal mental condition, and they also form the root of disagreement in the field of psychological theories. Although I am a medical man and therefore chiefly concerned with psychopathology, I am nevertheless convinced that this particular branch of psychology can only be benefited by a considerably deepened and more extensive knowledge of the normal psyche in general. The doctor especially should never lose sight of the fact that diseases are disturbed normal processes and not *entia per se* with a psychology exclusively their own. *Similia similibus curantur* is a remarkable truth of the old medicine, and as a great truth it is also liable to become great nonsense. Medical psychology, therefore, should be careful not to become morbid itself. One-sidedness and restriction of horizon are well-known neurotic peculiarities.

6   Whatever I may be able to tell you will undoubtedly remain a regrettably unfinished torso. Unfortunately I take little stock of new theories, as my empirical temperament is more eager for new facts than for what one might speculate about them, although this is, I must admit, an enjoyable intellectual pastime. Each new case is almost a new theory to me, and I am not quite

convinced that this standpoint is a thoroughly bad one, particularly when one considers the extreme youth of modern psychology, which to my mind has not yet left its cradle. I know, therefore, that the time for general theories is not yet ripe. It even looks to me sometimes as if psychology had not yet understood either the gigantic size of its task, or the perplexingly and distressingly complicated nature of its subject-matter: the psyche itself. It seems as if we were just waking up to this fact, and that the dawn is still too dim for us to realize in full what it means that the psyche, being the *object* of scientific observation and judgment, is at the same time its *subject,* the *means* by which you make such observations. The menace of so formidably vicious a circle has driven me to an extreme of caution and relativism which has often been thoroughly misunderstood.

7   I do not want to disturb our dealings by bringing up disquieting critical arguments. I only mention them as a sort of anticipatory excuse for seemingly unnecessary complications. I am not troubled by theories, but a great deal by facts; and I beg you therefore to keep in mind that the shortness of time at my disposal does not allow me to produce all the circumstantial evidence which would substantiate my conclusions. I especially refer here to the intricacies of dream-analysis and to the comparative method of investigating the unconscious processes. In short, I have to depend a great deal upon your goodwill, but I realize naturally it is my own task in the first place to make things as plain as possible.

8   Psychology is a science of consciousness, in the very first place. In the second place, it is the science of the products of what we call the unconscious psyche. We cannot directly explore the unconscious psyche because the unconscious is just unconscious, and we have therefore no relation to it. We can only deal with the conscious products which we suppose have originated in the field called the unconscious, that field of "dim representations" which the philosopher Kant in his *Anthropology*[1] speaks of as being half a world. Whatever we have to say about the unconscious is what the conscious mind says about it. Always the unconscious psyche, which is entirely of an unknown nature, is expressed by consciousness and in terms of consciousness, and

---

1 [*Anthropologie in pragmatischer Hinsicht* (1798), Pt. I, Bk. I, sec. 5.]

that is the only thing we can do. We cannot go beyond that, and we should always keep it in mind as an ultimate critique of our judgment.

9   Consciousness is a peculiar thing. It is an intermittent phenomenon. One-fifth, or one-third, or perhaps even one-half of our human life is spent in an unconscious condition. Our early childhood is unconscious. Every night we sink into the unconscious, and only in phases between waking and sleeping have we a more or less clear consciousness. To a certain extent it is even questionable how clear that consciousness is. For instance, we assume that a boy or girl ten years of age would be conscious, but one could easily prove that it is a very peculiar kind of consciousness, for it might be a consciousness without any consciousness of the *ego*. I know a number of cases of children eleven, twelve, and fourteen years of age, or even older, suddenly realizing "I am." For the first time in their lives they know that they themselves are experiencing, that they are looking back over a past in which they can remember things happening but cannot remember that they were in them.

10   We must admit that when we say "I" we have no absolute criterion whether we have a full experience of "I" or not. It might be that our realization of the ego is still fragmentary and that in some future time people will know very much more about what the ego means to man than we do. As a matter of fact, we cannot see where that process might ultimately end.

11   Consciousness is like a surface or a skin upon a vast unconscious area of unknown extent. We do not know how far the unconscious rules because we simply know nothing of it. You cannot say anything about a thing of which you know nothing. When we say "the unconscious" we often mean to convey something by the term, but as a matter of fact we simply convey that we do not know what the unconscious is. We have only indirect proofs that there is a mental sphere which is subliminal. We have some scientific justification for our conclusion that it exists. From the products which that unconscious mind produces we can draw certain conclusions as to its possible nature. But we must be careful not to be too anthropomorphic in our conclusions, because things might in reality be very different from what our consciousness makes them.

12   If, for instance, you look at our physical world and if you

8

compare what our consciousness makes of this same world, you find all sorts of mental pictures which do not exist as objective facts. For instance, we see colour and hear sound, but in reality they are oscillations. As a matter of fact, we need a laboratory with very complicated apparatus in order to establish a picture of that world apart from our senses and apart from our psyche; and I suppose it is very much the same with our unconscious— we ought to have a laboratory in which we could establish by objective methods how things really are when in an unconscious condition. So any conclusion or any statement I make in the course of my lectures about the unconscious should be taken with that critique in mind. It is always *as if*, and you should never forget that restriction.

13   The conscious mind moreover is characterized by a certain narrowness. It can hold only a few simultaneous contents at a given moment. All the rest is unconscious at the time, and we only get a sort of continuation or a general understanding or awareness of a conscious world through the *succession* of conscious moments. We can never hold an image of totality because our consciousness is too narrow; we can only see flashes of existence. It is always as if we were observing through a slit so that we only see a particular moment; all the rest is dark and we are not aware of it at that moment. The area of the unconscious is enormous and always continuous, while the area of consciousness is a restricted field of momentary vision.

14   Consciousness is very much the product of perception and orientation in the *external* world. It is probably localized in the cerebrum, which is of ectodermic origin and was probably a sense organ of the skin at the time of our remote ancestors. The consciousness derived from that localization in the brain therefore probably retains these qualities of sensation and orientation. Peculiarly enough, the French and English psychologists of the early seventeenth and eighteenth centuries tried to derive consciousness from the senses as if it consisted solely of sense data. That is expressed by the famous formula *Nihil est in intellectu quod non fuerit in sensu.*[2] You can observe something similar in

2 ["There is nothing in the mind that was not in the senses." Cf. Leibniz, *Nouveaux Essais sur l'Entendement humain*, Bk. II, ch. 1, sec. 2, in response to Locke. The formula was scholastic in origin; cf. Duns Scotus, *Super universalibus Porphyrii*, qu. 3.]

modern psychological theories. Freud, for instance, does not derive the conscious from sense data, but he derives the unconscious from the conscious, which is along the same rational line.

15   I would put it the reverse way: I would say the thing that comes first is obviously the unconscious and that consciousness really arises from an unconscious condition. In early childhood we are unconscious; the most important functions of an instinctive nature are unconscious, and consciousness is rather the product of the unconscious. It is a condition which demands a violent effort. You get tired from being conscious. You get exhausted by consciousness. It is an almost unnatural effort. When you observe primitives, for instance, you will see that on the slightest provocation or with no provocation whatever they doze off, they disappear. They sit for hours on end, and when you ask them, "What are you doing? What are you thinking?" they are offended, because they say, "Only a man that is crazy thinks—he has thoughts in his head. We do not think." If they think at all, it is rather in the belly or in the heart. Certain Negro tribes assure you that thoughts are in the belly because they only realize those thoughts which actually disturb the liver, intestines, or stomach. In other words, they are conscious only of emotional thoughts. Emotions and affects are always accompanied by obvious physiological innervations.

16   The Pueblo Indians told me that all Americans are crazy, and of course I was somewhat astonished and asked them why. They said, "Well, they say they think in their heads. No sound man thinks in the head. *We* think in the heart." They are just about in the Homeric age, when the diaphragm (*phren* = mind, soul) was the seat of psychic activity. That means a psychic localization of a different nature. *Our* concept of consciousness supposes thought to be in our most dignified head. But the Pueblo Indians derive consciousness from the intensity of feeling. Abstract thought does not exist for them. As the Pueblo Indians are sun-worshippers, I tried the argument of St. Augustine on them. I told them that God is not the sun but the one who made the sun.[3] They could not accept this because they cannot go beyond the perceptions of their senses and their feelings. There-

3 [*In Johannis Evang.*, XXXIV, 2. Cf. *Symbols of Transformation* (C.W., vol. 5), par. 162 and n. 69.]

fore consciousness and thought to them are localized in the heart. To us, on the other hand, psychic activities are nothing. We hold that dreams and fantasies are localized "down below," therefore there are people who speak of the *sub*-conscious mind, of the things that are *below* consciousness.

17 These peculiar localizations play a great role in so-called primitive psychology, which is by no means primitive. For instance if you study Tantric Yoga and Hindu psychology you will find the most elaborate system of psychic layers, of localizations of consciousness up from the region of the perineum to the top of the head. These "centres" are the so-called *chakras*,[4] and you not only find them in the teachings of yoga but can discover the same idea in old German alchemical books,[5] which surely do not derive from a knowledge of yoga.

18 The important fact about consciousness is that nothing can be conscious without an ego to which it refers. If something is not related to the ego then it is not conscious. Therefore you can define consciousness as a relation of psychic facts to the ego. What is that ego? The ego is a complex datum which is constituted first of all by a general awareness of your body, of your existence, and secondly by your memory data; you have a certain idea of having been, a long series of memories. Those two are the main constituents of what we call the ego. Therefore you can call the ego a complex of psychic facts. This complex has a great power of attraction, like a magnet; it attracts contents from the unconscious, from that dark realm of which we know nothing; it also attracts impressions from the outside, and when they enter into association with the ego they are conscious. If they do not, they are not conscious.

19 My idea of the ego is that it is a sort of complex. Of course, the nearest and dearest complex which we cherish is our ego. It is always in the centre of our attention and of our desires, and it is the absolutely indispensable centre of consciousness. If the ego becomes split up, as in schizophrenia, all sense of values is gone, and also things become inaccessible for voluntary reproduction

4 [Cf. "The Realities of Practical Psychotherapy" (C.W., vol. 16, 2nd edn.), pars. 558ff.]

5 [What Jung may have had in mind are the *melothesiae*, explained in "Psychology and Religion" (C.W., vol. 11), par. 113, n. 5; cf. *Psychology and Alchemy*, fig. 156.]

because the centre has split and certain parts of the psyche refer to one fragment of the ego and certain other contents to another fragment of the ego. Therefore, with a schizophrenic, you often see a rapid change from one personality into another.

20 You can distinguish a number of functions in consciousness. They enable consciousness to become oriented in the field of ectopsychic facts and endopsychic facts. What I understand by the *ectopsyche* is a system of relationship between the contents of consciousness and facts and data coming in from the environment. It is a system of orientation which concerns my dealing with the external facts given to me by the function of my senses. The *endopsyche,* on the other hand, is a system of relationship between the contents of consciousness and postulated processes in the unconscious.

21 In the first place we will speak of the ectopsychic functions. First of all we have *sensation,*[6] our sense function. By sensation I understand what the French psychologists call "la fonction du réel," which is the sum-total of my awareness of external facts given to me through the function of my senses. So I think that the French term "la fonction du réel" explains it in the most comprehensive way. Sensation tells me that something *is:* it does not tell me *what* it is and it does not tell me other things about that something; it only tells me that something is.

22 The next function that is distinguishable is *thinking.*[7] Thinking, if you ask a philosopher, is something very difficult, so never ask a philosopher about it because he is the only man who does not know what thinking is. Everybody else knows what thinking is. When you say to a man, "Now think properly," he knows exactly what you mean, but a philosopher never knows. Thinking in its simplest form tells you *what* a thing is. It gives a name to the thing. It adds a concept because thinking is perception and judgment. (German psychology calls it apperception.)[8]

23 The third function you can distinguish and for which ordinary language has a term is *feeling.*[9] Here minds become very confused and people get angry when I speak about feeling, be-

6 [*Psychological Types* (C.W., vol. 6), Definition 47.]
7 [Ibid., Def. 53.]
8 [Ibid., Def. 5.]
9 [Ibid., Def. 21.]

cause according to their view I say something very dreadful about it. Feeling informs you through its feeling-tones of the *values* of things. Feeling tells you for instance whether a thing is acceptable or agreeable or not. It tells you what a thing is *worth* to you. On account of that phenomenon, you cannot perceive and you cannot apperceive without having a certain feeling re-action. You always have a certain feeling-tone, which you can even demonstrate by experiment. We will talk of these things later on. Now the "dreadful" thing about feeling is that it is, like thinking, a *rational*[10] function. All men who think are abso-lutely convinced that feeling is never a rational function but, on the contrary, most irrational. Now I say: Just be patient for a while and realize that man cannot be perfect in every respect. If a man is perfect in his thinking he is surely never perfect in his feeling, because you cannot do the two things at the same time; they hinder each other. Therefore when you want to think in a dispassionate way, really scientifically or philosophically, you must get away from all feeling-values. You cannot be bothered with feeling-values at the same time, otherwise you begin to feel that it is far more important to think about the freedom of the will than, for instance, about the classification of lice. And cer-tainly if you approach from the point of view of feeling the two objects are not only different as to *facts* but also as to *value*. Val-ues are no anchors for the intellect, but they exist, and giving value is an important psychological function. If you want to have a complete picture of the world you must necessarily con-sider values. If you do not, you will get into trouble. To many people feeling appears to be most irrational, because you feel all sorts of things in foolish moods; therefore everybody is con-vinced, in this country particularly, that you should control your feelings. I quite admit that this is a good habit and wholly admire the English for that faculty. Yet there are such things as feelings, and I have seen people who control their feelings mar-vellously well and yet are terribly bothered by them.

24   Now the fourth function. Sensation tells us that a thing *is*. Thinking tells us *what* that thing is, feeling tells us what it is *worth* to us. Now what else could there be? One would assume one has a complete picture of the world when one knows there *is*

10 [Ibid., Def. 44.]

something, *what* it is, and what it is *worth*. But there is another category, and that is time. Things have a past and they have a future. They come from somewhere, they go to somewhere, and you cannot see where they came from and you cannot know where they go to, but you get what the Americans call a hunch. For instance, if you are a dealer in art or in old furniture you get a hunch that a certain object is by a very good master of 1720, you get a hunch that it is good work. Or you do not know what shares will do after a while, but you get the hunch that they will rise. That is what is called *intuition*,[11] a sort of divination, a sort of miraculous faculty. For instance, you do not know that your patient has something on his mind of a very painful kind, but you "get an idea," you "have a certain feeling," as we say, because ordinary language is not yet developed enough for one to have suitably defined terms. The word intuition becomes more and more a part of the English language, and you are very fortunate because in other languages that word does not exist. The Germans cannot even make a linguistic distinction between sensation and feeling. It is different in French; if you speak French you cannot possibly say that you have a certain "sentiment dans l'estomac," you will say "sensation"; in English you also have your distinctive words for sensation and feeling. But you can mix up *feeling* and *intuition* easily. Therefore it is an almost artificial distinction I make here, though for practical reasons it is most important that we make such a differentiation in scientific language. We must define what we mean when we use certain terms, otherwise we talk an unintelligible language, and in psychology this is always a misfortune. In ordinary conversation, when a man says feeling, he means possibly something entirely different from another fellow who also talks about feeling. There are any number of psychologists who use the word *feeling,* and they define it as a sort of crippled thought. "Feeling is nothing but an unfinished thought"—that is the definition of a well-known psychologist. But feeling is something genuine, it is something real, it is a function, and therefore we have a word for it. The instinctive natural mind always finds the words that designate things which really have existence. Only psychologists invent words for things that do not exist.

11 [Ibid., Def. 35.]

14

25   The last-defined function, intuition, seems to be very mysterious, and you know I am "very mystical," as people say. This then is one of my pieces of mysticism! Intuition is a function by which you see round corners, which you really cannot do; yet the fellow will do it for you and you trust him. It is a function which normally you do not use if you live a regular life within four walls and do regular routine work. But if you are on the Stock Exchange or in Central Africa, you will use your hunches like anything. You cannot, for instance, calculate whether when you turn round a corner in the bush you will meet a rhinoceros or a tiger—but you get a hunch, and it will perhaps save your life. So you see that people who live exposed to natural conditions use intuition a great deal, and people who risk something in an unknown field, who are pioneers of some sort, will use intuition. Inventors will use it and judges will use it. Whenever you have to deal with strange conditions where you have no established values or established concepts, you will depend upon that faculty of intuition.

26   I have tried to describe that function as well as I can, but perhaps it is not very good. I say that intuition is a sort of perception which does not go exactly by the senses, but it goes via the unconscious, and at that I leave it and say "I don't know how it works." I do not know what is happening when a man knows something he definitely should not know. I do not know how he has come by it, but he has it all right and he can act on it. For instance, anticipatory dreams, telepathic phenomena, and all that kind of thing are intuitions. I have seen plenty of them, and I am convinced that they do exist. You can see these things also with primitives. You can see them everywhere if you pay attention to these perceptions that somehow work through the subliminal data, such as sense-perceptions so feeble that our consciousness simply cannot take them in. Sometimes, for instance, in cryptomnesia, something creeps up into consciousness; you catch a word which gives you a suggestion, but it is always something that is unconscious until the moment it appears, and so presents itself as if it had fallen from heaven. The Germans call this an *Einfall*, which means a thing which falls into your head from nowhere. Sometimes it is like a revelation. Actually, intuition is a very natural function, a perfectly normal thing, and it is necessary, too, because it makes up for what you cannot perceive

15

or think or feel because it lacks reality. You see, the past is not real any more and the future is not as real as we think. Therefore we must be very grateful to heaven that we have such a function which gives us a certain light on those things which are round the corners. Doctors, of course, being often presented with the most unheard-of situations, need intuition a great deal. Many a good diagnosis comes from this "very mysterious" function.

27   Psychological functions are usually controlled by the will, or we hope they are, because we are afraid of everything that moves by itself. When the functions are controlled they can be excluded from use, they can be suppressed, they can be selected, they can be increased in intensity, they can be directed by will-power, by what we call intention. But they also can function in an involuntary way, that is, they think for you, they feel for you —very often they do this and you cannot even stop them. Or they function unconsciously so that you do not know what they have done, though you might be presented, for instance, with the result of a feeling process which has happened in the unconscious. Afterwards somebody will probably say, "Oh, you were very angry, or you were offended, and therefore you reacted in such and such a way." Perhaps you are quite unconscious that you have felt in that way, nevertheless it is most probable that you have. Psychological functions, like the sense functions, have their specific energy. You cannot dispose of feeling, or of thinking, or of any of the four functions. No one can say, "I will not think"—he will think inevitably. People cannot say, "I will not feel"—they will feel because the specific energy invested in each function expresses itself and cannot be exchanged for another.

28   Of course, one has preferences. People who have a good mind prefer to think about things and to adapt by thinking. Other people who have a good feeling function are good social mixers, they have a great sense of values; they are real artists in creating feeling situations and living by feeling situations. Or a man with a keen sense of objective observation will use his sensation chiefly, and so on. The dominating function gives each individual his particular kind of psychology. For example, when a man uses chiefly his intellect, he will be of an unmistakable type, and you can deduce from that fact the condition of his feeling. When thinking is the dominant or superior function,

16

feeling is necessarily in an inferior condition.[12] The same rule applies to the other three functions. But I will show you that with a diagram which will make it clear.

29   You can make the so-called cross of the functions (Figure 1).

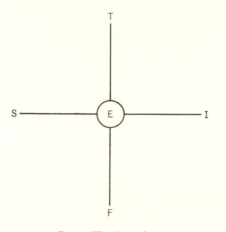

FIG. 1. The Functions

In the centre is the *ego* (E), which has a certain amount of energy at its disposal, and that energy is the will-power. In the case of the thinking type, that will-power can be directed to *thinking* (T). Then we must put *feeling* (F) down below, because it is, in this case, the *inferior function*.[13] That comes from the fact that when you think you must exclude feeling, just as when you feel you must exclude thinking. If you are thinking, leave feeling and feeling-values alone, because feeling is most upsetting to your thoughts. On the other hand people who go by feeling-values leave thinking well alone, and they are right to do so, because these two different functions contradict each other. People have sometimes assured me that their thinking was just as differentiated as their feeling, but I could not believe it, because an individual cannot have the two opposites in the same degree of perfection at the same time.

30   The same is the case with *sensation* (S) and *intuition* (I). How do they affect each other? When you are observing physical

12 [Ibid., Def. 30.]
13 [Ibid.]

facts you cannot see round corners at the same time. When you observe a man who is working by his sense function you will see, if you look at him attentively, that the axes of his eyes have a tendency to converge and to come together at one point. When you study the expression or the eyes of intuitive people, you will see that they only glance at things—they do not look, they radiate at things because they take in their fulness, and among the many things they perceive they get one point on the periphery of their field of vision and that is the *hunch*. Often you can tell from the eyes whether people are intuitive or not. When you have an intuitive attitude you usually do not as a rule observe the details. You try always to take in the whole of a situation, and then suddenly something crops up out of this wholeness. When you are a sensation type you will observe facts as they are, but then you have no intuition, simply because the two things cannot be done at the same time. It is too difficult, because the principle of the one function excludes the principle of the other function. That is why I put them here as opposites.

31   Now, from this simple diagram you can arrive at quite a lot of very important conclusions as to the structure of a given consciousness. For instance, if you find that *thinking* is highly differentiated, then feeling is undifferentiated. What does that mean? Does it mean these people have no feelings? No, on the contrary. They say, "I have very strong feelings. I am full of emotion and temperament." These people are under the sway of their emotions, they are caught by their emotions, they are overcome by their emotions at times. If, for instance, you study the private life of professors it is a very interesting study. If you want to be fully informed as to how the intellectual behaves at home, ask his wife and she will be able to tell you a story!

32   The reverse is true of the *feeling* type. The feeling type, if he is natural, never allows himself to be disturbed by thinking; but when he gets sophisticated and somewhat neurotic he is disturbed by thoughts. Then thinking appears in a compulsory way, he cannot get away from certain thoughts. He is a very nice chap, but he has extraordinary convictions and ideas, and his thinking is of an inferior kind. He is caught by this thinking, entangled in certain thoughts; he cannot disentangle because he cannot reason, his thoughts are not movable. On the other hand, an intellectual, when caught by his feelings, says, "I feel

18

just like that," and there is no argument against it. Only when he is thoroughly boiled in his emotion will he come out of it again. He cannot be reasoned out of his feeling, and he would be a very incomplete man if he could.

33   The same happens with the *sensation* type and the *intuitive* type. The intuitive is always bothered by the reality of things; he fails from the standpoint of realities; he is always out for the possibilities of life. He is the man who plants a field and before the crop is ripe is off again to a new field. He has ploughed fields behind him and new hopes ahead all the time, and nothing comes off. But the sensation type remains with things. He remains in a given reality. To him a thing is true when it is real. Consider what it means to an intuitive when something is real. It is just the wrong thing; it should not be, something else should be. But when a sensation type does not have a given reality—four walls in which to be—he is sick. Give the intuitive type four walls in which to be, and the only thing is how to get out of it, because to him a given situation is a prison which must be undone in the shortest time so that he can be off to new possibilities.

34   These differences play a very great role in practical psychology. Do not think I am putting people into this box or that and saying, "He is an intuitive," or "He is a thinking type." People often ask me, "Now, is So-and-So not a thinking type?" I say, "I never thought about it," and I did not. It is no use at all putting people into drawers with different labels. But when you have a large empirical material, you need critical principles of order to help you to classify it. I hope I do not exaggerate, but to me it is very important to be able to create a kind of order in my empirical material, particularly when people are troubled and confused or when you have to explain them to somebody else. For instance, if you have to explain a wife to a husband or a husband to a wife, it is often very helpful to have these objective criteria, otherwise the whole thing remains "He said"—"She said."

35   As a rule, the inferior function does not possess the qualities of a conscious differentiated function. The conscious differentiated function can as a rule be handled by intention and by the will. If you are a real thinker, you can direct your thinking by your will, you can control your thoughts. You are not the slave

of your thoughts, you can think of something else. You can say, "I can think something quite different, I can think the contrary." But the feeling type can never do that because he cannot get rid of his thought. The thought possesses him, or rather he is possessed by thought. Thought has a fascination for him, therefore he is afraid of it. The intellectual type is afraid of being caught by feeling because his feeling has an archaic quality, and there he is like an archaic man—he is the helpless victim of his emotions. It is for this reason that primitive man is extraordinarily polite, he is very careful not to disturb the feelings of his fellows because it is dangerous to do so. Many of our customs are explained by that archaic politeness. For instance, it is not the custom to shake hands with somebody and keep your left hand in your pocket, or behind your back, because it must be visible that you do not carry a weapon in that hand. The Oriental greeting of bowing with hands extended palms upward means "I have nothing in my hands." If you kowtow you dip your head to the feet of the other man so that he sees you are absolutely defenceless and that you trust him completely. You can still study the symbolism of manners with primitives, and you can also see why they are afraid of the other fellow. In a similar way, we are afraid of our inferior functions. If you take a typical intellectual who is terribly afraid of falling in love, you will think his fear very foolish. But he is most probably right, because he will very likely make foolish nonsense when he falls in love. He will be caught most certainly, because his feeling only reacts to an archaic or to a dangerous type of woman. This is why many intellectuals are inclined to marry beneath them. They are caught by the landlady perhaps, or by the cook, because they are unaware of their archaic feeling through which they get caught. But they are right to be afraid, because their undoing will be in their feeling. Nobody can attack them in their intellect. There they are strong and can stand alone, but in their feelings they can be influenced, they can be caught, they can be cheated, and they know it. Therefore never force a man into his feeling when he is an intellectual. He controls it with an iron hand because it is very dangerous.

36 The same law applies to each function. The inferior function is always associated with an archaic personality in ourselves; in the inferior function we are all primitives. In our differenti-

20

ated functions we are civilized and we are supposed to have free will; but there is no such thing as free will when it comes to the inferior function. There we have an open wound, or at least an open door through which anything might enter.

37   Now I am coming to the *endopsychic functions* of consciousness. The functions of which I have just spoken rule or help our conscious orientation in our relations with the environment; but they do not apply to the relation of things that are as it were below the ego. The ego is only a bit of consciousness which floats upon the ocean of the dark things. The dark things are the inner things. On that inner side there is a layer of psychic events that forms a sort of fringe of consciousness round the ego. I will illustrate it by a diagram:

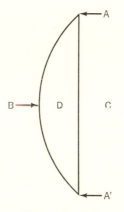

Fig. 2. The Ego

38   If you suppose AA′ to be the threshold of consciousness, then you would have in D an area of consciousness referring to the ectopsychic world B, the world ruled by those functions of which we were just speaking. But on the other side, in C, is the *shadow-world*. There the ego is somewhat dark, we do not see into it, we are an enigma to ourselves. We only know the ego in D, we do not know it in C. Therefore we are always discovering something new about ourselves. Almost every year something new turns up which we did not know before. We always think we are now at the end of our discoveries. We never are. We go on discovering that we are this, that, and other things, and some-

times we have astounding experiences. That shows there is always a part of our personality which is still unconscious, which is still becoming; we are unfinished; we are growing and changing. Yet that future personality which we are to be in a year's time is already here, only it is still in the shadow. The ego is like a moving frame on a film. The future personality is not yet visible, but we are moving along, and presently we come to view the future being. These potentialities naturally belong to the dark side of the ego. We are well aware of what we have been, but we are not aware of what we are going to be.

39 Therefore the *first* function on that endopsychic side is *memory*. The function of memory, or reproduction, links us up with things that have faded out of consciousness, things that became subliminal or were cast away or repressed. What we call memory is this faculty to reproduce unconscious contents, and it is the first function we can clearly distinguish in its relationship between our consciousness and the contents that are actually not in view.

40 The *second* endopsychic function is a more difficult problem. We are now getting into deep waters because here we are coming into darkness. I will give you the name first: *the subjective components of conscious functions*. I hope I can make it clear. For instance, when you meet a man you have not seen before, naturally you think something about him. You do not always think things you would be ready to tell him immediately; perhaps you think things that are untrue, that do not really apply. Clearly, they are subjective reactions. The same reactions take place with things and with situations. Every application of a conscious function, whatever the object might be, is always accompanied by subjective reactions which are more or less inadmissible or unjust or inaccurate. You are painfully aware that these things happen in you, but nobody likes to admit that he is subject to such phenomena. He prefers to leave them in the shadow, because that helps him to assume that he is perfectly innocent and very nice and honest and straightforward and "only too willing," etc.,—you know all these phrases. As a matter of fact, one is not. One has any amount of subjective reactions, but it is not quite becoming to admit these things. These reactions I call the subjective components. They are a very im-

portant part of our relations to our own inner side. There things get definitely painful. That is why we dislike entering this shadow-world of the ego. We do not like to look at the shadow-side of ourselves; therefore there are many people in our civilized society who have lost their shadow altogether, they have got rid of it. They are only two-dimensional; they have lost the third dimension, and with it they have usually lost the body. The body is a most doubtful friend because it produces things we do not like; there are too many things about the body which cannot be mentioned. The body is very often the personification of this shadow of the ego. Sometimes it forms the skeleton in the cupboard, and everybody naturally wants to get rid of such a thing. I think this makes sufficiently clear what I mean by subjective components. They are usually a sort of disposition to react in a certain way, and usually the disposition is not altogether favourable.

41   There is one exception to this definition: a person who is not, as we suppose we all are, living on the positive side, putting the right foot forward and not the wrong one, etc. There are certain individuals whom we call in our Swiss dialect "pitch-birds" [*Pechvögel*]; they are always getting into messes, they put their foot in it and always cause trouble, because they *live* their own shadow, they live their own negation. They are the sort of people who come late to a concert or a lecture, and because they are very modest and do not want to disturb other people, they sneak in at the end and then stumble over a chair and make a hideous racket so that everybody has to look at them. Those are the "pitch-birds."

42   Now we come to the *third* endopsychic component—I cannot say function. In the case of memory you can speak of a function, but even your memory is only to a certain extent a voluntary or controlled function. Very often it is exceedingly tricky; it is like a bad horse that cannot be mastered. It often refuses in the most embarrassing way. All the more is this the case with the subjective components and reactions. And now things begin to get worse, for this is where the *emotions* and *affects* come in. They are clearly not functions any more, they are just events, because in an emotion, as the word denotes, you are moved away, you are cast out, your decent ego is put aside, and something else

23

takes your place. We say, "He is beside himself," or "The devil is riding him," or "What has gotten into him today," because he is like a man who is possessed. The primitive does not say he got angry beyond measure; he says a spirit got into him and changed him completely. Something like that happens with emotions; you are simply possessed, you are no longer yourself, and your control is decreased practically to zero. That is a condition in which the inner side of a man takes hold of him, he cannot prevent it. He can clench his fists, he can keep quiet, but it has him nevertheless.

43   The *fourth* important endopsychic factor is what I call *invasion*. Here the shadow-side, the unconscious side, has full control so that it can break into the conscious condition. Then the conscious control is at its lowest. Those are the moments in a human life which you do not necessarily call pathological; they are pathological only in the old sense of the word when pathology meant the science of the passions. In that sense you can call them pathological, but it is really an extraordinary condition in which a man is seized upon by his unconscious and when anything may come out of him. One can lose one's mind in a more or less normal way. For instance, we cannot assume that the cases our ancestors knew very well are abnormal, because they are perfectly normal phenomena among primitives. They speak of the devil or an incubus or a spirit going into a man, or of his soul leaving him, one of his separate souls—they often have as many as six. When his soul leaves him, he is in an altered condition because he is suddenly deprived of himself; he suffers a loss of self. That is a thing you can often observe in neurotic patients. On certain days, or from time to time, they suddenly lose their energy, they lose themselves, and they come under a strange influence. These phenomena are not in themselves pathological; they belong to the ordinary phenomenology of man, but if they become habitual we rightly speak of a neurosis. These are the things that lead to neurosis; but they are also exceptional conditions among normal people. To have overwhelming emotions is not in itself pathological, it is merely undesirable. We need not invent such a word as pathological for an undesirable thing, because there are other undesirable things in the world which are not pathological, for instance, tax-collectors.

Discussion

Dr. J. A. Hadfield:

44   In what sense do you use the word "emotion"? You used the word "feeling" rather in the sense in which many people here use the word "emotion." Do you give the term "emotion" a special significance or not?

Professor Jung:

45   I am glad you have put that question, because there are usually great mistakes and misunderstandings concerning the use of the word emotion. Naturally everybody is free to use words as he likes, but in scientific language you are bound to cling to certain distinctions so that everyone knows what you are talking about. You will remember I explained "feeling" as a function of valuing, and I do not attach any particular significance to feeling. I hold that feeling is a rational function if it is differentiated. When it is not differentiated it just happens, and then it has all the archaic qualities which can be summed up by the word "unreasonable." But conscious feeling is a rational function of discriminating values.

46   If you study emotions you will invariably find that you apply the word "emotional" when it concerns a condition that is characterized by physiological innervations. Therefore you can measure emotions to a certain extent, not their psychic part but the physiological part. You know the James-Lange theory of affect.[14] I take emotion as affect, it is the same as "something affects you." It does something to you—it interferes with you. Emotion is the thing that carries you away. You are thrown out of yourself; you are beside yourself as if an explosion had moved you out of yourself and put you beside yourself. There is a quite tangible physiological condition which can be observed at the same time. So the difference would be this: feeling has no physical or tangible physiological manifestations, while emotion is characterized by an altered physiological condition. You know that the James-Lange theory of affect says that you only get really emotional when you are aware of the physiological altera-

[14] [The theory was independently advanced by William James and by the Danish physiologist C. G. Lange, and is commonly referred to by both their names.]

tion of your general condition. You can observe this when you are in a situation where you would most probably be angry. You know you are going to be angry, and then you feel the blood rushing up into your head, and *then* you are really angry, but not before. Before, you only know you are going to be angry, but when the blood rushes up into your head you are caught by your own anger, immediately the body is affected, and because you realize that you are getting excited, you are twice as angry as you ought to be. Then you are in a real emotion. But when you have *feeling* you have control. You are on top of the situation, and you can say, "I have a very nice feeling or a very bad feeling about it." Everything is quiet and nothing happens. You can quietly inform somebody, "I hate you," very nicely. But when you say it spitefully you have an emotion. To say it quietly will not cause an emotion, either in yourself or in the other person. Emotions are most contagious, they are the real carriers of mental contagion. For instance, if you are in a crowd that is in an emotional condition, you cannot help yourself, you are in it too, you are caught by that emotion. But the feelings of other people do not concern you in the least, and for this reason you will observe that the differentiated feeling type usually has a cooling effect upon you, while the emotional person heats you up because the fire is radiating out of him all the time. You see the flame of that emotion in his face. By sympathy your sympathetic system gets disturbed, and you will show very much the same signs after a while. That is not so with feelings. Do I make myself clear?

Dr. Henry V. Dicks:

47   May I ask, in continuation of that question, what is the relation in your view between affects and feelings?

Professor Jung:

48   It is a question of degree. If you have a value which is overwhelmingly strong for you it will become an emotion at a certain point, namely, when it reaches such an intensity as to cause a physiological innervation. All our mental processes probably cause slight physiological disturbances which are so small that we have not the means to demonstrate them. But we have a pretty sensitive method by which to measure emotions, or the physiological part of them, and that is the psychogalvanic

effect.[15] It is based on the fact that the electrical resistance of the skin decreases under the influence of emotion. It does not decrease under the influence of feeling.

49   I will give you an example. I made the following experiment with my former Professor at the Clinic. He functioned as my test partner, and I had him in the laboratory under the apparatus for measuring the psychogalvanic effect. I told him to imagine something which was intensely disagreeable to him but of which he knew I was not aware, something unknown to me yet known to him and exceedingly painful. So he did. He was well acquainted with such experiments and gifted with great power of concentration, so he concentrated on something, and there was almost no visible disturbance of the electrical resistance of the skin; the current did not increase at all. Then I thought I had a hunch. That very morning I had observed certain signs of something going on and I guessed it must be hellishly disagreeable to my chief. So I thought, "I am going to try something." I simply said to him, "Was not that the case of So-and-So?"—mentioning the name. Instantly there was a deluge of emotion. That was the *emotion;* the former reaction was the *feeling.*

50   It is a curious fact that hysterical pain does not cause contraction of the pupils, it is not accompanied by physiological innervation, and yet it is an intense pain. But physical pain causes contraction of the pupils. You can have an intense feeling and no physiological alteration; but as soon as you have physiological alteration you are possessed, you are dissociated, thrown out of your own house, and the house is then free for the devils.

Dr. Eric Graham Howe:

51   Could we equate emotion and feeling with conation and cognition respectively? Whereas feeling corresponds to cognition, emotion is conative.

Professor Jung:

52   Yes, one could say that in philosophical terminology. I have no objection.

15 [Jung and Peterson, "Psychophysical Investigations with the Galvanometer and Pneumograph in Normal and Insane Individuals" (1907); Jung and Ricksher, "Further Investigations on the Galvanic Phenomenon and Respiration in Normal and Insane Individuals" (1907) ; in C.W., vol. 2.]

Dr. Howe:

53   May I have another shot? Your classification into four functions, namely those of sensation, thinking, feeling, and intuition, seems to me to correspond with the one-, two-, three-, and four-dimensional classification. You yourself used the word "three-dimensional" referring to the human body, and you also said that intuition differed from the other three in that it was the function which included Time. Perhaps, therefore, it corresponds to a fourth dimension? In that case, I suggest that "sensation" corresponds with one-dimensional, "perceptual cognition" with two-dimensional, "conceptual cognition" (which would correspond perhaps with your "feeling") with three-dimensional, and "intuition" with four-dimensional on this system of classification.

Professor Jung:

54   You can put it like that. Since intuition sometimes seems to function as if there were no space, and sometimes as if there were no time, you might say that I add a sort of fourth dimension. But one should not go too far. The concept of the fourth dimension does not produce facts. Intuition is something like H. G. Wells's Time Machine. You remember the time machine, that peculiar motor, which when you sit on it moves off with you into time instead of into space. It consists of four columns, three of which are always visible, but the fourth is visible only indistinctly because it represents the time element. I am sorry but the awkward fact is that intuition is something like this fourth column. There is such a thing as unconscious perception, or perception by ways which are unconscious to us. We have the empirical material to prove the existence of this function. I am sorry that there are such things. My intellect would wish for a clear-cut universe with no dim corners, but there are these cobwebs in the cosmos. Nevertheless I do not think there is anything mystical about intuition. Can you explain beyond any possibility of doubt why, for instance, some birds travel enormous distances, or the doings of caterpillars, butterflies, ants, or termites? There you have to deal with quite a number of questions. Or take the fact of water having the greatest density at 4° Centigrade. Why such a thing? Why has energy a limitation to quantum? Well, it has, and that is awkward; it is not right that

such things should be, but they are. It is exactly like the old question, "Why has God made flies?"—He just has.

Dr. Wilfred R. Bion:

55   In your experiment why did you ask the Professor to think of an experience which was painful to himself and unknown to you? Do you think there is any significance in the fact that he knew you knew of the unpleasant experience in the second experiment and that this had some bearing on the difference of emotional reaction which he showed in the two examples you gave?

Professor Jung:

56   Yes, absolutely. My idea was based on the fact that when I know that my partner does not know, it is far more agreeable to me; but when I know that he knows too, it is a very different thing and is very disagreeable. In any doctor's life there are cases which are more or less painful when a colleague knows about them, and I knew almost for a certainty that if I gave him a hint that I knew, he would jump like a mine, and he did. That was my reason.

Dr. Eric B. Strauss:

57   Would Dr. Jung make clearer what he means when he says that feeling is a rational function? Further, I do not quite understand what Dr. Jung means by feeling. Most of us when we employ the term feeling understand polarities such as pleasure, pain, tension, and relaxation. Further, Dr. Jung claims that the distinction between feelings and emotions is only one of degree. If the distinction is only one of degree, how is it that he puts them on different sides of the frontier, so to speak? Still further, Dr. Jung claims that one of the criteria or the chief criterion would be that feelings are unaccompanied by physiological change, whereas emotions are accompanied by such changes. Experiments conducted by Professor Freudlicher[16] in Berlin have, I think, shown clearly that simple feelings, in the sense of pleasure, pain, tension, and relaxation, are as a matter of fact accompanied by physiological changes, such as changes in the blood pressure, which can now be recorded by very accurate apparatus.

16 [Possibly a stenographic slip for Jakob Freundlich, who conducted electrocardiogram experiments; see his article in *Deutsches Archiv für klinische Medizin* (Berlin), 177:4 (1934), 449–57.]

Professor Jung:

58   It is true that feelings, if they have an emotional character, are accompanied by physiological effects; but there are definitely feelings which do not change the physiological condition. These feelings are very mental, they are not of an emotional nature. That is the distinction I make. Inasmuch as feeling is a function of values, you will readily understand that this is not a physiological condition. It can be something as abstract as abstract thinking. You would not expect abstract thinking to be a physiological condition. Abstract thinking is what the term denotes. Differentiated thinking is rational; and so feeling can be rational in spite of the fact that many people mix up the terminology.

59   We must have a word for the giving of values. We must designate that particular function, as apart from others, and feeling is an apt term. Of course, you can choose any other word you like, only you must say so. I have absolutely no objection if the majority of thinking people come to the conclusion that feeling is a very bad word for it. If you say, "We prefer to use another term," then you must choose another term to designate the function of valuing, because the fact of values remains and we must have a name for it. Usually the sense of values is expressed by the term "feeling." But I do not cling to the term at all. I am absolutely liberal as to terms, only I give the definition of terms so that I can say what I mean when I use such and such a term. If anybody says that feeling is an emotion or that feeling is a thing that causes heightened blood pressure, I have no objection. I only say that I do not use the word in that sense. If people should agree that it ought to be forbidden to use the word feeling in such a way as I do, I have no objection. The Germans have the words *Empfindung* and *Gefühl*. When you read Goethe or Schiller you find that even the poets mix up the two functions. German psychologists have already recommended the suppression of the word *Empfindung* for feeling, and propose that one should use the word *Gefühl* (feeling) for values, while the word *Empfindung* should be used for sensation. No psychologist nowadays would say, "The feelings of my eyes or of my ears or of my skin." People of course say that they have feelings in their big toe or ear, but no scientific language of that kind is possible any more. Taking those two words as identical, one could ex-

press the most exalted moods by the word *Empfindung,* but it is exactly as if a Frenchman spoke of "les sensations les plus nobles de l'amour." People would laugh, you know. It would be absolutely impossible, shocking!

Dr. E. A. Bennet:

60   Do you consider that the superior function in the case of a person suffering from manic-depression remains conscious during the period of depression?

Professor Jung:

61   I would not say that. If you consider the case of manic-depressive insanity you occasionally find that in the manic phase one function prevails and in the depressive phase another function prevails. For instance, people who are lively, sanguine, nice and kind in the manic phase, and do not think very much, suddenly become very thoughtful when the depression comes on, and then they have obsessive thoughts, and vice versa. I know several cases of intellectuals who have a manic-depressive disposition. In the manic phase they think freely, they are productive and very clear and very abstract. Then the depressive phase comes on, and they have obsessive feelings; they are obsessed by terrible moods, just moods, not thoughts. Those are, of course, psychological details. You see these things most clearly in cases of men of forty and a little bit more who have led a particular type of life, an intellectual life or a life of values, and suddenly that thing goes under and up comes just the contrary. There are very interesting cases like that. We have the famous literary illustrations, Nietzsche for instance. He is a most impressive example of a change of psychology into its opposite at middle age. In younger years he was the aphorist in the French style; in later years, at 38, in *Thus Spake Zarathustra,* he burst out in a Dionysian mood which was absolutely the contrary of everything he had written before.

Dr. Bennet:

62   Is melancholia not extraverted?

Professor Jung:

63   You cannot say that, because it is an incommensurable consideration. Melancholia in itself could be termed an introverted condition but it is not an attitude of preference. When you call somebody an introvert, you mean that he prefers an introverted

habit, but he has his extraverted side too. We all have both sides, otherwise we could not adapt at all, we would have no influence, we would be beside ourselves. Depression is always an introverted condition. Melancholics sink down into a sort of embryonic condition, therefore you find that accumulation of peculiar physical symptoms.

Dr. Mary C. Luff:

64   As Professor Jung has explained emotion as an obsessive thing which possesses the individual, I am not clear how he differentiates what he calls "invasions" from "affects."

Professor Jung:

65   You experience sometimes what you call "pathological" emotions, and there you observe most peculiar contents coming through as emotion: thoughts you have never thought before, sometimes terrible thoughts and fantasies. For instance, some people when they are very angry, instead of having the ordinary feelings of revenge and so on, have the most terrific fantasies of committing murder, cutting off the arms and legs of the enemy, and such things. Those are invading fragments of the unconscious, and if you take a fully developed pathological emotion it is really a state of *eclipse* of consciousness when people are raving mad for a while and do perfectly crazy things. That is an invasion. That would be a pathological case, but fantasies of this kind can also occur within the limits of normal. I have heard innocent people say, "I could cut him limb from limb," and they actually do have these bloody fantasies; they would "smash the brains" of people, they imagine *doing* what in cold blood is merely *said* as a metaphor. When these fantasies get vivid and people are afraid of themselves, you speak of invasion.

Dr. Luff:

66   Is that what you call confusional psychosis?

Professor Jung:

67   It does not need to be a psychosis at all. It does not need to be pathological; you can observe such things in normal people when they are under the sway of a particular emotion. I once went through a very strong earthquake. It was the first time in my life I experienced an earthquake. I was simply overcome by the idea that the earth was not solid and that it was the skin of a huge animal that had shaken itself as a horse does. I was simply

caught by that idea for a while. Then I came out of the fantasy remembering that that is exactly what the Japanese say about earthquakes: that the big salamander has turned over or changed its position, the salamander that is carrying the earth.[17] Then I was satisfied that it was an archaic idea which had jumped into my consciousness. I thought it was remarkable; I did not quite think it was pathological.

Dr. B. D. Hendy:

68 Would Professor Jung say that affect, as he defined it, is *caused* by a characteristic physiological condition, or would he say that this physiological alteration is the *result* of, let us say, invasion?

Professor Jung:

69 The relation between body and mind is a very difficult question. You know that the James-Lange theory says that affect is the result of physiological alteration. The question whether the body or the mind is the predominating factor will always be answered according to temperamental differences. Those who by temperament prefer the theory of the supremacy of the body will say that mental processes are epiphenomena of physiological chemistry. Those who believe more in the spirit will say the contrary, to them the body is just the appendix of the mind and causation lies with the spirit. It is really a philosophical question, and since I am not a philosopher I cannot claim to make a decision. All we can know empirically is that processes of the body and processes of the mind happen together in some way which is mysterious to us. It is due to our most lamentable mind that we cannot think of body and mind as one and the same thing; probably they *are* one thing, but we are unable to think it. Modern physics is subject to the same difficulty; look at the regrettable things which happen with light! Light behaves as if it were oscillations, and it also behaves as if it were "corpuscles." It needed a very complicated mathematical formula by M. de Broglie to help the human mind to conceive the possibility that oscillations and corpuscles are two phenomena, observed under

17 [According to a Japanese legend, the *namazu,* a kind of catfish of monstrous size, carries on its back most of Japan, and when annoyed it moves its head or tail, thus provoking earthquakes. The legend is often depicted in Japanese art.]

different conditions, of one and the same ultimate reality.[18] You cannot *think* this, but you are forced to admit it as a postulate.

70   In the same way, the so-called psychophysical parallelism is an insoluble problem. Take for instance the case of typhoid fever with psychological concomitants. If the psychic factor were mistaken for a causation, you would reach preposterous conclusions. All we can say is that there are certain physiological conditions which are clearly caused by mental disorder, and certain others which are not caused but merely accompanied by psychic processes. Body and mind are the two aspects of the living being, and that is all we know. Therefore I prefer to say that the two things happen together in a miraculous way, and we had better leave it at that, because we cannot think of them together. For my own use I have coined a term to illustrate this being together; I say there is a peculiar principle of *synchronicity*[19] active in the world so that things happen together somehow and behave as if they were the same, and yet for us they are not. Perhaps we shall some day discover a new kind of mathematical method by which we can prove that it must be like that. But for the time being I am absolutely unable to tell you whether it is the body or the mind that prevails, or whether they just coexist.

Dr. L. J. Bendit:

71   I am not quite clear when invasion becomes pathological. You suggested in the first part of your talk this evening that invasion became pathological whenever it became habitual. What is the difference between a pathological invasion and an artistic inspiration and creation of ideas?

Professor Jung:

72   Between an artistic inspiration and an invasion there is absolutely no difference. It is exactly the same, therefore I avoid the word "pathological." I would never say that artistic inspiration is pathological, and therefore I make that exception for invasions too, because I consider that an inspiration is a perfectly normal fact. There is nothing bad in it. It is nothing out of the ordinary. Happily enough it belongs to the order of human beings that

18 [Louis Victor de Broglie, French physicist, recipient of Nobel Prize for physics (1929), discovered the wave character of electrons. In the preceding sentence of the text, instead of "oscillations" and "corpuscles" the more usual terms would be "waves" and "particles."]

19 [Cf. "Synchronicity: An Acausal Connecting Principle" (C.W., vol. 8).]

inspiration takes place occasionally—very rarely, but it does. But it is quite certain that pathological things come in pretty much the same way, so we have to draw the line somewhere. If you are all alienists and I present to you a certain case, then you might say that that man is insane. I would say that that man is not insane for this reason, that as long as he can explain himself to me in such a way that I feel I have a contact with him that man is not crazy. To be crazy is a very relative conception. For instance, when a Negro behaves in a certain way we say, "Oh well, he's only a Negro," but if a white man behaves in the same way we say, "That man is crazy," because a white man cannot behave like that. A Negro is expected to do such things but a white man does not do them. To be "crazy" is a social concept; we use social restrictions and definitions in order to distinguish mental disturbances. You can say that a man is peculiar, that he behaves in an unexpected way and has funny ideas, and if he happens to live in a little town in France or Switzerland you would say, "He is an original fellow, one of the most original inhabitants of that little place"; but if you bring that man into the midst of Harley Street, well, he is plumb crazy. Or if a certain individual is a painter, you think he is a very original artist, but let that man be the cashier of a big bank and the bank will experience something. Then they will say that fellow is surely crazy. But these are simply social considerations. We see the same thing in lunatic asylums. It is not an absolute increase in insanity that makes our asylums swell like monsters, it is the fact that we cannot stand abnormal people any more, so there are apparently very many more crazy people than formerly. I remember in my youth we had people whom I recognized later on as being schizophrenic, and we thought, "Well, Uncle So-and-So is a very original man." In my native town we had some imbeciles, but one did not say, "He is a terrible ass," or something like that, but "He is very nice." In the same way one called certain idiots "cretins," which comes from the saying "il est bon chrétien." You could not say anything else of them, but at least they were good Christians.

The Chairman:

73   Ladies and Gentlemen, I think we must let Professor Jung off any further activity for tonight, and we thank him very much indeed.

LECTURE II

The Chairman (Dr. J. A. Hadfield):

74   Ladies and Gentlemen, you have already been introduced to
Dr. Jung and that in the most eulogistic language, but I think
all who were here last night will recognize that even such a great
eulogy was in no sense exaggerated. Dr. Jung last night was referring to a number of the functions of the human mind, such as
feeling, thinking, intuition, and sensation, and I could not help
feeling that in him all these functions, contrary to what he told
us, seemed to be very well differentiated. I also had a hunch that
in him they were bound together in the centre by a sense of
humour. Nothing convinces me so much of the truth of any conception as when its creator is able to see it as a subject of humour, and that is what Dr. Jung did last night. Over-seriousness
in regard to any subject very often displays the fact that the individual is dubious and anxious about the truth of what he is
trying to convey.

Professor Jung:

75   Ladies and Gentlemen, yesterday we dealt with the functions of consciousness. Today I want to finish the problem of the
structure of the mind. A discussion of the human mind would
not be complete if we did not include the existence of unconscious processes. Let me repeat shortly the reflections which I
made last night.

76   We cannot deal with unconscious processes directly because
they are not reachable. They are not directly apprehended; they
appear only in their products, and we postulate from the peculiar quality of those products that there must be something behind them from which they originate. We call that dark sphere
the unconscious psyche.

77   The ectopsychic contents of consciousness derive in the first
place from the environment, through the data of the senses.

36

Then the contents also come from other sources, such as memory and processes of judgment. These belong to the endopsychic sphere. A third source for conscious contents is the dark sphere of the mind, the unconscious. We approach it through the peculiarities of the endopsychic functions, those functions which are not under the control of the will. They are the vehicle by which unconscious contents reach the surface of consciousness.

78 The unconscious processes, then, are not directly observable, but those of its products that cross the threshold of consciousness can be divided into two classes. The first class contains recognizable material of a definitely personal origin; these contents are individual acquisitions or products of instinctive processes that make up the personality as a whole. Furthermore, there are forgotten or repressed contents, and creative contents. There is nothing specially peculiar about them. In other people such things may be conscious. Some people are conscious of things of which other people are not. I call that class of contents the subconscious mind or the *personal unconscious,* because, as far as we can judge, it is entirely made up of personal elements, elements that constitute the human personality as a whole.

79 Then there is another class of contents of definitely unknown origin, or at all events of an origin which cannot be ascribed to individual acquisition. These contents have one outstanding peculiarity, and that is their mythological character. It is as if they belong to a pattern not peculiar to any particular mind or person, but rather to a pattern peculiar to *mankind in general.* When I first came across such contents I wondered very much whether they might not be due to heredity, and I thought they might be explained by racial inheritance. In order to settle that question I went to the United States and studied the dreams of pure-blooded Negroes, and I was able to satisfy myself that these images have nothing to do with so-called blood or racial inheritance, nor are they personally acquired by the individual. They belong to mankind in general, and therefore they are of a *collective* nature.

80 These collective patterns I have called *archetypes,* using an expression of St. Augustine's.[1] An archetype means a *typos* [imprint], a definite grouping of archaic character containing, in

1 [Cf. *The Archetypes and the Collective Unconscious* (C.W., vol. 9, i), par. 5.]

37

form as well as in meaning, *mythological motifs*. Mythological motifs appear in pure form in fairytales, myths, legends, and folklore. Some of the well-known motifs are: the figures of the Hero, the Redeemer, the Dragon (always connected with the Hero, who has to overcome him), the Whale or the Monster who swallows the Hero.[2] Another variation of the motif of the Hero and the Dragon is the Katabasis, the Descent into the Cave, the Nekyia. You remember in the Odyssey where Ulysses descends *ad inferos* to consult Tiresias, the seer. This motif of the Nekyia is found everywhere in antiquity and practically all over the world. It expresses the psychological mechanism of introversion of the conscious mind into the deeper layers of the unconscious psyche. From these layers derive the contents of an impersonal, mythological character, in other words, the archetypes, and I call them therefore the impersonal or *collective unconscious*.

81   I am perfectly well aware that I can give you only the barest outline of this particular question of the collective unconscious. But I will give you an example of its symbolism and of how I proceed in order to discriminate it from the personal unconscious. When I went to America to investigate the unconscious of Negroes I had in mind this particular problem: are these collective patterns racially inherited, or are they "a priori categories of imagination," as two Frenchmen, Hubert and Mauss,[3] quite independently of my own work, have called them. A Negro told me a dream in which occurred the figure of a man crucified on a wheel.[4] I will not mention the whole dream because it does not matter. It contained of course its personal meaning as well as allusions to impersonal ideas, but I picked out only that one motif. He was a very uneducated Negro from the South and not particularly intelligent. It would have been most probable, given the well-known religious character of the Negroes, that he should dream of a man crucified on a *cross*. The cross would have been a personal acquisition. But it is rather improbable that he should dream of the man crucified on a *wheel*. That is a very uncommon image. Of course I cannot prove to you that by some curious chance the Negro had not seen a

2 See *Psychology of the Unconscious* [or *Symbols of Transformation* (C.W., vol. 5), index, s.v.].

3 [Henri Hubert and Marcel Mauss, *Mélanges d'histoire des religions*, p. xxix.]

4 [Cf. *Symbols of Transformation*, par. 154.]

picture or heard something of the sort and then dreamt about it; but if he had not had any model for this idea it would be an *archetypal image,* because the crucifixion on the wheel is a *mythological motif.* It is the ancient sun-wheel, and the crucifixion is the sacrifice to the sun-god in order to propitiate him, just as human and animal sacrifices formerly were offered for the fertility of the earth. The sun-wheel is an exceedingly archaic idea, perhaps the oldest religious idea there is. We can trace it to the Mesolithic and Paleolithic ages, as the sculptures of Rhodesia prove. Now there were real wheels only in the Bronze Age; in the Paleolithic Age the wheel was not yet invented. The Rhodesian sun-wheel seems to be contemporary with very naturalistic animal-pictures, like the famous rhino with the tick-birds, a masterpiece of observation. The Rhodesian sun-wheel is therefore an original vision, presumably an archetypal sun-image.[5] But this image is not a naturalistic one, for it is always divided into four or eight partitions (Figure 3). This image, a sort of

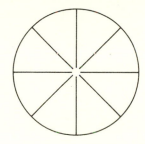

FIG. 3. Sun-wheel

divided circle, is a symbol which you find throughout the whole history of mankind as well as in the dreams of modern individuals. We might assume that the invention of the actual wheel started from this vision. Many of our inventions came from mythological anticipations and primordial images. For instance,

5 [Cf. "Psychology and Literature" (C.W., vol. 15), par. 150; "Psychology and Religion" (C.W., vol. 11), par. 100, and "Brother Klaus" (ibid.), par. 484. Documentation of the Rhodesian "sun-wheels" has not been possible, though such rock-carved forms are noted in Angola and South Africa: cf. Willcox, *The Rock Art of South Africa,* fig. 23 and pls. xvii–xx. Their dating is in doubt. The "rhino with tick-birds" is from the Transvaal and is in a museum in Pretoria. It was discovered in 1928 and widely publicized.]

the art of alchemy is the mother of modern chemistry. Our conscious scientific mind started in the matrix of the unconscious mind.

82   In the dream of the Negro, the man on the wheel is a repetition of the Greek mythological motif of Ixion, who, on account of his offence against men and gods, was fastened by Zeus upon an incessantly turning wheel. I give you this example of a mythological motif in a dream merely in order to convey to you an idea of the collective unconscious. One single example is of course no conclusive proof. But one cannot very well assume that this Negro had studied Greek mythology, and it is improbable that he had seen any representation of Greek mythological figures. Furthermore, figures of Ixion are pretty rare.

83   I could give you conclusive proof of a very elaborate kind of the existence of these mythological patterns in the unconscious mind. But in order to present my material I should need to lecture for a fortnight. I would have first to explain to you the meaning of dreams and dream-series and then give you all the historical parallels and explain fully their importance, because the symbolism of these images and ideas is not taught in public schools or universities, and even specialists very rarely know of it. I had to study it for years and to find the material myself, and I cannot expect even a highly educated audience to be *au courant* with such abstruse matters. When we come to the technique of dream-analysis I shall be forced to enter into some of the mythological material and you will get a glimpse of what this work of finding parallels to unconscious products is really like. For the moment I have to content myself with the mere statement that there are mythological patterns in that layer of the unconscious, that it produces contents which cannot be ascribed to the individual and which may even be in strict contradiction to the personal psychology of the dreamer. For instance, you are simply astounded when you observe a completely uneducated person producing a dream which really should not occur with such a person because it contains the most amazing things. And children's dreams often make you think to such a degree that you must take a holiday afterwards in order to recover from the shock, because these symbols are so tremendously profound and you think: How on earth is it possible that a child should have such a dream?

84   It is really quite simple to explain. Our mind has its history, just as our body has its history. You might be just as astonished that man has an appendix, for instance. Does he know he ought to have an appendix? He is just born with it. Millions of people do not know they have a thymus, but they have it. They do not know that in certain parts of their anatomy they belong to the species of the fishes, and yet it is so. Our unconscious mind, like our body, is a storehouse of relics and memories of the past. A study of the structure of the unconscious collective mind would reveal the same discoveries as you make in comparative anatomy. We do not need to think that there is anything mystical about it. But because I speak of a collective unconscious, I have been accused of obscurantism. There is nothing mystical about the collective unconscious. It is just a new branch of science, and it is really common sense to admit the existence of unconscious collective processes. For, though a child is not born conscious, his mind is not a *tabula rasa*. The child is born with a definite brain, and the brain of an English child will work not like that of an Australian blackfellow but in the way of a modern English person. The brain is born with a finished structure, it will work in a modern way, but this brain has its history. It has been built up in the course of millions of years and represents a history of which it is the result. Naturally it carries with it the traces of that history, exactly like the body, and if you grope down into the basic structure of the mind you naturally find traces of the archaic mind.

85   The idea of the collective unconscious is really very simple. If it were not so, then one could speak of a miracle, and I am not a miracle-monger at all. I simply go by experience. If I could tell you the experiences you would draw the same conclusions about these archaic motifs. By chance, I stumbled somehow into mythology and have read more books perhaps than you. I have not always been a student of mythology. One day, when I was still at the clinic, I saw a patient with schizophrenia who had a peculiar vision, and he told me about it. He wanted me to see it and, being very dull, I could not see it. I thought, "This man is crazy and I am normal and his vision should not bother me." But it did. I asked myself: What does it mean? I was not satisfied that it was just crazy, and later I came on a book by a German scholar,

41

Dieterich,[6] who had published part of a magic papyrus. I studied it with great interest, and on page 7 I found the vision of my lunatic "word for word." That gave me a shock. I said: "How on earth is it possible that this fellow came into possession of that vision?" It was not just one image, but a series of images and a literal repetition of them. I do not want to go into it now because it would lead us too far. It is a highly interesting case; as a matter of fact, I published it.[7]

86   This astonishing parallelism set me going. You probably have not come across the book of the learned professor Dieterich, but if you had read the same books and observed such cases you would have discovered the idea of the collective unconscious.

87   The deepest we can reach in our exploration of the unconscious mind is the layer where man is no longer a distinct individual, but where his mind widens out and merges into the mind of mankind—not the conscious mind, but the unconscious mind of mankind, where we are all the same. As the body has its anatomical conformity in its two eyes and two ears and one heart and so on, with only slight individual differences, so has the mind its basic conformity. On this collective level we are no longer separate individuals, we are all one. You can understand this when you study the psychology of primitives. The outstanding fact about the primitive mentality is this lack of distinctiveness between individuals, this oneness of the subject with the object, this *participation mystique,* as Lévy-Bruhl[8] terms it. Primitive mentality expresses the basic structure of the mind, that psychological layer which with us is the collective unconscious, that underlying level which is the same in all. Because the basic structure of the mind is the same in everybody, we cannot make distinctions when we experience on that level. There we do not know if something has happened to you or to me. In the underlying collective level there is a wholeness which cannot be dissected. If you begin to think about participation as a fact which means that fundamentally we are identical with everybody and

6 [Albrecht Dieterich, *Eine Mithrasliturgie.*]

7 [*Symbols of Transformation,* pars. 151ff.; *The Archetypes and the Collective Unconscious,* par. 105; *The Structure and Dynamics of the Psyche* (C.W. vol. 8), pars. 228 and 318f.]

8 *How Natives Think,* trans. by Lilian A. Clare.

everything, you are led to very peculiar theoretical conclusions. You should not go further than those conclusions because these things get dangerous. But some of the conclusions you should explore, because they can explain a lot of peculiar things that happen to man.

88   I want to sum up: I have brought a diagram (Figure 4). It looks very complicated but as a matter of fact it is very simple. Suppose our mental sphere to look like a lighted globe. The surface from which the light emanates is the function by which you chiefly adapt. If you are a person who adapts chiefly by thinking, your surface is the surface of a thinking man. You will tackle things with your thinking, and what you will show to people will be your thinking. It will be another function if you are of another type.[9]

89   In the diagram, *sensation* is given as the peripheral function. By it man gets information from the world of external objects. In the second circle, *thinking,* he gets what his senses have told him; he will give things a name. Then he will have a *feeling* about them; a feeling-tone will accompany his observation. And in the end he will get some consciousness of where a thing comes from, where it may go, and what it may do. That is *intuition,* by which you see round corners. These four functions form the ectopsychic system.

90   The next circle in the diagram represents the conscious ego-complex to which the functions refer. Inside the endopsyche you first notice *memory,* which is still a function that can be controlled by the will; it is under the control of your ego-complex. Then we meet the *subjective components of the functions.* They cannot be exactly directed by the will but they still can be suppressed, excluded, or increased in intensity by will-power. These components are no longer as controllable as memory, though even memory is a bit tricky as you know. Then we come to the *affects* and *invasions,* which are only controllable by sheer force. You can suppress them, and that is all you can do. You have to clench your fists in order not to explode, because they are apt to be stronger than your ego-complex.

91   This psychic system cannot really be expressed by such a crude diagram. The diagram is rather a scale of values showing

9 For general description of types and functions, see *Psychological Types,* Chap. X.

ECTOPSYCHIC
SPHERE

PERSONAL
UNCONSCIOUS

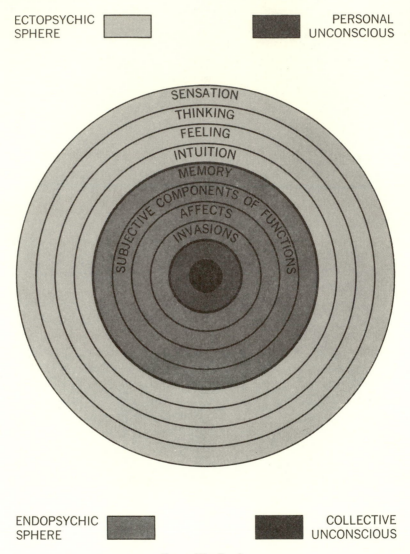

ENDOPSYCHIC
SPHERE

COLLECTIVE
UNCONSCIOUS

FIG. 4. The Psyche

44

how the energy or intensity of the ego-complex which manifests itself in will-power gradually decreases as you approach the darkness that is ultimately at the bottom of the whole structure —the *unconscious*. First we have the personal subconscious mind. The *personal unconscious* is that part of the psyche which contains all the things that could just as well be conscious. You know that many things are termed unconscious, but that is only a relative statement. There is nothing in this particular sphere that is necessarily unconscious in everybody. There are people who are conscious of almost anything of which man can be conscious. Of course we have an extraordinary amount of unconsciousness in our civilization, but if you go to other races, to India or to China, for example, you discover that these people are conscious of things for which the psychoanalyst in our countries has to dig for months. Moreover, simple people in natural conditions often have an extraordinary consciousness of things of which people in towns have no knowledge and of which townspeople begin to dream only under the influence of psychoanalysis. I noticed this at school. I had lived in the country among peasants and with animals, and I was fully conscious of a number of things of which other boys had no idea. I had the chance and I was not prejudiced. When you analyse dreams or symptoms or fantasies of neurotic or normal people, you begin to penetrate the unconscious mind, and you can abolish its artificial threshold. The personal unconscious is really something very relative, and its circle can be restricted and become so much narrower that it touches zero. It is quite thinkable that a man can develop his consciousness to such an extent that he can say: *Nihil humanum a me alienum puto*.[10]

92 Finally we come to the ultimate kernel which cannot be made conscious at all—the sphere of the archetypal mind. Its presumable contents appear in the form of images which can be understood only by comparing them with historical parallels. If you do not recognize certain material as historical, and if you do not possess the parallels, you cannot integrate these contents into consciousness and they remain projected. The contents of the *collective unconscious* are not subject to any arbitrary inten-

10 [Cf. Terence, *Heauton Timorumenos*, 1.1.25: "Homo sum; humani nil a me alienum puto" (I am a man; I count nothing human alien to me).]

tion and are not controllable by the will. They actually behave
as if they did not exist in yourself—you see them in your neighbours but not in yourself. When the contents of the collective
unconscious become activated, we become aware of certain
things in our fellow men. For instance, we begin to discover that
the bad Abyssinians are attacking Italy. You know the famous
story by Anatole France. Two peasants were always fighting
each other, and there was somebody who wanted to go into the
reasons for it, and he asked one man, "Why do you hate your
neighbour and fight him like this?" He replied, "Mais il est de
l'autre côté de la rivière!" That is like France and Germany. We
Swiss people, you know, had a very good chance during the
Great War to read newspapers and to study that particular
mechanism which behaved like a great gun firing on one side of
the Rhine and in exactly the same way on the other side, and it
was very clear that people saw in their neighbours the thing they
did not recognize in themselves.

93   As a rule, when the collective unconscious becomes really
constellated in larger social groups, the result is a public craze, a
mental epidemic that may lead to revolution or war or something of the sort. These movements are exceedingly contagious
—almost overwhelmingly contagious because, when the collective unconscious is activated, you are no longer the same person.
You are not only *in* the movement—you *are* it. If you lived in
Germany or were there for a while, you would defend yourself
in vain. It gets under your skin. You are human, and wherever
you are in the world you can defend yourself only by restricting
your consciousness and making yourself as empty, as soulless, as
possible. Then you lose your soul, because you are only a speck
of consciousness floating on a sea of life in which you do not
participate. But if you remain yourself you will notice that the
collective atmosphere gets under your skin. You cannot live in
Africa or any such country without having that country under
your skin. If you live with the yellow man you get yellow under
the skin. You cannot prevent it, because somewhere you are the
same as the Negro or the Chinese or whoever you live with, you
are all just human beings. In the collective unconscious you are
the same as a man of another race, you have the same archetypes,
just as you have, like him, eyes, a heart, a liver, and so on. It does
not matter that his skin is black. It matters to a certain extent,

46

sure enough—he has probably a whole historical layer less than you. The different strata of the mind correspond to the history of the races.

94   If you study races as I have done you can make very interesting discoveries. You can make them, for instance, if you analyse North Americans. The American, on account of the fact that he lives on virgin soil, has the Red Indian in him. The Red man, even if he has never seen one, and the Negro, though he may be cast out and the tram-cars reserved for white men only, have got into the American and you will realize that he belongs to a partly coloured nation.[11] These things are wholly unconscious, and you can only talk to very enlightened people about them. It is just as difficult to talk to Frenchmen or Germans when you have to tell them why they are so much against each other.

95   A little while ago I had a nice evening in Paris. Some very cultivated men had invited me, and we had a pleasant conversation. They asked me about national differences, and I thought I would put my foot in it, so I said: "What you value is *la clarté latine, la clarté de l'esprit latin*. That is because your thinking is inferior. The Latin thinker is inferior in comparison to the German thinker." They cocked their ears, and I said: "But your feeling is unsurpassable, it is absolutely differentiated." They said: "How is that?" I replied: "Go to a café or a vaudeville or a place where you hear songs and stage-plays and you will notice a very peculiar phenomenon. There are any number of very grotesque and cynical things and then suddenly something sentimental happens. A mother loses her child, there is a lost love, or something marvellously patriotic, and you must weep. For you, the salt and the sugar have to go together. But a German can stand a whole evening of sugar only. The Frenchman must have some salt in it. You meet a man and say: *Enchanté de faire votre connaissance*. You are not *enchanté de faire sa connaissance* at all; you are really feeling: 'Oh go to the devil.' But you are not disturbed, nor is he. But do not say to a German: *Enchanté de faire votre connaissance*, because he will believe it. A German will sell you a pair of sock-suspenders and not only expect, as is natural, to be paid for it. He also expects to be loved for it."

[11] [*Civilization in Transition* (C.W., vol. 10), pars. 94ff. and 946ff.]

96   The German nation is characterized by the fact that its feeling function is inferior, it is not differentiated. If you say that to a German he is offended. I should be offended too. He is very attached to what he calls *"Gemütlichkeit."* A room full of smoke in which everybody loves everybody—that is *gemütlich* and that must not be disturbed. It has to be absolutely clear, just one note and no more. That is *la clarté germanique du sentiment,* and it is inferior. On the other hand, it is a gross offence to a Frenchman to say something paradoxical, because it is not clear. An English philosopher has said, "A superior mind is never quite clear." That is true, and also superior feeling is never quite clear. You will only enjoy a feeling that is above board when it is slightly doubtful, and a thought that does not have a slight contradiction in it is not convincing.

97   Our particular problem from now on will be: How can we approach the dark sphere of man? As I have told you, this is done by three methods of analysis: the word-association test, dream-analysis, and the method of active imagination. First of all I want to say something about *word-association tests.*[12] To many of you perhaps these seem old-fashioned, but since they are still being used I have to refer to them. I use this test now not with patients but with criminal cases.

98   The experiment is made—I am repeating well-known things —with a list of say a hundred words. You instruct the test person to react with the first word that comes into his mind as quickly as possible after having heard and understood the stimulus word. When you have made sure that the test person has understood what you mean you start the experiment. You mark the time of each reaction with a stop-watch. When you have finished the hundred words you do another experiment. You repeat the stimulus words and the test person has to reproduce his former answers. In certain places his memory fails and reproduction becomes uncertain or faulty. These mistakes are important.

99   Originally the experiment was not meant for its present application at all; it was intended to be used for the study of mental association. That was of course a most Utopian idea. One can study nothing of the sort by such primitive means. But you can

12 *Studies in Word Association,* trans. by Eder. [Also in *Experimental Researches* (C.W., vol. 2).]

study something else when the experiment fails, when people make mistakes. You ask a simple word that a child can answer, and a highly intelligent person cannot reply. Why? That word has hit on what I call a complex, a conglomeration of psychic contents characterized by a peculiar or perhaps painful feeling-tone, something that is usually hidden from sight. It is as though a projectile struck through the thick layer of the *persona*[13] into the dark layer. For instance, somebody with a money complex will be hit when you say: "To buy," "to pay," or "money." That is a disturbance of reaction.

100   We have about twelve or more categories of disturbance and I will mention a few of them so that you will get an idea of their practical value. The prolongation of the reaction time is of the greatest practical importance. You decide whether the reaction time is too long by taking the average mean of the reaction times of the test person. Other characteristic disturbances are: reaction with more than one word, against the instructions; mistakes in reproduction of the word; reaction expressed by facial expression, laughing, movement of the hands or feet or body, coughing, stammering, and such things; insufficient reactions like "yes" or "no"; not reacting to the real meaning of the stimulus word; habitual use of the same words; use of foreign languages —of which there is not a great danger in England, though with us it is a great nuisance; defective reproduction, when memory begins to fail in the reproduction experiment; total lack of reaction.

101   All these reactions are beyond the control of the will. If you submit to the experiment you are done for, and if you do not submit to it you are done for too, because one knows why you are unwilling to do so. If you put it to a criminal he can refuse, and that is fatal because one knows why he refuses. If he gives in he hangs himself. In Zurich I am called in by the Court when they have a difficult case; I am the last straw.

102   The results of the association test can be illustrated very neatly by a diagram (Figure 5). The height of the columns represents the actual reaction time of the test person. The dotted horizontal line represents the average mean of reaction times. The unshaded columns are those reactions which show no signs

13 *Two Essays on Analytical Psychology* (C.W., vol. 7) , pars. 245f., 304f.

of disturbance. The shaded columns show disturbed reactions. In reactions 7, 8, 9, 10, you observe for instance a whole series of disturbances: the stimulus word at 7 was a critical one, and without the test person noticing it at all three subsequent reaction times are overlong on account of the perseveration of the

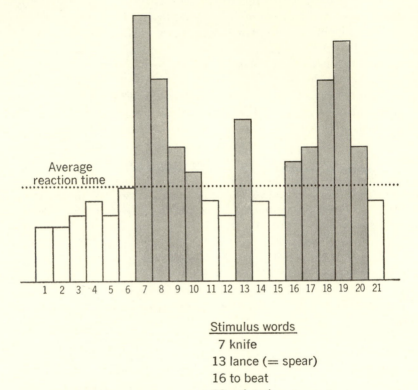

Average
reaction time

1 2 3 4 5 6 7 8 9 10 11 12 13 14 15 16 17 18 19 20 21

Stimulus words
7 knife
13 lance (= spear)
16 to beat
18 pointed
19 bottle

FIG. 5. Association Test

reaction to the stimulus word. The test person was quite unconscious of the fact that he had an emotion. Reaction 13 shows an isolated disturbance, and in 16–20 the result is again a whole series of disturbances. The strongest disturbances are in reactions 18 and 19. In this particular case we have to do with a so-called intensification of sensitiveness through the sensitizing effect of an unconscious emotion: when a critical stimulus word has aroused a perseverating emotional reaction, and when the next critical stimulus word happens to occur within the range of that perseveration, then it is apt to produce a greater effect than it would have been expected to produce if it had occurred in a series of indifferent associations. This is called the sensitizing effect of a perseverating emotion.

103   In dealing with criminal cases we can make use of the sensitizing effect, and then we arrange the critical stimulus words in such a way that they occur more or less within the presumable range of perseveration. This can be done in order to increase the effect of critical stimulus words. With a suspected culprit as a test person, the critical stimulus words are words which have a direct bearing upon the crime.

104   The test person for Figure 5 was a man about 35, a decent individual, one of my normal test persons. I had of course to experiment with a great number of normal people before I could draw conclusions from pathological material. If you want to know what it was that disturbed this man, you simply have to read the words that caused the disturbances and fit them together. Then you get a nice story. I will tell you exactly what it was.

105   To begin with, it was the word *knife* that caused four disturbed reactions. The next disturbance was *lance* (or *spear*) and then *to beat,* then the word *pointed* and then *bottle.* That was in a short series of fifty stimulus words, which was enough for me to tell the man point-blank what the matter was. So I said: "I did not know you had had such a disagreeable experience." He stared at me and said: "I do not know what you are talking about." I said: "You know you were drunk and had a disagreeable affair with sticking your knife into somebody." He said: "How do you know?" Then he confessed the whole thing. He came of a respectable family, simple but quite nice people. He had been abroad and one day got into a drunken quarrel, drew a knife and stuck it into somebody, and got a year in prison. That is a great secret which he does not mention because it would cast a shadow on his life. Nobody in his town or surroundings knows anything about it and I am the only one who by chance stumbled upon it. In my seminar in Zurich I also make these experiments. Those who want to confess are of course welcome to. However, I always ask them to

bring some material of a person *they* know and *I* do not know, and I show them how to read the story of that individual. It is quite interesting work; sometimes one makes remarkable discoveries.

106   I will give you other instances. Many years ago, when I was quite a young doctor, an old professor of criminology asked me about the experiment and said he did not believe in it. I said: "No, Professor? You can try it whenever you like." He invited me to his house and I began. After ten words he got tired and said: "What can you make of it? Nothing has come of it." I told him he could not expect a result with ten or twelve words; he ought to have a hundred and then we could see something. He said: "Can you do something with these words?" I said: "Little enough, but I can tell you something. Quite recently you have had worries about money, you have too little of it. You are afraid of dying of heart disease. You must have studied in France, where you had a love affair, and it has come back to your mind, as often, when one has thoughts of dying, old sweet memories come back from the womb of time." He said: "How do you know?" Any child could have seen it! He was a man of 72 and he had associated *heart* with *pain*—fear that he would die of heart failure. He associated *death* with *to die*—a natural reaction—and with *money* he associated *too little*, a very usual reaction. Then things became rather startling to me. To *pay*, after a long reaction time, he said *La Semeuse*, though our conversation was in German. That is the famous figure on the French coin. Now why on earth should this old man say *La Semeuse*? When he came to the word *kiss* there was a long reaction time and there was a light in his eyes and he said: *Beautiful*. Then of course I had the story. He would never have used French if it had not been associated with a particular feeling, and so we must think why he used it. Had he had losses with the French franc? There was no talk of inflation and devaluation in those days. That could not be the clue. I was in doubt whether it was money or love, but when he came to *kiss/beautiful* I knew it was love. He was not the kind of man to go to France in later life, but he had been a student in Paris, a lawyer, probably at the Sorbonne. It was relatively simple to stitch together the whole story.

107   But occasionally you come upon a real tragedy. Figure 6 is the case of a woman of about thirty years of age. She was in the

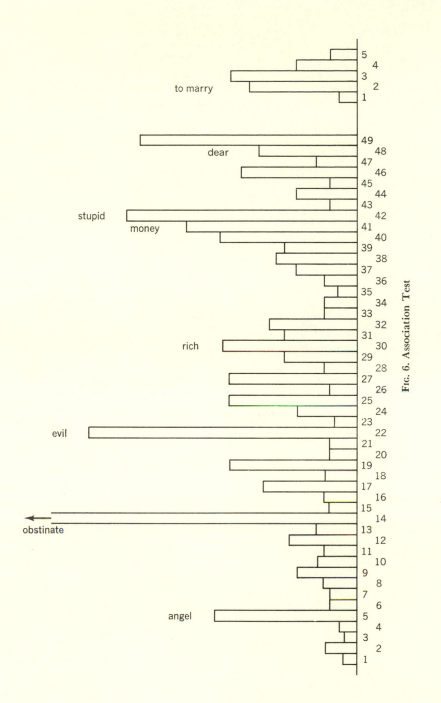

Fig. 6. Association Test

clinic, and the diagnosis was schizophrenia of a depressive character. The prognosis was correspondingly bad. I had this woman in my ward, and I had a peculiar feeling about her. I felt I could not quite agree with the bad prognosis, because already schizophrenia was a relative idea with me. I thought that we are all relatively crazy, but this woman was peculiar, and I could not accept the diagnosis as the last word. In those days one knew precious little. Of course I made an anamnesis, but nothing was discovered that threw any light on her illness. Therefore I put her to the association test and finally made a very peculiar discovery. The first disturbance was caused by the word *angel,* and a complete lack of reaction by the word *obstinate.* Then there were *evil, rich, money, stupid, dear,* and *to marry.* Now this woman was the wife of a well-to-do man in a very fine position and apparently happy. I had questioned her husband, and the only thing he could tell me, as she also did, was that the depression came on about two months after her eldest child had died— a little girl four years old. Nothing else could be found out about the aetiology of the case. The association test confronted me with a most baffling series of reactions which I could not put together. You will often be in such a situation, particularly if you have no routine with that kind of diagnosis. Then you first ask the test person about the words which are not going directly to the kernel. If you asked directly about the strongest disturbances you would get wrong answers, so you begin with relatively harmless words and you are likely to get an honest reply. I said: "What about *angel?* Does that word mean something to you?" She replied: "Of course, that is my child whom I have lost." And then came a great flood of tears. When the storm had blown over I asked: "What does *obstinate* mean to you?" She said: "It means nothing to me." But I said: "There was a big disturbance with the word and it means there is something connected with it." I could not penetrate it. I came to the word *evil* and could get nothing out of her. There was a severely negative reaction which showed that she refused to answer. I went on to *blue,* and she said: "Those are the eyes of the child I have lost." I said: "Did they make a particular impression on you?" She said: "Of course. They were so wonderfully blue when the child was born." I noticed the expression on her face, and I said: "Why are you upset?" and she replied: "Well, she did not have the eyes

54

of my husband." Finally it came out that the child had had the eyes of a former lover of hers. I said: "What is upsetting you with regard to that man?" And I was able to worm the story out of her.

108   In the little town in which she grew up there was a rich young man. She was of a well-to-do family but nothing grand. The man was of the moneyed aristocracy and the hero of the little town, and every girl dreamed of him. She was a pretty girl and thought she might have a chance. Then she discovered she had no chance with him, and her family said: "Why think of him? He is a rich man and does not think of you. Here is Mr. So-and-So, a nice man. Why not marry him?" She married him and was perfectly happy ever after until the fifth year of her marriage, when a former friend from her native town came to visit her. When her husband left the room he said to her: "You have caused pain to a certain gentleman" (meaning the hero). She said: "What? I caused pain?" The friend replied: "Didn't you know he was in love with you and was disappointed when you married another man?" That set fire to the roof. But she repressed it. A fortnight later she was bathing her boy, two years, and her girl, four years old. The water in the town—it was not in Switzerland—was not above suspicion, in fact it was infected with typhoid fever. She noticed that the little girl was sucking a sponge. But she did not interfere, and when the little boy said, "I want to drink some water," she gave him the possibly infected water. The little girl got typhoid fever and died, the little boy was saved. Then she had what she wanted—or what the devil in her wanted—the denial of her marriage in order to marry the other man. To this end she had committed murder. She did not know it; she only told me the facts and did not draw the conclusion that she was responsible for the death of the child since she knew the water was infected and there was danger. I was faced with the question whether I should tell her she had committed murder, or whether I should keep quiet. (It was only a question of telling *her*, there was no threat of a criminal case.) I thought that if I told her it might make her condition much worse, but there was a bad prognosis anyhow, whereas, if she could realize what she had done, the chance was that she might get well. So I made up my mind to tell her point-blank: "You killed your child." She went up in the air in an emotional state, but then

she came down to the facts. In three weeks we were able to discharge her, and she never came back. I traced her for fifteen years, and there was no relapse. That depression fitted her case psychologically: she was a murderess and under other circumstances would have deserved capital punishment. Instead of going to jail she was sent to the lunatic asylum. I practically saved her from the punishment of insanity by putting an enormous burden on her conscience. For if one can accept one's sin one can live with it. If one cannot accept it, one has to suffer the inevitable consequences.

Discussion

Question:

109   I want to refer to last night. Towards the end of his lecture Dr. Jung spoke of higher and lower functions and said the thinking type would use his feeling function archaically. I would like to know: is the reverse true? Does the feeling type, when he tries to think, think archaically? In other words, are thinking and intuition to be regarded always as higher functions than feeling and sensation? I ask this because . . . I gathered from lectures elsewhere that sensation was the lowest of conscious functions and thinking a higher one. It is certainly the case that in everyday life thinking seems to be the top-notch. The professor—not this Professor—thinking in his study regards himself and is regarded as the highest type, higher than the countryman who says: "Sometimes I sits and thinks and sometimes I just sits."

Professor Jung:

110   I hope I did not give you the impression that I was giving a preference to any of the functions. The dominating function in a given individual is always the most differentiated, and that can be *any* function. We have absolutely no criterion by which we can say this or that function in itself is the best. We can only say that the differentiated function in the individual is the best for adapting, and that the one that is most excluded by the superior function is inferior on account of being neglected. There are some modern people who say that intuition is the highest func-

tion. Fastidious individuals prefer intuition, it is classy! The sensation type always thinks that other people are very inferior because they are not so real as he is. He is the real fellow and everybody else is fantastic and unreal. Everybody thinks his superior function is the top of the world. In that respect we are liable to the most awful blunders. To realize the actual order of functions in our consciousness, severe psychological criticism is needed. There are many people who believe that world problems are settled by thinking. But no truth can be established without all four functions. When you have thought the world you have done one-fourth of it; the remaining three-fourths may be against you.

Dr. Eric B. Strauss:

111   Professor Jung said the word-association test was a means by which one could study the contents of the personal unconscious. In the examples he gave surely the matters revealed were matters in the patient's conscious mind and not in his unconscious. Surely if one wanted to seek for unconscious material one would have to go a step further and get the patient to associate freely on the anomalous reactions. I am thinking of the association with the word "knife," when Professor Jung so cleverly assumed the story of the unfortunate incident. That surely was in the patient's conscious mind, whereas, if the word "knife" had unconscious associations we might, if we were Freudian-minded, have assumed it was associated with an unconscious castration complex or something of that kind. I am not saying it is so, but I do not understand what Professor Jung means when he says the association test is to reach to the patient's unconscious. Surely in the instance given tonight it is used to reach the conscious, or what Freud would perhaps call the preconscious.

Professor Jung:

112   I should like very much if you would pay more attention to what I say. I told you that unconscious things are very *relative*. When I am unconscious of a certain thing I am only relatively unconscious of it; in some other respects I may know it. The contents of the personal unconscious are perfectly conscious in certain respects, but you do not know them under a *particular aspect* or at a *particular time*.

113   How can you establish whether the thing is conscious or un-

conscious? You simply ask people. We have no other criterion to establish whether something is conscious or unconscious. You ask: "Do you know whether you have had certain hesitations?" They say: "No, I had no hesitation; to my knowledge I had the same reaction time." "Are you conscious that something disturbed you?" "No, I am not." "Have you no recollection of what you answered to the word 'knife'?" "None at all." This unawareness of facts is a very common thing. When I am asked if I know a certain man I may say no, because I have no recollection of him and so I am not conscious of knowing him; but when I am told that I met him two years ago, that he is Mr. So-and-So who has done such and such a thing, I reply: "Certainly I know him." I know him and I do not know him. All the contents of the personal unconscious are *relatively* unconscious, even the castration complex and the incest complex. They are perfectly known under certain aspects, though they are unconscious under others. This relativity of being conscious of something becomes quite plain in hysterical cases. Quite often you find that things which seem unconscious are unconscious only to the doctor but not perhaps to the nurse or the relatives.

114   I had to see an interesting case once in a famous clinic in Berlin, a case of multiple sarcomatosis of the spinal cord, and because it was a very famous neurologist who had made the diagnosis I almost trembled, but I asked for the anamnesis and had a very nice one worked out. I asked when the symptoms began, and found it was the evening of the day when the only son of the woman had left her and married. She was a widow, quite obviously in love with her son, and I said: "This is no sarcomatosis but an ordinary hysteria, which we can prove presently." The professor was horrified at my lack of intelligence or tact or I don't know what, and I had to walk out. But somebody ran after me in the street. It was the nurse, who said: "Doctor, I want to thank you for saying that it *was* hysteria. I always thought so."

Dr. Eric Graham Howe:

115   May I return to what Dr. Strauss said? Last night Professor Jung reproved me for merely using words, but I think it is important to get these words clearly understood. I wonder if you have ever asked for the association experiment to be applied to the words "mystic" or "fourth dimension"? I believe you would

get a period of great delay and concentrated fury every time they were mentioned. I propose to return to the fourth-dimensional, because I believe it is a link badly needed to help our understanding. Dr. Strauss uses the word "unconscious," but I understand from Professor Jung that there is no such thing, there is only a relative unconsciousness which depends on a relative degree of consciousness. According to Freudians, there is a place, a thing, an entity called the unconscious. According to Professor Jung, as I understand him, there is no such thing. He is moving in a fluid medium of relationship and Freud in a static medium of unrelated entities. To get it clear Freud is *three-dimensional* and Jung is, in all his psychology, *four-dimensional*. For this reason, I would criticize if I may the whole diagrammatic system of Jung because he is giving you a three-dimensional presentation of a four-dimensional system, a static presentation of something that is functionally moving, and unless it is explained you get it confused with the Freudian terminology and you cannot understand it. I shall insist that there must be some clarification of words.

Professor Jung:

116   I could wish Dr. Graham Howe were not so indiscreet. You are right, but you should not say such things. As I explained, I tried to begin with the mildest propositions. You put your foot right into it and speak of four dimensions and of the word "mystic," and you tell me that all of us would have a long reaction time to such stimulus words. You are quite right, everybody would be stung because we are just beginners in our field. I agree with you that it is very difficult to let psychology be a living thing and not to dissolve it into static entities. Naturally you must express yourself in terms of the fourth dimension when you bring the time factor into a three-dimensional system. When you speak of dynamics and processes you need the time factor, and then you have all the prejudice of the world against you because you have used the word "four-dimensional." It is a taboo word that should not be mentioned. It has a history, and we should be exceedingly tactful with such words. The more you advance in the understanding of the psyche the more careful you will have to be with terminology, because it is historically coined and prejudiced. The more you penetrate the basic

problems of psychology the more you approach ideas which are philosophically, religiously, and morally prejudiced. Therefore certain things should be handled with the utmost care.

Dr. Howe:

117   This audience would like you to be provocative. I am going to say a rash thing. You and I do not regard the shape of the ego as a straight line. We would be prepared to regard the sphere as a true shape of the self in four dimensions, of which one is the three-dimensional outline. If so, will you answer a question: "What is the scope of that self which in four dimensions is a moving sphere?" I suggest the answer is: "The universe itself, which includes your concept of the collective racial unconscious."

Professor Jung:

118   I should be much obliged if you would repeat that question.

Dr. Howe:

119   How big is this sphere, which is the four-dimensional self? I could not help giving the answer and saying that it is the same bigness as the universe.

Professor Jung:

120   This is really a philosophical question, and to answer it requires a great deal of theory of cognition. The world is our picture. Only childish people imagine that the world is what we think it is. The image of the world is a projection of the world of the self, as the latter is an introjection of the world. But only the special mind of a philosopher will step beyond the ordinary picture of the world in which there are static and isolated things. If you stepped beyond that picture you would cause an earthquake in the ordinary mind, the whole cosmos would be shaken, the most sacred convictions and hopes would be upset, and I do not see why one should wish to disquiet things. It is not good for patients, nor for doctors; it is perhaps good for philosophers.

Dr. Ian Suttie:

121   I should like to go back to Dr. Strauss's question. I can understand what Dr. Strauss means and I think I can understand what Professor Jung means. As far as I can see, Professor Jung fails to make any link between his statement and Dr. Strauss's. Dr. Strauss wanted to know how the word-association test can

show the Freudian unconscious, the material that is actually pushed out of mind. As far as I understand Professor Jung, he means what Freud means by the "Id." It seems to me that we should define our ideas well enough to compare them and not merely use them, each in our own school.

Professor Jung:

122   I must repeat again that my methods do not discover *theories,* they discover *facts,* and I tell you what facts I discover with these methods. I cannot discover a castration complex or a repressed incest or something like that—I find only psychological *facts,* not theories. I am afraid you mix up too much theory with fact and you are perhaps disappointed that the experiments do not reveal a castration complex and such things, but a castration complex is a *theory.* What you find in the association method are definite facts which we did not know before and which the test person also did not know in this particular light. I do not say he did not know it under another light. You know many things when you are in your business that you do not know at home, and at home you know many things that you do not know in your official position. Things are known in one place and somewhere else they are not known. That is what we call unconscious. I must repeat that we cannot penetrate the unconscious *empirically* and then discover, for instance, the Freudian *theory* of the castration complex. The castration complex is a mythological idea, but it is not found as such. What we actually find are certain facts grouped in a specific way, and we name them according to mythological or historical parallels. You cannot find a mythological motif, you can only find a personal motif, and that never appears in the form of a theory but as a living fact of human life. You can abstract a theory from it, Freudian or Adlerian or any other. You can think what you please about the facts of the world, and there will be as many theories in the end as heads that think about it.

Dr. Suttie:

123   I protest! I am not interested in this or that theory or what facts are found or not, but I am interested in having a means of communication by which each can know what the others are thinking and for that end I hold that our conceptions must be defined. We must know what the other person means by a cer-

tain thing like the unconscious of Freud. As for the word "unconscious," it is becoming more or less known to everybody. It has therefore a certain social or illustrative value, but Jung refuses to recognize the word "unconscious" in the meaning Freud gives to it and uses "unconscious" in a way that we have come to consider as what Freud calls the "Id."

Professor Jung:

124   The word "unconscious" is not Freud's invention. It was known in German philosophy long before, by Kant and Leibniz and others, and each of them gives his definition of that term. I am perfectly well aware that there are many different conceptions of the unconscious, and what I was trying humbly to do was to say what *I* think about it. It is not that I undervalue the merits of Leibniz, Kant, von Hartmann, or any other great man, including Freud and Adler and so on. I was only explaining what *I* mean by the unconscious, and I presuppose that you are all aware of what Freud means by it. I did not think it was my task to explain things in such a way that somebody who is convinced of Freud's theory and prefers that point of view would be upset in his belief. I have no tendency to destroy your convictions or points of view. I simply exhibit my own point of view, and if anybody should be tempted to think that this also is reasonable, that is all I want. It is perfectly indifferent to me what one thinks about the unconscious in general, otherwise I should begin a long dissertation on the concept of the unconscious as understood by Leibniz, Kant, and von Hartmann.

Dr. Suttie:

125   Dr. Strauss asked about the relationship of the unconscious as conceived by you and by Freud. Is it possible to bring them into precise and definite relationship?

Professor Jung:

126   Dr. Graham Howe has answered the question. Freud is seeing the mental processes as static, while I speak in terms of dynamics and relationship. To me all is relative. There is nothing definitely unconscious; it is only not present to the conscious mind under a certain light. You can have very different ideas of why a thing is known under one aspect and not known under another aspect. The only exception I make is the mythological

pattern, which is profoundly unconscious, as I can prove by the facts.

Dr. Strauss:

127   Surely there is a difference between using your association test as a crime detector and for finding, let us say, unconscious guilt. Your criminal is conscious of his guilt and he is conscious that he is afraid of its being discovered. Your neurotic is unaware of his guilt and unaware that he is afraid of his guilt. Can the same kind of technique be used in these two very different kinds of cases?

The Chairman:

128   This woman was not conscious of her guilt though she had allowed the child to suck the sponge.

Professor Jung:

129   I will show you the difference experimentally. In Figure 7 you have a short illustration of respiration during the association test. You see four series of seven respirations registered after the stimulus words. The diagrams are condensations of respirations after indifferent and critical stimulus words in a greater number of test persons.

130   "A" gives respirations after indifferent stimulus words. The first inspirations after the stimulus words are restricted, while the following inspirations are of normal size.

131   In "B" where the stimulus word was a critical one the volume of breathing is definitely restricted, sometimes by more than half the normal size.

132   In "C" we have the behaviour of breathing after a stimulus word relating to a complex that was conscious to the test persons. The first inspiration is almost normal, and only later you find a certain restriction.

133   In "D" the respiration is after a stimulus word that was related to a complex of which the test persons were unconscious. In this case the first inspiration is remarkably small and the following are rather below normal.

134   These diagrams illustrate very clearly the difference of reaction between conscious and unconscious complexes. In "C," for instance, the complex is conscious. The stimulus word hits the test person, and there is a deep inspiration. But when the stimulus word hits an unconscious complex, the volume of breathing

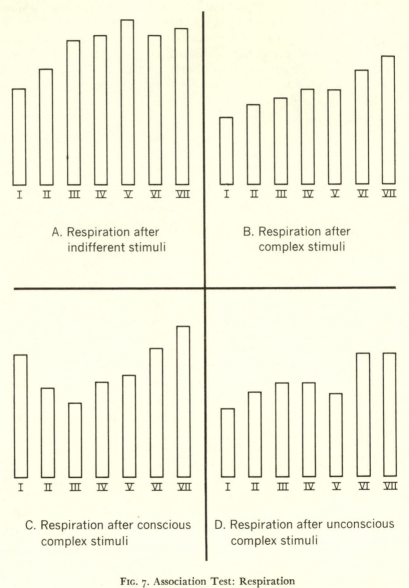

FIG. 7. Association Test: Respiration

is restricted, as shown in "D" *I*. There is a spasm in the thorax, so that almost no breathing takes place. In that way one has empirical proof of the physiological difference between conscious and unconscious reaction.[14]

Dr. Wilfred R. Bion:

135   You gave an analogy between archaic forms of the body and archaic forms of the mind. Is it purely an analogy or is there in fact a closer relationship? Last night you said something which suggested that you consider there is a connection between the mind and the brain, and there has lately been published in the *British Medical Journal* a diagnosis of yours from a dream of a physical disorder.[15] If that case was correctly reported it makes a very important suggestion, and I wondered whether you considered there was some closer connection between the two forms of archaic survival.

Professor Jung:

136   You touch again on the controversial problem of psychophysical parallelism for which I know of no answer, because it is beyond the reach of man's cognition. As I tried to explain yesterday, the two things—the psychic fact and the physiological fact—come together in a peculiar way. They happen together and are, so I assume, simply two different aspects to our *mind,* but not in reality. We see them as two on account of the utter incapacity of our mind to think them together. Because of that possible unity of the two things, we must expect to find dreams which are more on the physiological side than on the psychological, as we have other dreams that are more on the psycholog-

14 [Cf. supra, par. 48, n. 15.]
15 [Cf. T. M. Davie, "Comments upon a Case of 'Periventricular Epilepsy,'" *British Medical Journal,* no. 3893 (Aug. 17, 1935) , 293–297. The dream is reported by a patient of Davie as follows: "Someone beside me kept on asking me something about oiling some machinery. Milk was suggested as the best lubricant. Apparently I thought that oozy slime was preferable. Then a pond was drained, and amid the slime there were two extinct animals. One was a minute mastodon. I forgot what the other one was."

Davie's comment: "I thought it would be of interest to submit this dream to Jung to ask what his interpretation would be. He had no hesitation in saying that it indicated some organic disturbance, and that the illness was not primarily a psychological one, although there were numerous psychological derivatives in the dream. The drainage of the pond he interpreted as the damming-up of the cerebrospinal fluid circulation."]

ical than on the physical side. The dream to which you refer was very clearly a representation of an organic disorder. These "organic representations" are well known in ancient literature. The doctors of antiquity and of the Middle Ages used dreams for their diagnosis. I did not conduct a physical examination on the man you refer to. I only heard his history and was told the dream, and I gave my opinion on it. I have had other cases, for instance a very doubtful case of progressive muscular atrophy in a young girl. I asked about dreams and she had two dreams which were very colourful. A colleague, a man who knew something of psychology, thought it might be a case of hysteria. There were indeed hysterical symptoms, and it was still doubtful if it was progressive muscular atrophy or not; but on account of the dreams I came to the conclusion that it must be an organic disease, and the end proved my diagnosis. It was an organic disturbance, and the dreams were definitely referring to the organic condition.[16] According to my idea of the community of the psyche and the living body it should be like that, and it would be marvellous if it were not so.

Dr. Bion:

137 Will you be talking of that later when you speak on dreams?

Professor Jung:

138 I am afraid that I cannot go into such detail; it is too special. It is really a matter of special experience, and its presentation would be a very difficult job. It would not be possible to describe to you briefly the criteria by which I judge such dreams. The dream you mentioned, you may remember, was a dream of the little mastodon. To explain what that mastodon really means in an organic respect and why I must take that dream as an organic symptom would start such an argument that you would accuse me of the most terrible obscurantism. These things really are obscure. I had to speak in terms of the basic mind, which thinks in archetypal patterns. When I speak of archetypal patterns those who are aware of these things understand, but if you are not aware you think, "This fellow is absolutely crazy because he talks of mastodons and their difference from snakes and horses." I should have to give you a course of about four semesters about symbology first so that you could appreciate what I said.

16 [*The Practice of Psychotherapy* (C.W., vol. 16), pars. 344f.]

139   That is the great trouble: there is such a gap between what is usually known of these things and what I have worked on all these years. If I were to speak of this even before a medical audience I should have to talk of the peculiarities of the *niveau mental,* to quote Janet, and I might as well talk Chinese. For instance, I would say that the *abaissement du niveau mental* sank in a certain case to the level of the *manipura chakra,*[17] that is, to the level of the navel. We Europeans are not the only people on the earth. We are just a peninsula of Asia, and on that continent there are old civilizations where people have trained their minds in introspective psychology for thousands of years, whereas we began with our psychology not even yesterday but only this morning. These people have an insight that is simply fabulous, and I had to study Eastern things to understand certain facts of the unconscious. I had to go back to understand Oriental symbolism. I am about to publish a little book on one symbolic motif only,[18] and you will find it hair-raising. I had to study not only Chinese and Hindu but Sanskrit literature and medieval Latin manuscripts which are not even known to specialists, so that one must go to the British Museum to find the references. Only when you possess that apparatus of parallelism can you begin to make diagnoses and say that this dream is organic and that one is not. Until people have acquired that knowledge I am just a sorcerer. They say it is *un tour de passe-passe.* They said it in the Middle Ages. They said, "How can you see that Jupiter has satellites?" If you reply that you have a telescope, what is a telescope to a medieval audience?

140   I do not mean to boast about this. I am always perplexed when my colleagues ask: "How do you establish such a diagnosis or come to this conclusion?" I reply: "I will explain if you will allow me to explain what you ought to know to be able to understand it." I experienced this myself when the famous Einstein was Professor at Zurich. I often saw him, and it was when

17 [Cf. supra, par. 17, n. 4.]

18 [The mandala motif, in a lecture, "Traumsymbole des Individuationsprozesses," that Jung delivered a few weeks previously at the Eranos Tagung. It was published the next year in *Eranos-Jahrbuch 1935;* in translation, as "Dream Symbols of the Process of Individuation," *The Integration of the Personality,* 1939; revised as Part II of *Psychologie und Alchemie,* 1944 (= C.W., vol. 12). See also infra, par. 406, n. 15.]

he was beginning to work on his theory of relativity. He was often in my house, and I pumped him about his relativity theory. I am not gifted in mathematics and you should have seen all the trouble the poor man had to explain relativity to me. He did not know how to do it. I went fourteen feet deep into the floor and felt quite small when I saw how he was troubled. But one day he asked me something about psychology. Then I had my revenge.

141 Special knowledge is a terrible disadvantage. It leads you in a way too far, so that you cannot explain any more. You must allow me to talk to you about seemingly elementary things, but if you will accept them I think you will understand why I draw such and such conclusions. I am sorry that we do not have more time and that I cannot tell you everything. When I come to dreams I have to give myself away and to risk your thinking me a perfect fool, because I am not able to put before you all the historical evidence which led to my conclusions. I should have to quote bit after bit from Chinese and Hindu literature, medieval texts and all the things which you do not know. How could you? I am working with specialists in other fields of knowledge and they help me. There was my late friend Professor Wilhelm, the sinologist; I worked with him. He had translated a Taoist text, and he asked me to comment on it, which I did from the psychological side.[19] I am a terrible novelty to a sinologist, but what he has to tell us is a novelty to us. The Chinese philosophers were no fools. We think the old people were fools, but they were as intelligent as we are. They were frightfully intelligent people, and psychology can learn no end from old civilizations, particularly from India and China. A former President of the British Anthropological Society asked me: "Can you understand that such a highly intelligent people as the Chinese have no science?" I replied: "They have a science, but you do not understand it. It is not based on the principle of causality. The principle of causality is not the only principle; it is only relative."

142 People may say: What a fool to say causality is only relative! But look at modern physics! The East bases its thinking and its evaluation of facts on another principle. We have not even a

[19] *The Secret of the Golden Flower*. [The Chinese text was translated by Richard Wilhelm. The commentary by Jung is contained in *Alchemical Studies* (C.W., vol. 13).]

word for that principle. The East naturally has a word for it, but we do not understand it. The Eastern word is *Tao*. My friend McDougall[20] has a Chinese student, and he asked him: "What exactly do you mean by Tao?" Typically Western! The Chinese explained what Tao is and he replied: "I do not understand yet." The Chinese went out to the balcony and said: "What do you see?" "I see a street and houses and people walking and tramcars passing." "What more?" "There is a hill." "What more?" "Trees." "What more?" "The wind is blowing." The Chinese threw up his arms and said: "That is Tao."

143   There you are. Tao can be anything. I use another word to designate it, but it is poor enough. I call it *synchronicity*. The Eastern mind, when it looks at an ensemble of facts, accepts that ensemble as it is, but the Western mind divides it into entities, small quantities. You look, for instance, at this present gathering of people, and you say: "Where do they come from? Why should they come together?" The Eastern mind is not at all interested in that. It says: "What does it *mean* that these people are together?" That is not a problem for the Western mind. You are interested in what you come here for and what you are doing here. Not so the Eastern mind; it is interested in being together.

144   It is like this: you are standing on the sea-shore and the waves wash up an old hat, an old box, a shoe, a dead fish, and there they lie on the shore. You say: "Chance, nonsense!" The Chinese mind asks: "What does it mean that these things are together?" The Chinese mind experiments with that *being together* and *coming together at the right moment,* and it has an experimental method which is not known in the West, but which plays a large role in the philosophy of the East. It is a method of forecasting possibilities, and it is still used by the Japanese Government about political situations; it was used, for instance, in the Great War. This method was formulated in 1143 B.C.[21]

20 [William McDougall (1871–1938), American psychiatrist. Cf. Jung's "On the Psychogenesis of Schizophrenia" (C.W., vol. 3), par. 504, and "The Therapeutic Value of Abreaction" (C.W., vol. 16), par. 255.]
21 [Cf. *The I Ching, or Book of Changes*, trans. by Wilhelm/Baynes, 3rd edn., introduction, p. liii.]

LECTURE III

The Chairman (Dr. Maurice B. Wright):

145   Ladies and Gentlemen, it is my privilege to be the Chairman at Professor Jung's lecture at this evening's meeting. It was my privilege twenty-one years ago to meet Professor Jung when he came over to London to give a series of addresses,[1] but there was then a very small group of psychologically minded physicians. I remember very well how after the meetings we used to go to a little restaurant in Soho and talk until we were turned out. Naturally we were trying to pump Professor Jung as hard as we could. When I said goodbye to Professor Jung he said to me—he did not say it very seriously—"I think you are an extravert who has become an introvert." Frankly, I have been brooding about that ever since!

146   Now, ladies and gentlemen, just a word about last night. I think Professor Jung gave us a very good illustration of his views and of his work when he talked about the value of the telescope. A man with a telescope naturally can see a good deal more than anybody with unaided sight. That is exactly Professor Jung's position. With his particular spectacles, with his very specialized research, he has acquired a knowledge, a vision of the depth of the human psyche, which for many of us is very difficult to grasp. Of course, it will be impossible for him in the space of a few lectures to give us more than a very short outline of the vision he has gained. Therefore, in my opinion anything which might seem blurred or dark is not a question of obscurantism, it is a question of spectacles. My own difficulty is that, with my muscles of accommodation already hardening, it might be impossible for me ever to see that vision clearly, even if for the moment Professor Jung could lend me his spectacles. But however this may be,

1 [Cf. "On the Importance of the Unconscious in Psychopathology," and "On Psychological Understanding," both delivered in 1914 (C.W., vol. 3).]

I know that we are all thrilled with everything he can tell us, and we know how stimulating it is to our own thinking, especially in a domain where speculation is so easy and where proof is so difficult.

Professor Jung:

147   Ladies and Gentlemen, I ought to have finished my lecture on the association tests yesterday, but I would have had to overstep my time. So you must pardon me for coming back to the same thing once more. It is not that I am particularly in love with the association tests. I use them only when I must, but they are really the foundation of certain conceptions. I told you last time about the characteristic disturbances, and I think it would be a good thing, perhaps, if I were briefly to sum up all there is to say about the results of the experiment, namely about the complexes.

148   A complex is an agglomeration of associations—a sort of picture of a more or less complicated psychological nature—sometimes of traumatic character, sometimes simply of a painful and highly toned character. Everything that is highly toned is rather difficult to handle. If, for instance, something is very important to me, I begin to hesitate when I attempt to do it, and you have probably observed that when you ask me difficult questions I cannot answer them immediately because the subject is important and I have a long reaction time. I begin to stammer, and my memory does not supply the necessary material. Such disturbances are complex disturbances—even if what I say does not come from a personal complex of mine. It is simply an important affair, and whatever has an intense feeling-tone is difficult to handle because such contents are somehow associated with physiological reactions, with the processes of the heart, the tonus of the blood vessels, the condition of the intestines, the breathing, and the innervation of the skin. Whenever there is a high tonus it is just as if that particular complex had a body of its own, as if it were localized in my body to a certain extent, and that makes it unwieldy, because something that irritates my body cannot be easily pushed away because it has its roots in my body and begins to pull at my nerves. Something that has little tonus and little emotional value can be easily brushed aside because it has no roots. It is not adherent or adhesive.

149   Ladies and Gentlemen, that leads me to something very important—the fact that a complex with its given tension or energy has the tendency to form a little personality of itself. It has a sort of body, a certain amount of its own physiology. It can upset the stomach. It upsets the breathing, it disturbs the heart —in short, it behaves like a partial personality. For instance, when you want to say or do something and unfortunately a complex interferes with this intention, then you say or do something different from what you intended. You are simply interrupted, and your best intention gets upset by the complex, exactly as if you had been interfered with by a human being or by circumstances from outside. Under those conditions we really are forced to speak of the tendencies of complexes to act as if they were characterized by a certain amount of will-power. When you speak of will-power you naturally ask about the ego. Where then is the ego that belongs to the will-power of the complexes? We know our own ego-complex, which is supposed to be in full possession of the body. It is not, but let us assume that it is a centre in full possession of the body, that there is a focus which we call the ego, and that the ego has a will and can do something with its components. The ego also is an agglomeration of highly toned contents, so that in principle there is no difference between the ego-complex and any other complex.

150   Because complexes have a certain will-power, a sort of ego, we find that in a schizophrenic condition they emancipate themselves from conscious control to such an extent that they become visible and audible. They appear as visions, they speak in voices which are like the voices of definite people. This personification of complexes is not in itself necessarily a pathological condition. In dreams, for instance, our complexes often appear in a personified form. And one can train oneself to such an extent that they become visible or audible also in a waking condition. It is part of a certain yoga training to split up consciousness into its components, each of which appears as a specific personality. In the psychology of our unconscious there are typical figures that have a definite life of their own.[2]

151   All this is explained by the fact that the so-called unity of consciousness is an illusion. It is really a wish-dream. We like to

[2] For example, the figures of *anima* and *animus*. [See *Two Essays on Analytical Psychology* (C.W., vol. 7), pars. 296ff.]

think that we are one; but we are not, most decidedly not. We are not really masters in our house. We like to believe in our will-power and in our energy and in what we can do; but when it comes to a real show-down we find that we can do it only to a certain extent, because we are hampered by those little devils the complexes. Complexes are autonomous groups of associations that have a tendency to move by themselves, to live their own life apart from our intentions. I hold that our personal unconscious, as well as the collective unconscious, consists of an indefinite, because unknown, number of complexes or fragmentary personalities.

152   This idea explains a lot. It explains, for instance, the simple fact that a poet has the capacity to dramatize and personify his mental contents. When he creates a character on the stage, or in his poem or drama or novel, he thinks it is merely a product of his imagination; but that character in a certain secret way has made itself. Any novelist or writer will deny that these characters have a psychological meaning, but as a matter of fact you know as well as I do that they have one. Therefore you can read a writer's mind when you study the characters he creates.

153   The complexes, then, are partial or fragmentary personalities. When we speak of the ego-complex, we naturally assume that it has a consciousness, because the relationship of the various contents to the centre, in other words to the ego, is called consciousness. But we also have a grouping of contents about a centre, a sort of nucleus, in other complexes. So we may ask the question: Do complexes have a consciousness of their own? If you study spiritualism, you must admit that the so-called spirits manifested in automatic writing or through the voice of a medium do indeed have a sort of consciousness of their own. Therefore unprejudiced people are inclined to believe that the spirits are the ghosts of a deceased aunt or grandfather or something of the kind, just on account of the more or less distinct personality which can be traced in these manifestations. Of course, when we are dealing with a case of insanity we are less inclined to assume that we have to do with ghosts. We call it pathological then.

154   So much about the complexes. I insist on that particular point of consciousness within complexes only because complexes play a large role in dream-analysis. You remember my diagram

73

(Figure 4) showing the different spheres of the mind and the dark centre of the unconscious in the middle. The closer you approach that centre, the more you experience what Janet calls an *abaissement du niveau mental:* your conscious autonomy begins to disappear, and you get more and more under the fascination of unconscious contents. Conscious autonomy loses its tension and its energy, and that energy reappears in the increased activity of unconscious contents. You can observe this process in an extreme form when you carefully study a case of insanity. The fascination of unconscious contents gradually grows stronger and conscious control vanishes in proportion until finally the patient sinks into the unconscious altogether and becomes completely victimized by it. He is the victim of a new autonomous activity that does not start from his ego but starts from the dark sphere.

155   In order to deal with the association test thoroughly, I must mention an entirely different experiment. You will forgive me if for the sake of economizing time I do not go into the details of the researches, but these diagrams (Figs. 8, 9, 10, 11) illustrate the results of very voluminous researches into families.[3] They represent the quality of associations. For instance, the little summit in Figure 8 designated as number XI is a special class or category of association. The principle of classification is logical and linguistic. I am not going into this, and you will simply have to accept the fact that I have made fifteen categories into which I divide associations. We made tests with a great number of families, all for certain reasons uneducated people, and we found that the type of association and reaction is peculiarly parallel among certain members of the family; for instance, father and mother, or two brothers, or mother and child are almost identical in their type of reaction.

156   I shall explain this by Figure 8. The dotted line (. . . . .) represents the mother, the broken line (- - - - -) her sixteen-year-old daughter, and the unbroken line (———) the father. This was a very unfortunate marriage. The father was an alcoholic and the mother was a very peculiar type. You see that the sixteen-year-old daughter follows her mother's type closely. As much

3 "The Familial Constellations" (C.W., vol. 2) and "The Significance of the Father in the Destiny of the Individual" (C.W., vol. 4) , pars. 698–702.

as thirty per cent of all associations are identical words. This is a striking case of participation, of mental contagion. If you think about this case you can draw certain conclusions. The mother was forty-five years old, married to an alcoholic. Her life

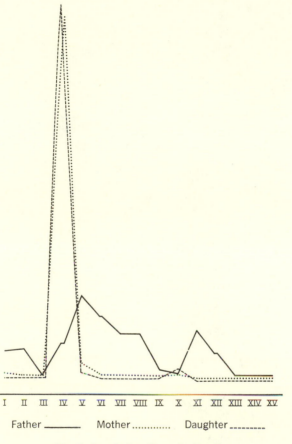

I II III IV V VI VII VIII IX X XI XII XIII XIV XV

Father _____   Mother ....   Daughter _____

Fig. 8. Association Test of a Family

was therefore a failure. Now the daughter has exactly the same reactions as the mother. If such a girl comes out into the world as though she were forty-five years old and married to an alcoholic, think what a mess she will get into! This participation explains why the daughter of an alcoholic who has had a hell of a

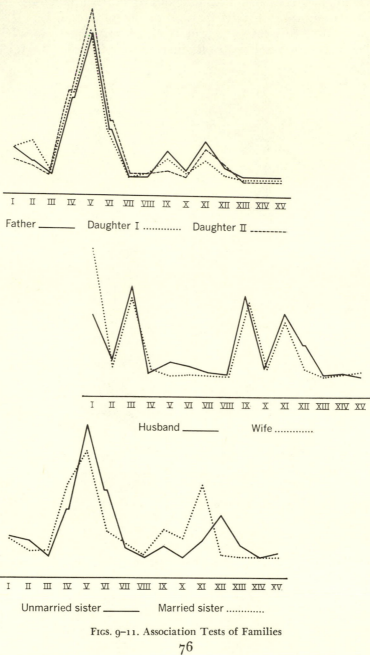

FIGS. 9–11. Association Tests of Families

youth will seek a man who is an alcoholic and marry him; and if by chance he should not be one, she will make him into one on account of that peculiar identity with one member of the family.

157   Figure 9 is a very striking case, too. The father, who was a widower, had two daughters who lived with him in complete identity. Of course, that also is most unnatural, because either he reacts like a girl or the two girls react like a man, even in the way they speak. The whole mental make-up is poisoned through the admixture of an alien element, because a young daughter is not in actual fact her father.

158   Figure 10 is the case of a husband and wife. This diagram gives an optimistic tone to my very pessimistic demonstrations. You see there is perfect harmony here; but do not make the mistake of thinking that this harmony is a paradise, for these people will kick against each other after a while because they are just too harmonious. A very good harmony in a family based on participation soon leads to frantic attempts on the part of the spouses to kick loose from each other, to liberate themselves, and then they invent irritating topics of discussion in order to have a reason for feeling misunderstood. If you study the ordinary psychology of marriage, you discover that most of the troubles consist in this cunning invention of irritating topics which have absolutely no foundation.

159   Figure 11 is also interesting. These two women are sisters living together; one is single and the other married. Their summit is found at number V. The wife in Figure 10 is the sister of these two women in Figure 11, and while most probably they were all of the same type originally, she married a man of another type. Their summit is at number III in Figure 10. The condition of identity or participation which is demonstrated in the association test can be substantiated by entirely different experiences, for instance, by graphology. The handwriting of many wives, particularly young wives, often resembles that of the husband. I do not know whether it is so in these days, but I assume that human nature remains very much the same. Occasionally it is the other way round because the so-called feeble sex has its strength sometimes.

160   Ladies and Gentlemen, we are now going to step over the border into dreams. I do not want to give you any particular in-

77

troduction to dream-analysis.[4] I think the best way is just to show you how I proceed with a dream, and then it does not need much explanation of a theoretical kind, because you can see what are my underlying ideas. Of course, I make great use of dreams, because dreams are an objective source of information in psychotherapeutic treatment. When a doctor has a case, he can hardly refrain from having ideas about it. But the more one knows about cases, the more one should make an heroic effort not to know in order to give the patient a fair chance. I always try not to know and not to see. It is much better to say you are stupid, or play what is apparently a stupid role, in order to give the patient a chance to come out with his own material. That does not mean that you should hide altogether.

161   This is a case of a man forty years old, a married man who has not been ill before. He looks quite all right; he is the director of a great public school, a very intelligent fellow who has studied an old-fashioned kind of psychology, Wundt psychology,[5] that has nothing to do with details of human life but moves in the stratosphere of abstract ideas. Recently he had been badly troubled by neurotic symptoms. He suffered from a peculiar kind of vertigo that seized upon him from time to time, palpitation, nausea, and peculiar attacks of feebleness and a sort of exhaustion. This syndrome presents the picture of a sickness which is well known in Switzerland. It is mountain sickness, a malady to which people who are not used to great heights are easily subject when climbing. So I asked, "Is it not mountain sickness you are suffering from?" He said, "Yes, you are right. It feels exactly like mountain sickness." I asked him if he had dreams, and he said that recently he had had three dreams.

162   I do not like to analyse one dream alone, because a single dream can be interpreted arbitrarily. You can speculate anything about an isolated dream; but if you compare a series of, say, twenty or a hundred dreams, then you can see interesting things. You see the process that is going on in the unconscious from night to night, and the continuity of the unconscious psyche extending through day and night. Presumably we are dreaming all the time, although we are not aware of it by day

4 "On the Practical Use of Dream Analysis" (C.W., vol. 16). [Also "General Aspects of Dream Psychology" and "On the Nature of Dreams" (C.W., vol. 8).]
5 [The reference is to Wilhelm Wundt, of Leipzig (1832–1920).]

because consciousness is much too clear. But at night, when there is that *abaissement du niveau mental,* the dreams can break through and become visible.

163   In the first dream *the patient finds himself in a small village in Switzerland. He is a very solemn black figure in a long coat; under his arm he carries several thick books. There is a group of young boys whom he recognizes as having been his classmates. They are looking at him and they say: "That fellow does not often make his appearance here."*

164   In order to understand this dream you have to remember that the patient is in a very fine position and has had a very good scientific education. But he started really from the bottom and is a self-made man. His parents were very poor peasants, and he worked his way up to his present position. He is very ambitious and is filled with the hope that he will rise still higher. He is like a man who has climbed in one day from sea-level to a level of 6,000 feet, and there he sees peaks 12,000 feet high towering above him. He finds himself in the place from which one climbs these higher mountains, and because of this he forgets all about the fact that he has already climbed 6,000 feet and immediately he starts to attack the higher peaks. But as a matter of fact though he does not realize it he is tired from his climbing and quite incapable of going any further at this time. This lack of realization is the reason for his symptoms of mountain sickness. The dream brings home to him the actual psychological situation. The contrast of himself as the solemn figure in the long black coat with thick books under his arm appearing in his native village, and of the village boys remarking that he does not often appear there, means that he does not often remember where he came from. On the contrary he thinks of his future career and hopes to get a chair as professor. Therefore the dream puts him back into his early surroundings. He ought to realize how much he has achieved considering who he was originally and that there are natural limitations to human effort.

165   The beginning of the second dream is a typical instance of the kind of dream that occurs when the conscious attitude is like his. *He knows that he ought to go to an important conference, and he is taking his portfolio. But he notices that the hour is rather advanced and that the train will leave soon, and so he gets into that well-known state of haste and of fear of being too*

late. He tries to get his clothes together, his hat is nowhere, his coat is mislaid, and he runs about in search of them and shouts up and down the house, "Where are my things?" Finally he gets everything together, and runs out of the house only to find that he has forgotten his portfolio. He rushes back for it, and looking at his watch finds how late it is getting; then he runs to the station, but the road is quite soft so that it is like walking on a bog and his feet can hardly move any more. Pantingly he arrives at the station only to see that the train is just leaving. His attention is called to the railway track, and it looks like this:

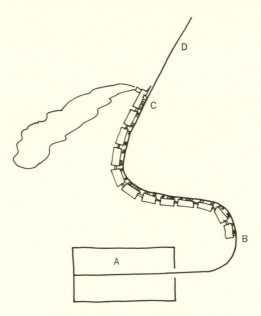

FIG. 12. Dream of the Train

166   *He is at A, the tail-end of the train is already at B and the engine is at C. He watches the train, a long one, winding round the curve, and he thinks, "If only the engine-driver, when he reaches point D, has sufficient intelligence not to rush full steam ahead; for if he does, the long train behind him which will still be rounding the curve will be derailed." Now the engine-driver arrives at D and he opens the steam throttle fully, the engine begins to pull, and the train rushes ahead. The dreamer sees*

*the catastrophe coming, the train goes off the rails, and he
shouts, and then he wakes up with the fear characteristic of
nightmare.*

167 Whenever one has this kind of dream of being late, of a hundred obstacles interfering, it is exactly the same as when one is in
such a situation in reality, when one is nervous about something. One is nervous because there is an unconscious resistance
to the conscious intention. The most irritating thing is that consciously you want something very much, and an unseen devil is
always working against it, and of course you are that devil too.
You are working against this devil and do it in a nervous way
and with nervous haste. In the case of this dreamer, that rushing
ahead is also against his will. He does not want to leave home,
yet he wants it very much, and all the resistance and difficulties
in his way are his own doing. He is that engine-driver who
thinks, "Now we are out of our trouble; we have a straight line
ahead, and now we can rush along like anything." The straight
line beyond the curve would correspond to the peaks 12,000 feet
high, and he thinks these peaks are accessible to him.

168 Naturally, nobody seeing such a chance ahead would refrain
from making the utmost use of it, so his reason says to him,
"Why not go on, you have every chance in the world." He does
not see why something in him should work against it. But this
dream gives him a warning that he should not be as stupid as
this engine-driver who goes full steam ahead when the tail-end
of the train is not yet out of the curve. That is what we always
forget; we always forget that our consciousness is only a surface,
our consciousness is the avant-garde of our psychological existence. Our head is only one end, but behind our consciousness is
a long historical "tail" of hesitations and weaknesses and complexes and prejudices and inheritances, and we always make our
reckoning without them. We always think we can make a
straight line in spite of our shortcomings, but they will weigh
very heavily and often we derail before we have reached our
goal because we have neglected our tail-ends.

169 I always say that our psychology has a long saurian's tail behind it, namely the whole history of our family, of our nation, of
Europe, and of the world in general. We are always human, and
we should never forget that we carry the whole burden of being
only human. If we were heads only we should be like little an-

gels that have heads and wings, and of course they can do what they please because they are not hindered by a body that can walk only on the earth. I must not omit to point out, not necessarily to the patient but to myself, that this peculiar movement of the train is like a snake. Presently we shall see why.

170   The next dream is the crucial dream, and I shall have to give certain explanations. In this dream we have to do with a peculiar animal which is half lizard and half crab. Before we go into the details of the dream, I want to make a few remarks about the method of working out the meaning of a dream. You know that there are many views and many misunderstandings as to the way in which you get at dreams.

171   You know, for instance, what is understood by free association. This method is a very doubtful one as far as my experience goes. Free association means that you open yourself to any amount and kind of associations and they naturally lead to your complexes. But then, you see, I do not want to know the complexes of my patients. That is uninteresting to me. I want to know what the *dreams* have to say about complexes, not what the complexes are. I want to know what a man's unconscious is doing *with* his complexes, I want to know what he is preparing himself for. *That* is what I read out of the dreams. If I wanted to apply the method of free association I would not need dreams. I could put up a signboard, for instance "Footpath to So-and-So," and simply let people meditate on that and add free associations, and they would invariably arrive at their complexes. If you are riding in a Hungarian or Russian train and look at the strange signs in the strange language, you can associate all your complexes. You have only to let yourself go and you naturally drift into your complexes.

172   I do not apply the method of free association because my goal is not to know the complexes; I want to know what the dream is. Therefore I handle the dream as if it were a text which I do not understand properly, say a Latin or a Greek or a Sanskrit text, where certain words are unknown to me or the text is fragmentary, and I merely apply the ordinary method any philologist would apply in reading such a text. My idea is that the dream does not conceal; we simply do not understand its language. For instance, if I quote to you a Latin or a Greek passage some of you will not understand it, but that is not because the text dis-

simulates or conceals; it is because you do not know Greek or Latin. Likewise, when a patient seems confused, it does not necessarily mean that he is confused, but that the doctor does not understand his material. The assumption that the dream wants to conceal is a mere anthropomorphic idea. No philologist would ever think that a difficult Sanskrit or cuneiform inscription conceals. There is a very wise word of the Talmud which says that the dream is its own interpretation. The dream is the whole thing, and if you think there is something behind it, or that the dream has concealed something, there is no question but that you simply do not understand it.

173   Therefore, first of all, when you handle a dream you say, "I do not understand a word of that dream." I always welcome that feeling of incompetence because then I know I shall put some good work into my attempt to understand the dream. What I do is this. I adopt the method of the philologist, which is far from being free association, and apply a logical principle which is called *amplification*. It is simply that of seeking the parallels. For instance, in the case of a very rare word which you have never come across before, you try to find parallel text passages, parallel applications perhaps, where that word also occurs, and then you try to put the formula you have established from the knowledge of other texts into the new text. If you make the new text a readable whole, you say, "Now we can read it." That is how we learned to read hieroglyphics and cuneiform inscriptions and that is how we can read dreams.

174   Now, how do I find the context? Here I simply follow the principle of the association experiment. Let us assume a man dreams about a simple sort of peasant's house. Now, do I know what a simple peasant's house conveys to that man's mind? Of course not; how could I? Do I know what a simple peasant's house means to him in general? Of course not. So I simply ask, "How does that thing appear to you?"—in other words, what is your context, what is the mental tissue in which that term "simple peasant's house" is embedded? He will tell you something quite astonishing. For instance, somebody says "water." Do I know what he means by "water"? Not at all. When I put that test word or a similar word to somebody, he will say "green." Another one will say "H_2O," which is something quite different. Another one will say "quicksilver," or "suicide." In each

case I know what tissue that word or image is embedded in. That is *amplification*. It is a well-known logical procedure which we apply here and which formulates exactly the technique of finding the context.

175   Of course, I ought to mention here the merit of Freud, who brought up the whole question of dreams and who has enabled us to approach the problem of dreams at all. You know his idea is that a dream is a distorted representation of a secret incompatible wish which does not agree with the conscious attitude and therefore is censored, that is, distorted, in order to become unrecognizable to the conscious and yet in a way to show itself and live. Freud logically says then: Let us redress that whole distortion; now be natural, give up your distorted tendencies and let your associations flow freely, then we will come to your natural facts, namely, your complexes. This is an entirely different point of view from mine. Freud is seeking the complexes, I am not. That is just the difference. I am looking for what the *unconscious is doing* with the complexes, because that interests me very much more than the fact that people have complexes. We all have complexes; it is a highly banal and uninteresting fact. Even the incest complex which you can find anywhere if you look for it is terribly banal and therefore uninteresting. It is only interesting to know what people do with their complexes; that is the practical question which matters. Freud applies the method of free association and makes use of an entirely different logical principle, a principle which in logic is called *reductio in primam figuram,* reduction to the first figure. The *reductio in primam figuram* is a so-called syllogism, a complicated sequence of logical conclusions, whose characteristic is that you start from a perfectly reasonable statement, and, through surreptitious assumptions and insinuations, you gradually change the reasonable nature of your first simple or prime figure until you reach a complete distortion which is utterly unreasonable. That complete distortion, in Freud's idea, characterizes the dream; the dream is a clever distortion that disguises the original figure, and you have only to undo the web in order to return to the first reasonable statement, which may be "I wish to commit this or that; I have such and such an incompatible wish." We start, for instance, with a perfectly reasonable assumption, such as "No unreasonable being is free"—in other words, has free will. This

is an example which is used in logic. It is a fairly reasonable statement. Now we come to the first fallacy, "Therefore, no free being is unreasonable." You cannot quite agree because there is already a trick. Then you continue, "All human beings are free" —they all have free will. Now you triumphantly finish up, "Therefore no human being is unreasonable." That is complete nonsense.

176   Let us assume that the dream is such an utterly nonsensical statement. This is perfectly plausible because obviously the dream is something like a nonsensical statement; otherwise you could understand it. As a rule you cannot understand it; you hardly ever come across dreams which are clear from beginning to end. The ordinary dream seems absolute nonsense and therefore one depreciates it. Even primitives, who make a great fuss about dreams, say that ordinary dreams mean nothing. But there are "big" dreams; medicine men and chiefs have big dreams, but ordinary men have no dreams. They talk exactly like people in Europe. Now you are confronted with that dream-nonsense, and you say, "This nonsense must be an insinuating distortion or fallacy which derives from an originally reasonable statement." You undo the whole thing and you apply the *reductio in primam figuram* and then you come to the initial undisturbed statement. So you see that the procedure of Freud's dream-interpretation is perfectly logical, if you assume that the statement of the dream is really nonsensical.

177   But do not forget when you make the statement that a thing is unreasonable that perhaps you do not understand because you are not God; on the contrary, you are a fallible human being with a very limited mind. When an insane patient tells me something, I may think: "What that fellow is talking about is all nonsense." As a matter of fact, if I am scientific, I say "I do not understand," but if I am unscientific, I say "That fellow is just crazy and I am intelligent." This argumentation is the reason why men with somewhat unbalanced minds often like to become alienists. It is humanly understandable because it gives you a tremendous satisfaction, when you are not quite sure of yourself, to be able to say "Oh, the others are much worse."

178   But the question remains: Can we safely say that a dream is nonsense? Are we quite sure that we know? Are we sure that the dream is a distortion? Are you absolutely certain when you dis-

cover something quite against your expectation that it is a mere distortion? Nature commits no errors. Right and wrong are human categories. The natural process is just what it is and nothing else—it is not nonsense and it is not unreasonable. We do not understand: that is the fact. Since I am not God and since I am a man of very limited intellectual capacities, I had better assume that I do not understand dreams. With that assumption I reject the prejudiced view that the dream is a distortion, and I say that if I do not understand a dream, it is my mind which is distorted, I am not taking the right view of it.

179   So I adopted the method which philologists apply to difficult texts, and I handle dreams in the same way. It is, of course, a bit more circumstantial and more difficult; but I can assure you that the results are far more interesting when you arrive at things that are human than when you apply a most dreadful monotonous interpretation. I hate to be bored. Above all we should avoid speculations and theories when we have to deal with such mysterious processes as dreams. We should never forget that for thousands of years very intelligent men of great knowledge and vast experience held very different views about them. It is only quite recently that we invented the theory that a dream is nothing. All other civilizations have had very different ideas about dreams.

180   Now I will tell you the big dream of my patient: *"I am in the country, in a simple peasant's house, with an elderly, motherly peasant woman. I talk to her about a great journey I am planning: I am going to walk from Switzerland to Leipzig. She is enormously impressed, at which I am very pleased. At this moment I look through the window at a meadow where there are peasants gathering hay. Then the scene changes. In the background appears a monstrously big crab-lizard. It moves first to the left and then to the right so that I find myself standing in the angle between them as if in an open pair of scissors. Then I have a little rod or a wand in my hand, and I lightly touch the monster's head with the rod and kill it. Then for a long time I stand there contemplating that monster."*

181   Before I go into such a dream I always try to establish a sequence, because this dream has a history before and will have a history afterwards. It is part of the psychic tissue that is continuous, for we have no reason to assume that there is no continuity

86

in the psychological processes, just as we have no reason to think that there is any gap in the processes of nature. Nature is a continuum, and so our psyche is very probably a continuum. This dream is just one flash or one observation of psychic continuity that became visible for a moment. As a continuity it is connected with the preceding dreams. In the previous dream we have already seen that peculiar snake-like movement of the train. This comparison is merely a hypothesis, but I have to establish such connections.

182   After the train-dream the dreamer is back in the surroundings of his early childhood; he is with a motherly peasant woman —a slight allusion to the mother, as you notice. In the very first dream, he impresses the village boys by his magnificent appearance in the long coat of the Herr Professor. In this present dream too he impresses the harmless woman with his greatness and the greatness of his ambitious plan to walk to Leipzig—an allusion to his hope of getting a chair there. The monster crablizard is outside our empirical experience; it is obviously a creation of the unconscious. So much we can see without any particular effort.

183   Now we come to the actual context. I ask him, "What are your associations to 'simple peasant's house'?" and to my enormous astonishment he says, "It is the lazar-house of St. Jacob near Basel." This house was a very old leprosery, and the building still exists. The place is also famous for a big battle fought there in 1444 by the Swiss against the troops of the Duke of Burgundy. His army tried to break into Switzerland but was beaten back by the avant-garde of the Swiss army, a body of 1,300 men who fought the Burgundian army consisting of 30,000 men at the lazar-house of St. Jacob. The 1,300 Swiss fell to the very last man, but by their sacrifice they stopped the further advance of the enemy. The heroic death of these 1,300 men is a notable incident in Swiss history, and no Swiss is able to talk of it without patriotic feeling.

184   Whenever the dreamer brings such a piece of information, you have to put it into the context of the dream. In this case it means that the dreamer is in a leprosery. The lazar-house is called "Siechenhaus," sick-house, in German, the "sick" meaning the lepers. So he has, as it were, a revolting contagious disease; he is an outcast from human society, he is in the sick-house.

And that sick-house is characterized, moreover, by that desperate fight which was a catastrophe for the 1,300 men and which was brought about by the fact that they did not obey orders. The avant-garde had strict instructions not to attack but to wait until the whole of the Swiss army had joined up with them. But as soon as they saw the enemy they could not hold back and, against the commands of their leaders, made a headlong rush and attacked, and of course they were all killed. Here again we come to the idea of this rushing ahead without establishing a connection with the bulk of the tail-end, and again the action is fatal. This gave me a rather uncanny feeling, and I thought, "Now what is the fellow after, what danger is he coming to?" The danger is not just his ambition, or that he wishes to be with the mother and commit incest, or something of the kind. You remember, the engine-driver is a foolish fellow too; he runs ahead in spite of the fact that the tail-end of the train is not yet out of the curve; he does not wait for it, but rushes along without thinking of the whole. That means that the dreamer has the tendency to rush ahead, not thinking of his tail; he behaves as if he were his head only, just as the avant-garde behaved as if it were the whole army, forgetting that it had to wait; and because it did not wait, every man was killed. This attitude of the patient is the reason for his symptoms of mountain sickness. He went too high, he is not prepared for the altitude, he forgets where he started from.

185   You know perhaps the novel by Paul Bourget, *L'Étape*. Its motif is the problem that a man's low origin always clings to him, and therefore there are very definite limitations to his climbing the social ladder. That is what the dream tries to remind the patient of. That house and that elderly peasant woman bring him back to his childhood. It looks, then, as if the woman might refer to the mother. But one must be careful with assumptions. His answer to my question about the woman was "That is my landlady." His landlady is an elderly widow, uneducated and old-fashioned, living naturally in a milieu inferior to his. He is too high up, and he forgets that the next part of his invisible self is the family in himself. Because he is a very intellectual man, feeling is his inferior function. His feeling is not at all differentiated, and therefore it is still in the form of the land-

88

lady, and in trying to impose upon that landlady he tries to impose upon himself with his enormous plan to walk to Leipzig.

186   Now what does he say about the trip to Leipzig? He says, "Oh, that is my ambition. I want to go far, I wish to get a Chair." Here is the headlong rush, here is the foolish attempt, here is the mountain sickness; he wants to climb too high. This dream was before the war, and at that time to be a professor in Leipzig was something marvellous. His feeling was deeply repressed; therefore it does not have right values and is much too naïve. It is still the peasant woman; it is still identical with his own mother. There are many capable and intelligent men who have no differentiation of feeling, and therefore their feeling is still contaminated with the mother, is still in the mother, identical with the mother, and they have mothers' feelings; they have wonderful feelings for babies, for the interiors of houses and nice rooms and for a very orderly home. It sometimes happens that these individuals, when they have turned forty, discover a masculine feeling and then there is trouble.

187   The feelings of a man are so to speak a woman's and appear as such in dreams. I designate this figure by the term *anima*, because she is the personification of the inferior functions which relate a man to the collective unconscious. The collective unconscious as a whole presents itself to a man in feminine form. To a woman it appears in masculine form, and then I call it the *animus*. I chose the term anima because it has always been used for that very same psychological fact. The anima as a personification of the collective unconscious occurs in dreams over and over again.[6] I have made long statistics about the anima figure in dreams. In this way one establishes these figures empirically.

188   When I ask my dreamer what he means when he says that the peasant woman is impressed by his plan, he answers, "Oh, well, that refers to my boasting. I like to boast before an inferior person to show who I am; when I am talking to uneducated people I like to put myself very much in the foreground. Unfortunately I have always to live in an inferior milieu." When a man resents the inferiority of his milieu and feels that he is too good for his surroundings, it is because the inferiority of the milieu *in himself* is projected into the outer milieu and therefore he begins to

[6] *Psychological Types,* Def. 48. See also *Two Essays,* pars. 296ff. [Also *Aion* (C.W., vol. 9, ii), ch. 3.]

mind those things which he should mind in himself. When he says, "I mind my inferior milieu," he ought to say, "I mind the fact that my own inner milieu is below the mark." He has no right values, he is inferior in his feeling-life. That is his problem.

189   At this moment he looks out of the window and sees the peasants gathering hay. That, of course, again is a vision of something he has done in the past. It brings back to him memories of similar pictures and situations; it was in summer and it was pretty hard work to get up early in the morning to turn the hay during the day and gather it in the evening. Of course, it is the simple honest work of such folk. He forgets that only the decent simple work gets him somewhere and not a big mouth. He also asserts, which I must mention, that in his present home he has a picture on the wall of peasants gathering hay, and he says, "Oh, that is the origin of the picture in my dream." It is as though he said, "The dream is nothing but a picture on the wall, it has no importance, I will pay no attention to it." At that moment the scene changes. When the scene changes you can always safely conclude that a representation of an unconscious thought has come to a climax, and it becomes impossible to continue that motif.

190   Now in the next part of the dream things are getting dark; the crab-lizard appears, apparently an enormous thing. I asked, "What about the crab, how on earth do you come to that?" He said, "That is a mythological monster which walks backwards. The crab walks backwards. I do not understand how I get to this thing—probably through some fairytale or something of that sort." What he had mentioned before were all things which you could meet with in real life, things which do actually exist. But the crab is not a personal experience, it is an archetype. When an analyst has to deal with an archetype he may begin to think. In dealing with the *personal* unconscious you are not allowed to think too much and to add anything to the associations of the patient. Can you add something to the personality of somebody else? You are a personality yourself. The other individual has a life of his own and a mind of his own inasmuch as he is a person. But inasmuch as he is not a person, inasmuch as he is also myself, he has the same basic structure of mind, and there I can begin to think, I can associate for him. I can even provide him with the

necessary context because he will have none, he does not know where that crab-lizard comes from and has no idea what it means, but I know and can provide the material for him.

191   I point out to him that the hero motif appears throughout the dreams. He has a hero fantasy about himself which comes to the surface in the last dream. He is the hero as the great man with the long coat and with the great plan; he is the hero who dies on the field of honour at St. Jacob; he is going to show the world who he is; and he is quite obviously the hero who overcomes the monster. The hero motif is invariably accompanied by the dragon motif; the dragon and the hero who fights him are two figures of the same myth.

192   The dragon appears in his dream as the crab-lizard. This statement does not, of course, explain what the dragon represents as an image of his psychological situation. So the next associations are directed round the monster. When it moves first to the left and then to the right the dreamer has the feeling that he is standing in an angle which could shut on him like open scissors. That would be fatal. He has read Freud, and accordingly he interprets the situation as an incest wish, the monster being the mother, the angle of the open scissors the legs of the mother, and he himself, standing in between, being just born or just going back into the mother.

193   Strangely enough, in mythology, the dragon *is* the mother. You meet that motif all over the world, and the monster is called the mother dragon.[7] The mother dragon eats the child again, she sucks him in after having given birth to him. The "terrible mother," as she is also called, is waiting with wide-open mouth on the Western Seas, and when a man approaches that mouth it closes on him and he is finished. That monstrous figure is the mother sarcophaga, the flesh-eater; it is, in another form, Matuta, the mother of the dead. It is the goddess of death.

194   But these parallels still do not explain why the dream chooses the particular image of the crab. I hold—and when I say I hold I have certain reasons for saying so—that representations of psychic facts in images like the snake or the lizard or the crab or the mastodon or analogous animals also represent organic facts. For instance, the serpent very often represents the cerebro-spinal

7 [E.g., *Symbols of Transformation*, Part II, ch. V, especially par. 395.]

91

system, especially the lower centres of the brain, and particularly
the medulla oblongata and spinal cord. The crab, on the other
hand, having a sympathetic system only, represents chiefly the
sympathicus and para-sympathicus of the abdomen; it is an abdominal thing. So if you translate the text of the dream it would
read: if you go on like this your cerebro-spinal system and your
sympathetic system will come up against you and snap you up.
That is in fact what is happening. The symptoms of his neurosis
express the rebellion of the sympathetic functions and of the
cerebro-spinal system against his conscious attitude.

195   The crab-lizard brings up the archetypal idea of the hero and
the dragon as deadly enemies. But in certain myths you find the
interesting fact that the hero is not connected with the dragon
only by his fight. There are, on the contrary, indications that the
hero is himself the dragon. In Scandinavian mythology the hero
is recognized by the fact that he has snake's eyes. He has snake's
eyes because he is a snake. There are many other myths and legends which contain the same idea. Cecrops, the founder of Athens, was a man above and a serpent below. The souls of heroes
often appear after death in the form of serpents.

196   Now in our dream the monstrous crab-lizard moves first to
the left, and I ask him about this left side. He says, "The crab
apparently does not know the way. Left is the unfavourable side,
left is sinister." Sinister does indeed mean left and unfavourable.
But the right side is also not good for the monster, because when
it goes to the right it is touched by the wand and is killed. Now
we come to his standing in between the angle of the monster's
movement, a situation which at first glance he interpreted as incest. He says, "As a matter of fact, I felt surrounded on either
side like a hero who is going to fight a dragon." So he himself
realizes the hero motif.

197   But unlike the mythical hero he does not fight the dragon
with a weapon, but with a wand. He says, "From its effect on the
monster it seems that it is a magical wand." He certainly does
dispose of the crab in a magical way. The wand is another mythological symbol. It often contains a sexual allusion, and sexual
magic is a means of protection against danger. You may remember, too, how during the earthquake at Messina[8] nature pro-

8 [The reference is to the disaster of 1908, when 90 per cent of the Sicilian city
was destroyed, with a loss of 60,000 lives.]

duced certain instinctive reactions against the overwhelming destruction.

198   The wand is an instrument, and instruments in dreams mean what they actually are, the devices of man to concretize his will. For instance, a knife is my will to cut; when I use a spear I prolong my arm, with a rifle I can project my action and my influence to a great distance; with a telescope I do the same as regards my sight. An instrument is a mechanism which represents my will, my intelligence, my capability, and my cunning. Instruments in dreams symbolize an analogous psychological mechanism. Now this dreamer's instrument is a magic wand. He uses a marvellous thing by which he can spirit away the monster, that is, his lower nervous system. He can dispose of such nonsense in no time, and with no effort at all.

199   What does this actually mean? It means that he simply thinks that the danger does not exist. That is what is usually done. You simply think that a thing is not and then it is no more. That is how people behave who consist of the head only. They use their intellect in order to think things away; they reason them away. They say, "This is nonsense, therefore it cannot be and therefore it is not." That is what he also does. He simply reasons the monster away. He says, "There is no such thing as a crab-lizard, there is no such thing as an opposing will; I get rid of it, I simply think it away. I think it is the mother with whom I want to commit incest, and that settles the whole thing, for I shall not do it." I said, "You have killed the animal—what do you think is the reason why you contemplate the animal for such a long time?" He said, "Oh, well, yes, naturally it is marvellous how you can dispose of such a creature with such ease." I said, "Yes, indeed it is very marvellous!"

200   Then I told him what I thought of the situation. I said, "Look here, the best way to deal with a dream is to think of yourself as a sort of ignorant child or ignorant youth, and to come to a two-million-year-old man or to the old mother of days and ask, 'Now, what do you think of me?' She would say to you, 'You have an ambitious plan, and that is foolish, because you run up against your own instincts. Your own restricted capabilities block the way. You want to abolish the obstacle by the magic of your thinking. You believe you can think it away by the artifices of your intellect, but it will be, believe me, matter for some

93

afterthought.' " And I also told him this: "Your dreams contain a warning. You behave exactly like the engine-driver or like the Swiss who were foolhardy enough to run up against the enemy without any support behind them, and if you behave in the same way you will meet with a catastrophe."

201   He was sure that such a point of view was much too serious. He was convinced that it is much more probable that dreams come from incompatible wishes and that he really had an unrealized incestuous wish which was at the bottom of this dream; that he was conscious now of this incestuous wish and had got rid of it and now could go to Leipzig. I said, "Well then, bon voyage." He did not return, he went on with his plans, and it took him just about three months to lose his position and go to the dogs. That was the end of him. He ran up against the fatal danger of that crab-lizard and would not understand the warning. But I do not want to make you too pessimistic. Sometimes there are people who really understand their dreams and draw conclusions which lead to a more favourable solution of their problems.

Discussion

Dr. Charles Brunton:

202   I do not know whether it is fair to ask about the dreams of someone who is not here, but I have a small daughter five and a half years old who has recently had two dreams which awakened her at night. The first dream occurred in the middle of August, and she told me this: "I see a wheel, and it is rolling down a road and it burns me." That was all I could get out of her. I wanted her to draw a picture of it the next day, but she did not want to be bothered, so I left it. The other dream was about a week ago, and this time it was "a beetle that was pinching me." That was all I could get about it. I do not know whether you would like to comment on them. The only thing I would like to add is that she knows the difference between a beetle and a crab. She is very fond of animals.

Professor Jung:

203   You have to consider that it is very difficult and not quite fair to comment on dreams of someone one does not know; but I will tell you as much as one can see from the symbolism. The

94

beetle would, according to my idea, have to do with the sympathetic system. Therefore I should conclude from that dream that there are certain peculiar psychological processes going on in the child, which touch upon her sympathetic system, and this might arouse some intestinal or other abdominal disorder. The most cautious statement one could make would be to say that there is a certain accumulation of energy in the sympathetic system which causes slight disturbances. This is also borne out by the symbol of the fiery wheel. The wheel in her dream seems to be a sun-symbol, and in Tantric philosophy fire corresponds to the so-called *manipura chakra,* which is localized in the abdomen. In the prodromal symptoms of epilepsy you sometimes find the idea of a wheel revolving inside. This too expresses a manifestation of a sympathetic nature. The image of the revolving wheel reminds us of the wheel upon which Ixion was crucified. The dream of the little girl is an archetypal dream, one of those strange archetypal dreams children occasionally have.

204   I explain these archetypal dreams of children by the fact that when consciousness begins to dawn, when the child begins to feel that *he is,* he is still close to the original psychological world from which he has just emerged: a condition of deep unconsciousness. Therefore you find with many children an awareness of the contents of the collective unconscious, a fact which in some Eastern beliefs is interpreted as reminiscence of a former existence. Tibetan philosophy, for instance, speaks of the "Bardo" existence and of the condition of the mind between death and birth.[9] The idea of former existence is a projection of the psychological condition of early childhood. Very young children still have an awareness of mythological contents, and if these contents remain conscious too long, the individual is threatened by an incapacity for adaptation; he is haunted by a constant yearning to remain with or to return to the original vision. There are very beautiful descriptions of these experiences by mystics and poets.

205   Usually at the age of four to six the veil of forgetfulness is drawn upon these experiences. However, I have seen cases of ethereal children, so to speak, who had an extraordinary awareness of these psychic facts and were living their life in archetypal

[9] Cf. W. Y. Evans-Wentz. *The Tibetan Book of the Dead.*

dreams and could not adapt. Recently I saw a case of a little girl of ten who had some most amazing mythological dreams.[10] Her father consulted me about these dreams. I could not tell him what I thought because they contained an uncanny prognosis. The little girl died a year later of an infectious disease. She had never been born entirely.

Dr. Leonard F. Browne:

206   I should like to ask Professor Jung a question with regard to the interpretation of the dreams he told us today. In view of the fact that the patient was unable to accept the interpretation, I should like to know whether that difficulty could have been overcome by some variation in the technique.

Professor Jung:

207   If I had had the intention of being a missionary, or a saviour, I should have used a clever trick. I should have said to the patient, "Yes, that is the mother complex all right," and we would have gone on talking that kind of jargon for several months and perhaps in the end I would have swung him round. But I know from experience that such a thing is not good; you should not cheat people even for their good. I do not want to cheat people out of their mistaken faith. Perhaps it was better for that man to go to the dogs than to be saved by wrong means. I never hinder people. When somebody says, "I am going to commit suicide if—," I say, "If that is your intention, I have no objection."

Dr. Browne:

208   Did you have any evidence that the symptoms of mountain sickness were cured?

Professor Jung:

209   The patient lost his neurosis in going down in life. That man did not belong at a height of 6,000 feet; he belonged lower down. He became inferior instead of being neurotic. Once I talked to the head of a great institution in America for the education of criminal children, and was told about a very interesting experience. They have two categories of children. The majority of them, when they come to the institution, feel ever so much better, they develop very nicely and normally and they

10 [Cf. infra, pars. 525ff. The case is also discussed in Jacobi, *Complex/Archetype/Symbol*, pp. 139ff.]

eventually grow out of whatever their original evil was. The other category, the minority, become hysterical when they try to be nice and normal. Those are the born criminals whom you cannot change. They are normal when they do wrong. We also do not feel quite right when we are behaving perfectly, we feel much better when we are doing a bit of wrong. That is because we are not perfect. The Hindus, when they build a temple, leave one corner unfinished; only the gods make something perfect, man never can. It is much better to know that one is not perfect, then one feels much better. So it is with these children, and so it is with our patients. It is wrong to cheat people out of their fate and to help them to go beyond their level. If a man has it in him to be adapted, help him by all means; but if it is really his task *not* to be adapted, help him by all means not to be adapted, because then he is all right.

210   What would the world be like if all people were adapted? It would be boring beyond endurance. There must be some people who behave in the wrong way; they act as scapegoats and objects of interest for the normal ones. Think how grateful you are for detective novels and newspapers, so that you can say, "Thank heaven I am not that fellow who has committed the crime, I am a perfectly innocent creature." You feel satisfaction because the evil people have done it for you. This is the deeper meaning of the fact that Christ as the redeemer was crucified between two thieves. These thieves in their way were also redeemers of mankind, they were the scapegoats.

Question:

211   I would like to ask a question about the psychological functions, if that is not going too far back. In answering a question last night you said that there was no criterion for considering either of the four functions as being superior in itself and you further said that all the four functions would have to be equally differentiated in order to obtain full and adequate knowledge of the world. Do you mean, therefore, that it is possible in any given case for all the four functions to be equally differentiated or to be arrived at by education?

Professor Jung:

212   I do not believe that it is humanly possible to differentiate all four functions alike, otherwise we would be perfect like God,

and that surely will not happen. There will always be a flaw in the crystal. We can never reach perfection. Moreover, if we could differentiate the four functions equally we should only make them into consciously disposable functions. Then we would lose the most precious connection with the unconscious through the inferior function, which is invariably the weakest; only through our feebleness and incapacity are we linked up with the unconscious, with the lower world of the instincts and with our fellow beings. Our virtues only enable us to be independent. There we do not need anybody, there we are kings; but in our inferiority we are linked up with mankind as well as with the world of our instincts. It would not even be an advantage to have all the functions perfect, because such a condition would amount to complete aloofness. I have no perfection craze. My principle is: for heaven's sake do not be perfect, but by all means try to be complete—whatever that means.

Question:

213   May I ask what it means to be complete? Will you enlarge upon that?

Professor Jung:

214   I must leave something to your own mental efforts. It is surely a most amusing enterprise, for instance, to think on your way home what it possibly means to be complete. We should not deprive people of the pleasure of discovering something. To be complete is a very great problem, and to talk of it is amusing, but to be it is the main thing.

Question:

215   How do you fit mysticism into your scheme?

Professor Jung:

216   Into what scheme?

Reply:

217   The scheme of psychology and the psyche.

Professor Jung:

218   Of course you should define what you mean by mysticism. Let us assume that you mean people who have mystical experience. Mystics are people who have a particularly vivid experience of the processes of the collective unconscious. Mystical experience is experience of archetypes.

Question:

219   Is there any difference between archetypal forms and mystical forms?

Professor Jung:

220   I make no distinction between them. If you study the phenomenology of mystical experience you will come across some very interesting things. For instance, you all know that our Christian heaven is a masculine heaven and that the feminine element is only tolerated. The Mother of God is not divine, she is only the arch-saint. She intercedes for us at the throne of God but she is not part of the Deity. She does not belong to the Trinity.

221   Now some Christian mystics have a different experience. For instance we have a Swiss mystic, Niklaus von der Flüe.[11] He experienced a God and a Goddess. Then there was a mystic of the thirteenth century, Guillaume de Digulleville, who wrote the *Pèlerinage de l'âme de Jésus Christ.*[12] Like Dante, he had a vision of the highest paradise as "le ciel d'or," and there upon a throne one thousand times more bright than the sun sat le Roi, who is God himself, and beside him on a crystal throne of brownish hue, la Reine, presumably the Earth. This is a vision outside the Trinity idea, a mystical experience of an archetypal nature which includes the feminine principle. The Trinity is a dogmatic image based on an archetype of an exclusively masculine nature. In the Early Church the Gnostic interpretation of the Holy Ghost as feminine was declared a heresy.

222   Dogmatic images, such as the Trinity, are archetypes which have become abstract ideas. But there are a number of mystical experiences inside the Church whose archetypal character is still visible. Therefore they sometimes contain a heretical or pagan element. Remember, for instance, St. Francis of Assisi. Only through the great diplomatic ability of Pope Boniface VIII could St. Francis be assimilated into the Church. You have only to think of his relation to animals to understand the difficulty. Animals, like the whole of Nature, were taboo to the Church. Yet there are sacred animals like the Lamb, the Dove, and, in the Early Church, the Fish, which are worshipped.

11 ["Brother Klaus" (C.W., vol. 11).]

12 [*Psychology and Alchemy* (C.W., vol. 12), pars. 315ff.]

Question:

223   Will Professor Jung give us his view on the psychological differences between the dissociation in hysteria and the dissociation in schizophrenia?

Professor Jung:

224   In hysteria the dissociated personalities are still in a sort of interrelation, so that you always get the impression of a total person. With a hysterical case you can establish a rapport, you get a feeling reaction from the whole person. There is only a superficial division between certain memory compartments, but the basic personality is always present. In the case of schizophrenia that is not so. There you encounter only fragments, there is nowhere a whole. Therefore, if you have a friend or a relative whom you have known well and who becomes insane, you will get a tremendous shock when you are confronted with a fragmentary personality which is completely split up. You can only deal with one fragment at a time; it is like a splinter of glass. You do not feel the continuity of the personality any longer. While with a hysterical case you think: if I could only wipe away that sort of obscuration or that sort of somnambulism then we should have the sum-total of the personality. But with schizophrenia it is a deep dissociation of personality; the fragments cannot come together any more.

Question:

225   Are there any more strictly psychological conceptions by which that difference can be expressed?

Professor Jung:

226   There are certain borderline cases where you can stitch the parts together if you can reintegrate the lost contents. I will tell you of a case I had. A woman had been twice in a lunatic asylum with a typical schizophrenic attack. When she was brought to me she was better, but still in a state of hallucination. I saw that it was possible to reach the split-off parts. Then I began to go through every detail of the experiences which she had had in the lunatic asylum with her; we went through all the voices and all the delusions, and I explained every fact to her so that she could associate them with her consciousness. I showed her what these unconscious contents were that came up during her insanity, and because she was an intelligent person, I gave her books to

100

read so that she acquired a great deal of knowledge, chiefly mythological knowledge, by which she herself could stitch the parts together. The breaking lines were still there, of course, and whenever afterwards she had a new wave of disintegration I told her to try to draw or paint a picture of that particular situation in order to have a picture of the whole of herself which objectified her condition, and so she did. She brought me quite a number of pictures she had made, which had helped her whenever she felt she was falling apart again. In this way I have kept her afloat for about twelve years, and she has had no more attacks which necessitated her seclusion in an asylum. She could always manage to ward off the attacks by objectifying their contents. She told me, moreover, that when she had made such a picture she went to her books and read a chapter about some of its main features, in order to bring it into general connection with mankind, with what people know, with the collective consciousness, and then she felt right again. She said she felt adapted and she was no longer at the mercy of the collective unconscious.

227   All cases are not as accessible as that one, as you will realize. I cannot cure schizophrenia in principle. Occasionally by great good chance I can synthetize the fragments. But I do not like to do it because it is frightfully difficult work.

LECTURE IV

The Chairman (Dr. Emanuel Miller):

228   I shall not take any of Professor Jung's time away from you but will merely express my great pleasure at the opportunity of being Chairman this evening. Only I am put to a grave disadvantage: I have not been able to attend the previous lectures and therefore I do not know to what depths of the unconscious Professor Jung has already led you, but I think he is going to continue tonight the presentation of his method of dream-analysis.

Professor Jung:

229   The interpretation of a profound dream, such as our last one was, is never sufficient when it is left in the personal sphere. This dream contains an archetypal image, and that is always an indication that the psychological situation of the dreamer extends beyond the mere personal layer of the unconscious. His problem is no more entirely a personal affair, but something which touches upon the problems of mankind in general. The symbol of the monster is an indication of this. This symbol brings up the hero myth, and furthermore the association with the battle of St. Jacob, which characterizes the localization of the scene, appeals also to a general interest.

230   The ability to apply a general point of view is of great therapeutic importance. Modern therapy is not much aware of this, but in ancient medicine it was well known that the raising of the personal disease to a higher and more impersonal level had a curative effect. In ancient Egypt, for instance, when a man was bitten by a snake, the priest-physician was called in, and he took from the temple library the manuscript about the myth of Rā and his mother Isis, and recited it. Isis had made a poisonous worm and hidden it in the sand, and the god Rā had stepped on

the serpent and was bitten by it, so that he suffered terrible pain and was threatened with death. Therefore the gods caused Isis to work a spell which drew the poison out of him.[1] The idea was that the patient would be so impressed by this narrative that he would be cured. To us this sounds quite impossible. We could not imagine that the reading of a story from *Grimm's Fairy Tales,* for instance, would cure typhoid fever or pneumonia. But we only take into account our rational modern psychology. To understand the effect we have to consider the psychology of the ancient Egyptians, which was quite different. And yet those people were not so very different. Even with us certain things can work miracles; sometimes spiritual consolation or psychological influence alone can cure, or at least will help to cure an illness. And of course it is all the more so with a person on a more primitive level and with a more archaic psychology.

231 In the East a great amount of practical therapy is built upon this principle of raising the mere personal ailment into a generally valid situation, and ancient Greek medicine also worked with the same method. Of course the collective image or its application has to be in accordance with the particular psychological condition of the patient. The myth or legend arises from the archetypal material which is constellated by the disease, and the psychological effect consists in connecting the patient with the general human meaning of his particular situation. Snakebite, for instance, is an archetypal situation, therefore you find it as a motif in any number of tales. If the archetypal situation underlying the illness can be expressed in the right way the patient is cured. If no adequate expression is found, the individual is thrown back upon himself, into the isolation of being ill; he is alone and has no connection with the world. But if he is shown that his particular ailment is not his ailment only, but a general ailment—even a god's ailment—he is in the company of men and gods, and this knowledge produces a healing effect. Modern spiritual therapy uses the same principle: pain or illness is com-

---

[1] "And Isis, the great lady of enchantments, said, 'Flow on, poison, and come forth from Rā. . . . I have worked, and I make the poison to fall on the ground, for the venom hath been mastered. . . . Let Rā live, and let the poison die; and if the poison live then Rā shall die.' And similarly, a certain man, the son of a certain man, shall live, and the poison shall die." E. A. Wallis Budge, *Egyptian Literature,* I, p. 55.

pared with the sufferings of Christ, and this idea gives consolation. The individual is lifted out of his miserable loneliness and represented as undergoing a heroic meaningful fate which is ultimately good for the whole world, like the suffering and death of a god. When an ancient Egyptian was shown that he was undergoing the fate of Ra, the sun-god, he was immediately ranked with the Pharaoh, who was the son and representative of the gods, and so the ordinary man was a god himself, and this brought such a release of energy that we can understand quite well how he was lifted out of his pain. In a particular frame of mind people can endure a great deal. Primitives can walk on glowing coals and inflict the most terrible injuries on themselves under certain circumstances without feeling any pain. And so it is quite likely that an impressive and adequate symbol can mobilize the forces of the unconscious to such an extent that even the nervous system becomes affected and the body begins to react in a normal way again.

232   In the case of psychological suffering, which always isolates the individual from the herd of so-called normal people, it is also of the greatest importance to understand that the conflict is not a personal failure only, but at the same time a suffering common to all and a problem with which the whole epoch is burdened. This general point of view lifts the individual out of himself and connects him with humanity. The suffering does not even have to be a neurosis; we have the same feeling in very ordinary circumstances. If for instance you live in a well-to-do community, and you suddenly lose all your money, your natural reaction will be to think that it is terrible and shameful and that you are the only one who is such an ass as to lose his money. But if everybody loses his money it is quite another matter and you feel reconciled to it. When other people are in the same hole as I am I feel much better. If a man is lost in the desert or quite alone on a glacier, or if he is the responsible leader of a group of men in a precarious situation, he will feel terrible. But when he is a soldier in a whole battalion that is lost, he will join the rest in cheering and making jokes, and will not realize the danger. The danger is not less, but the individual feels quite differently about it in a group than when he has to face it alone.

233   Whenever archetypal figures appear in dreams, especially in the later stages of analysis, I explain to the patient that his case is

not particular and personal, but that his psychology is approaching a level which is universally human. That outlook is very important, because a neurotic feels tremendously isolated and ashamed of his neurosis. But if he knows his problem to be general and not merely personal, it makes all the difference. In the case of our dreamer, if I had been going on with the treatment I would have called the patient's attention to the fact that the motif in his last dream was a general human situation. He himself in his associations had realized the hero-dragon conflict.

234 The hero's fight with the dragon, as the symbol of a typical human situation, is a very frequent mythological motif. One of the most ancient literary expressions of it is the Babylonian Creation Myth, where the hero-god Marduk fights the dragon Tiamat. Marduk is the spring-god and Tiamat is the mother-dragon, the primordial chaos. Marduk kills her and splits her in two parts. From one half he makes the heavens and from the other he makes the earth.[2]

235 A more striking parallel to our case is the great Babylonian epos of Gilgamesh.[3] Gilgamesh is really an *arriviste par excellence,* a man of ambitious plans, like our dreamer, and a great king and hero. All the men are working for him like slaves to build a town with mighty walls. The women feel neglected and complain to the gods about their reckless tyrant. So the gods decide that something has to be done about it. Translated into psychological language this means: Gilgamesh is using his consciousness only, his head has wings and is detached from the body, and his body is going to say something about it. It will react with a neurosis, that is, by constellating a very opposite factor. How is this neurosis described in the poem? The gods decide to "call up," that is to make, a man like Gilgamesh. They create Enkidu; yet he is in some ways different. The hair of his head is long, he looks like a cave-man, and he lives with the wild animals in the plains and drinks from the water-wells of the gazelles. Gilgamesh, being normal so far, has a perfectly normal dream about the intention of the gods. He dreams that a star falls down on his back, a star like a mighty warrior, and Gilgamesh is wrestling with him but cannot shake himself free. Finally he overcomes him and puts him down at his mother's feet,

2 [*Symbols of Transformation,* pars. 375ff.]

3 R. Campbell Thompson, *The Epic of Gilgamish.*

and the mother "makes him equal" to Gilgamesh. The mother is a wise woman and interprets the dream for Gilgamesh so that he is ready to meet the danger. Enkidu is meant to fight Gilgamesh and bring him down, but Gilgamesh in a very clever way makes him his friend. He has conquered the reaction of his unconscious by cunning and will-power and he persuades his opponent that they are really friends and that they can work together. Now things are going worse than ever.

236 Although right in the beginning Enkidu has an oppressive dream, a vision of the underworld where the dead live, Gilgamesh is preparing for a great adventure. Like heroes, Gilgamesh and Enkidu start out together to overcome Humbaba, a terrible monster whom the gods have made guardian of their sanctuary on the cedar mountain. His voice roars like the tempest, and everybody who approaches the wood is overcome by weakness. Enkidu is brave and very strong, but he is nervous about the enterprise. He is depressed by bad dreams and pays a lot of attention to them, like the inferior man in ourselves whom we ridicule when that inferior part of ourselves feels superstitious about certain dates, and so on; the inferior man nevertheless continues to be nervous about certain things. Enkidu is very superstitious, he has had bad dreams on the way to the forest and has forebodings that things will go wrong. But Gilgamesh interprets the dreams optimistically. Again the reaction of the unconscious is cheated, and they succeed in bringing back Humbaba's head triumphantly to their city.

237 Now the gods decide to interfere, or rather it is a goddess, Ishtar, who tries to defeat Gilgamesh. The ultimate principle of the unconscious is the Eternal Feminine, and Ishtar, with true feminine cunning, makes wonderful promises to Gilgamesh if he will become her lover: he would be like a god and his power and wealth would increase beyond measure. But Gilgamesh does not believe a word of it, he refuses with insulting words and reproaches her for all her faithlessness and cruelty towards her lovers. Ishtar in her rage and fury persuades the gods to create an enormous bull, which descends from the heavens and devastates the country. A great fight begins, and hundreds of men are killed by the poisonous breath of the divine bull. But again Gilgamesh, with the help of Enkidu, slay him, and the victory is celebrated.

238   Ishtar, overcome by rage and pain, descends to the wall of the city, and now Enkidu himself commits an outrage against her. He curses her and throws the member of the dead bull in her face. This is the climax, and now the peripeteia sets in. Enkidu has more dreams of an ominous nature and becomes seriously ill and dies.

239   This means that the conscious separates from the unconscious altogether; the unconscious withdraws from the field, and Gilgamesh is now alone and overcome with grief. He can hardly accept the loss of his friend, but what torments him most is the fear of death. He has seen his friend die and is faced with the fact that he is mortal too. One more desire tortures him—to secure immortality. He sets out heroically to find the medicine against death, because he knows of an old man, his ancestor, who has eternal life and who lives far away in the West. So the journey to the underworld, the Nekyia, begins, and he travels to the West like the sun, through the door of the heavenly mountain. He overcomes enormous difficulties, and even the gods do not oppose his plan, although they tell him that he will seek in vain. Finally he comes to his destination and persuades the old man to tell him of the remedy. At the bottom of the sea he acquires the magic herb of immortality, the *pharmakon athanasias,* and he is bringing the herb home. Although he is tired of travelling he is full of joy because he has the wonderful medicine and does not need to be afraid of death any more. But while he is refreshing himself by bathing in a pool, a snake smells out the herb of immortality and steals it from him. After his return, he takes up new plans for the fortification of his city, but he finds no peace. He wants to know what happens to man after death and he finally succeeds in evoking Enkidu's spirit, which comes up from a hole in the earth and gives Gilgamesh very melancholy information. With this the epos ends. The ultimate victory is won by the cold-blooded animal.

240   There are quite a number of dreams recorded from antiquity with parallel motifs, and I will give you a short example of how our colleagues of old—the dream interpreters of the first century A.D.—proceeded. The story is told by Flavius Josephus in his history of the Jewish war,[4] where he also records the destruction of Jerusalem.

4 [Josephus, *The Jewish War* 2.111–115.]

241 There was a Tetrarch of Palestine by the name of Archelaos, a Roman governor who was very cruel and who, like practically all of those provincial governors, regarded his position as an opportunity to enrich himself and steal what he could lay his hands on. Therefore a delegation was sent to the emperor Augustus to complain about him. This was in the tenth year of Archelaos' governorship. About this time he had a dream in which he saw nine big ripe ears of wheat which were eaten up by hungry oxen. Archelaos was alarmed and instantly called in his court psychoanalyst. But the psychoanalyst did not know what the dream meant, or he was afraid to tell the truth and wriggled out of it. Archelaos called in other psychoanalysts for consultation, and they in the same way refused to know anything about the dream.

242 But there was a peculiar sect of people, the Essenes or Therapeutai, with more independent minds. They lived in Egypt and near the Dead Sea, and it is not impossible that John the Baptist as well as Simon Magus belonged to such circles. So as a last resort a man called Simon the Essene was sent for, and he told Archelaos: "The ears of wheat signify the years of your reign, and the oxen the change of things. The nine years are fulfilled and there will be a great change in your fate. The hungry oxen mean your destruction." In those countries such a dream-image would be perfectly understandable. The fields have to be guarded carefully against foraging cattle. There is little grass, and it is a catastrophe when during the night the oxen break through the fence into the field and trample down and eat the growing grain, so that in the morning the whole bread of a year is gone. Now for the confirmation of the interpretation. A few days later a Roman ambassador arrived to investigate, dismissed Archelaos, took all his property from him, and exiled him to Gaul.

243 Archelaos was married, and his wife, Glaphyra, also had a dream. Naturally she was impressed by what had happened to her husband. She dreamt of her first husband—Archelaos was her third marriage—who had been disposed of in a very impolite way: he had been murdered, and Archelaos was most probably the murderer. Things were a bit rough in those days. This former husband, Alexandros, appeared to her in the dream and blamed her for her conduct and told her that he was going to

take her back into his household. Simon did not interpret this dream, so the analysis is left to our discretion. The important fact is that Alexandros was dead, and that Glaphyra saw the dead husband in her dream. This, of course, in those days, meant the ghost of that person. So when he told her that he was going to take her back to his household it signified that he was going to fetch her to Hades. And indeed, a few days later she committed suicide.

244   The way the dream-interpreter proceeded with the dream of Archelaos was very sensible. He understood the dream exactly as we would, although these dreams are of a much simpler nature than most of our dreams. I have noticed that dreams are as simple or as complicated as the dreamer is himself, only they are always a little bit ahead of the dreamer's consciousness. I do not understand my own dreams any better than any of you, for they are always somewhat beyond my grasp and I have the same trouble with them as anyone who knows nothing about dream-interpretation. Knowledge is no advantage when it is a matter of one's own dreams.

245   Another interesting parallel to our case is the story you all know in the fourth chapter of the Book of Daniel.[5] When the king Nebuchadnezzar had conquered the whole of Mesopotamia and Egypt, he thought he was very great indeed because he possessed the whole known world. Then he had the typical dream of the *arriviste* who has climbed too high. He dreamed of an enormous tree growing up to heaven and casting a shadow over the whole earth. But then a watcher and holy one from heaven ordered the tree to be hewn down, and his branches cut off, and his leaves shaken, so that only his stump remained; and that he should live with the beasts and his human heart be taken from him and a beast's heart given to him.

246   Of course all the astrologers and wise men and dream-interpreters refused to understand the dream. Only Daniel, who already in the second chapter had proved himself a courageous analyst—he even had a vision of a dream which Nebuchadnezzar could not remember—understood its meaning. He warned the king to repent of his avarice and injustice, otherwise the dream would come true. But the king went on as before,

5 [Cf. *The Structure and Dynamics of the Psyche* (C.W., vol. 8), frontispiece and refs. with it.]

very proud of his power. Then a voice from heaven cursed him and repeated the prophecy of the dream. And it all happened as foretold. Nebuchadnezzar was cast out to the beasts and he became like an animal himself. He ate grass as the oxen and his body was wet with the dew of heaven, his hair grew long like eagles' feathers and his nails like birds' claws. He was turned back into a primitive man and all his conscious reason was taken away because he had misused it. He regressed even further back than the primitive and became completely inhuman; he was Humbaba, the monster, himself. All this symbolized a complete regressive degeneration of a man who has overreached himself.

247   His case, like our patient's, is the eternal problem of the successful man who has overreached himself and is contradicted by his unconscious. The contradiction is first shown in the dreams and, if not accepted, must be experienced in reality in a fatal way. These historical dreams, like all dreams, have a *compensatory function:* they are an indication—a symptom, if you prefer to say so—that the individual is at variance with unconscious conditions, that somewhere he has deviated from his natural path. Somewhere he has fallen a victim to his ambition and his ridiculous designs, and, if he does not pay attention, the gap will widen and he will fall into it, as our patient has.

248   I want to emphasize that it is not safe to interpret a dream without going into careful detail as to the context. Never apply any theory, but always ask the patient how *he* feels about his dream-images. For dreams are always about a particular problem of the individual about which he has a wrong conscious judgment. The dreams are the reaction to our conscious attitude in the same way that the body reacts when we overeat or do not eat enough or when we ill-treat it in some other way. *Dreams are the natural reaction of the self-regulating psychic system.* This formulation is the nearest I can get to a theory about the structure and function of dreams. I hold that dreams are just as manifold and unpredictable and incalculable as a person you observe during the day. If you watch an individual at one moment and then at another you will see and hear the most varied reactions, and it is exactly the same with dreams. In our dreams we are just as many-sided as in our daily life, and just as you cannot form a theory about those many aspects of the conscious personality you

cannot make a general theory of dreams. Otherwise we would have an almost divine knowledge of the human mind, which we certainly do not possess. We know precious little about it, therefore we call the things we do not know unconscious.

249   But today I am going to contradict myself and break all my rules. I am going to interpret a single dream, not one out of a series; moreover I do not know the dreamer, and further, I am not in possession of the associations. Therefore I am interpreting the dream arbitrarily. There is a justification for this procedure. If a dream is clearly formed of *personal* material you have to get the individual associations; but if the dream is chiefly a *mythological* structure—a difference which is obvious at once— then it speaks a universal language, and you or I can supply parallels with which to construct the context as well as anybody else, always provided we possess the necessary knowledge. For instance, when the dream takes up the hero-dragon conflict, everybody has something to say about it, because we have all read fairytales and legends and know something of heroes and dragons. On the collective level of dreams there is practically no difference in human beings, while there is all the difference on the personal level.

250   The main substance of the dream I am going to speak of is mythological. Here we are confronted with the question: Under what conditions does one have mythological dreams? With us they are rather rare, as our consciousness is to a great extent detached from the underlying archetypal mind. Mythological dreams therefore are felt by us as a very alien element. But this is not so with a mentality nearer to the primordial psyche. Primitives pay great attention to such dreams and call them "big dreams" in contradistinction to ordinary ones. They feel that they are important and contain a general meaning. Therefore in a primitive community the dreamer feels bound to announce a big dream to the assembly of men, and a palaver is held over it. Such dreams were also announced to the Roman Senate. There is a story of a senator's daughter in the first century B.C. who dreamed that the goddess Minerva had appeared to her and complained that the Roman people were neglecting her temple. The lady felt obliged to report the dream to the Senate, and the Senate voted a certain sum of money for the restoration of the temple. A similar case is told of Sophocles, when a precious

golden vessel had been stolen from the temple of Herakles. The god appeared to Sophocles in a dream and told him the name of the thief.[6] After the third repetition of the dream, Sophocles felt obliged to inform the Areopagus. The man in question was seized, and in the course of the investigation he confessed and brought back the vessel. These mythological or collective dreams have a character which forces people instinctively to tell them. This instinct is quite appropriate, because such dreams do not belong to the individual; they have a collective meaning. They are true in themselves in general, and in particular they are true for people in certain circumstances. That is the reason why in antiquity and in the Middle Ages dreams were held in great esteem. It was felt that they expressed a collective human truth.

251   Now I will tell you the dream. It was sent to me by a colleague of mine years ago with a few remarks about the dreamer. My colleague was an alienist at a clinic, and the patient was a distinguished young Frenchman, twenty-two years of age, highly intelligent, and vesy aesthetic. He had travelled in Spain and had come back with a depression which was diagnosed as manic-depressive insanity, depressive form. The depression was not very bad, but bad enough for him to be sent to the clinic. After six months he was released from confinement, and a few months later he committed suicide. He was no longer under the depression, which was practically cured; he committed suicide apparently in a state of calm reasoning. We shall understand from the dream why he committed suicide. This is the dream, and it occurred at the beginning of the depression:

Underneath the great cathedral of Toledo there is a cistern filled with water which has a subterranean connection with the river Tagus, which skirts the city. This cistern is a small dark room. In the water there is a huge serpent whose eyes sparkle like jewels. Near it there is a golden bowl containing a golden dagger. This dagger is the key to Toledo, and its owner commands full power over the city. The dreamer knows the serpent to be the friend and protector of B— C—, a young friend of his who is present. B— C— puts his naked foot into the serpent's jaws. The serpent licks it in a friendly way and B— C— enjoys

6 [Thus far, the dream is documented in the "Life of Sophocles," sec. 12, in *Sophoclis Fabulae,* ed. Pearson, p. xix.]

playing with the serpent; he has no fear of it because he is a child without guile. In the dream B— C— appears to be about the age of seven; he had indeed been a friend of the dreamer's early youth. Since this time, the dream says, the serpent has been forgotten and nobody dared to descend into its haunts.

252   This part is a sort of introduction, and now the real action begins.

The dreamer is alone with the serpent. He talks to it respectfully, but without fear. The serpent tells the dreamer that Spain belongs to him as he is B— C—'s friend, and asks him to give back the boy. The dreamer refuses to do this and promises instead that he himself will descend into the darkness of the cave to be the friend of the serpent. But then he changes his mind, and instead of fulfilling his promise he decides to send another friend, a Mr. S—, to the serpent. This friend is descended from the Spanish Moors, and to risk the descent into the cistern he has to recover the original courage of his race. The dreamer advises him to get the sword with the red hilt which is to be found in the weapons factory on the other bank of the Tagus. It is said to be a very ancient sword, dating back to the old Phocaeans.[7] S— gets the sword and descends into the cistern, and the dreamer tells him to pierce his left palm with the sword. S— does so, but he is not able to keep his countenance in the powerful presence of the serpent. Overcome by pain and fear, he cries out and staggers up the stairs again without having taken the dagger. Thus the dreamer cannot hold Toledo, and he could do nothing about it and had to leave his friend there as a mere wall decoration.

252a   That is the end of the dream. The original of course is in French. Now for the context. We have certain hints as to these friends. B— C— is a friend of the dreamer's early youth, a little bit older than himself, and he projected everything that was wonderful and charming into this boy and made him a sort of hero. But he lost sight of him later; perhaps the boy died. S— is a friend of more recent date. He is said to be descended from the Spanish Moors. I do not know him personally, but I know his family. It is a very old and honourable family from the South of

7 [The people of ancient Phocaea, on the western coast of Asia Minor, founded Massilia (Marseilles) and colonies on the east coast of Spain.]

France, and the name might easily be a Moorish name. The dreamer knew this legend about the family of S—.

253   As I told you, the dreamer had recently been to Spain and of course had seen Toledo, and he had the dream after he got back and had been taken to the clinic. He was in a bad state, practically in despair, and he could not help telling the dream to his doctor. My colleague did not know what to do with it, but he felt an urge to send me the dream because he felt it to be very important. But at the time I received the dream I could not understand it. Nevertheless I had the feeling that if I had known something more about such dreams, and if I could have handled the case myself, I might have been able to help the young man and his suicide might not have occurred. Since then I have seen many cases of a similar nature. Often one can turn a difficult corner by a real understanding of dreams like this one. With such a sensitive, refined individual who had studied the history of art and was an unusually artistic and intelligent person, one must be exceedingly careful. Banalities are no use in such a case; one has to be serious and enter into the real material.

253a   We make no mistake when we assume that the dreamer has picked out Toledo for a particular reason—both as the object of his trip and of his dream; and the dream brings up material which practically everybody would have who had seen Toledo with the same mental disposition, the same education and refinement of aesthetic perception and knowledge. Toledo is an extremely impressive city. It contains one of the most marvellous Gothic cathedrals of the world. It is a place with an immensely old tradition; it is the old Roman Toletum, and for centuries has been the seat of the Cardinal Archbishop and Primate of Spain. From the sixth to the eighth century it was the capital of the Visigoths; from the eighth to the eleventh it was a provincial capital of the Moorish kingdom; and from the eleventh to the sixteenth century it was the capital of Castile. The cathedral of Toledo, being such an impressive and beautiful building, naturally suggests all that it represents: the greatness, the power, the splendour, and the mystery of medieval Christianity, which found its essential expression in the Church. Therefore the cathedral is the embodiment, the incarnation, of the spiritual kingdom, for in the Middle Ages the world was ruled by the Emperor *and* by God. So the cathedral expresses the Christian philosophy or *Weltanschauung* of the Middle Ages.

254   The dream says that underneath the cathedral there is a mysterious place, which in reality is not in tune with a Christian church. What is beneath a cathedral of that age? There is always the so-called under-church or crypt. You have probably seen the great crypt at Chartres; it gives a very good idea of the mysterious character of a crypt. The crypt at Chartres was previously an old sanctuary with a well, where the worship of a virgin was celebrated—not of the Virgin Mary, as is done now—but of a Celtic goddess. Under every Christian church of the Middle Ages there is a secret place where in old times the mysteries were celebrated. What we now call the sacraments of the Church were the *mysteria* of early Christianity. In Provençal the crypt is called *le musset,* which means a secret; the word perhaps originates from *mysteria* and could mean mystery-place. In Aosta, where they speak a Provençal dialect, there is a *musset* under the cathedral.

255   The crypt is probably taken over from the cult of Mithras. In Mithraism the main religious ceremony took place in a vault half sunk into the earth, and the community remained separated in the main church above. There were peepholes so that they could see and hear the priests and the elect ones chanting and celebrating their rites below, but they were not admitted to them. That was a privilege for the initiates. In the Christian church the separation of the baptistry from the main body of the building derives from the same idea, for baptism as well as the communion were mysteria of which one could not speak directly. One had to use a sort of allegorical allusion so as not to betray the secrets. The mystery also attached to the name of Christ, which therefore was not allowed to be mentioned; instead, he was referred to by the name of Ichthys, the Fish. You have probably seen reproductions of very early Christian paintings where Christ appears as the Fish. This secrecy connected with the holy name is probably the reason why the name of Christ is not mentioned in an early Christian document of about A.D. 140 known as *The Shepherd* of Hermas,[8] which was an important part of the body of Christian literature recognized

---

[8] [Cf. *Psychological Types*, ch. V, 4a.]

by the Church till about the fifth century. The writer of this book of visions, Hermas, is supposed to have been the brother of the Roman bishop Pius. The spiritual teacher who appears to Hermas is called the Poimen, the Shepherd, and not the Christ.

256   The idea of the crypt or mystery-place leads us to something below the Christian *Weltanschauung*, something older than Christianity, like the pagan well below the cathedral at Chartres, or like an antique cave inhabited by a serpent. The well with the serpent is of course not an actual fact which the dreamer saw when he travelled in Spain. This dream-image is not an individual experience and can therefore only be paralleled by archaeological and mythological knowledge. I have to give you a certain amount of that parallelism so that you can see in what context or tissue such a symbolical arrangement appears when looked at in the light of comparative research work. You know that every church still has its baptismal font. This was originally the *piscina*, the pond, in which the initiates were bathed or symbolically drowned. After a figurative death in the baptismal bath they came out transformed *quasi modo geniti,* as reborn ones. So we can assume that the crypt or baptismal font has the meaning of a place of terror and death and also of rebirth, a place where dark initiations take place.

257   The serpent in the cave is an image which often occurs in antiquity. It is important to realize that in classical antiquity, as in other civilizations, the serpent not only was an animal that aroused fear and represented danger, but also signified healing. Therefore Asklepios, the god of physicians, is connected with the serpent; you all know his emblem which is still in use. In the temples of Asklepios, the Asklepieia, which were the ancient clinics, there was a hole in the ground, covered by a stone, and in that hole lived the sacred serpent. There was a slot in the stone through which the people who came to the place of healing threw down the fee for the doctors. The snake was at the same time the cashier of the clinic and collector of gifts that were thrown down into its cave. During the great pestilence in the time of Diocletian the famous serpent of the Asklepieion at Epidaurus was brought to Rome as an antidote to the epidemic. It represented the god himself.

258   The serpent is not only the god of healing; it also has the quality of wisdom and prophecy. The fountain of Castalia at

Delphi was originally inhabited by a python. Apollo fought and overcame the python, and from that time Delphi was the seat of the famous oracle and Apollo its god, until he left half his powers to Dionysus, who later came in from the East. In the underworld, where the spirits of the dead live, snakes and water are always together, as we can read in Aristophanes' *The Frogs*. The serpent in legend is often replaced by the dragon; the Latin *draco* simply means snake. A particularly suggestive parallel to our dream symbol is a Christian legend of the fifth century about St. Sylvester:[9] there was a terrible dragon in a cave under the Tarpeian rock in Rome to whom virgins were sacrificed. Another legend says that the dragon was not a real one but artificial, and that a monk went down to prove it was not real and when he got down to the cave he found that the dragon had a sword in his mouth and his eyes consisted of sparkling jewels.

259   Very often these caves, like the cave of Castalia, contain springs. These springs played a very important role in the cult of Mithras, from which many elements of the early Church originated. Porphyry relates that Zoroaster, the founder of the Persian religion, dedicated to Mithras a cave containing many springs. Those of you who have been to Germany and seen the Saalburg near Frankfurt will have noticed the spring near the grotto of Mithras. The cult of Mithras is always connected with a spring. There is a beautiful Mithraeum in Provence which has a large piscina with wonderful crystal-clear water, and in the background a rock on which is carved the Mithras Tauroktonos —the bull-killing Mithras. These sanctuaries were always a great scandal to the early Christians. They hated all these natural arrangements because they were no friends of nature. In Rome a Mithraeum has been discovered ten feet below the surface of the Church of San Clemente. It is still in good condition but filled with water, and when it is pumped out it fills again. It is always under water because it adjoins a spring which floods the interior. The spring has never been found. We know of other religious ideas in antiquity, for instance of the Orphic cult, which always associate the underworld with water.

260   This material will give you an idea that the serpent in the cave full of water is an image that was generally known and

9 [*Symbols of Transformation*, pars. 572f.]

117

played a great role in antiquity. As you have noticed, I have chosen all my examples exclusively from antiquity; I could have chosen other parallels from other civilizations, and you would find it was the same. The water in the depths represents the unconscious. In the depths as a rule is a treasure guarded by a serpent or a dragon; in our dream the treasure is the golden bowl with the dagger in it. In order to recover the treasure the dragon has to be overcome. The treasure is of a very mysterious nature. It is connected with the serpent in a strange way; the peculiar nature of the serpent denotes the character of the treasure as though the two things were one. Often there is a golden snake with the treasure. Gold is something that everyone is seeking, so we could say that it looks as if the serpent himself were the great treasure, the source of immense power. In early Greek myths, for instance, the dweller in the cave is a hero, such as Cecrops, the founder of Athens. Above he is half man and half woman, a hermaphrodite, but the lower part of his body is a serpent; he is clearly a monster. The same is said of Erechtheus, another mythical king of Athens.

261   That prepares us a little for understanding the golden bowl and the dagger in our dream. If you have seen Wagner's *Parsifal* you know that the bowl corresponds to the Grail and the dagger to the spear and that the two belong together; they are the male and the female principle which form the union of opposites. The cave or underworld represents a layer of the unconscious where there is no discrimination at all, not even a distinction between the male and the female, which is the first differentiation primitives make. They distinguish objects in this way, as we still do occasionally. Some keys, for instance, have a hole in the front, and some are solid. They are often called male and female keys. You know the Italian tiled roofs. The convex tiles are placed above and the concave ones underneath. The upper ones are called monks and the under ones the nuns. This is not an indecent joke to the Italians, but the quintessence of discrimination.

262   When the unconscious brings together the male and the female, things become utterly indistinguishable and we cannot say any more whether they are male or female, just as Cecrops came from such a mythical distance that one could not say whether he was man or woman, human or serpent. So we see that the bot-

tom of the cistern in our dream is characterized by a complete union of opposites. This is the primordial condition of things, and at the same time a most ideal achievement, because it is the union of elements eternally opposed. Conflict has come to rest, and everything is still or once again in the original state of indistinguishable harmony. You find the same idea in ancient Chinese philosophy. The ideal condition is named Tao, and it consists of the complete harmony between heaven and earth. Figure 13 represents the symbol for Tao. On one side it is white with a

FIG. 13. Tao

black spot, and on the other it is black with a white spot. The white side is the hot, dry, fiery principle, the south; the black side is the cold, humid, dark principle, the north. The condition of Tao is the beginning of the world where nothing has yet begun—and it is also the condition to be achieved by the attitude of superior wisdom. The idea of the union of the two opposite principles, of male and female, is an archetypal image. I once had a very nice example of its still-living primitive form. When on military duty with the army during the war, I was with the mountain artillery, and the soldiers had to dig a deep hole for the position of a heavy gun. The soil was very refractory, and they cursed a good deal while they were digging up the heavy blocks. I was sitting hidden behind a rock, smoking my pipe and listening to what they said. One man said: "Now, damn it all, we have dug into the depths of this blooming old valley where the old lake-dwellers lived and where father and mother are still sleeping together." That is the same idea, very naïvely expressed. A Negro myth says that the primordial man and the primordial woman were sleeping together in the calabash; they were quite unconscious until they found they were torn asunder and what was in between was the son. Man was in between, and

119

from that time they were separated, and then they knew each other. The original condition of absolute unconsciousness is expressed as a completely restful condition where nothing happens.

263 When the dreamer comes to these symbols he reaches the layer of complete unconsciousness, which is represented as the greatest treasure. It is the central motif in Wagner's *Parsifal* that the spear should be restored to the Grail because they belong eternally together. This union is a symbol of complete fulfilment—eternity before and after the creation of the world, a dormant condition. That is probably the thing which the desire of man is seeking. That is why he ventures into the cave of the dragon, to find that condition where consciousness and the unconscious are so completely united that he is neither conscious nor unconscious. Whenever the two are too much separated, consciousness seeks to unite them again by going down into the depths where they once were one. Thus you find in Tantric Yoga or Kundalini Yoga an attempt to reach the condition where Shiva is in eternal union with Shakti. Shiva is the eternally unextended point, and he is encircled by the female principle, Shakti, in the form of a serpent.

264 I could give you many more instances of this idea. It played a great role in the secret tradition of the Middle Ages. In medieval alchemical texts there are pictures of the process of the union of Sol and Luna, the male and the female principle. We have traces of an analogous symbolism in Christian reports about the ancient mysteries. There is a report by a Bishop Asterios about Eleusis, and it says that every year the priest made the *katabasis* or descent into the cave. And the priest of Apollo and the priestess of Demeter, the earth mother, celebrated the *hierosgamos*, the sacred nuptials, for the fertilization of the earth. This is a Christian statement which is not substantiated. The initiates of the Eleusinian mysteries were sworn to the strictest secrecy; if they betrayed anything, they were punished with death. So we have practically no knowledge of their rites. We know, on the other hand, that during the mysteries of Demeter certain obscenities took place because they were thought good for the fertility of the earth. The distinguished ladies of Athens assembled, with the priestess of Demeter presiding. They had a good meal

and plenty of wine and afterwards performed the rite of the *aischrologia*. That is, they had to tell indecent jokes. This was considered a religious duty because it was good for the fertility of the next season.[10] A similar rite took place in Bubastis in Egypt at the time of the Isis mysteries. The inhabitants of the villages on the upper Nile came down in parties, and the women on the barges used to expose themselves to the women on the banks of the Nile. It was probably done for the same reason as the *aischrologia*, to ensure the fertility of the earth. You can read about it in Herodotus.[11] In southern Germany as late as the nineteenth century, in order to increase the fertility of the soil, the peasant used to take his wife to his fields and have intercourse with her in a furrow. This is called sympathetic magic.

265   The bowl is a vessel that receives or contains, and is therefore female. It is a symbol of the body which contains the anima, the breath and liquid of life, while the dagger has piercing, penetrating qualities and is therefore male. It cuts, it discriminates and divides, and so is a symbol of the masculine Logos principle.

266   In our dream the dagger is said to be the key to Toledo. The idea of the key is often associated with the mysteries in the cave. In the cult of Mithras there is a peculiar kind of god, the key god Aion, whose presence could not be explained; but I think it is quite understandable. He is represented with the winged body of a man and the head of a lion, and he is encoiled by a snake which rises up over his head.[12] You have a figure of him in the British Museum. He is Infinite Time and Long Duration; he is the supreme god of the Mithraic hierarchy and creates and destroys all things, the *durée créatrice* of Bergson. He is a sun-god. Leo is the zodiacal sign where the sun dwells in summer, while

---

[10] [Cf. *Psychology and Alchemy*, par. 105, n. 35, citing Foucart, *Les Mystères d'Eleusis*. According to classicists, Asterios' report referred to rituals of Demeter celebrated at Alexandria in which a priest (not of Apollo) and a priestess performed the *hierosgamos*. The narration of *aischrologia* to please Demeter occurred during the Thesmophoria, an autumn festival in her honour, the Stenia, celebrating her return, and the mid-winter Haloa, sacred to Demeter and Dionysus. Cf. Harrison, *Prolegomena*, ch. IV, esp. pp. 136, 148f.]

[11] [Herodotus 2.60 (Penguin edn., pp. 125f.).]

[12] [See *Aion* (C.W., vol. 9, ii), frontispiece, and *Symbols of Transformation*, index, s.v.]

the snake symbolizes the winter or wet time. So Aion, the lion-headed god with the snake round his body, again represents the union of opposites, light and darkness, male and female, creation and destruction. The god is represented as having his arms crossed and holding a key in each hand. He is the spiritual father of St. Peter, for he too holds the keys. The keys which Aion is holding are the keys to the past and future.

267   The ancient mystery cults are always connected with psychopompic deities. Some of these deities are equipped with the keys to the underworld, because as the guardians of the door they watch over the descent of the initiates into the darkness and are the leaders into the mysteries. Hecate is one of them.

268   In our dream the key is the key to the city of Toledo, so we have to consider the symbolic meaning of Toledo and of the city. As the old capital of Spain, Toledo was a very strong fortification and the very ideal of a feudal city, a refuge and stronghold which could not easily be touched from outside. The city represents a totality, closed in upon itself, a power which cannot be destroyed, which has existed for centuries and will exist for many centuries more. Therefore the city symbolizes the totality of man, an attitude of wholeness which cannot be dissolved.

269   The city as a synonym for the self, for psychic totality, is an old and well-known image. We read for instance in the Oxyrhynchus sayings of Jesus:[13] "A city built upon the top of a high hill and stablished, can neither fall nor be hid." And: "Strive therefore to know yourselves, and ye shall be aware that ye are the sons of the almighty Father; and ye shall know that ye are in the city of God and ye are the city." There is a Coptic treatise in the Codex Brucianus in which we find the idea of the Monogenes, or only son of God, who is also the Anthropos, Man.[14] He is called the city with the four gates. The city with the four gates symbolizes the idea of totality; it is the individual who possesses the four gates to the world, the four psychological functions, and so is contained in the self. The city with the four gates is his indestructible wholeness—consciousness and the unconscious united.

13 *New Sayings of Jesus and Fragment of a Lost Gospel,* ed. by Grenfell and Hunt [pp. 36 and 15].
14 [It is MS. Bruce 96, Bodleian Library, Oxford. Cf. *Psychology and Alchemy,* par. 138f.]

270   So these depths, that layer of utter unconsciousness in our dream, contain at the same time the key to individual completeness and wholeness, in other words to healing. The meaning of "whole" or "wholeness" is to make holy or to heal. The descent into the depths will bring healing. It is the way to the total being, to the treasure which suffering mankind is forever seeking, which is hidden in the place guarded by terrible danger. This is the place of primordial unconsciousness and at the same time the place of healing and redemption, because it contains the jewel of wholeness. It is the cave where the dragon of chaos lives and it is also the indestructible city, the magic circle or *temenos*, the sacred precinct where all the split-off parts of the personality are united.

271   The use of a magic circle or mandala, as it is called in the East, for healing purposes is an archetypal idea. When a man is ill the Pueblo Indians of New Mexico make a sand-painting of a mandala with four gates. In the centre of it they build the so-called sweat-house or medicine-lodge, where the patient has to undergo the sweat-cure. On the floor of the medicine-lodge is painted another magic circle—being thus placed in the centre of the big mandala—and in the midst of it is the bowl with the healing water. The water symbolizes the entrance to the underworld. The healing process in this ceremony is clearly analogous to the symbolism which we find in the collective unconscious. It is an individuation process, an identification with the totality of the personality, with the self. In Christian symbolism the totality is Christ, and the healing process consists of the *imitatio Christi*. The four gates are replaced by the four arms of the cross.

272   The serpent in the cave in our dream is the friend of B— C—, the hero of the dreamer's early days, into whom he projected everything he wanted to become and all the virtues to which he was aspiring. That young friend is at peace with the serpent. He is a child without guile, he is innocent and knows as yet of no conflict. Therefore he has the key to Spain and the power over the four gates.[15]

---

15 [For further analysis of this dream, from the Basel Seminar (supra, p. 3), see Jung's *L'Homme à la découverte de son âme*, pp. 214ff.]

Discussion

Dr. David Yellowlees:

273   I need hardly mention that I shall not attempt to discuss anything that has been said tonight. We are all glad Professor Jung has given us such an extraordinarily fascinating account of his own views, rather than spend time on controversial matters. But I think some of us would be grateful if he would recognize that we approach psychology and psychotherapy along lines not exclusively Freudian perhaps, but in accordance with certain fundamental principles with which Freud's name is associated, though he may not have originated them. We are very grateful that Professor Jung has given us what we believe to be a wider view. Some of us prefer that view, and perhaps the Freudians would be able to tell us why. But the question was raised the other night as to the relationship between the concept of the unconscious which Professor Jung has been laying before us and Freud's concept of it, and I think if Professor Jung will be so good he could help us a little in that direction. I know quite well I may be misinterpreting him, but the impression I got on Tuesday night was almost as if he had said that he was dealing with facts and Freud with theories. He knows as well as I do that this bald statement really requires some amplification and I wish he could tell us, for example, what we ought to do from a therapeutic point of view when faced with a patient who produces spontaneously what I would call Freudian material, and how far we should regard Freudian theories simply as theories in view of the evidence which can be proved by such material as infantile fixation of the libido—oral, anal, phallic, and so on. If Professor Jung would say a little to give us some kind of correlation we would be very grateful.

Professor Jung:

274   I told you at the beginning that I do not want to be critical. I just want to give you a point of view of my own, of how I envisage psychological material, and I suppose that when you have heard what I have to contribute you will be able to make up your minds about these questions, and how much of Freud, how much of Adler, or myself, or I do not know whom, you will want

to follow. If you want me to elucidate the question of the connection with Freud, I am quite glad to do it. I started out entirely on Freud's lines. I was even considered to be his best disciple. I was on excellent terms with him until I had the idea that certain things are symbolical. Freud would not agree to this, and he identified his method with the theory and the theory with the method. That is impossible, you cannot identify a method with science. I said that in view of these things I could not keep on publishing the *Jahrbuch*[15] and I withdrew.

275   But I am perfectly well aware of the merits of Freud and I do not want to diminish them. I know that what Freud says agrees with many people, and I assume that these people have exactly the kind of psychology that he describes. Adler, who has entirely different views, also has a large following, and I am convinced that many people have an Adlerian psychology. I too have a following—not so large as Freud's—and it consists presumably of people who have my psychology. I consider my contribution to psychology to be my subjective confession. It is my personal psychology, my prejudice that I see psychological facts as I do. I admit that I see things in such and such a way. But I expect Freud and Adler to do the same and confess that their ideas are their subjective point of view. So far as we admit our personal prejudice, we are really contributing towards an objective psychology. We cannot help being prejudiced by our ancestors, who want to look at things in a certain way, and so we instinctively have certain points of view. It would be neurotic if I saw things in another way than my instinct tells me to do; my snake, as the primitives say, would be all against me. When Freud said certain things, my snake did not agree. And I take the route that my snake prescribes, because that is good for me. But I have patients with whom I have to make a Freudian analysis and go into all the details which Freud has correctly described. I have other cases that force me to an Adlerian point of view, because they have a power complex. People who have the capacity to adapt and are successful are more inclined to have a Freudian psychology, because a man in that position is looking for the gratification of his desires, while the man who has not been suc-

15 [*Jahrbuch für psychoanalytische und psychopathologische Forschungen* (Leipzig and Vienna); Jung withdrew from the editorship in 1913.]

cessful has no time to think about desires. He has only one desire—to succeed, and he will have an Adlerian psychology, because a man who always falls into the second place will develop a power complex.

276   I have no power complex in that sense because I have been fairly successful and in nearly every respect I have been able to adapt. If the whole world disagrees with me it is perfectly indifferent to me. I have a perfectly good place in Switzerland, I enjoy myself, and if nobody enjoys my books I enjoy them. I know nothing better than being in my library, and if I make discoveries in my books, that is wonderful. I cannot say I have a Freudian psychology because I never had such difficulties in relation to desires. As a boy I lived in the country and took things very naturally, and the natural and unnatural things of which Freud speaks were not interesting to me. To talk of an incest complex just bores me to tears. But I know exactly how I could make myself neurotic: if I said or believed something that is not myself. I say what I see, and if somebody agrees with me it pleases me and if nobody agrees it is indifferent to me. I can join neither the Adlerian nor the Freudian confession. I can agree only with the Jungian confession because I see things that way even if there is not a single person on earth who shares my views. The only thing I hope for is to give you some interesting ideas and let you see how I tackle things.

277   It is always interesting to me to see a craftsman at work. His skill makes the charm of a craft. Psychotherapy is a craft and I deal in my individual way—a very humble way with nothing particular to show—with the things I have to do. Not that I believe for a moment that I am absolutely right. Nobody is absolutely right in psychological matters. Never forget that in psychology the *means* by which you judge and observe the psyche is the *psyche* itself. Have you ever heard of a hammer beating itself? In psychology the observer is the observed. The psyche is not only the *object* but also the *subject* of our science. So you see, it is a vicious circle and we have to be very modest. The best we can expect in psychology is that everybody puts his cards on the table and admits: "I handle things in such and such a way, and this is how I see them." Then we can compare notes.

278   I have always compared notes with Freud and Adler. Three books have been written by pupils of mine who tried to give a

synopsis of the three points of view.[16] You have never heard this from the other side. That is our Swiss temperament. We are liberal and we try to see things side by side, together. From my point of view the best thing is to say that obviously there are thousands of people who have a Freudian psychology and thousands who have an Adlerian psychology. Some seek gratification of desire and some others fulfilment of power and yet others want to see the world as it is and leave things in peace. We do not want to change anything. The world is good as it is.

279   There are many different psychologies in existence. A certain American university, year after year, issues a volume of the psychologies of 1934, 1935, and so on. There is a total chaos in psychology, so do not be so frightfully serious about psychological theories. Psychology is not a religious creed but a point of view, and when we are human about it we may be able to understand each other. I admit that some people have sexual trouble and others have other troubles. I have chiefly other troubles. You now have an idea of how I look at things. My problem is to wrestle with the big monster of the historical past, the great snake of the centuries, the burden of the human mind, the problem of Christianity. It would be so much simpler if I knew nothing; but I know too much, through my ancestors and my own education. Other people are not worried by such problems, they do not care about the historical burdens Christianity has heaped upon us. But there are people who are concerned with the great battle between the present and the past or the future. It is a tremendous human problem. Certain people make history and others build a little house in the suburbs. Mussolini's case is not settled by saying he has a power complex. He is concerned with politics, and that is his life and death. The world is huge and there is not one theory only to explain everything.

280   To Freud the unconscious is chiefly a receptacle for things repressed. He looks at it from the corner of the nursery. To me it is a vast historical storehouse. I acknowledge I have a nursery too, but it is small in comparison with the vast spaces of history which were more interesting to me from childhood than the nursery. There are many people like myself, I am optimistic in that respect. Once I thought there were no people like myself; I

16 W. M. Kranefeldt, *Secret Ways of the Mind;* G. R. Heyer, *The Organism of the Mind;* Gerhard Adler, *Entdeckung der Seele.*

was afraid it was megalomania to think as I did. Then I found many people who fitted in with my point of view, and I was satisfied that I represented perhaps a minority of people whose basic psychological facts are expressed more or less happily by my formulation, and when you get these people under analysis you will find they do not agree with Freud's or Adler's point of view, but with mine. I have been reproached for my naïveté. When I am not sure about a patient I give him books by Freud and Adler and say, "Make your choice," in the hope that we are going on the right track. Sometimes we are on the wrong track. As a rule, people who have reached a certain maturity and who are philosophically minded and fairly successful in the world and not too neurotic, agree with my point of view. But you must not conclude from what I present to you that I always lay my cards on the table and tell the patient all I mention here. Time would not allow me to go into all those details of interpretation. But a few cases need to acquire a great amount of knowledge and are grateful when they see a way to enlarge their point of view.

281　　　I cannot say where I could find common ground with Freud when he calls a certain part of the unconscious the Id. Why give it such a funny name? It is the unconscious and that is something we do not know. Why call it the Id? Of course the difference of temperament produces a different outlook. I never could bring myself to be so frightfully interested in these sex cases. They do exist, there are people with a neurotic sex life and you have to talk sex stuff with them until they get sick of it and you get out of that boredom. Naturally, with my temperamental attitude, I hope to goodness we shall get through with the stuff as quickly as possible. It is neurotic stuff and no reasonable normal person talks of it for any length of time. It is not natural to dwell on such matters. Primitives are very reticent about them. They allude to sexual intercourse by a word that is equivalent to "hush." Sexual things are taboo to them, as they really are to us if we are natural. But taboo things and places are always apt to be the receptacle for all sorts of projections. And so very often the real problem is not to be found there at all. Many people make unnecessary difficulties about sex when their actual troubles are of quite a different nature.

282　　　Once a young man came to me with a compulsion neurosis.

He brought me a manuscript of his of a hundred and forty pages, giving a complete Freudian analysis of his case. It was quite perfect according to the rules, it could have been published in the *Jahrbuch*. He said: "Will you read this and tell me why I am not cured although I made a complete psychoanalysis?" I said: "So you have, and I do not understand it either. You ought to be cured according to all the rules of the art, but when you say you are not cured I have to believe you." He repeated: "Why am I not cured, having a complete insight into the structure of my neurosis?" I said: "I cannot criticize your thesis. The whole thing is marvellously well demonstrated. There remains only one, perhaps quite foolish, question: you do not mention where you come from and who your parents are. You say you spent last winter on the Riviera and the summer in St. Moritz. Were you very careful in the choice of your parents?" "Not at all." "You have an excellent business and are making a good deal of money?" "No, I cannot make money." "Then you have a big fortune from an uncle?" "No." "Then where does the money come from?" He replied: "I have a certain arrangement. I have a friend who gives me the money." I said: "It must be a wonderful friend," and he replied, "It is a woman." She was much older than himself, aged thirty-six, a teacher in an elementary school with a small salary, who, as an elderly spinster, fell in love with the fellow who was twenty-eight. She lived on bread and milk so that he could spend his winter on the Riviera and his summer in St. Moritz. I said: "And you ask why you are ill!" He said: "Oh, you have a moralistic point of view; that is not scientific." I said: "The money in your pocket is the money of the woman you cheat." He said, "No, we agreed upon it. I had a serious talk with her and it is not a matter for discussion that I get the money from her." I said: "You are pretending to yourself that it is not her money, but you live by it, and that is immoral. That is the cause of your compulsion neurosis. It is a compensation and a punishment for an immoral attitude." An utterly unscientific point of view, of course, but it is my conviction that he deserves his compulsion neurosis and will have it to the last day of his life if he behaves like a pig.

Dr. T. A. Ross:

283   Did not that come out in the analysis?

Professor Jung:

284   He went right away like a god and thought: "Dr. Jung is only a moralist, not a scientist. Anybody else would have been impressed by the interesting case instead of looking for simple things." He commits a crime and steals the savings of a lifetime from an honest woman in order to be able to have a good time. That fellow belongs in gaol, and his compulsion neurosis provides it for him all right.

Dr. P. W. L. Camps:

285   I am a humble general practitioner, not a psychologist, and may be labelled as a suburban villa. I am an outsider in this place. The first night I thought I had no right to be here; the second night I was here again; the third night I was glad to be here; and the fourth night I am in a maze of mythology.

286   I would like to ask something about last night. We were sent away with the idea that perfection was most undesirable and completion the end and aim of existence. I slept soundly last night but I felt that I had had an ethical shock. Perhaps I am not gifted with much intellect and it was an intellectual shock too. Professor Jung declares himself a determinist or fatalist. After he had analysed a young man who went away disappointed and then went to bits, Professor Jung felt it was only right that he should go to bits. You as psychologists, I take it, are endeavouring to cure people, and you have a purpose in life, not merely to enjoy your interests, whether it be mythology or the study of human nature. You want to get at the bottom of human nature and try to build it up to something better.

287   I listened with the greatest interest to Professor Jung's simple English terms and rejoiced in them. I have been confounded with all this new terminology. To hear of our sensation and thinking and feeling and intuition—to which possibly an X may be added for something else—was most illuminating to me as an ordinary individual.

288   But I feel that we did not hear where the conscious or rather where the unconscious of the child develops. I fear that we did not hear enough about children. I should like to ask Professor Jung where the unconscious in the child does become the conscious.

289   I should also like to know whether we are not misled some-

what by this multitude of diagrams, barriers, Egos, and Ids, and other things I have seen portrayed; whether we could not improve on these diagrams by having a gradation of stages.

290   As Professor Jung has pointed out, we have inherited faces and eyes and ears and there are a multitude of faces and in psychology there are a multitude of types also. Is it not reasonable to suppose that there is an enormous possibility of varieties planted on that inheritance, that they are a sort of mesh, a sieve as it were, that will receive impressions and select them in the unconscious years of early life and reach through into consciousness later? I should like to ask Professor Jung whether these thoughts have crossed the mind of an eminent psychologist such as he is—the very greatest psychologist in my view—tonight?

Professor Jung:

291   After that severe reproach for immorality I owe an explanation of my cynical remarks of yesterday. I am not as bad as all that. I naturally try to do my best for my patients, but in psychology it is very important that the doctor should not strive to heal at all costs. One has to be exceedingly careful not to impose one's own will and conviction on the patient. We have to give him a certain amount of freedom. You can't wrest people away from their fate, just as in medicine you cannot cure a patient if nature means him to die. Sometimes it is really a question whether you are allowed to rescue a man from the fate he must undergo for the sake of his further development. You cannot save certain people from committing terrible nonsense because it is in their grain. If I take it away they have no merit. We only gain merit and psychological development by accepting ourselves as we are and by being serious enough to live the lives we are trusted with. Our sins and errors and mistakes are necessary to us, otherwise we are deprived of the most precious incentives to development. When a man goes away, having heard something which might have changed his mind, and does not pay attention, I do not call him back. You may accuse me of being unchristian, but I do not care. I am on the side of nature. The old Chinese Book of Wisdom says: "The Master says it once." He does not run after people, it is no good. Those who are meant to hear will understand, and those who are not meant to understand will not hear.

292   I was under the impression that my audience consisted chiefly of psychotherapists. If I had known that medical men were present I would have expressed myself more civilly. But psychotherapists will understand. Freud—to quote the master's own words—says it is not good to try to cure at all costs. He often repeated that to me, and he is right.

293   Psychological truths are two-edged, and whatever I say can be used in such a way that it can work the greatest evil, the greatest devastation and nonsense. There is not one statement I have made which has not been twisted into its opposite. So I do not insist on any statement. You can take it, but if you do not take it, all right. You may perhaps blame me for that, but I trust that there is a will to live in everybody which will help them to choose the thing that is right for them. When I am treating a man I must be exceedingly careful not to knock him down with my views or my personality, because he has to fight his lonely fight through life and he must be able to trust in his perhaps very incomplete armour and in his own perhaps very imperfect aim. When I say, "That is not good and should be better," I deprive him of courage. He must plough his field with a plough that is not good perhaps; mine may be better, but what good is it to him? He has not got my plough, I have it and he cannot borrow it; he must use his own perhaps very incomplete tools and has to work with his own inherited capacities, whatever they are. I help him of course, I may say for instance: "Your thinking is perfectly good, but perhaps in another respect you could improve." If he does not want to hear it, I shall not insist because I do not want to make him deviate.

Dr. Marion Mackenzie:

294   In the same way that the rich young man was not called back but went away sorrowful?

Professor Jung:

295   Yes, it is the same technique. If I were to say to a man, "You should not go away," he would never come back. I have to say, "Have your own way." Then he will trust me.

296   As to the question about children, there has been in the last decades such a noise about children that I often scratch my head at a meeting and say: "Are they all midwives and nurses?" Does not the world consist chiefly of parents and grandparents? The

adults have the problems. Leave the poor children alone. I get the mother by the ears and not the child. The parents make the neuroses of children.

297 It is certainly interesting to make researches into the development of consciousness. The beginning of consciousness is a fluid condition, and you cannot say when the child has become really conscious and when it has not yet. But that belongs to an entirely different chapter: the psychology of the ages. There is a psychology of childhood, which apparently consists in the psychology of the respective parents; a psychology from infancy to puberty; a psychology of puberty, of the young man, of the adult man of thirty-five, of the man in the second half of life, of the man in old age. That is a science in itself, and I could not possibly bring in all that too. I have a most difficult time as it is to illustrate one single dream. Science is large. It is as if you expected a physicist, when he talks of the theory of light, to elucidate at the same time the whole of mechanical physics. It is simply not possible. Psychology is not an introductory course for nurses; it is a very serious science and consists of a heap of knowledge, so you should not expect too much from me. I am doing my level best to grapple with dreams and to tell you something about them, and I naturally cannot fulfil all expectations.

298 As to the question about perfection: to strive for perfection is a high ideal. But I say: "Fulfil something you are able to fulfil rather than run after what you will never achieve." Nobody is perfect. Remember the saying: "None is good but God alone," [17] and nobody can be. It is an illusion. We can modestly strive to fulfil ourselves and to be as complete human beings as possible, and that will give us trouble enough.

Dr. Eric B. Strauss:

299 Does Professor Jung intend to publish the reasons which led him to identify certain archetypal symbols with physiological processes?

Professor Jung:

300 The case you refer to was submitted to me by Dr. Davie, and afterwards he published it without my knowledge.[18] I do not

17 [Luke 18:19.]
18 [See supra, par. 135, n. 15.]

wish to say more about this correlation because I do not yet feel on very safe ground. Questions of differential diagnosis between organic disease and psychological symbols are very difficult, and I prefer not to say anything about it for the time being.

Dr. Strauss:

301   But your diagnosis was made from the facts of the dream?

Professor Jung:

302   Yes, because the organic trouble disturbed the mental functioning. There was a serious depression and presumably a profound disturbance of the sympathetic system.

Dr. H. Crichton-Miller:

303   Tomorrow is the last seminar, and there is a point that interests us that has not been referred to. That is the difficult problem of transference. I wonder if Professor Jung would think it proper to give us his view tomorrow—without dealing necessarily with other schools—as to transference and the proper handling of it?

LECTURE V

The Chairman (Dr. J. R. Rees):

304   Ladies and Gentlemen: You will have noticed that the Chairman's remarks have been growing shorter each evening. Yesterday Professor Jung was in the middle of a continuous story, and I think we all want him to get on with it straight away.

Professor Jung:

305   Ladies and Gentlemen: You remember that I began to give you the material belonging to this dream. I am now in the middle of it and there is a great more to come. But at the end of yesterday's lecture I was asked by Dr. Crichton-Miller to speak about the problem of transference. That showed me something which seems to be of practical interest. When I analyse such a dream carefully and put in a great deal of work, it often happens that my colleagues wonder why I am heaping up such a quantity of learned material. They think, "Well, yes, it shows his zeal and his goodwill to make something of a dream. But what is the practical use of all these parallels?"

306   I do not mind these doubts in the least. But I was really just about to bring in something belonging to the problem, and Dr. Crichton-Miller has caught me in this attempt and asked just that question which any practical doctor would ask. Practical doctors are troubled by practical problems, and not by theoretical questions; therefore they always get a bit impatient when it comes to theoretical elucidations. They are particularly troubled by the half-amusing, half-painful, even tragic problems of transference. If you had been a little bit more patient, you would have seen that I was handling the very material by which transference can be analysed. But since the question has been raised I think I should rather give way to your wish and talk about the psychology and treatment of transference. But the

135

choice is up to you. My feeling was that Dr. Crichton-Miller had spoken the mind of the majority of you. Am I right in this assumption?

Members:

307   Yes.

Professor Jung:

308   I think you are right in your decision, for if I am going to speak about transference I shall have the opportunity to lead back to what I had originally intended with the analysis of that dream. I am afraid we will not have time to finish it; but I think it is better if I start from your actual problems and your actual difficulties.

309   I would never have been forced to work out that elaborate symbolism and this careful study of parallels if I had not been terribly worried by the problem of transference. So, in discussing the question of transference, an avenue will open to the kind of work I was trying to describe to you in my lecture last night. I told you in the beginning that my lectures will be a sorry torso. I am simply unable, in five evenings, even if I compress things together as I have done, to give you a complete summary of what I have to tell.

310   Speaking about the transference makes it necessary first to define the concept so that we really understand what we are talking about. You know that the word transference, originally coined by Freud, has become a sort of colloquial term; it has even found its way into the larger public. One generally means by it an awkward hanging-on, an adhesive sort of relationship.

311   The term "transference" is the translation of the German word *Übertragung*. Literally *Übertragung* means: to carry something over from one place to another. The word *Übertragung* is also used in a metaphorical sense to designate the carrying over from one form into another. Therefore in German it is synonymous with *Übersetzung*—that is, translation.

312   The psychological process of transference is a specific form of the more general process of projection. It is important to bring these two concepts together and to realize that transference is a special case of projection—at least that is how I understand it. Of course, everybody is free to use the term in his own way.

313   Projection is a general psychological mechanism that carries over subjective contents of any kind into the object. For instance, when I say, "The colour of this room is yellow," that is a projection, because in the object itself there is no yellow; yellow is only in us. Colour is our subjective experience as you know. The same when I hear a sound, that is a projection, because sound does not exist in itself; it is a sound in my head, it is a psychic phenomenon which I project.

314   Transference is usually a process that happens between two people and not between a human subject and a physical object, though there are exceptions; whereas the more general mechanism of projection, as we have seen, can just as well extend to physical objects. The mechanism of projection, whereby subjective contents are carried over into the object and appear as if belonging to it, is never a voluntary act, and transference, as a specific form of projection, is no exception to this rule. You cannot consciously and intentionally project, because then you know all the time that you are projecting your subjective contents; therefore you cannot locate them in the object, for you know that they really belong to you. In projection the apparent fact you are confronted with in the object is in reality an illusion; but you assume what you observe in the object not to be subjective, but objectively existing. Therefore, a projection is abolished when you find out that the apparently objective facts are really subjective contents. Then these contents become associated with your own psychology, and you cannot attribute them to the object any more.

315   Sometimes one is apparently quite aware of one's projections though one does not know their full extent. And that portion of which one is not aware remains unconscious and still appears as if belonging to the object. This often happens in practical analysis. You say, for instance: "Now, look here, you simply project the image of your father into that man, or into myself," and you assume that this is a perfectly satisfactory explanation and quite sufficient to dissolve the projection. It is satisfactory to the doctor, perhaps, but not to the patient. Because, if there is still something more in that projection, the patient will keep on projecting. It does not depend upon his will; it is simply a phenomenon that produces itself. Projection is an automatic, spontaneous fact. It is simply there; you do not know how it happens.

You just find it there. And this rule, which holds good for projection in general, is also true of transference. Transference is something which is just there. If it exists at all, it is there *a priori*. Projection is always an *unconscious* mechanism, therefore consciousness, or conscious realization, destroys it.

316   Transference, strictly, as I have already said, is a projection which happens between two individuals and which, as a rule, is of an emotional and compulsory nature. Emotions in themselves are always in some degree overwhelming for the subject, because they are involuntary conditions which override the intentions of the ego. Moreover, they cling to the subject, and he cannot detach them from himself. Yet this involuntary condition of the subject is at the same time projected into the object, and through that a bond is established which cannot be broken, and exercises a compulsory influence upon the subject.

317   Emotions are not detachable like ideas or thoughts, because they are identical with certain physical conditions and are thus deeply rooted in the heavy matter of the body. Therefore the emotion of the projected contents always forms a link, a sort of dynamic relationship, between the subject and the object—and that is the transference. Naturally, this emotional link or bridge or elastic string can be positive or negative, as you know.

318   The projection of emotional contents always has a peculiar influence. Emotions are contagious, because they are deeply rooted in the sympathetic system; hence the word "sympathicus." Any process of an emotional kind immediately arouses similar processes in others. When you are in a crowd which is moved by an emotion, you cannot fail to be roused by that same emotion. Suppose you are in a country where a language is spoken which you don't understand, and somebody makes a joke and people laugh, then you laugh too in an idiotic way, simply because you can't refrain from laughing. Also when you are in a crowd which is politically excited you can't help being excited too, even when you do not share their opinion at all, because emotion has this suggestive effect. The French psychologists have dealt with this "contagion mentale"; there are some very good books on the subject, especially *The Crowd: A Study of the Popular Mind,* by Le Bon.

319   In psychotherapy, even if the doctor is entirely detached from the emotional contents of the patient, the very fact that the

patient has emotions has an effect upon him. And it is a great mistake if the doctor thinks he can lift himself out of it. He cannot do more than become conscious of the fact that he is affected. If he does not see that, he is too aloof and then he talks beside the point. It is even his duty to accept the emotions of the patient and to mirror them. That is the reason why I reject the idea of putting the patient upon a sofa and sitting behind him. I put my patients in front of me and I talk to them as one natural human being to another, and I expose myself completely and react with no restriction.

320 I remember very well a case of an elderly woman of about fifty-eight—a doctor too—from the United States. She arrived in Zurich in a state of utter bewilderment. She was so confused at first I thought her half crazy, until I discovered that she had been in an analysis. She told me certain things she had done in her bewilderment, and it was quite obvious that she would never have done these things if her analyst had been a human being and not a mystical cipher who was sitting behind her, occasionally saying a wise word out of the clouds and never showing an emotion. So she got quite lost in her own mists and did some foolish things which he could easily have prevented her from doing if he had behaved like a human being. When she told me all that, I naturally had an emotional reaction and swore, or something like that. Upon which she shot out of her chair and said reproachfully, "But you have an emotion!" I answered, "Why, of course I have an emotion." She said, "But you should not have an emotion." I replied, "Why not? I have a good right to an emotion." She objected, "But you are an analyst!" I said, "Yes, I am an analyst, and I have emotions. Do you think that I am an idiot or a catatonic?" "But analysts have no emotions." I remarked, "Well, your analyst apparently had no emotions, and, if I may say so, he was a fool!" That one moment cleared her up completely; she was absolutely different from then on. She said, "Thank heaven! Now I know where I am. I know there is a human being opposite me who has human emotions!" My emotional reaction had given her orientation. She wasn't a thinking type, she was a feeling type and therefore needed that kind of orientation. But her analyst was a man who simply thought and existed in his intellect, and had no connection with her feeling-life. She was a highly emotional sanguine

sort of person who needed the emotionality and the feeling gesture of another human being in order not to feel alone. When you have to treat a feeling type and you talk intellectual stuff exclusively it is the same as if you, as the only intellectual, were talking to a company of feeling types. You would be utterly lost; you would feel as if you were at the North Pole, because you wouldn't be understood; nobody would react to your ideas. People would all be frightfully nice—and you would feel utterly foolish because they would not respond to your way of thinking.

321 One always has to answer people in their main function, otherwise no contact is established. So, in order to be able to show my patients that their reactions have arrived in my system, I have to sit opposite them so that they can read the reactions in my face and can see that I am listening. If I sit behind them, then I can yawn, I can sleep, I can go off on my own thoughts, and I can do what I please. They never know what is happening to me, and then they remain in an auto-erotic and isolated condition which is not good for ordinary people. Of course, if they were going to prepare for an existence as hermits on the Himalayas, it would be a different matter.

322 The emotions of patients are always slightly contagious, and they are very contagious when the contents which the patient projects into the analyst are identical with the analyst's own unconscious contents. Then they both fall into the same dark hole of unconsciousness, and get into the condition of participation. This is the phenomenon which Freud has described as counter-transference. It consists of mutual projecting into each other and being fastened together by mutual unconsciousness. Participation, as I have told you, is a characteristic of primitive psychology, that is, of a psychological level where there is no conscious discrimination between subject and object. Mutual unconsciousness is of course most confusing both to the analyst and to the patient; all orientation is lost, and the end of such an analysis is disaster.

323 Even analysts are not absolutely perfect, and it can happen that they are occasionally unconscious in certain respects. Therefore long ago I stipulated that analysts ought to be analysed themselves; they should have a father confessor or a mother confessor. Even the Pope, for all his infallibility, has to

confess regularly, and not to a monsignor or a cardinal but to an ordinary priest. If the analyst does not keep in touch with his unconscious objectively, there is no guarantee whatever that the patient will not fall into the unconscious of the analyst. You probably all know certain patients who possess a diabolical cunning in finding out the weak spot, the vulnerable place in the analyst's psyche. To that spot they seek to attach the projections of their own unconscious. One usually says that it is a characteristic of women, but that is not true, men do just the same. They always find out this vulnerable spot in the analyst, and he can be sure that, whenever something gets into him, it will be exactly in that place where he is without defence. That is the place where he is unconscious himself and where he is apt to make exactly the same projections as the patient. Then the condition of participation happens, or, more strictly speaking, a condition of personal contamination through mutual unconsciousness.

324   One has, of course, all sorts of ideas about transference, and we are all somewhat prejudiced by the definition which Freud has given; one is inclined to think that it is always a matter of erotic transference. But my experience has not confirmed the theory that it is erotic contents or infantile things exclusively that are projected. According to my experience, anything can be a matter for projection, and the erotic transference is just one of the many possible forms of transference. There are many other contents in the human unconscious which are also of a highly emotional nature, and they can project themselves just as well as sexuality. All activated contents of the unconscious have the tendency to appear in projection. It is even the rule that an unconscious content which is constellated shows itself first as a projection. Any activated archetype can appear in projection, either into an external situation, or into people, or into circumstances —in short, into all sorts of objects. There are even transferences to animals and to things.

325   Not very long ago I had an interesting case of an unusually intelligent man. I explained to him a projection he had "made": he had projected his unconscious image of woman into a real woman, and the dreams showed very clearly just where the real person was utterly different from what he expected her to be.

The fact went home. Then he said, "If I had known that two years ago it would have saved me 40,000 francs!" I asked, "How is that?" "Well, somebody showed me an old Egyptian sculpture, and I instantly fell in love with it. It was an Egyptian cat, a very beautiful thing." He instantly bought it for 40,000 francs and put it on the mantelpiece in his drawing-room. But then he found that he had lost his peace of mind. His office was on the floor below, and nearly every hour he had to jump up from his work to look at the cat, and when he had satisfied his desire he went back to work only to go upstairs again after some time. This restlessness became so disagreeable that he put the cat on his desk right opposite him—to find that he couldn't work any more! Then he had to lock it away in the attic in order to be liberated from its influence, and he had to fight down a continuous temptation to open the box and look at the cat again. When he understood his general projection of the feminine image—for, of course, the cat symbolized the woman—then the whole charm and fascination of the sculpture was gone.

326   That was a projection into a physical object, and it made the cat into a living being to whom he always had to return as some people return to the analyst. As you know, the analyst is often accused of having snake's eyes, of magnetizing or hypnotizing people, of forcing them to come back to him, of not letting them go. There *are* certain exceptionally bad cases of counter-transference when the analyst really cannot let go of the patient; but usually such accusations are the expression of a very disagreeable kind of projection which may even amount to ideas of persecution.

327   The intensity of the transference relationship is always equivalent to the importance of its contents to the subject. If it is a particularly intense transference, we can be sure that the contents of the projection, once they are extracted and made conscious, will prove to be just as important to the patient as the transference was. When a transference collapses it does not vanish into the air; its intensity, or a corresponding amount of energy, will appear in another place, for instance in another relationship, or in some other important psychological form. For the intensity of the transference is an intense emotion which is really the property of the patient. If the transference is dissolved, all that projected energy falls back into the subject, and

he is then in possession of the treasure which formerly, in the transference, had simply been wasted.

328   Now we have to say a few words about the *aetiology* of the transference. Transference can be an entirely spontaneous and unprovoked reaction, a sort of "love at first sight." Of course transference should never be misunderstood as love; it has nothing to do with love whatever. Transference only misuses love. It may appear as if transference were love, and inexperienced analysts make the mistake of taking it for love, and the patient makes the same mistake and says that he is in love with the analyst. But he is not in love at all.

329   Occasionally a transference can even spring up before the first sight, that is before or outside the treatment. And if it happens to a person who does not come for analysis afterwards, we cannot find out the reasons. But this shows all the more that it has nothing whatever to do with the real personality of the analyst.

330   Once a lady came to me whom I had seen about three weeks before at a social reception. I had not even spoken to her then, I had only talked to her husband, and I knew him only rather superficially. The lady then wrote for a consultation, and I gave her an appointment. She came, and when she was at the door of my consulting room she said, "I don't want to enter." I replied, "You don't have to enter; you can go away, of course! I have absolutely no interest in having you here if you don't want to come." Then she said, "But I must!" I answered, "I'm not forcing you." "But you forced me to come." "How did I do that?" I thought she was crazy, but she was not crazy at all, she merely had a transference which pulled her to me. She had made some kind of projection in the meantime, and that projection had such a high emotional value for her that she could not resist it; she was magically drawn to come to me because that elastic string was too strong for her. In the course of her analysis we naturally found out what the contents of that non-provoked transference were.

331   Usually a transference establishes itself only during the analysis. Very often it is caused by a difficulty in making contact, in establishing emotional harmony between the doctor and the patient—what the French psychologists at the time of hypnotic

and suggestion therapy used to call "le rapport." A good rapport means that the doctor and patient are getting on well together, that they can really talk to each other and that there is a certain amount of mutual confidence. Of course, at the time of the hypnotic therapists, the whole hypnotic and suggestive effect depended on the existence or non-existence of the rapport. In analytical treatment, if the rapport between analyst and patient is difficult on account of differences of personality, or if there are other psychological distances between them that hinder the therapeutic effect, that lack of contact causes the unconscious of the patient to try to cover the distance by building a compensatory bridge. Since there is no common ground, no possibility of forming any kind of relationship, a passionate feeling or an erotic fantasy attempts to fill the gap.

332   This often happens to people who habitually resist other human beings—either because of an inferiority complex or because of megalomania, or for other reasons—and who are psychologically very isolated. Then, out of fear of getting lost, their nature causes a violent effort of the emotions to attach themselves to the analyst. They are in despair that perhaps he too will not understand them; so they try to propitiate either the circumstances, or the analyst, or their own unwillingness by a sort of sexual attraction.

333   All these compensatory phenomena can be turned round and be applied to the analyst as well. Suppose, for instance, that an analyst has to treat a woman who does not particularly interest him, but suddenly he discovers that he has a sexual fantasy about her. Now I don't wish it on analysts that they should have such fantasies, but if they do they had better realize it, because it is important information from their unconscious that their human contact with the patient is not good, that there is a disturbance of rapport. Therefore the analyst's unconscious makes up for the lack of a decent human rapport by forcing a fantasy upon him in order to cover the distance and to build a bridge. These fantasies can be visual, they can be a certain feeling or a sensation—a sexual sensation, for instance. They are invariably a sign that the analyst's attitude to the patient is wrong, that he overvalues him or undervalues him or that he does not pay the right attention. That correction of his attitude can also be expressed by dreams. So if you dream of a patient, always pay attention

and try to see whether the dream is showing you where you may be wrong. Patients are tremendously grateful when you are honest in that respect, and they feel it very much when you are dishonest or neglectful.

334   I once had a most instructive case of that sort. I was treating a young girl of about twenty or twenty-four. She had had a very peculiar childhood; she was born in Java of a very good European family, and had a native nurse.[1] As happens with children born in the colonies, the exotic environment and that strange and, in this case, even barbarous civilization got under her skin, and the whole emotional and instinctual life of the child became tainted with that peculiar atmosphere. That atmosphere is something the white man in the East hardly ever realizes; it is the psychic atmosphere of the native in regard to the white man, an atmosphere of intense fear—fear of the cruelty, the recklessness, and the tremendous and unaccountable power of the white man. That atmosphere infects children born in the East; the fear creeps into them and fills them with unconscious fantasies about the cruelty of the white man, and their psychology gets a peculiar twist and their sex life often goes completely wrong. They suffer from unaccountable nightmares and panics and cannot adapt themselves to normal circumstances when it comes to the problem of love and marriage and so on.

335   That was the case with this girl. She went hopelessly astray and got into the most risky erotic situations, and she acquired a very bad reputation. She adopted inferior ways; she began to paint and powder herself in a rather conspicuous fashion, also to wear big ornaments in order to satisfy the primitive woman in her blood, or rather in her skin, so that *she* could join in and help her to live. Because she could not and naturally would not live without her instincts, she had to do all sorts of things which went too low. For instance, she easily succumbed to bad taste; she wore terrible colours to please the primitive unconscious in her so that it would join in when she wanted to interest a man. But naturally her choice of men was also below the mark, and so she got into a frightful tangle. Her nickname was "the great

1 [The case is discussed more fully in "The Realities of Practical Psychotherapy" (C.W., vol. 16, 2nd edn.), appendix. See also "Concerning Mandala Symbolism" (C.W., vol. 9, i), pars. 656–659 and figs. 7, 8, and 9, showing mandalas painted by this patient.]

whore of Babylon." All this was, of course, most unfortunate for an otherwise decent girl. When she came to me she really looked absolutely forbidding, so that I felt pretty awkward on account of my own maids when she was in my office for an hour. I said, "Now, you simply can't look like that, you look like—" and I said something exceedingly drastic. She was very sad over it but she couldn't help it.

336   At this point I dreamed of her in the following way: *I was on a highway at the foot of a high hill, and upon the hill was a castle, and on that castle was a high tower, the donjon. On top of that high tower was a loggia, a beautiful open contrivance with pillars and a beautiful marble balustrade, and upon that balustrade sat an elegant figure of a woman. I looked up—and I had to look up so that I felt the pain in my neck even afterwards— and the figure was my patient!* Then I woke up and instantly I thought, "Heavens! Why does my unconscious put that girl so high up?" And immediately the thought struck me, "I have looked down on her." For I really thought that she was bad. My dream showed me that this was a mistake, and I knew that I had been a bad doctor. So I told her the next day: "I have had a dream about you where I had to look up to you so that my neck hurt me, and the reason for this compensation is that I have looked down on you." That worked miracles, I can tell you! No trouble with the transference any more, because I simply got right with her and met her on the right level.

337   I could tell you quite a number of informative dreams like that about the doctor's own attitude. And when you really try to be on a level with the patient, not too high nor too low, when you have the right attitude, the right appreciation, then you have much less trouble with the transference. It won't save you from it entirely, but sure enough you won't have those bad forms of transference which are mere over-compensations for a lack of rapport.

338   There is another reason for over-compensation by transference in the case of patients with an utterly auto-erotic attitude; patients who are shut away in auto-erotic insulation and have a thick coat of armour, or a thick wall and moat around them. Yet they have a desperate need for human contact, and they naturally begin to crave for a human being outside the walls. But

they don't do anything about it. They won't lift a finger, and neither will they allow anybody to approach them, and from this attitude they get a terrible transference. Such transferences cannot be touched, because the patients are too well defended on all sides. On the contrary, if you try to do something about the transference, they feel it as a sort of aggression, and they defend themselves still more. So you must leave these people to roast in their own fat until they are satisfied and come voluntarily out of their fortress. Of course they will complain like anything about your lack of understanding and so on, but the only thing you can do is to be patient and say, "Well, you are inside, you show nothing, and as long as you don't show anything I can do nothing either."

339   In such a case the transference can come almost to the boiling point, because only a strong flame will cause the person to leave his castle. Of course that means a great outburst; but the outburst must be borne quietly by the doctor, and the patient will later on be very thankful that he has not been taken literally. I remember the case of a colleague of mine—and I can safely tell you of this case because she is dead—an American woman who came to me under very complicated circumstances. In the beginning she was on her high horse. You know there are peculiar institutions in America called universities and colleges for women; in our technical language we call them animus incubators, and they turn out annually a large number of fearful persons. Now she was such a bird. She was "very competent," and she had got into a disagreeable transference situation. She was an analyst and had a case of a married man who fell wildly in love with her, apparently. It was not, of course, love, it was transference. He projected into her that she wanted to marry him but would not admit that she was in love with him and so wasted no end of flowers and chocolates and finery over her, and finally he even threatened her with a revolver. So she had to leave at once and come to me.

340   It soon turned out that she had no idea of a woman's feeling-life. She was O.K. as a doctor, but whatever touched the sphere of a man was absolutely and utterly strange to her. She was even blissfully ignorant of a man's anatomy, because at the university where she had studied one only dissected female bodies. So you can imagine the situation with which I was confronted.

147

341   Naturally I saw it coming, and I saw right away why the man had fallen into the trap. She was totally unconscious of herself as a woman; she was just a man's mind with wings underneath, and the whole woman's body was non-existent, and her patient was forced by nature to fill the gap. He had to prove to her that a man does exist and that a man has a claim, that she was a woman and that she should respond to him. It was her female non-existence that baited the trap. He was, of course, equally unconscious, because he did not see at all that she did not exist as a woman. You see, he also was such a bird, consisting of only a head with wings underneath. He also was not a man. We often discover with Americans that they are tremendously unconscious of themselves. Sometimes they suddenly grow aware of themselves, and then you get these interesting stories of decent young girls eloping with Chinamen or with Negroes, because in the American that primitive layer, which with us is a bit difficult, with them is decidedly disagreeable, as it is much lower down. It is the same phenomenon as "going black" or "going native" in Africa.

342   Now these two people both came into this awful transference situation, and one could say they were both entirely crazy, and therefore the woman had to run away. The treatment was, of course, perfectly clear. One had to make her conscious of herself as a woman, and a woman never becomes conscious of herself as long as she cannot accept the fact of her feelings. Therefore her unconscious arranged a marvellous transference to me, which naturally she would not accept, and I did not force it upon her. She was just such a case of complete insulation, and facing her with her transference would merely have forced her into a position of defence which of course would have defeated the whole purpose of the treatment. So I never spoke of it and just let things go, and quietly worked along with the dreams. The dreams, as they always do, were steadily informing us of the progress of her transference. I saw the climax coming and knew that one day a sudden explosion would take place. Of course, it would be a bit disagreeable and of a very emotional nature, as you have perhaps noticed in your own experience, and I foresaw a highly sentimental situation. Well, you just have to put up with it; you cannot help it. After six months of very quiet and painstaking systematic work she couldn't hold herself in any

longer, and suddenly she almost shouted: "But I love you!" and then she broke down and fell upon her knees and made an awful mess of herself.

343   You just have to stand such a moment. It is really awful to be thirty-four years old and to discover suddenly that you are human. Then it comes, of course, as a big lump to you and that lump is often indigestible. If I had told her six months before that the moment would come when she would make declarations of love, she would have jumped off to the moon. Hers was a condition of auto-erotic insulation, and the rising flame, the increasing fire of her emotions finally burned through the walls, and naturally it all came out as a sort of organic eruption. She was the better for its happening, and in that moment even the transference situation in America was settled.

344   You probably think that all this sounds pretty cold-blooded. As a matter of fact, you can only cope decently with such a situation when you do not behave as if you were superior. You have to accompany the process and lower your consciousness and feel along the situation, in order not to differ too much from your patient; otherwise he feels too awkward and will have the most terrible resentment afterwards. So it is quite good to have a reserve of sentiments which you can allow to play on such an occasion. Of course it requires some experience and routine to strike the right note. It is not always quite easy, but one has to bridge over these painful moments so that the reactions of the patient will not be too bad.

345   I have already mentioned a further reason for the transference, and that is mutual unconsciousness and contamination.[2] The case which I just told you about provides an example of this. Contamination through mutual unconsciousness happens as a rule when the analyst has a similar lack of adaptation to that of the patient; in other words, when he is neurotic. In so far as the analyst is neurotic, whether his neurosis be good or bad, he has an open wound, somewhere there is an open door which he does not control, and there a patient will get in, and then the analyst will be contaminated. Therefore it is an important postulate that the analyst should know as much as possible about himself.

2 [Supra, pars. 322f.]

346   I remember the case of a young girl who had been with two analysts before she came to me, and when she came to me she had the identical dream she had had when she was with those analysts.[3] Each time at the very beginning of her analysis she had a particular dream: *She came to the frontier and she wanted to cross it, but she could not find the custom-house where she should have gone to declare whatever she carried with her.* In the first dream she was seeking the frontier, but she did not even come to it. That dream gave her the feeling that she would never be able to find the proper relation to her analyst; but because she had feelings of inferiority and did not trust her judgment, she remained with him, and nothing came of it at all. She worked with him for two months and then she left.

347   She then went to another analyst. Again she dreamed that *she came to the frontier; it was a black night, and the only thing she could see was a faint little light. Somebody said that that was the light in the custom-house, and she tried to get to it. On the way she went down a hill and crossed a valley. In the depths of the valley was a dark wood and she was afraid to go on, but nevertheless she went through it, and suddenly she felt that somebody was clinging to her in the darkness. She tried to shake herself free, but that somebody clung to her still more, and she suddenly discovered that it was her analyst.* Now what happened was that after about three months of work this analyst developed a violent counter-transference to her, which the initial dream had foreseen.

348   When she came to me—she had seen me before at a lecture and had made up her mind to work with me—she dreamed that *she was coming to the Swiss frontier. It was day and she saw the custom-house. She crossed the frontier and she went into the custom-house, and there stood a Swiss customs official. A woman went in front of her and he let that woman pass, and then her turn came. She had only a small bag with her, and she thought she would pass unnoticed. But the official looked at her and said: "What have you got in your bag?" She said: "Oh, nothing at all," and opened it. He put his hand in and pulled out something that grew bigger and bigger, until it was two complete beds.* Her problem was that she had a resistance against mar-

3 [This is actually the same case that was discussed supra, pars. 334f.]

riage; she was engaged and would not marry for certain reasons, and those beds were the marriage-beds. I pulled that complex out of her and made her realize the problem, and soon after she married.

349   These initial dreams are often most instructive. Therefore I always ask a new patient when he first comes to me: "Did you know some time ago that you were coming? Have you met me before? Have you had a dream lately, perhaps last night?"—because if he did, it gives me most valuable information about his attitude. And when you keep in close touch with the unconscious you can turn many a difficult corner. A transference is always a hindrance; it is never an advantage. You cure in spite of the transference, not because of it.

350   Another reason for the transference, particularly for bad forms of it, is provocation on the part of the analyst. There are certain analysts, I am sorry to say, who work for a transference because they believe, I don't know why, that transference is a useful and even necessary part of the treatment; therefore patients *ought* to have a transference. Of course this is an entirely mistaken idea. I have often had cases who came to me after a previous analysis and who after a fortnight or so became almost desperate. So far things had gone on very nicely and I was fully confident that the case would work out beautifully—and suddenly the patients informed me that they could not go on, and then the tears came. I asked, "Why can't you go on? Have you got no money, or what is the matter?" They said, "Oh, no, that is not the reason. I have no transference." I said, "Thank heaven you have no transference! A transference is an illness. It is abnormal to have a transference. Normal people never have transferences." Then the analysis goes on again quietly and nicely.

351   We do not need transference just as we do not need projection. Of course, people will have it nevertheless. They always have projections but not the kind they expect. They have read Freud on transference, or they have been with another analyst, and it has been pumped into them that they ought to have a transference or they will never be cured. This is perfect nonsense. Transference or no transference, that has nothing to do with the cure. It is simply due to a peculiar psychological condition that there are these projections, and, just as one dis-

151

solves other projections by making them conscious, one has to dissolve the transference by making it conscious too. If there is no transference, so much the better. You get the material just the same. It is not transference that enables the patient to bring out his material; you get all the material you could wish for from dreams. The dreams bring out everything that is necessary. If you work for a transference, most likely you will provoke one, and the result of the analysis will be bad; for you can only provoke a transference by insinuating the wrong things, by arousing expectations, by making promises in a veiled way, which you do not mean to keep because you could not. You cannot possibly have affairs with eleven thousand virgins, and so you cheat people. An analyst is not allowed to be too friendly, otherwise he will be caught by it; he will produce an effect which goes beyond him. He cannot pay the bill when it is presented, and he should not provoke something for which he is not willing to pay. Even if the analyst means to do it for the good of the patient, it is a very misguided way, and it is always a great mistake. Leave people where they are. It does not matter whether they love the analyst or not. We are not all Germans who want to be loved when they sell you a pair of sock-suspenders. It is too sentimental. The patient's main problem is precisely to learn how to live his own life, and you don't help him when you meddle with it.

352   Those are some of the reasons for a transference. The general psychological reason for projection is always an activated unconscious that seeks expression. The intensity of the transference is equivalent to the importance of the projected content. A strong transference of a violent nature corresponds to a fiery content; it contains something important, something of great value to the patient. But as long as it is projected, the analyst seems to embody this most precious and important thing. He can't help being in this unfortunate position, but he has to give that value back to the patient, and the analysis is not finished until the patient has integrated the treasure. So, if a patient projects the saviour complex into you, for instance, you have to give back to him nothing less than a saviour—whatever that means. But *you* are not the saviour—most certainly not.

353   Projections of an archetypal nature involve a particular diffi-

culty for the analyst. Each profession carries its respective difficulties, and the danger of analysis is that of becoming infected
by transference projections, in particular by archetypal contents. When the patient assumes that his analyst is the fulfilment
of his dreams, that he is not an ordinary doctor but a spiritual
hero and a sort of saviour, of course the analyst will say, "What
nonsense! This is just morbid. It is a hysterical exaggeration."
Yet—it tickles him; it is just too nice. And, moreover, he has the
same archetypes in himself. So he begins to feel, "If there are
saviours, well, perhaps it is just possible that I am one," and he
will fall for it, at first hesitantly, and then it will become more
and more plain to him that he really is a sort of extraordinary
individual. Slowly he becomes fascinated and exclusive. He is
terribly touchy, susceptible, and perhaps makes himself a nuisance in medical societies. He cannot talk with his colleagues
any more because he is—I don't know what. He becomes very
disagreeable or withdraws from human contacts, isolates himself, and then it becomes more and more clear to him that he is a
very important chap really and of great spiritual significance,
probably an equal of the Mahatmas on the Himalayas, and it is
quite likely that he also belongs to the great brotherhood. And
then he is lost to the profession.

354   We have very unfortunate examples of this kind. I know
quite a number of colleagues who have gone that way. They
could not resist the continuous onslaught of the patients' collective unconscious—case after case projecting the saviour complex
and religious expectations and the hope that perhaps this analyst with his "secret knowledge" might own the key that has
been lost by the Church, and thus could reveal the redeeming
truth. All this is a subtle and very alluring temptation and they
have given way to it. They identify with the archetype, they discover a creed of their own, and as they need disciples who believe in them they will found a sect.

355   The same problem also accounts for the peculiar difficulty psychologists of different schools have in discussing their
divergent ideas in a reasonably amicable way, and for a tendency, peculiar to our branch of science, to lock themselves
into little groups and scientific sects with a faith of their own.
All these groups really doubt their exclusive truth, and therefore they all sit together and say the same thing continually

until they finally believe it. Fanaticism is always a sign of repressed doubt. You can study that in the history of the Church. Always in those times when the Church begins to waver the style becomes fanatical, or fanatical sects spring up, because the secret doubt has to be quenched. When one is really convinced, one is perfectly calm and can discuss one's belief as a personal point of view without any particular resentment.

356   It is a typical occupational hazard of the psychotherapist to become psychically infected and poisoned by the projections to which he is exposed. He has to be continually on his guard against inflation. But the poison does not only affect him psychologically; it may even disturb his sympathetic system. I have observed quite a number of the most extraordinary cases of physical illness among psychotherapists, illness which does not fit in with the known medical symptomatology, and which I ascribe to the effect of this continuous onslaught of projections from which the analyst does not discriminate his own psychology. The peculiar emotional condition of the patient does have a contagious effect. One could almost say it arouses similar vibrations in the nervous system of the analyst, and therefore, like alienists, psychotherapists are apt to become a little queer. One should bear that problem in mind. It very definitely belongs to the problem of transference.

357   We now have to speak of the *therapy* of the transference.[4] This is an enormously difficult and complicated subject, and I am afraid I shall tell you certain things which you know just as well as I do, but in order to be systematic I cannot omit them.

358   It is obvious that the transference has to be dissolved and dealt with in the same way as the analyst would deal with any other projection. That means in practical terms: you have to make the patient realize the *subjective value* of the personal and impersonal contents of his transference. For it is not only personal material which he projects. As you have just heard, the contents can just as well be of an impersonal, that is archetypal, nature. The saviour complex is certainly not a personal motif; it is a world-wide expectation, an idea which you find all over the

4 [For Jung's later views on this problem, see "The Psychology of the Transference" (C.W., vol. 16).]

world and in every epoch of history. It is the archetypal ideas of the magic personality.[5]

359   In the beginning of an analysis, transference projections are inevitable repetitions of former personal experiences of the patient's. At this stage you have to treat all the relationships which the patient has had before. For instance, if you have a case who has been in many health-resorts with the typical doctors you find in such places, the patient will project these experiences into the analyst; so you have first to work through the figures of all those colleagues in seaside places and sanatoria, with enormous fees and the necessary theatrical display, and the patient quite naturally assumes that you too are such a bird. You have to work through the whole series of people that the patient has experienced—the doctors, the lawyers, the teachers in schools, the uncles, the cousins, the brothers, and the father. And when you have gone through the whole procession and come right down to the nursery you think that now you are through with it, but you are not. It is just as if behind the father there was still more, and you even begin to suspect that the grandfather is being projected. That is possible; I never knew of a great-grandfather that was projected into me, but I know of a grandfather that was. When you have got down to the nursery, so that you almost peep out of the other side of existence, then you have exhausted the possibilities of *consciousness;* and if the transference does not come to an end there, despite all your efforts, it is on account of the projection of *impersonal* contents. You recognize the existence of impersonal projections by the peculiar impersonal nature of their contents; as for instance the saviour complex or an archaic God-image. The archetypal character of these images produces a "magic," that is, an overpowering effect. With our rational consciousness we can't see why this should happen. God, for instance, is spirit, and spirit to us is nothing substantial or dynamic. But if you study the original meaning of these terms, you get at the real nature of the underlying experience, and you understand how they affect the primitive mind, and, in a similar way, the primitive psyche in ourselves. Spirit, *spiritus,* or *pneuma* really means air, wind, breath; *spiritus* and *pneuma* in their archetypal character are dynamic and half-

5 *Two Essays* (C.W., vol. 7), pars. 374ff.

substantial agencies; you are moved by them as by a wind, they are breathed into you, and then you are inflated.

360   The projected archetypal figures can just as well be of negative character, like images of the sorcerer, the devil, of demons and so on. Even analysts are not at all quite fireproof in that respect. I know colleagues who produce the most marvellous fantasies about myself and believe that I am in league with the devil and work black magic. And with people who never before thought that there was such a thing as the devil, the most incredible figures appear in the transference of impersonal contents. The projection of images of parental influence can be dissolved with the ordinary means of normal reasoning and common sense; but you cannot destroy the hold of impersonal images by mere reason. It would not even be right to destroy them, because they are tremendously important. In order to explain this, I am afraid I shall have to refer again to the history of the human mind.

361   It is no new discovery that archetypal images are projected. They actually have to be projected, otherwise they inundate consciousness. The problem is merely to have a form which is an adequate container. There is, as a matter of fact, an age-old institution which helps people to project impersonal images. You know it very well; you all probably have gone through the procedure, but unfortunately you were too young to recognize its importance. This institution is religious initiation, and with us it is baptism. When the fascinating and unique influence of the parental images has to be loosened, so that the child is liberated from his original biological participation with the parents, then Nature, that is the unconscious nature in man, in her infinite wisdom produces a certain kind of initiation. You find it with very primitive tribes—it is the initiation into manhood, into participation in the spiritual and social life of the tribe. In the course of the differentiation of consciousness, initiation has undergone many changes of form, until with us it was elaborated into the Christian institution of baptism. In baptism, there are two necessary functionaries, godfather and godmother. In our Swiss dialect we call them by the names of God, "Götti" and "Gotte." "Götti" is the masculine form, it means the begetter; "Gotte" is the feminine form. The word "God" has nothing to do with "good"; it really means the Begetter. Baptism and the

spiritual parents in the form of godfather and godmother express the mysterium of being twice-born. You know that all the higher castes in India have the honorific title of "Twice-born." It was also the prerogative of the Pharaoh to be twice-born. Therefore very often you find in Egyptian temples beside the main room the so-called birth-chamber where one or two rooms were reserved for the rite. In them the Pharaoh's twofold birth is described, how he is born in the flesh as a human being from ordinary parents, but is also generated by the god and carried and given birth to by the goddess. He is born the son of man and of God.

362 Our baptism means the detaching of the child from the merely natural parents and from the overpowering influence of the parental images. For this purpose, the biological parents are replaced by spiritual parents; godfather and godmother represent the *intercessio divina* through the medium of the Church, which is the visible form of the spiritual kingdom. In the Catholic rite even marriage—where we would suppose it to be all-important that this particular man and this particular woman become united and are confronted with each other—is interfered with by the Church; the *intercessio sacerdotis* prevents the immediate contact of the couple. The priest represents the Church, and the Church is always in between in the form of confession, which is obligatory. This intervention is not due to the particular cunning of the Church; it is rather her great wisdom, and it is an idea going back to the very origins of Christianity that we are not married merely as man and woman; we are married *in Christo*. I own an antique vase upon which an early Christian marriage is represented. The man and the woman hold each other's hand in the Fish; the Fish is between them, and the Fish is Christ. In this way the couple is united in the Fish. They are separated and united by Christ; Christ is in between, he is the representative of the power which is meant to separate man from merely natural forces.

363 This process of separation from nature is undergone in the well-known initiation rites or puberty rites of primitive tribes. When they approach puberty, the boys are called away suddenly. In the night they hear the voice of the spirits, the bull-roarers, and no woman is allowed to appear out of the house, or she is killed instantly. Then the boys are brought out to the

bush-house, where they are put through all sorts of gruesome performances. They are not allowed to speak; they are told that they are dead, and then they are told that they are now reborn. They are given new names in order to prove that they are no more the same personalities as before, and so they are no longer the children of their parents. The initiation can even go so far that, after they return, the mothers are not allowed to talk to their sons any more, because the young men are no longer their children. Formerly, with the Hottentots, the boy had occasionally even to perform incest once with his mother in order to prove that she was not his mother any more, but just a woman like the rest.

364   Our corresponding Christian rite has lost much of its importance, but if you study the symbolism of baptism you still see traces of the original meaning. Our birth-chamber is the baptismal font; this is really the piscina, the fish-pond in which one is like a little fish; one is symbolically drowned and then revived. You know that the early Christians were actually plunged into the baptismal font, and this used to be much larger than it is now; in many old churches the baptistry was a building on its own, and it was always built on the ground-plan of a circle. On the day before Easter, the Catholic Church has a special ceremony for the consecration of the baptismal font, the Benedictio Fontis. The merely natural water is exorcised from the admixture of all malign powers and transformed into the regenerating and purifying fountain of life, the immaculate womb of the divine source. Then the priest divides the water in the fourfold form of the cross, breathes upon it three times, plunges the consecrated Easter candle three times into it, as a symbol of the eternal light, and at the same time his incantation brings the virtue, the power of the Spiritus Sanctus to descend into the font. From this *hierosgamos,* from the holy marriage between the Spiritus Sanctus and the baptismal water as the womb of the Church, man is reborn in the true innocence of new childhood. The maculation of sin is taken from him and his nature is joined with the image of God. He is no longer contaminated by merely natural forces, he is regenerated as a spiritual being.

365   We know of other institutions for detaching man from natural conditions. I can't go into much detail, but if you study the

psychology of primitives, you find that all important events of life are connected with elaborate ceremonies whose purpose is to detach man from the preceding stage of existence and to help him to transfer his psychic energy into the next phase. When a girl marries, she ought to be detached from the parental images and should not become attached to a projection of the father-image into the husband. Therefore in Babylon a peculiar ritual was observed whose purpose was to detach the young girl from the father-image. This is the rite of temple prostitution, in which girls of good families had to hand themselves over to a stranger visiting the temple, who presumably would never return, and had to spend a night with him. We know of a similar institution in the Middle Ages, the *jus primae noctis,* the right of the first night which the feudal lord had in regard to his serfs. The bride had to spend her wedding-night with her feudal lord. By the rite of temple prostitution, a most impressive image was created which collided with the image of the man the young woman was going to marry, and so when there was trouble in marriage—for even in those days trouble occasionally arose— the regression which is the natural result would not go back to the father-image but to the stranger she had once met, the lover who came from unknown lands. Then she did not fall back into childhood but upon a human being suited to her age, and so was sufficiently protected against infantile regression.

366   This ritual shows a very beautiful observation of the human psyche. For there is an archetypal image in women of a lover in a remote, unknown land, a man coming over the seas who meets her once and then goes away again. You know this motif from Wagner's *Flying Dutchman* and from Ibsen's *Lady from the Sea.* In both dramas the heroine is waiting for the stranger who will come from far over the seas to have the great love experience with her. In Wagner's opera she has fallen in love with the actual image of him and knows him even before he arrives. The Lady from the Sea has met him once before and is under the compulsion of always going to the sea to await his return. In that Babylonian rite this archetypal image is lived concretely in order to detach the woman from the parental images which are real archetypal images and therefore exceedingly powerful. I have written a little book about the relations between the ego

159

and the unconscious,[6] where I have described a case of projection of the father-image by a woman who was under my treatment, and how the problem then developed through the analysis of the archetypal image which was at the basis of this father transference.

367   The first stage of the treatment of the transference does not involve only the realization by the patient that he is still looking at the world from the angle of the nursery, school-room, and so on, by projecting and expecting all the positive and negative authoritative figures of his personal experience; this realization merely deals with the objective side. To establish a really mature attitude, he has to see the *subjective value* of all these images which seem to create trouble for him. He has to assimilate them into his own psychology; he has to find out in what way they are part of himself; how he attributes for instance a positive value to an *object,* when as a matter of fact it is he who could and should develop this value. And in the same way, when he projects negative qualities and therefore hates and loathes the object, he has to discover that he is projecting his own inferior side, his shadow, as it were, because he prefers to have an optimistic and one-sided image of himself. Freud, as you know, deals only with the objective side. But you cannot really help a patient to assimilate the contents of his neurosis by indulgence in a childish lack of responsibility, or by resignation to a blind fate of which he is the victim. His neurosis means him to become a total personality, and that includes recognition of and responsibility for his whole being, his good and his bad sides, his superior as well as his inferior functions.

368   Let us now assume that the projection of personal images has been worked through and is sufficiently dealt with, but there is still a transference which you simply cannot dissolve. Then we come to the *second stage* in the therapy of transference. That is the *discrimination between personal and impersonal contents.* The personal projections, as we have seen, must be dissolved; and they can be dissolved through conscious realization. But the impersonal projections cannot be destroyed because they belong to the structural elements of the psyche. They are not relics of a

6 *Two Essays,* pars. 206ff.

past which has to be outgrown; they are, on the contrary, purposive and compensatory functions of the utmost importance. They are an important protection against situations in which a man might lose his head. In any situation of panic, whether external or internal, the archetypes intervene and allow a man to react in an instinctively adapted way, just as if he had always known the situation: he reacts in the way mankind has always reacted. Therefore the mechanism is of vital importance.

369   It goes without saying that the projection of these impersonal images upon the analyst has to be withdrawn. But you merely dissolve the *act* of projection; you should not, and really cannot, dissolve its *contents*. Neither, of course, can the patient assimilate the impersonal contents into his personal psychology. The fact that they are *impersonal* contents is just the reason for projecting them; one feels that they do not belong to one's subjective mind, they must be located somewhere outside one's ego, and, for lack of a suitable form, a human object is made their receptacle. So you have to be exceedingly careful in handling impersonal projections. It would, for instance, be a great mistake to say to a patient: "You see, you simply project the saviour-image into me. What nonsense to expect a saviour and to make me responsible." If you meet such an expectation, take it seriously; it is by no means nonsense. The whole world has a saviour expectation; you find it everywhere. Look at Italy, for instance, or look at Germany. At present you have no saviour in England, and in Switzerland we have none; but I don't believe that we are so very different from the rest of Europe. The situation with us is slightly different from that of the Italians and Germans; they are perhaps a little bit less balanced; but even with us it would need precious little. In those countries you have the saviour complex as mass psychology. The saviour complex is an archetypal image of the collective unconscious, and it quite naturally becomes activated in an epoch so full of trouble and disorientation as ours. In these collective events, we merely see, as through a magnifying glass, what can also happen within the individual. It is in just such a moment of panic that the compensatory psychic elements come into action. It is not at all an abnormal phenomenon. It is perhaps strange to us that it should be expressed in political form. But the collective unconscious is a very irrational factor, and our rational consciousness cannot dictate to it

how it should make its appearance. Of course, if left entirely to itself, its activation can be very destructive; it can, for instance, be a psychosis. Therefore, man's relation to the collective unconscious has always been regulated; there is a characteristic form by which the archetypal images are expressed. For the collective unconscious is a function that always operates, and man has to keep in touch with it. His psychic and spiritual health is dependent on the co-operation of the impersonal images. Therefore man has always had his religions.

370   What are religions? Religions are psychotherapeutic systems. What are we doing, we psychotherapists? We are trying to heal the suffering of the human mind, of the human psyche or the human soul, and religions deal with the same problem. Therefore our Lord himself is a healer; he is a doctor; he heals the sick and he deals with the troubles of the soul; and that is exactly what we call psychotherapy. It is not a play on words when I call religion a psychotherapeutic system. It is the most elaborate system, and there is a great practical truth behind it. I have a clientele which is pretty large and extends over a number of continents, and where I live we are practically surrounded by Catholics; but during the last thirty years I have not had more than about six practising Catholics among my patients. The vast majority were Protestants and Jews. I once sent round a questionnaire to people whom I did not know, asking: "If you were in psychological trouble what would you do? Would you go to the doctor or would you go to the priest or parson?" I cannot remember the actual figures; but I remember that about twenty per cent of the Protestants said they would go to the parson. All the rest were most emphatically against the parson and for the doctor, and the most emphatic were the relatives and children of parsons. There was one Chinese who replied, and he put it very nicely. He remarked: "When I am young I go to the doctor, and when I am old I go to the philosopher." But about fifty-eight or sixty per cent of the Catholics answered that they would certainly go to the priest. That proves that the Catholic Church in particular, with its rigorous system of confession and its director of conscience, is a therapeutic institution. I have had some patients who, after having had analysis with me, even joined the Catholic Church, just as I have had some patients who now go to the so-called Oxford Group Movement—with my blessing! I think it

is perfectly correct to make use of these psychotherapeutic institutions which history has given to us, and I wish I were still a medieval man who could join such a creed. Unfortunately it needs a somewhat medieval psychology to do it, and I am not sufficiently medieval. But you see from this that I take the archetypal images and a suitable form for their projection seriously, because the collective unconscious is really a serious factor in the human psyche.

371   All those personal things like incestuous tendencies and other childish tunes are mere surface; what the unconscious really contains are the great collective events of the time. In the collective unconscious of the individual, history prepares itself; and when the archetypes are activated in a number of individuals and come to the surface, we are in the midst of history, as we are at present. The archetypal image which the moment requires gets into life, and everybody is seized by it. That is what we see today. I saw it coming, I said in 1918 that the "blond beast" is stirring in its sleep and that something will happen in Germany.[7] No psychologist then understood at all what I meant, because people had simply no idea that our personal psychology is just a thin skin, a ripple upon the ocean of collective psychology. The powerful factor, the factor which changes our whole life, which changes the surface of our known world, which makes history, is collective psychology, and collective psychology moves according to laws entirely different from those of our consciousness. The archetypes are the great decisive forces, they bring about the real events, and not our personal reasoning and practical intellect. Before the Great War all intelligent people said: "We shall not have any more war, we are far too reasonable to let it happen, and our commerce and finance are so interlaced internationally that war is absolutely out of the question." And then we produced the most gorgeous war ever seen. And now they begin to talk that foolish kind of talk about reason and peace plans and such things; they blindfold themselves by clinging to a childish optimism—and now look at reality! Sure enough, the archetypal images decide the fate of man. Man's unconscious psychology decides, and not what we think and talk in the brain-chamber up in the attic.

---

[7] "The Role of the Unconscious" (C.W., vol. 10), par. 17.

372   Who would have thought in 1900 that it would be possible thirty years later for such things to happen in Germany as are happening today? Would you have believed that a whole nation of highly intelligent and cultivated people could be seized by the fascinating power of an archetype? I saw it coming, and I can understand it because I know the power of the collective unconscious. But on the surface it looks simply incredible. Even my personal friends are under that fascination, and when I am in Germany, I believe it myself, I understand it all, I know it has to be as it is. One cannot resist it. It gets you below the belt and not in your mind, your brain just counts for nothing, your sympathetic system is gripped. It is a power that fascinates people from within, it is the collective unconscious which is activated, it is an archetype which is common to them all that has come to life. And because it is an archetype, it has historical aspects and we cannot understand the events without knowing history.[8] It is German history that is being lived today, just as Fascism is living Italian history. We cannot be children about it, having intellectual and reasonable ideas and saying: this should not be. That is just childish. This is real history, this is what really happens to man and has always happened, and it is far more important than our personal little woes and our personal convictions. I know highly educated Germans who were just as reasonable as I think I am or as you think you are. But a wave went over them and just washed their reason away, and when you talk to them you have to admit that they could not do anything about it. An incomprehensible fate has seized them, and you cannot say it is right, or it is wrong. It has nothing to do with rational judgment, it is just history. And when your patient's transference touches upon the archetypes, you touch upon a mine that may explode, just as we see it explode collectively. These impersonal images contain enormous dynamic power. Bernard Shaw says in *Man and Superman:* "This creature Man, who in his own selfish affairs is a coward to the backbone, will fight for an idea like a hero." [9] Of course, we would not call Fascism or Hitlerism ideas. They are archetypes, and so we would say: Give an archetype to the people and the whole crowd moves like one man, there is no resisting it.

8 "Wotan" (C.W., vol. 10).
9 [Act III, in a speech by Don Juan (Penguin edn., 1952, p. 149).]

373   On account of this tremendous dynamic power of archetypal images you cannot reason them away. Therefore the only thing to do at the *third stage* of the therapy of the transference is *to differentiate the personal relationship to the analyst from impersonal factors.* It is perfectly understandable that when you have carefully and honestly worked for a patient, he likes you, and because you have done a decent bit of work on a patient, you like him, whether it is a man or a woman. That is quite self-evident. It would be most unnatural and neurotic if there were not some personal recognition on the patient's part for what you have done for him. A personal human reaction to you is normal and reasonable, therefore let it be, it deserves to live; it is not transference any more. But such an attitude to the analyst is possible in a human and decent form only when it is not vitiated by unrecognized impersonal values. This means that there has to be, on the other side, a full recognition of the importance of the archetypal images, many of which have a religious character. Whether you assume that the Nazi storm in Germany has a religious value or not does not matter. It has. Whether you think that the Duce is a religious figure or not does not matter, because he is a religious figure. You could even read the affirmation of it in a newspaper these days, when they quoted that verse about a Roman Caesar: "Ecce deus, deus ille, Menalca." [10] Fascism is the Latin form of religion, and its religious character explains why the whole thing has such a tremendous fascination.

374   The consequence of this recognition of the importance of impersonal values may be that your patient joins a Church or a religious creed or whatever it may be. If he cannot bring together his experience of the collective unconscious within a given religious form, then the difficulty begins. Then the impersonal factors have no receptacle, and so the patient falls back into the transference, and the archetypal images spoil the human relation to the analyst. Then the analyst *is* the saviour, or curse him, he is not when he ought to be! For he is only a human being; he cannot be the saviour nor any other archetypal image which is activated in the patient's unconscious.

375   On account of that enormously difficult and important prob-

10 [Cf. Virgil, *Eclogue V*, 64: "ipsa sonant arbusta: 'deus, deus ille, Menalca!'" (the very groves ring out: "A god is he, a god, Menalcas!").]

lem I have worked out a particular technique for restoring these projected impersonal values to the individual himself. It is a rather complicated technique, and last night I was just about to show you something of it in relation to that dream. For when the unconscious says that below the Christian Church is the secret chamber with the golden bowl and the golden dagger, it does not lie. The unconscious is nature, and nature never lies. There *is* gold, there *is* the treasure and the great value.

376   If I had had the opportunity I would have gone on and told you something about that treasure and the means to secure it. And then you would have seen the justification for the method which enables the individual to keep in touch with his impersonal images. As it is, I can only allude to it and must refer you to my books for further material.[11]

377   I call this *fourth stage* of the therapy of transference the *objectivation of impersonal images*. It is an essential part of the process of individuation.[12] Its goal is to detach consciousness from the object so that the individual no longer places the guarantee of his happiness, or of his life even, in factors outside himself, whether they be persons, ideas, or circumstances, but comes to realize that everything depends on whether he holds the treasure or not. If the possession of that gold is realized, then the centre of gravity is *in* the individual and no longer in an object on which he depends. To reach such a condition of detachment is the aim of Eastern practices, and it is also the aim of all the teachings of the Church. In the various religions the treasure is projected into the sacred figures, but this hypostasis is no longer possible for the modern enlightened mind. A great number of individuals cannot express their impersonal values in historical symbols any more.

378   They are therefore faced with the necessity of finding an individual method by which the impersonal images are given shape. For they have to take on form, they have to live their characteristic life, otherwise the individual is severed from the basic function of the psyche, and then he is neurotic, he is disorientated and in conflict with himself. But if he is able to objectify

11 See particularly the "Commentary on *The Secret of the Golden Flower*" (C.W., vol. 13) and "The Aims of Psychotherapy" (C.W., vol. 16).
12 See *Psychological Types*, Def. 29, and *Two Essays*, pars. 266ff. [Also "A Study in the Process of Individuation" (C.W., vol. 9, i).]

the impersonal images and relate to them, he is in touch with that vital psychological function which from the dawn of consciousness has been taken care of by religion.

379   It is impossible for me to go into details of the problem, not only because the time for my lecture is over, but because it is beyond scientific conceptions to give adequate expression to a living psychic experience. All we can say rationally about this condition of detachment is to define it as a sort of centre within the psyche of the individual, but not within the ego. It is a non-ego centre. I am afraid I should have to give you a long dissertation on comparative religion in order to convey to you fully what I mean by a non-ego centre.[13] So I can only mention the existence of this problem. It is really the essential problem of a great number of individuals who come to analysis, and therefore the psychotherapist has to try to find a method by which he can help them to solve it.

380   If we adopt such a method, we take up the torch that was abandoned by our old colleagues of the seventeenth century when they put it down in order to become chemists. In so far as we psychologists are emerging from chemical and material conceptions of the psyche, we are taking up that torch again, century—for alchemy was the work of the doctors who were busy with the mind.

Discussion

Question:

381   May I ask Professor Jung a very elementary question: Would he give us a definition of neurosis?

Professor Jung:

382   A neurosis is a dissociation of personality due to the existence of complexes. To have complexes is in itself normal; but if the complexes are incompatible, that part of the personality which is too contrary to the conscious part becomes split off. If the split reaches the organic structure, the dissociation is a psychosis, a schizophrenic condition, as the term denotes. Each complex then lives an existence of its own, with no personality left to tie them together.

13 [Cf. *Psychology and Alchemy*, pars. 44, 126, 129, 135, 325ff.]

383　　As the split-off complexes are unconscious, they find only an indirect means of expression, that is, through neurotic symptoms. Instead of suffering from a psychological conflict, one suffers from a neurosis. Any incompatibility of character can tinuing a process which began in the West in the twelfth cen cause dissociation, and too great a split between the thinking and the feeling function, for instance, is already a slight neurosis. When you are not quite at one with yourself in a given matter, you are approaching a neurotic condition. The idea of psychic dissociation is the most general and cautious way I can define a neurosis. Of course it does not cover the symptomatology and phenomenology of neurosis; it is only the most general psychological formulation I am able to give.

Dr. H. G. Baynes:

384　　You said that transference is of no practical value in analysis. Is it not possible to give it a teleological value?

Professor Jung:

385　　I have not said it in so many words, but the teleological value of transference becomes apparent from an analysis of its archetypal contents. Its purposive value is also shown in what I said about transference as a function of compensation for a lack of rapport between the analyst and the patient—at least if one assumes that it is normal for human beings to be *en rapport* with each other. Of course I could imagine that an introverted philosopher is rather inclined to think that people have no contacts. For instance, Schopenhauer says that human egotism is so great that a man can kill his brother in order to smear his boots with his brother's fat.

Dr. Henry V. Dicks:

386　　I think we can assume then, Professor Jung, that you regard the outbreak of a neurosis as an attempt at self-cure, as an attempt at compensation by bringing out the inferior function?

Professor Jung:

387　　Absolutely.

Dr. Dicks:

388　　I understand, then, that the outbreak of a neurotic illness, from the point of view of man's development, is something favourable?

Professor Jung:

389   That is so, and I am glad you bring up that idea. That is really my point of view. I am not altogether pessimistic about neurosis. In many cases we have to say: "Thank heaven he could make up his mind to be neurotic." Neurosis is really an attempt at self-cure, just as any physical disease is part an attempt at self-cure. We cannot understand a disease as an *ens per se* any more, as something detached which not so long ago it was believed to be. Modern medicine—internal medicine, for instance—conceives of disease as a system composed of a harmful factor and a healing factor. It is exactly the same with neurosis. It is an attempt of the self-regulating psychic system to restore the balance, in no way different from the function of dreams—only rather more forceful and drastic.

Dr. J. A. Hadfield:

390   Would Professor Jung give us a short account of the technique of active imagination?

Professor Jung:

391   That was the subject I really wanted to tell you about today in consequence of the analysis of the Toledo dream, so I am very glad to take it up. You will realize that I shall not be able to present any empirical material, but I may succeed in giving you an idea of the method. I believe that the best way is to tell you of a case where it was very difficult to teach the patient the method.

392   I was treating a young artist, and he had the greatest trouble in understanding what I meant by active imagination. He tried all sorts of things but he could not get at it. The difficulty with him was that he could not think. Musicians, painters, artists of all kinds, often can't think at all, because they never intentionally use their brain. This man's brain too was always working for itself; it had its artistic imaginations and he couldn't use it psychologically, so he couldn't understand. I gave him every chance to try, and he tried all sorts of stunts. I cannot tell you all the things he did, but I will tell you how he finally succeeded in using his imagination psychologically.

393   I live outside the town, and he had to take the train to get to my place. It starts from a small station, and on the wall of that station was a poster. Each time he waited for his train he looked

at that poster. The poster was an advertisement for Mürren in the Bernese Alps, a colourful picture of the waterfalls, of a green meadow and a hill in the centre, and on that hill were several cows. So he sat there staring at that poster and thinking that he could not find out what I meant by active imagination. And then one day he thought: "Perhaps I could start by having a fantasy about that poster. I might for instance imagine that I am myself in the poster, that the scenery is real and that I could walk up the hill among the cows and then look down on the other side, and then I might see what there is behind that hill."

394 So he went to the station for that purpose and imagined that he was in the poster. He saw the meadow and the road and walked up the hill among the cows, and then he came up to the top and looked down, and there was the meadow again, sloping down, and below was a hedge with a stile. So he walked down and over the stile, and there was a little footpath that ran round a ravine, and a rock, and when he came round that rock, there was a small chapel, with its door standing a little ajar. He thought he would like to enter, and so he pushed the door open and went in, and there upon an altar decorated with pretty flowers stood a wooden figure of the Mother of God. He looked up at her face, and in that exact moment something with pointed ears disappeared behind the altar. He thought, "Well, that's all nonsense," and instantly the whole fantasy was gone.

395 He went away and said, "Now again I haven't understood what active imagination is." And then, suddenly, the thought struck him: "Well, perhaps that really *was* there; perhaps that thing behind the Mother of God, with the pointed ears, that disappeared like a flash, really happened." Therefore he said to himself: "I will just try it all over as a test." So he imagined that he was back in the station looking at the poster, and again he fantasied that he was walking up the hill. And when he came to the top of the hill, he wondered what he would see on the other side. And there was the hedge and the stile and the hill sloping down. He said, "Well, so far so good. Things haven't moved since, apparently." And he went round the rock, and there was the chapel. He said: "There is the chapel, that at least is no illusion. It is all quite in order." The door stood ajar and he was quite pleased. He hesitated a moment and said: "Now, when I

push that door open and I see the Madonna on the altar, then that thing with the pointed ears should jump down behind the Madonna, and if it doesn't, then the whole thing is bunk!" And so he pushed the door open and looked—and there it all was and the thing jumped down, as before, and then he was convinced. From then on he had the key and knew he could rely on his imagination, and so he learned to use it.

396   There is no time to tell you about the development of his images, nor how other patients arrive at the method. For of course everybody gets at it in his own way. I can only mention that it might also be a dream or an impression of a hypnagogic nature from which active imagination can start. I really prefer the term "imagination" to "fantasy," because there is a difference between the two which the old doctors had in mind when they said that "opus nostrum," our work, ought to be done "per veram imaginationem et non phantastica"—by true imagination and not by a fantastical one.[13] In other words, if you take the correct meaning of this definition, fantasy is mere nonsense, a phantasm, a fleeting impression; but imagination is active, purposeful creation. And this is exactly the distinction I make too.

397   A fantasy is more or less your own invention, and remains on the surface of personal things and conscious expectations. But active imagination, as the term denotes, means that the images have a life of their own and that the symbolic events develop according to their own logic—that is, of course, if your conscious reason does not interfere. You begin by concentrating upon a starting point. I will give you an example from my own experience. When I was a little boy, I had a spinster aunt who lived in a nice old-fashioned house. It was full of beautiful old coloured engravings. Among them was a picture of my grandfather on my mother's side. He was a sort of bishop, and he was represented as coming out of his house and standing on a little terrace. There were handrails and stairs coming down from the terrace, and a footpath leading to the cathedral. He was in full regalia, standing there at the top of the terrace. Every Sunday morning I was allowed to pay a call on my aunt, and then I knelt on a chair and looked at that picture until grandfather came down the steps. And each time my aunt would say, "But, my dear, he

[13] [Cf. *Psychology and Alchemy* (C.W., vol. 12), par. 360.]

doesn't walk, he is still standing there." But I knew I had seen him walking down.

398   You see how it happened that the picture began to move. And in the same way, when you concentrate on a mental picture, it begins to stir, the image becomes enriched by details, it moves and develops. Each time, naturally, you mistrust it and have the idea that you have just made it up, that it is merely your own invention. But you have to overcome that doubt, because it is not true. We can really produce precious little by our conscious mind. All the time we are dependent upon the things that literally fall into our consciousness; therefore in German we call them *Einfälle*. For instance, if my unconscious should prefer not to give me ideas, I could not proceed with my lecture, because I could not invent the next step. You all know the experience when you want to mention a name or a word which you know quite well, and it simply does not present itself; but some time later it drops into your memory. We depend entirely upon the benevolent co-operation of our unconscious. If it does not co-operate, we are completely lost. Therefore I am convinced that we cannot do much in the way of conscious invention; we over-estimate the power of intention and the will. And so when we concentrate on an inner picture and when we are careful not to interrupt the natural flow of events, our unconscious will produce a series of images which make a complete story.

399   I have tried that method with many patients and for many years, and I possess a large collection of such "opera." It is most interesting to watch the process. Of course I don't use active imagination as a panacea; there have to be definite indications that the method is suitable for the individual, and there are a number of patients with whom it would be wrong to force it upon them. But often in the later stage of analysis, the objectivation of images replaces the dreams. The images anticipate the dreams, and so the dream-material begins to peter out. The unconscious becomes deflated in so far as the conscious mind relates to it. Then you get all the material in a creative form and this has great advantages over dream-material. It quickens the process of maturation, for analysis is a process of quickened maturation. This definition is not my own invention; the old professor Stanley Hall invented the term.

400   Since by active imagination all the material is produced in a

conscious state of mind, the material is far more rounded out than the dreams with their precarious language. And it contains much more than dreams do; for instance, the feeling-values are in it, and one can judge it by feeling. Quite often, the patients themselves feel that certain material contains a tendency to visibility. They say, for instance: "That dream was so impressive, if I only could paint I would try to express its atmosphere." Or they feel that a certain idea should be expressed not rationally but in symbols. Or they are gripped by an emotion which, if given form, would be explainable, and so on. And so they begin to draw, to paint, or to shape their images plastically, and women sometimes do weaving. I have even had one or two women who danced their unconscious figures. Of course, they can also be expressed in writing.

401   I have many complete series of such pictures. They yield an enormous amount of archetypal material. Just now I am about to work out the historical parallels of some of them. I compare them with the pictorial material produced in similar attempts in past centuries, particularly in the early Middle Ages. Certain elements of the symbolism go back to Egypt. In the East we find many interesting parallels to our unconscious material, even down to the last details. This comparative work gives us a most valuable insight into the structure of the unconscious. You have to hand the necessary parallels to the patients too, not of course in such an elaborate way as you would present it in a scientific study, but as much as each individual needs in order to understand his archetypal images. For he can see their real meaning only when they are not just a queer subjective experience with no external connections, but a typical, ever-recurring expression of the objective facts and processes of the human psyche. By objectifying his impersonal images, and understanding their inherent ideas, the patient is able to work out all the values of his archetypal material. Then he can really see it, and the unconscious becomes understandable to him. Moreover, this work has a definite effect upon him. Whatever he has put into it works back on him and produces a change of attitude which I tried to define by mentioning the non-ego centre.

402   I will give you an interesting example. I had a case, a university man, a very one-sided intellectual. His unconscious had become troubled and activated; so it projected itself into other

men who appeared to be his enemies, and he felt terribly lonely, because everybody seemed to be against him. Then he began to drink in order to forget his troubles, but he got exceedingly irritable and in these moods he began to quarrel with other men, and several times he had very disagreeable encounters, and once he was thrown out of a restaurant and got beaten up. And there were more incidents of that sort. Then things became really too thick for his endurance, and he came to me to ask my advice about what he should do. In that interview, I got a very definite impression of him: I saw that he was chock-full of archaic material, and I said to myself: "Now I am going to make an interesting experiment to get that material absolutely pure, without any influence from myself, and therefore I won't touch it." So I sent him to a woman doctor who was then just a beginner and who did not know much about archetypal material. Thus I was absolutely sure that she would not tamper with it. The patient was in such low spirits that he did not object to my proposition. So he worked with her and did everything she said.[14]

403   She told him to watch his dreams, and he wrote them all down carefully, from the first to the last. I now have a series of about thirteen hundred dreams of his. They contain the most marvellous series of archetypal images. And quite naturally, without being told to do so, he began to draw a number of pictures which he saw in his dreams, because he felt them to be very important. And in this work on his dreams and on these pictures he did exactly the kind of work which other patients do by active imagination. He even invented active imagination for himself in order to work out certain most intricate problems which his dreams presented him with, as for instance how to balance the contents of a circle, and more things like this. He worked out the problem of the *perpetuum mobile,* not in a crazy way but in a symbolic way. He worked on all the problems which medieval philosophy was so keen on and of which our rational mind says, "That is all nonsense." Such a statement only shows that we do not understand. They did understand; we are the fools, not they.

404   In the course of this analysis, which took him through about the first four hundred dreams, he was not under my surveil-

14 [This case provided the material for Part II of *Psychology and Alchemy.*]

lance. After the first interview I did not see him at all for eight months. He was five months with that doctor, and then for three months he was doing the work all by himself, continuing the observation of his unconscious with minute accuracy. He was very gifted in this respect. In the end, for about two months, he had a number of interviews with me. But I did not have to explain much of the symbolism to him.

405   The effect of this work with his unconscious was that he became a perfectly normal and reasonable person. He did not drink any more, he became completely adapted and in every respect completely normal. The reason for this is quite obvious: that man—he was not married—had lived in a very one-sided intellectual way, and naturally had certain desires and needs also. But he had no chance with women at all, because he had no differentiation of feeling whatsoever. So he made a fool of himself with women at once, and of course they had no patience with him. And he made himself very disagreeable to men, so he was frightfully lonely. But now he had found something that fascinated him; he had a new centre of interest. He soon discovered that his dreams pointed to something very meaningful, and so his whole intuitive and scientific interest was aroused. Instead of feeling like a lost sheep, he thought: "Ah, when I am through with my work in the evening, I go to my study, and then I shall see what happens. I will work over my dreams, and then I shall discover extraordinary things." And so it was. Of course rational judgment would say that he just fell violently into his fantasies. But that was not the case at all. He did a real bit of hard work on his unconscious, and he worked out his images scientifically. When he came to me after his three months alone, he was already almost normal. Only he still felt uncertain; he was troubled because he could not understand some of the material he had dug up from the unconscious. He asked my advice about it, and I most carefully gave him certain hints as to its meaning, but only so far as this could help him to keep on with the work and carry it through.

406   At the end of the year I am going to publish a selection from his first four hundred dreams, where I show the development of one motif only, the central motif of these archetypal images.[15]

15 "Traumsymbole des Individuationsprozesses," in the Eranos-Jahrbuch 1935. [Now Part II of Psychology and Alchemy.]

There will be an English translation later, and then you will have the opportunity to see how the method works in a case absolutely untouched by myself, or by any other outside suggestion. It is a most amazing series of images and really shows what active imagination can do. You understand, in this case it was only partially a method for objectifying the images in plastic form, because many of the symbols appeared directly in the dreams; but all the same it shows the kind of atmosphere which active imagination can produce. I have patients who, evening after evening, work at these images, painting and shaping their observations and experiences. The work has a fascination for them; it is the fascination which the archetypes always exert upon consciousness. But by objectifying them, the danger of their inundating consciousness is averted and their positive effect is made accessible. It is almost impossible to define this effect in rational terms; it is a sort of "magical" effect, that is, a suggestive influence which goes out from the images to the individual, and in this way his unconscious is extended and is changed.

407   I am told that Dr. Bennet has brought some pictures by a patient. Will he be so kind as to show them?

This picture (Figure 14) is meant to represent a bowl or vase. Of course it is very clumsily expressed and is a mere attempt, a suggestion of a vase or bowl. The motif of the vessel is itself an archetypal image which has a certain purpose, and I can prove from this picture what the purpose is. A vessel is an instrument for containing things. It contains for instance liquids, and prevents them from getting dispersed. Our German word for vessel is *Gefäss*, which is the noun of *fassen*, that is, to set, to contain, to take hold of. The word *Fassung* means the setting, and also, metaphorically, composure, to remain collected. So the vessel in this picture indicates the movement of containing in order to gather in and to hold together. You have to hold something together which otherwise would fall asunder. From the way this picture is composed, and from certain features in it, it is obvious that the psychology of this man contains a number of disparate elements. It is a picture characteristic of a schizophrenic condition. I do not know the case at all, but Dr. Bennet confirms that my conclusion is correct. You see the disparate elements all over

the picture; there are a number of things which are not motivated and which don't belong together. Moreover, you see peculiar lines dividing the field. These lines are characteristic of a
schizophrenic mentality; I call them the breaking lines. When a
schizophrenic paints a picture of himself, he naturally expresses

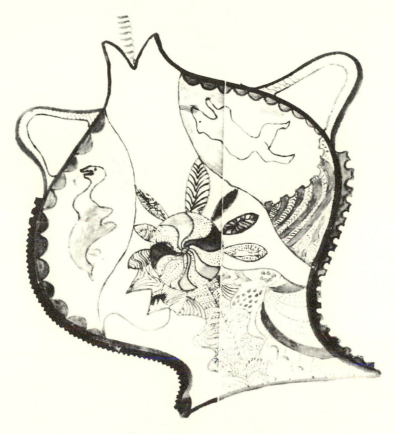

FIG. 14. Painting by a patient

the schizophrenic split in his own mental structure, and so you
find these breaking lines which often go right through a particular figure, like the breaking lines in a mirror. In this picture, the
figures themselves show no breaking lines; they only go all over
the field.

408   This man, then, tries to gather in all the disparate elements into the vessel. The vessel is meant to be the receptacle for his whole being, for all the incompatible units. If he tried to gather them into his ego, it would be an impossible task, because the ego can be identical only with one part at a time. So he indicates by the symbol of the vessel that he is trying to find a container for everything, and therefore he gives a hint at a non-ego centre by that sort of ball or globe in the middle.

409   The picture is an attempt at self-cure. It brings all the disparate elements into the light, and it also tries to put them together into that vessel. This idea of a receptacle is an archetypal idea. You find it everywhere, and it is one of the central motifs of unconscious pictures. It is the idea of the magic circle which is drawn round something that has to be prevented from escaping or protected against hostile influences. The magic circle as an apotropaic charm is an archaic idea which you still find in folklore. For instance, if a man digs for a treasure, he draws the magic circle round the field in order to keep the devil out. When the ground-plan of a city was set out, there used to be a ritual walk or ride round the circumference in order to protect the place within. In some Swiss villages, it is still the custom for the priest and the town council to ride round the fields when the blessing is administered for the protection of the harvest. In the centre of the magic circle or sacred precinct is the temple. One of the most wonderful examples of this idea is the temple of Borobudur in Java. The walk round, the *circumambulatio,* is done in a spiral; the pilgrims pass the figures of all the different lives of the Buddha, until on the top there is the invisible Buddha, the Buddha yet to come. The ground-plan of Borobudur is a circle within a square. This structure is called in Sanskrit a mandala. The word means a circle, particularly a magic circle. In the East, you find the mandala not only as the ground-plan of temples, but as pictures in the temples, or drawn for the day of certain religious festivals. In the very centre of the mandala there is the god, or the symbol of divine energy, the diamond thunderbolt. Round this innermost circle is a cloister with four gates. Then comes a garden, and round this there is another circle which is the outer circumference.

410   The symbol of the mandala has exactly this meaning of a holy place, a *temenos,* to protect the centre. And it is a symbol

178

which is one of the most important motifs in the objectivation of unconscious images.[16] It is a means of protecting the centre of the personality from being drawn out and from being influenced from outside.

411   This picture by Dr. Bennet's patient is an attempt to draw such a mandala. It has a centre, and it contains all his psychic elements, and the vase would be the magic circle, the *temenos*, round which he has to do the *circumambulatio*. Attention is thus directed towards the centre, and at the same time all the disparate elements come under observation and an attempt is made to unify them. The *circumambulatio* had always to be done clockwise. If one turned round in the other direction it was very unfavourable. The idea of the *circumambulatio* in this picture is the patient's first attempt to find a centre and a container for his whole psyche. But he does not succeed. The design shows no balance, and the vase is toppling over. It even topples over towards the left, towards the side of the unconscious. So the unconscious is still too powerful. If he wants his apotropaic magic to work, he must do it in a different way. We shall see what he does in the next picture.

412   In this picture (Figure 15) he makes an attempt at symmetry. Now these disparate, monstrous things which he could not grasp before are collected and assimilated into more favourable, less pathological forms. He can now gather the living units of his unconscious, in the form of snakes, into the sacred vase. And the vase stands firm, it does not topple over any more, and its shape has improved. He does not succeed yet with his intention; but at least he can give his animals some form. They are all animals of the underworld, fishes that live in the deep sea, and snakes of the darkness. They symbolize the lower centres of his psychology, the sympathetic system. A most remarkable thing is that he also gathers in the stars. That means that the cosmos, his world, is collected into the picture. It is an allusion to the unconscious astrology which is in our bones, though we are unaware of it. At the top of the whole picture is the personification of the unconscious, a naked anima-figure who turns her back. That is a typical position; in the beginning of the objectivation of these images the anima-figure often turns her back. At the foot of the

16 [Cf. "Commentary on *The Secret of the Golden Flower*" (C.W., vol. 13) and "Concerning Mandala Symbolism" (C.W. vol. 9, 1).]

vase are eight figures of the crescent moon; the moon is also a symbol of the unconscious. A man's unconscious is the lunar world, for it is the night world, and this is characterized by the

FIG. 15. Painting by a patient

moon, and Luna is a feminine designation, because the unconscious is feminine. There are still various breaking lines which disturb the harmony. But I should assume that if no particular trouble interferes, the patient will most likely continue along this constructive line. I should say that there is hope that he might come round altogether, because the appearance of the anima is rather a positive sign. She also is a sort of vase, for in the beginning she incorporates the whole of the unconscious, instead of its being scattered in all the various units. Also, the patient tries to separate the motifs to the right and to the left, and this indicates an attempt at conscious orientation. The ball or globe in the first picture has disappeared, but this is not a negative sign. The whole vessel is the centre, and he has corrected the toppling over of the vase, it stands quite firmly on its base. All this shows that he is really making an attempt to put himself right.

413 The pictures should be given back to the patient because they are very important. You can get copies; patients like to do copies for the doctor. But he should leave the originals with the patients, because they want to look at them; and when they look at them they feel that their unconscious is expressed. The objective form works back on them and they become enchanted. The suggestive influence of the picture reacts on the psychological system of the patient and induces the same effect which he put into the picture. That is the reason for idols, for the magic use of sacred images, of icons. They cast their magic into our system and put us right, provided we put ourselves into them. If you put yourself into the icon, the icon will speak to you. Take a Lamaic mandala which has a Budda in the centre, or a Shiva, and, to the extent that you can put yourself into it, it answers and comes into you. It has a magic effect.

414 Because these pictures of the unconscious express the actual psychological condition of the individual, you can use them for the purpose of diagnosis. You can tell right away from such a picture where the patient stands, whether he has a schizophrenic disposition or is merely neurotic. You can even tell what his prognosis is. It only needs some experience to make these paintings exceedingly helpful. Of course, one should be careful. One should not be dogmatic and say to every patient, "Now you paint." There are people who think: "Dr. Jung's treatment consists in telling his patients to paint," just as formerly they thought: "He divides them into introverts and extraverts and says 'you should live in such and such a way, because you belong to this type or that.'" That is certainly not treatment. Each pa-

tient is a new problem for the doctor, and he will only be cured of his neurosis if you help him to find his individual way to the solution of his conflicts.

The Chairman:

415   Ladies and Gentlemen, you have been expressing by your applause something of what you feel about Professor Jung. This is the last time in this group of talks that we will have the honour and pleasure and privilege of hearing Professor Jung. We have only inadequate ways of expressing our thanks to him for these lectures which have been so stimulating, so challenging, which have left us with so many things to think about in the future, things which to all of us, especially those who are practising psychotherapy, are enormously suggestive. I think that is what you meant to do for us, Sir, and that is what you have done. We in this Institute are extremely proud to have had you here talking to us, and all of us, I think, are harbouring the idea that before long you will be back in England to talk to us again and make us think more about these great problems.

II

SYMBOLS AND THE
INTERPRETATION OF DREAMS

[This essay was composed in English and completed shortly before Jung's death in June 1961. Without title, it was written to introduce a symposium, *Man and His Symbols* (© 1964 Aldus Books, London), consisting of essays by Jung and four colleagues, edited by Jung and after his death by Dr. Marie-Louise von Franz, with John Freeman as co-ordinating editor. The symposium was conceived as a popular presentation of Jung's ideas, and accordingly its contents were, with the authors' agreement, extensively reworked under the supervision of John Freeman in collaboration with Dr. von Franz. Jung's essay was largely rewritten and, particularly in the opening sections, rearranged; a number of deletions were made, some explanatory passages were added, and it was given the title "Approaching the Unconscious." The present version is Jung's original text, revised by R. F. C. Hull; except for some minor transpositions the original arrangement has been preserved. The illustrations (122 in the original edn.) have been omitted. Chapter divisions and titles have been introduced in consultation with Dr. von Franz. Acknowledgment is made to Aldus Books and Doubleday and Co. for permission to incorporate some stylistic improvements from the 1964 version.—EDITORS.]

1. THE SIGNIFICANCE OF DREAMS

416   Through his language, man tries to designate things in such a way that his words will convey the meaning of what he intends to communicate. But sometimes he uses terms or images that are not strictly descriptive and can be understood only under certain conditions. Take, for instance, the many abbreviations like UN, UNESCO, NATO, etc., which infest our newspapers, or trademarks or the names of patent medicines. Although one cannot see what they mean, they yet have a definite meaning if you know it. Such designations are not *symbols,* they are *signs.* What we call a symbol is a term, a name, or an image which in itself may be familiar to us, but its connotations, use, and application are specific or peculiar and hint at a hidden, vague, or unknown meaning. Take as an example the image of the double adze that occurs frequently on Cretan monuments. We know the object, but we do not know its specific meaning. Again, a Hindu who had been on a visit to England told his friends at home that the English worshipped animals, because he had found eagles, lions, and oxen in their old churches and cathedrals, and he was not aware that these animals were the symbols of the evangelists. There are even many Christians who do not know that they are derived from the vision of Ezekiel, which in turn offers a parallel to the Egyptian Horus and his four sons. Other examples are the wheel and the cross, which are universally known objects, yet under certain conditions they are symbolic and mean something that is still a matter for controversial speculation.

417   A term or image is symbolic when it means more than it denotes or expresses. It has a wider "unconscious" aspect—an aspect that can never be precisely defined or fully explained. This peculiarity is due to the fact that, in exploring the symbol, the mind is finally led towards ideas of a transcendent nature, where

our reason must capitulate. The wheel, for instance, may lead our thoughts to the idea of a "divine" sun, but at this point reason has to admit its inadequacy, for we are unable to define or to establish the existence of a "divine" being. We are merely human, and our intellectual resources are correspondingly limited. We may call something "divine," but this is simply a name, a *façon de parler,* based perhaps on a creed, yet never amounting to a proof.

418   Because there are innumerable things beyond the range of human understanding, we constantly use symbolic expressions and images when referring to them (ecclesiastical language in particular is full of symbols). But this conscious use of symbolism is only one aspect of a psychological fact of great importance: we also produce symbols unconsciously and spontaneously in our dreams.

419   Each act of apperception, or cognition, accomplishes its task only partially; it is never complete. First of all, sense-perception, fundamental to all experience, is restricted by the limited number and quality of our senses, which can however be compensated to a certain extent by the use of instruments, but not sufficiently to eliminate entirely a fringe of uncertainty. Moreover apperception translates the observed fact into a seemingly incommensurable medium—into a psychic event, the nature of which is unknowable. Unknowable, because cognition cannot cognize itself—the psyche cannot know its own psychic substance. There is thus an indefinite number of unknown factors in every experience, in addition to which the object of cognition is always unknown in certain respects since we cannot know the ultimate nature of matter itself.

420   Every conscious act or event thus has an unconscious aspect, just as every sense-perception has a subliminal aspect: for instance, sound below or above audibility, or light below or above visibility. The unconscious part of a psychic event reaches consciousness only indirectly, if at all. The event reveals the existence of its unconscious aspect inasmuch as it is characterized either by emotionality or by a vital importance that has not been realized consciously. The unconscious part is a sort of afterthought, which may become conscious in the course of time by means of intuition or by deeper reflection. But the event can also manifest its unconscious aspect—and this is usually the case

186

—in a dream. The dream shows this aspect in the form of a symbolic image and not as a rational thought. It was the understanding of dreams that first enabled us to investigate the unconscious aspect of conscious psychic events and to discover its nature.

421   It has taken the human mind a long time to arrive at a more or less rational and scientific understanding of the functional meaning of dreams. Freud was the first who tried to elucidate the unconscious background of consciousness in an empirical way. He worked on the general assumption that dream-contents are related to conscious representations through the law of association, i.e., by causal dependence, and are not merely chance occurrences. This assumption is by no means arbitrary but is based on the empirical fact, observed long ago by neurologists and especially by Pierre Janet, that neurotic symptoms are connected with some conscious experience. They even appear to be split-off areas of the conscious mind which, at another time and under different conditions, can be conscious, just as an hysterical anaesthesia can be there one moment and gone the next, only to reappear again after a while. Breuer and Freud recognized more than half a century ago that neurotic symptoms are meaningful and make sense inasmuch as they express a certain thought. In other words, they function in the same manner as dreams: they *symbolize*. A patient, for instance, confronted with an intolerable situation, develops a spasm whenever he tries to swallow: "He can't swallow it." Under similar conditions another patient develops asthma: "He can't breathe the atmosphere at home." A third suffers from a peculiar paralysis of the legs: "He can't go on any more." A fourth vomits everything he eats: "He can't stomach it." And so on. They could all just as well have had dreams of a similar kind.

422   Dreams, of course, display a greater variety and are often full of picturesque and luxuriant fantasy, but they boil down eventually to the same basic thought if one follows Freud's original method of "free association." This method consists in letting the patient go on talking about his dream-images. That is precisely what the non-psychological doctor omits to do. Being always pressed for time, he loathes letting his patient babble on about his fantasies seemingly without end. Yet, if he only knew, his patient is just about to give himself away and to reveal the unconscious background of his ailment. Anyone who talks long

enough will inevitably betray himself by what he says and what he purposely refrains from saying. He may try very hard to lead the doctor and himself away from the real facts, but after a while it is quite easy to see which point he is trying to steer away from. Through apparently rambling and irrational talk, he unconsciously circumscribes a certain area to which he continually returns in ever-renewed attempts to hide it. In his circumlocutions he even makes use of a good deal of symbolism, apparently serving his purpose of hiding and avoiding yet pointing all the time to the core of his predicament.

423   Thus, if the doctor is patient enough, he will hear a wealth of symbolic talk, seemingly calculated to hide something, a secret, from conscious realization. A doctor sees so many things from the seamy side of life that he is seldom far from the truth when he interprets the hints which his patient is emitting as signs of an uneasy conscience. What he eventually discovers, unfortunately, confirms his expectations. Thus far nobody can say anything against Freud's theory of repression and wish-fulfilment as apparent causes of dream symbolism.

424   If one considers the following experience, however, one becomes sceptical. A friend and colleague of mine, travelling for long hours on a train journey through Russia, passed the time by trying to decipher the Cyrillic script of the railway notices in his compartment. He fell into a sort of reverie about what the letters might mean and—following the principle of "free association"—what they reminded him of, and soon he found himself in the midst of all sorts of reminiscences. Among them, to his great displeasure, he did not fail to discover those old and disagreeable companions of sleepless nights, his "complexes"—repressed and carefully avoided topics which the doctor would joyously point to as the most likely causes of a neurosis or the most convincing meaning of a dream.

425   There was no dream, however, merely "free associations" to incomprehensible letters, which means that from any point of the compass you can reach the centre directly. Through free association you arrive at the critical secret thoughts, no matter where you start from, be it symptoms, dreams, fantasies, Cyrillic letters or examples of modern art. At all events, this fact proves nothing with regard to dreams and their real meaning. It only shows the existence of associable material floating about. Very

often dreams have a very definite, as if purposeful, structure, indicating the underlying thought or intention though, as a rule, the latter is not immediately comprehensible.

426   This experience was an eye-opener to me, and, without dismissing the idea of "association" altogether, I thought one should pay more attention to the dream itself, i.e., to its actual form and statement. For instance, a patient of mine dreamed of a drunken, dishevelled, vulgar woman called his "wife" (though in reality his wife was totally different). The dream statement, therefore, is shocking and utterly unlike reality, yet that is what the dream says. Naturally such a statement is not acceptable and is immediately dismissed as dream nonsense. If you let the patient associate freely to the dream, he will most likely try to get away as far as possible from such a shocking thought in order to end up with one of his staple complexes, but you will have learnt nothing about the meaning of this particular dream. What is the unconscious trying to convey by such an obviously untrue statement?

427   If somebody with little experience and knowledge of dreams should think that dreams are just chaotic occurrences without meaning, he is at liberty to do so. But if one assumes that they are normal events, which as a matter of fact they are, one is bound to consider that they are either causal—i.e., that there is a rational cause for their existence—or in some way purposive, or both; in other words, that they make sense.

428   Clearly, the dream is seeking to express the idea of a degenerate female who is closely connected with the dreamer. This idea is projected upon his wife, where the statement becomes untrue. What does it refer to, then?

429   Subtler minds in the Middle Ages already knew that every man "carries Eve, his wife, hidden in his body." [1] It is this feminine element in every man (based on the minority of female genes in his biological make-up) which I have called the *anima.* "She" consists essentially in a certain inferior kind of relatedness to the surroundings and particularly to women, which is kept carefully concealed from others as well as from oneself. A man's visible personality may seem quite normal, while his anima side is sometimes in a deplorable state. This was the case with our

1 [Dominicus Gnosius, *Hermetis Trismegisti Tractatus vere Aureus de Lapide philosophici secreto* (1610), p. 101.—EDITORS.]

dreamer: his female side was not nice. Applied to his anima, the dream-statement hits the nail on the head when it says: you are behaving like a degenerate female. It hits him hard as indeed it should. One should not, however, understand such a dream as evidence for the *moral nature* of the unconscious. It is merely an attempt to balance the lopsidedness of the conscious mind, which had believed the fiction that one was a perfect gentleman throughout.

430   Such experiences taught me to mistrust free association. I no longer followed associations that led far afield and away from the manifest dream-statement. I concentrated rather on the actual dream-text as the thing which was intended by the unconscious, and I began to circumambulate the dream itself, never letting it out of my sight, or as one turns an unknown object round and round in one's hands to absorb every detail of it.

431   But why should one consider dreams, those flimsy, elusive, unreliable, vague, and uncertain phantasms, at all? Are they worthy of our attention? Our rationalism would certainly not recommend them, and the history of dream interpretation before Freud was a sore point anyway; most discouraging in fact, most "unscientific" to say the least of it. *Yet dreams are the commonest and universally accessible source for the investigation of man's symbolizing faculty,* apart from the contents of psychoses, neuroses, myths, and the products of the various arts. All these, however, are more complicated and more difficult to understand, because, when it comes to the question of their individual nature, one cannot venture to interpret such unconscious products without the aid of the originator. Dreams are indeed the chief source of all our knowledge about symbolism.

432   One cannot *invent* symbols; wherever they occur, they have not been devised by conscious intention and wilful selection, because, if such a procedure had been used, they would have been nothing but signs and abbreviations of conscious thoughts. Symbols occur to us spontaneously, as one can see in our dreams, which are not invented but which happen to us. They are not immediately understandable, they need careful analysis by means of association, but, as I have said, not of "free association," which we know always leads back eventually to the emotional thoughts or complexes that are unconsciously captivating our mind. To get there, we have no need of dreams. But in the

early days of medical psychology the general assumption was that dreams were analysed for the purpose of discovering complexes. For this purpose, however, it is sufficient to conduct an association test, which supplies all the necessary hints as I have shown long ago. And not even this test is necessary, because one can obtain the same result by letting people talk long enough.

433   There can be no doubt that dreams often arise from an emotional disturbance in which the habitual complexes are involved. The habitual complexes are the tender spots of the psyche, which react most quickly to a problematical external situation. But I began to suspect that dreams might have another, more interesting function. The fact that they eventually lead back to the complexes is not the specific merit of dreams. If we want to learn what a dream means and what specific function it fulfils, we must disregard its inevitable outcome, the complex. We must put a check on limitless "free" association, a restriction provided by the dream itself. By free association, we move away from the individual dream-image and lose sight of it. We must, on the contrary, keep close to the dream and its individual form. The dream is its own limitation. It is itself the criterion of what belongs to it and of what leads away from it. All material that does not lie within the scope of the dream, or that oversteps the boundaries set by its individual form, leads astray and produces nothing but the complexes, and we do not know whether they belong to the dream or not since they can be produced in so many other ways. There is, for instance, an almost infinite variety of images by which the sexual act can be "symbolized," or rather allegorized. But the dream obviously intends its own specific expression in spite of the fact that the resultant associations will lead to the idea of sexual intercourse. This is no news and is easy to see, but the real task is to understand why the dream has chosen its own individual expression.

434   Only the material that is clearly and visibly indicated as belonging to the dream by the dream-images themselves should be used for interpretation. While free association moves away from the theme of the dream in something like a zigzag line, the new method, as I have always said, is more like a circumambulation, the centre of which is the dream-image. One concentrates on the specific topics, on the dream itself, and disregards the frequent attempts of the dreamer to break away from it. This ever-

present "neurotic" dissociative tendency has many aspects, but at bottom it seems to consist in a basic resistance of the conscious mind to anything unconscious and unknown. As we know, this often fierce resistance is typical of the psychology of primitive societies, which are as a rule conservative and show pronounced misoneistic tendencies. Anything new and unknown causes distinct and even superstitious fear. The primitive manifests all the reactions of a wild animal to untoward events. Our highly differentiated civilization is not at all free from such primitive behaviour. A new idea that is not exactly in line with general expectations meets with the severest obstacles of a psychological kind. It is given no credit, but is feared, combatted, and abhorred in every way. Many pioneers can tell a story of misery, all due to the primitive misoneism of their contemporaries. When it comes to psychology, one of the youngest of the sciences, you can see misoneism at work, and in dealing with your own dreams you can easily observe your reactions when you have to admit a disagreeable thought. It is chiefly and above all fear of the unexpected and unknown that makes people eager to use free association as a means of escape. I do not know how many times in my professional work I have had to repeat the words: "Now let's get back to your dream. What does the *dream* say?"

435   If one wants to understand a dream it must be taken seriously, and one must also assume that it means what it manifestly says, since there is no valid reason to suppose that it is anything other than it is. Yet the apparent futility of dreams is so overwhelming that not only the dreamer but the interpreter as well may easily succumb to the prejudice of the "nothing but" explanation. Whenever a dream gets difficult and obstinate, the temptation to dismiss it altogether is not far away.

436   When I was doing fieldwork with a primitive tribe in East Africa, I discovered to my amazement that they denied having dreams at all. But by patient indirect talk I soon found that they had dreams all right, like everybody else, but were convinced that their dreams meant nothing. "Dreams of ordinary men mean nothing," they said. The only dreams that mattered were those of the chief and the medicine-man, which concerned the welfare of the tribe. Such dreams were highly appreciated. The only drawback was that the chief as well as the medicine-man denied having any more dreams "since the British were in the

country." The District Commissioner had taken over the function of the "big dream."

437   This incident shows that even in a primitive society opinions about dreams are ambivalent, just as in our society, where most people see nothing in dreams while a minority thinks very highly of them. The Church, for instance, has long known of *somnia a Deo missa* (dreams sent by God), and in our own time we have watched the growth of a scientific discipline which aims at exploring the vast field of unconscious processes. Yet the average man thinks little or nothing about dreams, and even a thoroughly educated person shares the common ignorance and underrates everything remotely connected with the "unconscious."

438   The very existence of an unconscious psyche is denied by a great number of scientists and philosophers, who often use the naïve argument that if there were an unconscious psyche there would be two subjects in the individual instead of one. But that is precisely the case, in spite of the supposed unity of the personality. It is, indeed, the great trouble of our time that so many people exist whose right hand does not know what their left is doing. It is by no means the neurotic alone who finds himself in this predicament. It is not a recent development, nor can it be blamed on Christian morality; it is, on the contrary, the symptom of a general unconsciousness that is the heritage of all mankind.

439   The development of consciousness is a slow and laborious process that took untold ages to reach the civilized state (which we date somewhat arbitrarily from the invention of writing, about 4000 B.C.). Although the development since that date seems to be considerable, it is still far from complete. Indefinitely large areas of the mind still remain in darkness. What we call "psyche" is by no means identical with consciousness and its contents. Those who deny the existence of the unconscious do not realize that they are actually assuming our knowledge of the psyche to be complete, with nothing left for further discoveries. It is exactly as if they declared our present knowledge of nature to be the summit of all possible knowledge. Our psyche is part of nature, and its enigma is just as limitless. We cannot define "nature" or "psyche," but can only state what, at present, we understand them to be. No man in his senses, therefore, could make

such a statement as "there is no unconscious," i.e., no psychic contents of which he and others are unconscious—not to mention the mountain of convincing evidence that medical science has accumulated. It is not, of course, scientific responsibility or honesty that causes such resistance, but age-old misoneism, fear of the new and unknown.

440   This peculiar resistance to the unknown part of the psyche has its historical reasons. Consciousness is a very recent acquisition and as such is still in an "experimental state"—frail, menaced by specific dangers, and easily injured. As a matter of fact one of the most common mental derangements among primitives consists in the "loss of a soul," which, as the term indicates, means a noticeable dissociation of consciousness. On the primitive level the psyche or soul is by no means a unit, as is widely supposed. Many primitives assume that, as well as his own, a man has a "bush-soul," incarnate in a wild animal or a tree, with which he is connected by a kind of psychic identity. This is what Lévy-Bruhl called *participation mystique*.[2] In the case of an animal it is a sort of brother, so much so that a man whose brother is a crocodile is supposed to be safe while swimming across a crocodile-infested river. In the case of a tree, the tree is supposed to have authority over the individual like a parent. Injury to the bush-soul means an equal injury to the man. Others assume that a man has a number of souls, which shows clearly that the primitive often feels that he consists of several units. This indicates that his psyche is far from being safely synthesized; on the contrary, it threatens to fall asunder only too easily under the onslaught of unchecked emotions.

441   What we observe in the seemingly remote sphere of the primitive mind has by no means vanished in our advanced civilization. Only too often, as I have said, the right hand does not know what the left is doing, and in a state of violent affect one frequently forgets who one is, so that people can ask: "What the devil has got into you?" We are possessed and altered by our moods, we can suddenly be unreasonable, or important facts unaccountably vanish from our memory. We talk about being able to "control ourselves," but self-control is a rare and remarkable

2 Lévy-Bruhl later retracted this term under the pressure of adverse criticism, to which he unfortunately succumbed. His critics were wrong inasmuch as unconscious identity is a well-known psychological fact.

virtue. If you ask your friends or relatives they may be able to tell you things about yourself of which you have no knowledge. One almost always forgets or omits to apply to oneself the criticism that one hands out so freely to others, fascinated by the mote in one's brother's eye.

442   All these well-known facts show beyond a doubt that, on the heights of our civilization, human consciousness has not yet attained a reasonable degree of continuity. It is still dissociable and vulnerable, in a way fortunately so, since the dissociability of the psyche is also an advantage in that it enables us to concentrate on one point by dismissing everything else that might claim attention. It makes a great difference, however, whether your consciousness purposely splits off and suppresses a part of the psyche temporarily, or whether the same thing *happens* to you, so that the psyche splits spontaneously without your consent and knowledge, or perhaps even against your will. The first is a civilized achievement, the second a primitive and archaic condition or a pathological event and the cause of a neurosis. It is the "loss of a soul," the symptom of a still existing mental primitivity.

443   It is a long way indeed from primitivity to a reliable cohesion of consciousness. Even in our days the unity of consciousness is a doubtful affair, since only a little affect is needed to disrupt its continuity. On the other hand the perfect control of emotion, however desirable from one point of view, would be a questionable accomplishment, for it would deprive social intercourse of all variety, colour, warmth, and charm.

2. THE FUNCTIONS OF THE UNCONSCIOUS

444   Our new method treats the dream as a spontaneous product of the psyche about which there is no previous assumption except that it somehow makes sense. This is no more than every science assumes, namely that its object is worthy of investigation. No matter how low one's opinion of the unconscious may be, the unconscious is at least on a level with the louse, which, after all, enjoys the honest interest of the entomologist. As to the alleged boldness of the hypothesis that an unconscious psyche exists, I must emphasize that a more modest formulation could hardly be imagined. It is so simple that it amounts to a tautology: a content of consciousness disappears and cannot be reproduced. The best we can say of it is: the thought (or whatever it was) has become unconscious, or is cut off from consciousness, so that it cannot even be remembered. Or else it may happen that we have an inkling or hunch of something which is about to break into consciousness: "something is in the air," "we smell a rat," and so on. To speak under these conditions of latent or unconscious contents is hardly a daring hypothesis.

445   When something vanishes from consciousness it does not dissolve into thin air or cease to exist, any more than a car disappearing round a corner becomes non-existent. It is simply out of sight, and, as we may meet the car again, so we may come across a thought again which was previously lost. We find the same thing with sensation, as the following experiment proves. If you produce a continuous note on the edge of audibility, you will observe in listening to it that at regular intervals it is audible and inaudible. These oscillations are due to a periodic increase and decrease of attention. The note never ceases to exist with static intensity. It is merely the decrease of attention that causes its apparent disappearance.

446   The unconscious, therefore, consists in the first place of a

multitude of temporarily eclipsed contents which, as experience shows, continue to influence the conscious processes. A man in a distracted state of mind goes to a certain place in his room, obviously to fetch something. Then he suddenly stops perplexed: he has forgotten why he got up and what he was after. He gropes absent-mindedly among a whole collection of objects, completely at sea as to what he wants to find. Suddenly he wakes up, having discovered the thing he wants. He behaves like a man walking in his sleep oblivious of his original purpose, yet unconsciously guided by it. If you observe the behaviour of a neurotic, you can see him performing apparently conscious and purposeful acts yet, when you ask him about them, you discover to your surprise that he is either unconscious of them or has something quite different in mind. He hears and does not hear, he sees yet is blind, he knows and does not know at the same time. Thousands of such observations have convinced the specialist that unconscious contents behave as if they were conscious, and that you can never be sure whether thought, speech, or action is conscious or not. Something so obvious to yourself that you cannot imagine it to be invisible to anybody can be as good as nonexistent to your fellows, and yet they behave as if they were just as conscious of it as you are yourself.

447   This kind of behaviour has given rise to the medical prejudice that hysterical patients are confirmed liars. Yet the surplus of lies they seem to produce is due to the uncertainty of their mental state, to the dissociability of their consciousness, which is liable to unpredictable eclipses, just as their skin shows unexpected and changing areas of anaesthesia. There is no certainty whether a needle-prick will be registered or not. If their attention can be focused on a certain point, the whole surface of their body may be completely anaesthetized, and, when attention relaxes, sense-perception is instantly restored. Moreover when one hypnotizes such cases one can easily demonstrate that they are aware of everything that has been done in an anaesthetized area or during an eclipse of consciousness. They can remember every detail just as if they had been fully conscious during the experiment. I recall a similar case of a woman who was admitted to the clinic in a state of complete stupor. Next day when she came to, she knew who she was, but did not know where she was nor how or why she had come there, nor did she know the date. I hypno-

tized her, and she could tell me a verifiable story of why she fell ill, how she had got to the clinic, and who had received her, with all the details. As there was a clock in the entrance hall, though not in a very conspicuous place, she could also remember the time of her admission to the minute. Everything happened as if she had been in a completely normal condition and not deeply unconscious.

448   It is true that the bulk of our evidential material comes from clinical observation. That is the reason why many critics assume that the unconscious and its manifestations belong to the sphere of psychopathology as neurotic or psychotic symptoms and that they do not occur in a normal mental state. But, as has been pointed out long ago, neurotic phenomena are not by any means the exclusive products of disease. They are as a matter of fact *normal occurrences pathologically exaggerated,* and therefore just more obvious than their normal parallels. One can indeed observe all hysterical symptoms in a diminutive form in normal individuals, but they are so slight that they usually pass unnoticed. In this respect, everyday life is a mine of evidential material.

449   Just as conscious contents can vanish into the unconscious, other contents can also arise from it. Besides a majority of mere recollections, really new thoughts and creative ideas can appear which have never been conscious before. They grow up from the dark depths like a lotus, and they form an important part of the subliminal psyche. This aspect of the unconscious is of particular relevance in dealing with dreams. One must always bear in mind that dream material does not necessarily consist of memories; it may just as well contain new thoughts that are not yet conscious.

450   Forgetting is a normal process, in which certain conscious contents lose their specific energy through a deflection of attention. When interest turns elsewhere, it leaves former contents in the shadow, just as a searchlight illuminates a new area by leaving another to disappear in the darkness. This is unavoidable, for consciousness can keep only a few images in full clarity at one time, and even this clarity fluctuates, as I have mentioned. "Forgetting" may be defined as temporarily subliminal contents remaining outside the range of vision against one's will. But the forgotten contents have not ceased to exist. Although they cannot be reproduced they are present in a subliminal state, from

which they can rise up spontaneously at any time, often after many years of apparently total oblivion, or they can be fetched back by hypnosis.

451   Besides normal forgetting, there are the cases described by Freud of disagreeable memories which one is only too ready to lose. As Nietzsche has remarked, when pride is insistent enough, memory prefers to give way. Thus among the lost memories we encounter not a few that owe their subliminal state (and their incapacity to be reproduced at will) to their disagreeable and incompatible nature. These are the *repressed* contents.

452   As a parallel to normal forgetting, *subliminal sense-perceptions* should be mentioned, because they play a not unimportant role in our daily life. We see, hear, smell and taste many things without noticing them at the time, either because our attention is deflected or because the stimulus is too slight to produce a conscious impression. But in spite of their apparent non-existence they can influence consciousness. A well-known example is the case of the professor walking in the country with a pupil, deep in serious conversation. Suddenly he notices that his thoughts are interrupted by an unexpected flow of memories from his early childhood. He cannot account for it, as he is unable to discover any associative connection with the subject of his conversation. He stops and looks back: there at a little distance is a farm, through which they had passed a short while ago, and he remembers that soon afterwards images of his childhood began to surge up. "Let us go back to the farm," he says to his pupil; "it must be about there that my fantasies started." Back at the farm, the professor notices the smell of geese. Instantly he recognizes it as the cause of the interruption: in his early youth he had lived on a farm where there were geese, whose characteristic smell had formed a lasting impression and caused the reproduction of the memory-images. He had noticed the smell while passing the farmyard, subliminally, and the unconscious perception had called back long-forgotten memories.

453   This example illustrates how the subliminal perception released early childhood memories, the energic tension of which proved to be strong enough to interrupt the conversation. The perception was subliminal because the attention was engaged elsewhere, and the stimulus was not strong enough to deflect it and to reach consciousness directly. Such phenomena are frequent in everyday life, but mostly they pass unnoticed.

454   A relatively rare but all the more astonishing phenomenon that falls into the same category is *cryptomnesia,* or the "concealed recollection." It consists in the fact that suddenly, mostly in the flow of creative writing, a word, a sentence, an image, a metaphor, or even a whole story appears which may exhibit a strange or otherwise remarkable character. If you ask the author where this fragment comes from, he does not know, and it becomes obvious that he has not even noticed it as anything peculiar. I will quote one such example from Nietzsche's *Thus Spake Zarathustra.* The author describes Zarathustra's "descent to hell" with certain characteristic details which coincide almost word for word with the narration in a ship's log from the year 1686.

455   Nietzsche, *Thus Spake Zarathustra* (1883) [1]

Now about the time that Zarathustra sojourned on the Happy Isles, it happened that a ship anchored at the isle on which the smoking mountain stands, and the crew went ashore to shoot rabbits. About the noontide hour, however, when the captain and his men were together again, they suddenly saw a man coming towards them through the air, and a voice said distinctly: "It is time! It is highest time!" But when the figure drew close to them, flying past quickly like a shadow in the direction of the volcano, they recognized with the greatest dismay that it was Zarathustra. . . . "Behold," said the old helmsman, "Zarathustra goes down to hell!"

Justinus Kerner, *Blätter aus Prevorst* (1831-39) [2]

The four captains and a merchant, Mr. Bell, went ashore on the island of Mount Stromboli to shoot rabbits. At three o'clock they mustered the crew to go aboard, when, to their inexpressible astonishment, they saw two men flying rapidly towards them through the air. One was dressed in black, the other in grey. They came past them very closely, in the greatest haste, and to their utmost dismay descended into the crater of the terrible volcano, Mount Stromboli. They recognized the pair as acquaintances from London.

[1] Ch. XL, "Great Events" (trans. Common, p. 180, slightly modified). [For other discussions, see *Psychiatric Studies,* pars. 140ff. and 180ff.—EDITORS.]
[2] Vol. IV, p. 57, headed "An Extract of Awe-Inspiring Import from the Log of the Ship *Sphinx* in the Year 1686, in the Mediterranean."

456   When I read Nietzsche's story I was struck by its peculiar style, which is different from Nietzsche's usual language, and by the strange images of a ship anchored off a mythological island, of a captain and his crew shooting rabbits, and of the descent to hell of a man who was recognized as an old acquaintance. The parallels with Kerner could not be a mere coincidence. Kerner's collection dates from about 1835 and is probably the only extant source of the seaman's yarn. At least I was certain that Nietzsche must have gleaned it from there. He retells the story with a few significant variations and as if it were his own invention. As it was in the year 1902 that I came across this case, I still had the opportunity to write to Elizabeth Förster-Nietzsche, the author's sister, and she remembered that she and her brother had read the *Blätter aus Prevorst* when Nietzsche was eleven years old, though she did not remember this particular story. The reason why I remembered it was that I had come across Kerner's collection four years before, in a private library; and, as I was interested in the writings of the physicians of that time as the forerunners of medical psychology, I had read through all the volumes of the *Blätter*. Naturally I should have forgotten the yarn in the course of time, because it did not interest me in any way. But in reading Nietzsche I suddenly had a *sentiment du déjà vu*, followed by a dim recollection of old-fashioned cut, and gradually the picture of Kerner's book filtered into my consciousness.

457   Benoît, who produced a surprising parallel to Rider Haggard's *She* in his novel *L'Atlantide*, when accused of plagiarism had to answer that he had never come across Rider Haggard's book and was entirely unaware of its existence. This case could also have been one of cryptomnesia, if it had not been an elaboration of a sort of *représentation collective*, as Lévy-Bruhl has named certain general ideas characteristic of primitive societies. I shall be dealing with these later on.

458   What I have said about the unconscious will give the reader a fair idea of the subliminal material on which the spontaneous production of dream-symbols is based. It is evidently material that owes its unconsciousness chiefly to the fact that certain conscious contents must necessarily lose their energy, i.e., the attention bestowed on them, or their specific emotional tone, in order to make room for new contents. If they were to retain their en-

ergy, they would remain above the threshold and one could not get rid of them. It is as if consciousness were a sort of projector that casts its light (of attention or interest) on new perceptions —due to arrive presently—as well as on the traces of former ones in a dormant state. As a conscious act, this process can be understood as an intentional and voluntary event. Yet just as often consciousness is forced to turn on its light by the intensity of an external or internal stimulus.

459   This observation is not superfluous, for there are many people who overestimate the role of will-power and think nothing can happen in their minds that they do not intend. But, for the sake of psychological understanding, one should learn to discriminate carefully between *intentional and unintentional contents*. The former are derived from the ego-personality, while the latter arise from a source which is not identical with the ego, that is, from a subliminal part of the ego, from its "other side," which is in a way another subject. The existence of this other subject is by no means a pathological symptom, but a normal fact that can be observed at any time anywhere.

460   I once had a discussion with one of my colleagues about another doctor who had done something I had qualified as "utterly idiotic." This doctor was my colleague's personal friend, and moreover a believer in the somewhat fanatical creed to which my colleague subscribed. Both were teetotalers. He impulsively replied to my criticism: "Of course he is an ass"—pulling himself up short—"a highly intelligent man, I meant to say." I mildly remarked that the ass came first, whereupon he angrily denied ever having said such a thing about his friend, and to an unbeliever at that. This man was highly regarded as a scientist, but his right hand did not know what his left was doing. Such people are not fit for psychology and, as a matter of fact, do not like it. But that is the way the voice from the other side is usually treated: "I didn't mean it, I never said so." And in the end, as Nietzsche says, memory prefers to give way.

3. THE LANGUAGE OF DREAMS

461   All contents of consciousness have been or can become subliminal, thus forming part of the psychic sphere which we call
the unconscious. All urges, impulses, intentions, affects, all perceptions and intuitions, all rational and irrational thoughts,
conclusions, inductions, deductions, premises, etc., as well as all
categories of feeling, have their subliminal equivalents, which
may be subject to partial, temporary, or chronic unconsciousness. One uses a word or a concept, for instance, that in another
connection has an entirely different meaning of which one is
momentarily unconscious, and this can lead to a ridiculous or
even disastrous misunderstanding. Even a most carefully defined
philosophical or mathematical concept, which we are sure does
not contain more than we have put into it, is nevertheless more
than we assume. It is at the least a psychic event, the nature of
which is actually unknowable. The very numbers you use in
counting are more than you take them for. They are at the same
time mythological entities (for the Pythagoreans they were even
divine), but you are certainly unaware of this when you use
numbers for a practical purpose.

462   We are also unconscious of the fact that general terms like
"state," "money," "health," "society" etc. usually mean more
than they are supposed to signify. They are general only because
we assume them to be so, but in practical reality they have all
sorts of nuances of meaning. I am not thinking of the deliberate
twisting of such concepts in their Communist usage, but of the
fact that even when they are understood in their proper sense
they nevertheless vary slightly from person to person. The reason for this variation is that a general notion is received into an
individual context and is therefore understood and used in an
individual way. As long as concepts are identical with mere
words, the variation is almost imperceptible and of no practical

importance. But when an exact definition or a careful explanation is needed, one can occasionally discover the most amazing variations, not only in the purely intellectual understanding of the term, but particularly in its emotional tone and its application. As a rule these variations are subliminal and therefore never realized.

463   One may dismiss such differences as redundant or over-nice distinctions, but the fact that they exist shows that even the most banal contents of consciousness have a penumbra of uncertainty around them, which justifies us in thinking that each of them carries a definite subliminal charge. Although this aspect plays little role in everyday life, one must bear it in mind when analysing dreams. I recall a dream of my own that baffled me for a while. In this dream, a certain Mr. X was desperately trying to get behind me and jump on my back. I knew nothing of this gentleman except that he had succeeded in twisting something I had said into a rather grotesque travesty of my meaning. This kind of thing had frequently happened to me in my professional life, and I had never bothered to realize whether it made me angry or not. But as it is of practical importance to maintain conscious control of one's emotions, the dream pointedly brought up the incident again in the apparent "disguise" of a colloquialism. This saying, common enough in ordinary speech, is "Du kannst mir auf den Buckel steigen" (you can climb on my back), which means "I don't give a damn what you say."

464   One could say that this dream-image was symbolic, for it did not state the situation directly but in a roundabout way, through a concretized colloquial metaphor which I did not understand at first sight. Since I have no reason to believe that the unconscious has any intention of concealing things, I must be careful not to project such a device on its activity. It is characteristic of dreams to prefer pictorial and picturesque language to colourless and merely rational statements. This is certainly not an intentional concealment; it simply emphasizes our inability to understand the emotionally charged picture-language of dreams.

465   As daily adaptation to the reality of things demands accurate statements, we have learnt to discard the trimming of fantasy, and have thus lost a quality that is still characteristic of the primitive mind. Primitive thinking sees its object surrounded

by a fringe of associations which have become more or less unconscious in civilized man. Thus animals, plants, and inanimate
objects can acquire properties that are most unexpected to the
white man. A nocturnal animal seen by day is, for the primitive,
quite obviously a medicine-man who has temporarily changed
his shape; or else it is a doctor-animal or an animal-ancestor, or
somebody's bush-soul. A tree can be part of a man's life, it has a
soul and a voice, and the man shares its fate, and so on. Certain
South American Indians assure you that they are red *araras*
(parrots), although they are quite aware that they have no
feathers and don't look like birds. In the primitive's world,
things do not have the same sharp boundaries they do in ours.
What we call psychic identity or *participation mystique* has
been stripped off our world of things. It is exactly this halo, or
"fringe of consciousness," as William James calls it, which gives
a colourful and fantastic aspect to the primitive's world. We
have lost it to such a degree that we do not recognize it when we
meet it again, and are baffled by its incomprehensibility. With us
such things are kept below the threshold; and when they occasionally reappear, we are convinced that something is wrong.

466   I have more than once been consulted by highly educated
and otherwise intelligent people because they had peculiar
dreams, involuntary fantasies, or even visions, which shocked or
frightened them. They assumed that nobody in a sound mental
condition could suffer from such phenomena, and that a person
who had a vision was certainly pathological. A theologian I
knew once avowed his belief that Ezekiel's visions were morbid
symptoms, and that when Moses and other prophets heard
"voices" they were suffering from hallucinations. Naturally he
got into a panic when some spontaneous events of this kind happened to him. We are so used to the rational surface of our
world that we cannot imagine anything untoward happening
within the confines of common sense. If our mind once in a
while does something thoroughly unexpected, we are terrified
and immediately think of a pathological disturbance, whereas
primitive man would think of fetishes, spirits, or gods but would
never doubt his sanity. Modern man is very much in the situation of the old doctor who was himself a psychotic patient.
When I asked him how he was, he replied that he had had a
wonderful night disinfecting the whole heaven with chloride of

mercury but had found no trace of God. What we find instead of God is a neurosis or something worse, and the fear of God has changed into a phobia or anxiety neurosis. The emotion remains the same, only its object has changed its name and nature for the worse.

467   I remember a professor of philosophy and psychology who consulted me about his cancer phobia. He suffered from a compulsive conviction that he had a malignant tumour, although nothing of the sort was ever found in dozens of X-ray pictures. "Oh, I know there is nothing," he would say, "but there still *might* be something." Such a confession is certainly far more humiliating to a strong intellect than the belief of a primitive that he is plagued by a ghost. Malevolent spirits are at least a perfectly admissible hypothesis in a primitive society, but it is a shattering experience for a civilized person to have to admit that he is the victim of nothing more than a foolish prank of the imagination. The primitive phenomenon of obsession has not vanished, it is the same as ever. It is only interpreted in a different and more obnoxious way.

468   Many dreams present images and associations that are analogous to primitive ideas, myths, and rites. These dream-images were called "archaic remnants" by Freud. The term suggests that they are psychic elements left over from times long ago and still adhering to our modern mind. This point of view forms part of the prevailing depreciation of the unconscious as a mere appendix of consciousness or, to put it more drastically, a dustbin which collects all the refuse of the conscious mind—all things discarded, disused, worthless, forgotten, and repressed.

469   This opinion had to be abandoned in more recent times, since further investigation has shown that such images and associations belong to the regular structure of the unconscious and can be observed more or less everywhere, in the dreams of highly educated as well as illiterate people, of the intelligent as well as the stupid. They are in no sense dead or meaningless "remnants"; on the contrary, they still continue to function and are therefore of vital value just because of their "historical" nature. They are a sort of language that acts as a bridge between the way in which we consciously express our thoughts and a more primitive, more colourful and pictorial form of expression—a language that appeals directly to feeling and emotion. Such a lan-

guage is needed to translate certain truths from their "cultural" form (where they are utterly ineffectual) into a form that hits the nail on the head. For instance, there is a lady well known for her stupid prejudices and stubborn arguments. The doctor tries in vain to instil some insight. He says: "My dear lady, your views are indeed very interesting and original. But you see, there are many people who unfortunately lack your assumptions and have need of your forbearance. Couldn't you . . ." etc. He could just as well talk to a stone. But the dream follows a different method. She dreams: there is a great social affair to which she is invited. She is received by her hostess (a very bright woman) at the door with the words: "Oh, how nice that you have come, all your friends are already here and are expecting you." She leads her to a door, opens it, and the lady steps into—a cowshed.

470   This is a more concrete and drastic language, simple enough to be understood even by a blockhead. Although the lady would not admit the point of the dream, it nevertheless went home, and after a time she was forced to accept it because she could not help seeing the self-inflicted joke.

471   The message of the unconscious is of greater importance than most people realize. As consciousness is exposed to all sorts of external attractions and distractions, it is easily led astray and seduced into following ways that are unsuited to its individuality. The general function of dreams is to balance such disturbances in the mental equilibrium by producing contents of a complementary or compensatory kind. Dreams of high vertiginous places, balloons, aeroplanes, flying and falling, often accompany states of consciousness characterized by fictitious assumptions, overestimation of oneself, unrealistic opinions, and grandiose plans. If the warning of the dream is not heeded, real accidents take its place. One stumbles, falls downstairs, runs into a car, etc. I remember the case of a man who was inextricably involved in a number of shady affairs. He developed an almost morbid passion for dangerous mountain-climbing as a sort of compensation: he was trying to "get above himself." In one dream he saw himself stepping off the summit of a high mountain into the air. When he told me his dream, I instantly saw the risk he was running, and I tried my best to emphasize the warning and convince him of the need to restrain himself. I even told him that the dream meant his death in a mountain accident. It

was in vain. Six months later he "stepped off into the air." A mountain guide watched him and a young friend letting themselves down on a rope in a difficult place. The friend had found a temporary foothold on a ledge, and the dreamer was following him down. Suddenly he let go of the rope "as if he were jumping into the air," as the guide reported afterwards. He fell on his friend, and both went down and were killed.

472 Another typical case was that of a lady who was living above herself in a fantasy of distinction and austerity. But she had shocking dreams, reminding her of all sorts of unsavoury things. When I put my finger on them, she indignantly refused to acknowledge them. The dreams then became menacing, full of references to the long lonely walks she took in the woods near the town, where she indulged in soulful musings. I saw the danger and warned her insistently, but she would not listen. A week later a sexual pervert attacked her murderously, and only in the nick of time was she rescued by some people who had heard her screams. Obviously she had a secret longing for some such adventure and preferred to pay the price of two broken ribs and the fracture of a laryngeal cartilage, just as the mountain climber at least had the satisfaction of finding a definite way out of his predicament.

473 Dreams prepare, announce, or warn about certain situations, often long before they actually happen. This is not necessarily a miracle or a precognition. Most crises or dangerous situations have a long incubation, only the conscious mind is not aware of it. Dreams can betray the secret. They often do, but just as often, it seems, they do not. Therefore our assumption of a benevolent hand restraining us in time is doubtful. Or, to put it more positively, it seems that a benevolent agency is at work sometimes but at other times not. The mysterious finger may even point the way to perdition. One cannot afford to be naïve in dealing with dreams. They originate in a spirit that is not quite human, but is rather the breath of nature—of the beautiful and generous as well as the cruel goddess. If we want to characterize this spirit, we would do better to turn to the ancient mythologies and the fables of the primeval forest. Civilization is a most expensive process and its acquisitions have been paid for by enormous losses, the extent of which we have largely forgotten or have never appreciated.

474   Through our efforts to understand dreams we become acquainted with what William James has aptly called the "fringe of consciousness." What appear to be redundant and unwelcome accessories are, if studied more closely, the almost invisible roots of conscious contents, i.e., their subliminal aspects. They form the psychic material that must be considered as the intermediary between unconscious and conscious contents, or the bridge that spans the gap between consciousness and the ultimately physiological foundations of the psyche. The practical importance of such a bridge can hardly be overrated. It is the indispensable link between the rational world of consciousness and the world of instinct. The more our consciousness is influenced by prejudices, fantasies, infantile wishes, and the lure of external objects, the more the already existing gap will widen out into a neurotic dissociation and lead to an artificial life far removed from healthy instincts, nature, and truth. Dreams try to re-establish the equilibrium by restoring the images and emotions that express the state of the unconscious. One can hardly ever restore the original condition by rational talk, which is far too flat and colourless. But, as my examples have shown, the language of dreams provides just those images which appeal to the deeper strata of the psyche. One could even say that the interpretation of dreams enriches consciousness to such an extent that it relearns the forgotten language of the instincts.

475   In so far as instincts are physiological urges, they are perceived by the senses and at the same time manifest themselves as fantasies. But in so far as they are not perceived sensually, they reveal their presence only in images. The vast majority of instinctive phenomena consists, however, of images, many of which are of a symbolic nature whose meaning is not immediately recognizable. One finds them chiefly in that twilight realm between dim consciousness and the unconscious background of the dream. Sometimes a dream is of such vital importance that its message reaches consciousness no matter how uncomfortable or shocking it may be. From the standpoint of mental equilibrium and physiological health in general, it is much better for the conscious and the unconscious to be connected and to move on parallel lines than for them to be dissociated. In this respect the production of symbols can be considered a most valuable function.

476   One will naturally ask what is the point of this function if its symbols should pass unnoticed or prove to be incomprehensible? But lack of conscious understanding does not mean that the dream has no effect at all. Even civilized man can occasionally observe that a dream which he cannot remember can slightly alter his mood for better or worse. Dreams can be "understood" to a certain extent in a subliminal way, and that is mostly how they work. Only when a dream is very impressive, or repeats itself often, do interpretation and conscious understanding become desirable. But in pathological cases an interpretation is imperative and should be undertaken if there are no counter-indications, such as the existence of a latent psychosis, which is, as it were, only waiting for a suitable releasing agent to burst forth in full force. Unintelligent and incompetent application of dream analysis and interpretation is indeed not advisable, and particularly not when there is a dissociation between a very one-sided consciousness and a correspondingly irrational or "crazy" unconscious.

477   Owing to the infinite variety of conscious contents and their deviation from the ideal middle line, the unconscious compensation is equally varied, so that one would be hard put to it to say whether dreams and their symbols are classifiable or not. Though there are dreams and occasional symbols—better called motifs in this case—which are typical and occur often, most dreams are individual and atypical. Typical motifs are falling, flying, being chased by dangerous animals or men, being insufficiently or absurdly clothed in public places, being in a hurry or lost in a milling crowd, fighting with useless weapons or being utterly defenceless, running and getting nowhere, and so on. A typical infantile motif is the dream of growing infinitely small or infinitely big, or of being transformed from the one into the other.

478   A noteworthy phenomenon is the recurrent dream. There are cases of dreams repeating themselves from the days of childhood to the advanced years of adult life. Such dreams usually compensate a defect in one's conscious attitude, or they date from a traumatic moment that has left behind some specific prejudice, or they anticipate a future event of some importance. I myself dreamt of a motif that was repeated many times over a period of years. It was that I discovered a part of a wing of my

house which I did not know existed. Sometimes it was the place where my parents lived—who had died long ago—where my father, to my great surprise, had a laboratory in which he studied the comparative anatomy of fishes, and where my mother ran a hostelry for ghostly visitors. Usually the wing or independent guest-house was an historical building several hundred years old, long forgotten, yet my ancestral property. It contained interesting old furniture, and towards the end of this series of recurrent dreams I discovered an old library whose books were unknown to me. Finally, in the last dream, I opened one of the old volumes and found in it a profusion of the most marvellous symbolic pictures. When I awoke, my heart was pounding with excitement.

479 Some time before this dream I had placed an order with an antiquarian bookseller abroad for one of the Latin alchemical classics, because I had come across a quotation that I thought might be connected with early Byzantine alchemy, and I wished to verify it. Several weeks after my dream a parcel arrived containing a parchment volume of the sixteenth century with many most fascinating symbolic pictures. They instantly reminded me of my dream library. As the rediscovery of alchemy forms an important part of my life as a pioneer of psychology, the motif of the unknown annex of my house can easily be understood as an anticipation of a new field of interest and research. At all events, from that moment thirty years ago the recurrent dream came to an end.

480 Symbols, like dreams, are natural products, but they do not occur only in dreams. They can appear in any number of psychic manifestations: there are symbolic thoughts and feelings, symbolic acts and situations, and it often looks as if not only the unconscious but even inanimate objects were concurring in the arrangement of symbolic patterns. There are numerous well-authenticated stories of a clock that stopped at the moment of its owner's death, like Frederick the Great's pendulum clock at Sans Souci; of a mirror that broke, or a boiling coffee-pot that exploded, just before or during a crisis; and so on. Even if the sceptic refuses to credit such reports, stories of this kind are ever renewed and are told again and again, which is ample proof of their psychological importance, even though ignorant people deny their factual existence.

481   The most important symbols, however, are not individual but collective in their nature and origin. They are found principally in the religions. The believer assumes that they are of divine origin—that they are revealed. The sceptic thinks they are invented. Both are wrong. It is true that, on the one hand, such symbols have for centuries been the objects of careful and quite conscious elaboration and differentiation, as in the case of dogmas. But, on the other hand, they are *représentations collectives* dating from dim and remote ages, and these are "revelations" only in the sense that they are images originating in dreams and creative fantasies. The latter are involuntary, spontaneous manifestations and by no means arbitrary and intentional inventions.

482   There was never a genius who sat down with his pen or brush and said: "Now I am going to invent a symbol." No one can take a more or less rational thought, reached as a logical conclusion or deliberately chosen, and then disguise it as a "symbolic" phantasmagoria. No matter how fantastic the trappings may look, it would still be a *sign* hinting at a conscious thought, and not a symbol. A sign is always less than the thing it points to, and a symbol is always more than we can understand at first sight. Therefore we never stop at the sign but go on to the goal it indicates; but we remain with the symbol because it promises more than it reveals.

483   If the contents of dreams agree with a sex theory, then we know their essence already, but if they are symbolic we at least know that we do not understand them yet. *A symbol does not disguise, it reveals in time.* It is obvious that dream interpretation will yield one result when you consider the dream to be symbolic, and an entirely different one when you assume that the essential thought is merely disguised but already known in principle. In the latter case, dream interpretation makes no sense whatever, for you find only what you know already. Therefore I always advise my pupils: "Learn as much as you can about symbolism and forget it all when you are analysing a dream." This advice is so important in practice that I myself have made it a rule to admit that I never understand a dream well enough to interpret it correctly. I do this in order to check the flow of my own associations and reactions, which might otherwise prevail over my patient's uncertainties and hesitations. As it is of the

highest therapeutic importance for the analyst to get the message of the dream as accurately as possible, it is essential for him to explore the context of the dream-images with the utmost thoroughness. I had a dream while I was working with Freud that illustrates this very clearly.

484   I dreamt that I was in "my house," apparently on the first floor, in a cosy, pleasant drawing-room furnished in the style of the eighteenth century. I was rather astonished because I realized I had never seen this room before, and began to wonder what the ground floor was like. I went downstairs and found it rather dark, with panelled walls and heavy furniture dating from the sixteenth century or even earlier. I was greatly surprised and my curiosity increased, because it was all a very unexpected discovery. In order to become better acquainted with the whole structure of the house, I thought I would go down to the cellar. I found a door, with a flight of stone steps that led down to a large vaulted room. The floor consisted of large slabs of stone, and the walls struck me as very ancient. I examined the mortar and found it was mixed with splinters of brick. Obviously it was an old Roman wall. I began to grow excited. In a corner, I saw an iron ring in one of the stone slabs. I lifted it up and saw yet another narrow flight of steps leading down to a sort of cave which was obviously a prehistoric tomb. It contained two skulls, some bones, and broken shards of pottery. Then I woke up.

485   If Freud, when analysing this dream, had followed my method of exploring the context, he would have heard a far-reaching story. But I am afraid he would have dismissed it as a mere attempt to escape from a problem that was really his own. The dream is in fact a short summary of my life—the life of my mind. I grew up in a house two hundred years old, our furniture consisted mostly of pieces about a hundred years old, and mentally my greatest adventure had been the study of Kant and Schopenhauer. The great news of the day was the work of Charles Darwin. Shortly before this I had been living in a still medieval world with my parents, where the world and man were still presided over by divine omnipotence and providence. This world had become antiquated and obsolete. My Christian faith had been relativized by my encounter with Eastern religions and

Greek philosophy. It is for this reason that the ground floor was so still, dark, and obviously uninhabited.

486   My then historical interests had developed from my original preoccupation with comparative anatomy and paleontology when I worked as an assistant at the Anatomical Institute. I was fascinated by the bones of fossil man, particularly by the much-discussed *Neanderthalensis* and the still more controversial skull of Dubois' *Pithecanthropus*. As a matter of fact, these were my real associations to the dream. But I did not dare mention the subject of skulls, skeletons, or corpses to Freud, because I had learned that this theme was not popular with him. He cherished the peculiar idea that I anticipated his early death. He drew this conclusion from the fact that I was interested in the mummified corpses in the so-called Bleikeller in Bremen, which we had visited together in 1909 on our trip to America.[1]

487   Thus I was reluctant to come out with my thoughts, since through recent experience I was deeply impressed by the almost unbridgeable gap between Freud's mental outlook and background and my own. I was afraid of losing his friendship if I should open up to him about my inner world, which, I surmised, would look very queer to him. Feeling quite uncertain about my own psychology, I almost automatically told him a lie about my "free associations" in order to escape the impossible task of enlightening him about my very personal and utterly different mental constitution.

488   I soon realized that Freud was seeking for some incompatible wish of mine. And so I suggested tentatively that the skulls might refer to certain members of my family whose death, for some reason, I might desire. This proposal met with his approval, but I was not satisfied with such a "phoney" solution.

489   While I was trying to find a suitable answer to Freud's questions, I was suddenly confounded by an intuition about the role which the subjective factor plays in psychological understanding. My intuition was so overwhelming that my only thought was how to get out of this impossible snarl, and I took the easy way out by a lie. This was neither elegant nor morally defensible, but otherwise I should have risked a fatal row with Freud —and I did not feel up to that for many reasons.

[1] For further details, see my *Memories, Dreams, Reflections*, pp. 156ff. (London edn., pp. 152ff.).

490   My intuition consisted in a sudden and most unexpected insight into the fact that my dream meant myself, *my* life and *my* world, my whole reality as against a theoretical structure erected by another, alien mind for reasons and purposes of its own. It was not Freud's dream, it was mine; and suddenly I understood in a flash what my dream meant.

491   I must apologize for this rather lengthy narration of the jam I got into through telling Freud my dream. But it is a good example of the difficulties in which one gets involved in the course of a real dream analysis. So much depends on the personal differences between the analyst and the analysand.

492   Dream analysis on this level is less a technique than a dialectical process between two personalities. If it is handled as a technique, the peculiarity of the subject as an individual is excluded and the therapeutic problem is reduced to the simple question: who will dominate whom? I had given up hypnotic treatment for this very reason, because I did not want to impose my will on others. I wanted the healing processes to grow out of the patient's own personality, and not out of suggestions of mine that would have only a passing effect. I wanted to protect and preserve my patient's dignity and freedom so that he could live his life by his own volition.

493   I could not share Freud's almost exclusive interest in sex. Assuredly sex plays no small role among human motives, but in many cases it is secondary to hunger, the power drive, ambition, fanaticism, envy, revenge, or the devouring passion of the creative impulse and the religious spirit.

494   For the first time it dawned on me that before we construct general theories about man and his psyche we should learn a great deal more about the real human being, rather than an abstract idea of *Homo sapiens.*

4. THE PROBLEM OF TYPES IN
DREAM INTERPRETATION

495   In all other branches of science, it is a legitimate procedure to apply an hypothesis to an impersonal object. Psychology, however, inescapably confronts us with the living relationship between two individuals, neither of whom can be divested of his subjectivity or depersonalized in any way. They can mutually agree to deal with a chosen theme in an impersonal, objective manner, but when the whole of the personality becomes the object of their discussion, two individual subjects confront one another and the application of a one-way rule is excluded. Progress is possible only if mutual agreement can be reached. The objectivity of the final result can be established only by comparison with the standards that are generally valid in the social milieu to which the individuals belong, and we must also take their own mental equilibrium, or "sanity," into account. This does not mean that the final result must be the complete collectivization of the individual, for this would be a most unnatural condition. On the contrary, a sane and normal society is one in which people habitually disagree. General agreement is relatively rare outside the sphere of the instinctive qualities. Disagreement functions as a vehicle of mental life in a society, but it is not a goal; agreement is equally important. Because psychology basically depends upon balanced opposites, no judgment can be considered final unless allowance is made for its reversibility. The reason for this peculiarity lies in the fact that there is no standpoint above or outside psychology that would enable us to form a final judgment as to what the psyche is. Everything we can imagine is in a psychic state, i.e., in the state of a conscious representation. To get outside this is the whole difficulty of the physical sciences.

496   In spite of the fact that the only reality is the individual, some generalities are necessary in order to clarify and classify the empirical material, for it would obviously be impossible to formulate any psychological theory, or to teach it, by describing individuals. As a principle of classification, one can choose any likeness or unlikeness if only it is general enough, be it anatomical, physiological, or psychological. For our purpose, which is mainly concerned with psychology, it will be a psychological one, namely the widespread and easily observable fact that a great number of people are *extraverted* and others *introverted*. There is no need for a special explanation of these terms as they have passed into common speech.

497   This is one of the many generalities from which one can choose, and it is fairly suitable for our purpose in so far as we are seeking to describe the method of, and approach to, an understanding of dreams as the main source of natural symbols. As I have said, the process of interpretation consists in the confrontation of two minds, the analyst's and the analysand's, and not in the application of a preconceived theory. The analyst's mind is characterized by a number of individual peculiarities, perhaps just as many as the analysand's. They have the effect of prejudices. It cannot be assumed that the analyst is a superman just because he is a doctor and possesses a theory and a corresponding technique. He can only imagine himself to be superior if he assumes that his theory and technique are absolute truths, capable of embracing the whole of the psyche. Since such an assumption is more than doubtful, he cannot really be sure of it. Consequently he will be assailed by secret doubts in adopting such an attitude, i.e., in confronting the human wholeness of the analysand with a theory and a technique (which are mere hypotheses) instead of with his own living wholeness. This alone is the equivalent of his analysand's personality. Psychological experience and knowledge are nothing more than professional advantages on the part of the analyst that do not keep him safely outside the fray. He will be tested just as much as the analysand.

498   Since the systematic analysis of dreams demands the confrontation of two individuals, it will make a great difference whether their type of attitude is the same or not. If both belong to the same type, they may sail along happily for a long time. But if one is an extravert and the other an introvert, their different

and contradictory standpoints may clash right away, particularly when they are unconscious of their own type or are convinced that it is the only right one. Such a mistake is easily made, because the value of the one is the non-value of the other. The one will choose the majority view, the other will reject it just because it is everybody's taste. Freud himself interpreted the introverted type as an individual morbidly engrossed in himself. But introspection and self-knowledge can just as well be of the greatest value.

499 The apparently trifling difference between the extravert, with his emphasis on externals, and the introvert, who puts the emphasis on the way he takes a situation, plays a very great role in the analysis of dreams. From the start you must bear in mind that what the one appreciates may be very negative to the other, and the high ideal of the one can be an object of repulsion to the other. This becomes more and more obvious the further you go into the details of type differences. Extraversion and introversion are just two among many peculiarities of human behaviour, but they are often rather obvious and easily recognizable. If one studies extraverted individuals, for instance, one soon discovers that they differ from one another in many ways, and that being extraverted is a superficial and too general criterion to be really characteristic. That is why, long ago, I tried to find some further basic peculiarities that might serve the purpose of getting some order into the apparently limitless variations of human personality.

500 I had always been impressed by the fact that there are surprisingly many individuals who never use their minds if they can avoid it, and yet are not stupid, and an equal number who obviously do use their minds but in an amazingly stupid way. I was also surprised to find many intelligent and wide-awake people who lived (as far as one could make out) as if they had never learned to use their sense organs. They did not see the things before their eyes, hear the words sounding in their ears, notice the things they touched or tasted, and lived without being aware of their own bodies. There were others who seemed to live in a most curious condition of consciousness, as if the state they had arrived at today were final, with no change in sight, or as if the world and the psyche were static and would remain so for ever. They seemed devoid of all imagination, and entirely and exclu-

sively dependent on sense perception. Chances and possibilities did not exist in their world, and in their "today" there was no real "tomorrow." The future was just the repetition of the past.

501 What I am trying to convey to the reader is the first glimpse of the impressions I received when I began to observe the many people I met. It soon became clear to me that the people who used their minds were those who *thought,* who employed their intellectual faculty in trying to adapt to people and circumstances; and that the equally intelligent people, who yet did not think, were those who sought and found their way by *feeling.* Now "feeling" is a word that needs some explanation. For instance, one speaks of "feeling" when it is a matter of "sentiment" (corresponding to the French *sentiment*). But one also applies the same word to an opinion; a communication from the White House may begin: "The President feels . . ." Or one uses it to express an intuition: "I had a feeling . . ." Finally, feeling is often confused with sensation.

502 What I mean by feeling in contrast to thinking is a *judgment of value:* agreeable or disagreeable, good or bad, and so on. Feeling so defined is not an emotion or affect, which is, as the words convey, an involuntary manifestation. Feeling as I mean it is a judgment without any of the obvious bodily reactions that characterize an emotion. Like thinking, it is a *rational* function; whereas intuition, like sensation, is *irrational.* In so far as intuition is a "hunch" it is not a product of a voluntary act; it is rather an involuntary event, which depends on different external or internal circumstances instead of an act of judgment. Intuition is more like sense perception, which is also an irrational event in so far as it depends essentially on external or internal stimuli deriving from physical and not mental causes.

503 These four functional types correspond to the obvious means by which consciousness obtains its orientation. *Sensation* (or sense perception) tells you that something exists; *thinking* tells you what it is; *feeling* tells you whether it is agreeable or not; and *intuition* tells you where it comes from and where it is going.

504 The reader should understand that these four criteria are just so many viewpoints among others, such as will-power, temperament, imagination, memory, morality, religiousness, etc.

There is nothing dogmatic about them, nor do they claim to be the ultimate truth about psychology; but their basic nature recommends them as suitable principles of classification. Classification has little value if it does not provide a means of orientation and a practical terminology. I find classification into types particularly helpful when I am called upon to explain parents to children or husbands to wives, and vice versa. It is also useful in understanding one's own prejudices.

505   Thus, if you want to understand another person's dream, you have to sacrifice your own predilections and suppress your prejudices, at least for the time being. This is neither easy nor comfortable, because it means a moral effort that is not everyone's cup of tea. But, if you do not make the effort to criticize your own standpoint and to admit its relativity, you will get neither the right information about, nor sufficient insight into, your analysand's mind. As you expect at least some willingness on his part to listen to your opinion and to take it seriously, the patient must be granted the same right too. Although such a relationship is indispensable for any understanding and is therefore a self-evident necessity, one has to remind oneself again and again that in therapy it is more important for the patient to understand than for the analyst's theoretical expectations to be satisfied. The patient's resistance to the analyst is not necessarily wrong; it is rather a sign that something does not "click." Either the patient is not yet at a point where he would be able to understand, or the interpretation does not fit.

506   In our efforts to interpret the dream symbols of another person, we are particularly hampered by an almost invincible tendency to fill the gaps in our understanding by *projection*—that is, by the assumption that what I think is also my partner's thought. This source of error can be avoided by establishing the context of the dream-images and excluding all theoretical assumptions—except for the heuristic hypothesis that dreams somehow make sense.

507   There is no rule, let alone a law, of dream interpretation, although it does look as if the general purpose of dreams is *compensation*. At least, compensation can be said to be the most promising and most fertile hypothesis. Sometimes the manifest dream demonstrates its compensatory character from the start. For instance, a patient with no small idea of himself and his

moral superiority dreamt of a drunken tramp wallowing in a ditch beside the road. The dreamer says (in the dream): "It's awful to see how low a man can fall!" It is evident that the dream was attempting to deflate his exalted opinion of himself. But there was more to it than that. It turned out that he had a black sheep in the family, a younger brother who was a degenerate alcoholic. What the dream also revealed was that his superior attitude compensated the inferiority of his brother—and of the brother who was also himself.

508   In another case, a lady who was proud of her intelligent understanding of psychology kept on dreaming about a certain woman whom she occasionally met in society. In real life she did not like her, thinking her vain, dishonest, and an intriguer. She wondered why she should dream of a person so unlike herself and yet, in the dream, so friendly and intimate, like a sister. The dream obviously wanted to convey the idea that she was "shadowed" by an unconscious character resembling that woman. As she had a very definite idea of herself, she was unaware of her own power-complex and her own shady motives, which had more than once led to disagreeable scenes that were always attributed to others but never to her own machinations.

509   It is not only the shadow-side that is overlooked, disregarded and repressed; positive qualities can also be subjected to the same treatment. An instance of this would be an apparently modest, self-effacing man with winning, apologetic or deprecatory manners, who always takes a back seat though with seeming politeness he never misses an opportunity to be present. His judgment is well-informed, even competent and apparently appreciative, yet it hints at a certain higher level from which the matter in question could be dealt with in a far superior way. In his dreams he constantly meets great men such as Napoleon and Alexander the Great. His obvious inferiority complex is clearly compensated by such momentous visitors, but at the same time the dreams raise the critical question: what sort of man must I be to have such illustrious callers? In this respect, they show that the dreamer nurses a secret megalomania as an antidote to his inferiority complex. Without his knowing it, the idea of grandeur enables him to immunize himself against all influences from his surroundings; nothing penetrates his skin, and he can thus keep aloof from obligations that would be binding to other

people. He does not feel in any way called upon to prove to himself or his fellows that his superior judgment is based on corresponding merits. He is not only a bachelor, but mentally sterile as well. He only understands the art of spreading hints and whisperings about his importance, but no monument witnesses to his deeds. He plays this inane game all unconsciously, and the dreams try to bring it home to him in a curiously ambiguous way, as the old saying goes: *Ducunt volentem fata, nolentem trahunt* (the fates lead the willing, but drag the unwilling). Hobnobbing with Napoleon or being on speaking terms with Alexander the Great is just the thing a man with an inferiority complex could wish for—a wholesale confirmation of the greatness behind the scenes. It is true wish-fulfilment, which anticipates an achievement without the merits that should lead to it. But why, one will ask, can't dreams be open and direct about it, and say it clearly without subterfuges that seem to mislead in an almost cunning way?

510   I have frequently been asked this question and I have asked it myself. I am often surprised at the tantalizing way dreams seem to evade definite information or omit the decisive point. Freud assumed the existence of a special factor, called the "censor," which was supposed to twist the dream-images and make them unrecognizable or misleading in order to deceive the dreaming consciousness about the real subject of the dream: the incompatible wish. Through the concealment of the critical point, it was supposed that the dreamer's sleep would be protected against the shock of a disagreeable reminiscence. But the dream as a guardian of sleep is an unlikely hypothesis, since dreams just as often disturb sleep.

511   It looks rather as if, instead of an unconscious censor, consciousness, or the dreamer's approach to consciousness, had itself a blotting-out effect on the subliminal contents. Subliminality corresponds to what Janet calls *abaissement du niveau mental*. It is a lowering of the energic tension, in which psychic contents sink below the threshold and lose the qualities they possess in their conscious state. They lose their definiteness and clearness, and their relations become vaguely analogous instead of rational and comprehensible. This is a phenomenon that can be observed in all dreamlike conditions, whether due to fatigue, fever, or toxins. But as soon as their tension increases, they become less

subliminal, more definite, and thus more conscious. There is no reason to believe that the *abaissement* shields incompatible wishes from discovery, although it may incidentally happen that an incompatible wish disappears along with the vanishing consciousness. The dream, being essentially a subliminal process, cannot produce a definite thought, unless it should cease to be a dream by instantly becoming a conscious content. The dream cannot but skip all those points that are particularly important to the conscious mind. It manifests the "fringe of consciousness," like the faint glimmer of the stars during a total eclipse of the sun.

512   Dream symbols are for the most part manifestations of a psyche that is beyond the control of consciousness. Meaning and purposefulness are not prerogatives of the conscious mind; they operate through the whole of living nature. There is no difference in principle between organic and psychic formations. As a plant produces its flower, so the psyche creates its symbols. Every dream is evidence of this process. Thus, through dreams, intuitions, impulses, and other spontaneous happenings, instinctive forces influence the activity of consciousness. Whether that influence is for better or worse depends on the actual contents of the unconscious. If it contains too many things that normally ought to be conscious, then its function becomes twisted and prejudiced; motives appear that are not based on true instincts, but owe their activity to the fact that they have been consigned to the unconscious by repression or neglect. They overlay, as it were, the normal unconscious psyche and distort its natural symbol-producing function.

513   Therefore it is usual for psychotherapy, concerned as it is with the causes of a disturbance, to begin by eliciting from the patient a more or less voluntary confession of all the things he dislikes, is ashamed of, or fears. This is like the much older confession in the Church, which in many ways anticipated modern psychological techniques. In practice, however, the procedure is often reversed, since overpowering feelings of inferiority or a serious weakness may make it very difficult, if not impossible, for the patient to face a still deeper darkness and worthlessness. I have often found it more profitable first to give a positive outlook to the patient, a foundation on which he could stand, before we approached more painful and debilitating insights.

514   Take as a simple example the dream of "personal exaltation," in which one has tea with the Queen of England, or is on
intimate terms with the Pope. If the dreamer is not a schizophrenic, the practical interpretation of the symbol depends very
much on the state of his consciousness. If he is obviously convinced of his greatness a damper will be indicated, but if it is a
matter of a worm already crushed by the weight of his inferiority, a further lowering of his values would amount to cruelty. In
the former case a reductive treatment will recommend itself,
and it will be easy to show from the associative material how
inappropriate and childish the dreamer's intentions are, and
how much they emanate from infantile wishes to be equal or
superior to his parents. But in the latter case, where an all-
pervading feeling of worthlessness has already devalued every
positive aspect, to show the dreamer, on top of it all, how infantile, ridiculous, or even perverse he is would be quite unfitting.
Such a procedure would only increase his inferiority, as well as
cause an unwelcome and quite unnecessary resistance to the
treatment.

515   There is no therapeutic technique or doctrine that is generally applicable, since every case that comes for treatment is an
individual in a specific condition. I remember a patient I had to
treat over a period of nine years. I saw him only for a few weeks
each year, as he lived abroad. From the start I knew what his real
trouble was, but I also saw how the least attempt to get closer to
the truth was met by a violent reaction and a self-defence that
threatened complete rupture between us. Whether I liked it or
not, I had to do my best to maintain the rapport and to follow
his inclination, supported by his dreams, though this led the discussion away from the central problem that, according to all reasonable expectations, should have been discussed. It went so far
that I often accused myself of leading my patient astray, and
only the fact that his condition slowly but clearly improved prevented me from confronting him brutally with the truth.

516   In the tenth year, however, the patient declared himself
cured and freed from all symptoms. I was surprised and ready to
doubt his statement, because theoretically he could not be
cured. Noticing my astonishment, he smiled and said: "And now
I want to thank you quite particularly for your unfailing tact
and patience in helping me to circumvent the painful cause of

my neurosis. I am now ready to tell you everything about it. If I had been able to do so I would have told you right out at the first consultation. But that would have destroyed my rapport with you, and where would I have been then? I would have been morally bankrupt and would have lost the ground from under my feet, having nothing to stand on. In the course of the years I have learnt to trust you, and as my confidence grew my condition improved. I improved because my belief in myself was restored, and now I am strong enough to discuss the problem that was destroying me."

517   He then made a devastatingly frank confession, which showed me the reasons for the peculiar course our treatment had followed. The original shock had been such that he could not face it alone. It needed the two of us, and that was the therapeutic task, not the fulfilment of theoretical presuppositions.

518   From cases like this I learnt to follow the lines already indicated in the material presented by the patient and in his disposition, rather than commit myself to general theoretical considerations that might not be applicable to that particular case. The practical knowledge of human nature I have accumulated in the course of sixty years has taught me to regard each case as a new experience, for which, first of all, I have to seek the individual approach. Sometimes I have not hesitated to plunge into a careful study of infantile events and fantasies; at other times I have begun at the top, even if this meant soaring into a mist of most unlikely metaphysical speculations. It all depends on whether I am able to learn the language of the patient and to follow the gropings of his unconscious towards the light. Some demand one thing and some another. Such are the differences between individuals.

519   This is eminently true of the interpretation of symbols. Two different individuals can have almost the same dream, yet if one is young and the other old, the problems disturbing them will be correspondingly different, and it would be absurd to interpret both dreams in the same way. An example that comes to mind is a dream in which a company of young men are riding on horseback across a wide field. The dreamer is in the lead and jumps a ditch of water, just clearing it. The others fall into the ditch. The young man who told me this dream was a cautious, introverted type and rather afraid of adventure. But the old

man, who also had this dream, was bold and fearless, and had lived an active and enterprising life. At the time of the dream, he was an invalid who would not settle down, gave much trouble to his doctor and nurse, and had injured himself by his disobedience and restlessness. Obviously the dream was telling the young man what he *ought* to do, and the old man what he was *still doing*. While it encouraged the hesitant young man, the old one would be only too glad to risk the jump. But that still-flickering spirit of adventure was just his greatest trouble.

520 This example shows how the interpretation of dreams and symbols depends largely on the individual disposition of the dreamer. Symbols have not one meaning only but several, and often they even characterize a pair of opposites, as does, for instance, the *stella matutina,* the morning star, which is a well-known symbol of Christ and at the same time of the devil (Lucifer). The same applies to the lion. The correct interpretation depends on the context, i.e., the associations connected with the image, and on the actual condition of the dreamer's mind.

5. THE ARCHETYPE IN DREAM SYMBOLISM

The hypothesis we have advanced, that dreams serve the purpose of *compensation,* is a very broad and comprehensive assumption. It means that we believe the dream to be a normal psychic phenomenon that transmits unconscious reactions or spontaneous impulses to the conscious mind. Since only a small minority of dreams are manifestly compensatory, we must pay particular attention to the language of dreams that we consider to be symbolic. The study of this language is almost a science in itself. It has, as we have seen, an infinite variety of individual expressions. They can be read with the help of the dreamer, who himself provides the associative material, or context of the dream-image, so that we can look at all its aspects as if circumambulating it. This method proves to be sufficient in all ordinary cases, such as when a relative, a friend, or a patient tells you a dream more or less conversationally. But when it is a matter of outstanding dreams, of obsessive or recurrent dreams, or dreams that are highly emotional, the personal associations produced by the dreamer no longer suffice for a satisfactory interpretation. In such cases, we have to take into consideration the fact, already observed and commented on by Freud, that elements often occur in a dream that are not individual and cannot be derived from personal experience. They are what Freud called "archaic remnants"—thought-forms whose presence cannot be explained by anything in the individual's own life, but seem to be aboriginal, innate, and inherited patterns of the human mind.

522   Just as the human body represents a whole museum of organs, with a long evolutionary history behind them, so we should expect the mind to be organized in a similar way rather than to be a product without history. By "history" I do not mean the fact that the mind builds itself up through conscious tradition (language, etc.), but rather its biological, prehistoric,

and unconscious development beginning with archaic man, whose psyche was still similar to that of an animal. This immensely old psyche forms the basis of our mind, just as the structure of our body is erected upon a generally mammalian anatomy. Wherever the trained eye of the morphologist looks, it recognizes traces of the original pattern. Similarly, the experienced investigator of the psyche cannot help seeing the analogies between dream-images and the products of the primitive mind, its *représentations collectives,* or mythological motifs. But just as the morphologist needs the science of comparative anatomy, so the psychologist cannot do without a "comparative anatomy of the psyche." He must have a sufficient experience of dreams and other products of the unconscious on the one hand, and on the other of mythology in its widest sense. He cannot even see the analogy between a case of compulsion neurosis, schizophrenia, or hysteria and that of a classical demonic possession if he has not sufficient knowledge of both.

523   My views about the "archaic remnants," which I have called "archetypes" [1] or "primordial images," are constantly criticized by people who lack a sufficient knowledge both of the psychology of dreams and of mythology. The term "archetype" is often misunderstood as meaning a certain definite mythological image or motif. But this would be no more than a conscious representation, and it would be absurd to assume that such variable representations could be inherited. The archetype is, on the contrary, an inherited *tendency* of the human mind to form representations of mythological motifs—representations that vary a great deal without losing their basic pattern. There are, for instance, numerous representations of the motif of the hostile brothers, but the motif remains the same. This inherited tendency is instinctive, like the specific impulse of nest-building, migration, etc. in birds. One finds these *représentations collectives* practically everywhere, characterized by the same or similar motifs. They cannot be assigned to any particular time or region or race. They are without known origin, and they can reproduce themselves even where transmission through migration must be ruled out.

524   My critics have also incorrectly assumed that by archetypes I

1 From Gk. *archē,* 'origin', and *tupos,* 'blow, imprint'.

mean "inherited ideas," and on this ground have dismissed the concept of the archetype as a mere superstition. But if archetypes were ideas that originated in our conscious mind or were acquired by it, one would certainly understand them, and would not be astonished and bewildered when they appear in consciousness. I can remember many cases of people who have consulted me because they were baffled by their own or their children's dreams. The reason was that the dreams contained images that could not be traced to anything they remembered, and they could not explain where their children could have picked up such strange and incomprehensible ideas. These people were highly educated persons, sometimes psychiatrists themselves. One of them was a professor who had a sudden vision and thought he was crazy. He came to me in a state of complete panic. I simply took a four-hundred-year-old volume from the shelf and showed him an old woodcut that depicted his vision. "You don't need to be crazy," I told him. "They knew all about your vision four hundred years ago." Whereupon he sat down entirely deflated but once more normal.

525   I particularly remember the case of a man who was himself a psychiatrist. He brought me a handwritten booklet he had received as a Christmas present from his ten-year-old daughter. It contained a whole series of dreams she had had when she was eight years old. It was the weirdest series I had ever seen, and I could well understand why her father was more than puzzled by the dreams. Childlike though they were, they were a bit uncanny, containing images whose origin was wholly incomprehensible to her father. Here are the salient motifs from the dreams:[2]

1. The "bad animal": a snakelike monster with many horns, that kills and devours all other animals. But God comes from the four corners, being really four gods, and gives rebirth to all the animals.
2. Ascent into heaven where pagan dances are being celebrated, and descent to hell where angels are doing good deeds.
3. A horde of small animals frightens the dreamer. The animals grow to enormous size, and one of them devours her.
4. A small mouse is penetrated by worms, snakes, fishes, and hu-

2 [For another analysis of this case, see Jacobi, *Complex/Archetype/Symbol*, Part II.—Editors.]

man beings. Thus the mouse becomes human. This is the origin of mankind in four stages.

5. A drop of water is looked at through a microscope: it is full of branches. This is the origin of the world.

6. A bad boy with a clod of earth. He throws bits of it at the passers-by, and they all become bad too.

7. A drunken woman falls into the water and comes out sober and renewed.

8. In America many people are rolling in an ant heap, attacked by the ants. The dreamer, in a panic, falls into a river.

9. The dreamer is in a desert on the moon. She sinks so deep into the ground that she reaches hell.

10. She touches a luminous ball seen in a vision. Vapours come out of it. Then a man comes and kills her.

11. She is dangerously ill. Suddenly birds come out of her skin and cover her completely.

12. Swarms of gnats hide the sun, moon, and stars, all except one star which then falls on the dreamer.

526   In the unabridged German original, each dream begins with the words of the fairytale: "Once upon a time . . ." With these words the little dreamer suggests that she feels as if each dream were a sort of fairytale, which she wants to tell her father as a Christmas present. Her father was unable to elucidate the dreams through their context, for there seemed to be no personal associations. Indeed, this kind of childhood dream often seems to be a "Just So Story," with very few or no spontaneous associations. The possibility that these dreams were conscious elaborations can of course be ruled out only by someone who had an intimate knowledge of the child's character and did not doubt her truthfulness. They would, however, remain a challenge to our understanding even if they were fantasies that originated in the waking state. The father was convinced that they were authentic, and I have no reason to doubt it. I knew the little girl myself, but this was before she gave the dreams to her father, and I had no chance to question her about them, for she lived far away from Switzerland and died of an infectious disease about a year after that Christmas.

527   The dreams have a decidedly peculiar character, for their leading thoughts are in a way like philosophical problems. The first dream, for instance, speaks of an evil monster killing all other animals, but God gives rebirth to them through a kind of

apocatastasis, or restitution. In the Western world this idea is known through Christian tradition. It can be found in the Acts of the Apostles 3:21: "(Christ,) whom the heaven must receive until the times of restitution of all things . . ." The early Greek Fathers of the Church (Origen, for instance) particularly insisted on the idea that, at the end of time, everything will be restored by the Redeemer to its original and perfect state. According to Matthew 17:11, there was already an old Jewish tradition that Elias "truly shall first come, and restore all things." I Corinthians 15:22 refers to the same idea in the following words: "For as in Adam all die, even so in Christ shall all be made alive."

528   One might argue that the child had met with this thought in her religious education. But she had had very little of this, as her parents (Protestants) belonged to those people, common enough in our days, who know the Bible only from hearsay. It is particularly unlikely that the idea of *apocatastasis* had been explained to her, and had become a matter of vital interest. Her father, at any rate, was entirely unaware of this mythical idea.

529   Nine of the twelve dreams are concerned with the theme of destruction and restoration. We find the same connection in I Corinthians 15:22, where Adam and Christ, i.e., death and resurrection, are linked together. None of these dreams, however, shows anything more than superficial traces of a specifically Christian education or influence. On the contrary, they show more analogy with primitive tales. This is corroborated by the other motif—the cosmogonic myth of the creation of the world and of man, which appears in dreams 4 and 5.

530   The idea of Christ the Redeemer belongs to the world-wide and pre-Christian motif of the hero and rescuer who, although devoured by the monster, appears again in a miraculous way, having overcome the dragon or whale or whatever it was that swallowed him. How, when, and where such a motif originated nobody knows. We do not even know how to set about investigating the problem in a sound way. Our only certainty is that every generation, so far as we can see, has found it as an old tradition. Thus we can safely assume that the motif "originated" at a time when man did not yet know that he possessed a hero myth—in an age, therefore, when he did not yet reflect con-

sciously on what he was saying. The hero figure is a typical image, an archetype, which has existed since time immemorial.

531 The best examples of the spontaneous production of archetypal images are presented by individuals, particularly children, who live in a milieu where one can be sufficiently certain that any direct knowledge of the tradition is out of the question. The milieu in which our little dreamer lived was acquainted only with the Christian tradition, and very superficially at that. Christian traces may be represented in her dreams by such ideas as God, angels, heaven, hell, and evil, but the way in which they are treated points to a tradition that is entirely non-Christian.

532 Let us take the first dream, of the God who really consists of four gods, coming from the "four corners." The corners of what? There is no room mentioned in the dream. A room would not even fit in with the picture of what is obviously a cosmic event, in which the Universal Being himself intervenes. The quaternity itself is a strange idea, but one that plays a great role in Eastern religions and philosophies. In the Christian tradition it has been superseded by the Trinity, a notion that we must assume was known to the child. But who in an ordinary middle-class milieu would be likely to know of a divine quaternity? It is an idea that was once current in circles acquainted with Hermetic philosophy in the Middle Ages, but it petered out at the beginning of the eighteenth century and has been entirely obsolete for at least two hundred years. Where, then, did the little girl pick it up? From Ezekiel's vision? But there is no Christian teaching that identifies the seraphim with God.

533 The same question may be asked about the horned serpent. In the Bible, it is true, there are many horned animals, for instance in the Book of Revelation (ch. 13). But they seem to be quadrupeds, although their overlord is the dragon, which in Greek (*drakon*) means serpent. The horned serpent appears in Latin alchemy as the *quadricornutus serpens* (four-horned serpent), a symbol of Mercurius and an antagonist of the Christian Trinity. But this is an obscure reference, and, as far as I can discover, it occurs only in one author.[3]

534 In dream 2 a motif appears that is definitely non-Christian and a reversal of values: pagan dances by men in heaven and

3 [Gerard Dorn, of Frankfurt, a 17th-century physician and alchemist.]

good deeds by angels in hell. This suggests, if anything, a relativization of moral values. Where did the child hit on such a revolutionary and modern idea, worthy of Nietzsche's genius? Such an idea is not strange to the philosophical mind of the East, but where could we find it in the child's milieu, and what is its place in the mind of an eight-year-old girl?

535   This question leads to a further one: what is the compensatory meaning of the dreams, to which the little girl obviously attributed so much importance that she gave them to her father as a Christmas present?

536   If the dreamer had been a primitive medicine-man, one would not go far wrong in supposing them to be variations on the philosophical themes of death, resurrection, or restitution, the origin of the world, the creation of man, and the relativity of values (Lao-tze: "high stands on low"). One might well give up such dreams as hopeless if one tried to interpret them from a personal standpoint. But, as I have said, they undoubtedly contain *représentations collectives,* and they are in a way analogous to the doctrines taught to young people in primitive tribes when they are initiated into manhood. At such times they learn about what God or the gods or the "founding" animals have done, how the world and man were created, what the end of the world will be, and the meaning of death. And when do we, in our Christian civilization, hand out similar instructions? At the beginning of adolescence. But many people begin to think of these things again in old age, at the approach of death.

537   Our dreamer, as it happened, was in both these situations, for she was approaching puberty and at the same time the end of her life. Little or nothing in the symbolism of the dreams points to the beginning of a normal adult life, but there are many allusions to destruction and restoration. When I first read the dreams, I had the uncanny feeling that they foreboded disaster. The reason I felt like that was the peculiar nature of the compensation that I deduced from the symbolism. It was the opposite of what one would expect to find in the consciousness of a girl of that age. These dreams open up a new and rather terrifying vision of life and death, such as one might expect in someone who looks back upon life rather than forward to its natural continuation. Their atmosphere recalls the old Roman saying, *vita somnium breve* (life is a short dream), rather than the joy and

exuberance of life's springtime. For this child, life was a *ver sacrum vovendum,* a vow of a vernal sacrifice. Experience shows that the unknown approach of death casts an *adumbratio,* an anticipatory shadow, over the life and dreams of the victim. Even the altar in our Christian churches represents, on the one hand, a tomb, and on the other a place of resurrection—the transformation of death into eternal life.

538   Such are the thoughts that the dreams brought home to the child. They were a preparation for death, expressed through short stories, like the instruction at primitive initiations, or the *koans* of Zen Buddhism. It is an instruction that does not resemble the orthodox Christian doctrine but is more like primitive thought. It seems to have originated outside the historical tradition, in the matrix that, since prehistoric times, has nourished philosophical and religious speculations about life and death.

539   In the case of this girl, it was as if future events were casting their shadow ahead by arousing thought-forms that, though normally dormant, are destined to describe or accompany the approach of a fatal issue. They are to be found everywhere and at all times. Although the concrete shape in which they express themselves is more or less personal, their general pattern is collective, just as animal instincts vary a good deal in different species and yet serve the same general purpose. We do not assume that each newborn animal creates its own instincts as an individual acquisition, and we cannot suppose, either, that human beings invent and produce their specifically human modes of reaction with every new birth. Like the instincts, the collective thought-patterns of the human mind are innate and inherited; and they function, when occasion arises, in more or less the same way in all of us.

540   Emotional manifestations are based on similar patterns, and are recognizably the same all over the earth. We understand them even in animals, and the animals themselves understand each other in this respect, even if they belong to different species. And what about insects, with their complicated symbiotic functions? Most of them do not even know their parents and have nobody to teach them. Why should we suppose, then, that man is the only living creature deprived of specific instincts, or that his psyche is devoid of all traces of its evolution? Naturally, if you identify the psyche with consciousness, you can easily suc-

cumb to the erroneous idea that the psyche is a *tabula rasa,* completely empty at birth, and that it later contains only what it has learnt by individual experience. But the psyche is more than consciousness. Animals have little consciousness, but they have many impulses and reactions that denote the existence of a psyche, and primitives do a lot of things whose meaning is unknown to them. You may ask many civilized people in vain for the reason and meaning of the Christmas tree or of the coloured eggs at Easter, because they have no idea about the meaning of these customs. The fact is, they do things without knowing why they do them. I am inclined to believe that things were generally done first and that only a long time afterwards somebody asked a question about them, and then eventually discovered why they were done. The medical psychologist is constantly confronted with otherwise intelligent patients who behave in a peculiar way and have no inkling of what they say or do. We have dreams whose meaning escapes us entirely, even though we may be firmly convinced that the dream has a definite meaning. We feel it is important or even terrifying, but why?

541 Regular observation of such facts has enforced the hypothesis of an unconscious psyche, the contents of which seem to be of approximately the same variety as those of consciousness. We know that consciousness depends in large measure on the collaboration of the unconscious. When you make a speech, the next sentence is being prepared while you speak, but this preparation is mostly unconscious. If the unconscious does not collaborate and withholds the next sentence you are stuck. You want to quote a name, or a term otherwise familiar to you, but nothing is forthcoming. The unconscious does not deliver it. You want to introduce somebody whom you know well, but his name has vanished, as if you had never known it. Thus you depend on the goodwill of your unconscious. Any time the unconscious chooses, it can defeat your otherwise good memory, or put something into your mouth that you did not intend at all. It can produce unpredictable and unreasonable moods and affects and thus cause all sorts of complications.

542 Superficially, such reactions and impulses seem to be of an intimately personal nature and are therefore believed to be entirely individual. In reality, they are based on a preformed and ever-ready instinctive system with its own characteristic and uni-

versally understandable thought-forms, reflexes, attitudes, and gestures. These follow a pattern that was laid down long before there was any trace of a reflective consciousness. It is even conceivable that the latter originated in violent emotional clashes and their often disastrous consequences. Take the case of the savage who, in a moment of anger and disappointment at having caught no fish, strangles his much beloved only son, and is then seized with immeasurable regret as he holds the little dead body in his arms. Such a man has a great chance to remember the agony of this moment for ever. This could have been the beginning of a reflective consciousness. At all events, the shock of a similar emotional experience is often needed to make people wake up and pay attention to what they are doing. I would mention the famous case of the Spanish hidalgo, Ramón Lull, who after a long chase finally succeeded in meeting his lady at a secret rendezvous. Silently she opened her garment and showed him her cancer-eaten bosom. The shock changed his life: he became a holy man.

543   Often in the case of these sudden transformations one can prove that an archetype has been at work for a long time in the unconscious, skilfully arranging circumstances that will unavoidably lead to a crisis. It is not rare for the development to manifest itself so clearly (for instance in a series of dreams) that the catastrophe can be predicted with reasonable certainty. One can conclude from experiences such as these that archetypal forms are not just static patterns, but dynamic factors that manifest themselves in spontaneous impulses, just as instincts do. Certain dreams, visions, or thoughts can suddenly appear, and in spite of careful investigation one cannot find out what causes them. This does not mean that they have no cause; they certainly have, but it is so remote or obscure that one cannot see what it is. One must wait until the dream and its meaning are sufficiently understood, or until some external event occurs that will explain the dream.

544   Our conscious thoughts often concern themselves with the future and its possibilities, and so does the unconscious and its dreams. There has long been a world-wide belief that the chief function of dreams is prognostication of the future. In antiquity, and still in the Middle Ages, dreams played their part in medical prognosis. I can confirm from a modern dream the

prognosis, or rather precognition, in an old dream quoted by Artemidoros of Daldis, in the second century A.D. He relates that a man dreamt he saw his father die in the flames of a house on fire. Not long afterwards, he himself died of a *phlegmone* (fire, high fever), presumably pneumonia. Now it so happened that a colleague of mine was suffering from a deadly gangrenous fever —in fact, a *phlegmone*. A former patient of his, who had no knowledge of the nature of the doctor's illness, dreamt that the doctor was perishing in a great fire. The dream occurred three weeks before the doctor died, at a time when he had just entered hospital and the disease was only at its beginning. The dreamer knew nothing but the bare fact that the doctor was ill and had entered hospital.

545   As this example shows, dreams can have an anticipatory or prognostic aspect, and their interpreter will be well advised to take this aspect into account, particularly when an obviously meaningful dream does not yield a context sufficient to explain it. Such a dream often comes right out of the blue, and one wonders what could have prompted it. Of course, if one knew its ultimate outcome, the cause would be clear. It is only our conscious mind that does not know; the unconscious seems already informed, and to have submitted the case to a careful prognostic examination, more or less in the way consciousness would have done if it had known the relevant facts. But, precisely because they were subliminal, they could be perceived by the unconscious and submitted to a sort of examination that anticipates their ultimate result. So far as one can make out from dreams, the unconscious in its "deliberations" proceeds in an instinctive way rather than along rational lines. The latter way is the prerogative of consciousness, which selects with reason and knowledge. But the unconscious is guided chiefly by instinctive trends, represented by corresponding thought-forms—the archetypes. It looks as if it were a poet who had been at work rather than a rational doctor, who would speak of infection, fever, toxins, etc., whereas the dream describes the diseased body as a man's earthly house, and the fever as the heat of a conflagration that is destroying the house and its inhabitant.

546   As this dream shows, the archetypal mind has handled the situation in the same way as it did at the time of Artemidoros. A situation of a more or less unknown nature has been intuitively

grasped by the unconscious and submitted to an archetypal treatment. This shows clearly that, in place of the *raisonnement* which consciousness would have applied, the archetypal mind has autonomously taken over the task of prognostication. The archetypes have their own initiative and their own specific energy, which enable them not only to produce a meaningful interpretation (in their own style) but also to intervene in a given situation with their own impulses and thought-forms. In this respect they function like complexes, which also enjoy a certain autonomy in everyday life. They come and go very much as they please, and they often interfere with our conscious intentions in an embarrassing way.

547   One can perceive the specific energy of the archetypes when one experiences the peculiar feeling of numinosity that accompanies them—the fascination or spell that emanates from them. This is also characteristic of the personal complexes, whose behaviour may be compared with the role played by the archetypal *représentations collectives* in the social life of all times. As personal complexes have their individual history, so do social complexes of an archetypal character. But while personal complexes never produce more than a personal bias, archetypes create myths, religions, and philosophical ideas that influence and set their stamp on whole nations and epochs. And just as the products of personal complexes can be understood as compensations of onesided or faulty attitudes of consciousness, so myths of a religious nature can be interpreted as a sort of mental therapy for the sufferings of mankind, such as hunger, war, disease, old age, and death.

548   The universal hero myth, for example, shows the picture of a powerful man or god-man who vanquishes evil in the form of dragons, serpents, monsters, demons, and enemies of all kinds, and who liberates his people from destruction and death. The narration or ritual repetition of sacred texts and ceremonies, and the worship of such a figure with dances, music, hymns, prayers, and sacrifices, grip the audience with numinous emotions and exalt the participants to identification with the hero. If we contemplate such a situation with the eyes of a believer, we can understand how the ordinary man is gripped, freed from his impotence and misery, and raised to an almost superhuman status, at least for the time being, and often enough he is sus-

tained by such a conviction for a long time. An initiation of this kind produces a lasting impression, and may even create an attitude that gives a certain form and style to the life of a society. I would mention as an example the Eleusinian mysteries, which were finally suppressed at the beginning of the seventh century. They formed, together with the Delphic oracle, the essence and spirit of ancient Greece. On a much greater scale the Christian era owes its name and significance to another antique mystery, that of the god-man, which has its roots in the archetypal Osiris-Horus myth of ancient Egypt.

549   It is nowadays a common prejudice to assume that once, in an obscure prehistoric time, the basic mythological ideas were "invented" by a clever old philosopher or prophet, and ever afterwards "believed" by credulous and uncritical people, although the stories told by a power-seeking priesthood were not really "true" but mere "wishful thinking." The word "invent" is derived from the Latin *invenire* and means, in the first place, to "come upon" or to "find" something and, in the second, to find something by *seeking* for it. In the latter case, it is not a matter of finding or coming upon something by mere chance, for there is a sort of foreknowledge or a faint inkling of the thing you are going to find.

550   When we contemplate the strange ideas in the dreams of the little girl, it seems unlikely that she *sought* them, as she was rather surprised at finding them. They occurred to her rather as strange and unexpected stories that seemed noteworthy and interesting enough to be given to her father as a Christmas present. In doing so, she lifted them up into the sphere of our still living Christian mystery, the birth of our Lord, blended with the secret of the evergreen tree that carries the newborn Light. Although there is ample historical evidence for the symbolic relationship between Christ and the tree symbol, the little girl's parents would have been badly embarrassed had they been asked to explain exactly what they meant by decorating a tree with burning candles to celebrate the nativity of Christ. "Oh, it's just a Christmas custom!" they would have said. A serious answer would require a far-reaching dissertation on the symbolism of the dying god in antiquity, in the Near East, and its relation to the cult of the Great Mother and her symbol, the tree—to mention only one aspect of this complicated problem.

239

551   The further we delve into the origins of a *représentation collective* or, in ecclesiastical language, of a dogma, the more we uncover a seemingly limitless web of archetypal patterns that, before modern times, were never the object of conscious reflection. Thus, paradoxically enough, we know more about mythological symbolism than did any age before our own. The fact is that in former times men *lived* their symbols rather than reflected upon them. I will illustrate this by an experience I once had with the primitives on Mount Elgon in East Africa. Every morning at dawn they leave their huts and breathe or spit into their hands, stretching them out to the first rays of the sun, as if they were offering either their breath or their spittle to the rising god—to *mungu*. (This Swahili word, which they used in explaining the ritual act, is derived from a Polynesian root equivalent to *mana* or *mulungu*. These and similar terms designate a "power" of extraordinary efficacy, an all-pervading essence which we would call divine. Thus the word *mungu* is their equivalent for Allah or God.) When I asked them what they meant by this act and why they did it, they were completely baffled. They could only say: "We have always done it. It has always been done when the sun rises." They laughed at the obvious conclusion that the sun is *mungu*. The sun is not *mungu* when it is above the horizon; *mungu* is the actual moment of the sunrise.

552   What they were doing was obvious to me but not to them. They just do it, they never reflect on what they are doing, and are consequently unable to explain themselves. They are evidently just repeating what they have "always" done at sunrise, no doubt with a certain emotion and by no means merely mechanically, for they *live* it while we *reflect* on it. Thus I knew that they were offering their *souls* to *mungu,* because the breath (of life) and the spittle mean "soul substance." Breathing or spitting on something conveys a "magical" effect, as, for instance, when Christ used spittle to heal the blind, or when a son inhales his dying father's last breath in order to take over the father's soul. It is most unlikely that these primitives ever, even in the remote past, knew any more about the meaning of their ceremony. On the contrary, their ancestors probably knew even less, because they were more profoundly unconscious and thought if possible even less about their doings.

553   Faust aptly says: "Im Anfang war die Tat" (in the beginning was the deed). Deeds were never invented, they were done. Thoughts, on the other hand, are a relatively late discovery; they were found, and then they were sought and found. Yet unreflected life existed long before man; it was not invented, but in it man found himself as an afterthought. First he was moved to deeds by unconscious factors, and only a long time afterwards did he begin to reflect about the causes that had moved him; then it took him a very long time indeed to arrive at the preposterous idea that he must have moved himself—his mind being unable to see any other motivating force than his own. We would laugh at the idea of a plant or an animal inventing itself, yet there are many people who believe that the psyche or the mind invented itself and thus brought itself into being. As a matter of fact, the mind has grown to its present state of consciousness as an acorn grows into an oak or as saurians developed into mammals. As it has been, so it is still, and thus we are moved by forces from within as well as from without.

554   In a mythological age these forces were called *mana*, spirits, demons, and gods, and they are as active today as they ever were. If they conform to our wishes, we call them happy hunches or impulses and pat ourselves on the back for being smart fellows. If they go against us, then we say it is just bad luck, or that certain people have it in for us, or it must be pathological. The one thing we refuse to admit is that we are dependent on "powers" beyond our control.

555   It is true that civilized man has acquired a certain amount of will-power which he can apply where he pleases. We have learnt to do our work efficiently without having recourse to chanting and drumming to hypnotize us into the state of doing. We can even dispense with the daily prayer for divine aid. We can carry out what we propose to do, and it seems self-evident that an idea can be translated into action without a hitch, whereas the primitive is hampered at every step by doubts, fears, and superstitions. The motto "Where there's a will there's a way" is not just a Germanic prejudice; it is the superstition of modern man in general. In order to maintain his credo, he cultivates a remarkable lack of introspection. He is blind to the fact that, with all his rationality and efficiency, he is possessed by powers beyond his control. The gods and demons have not disappeared at all, they

have merely got new names. They keep him on the run with restlessness, vague apprehensions, psychological complications, an invincible need for pills, alcohol, tobacco, dietary and other hygienic systems—and above, all, with an impressive array of neuroses.

556   I once met a drastic example of this in a professor of philosophy and "psychology"—a psychology in which the unconscious had not yet arrived. He was the man I mentioned who was obsessed by the idea that he had cancer, although X-rays had proved to him that it was all imaginary. Who or what caused this idea? It obviously derived from a fear that was not caused by observation of the facts. It suddenly overcame him and then remained. Symptoms of this kind are extraordinarily obstinate and often enough hinder the patient from getting the proper treatment. For what good would psychotherapy be in dealing with a malignant tumour? Such a dangerous thing could only be operated on without delay. To the professor's ever-renewed relief, every new authority assured him that there was no trace of cancer. But the very next day the doubt began nagging again, and he was plunged once more into the night of unmitigated fear.

557   The morbid thought had a power of its own that he could not control. It was not foreseen in his philosophical brand of psychology, where everything flowed neatly from consciousness and sense-perception. The professor admitted that his case was pathological, but there his thinking stopped, because it had arrived at the sacrosanct border-line between the philosophical and the medical faculty. The one deals with normal and the other with abnormal contents, unknown in the philosopher's world.

558   This compartment psychology reminds me of another case. It was that of an alcoholic who had come under the laudable influence of a certain religious movement and, fascinated by its enthusiasm, had forgotten he needed a drink. He was obviously and miraculously cured by Jesus, and accordingly was held up as a witness to divine grace or to the efficacy of the said organization. After a few weeks of public confession, the novelty began to wear off and some alcoholic refreshment seemed to be indicated. But this time the helpful organization came to the conclusion that the case was "pathological" and not suitable for an

intervention by Jesus. So they put him in a clinic to let the doctor do better than the divine healer.

559   This is an aspect of the modern "cultural" mind that is well worth looking into. It shows an alarming degree of dissociation and psychological confusion. We believe exclusively in consciousness and free will, and are no longer aware of the powers that control us to an indefinite degree, outside the narrow domain where we can be reasonable and exercise a certain amount of free choice and self-control. In our time of general disorientation, it is necessary to know about the true state of human affairs, which depends so much on the mental and moral qualities of the individual and on the human psyche in general. But if we are to see things in their right perspective, we need to understand the past of man as well as his present. That is why a correct understanding of myths and symbols is of essential importance.

6. THE FUNCTION OF RELIGIOUS SYMBOLS

560   Although our civilized consciousness has separated itself from the instincts, the instincts have not disappeared; they have merely lost their contact with consciousness. They are thus forced to assert themselves in an indirect way, through what Janet called automatisms. These take the form of symptoms in the case of a neurosis or, in normal cases, of incidents of various kinds, like unaccountable moods, unexpected forgetfulness, mistakes in speech, and so on. Such manifestations show very clearly the *autonomy* of the archetypes. It is easy to believe that one is master in one's own house, but, as long as we are unable to control our emotions and moods, or to be conscious of the myriad secret ways in which unconscious factors insinuate themselves into our arrangements and decisions, we are certainly not the masters. On the contrary, we have so much reason for uncertainty that it will be better to look twice at what we are doing.

561   The exploration of one's conscience, however, is not a popular pastime, although it would be most necessary, particularly in our time when man is threatened with self-created and deadly dangers that are growing beyond his control. If, for a moment, we look at mankind as one individual, we see that it is like a man carried away by unconscious powers. He is dissociated like a neurotic, with the Iron Curtain marking the line of division. Western man, representing the kind of consciousness hitherto regarded as valid, has become increasingly aware of the aggressive will to power of the East, and he sees himself forced to take extraordinary measures of defence. What he fails to see is that it is his own vices, publicly repudiated and covered up by good international manners, that are thrown back in his face through their shameless and methodical application by the East. What the West has tolerated, but only secretly, and indulged in a bit shamefacedly (the diplomatic lie, the double-cross, veiled

244

threats), comes back openly and in full measure and gets us tied up in knots—exactly the case of the neurotic! It is the face of our own shadow that glowers at us across the Iron Curtain.

562   This state of affairs explains the peculiar feeling of helplessness that is creeping over our Western consciousness. We are beginning to realize that the conflict is in reality a moral and mental problem, and we are trying to find some answer to it. We grow increasingly aware that the nuclear deterrent is a desperate and undesirable answer, as it cuts both ways. We know that moral and mental remedies would be more effective because they could provide us with a psychic immunity to the ever-increasing infection. But all our attempts have proved to be singularly ineffectual, and will continue to do so as long as we try to convince ourselves and the world that it is only *they,* our opponents, who are all wrong, morally and philosophically. We expect *them* to see and understand where they are wrong, instead of making a serious effort ourselves to recognize our own shadow and its nefarious doings. If we could only see our shadow, we should be immune to any moral and mental infection and insinuation. But as long as this is not so, we lay ourselves open to every infection because we are doing practically the same things as *they* are, only with the additional disadvantage that we neither see nor want to understand what we are doing under the cloak of good manners.

563   The East has one big myth—which we call an illusion in the vain hope that our superior judgment will make it disappear. This myth is the time-hallowed archetypal dream of a Golden Age or a paradise on earth, where everything is provided for everybody, and one great, just, and wise Chief rules over a human kindergarten. This powerful archetype in its infantile form has got them all right, but it won't disappear from the world at the mere sight of our superior point of view. We even support it by our own childishness, for our Western civilization is in the grip of the same mythology. We cherish the same prejudices, hopes, and expectations. We believe in the Welfare State, in universal peace, in more or less equality for man, in his eternal human rights, in justice and truth, and (not too loud) in the Kingdom of God on earth.

564   The sad truth is that man's real life consists of inexorable opposites—day and night, wellbeing and suffering, birth and

death, good and evil. We are not even sure that the one will prevail against the other, that good will overcome evil, or joy defeat pain. Life and the world are a battleground, have always been and always will be, and, if it were not so, existence would soon come to an end. It is for this reason that a superior religion like Christianity expected an early end to this world, and Buddhism actually puts an end to it by turning its back on all desires. These categorical answers would be frankly suicidal if they were not bound up with the peculiar moral ideas and practices that constitute the body of both religions.

565   I mention this because in our time there are countless people who have lost faith in one or other of the world religions. They do not understand them any longer. While life runs smoothly, the loss remains as good as unnoticed. But when suffering comes, things change very rapidly. One seeks the way out and begins to reflect about the meaning of life and its bewildering experiences. It is significant that, according to the statistics, the psychiatrist is consulted more by Protestants and Jews than by Catholics. This might be expected, for the Catholic Church still feels responsible for the *cura animarum*, the care of souls. But in this scientific age, the psychiatrist is apt to be asked questions that once belonged to the domain of the theologian. People feel that it makes, or would make, a great difference if only they had a positive belief in a meaningful way of life or in God and immortality. The spectre of death looming up before them often gives a powerful incentive to such thoughts. From time immemorial, men have had ideas about a Supreme Being (one or several) and about the Land of the Hereafter. Only modern man thinks he can do without them. Because he cannot discover God's throne in heaven with a telescope or radar, or establish for certain that dear father or mother are still about in a more or less corporeal form, he assumes that such ideas are not "true." I would rather say that they are not "true" enough. They have accompanied human life since prehistoric times and are still ready to break through into consciousness at the slightest provocation.

566   One even regrets the loss of such convictions. Since it is a matter of invisible and unknowable things (God is beyond human understanding, and immortality cannot be proved), why should we bother about evidence or truth? Suppose we did not

246

know and understand the need for salt in our food, we would nevertheless profit from its use. Even if we should assume that salt is an illusion of our taste-buds, or a superstition, it would still contribute to our wellbeing. Why, then, should we deprive ourselves of views that prove helpful in crises and give a meaning to our existence? And how do we know that such ideas are not true? Many people would agree with me if I stated flatly that such ideas are illusions. What they fail to realize is that this denial amounts to a "belief" and is just as impossible to prove as a religious assertion. We are entirely free to choose our standpoint; it will in any case be an arbitrary decision. There is, however, a strong empirical reason why we should hold beliefs that we know can never be proved. It is that they are known to be useful. Man positively needs general ideas and convictions that will give a meaning to his life and enable him to find his place in the universe. He can stand the most incredible hardships when he is convinced that they make sense; but he is crushed when, on top of all his misfortunes, he has to admit that he is taking part in a "tale told by an idiot."

567   It is the purpose and endeavour of religious symbols to give a meaning to the life of man. The Pueblo Indians believe that they are the sons of Father Sun, and this belief gives their life a perspective and a goal beyond their individual and limited existence. It leaves ample room for the unfolding of their personality, and is infinitely more satisfactory than the certainty that one is and will remain the underdog in a department store. If St. Paul had been convinced that he was nothing but a wandering weaver of carpets, he would certainly not have been himself. His real and meaningful life lay in the certainty that he was the messenger of the Lord. You can accuse him of megalomania, but your opinion pales before the testimony of history and the *consensus omnium*. The myth that took possession of him made him something greater than a mere craftsman.

568   Myths, however, consist of symbols that were not invented but happened. It was not the man Jesus who created the myth of the God-man; it had existed many centuries before. He himself was seized by this symbolic idea, which, as St. Mark tells us, lifted him out of the carpenter's shop and the mental narrowness of his surroundings. Myths go back to primitive story-tellers and their dreams, to men moved by the stirrings of their fanta-

sies, who were not very different from poets and philosophers in later times. Primitive story-tellers never worried about the origin of their fantasies; it was only much later that people began to wonder where the story came from. Already in ancient Greece they were advanced enough to surmise that the stories about the gods were nothing but old and exaggerated traditions of ancient kings and their deeds. They assumed even then that the myth did not mean what it said because it was obviously improbable. Therefore they tried to reduce it to a generally understandable yarn. This is exactly what our time has tried to do with dream symbolism: it is assumed that it does not mean what it seems to say, but something that is generally known and understood, though not openly admitted because of its inferior quality. For those who had got rid of their conventional blinkers there were no longer any riddles. It seemed certain that dreams meant something different from what they said.

569 This assumption is wholly arbitrary. The Talmud says more aptly: "The dream is its own interpretation." Why should dreams mean something different from what appears in them? Is there anything in nature that is other than what it is? For instance, the duck-billed platypus, that original monster which no zoologist would ever have invented, is it not just what it is? The dream is a normal and natural phenomenon, which is certainly just what it is and does not mean something it is not. We call its contents symbolic because they have obviously not only one meaning, but point in different directions and must therefore mean something that is unconscious, or at least not conscious in all its aspects.

570 To the scientific mind, such phenomena as symbolic ideas are most irritating, because they cannot be formulated in a way that satisfies our intellect and logic. They are by no means the only instance of this in psychology. The trouble begins already with the phenomenon of affect or emotion, which evades all the attempts of the psychologist to pin it down in a hard-and-fast concept. The cause of the difficulty is the same in both cases—the intervention of the unconscious. I know enough of the scientific standpoint to understand that it is most annoying to have to deal with facts that cannot be grasped completely or at any rate adequately. The trouble with both phenomena is that the facts are undeniable and yet cannot be formulated in intellectual terms.

248

Instead of observable details with clearly discernible features, it is life itself that wells up in emotions and symbolic ideas. In many cases emotion and symbol are actually one and the same thing. There is no intellectual formula capable of representing such a complex phenomenon in a satisfactory way.

571   The academic psychologist is perfectly free to dismiss the emotions or the unconscious, or both, from his consideration. Yet they remain facts to which at least the medical psychologist has to pay ample attention, for emotional conflicts and the interventions of the unconscious are the classical features of his science. If he treats a patient at all, he is confronted with irrationalities of this kind whether he can formulate them intellectually or not. He has to acknowledge their only too troublesome existence. It is therefore quite natural that people who have not had the medical psychologist's experience find it difficult to follow what he is talking about. Anyone who has not had the chance, or the misfortune, to live through the same or similar experiences is hardly capable of understanding what happens when psychology ceases to be a tranquil pursuit for the scientist in his laboratory and becomes a real life adventure. Target practice on a shooting range is far from being a battlefield, but the doctor has to deal with casualties in a real war. Therefore he has to concern himself with psychic realities even if he cannot define them in scientific terms. He can name them, but he knows that all the terms he uses to designate the essentials of life do not pretend to be more than names for facts that have to be experienced in themselves, because they cannot be reproduced by their names. No textbook can teach psychology; one learns only by actual experience. No understanding is gained by memorizing words, for symbols are the living facts of life.

572   The cross in the Christian religion, for instance, is a meaningful symbol that expresses a multitude of aspects, ideas, and emotions, but a cross before somebody's name simply indicates that that individual is dead. The *lingam* or phallus functions as an all-embracing symbol in the Hindu religion, but if a street urchin draws one on a wall, it just means an interest in his penis. Because infantile and adolescent fantasies often continue far into adult life, many dreams contain unmistakable sexual allusions. It would be absurd to understand them as anything else.

But when a mason speaks of monks and nuns to be laid upon each other, or a locksmith of male and female keys, it would be nonsensical to suppose that he is indulging in glowing adolescent fantasies. He simply means a particular kind of tile or key that has been given a colourful name. But when an educated Hindu talks to you about the *lingam,* you will hear things we Westerners would never connect with the penis. You may even find it most difficult to guess what he actually means by this term, and you will naturally conclude that the lingam *symbolizes* a good many things. It is certainly not an obscene allusion; nor is the cross a mere sign for death but a symbol for a great many other ideas. Much, therefore, depends on the maturity of the dreamer who produces such an image.

573　　The interpretation of dreams and symbols requires some intelligence. It cannot be mechanized and crammed into stupid and unimaginative brains. It demands an ever-increasing knowledge of the dreamer's individuality as well as an ever-increasing self-awareness on the part of the interpreter. No experienced worker in this field will deny that there are rules of thumb that can prove helpful, but they must be applied with prudence and intelligence. Not everybody can master the "technique." You may follow all the right rules and the apparently safe path of knowledge and yet you get stuck in the most appalling nonsense, simply by overlooking a seemingly unimportant detail that a better intelligence would not have missed. Even a man with a highly developed intellect can go badly astray because he has never learnt to use his intuition or his feeling, which might be at a regrettably low level of development.

574　　The attempt to understand symbols does not only bring you up against the symbol itself, but up against the wholeness of the symbol-producing individual. If one is really up to this challenge, one may meet with success. But as a rule it will be necessary to make a special study of the individual and his or her cultural background. One can learn a lot in this way and so get a chance to fill in the gaps in one's education. I have made it a rule myself to consider every case an entirely new proposition about which I do not even know the ABC. Routine may be and often is practical, and quite useful as long as one skates on the surface, but as soon as one gets in touch with the vital problems, life itself takes over and even the most brilliant theoretical premises become ineffectual words.

575   This makes the teaching of methods and techniques a major problem. As I have said, the pupil has to acquire a good deal of specialized knowledge. This provides him with the necessary mental tool-shop, but the main thing, the handling of the tools, can be acquired only if the pupil undergoes an analysis that acquaints him with his own conflict. This can be quite a task with some so-called normal but unimaginative individuals. They are just incapable of realizing, for instance, the simple fact that psychic events happen to us spontaneously. Such people prefer to cling to the idea that whatever occurs either is done by themselves or else is pathological and must be cured by pills or injections. They show how close dull normality is to a neurosis, and as a matter of fact such people succumb most easily to psychic epidemics.

576   In all the higher grades of science, imagination and intuition play an increasingly important role over and above intellect and its capacity for application. Even physics, the most rigorous of all the applied sciences, depends to an astonishing degree on intuition, which works by way of the unconscious processes and not by logical deductions, although it is possible to demonstrate afterwards what logical procedure might have led to the same result.

577   Intuition is almost indispensable in the interpretation of symbols, and can cause an immediate acceptance on the part of the dreamer. But, subjectively convincing as such a lucky hunch may be, it is also somewhat dangerous, because it leads to a false sense of security. It may even seduce both the interpreter and the dreamer into continuing this rather facile exchange of ideas, which may end in a sort of mutual dream. The secure basis of real intellectual and moral knowledge gets lost if one is satisfied with a vague feeling of having understood. Usually when one asks people the reasons for their so-called understanding, they are unable to give an explanation. One can understand and explain only when one has brought intuitions down to the safe basis of real knowledge of the facts and their logical connections. An honest investigator will have to admit that this is not possible in certain cases, but it would be dishonest of him to dismiss them on that account. Even a scientist is a human being, and it

is quite natural that he, like others, hates the things he cannot explain and thus falls victim to the common illusion that what we know today represents the highest summit of knowledge. Nothing is more vulnerable and ephemeral than scientific theories, which are mere tools and not everlasting truths.

7. HEALING THE SPLIT

578   When the medical psychologist takes an interest in symbols, he is primarily concerned with "natural" symbols as distinct from "cultural" symbols. The former are derived from the unconscious contents of the psyche, and they therefore represent an enormous number of variations on the basic archetypal motifs. In many cases, they can be traced back to their archaic roots, i.e., to ideas and images that we meet in the most ancient records and in primitive societies. In this respect, I should like to call the reader's attention to such books as Mircea Eliade's study of shamanism,[1] where a great many illuminating examples may be found.

579   "Cultural" symbols, on the other hand, are those that have expressed "eternal truths" or are still in use in many religions. They have gone through many transformations and even a process of more or less conscious elaboration, and in this way have become the *représentations collectives* of civilized societies. Nevertheless, they have retained much of their original numinosity, and they function as positive or negative "prejudices" with which the psychologist has to reckon very seriously.

580   Nobody can dismiss these numinous factors on merely rational grounds. They are important constituents of our mental make-up and vital forces in the building up of human society, and they cannot be eradicated without serious loss. When they are repressed or neglected, their specific energy disappears into the unconscious with unpredictable consequences. The energy that appears to have been lost revives and intensifies whatever is uppermost in the unconscious—tendencies, perhaps, that have hitherto had no chance to express themselves, or have not been allowed an uninhibited existence in our consciousness. They

1 *Shamanism: Archaic Techniques of Ecstasy.*

form an ever-present destructive "shadow." Even tendencies that might be able to exert a beneficial influence turn into veritable demons when they are repressed. This is why many well-meaning people are understandably afraid of the unconscious, and incidentally of psychology.

581   Our times have demonstrated what it means when the gates of the psychic underworld are thrown open. Things whose enormity nobody could have imagined in the idyllic innocence of the first decade of our century have happened and have turned the world upside down. Ever since, the world has remained in a state of schizophrenia. Not only has the great civilized Germany disgorged its primitivity, but Russia also is ruled by it, and Africa has been set on fire. No wonder the Western world feels uneasy, for it does not know how much it plays into the hands of the uproarious underworld and what it has lost through the destruction of its numinosities. It has lost its moral and spiritual values to a very dangerous degree. Its moral and spiritual tradition has collapsed, and has left a worldwide disorientation and dissociation.

582   We could have seen long ago from primitive societies what the loss of numinosity means: they lose their *raison d'être*, the order of their social organizations, and then they dissolve and decay. We are now in the same condition. We have lost something we have never properly understood. Our spiritual leaders cannot be spared the blame for having been more interested in protecting their institutions than in understanding the mystery that symbols present. Faith does not exclude thought (which is man's strongest weapon), but unfortunately many believers are so afraid of science, and also of psychology, that they turn a blind eye to the numinous psychic powers that forever control man's fate. We have stripped all things of their mystery and numinosity; nothing is holy any longer.

583   The masses and their leaders do not realize that it makes no substantial difference whether you call the world principle male and a father (spirit), or female and a mother (matter). Essentially, we know as little of the one as of the other. Since the beginning of the human mind, both were numinous symbols, and their importance lay in their numinosity and not in their sex or other chance attributes. Since energy never vanishes, the emotional energy that manifests itself in all numinous phenom-

ena does not cease to exist when it disappears from consciousness. As I have said, it reappears in unconscious manifestations, in symbolic happenings that compensate the disturbances of the conscious psyche. Our psyche is profoundly disturbed by the loss of moral and spiritual values that have hitherto kept our life in order. Our consciousness is no longer capable of integrating the natural afflux of concomitant, instinctive events that sustains our conscious psychic activity. This process can no longer take place in the same way as before, because our consciousness has deprived itself of the organs by which the auxiliary contributions of the instincts and the unconscious could be assimilated. These organs were the numinous symbols, held holy by common consent.

584   A concept like "physical matter," stripped of its numinous connotation of the "Great Mother," no longer expresses the vast emotional meaning of "Mother Earth." It is a mere intellectual term, dry as dust and entirely inhuman. In the same way, "spirit" identified with "intellect" ceases to be the Father of All. It degenerates into the limited mind of man, and the immense emotional energy expressed in the image "our Father" vanishes in the sand of an intellectual desert.

585   Through scientific understanding, our world has become dehumanized. Man feels himself isolated in the cosmos. He is no longer involved in nature and has lost his emotional participation in natural events, which hitherto had a symbolic meaning for him. Thunder is no longer the voice of a god, nor is lightning his avenging missile. No river contains a spirit, no tree means a man's life, no snake is the embodiment of wisdom, and no mountain still harbours a great demon. Neither do things speak to him nor can he speak to things, like stones, springs, plants, and animals. He no longer has a bush-soul identifying him with a wild animal. His immediate communication with nature is gone for ever, and the emotional energy it generated has sunk into the unconscious.

586   This enormous loss is compensated by the symbols in our dreams. They bring up our original nature, its instincts and its peculiar thinking. Unfortunately, one would say, they also express their contents in the language of nature, which is strange and incomprehensible to us. It sets us the task of translating its images into the rational words and concepts of modern speech,

which has liberated itself from its primitive encumbrances—
notably from its mystical participation with things. Nowadays,
talking of ghosts and other numinous figures is no longer the
same as conjuring them up. We have ceased to believe in magical formulas; not many taboos and similar restrictions are left;
and our world seems to be disinfected of all such superstitious
numina as "witches, warlocks, and worricows," to say nothing of
werewolves, vampires, bush-souls, and all the other bizarre beings that populate the primeval forest.

587   At least the surface of our world seems to be purified of all
superstitious and irrational admixtures. Whether, however, the
real inner world of man—and not our wish-fulfilling fiction
about it—is also freed from primitivity is another question. Is
not the number 13 still taboo for many people? Are there not
still many individuals possessed by funny prejudices, projections, and illusions? A realistic picture of the human mind reveals many primitive traits and survivals, which are still playing
their roles just as if nothing had happened during the last five
hundred years. The man of today is a curious mixture of characteristics acquired over the long ages of his mental development.
This is the man and his symbols we have to deal with, and we
must scrutinize his mental products very carefully indeed. Sceptical viewpoints and scientific convictions exist in him side by
side with old-fashioned prejudices, outdated habits of thought
and feeling, obstinate misinterpretations, and blind ignorance.

588   Such are the people who produce the symbols we are investigating in their dreams. In order to explain the symbols and their
meaning, it is essential to learn whether these representations
are still the same as they ever were, or whether they have been
chosen by the dream for its particular purpose from a store of
general conscious knowledge. If, for instance, one has to deal
with a dream in which the number 13 occurs, the question is:
Does the dreamer habitually believe in the unfavourable nature
of the number, or does the dream merely allude to people who
still indulge in such superstitions? The answer will make a great
difference to the interpretation. In the former case, the dreamer
is still under the spell of the unlucky 13, and will therefore feel
most uncomfortable in room no. 13 or sitting at a table with
thirteen people. In the latter case, 13 may not be more than a
chiding or disparaging remark. In one case it is a still numinous

representation; in the other it is stripped of its original emotionality and has assumed the innocuous character of a mere piece of indifferent information.

589   This illustrates the way in which archetypes appear in practical experience. In the first case they appear in their original form—they are images and at the same time emotions. One can speak of an archetype only when these two aspects coincide. When there is only an image, it is merely a word-picture, like a corpuscle with no electric charge. It is then of little consequence, just a word and nothing more. But if the image is charged with numinosity, that is, with psychic energy, then it becomes dynamic and will produce consequences. It is a great mistake in practice to treat an archetype as if it were a mere name, word, or concept. It is far more than that: it is a piece of life, an image connected with the living individual by the bridge of emotion. The word alone is a mere abstraction, an exchangeable coin in intellectual commerce. But the archetype is living matter. It is not limitlessly exchangeable but always belongs to the economy of a living individual, from which it cannot be detached and used arbitrarily for different ends. It cannot be explained in just any way, but only in the one that is indicated by that particular individual. Thus the symbol of the cross, in the case of a good Christian, can be interpreted only in the Christian way unless the dream produces very strong reasons to the contrary, and even then the specifically Christian meaning should not be lost sight of.

590   The mere use of words is futile if you do not know what they stand for. This is particularly true in psychology, where we speak of archetypes like the anima and animus, the wise old man, the great mother, and so on. You can know about all the saints, sages, prophets, and other godly men, and all the great mothers of the world, but if they are mere images whose numinosity you have never experienced, it will be as if you were talking in a dream, for you do not know what you are talking about. The words you use are empty and valueless, and they gain life and meaning only when you try to learn about their numinosity, their relationship to the living individual. Then only do you begin to understand that the names mean very little, but that the way they are related to you is all-important.

591   The symbol-producing function of our dreams is an attempt

to bring our original mind back to consciousness, where it has never been before, and where it has never undergone critical self-reflection. We *have been* that mind, but we have never *known* it. We got rid of it before understanding it. It rose from its cradle, shedding its primitive characteristics like cumbersome and valueless husks. It looks as if the unconscious represented the deposit of these remnants. Dreams and their symbols continually refer to them, as if they intended to bring back all the old primitive things from which the mind freed itself in the course of its evolution: illusions, childish fantasies, archaic thought-forms, primitive instincts. This is in reality the case, and it explains the resistance, even fear and horror, one experiences in approaching the unconscious. One is shocked less by the primitivity of its contents than by their emotionality. They are not merely neutral or indifferent, they are so charged with affect that they are often exceedingly uncomfortable. They can even cause real panic, and the more they are repressed the more they spread through the whole personality in the form of a neurosis.

592   It is just their emotionality, however, that gives them such a vital importance. It is as if a man who has lived through a period of life in an unconscious state should suddenly realize that there is a gap in his memory—that important events seem to have taken place that he cannot remember. In so far as he assumes that the psyche is an exclusively personal affair (and this is the usual assumption), he will try to retrieve the apparently lost infantile memories. But the gaps in his childhood memories are merely the symptoms of a much greater loss, the loss of the primitive psyche—the psyche that lived and functioned before it was reflected by consciousness.

593   As the evolution of the embryonic body repeats its prehistory, so the mind grows up through the series of its prehistoric stages. Dreams seem to consider it their main task to bring back a sort of recollection of the prehistoric as well as the infantile world, right down to the level of the most primitive instincts, as if such memories were a priceless treasure. And these memories can indeed have a remarkably healing effect in certain cases, as Freud saw long ago. This observation confirms the view that an infantile memory-gap (a so-called amnesia) amounts to a definite loss and that its recovery brings an increase in vitality and well-being. Since we measure a child's psychic life by the

paucity and simplicity of its conscious contents, we do not appreciate the far-reaching complexities of the infantile mind that stem from its original identity with the prehistoric psyche. That "original mind" is just as much present and still functioning in the child as the evolutionary stages are in the embryo. If the reader remembers what I said earlier about the child who made a present of her dreams to her father, he will get a good idea of what I mean.

594   In infantile amnesia, one finds strange admixtures of mythological fragments that also often appear in later psychoses. Images of this kind are highly numinous and therefore very important. If such recollections reappear in adult life, they may in some cases cause profound psychological disturbances, while in other people they can produce astonishing cures or religious conversions. Often they bring back a piece of life, missing for a long time, that enriches the life of an individual.

595   The recollection of infantile memories and the reproduction of archetypal modes of psychic functioning create a wider horizon and a greater extension of consciousness, provided that one succeeds in assimilating and integrating the lost and regained contents. Since they are not neutral, their assimilation will modify the personality, even as they themselves will have to undergo certain alterations. In this part of the individuation process the interpretation of symbols plays an important practical role; for the symbols are natural attempts to reconcile and reunite often widely separated opposites, as is apparent from the contradictory nature of many symbols. It would be a particularly obnoxious error in this work of assimilation if the interpreter were to take only the conscious memories as "true" or "real," while considering the archetypal contents as merely fantastic representations. Dreams and their ambiguous symbols owe their forms on the one hand to repressed contents and on the other to archetypes. They thus have two aspects and enable one to interpret in two ways: one lays the emphasis either on their personal or on their archetypal aspect. The former shows the morbid influence of repression and infantile wishes, while the latter points to the sound instinctive basis. However fantastic the archetypal contents may be, they represent emotional powers or "numinosities." If one should try to brush them aside, they would only get repressed and would create the same neurotic condition as be-

fore. Their numinosity gives the contents an autonomous nature. This is a psychological fact that cannot be denied. If it is nevertheless denied, the regained contents are annihilated and any attempt at a synthesis is futile. But it appears to be a tempting way out and therefore it is often chosen.

596   Not only is the existence of archetypes denied, but even those people who do admit their existence usually treat them as if they were mere images and forget that they are living entities that make up a great part of the human psyche. As soon as the interpreter strips them of their numinosity, they lose their life and become mere words. It is then easy enough to link them together with other mythological representations, and so the process of limitless substitution begins; one glides from archetype to archetype, everything means everything, and one has reduced the whole process to absurdity. All the corpses in the world are chemically identical, but living individuals are not. It is true that the forms of archetypes are to a considerable extent interchangeable, but their numinosity is and remains a fact. It represents the *value* of an archetypal event. This emotional value must be kept in mind and allowed for throughout the whole intellectual process of interpretation. The risk of losing it is great, because thinking and feeling are so diametrically opposed that thinking abolishes feeling-values and vice versa. Psychology is the only science that has to take the factor of value (feeling) into account, since it forms the link between psychic events on the one hand, and meaning and life on the other.

597   Our intellect has created a new world that dominates nature, and has populated it with monstrous machines. The latter are so indubitably useful and so much needed that we cannot see even a possibility of getting rid of them or of our odious subservience to them. Man is bound to follow the exploits of his scientific and inventive mind and to admire himself for his splendid achievements. At the same time, he cannot help admitting that his genius shows an uncanny tendency to invent things that become more and more dangerous, because they represent better and better means for wholesale suicide. In view of the rapidly increasing avalanche of world population, we have already begun to seek ways and means of keeping the rising flood at bay. But nature may anticipate all our attempts by turning against man his own creative mind, and, by releasing the H-bomb or some

equally catastrophic device, put an effective stop to over-population. In spite of our proud domination of nature we are still her victims as much as ever and have not even learnt to control our own nature, which slowly and inevitably courts disaster.

598   There are no longer any gods whom we can invoke to help us. The great religions of the world suffer from increasing anaemia, because the helpful numina have fled from the woods, rivers, mountains, and animals, and the God-men have disappeared underground into the unconscious. There we suppose they lead an ignominious existence among the relics of our past, while we remain dominated by the great *Déesse Raison,* who is our overwhelming illusion. With her aid we are doing laudable things: we rid the world of malaria, we spread hygiene everywhere, with the result that under-developed populations increase at such a rate that food is becoming a problem. "We have conquered nature" is a mere slogan. In reality we are confronted with anxious questions, the answers to which seem nowhere in sight. The so-called conquest of nature overwhelms us with the natural fact of over-population and makes our troubles more or less unmanageable because of our psychological incapacity to reach the necessary political agreements. It remains quite natural for men to quarrel and fight and struggle for superiority over one another. Where indeed have we "conquered nature"?

599   As any change must begin somewhere, it is the single individual who will undergo it and carry it through. The change must begin with one individual; it might be any one of us. Nobody can afford to look around and to wait for somebody else to do what he is loath to do himself. As nobody knows what he could do, he might be bold enough to ask himself whether by any chance his unconscious might know something helpful, when there is no satisfactory conscious answer anywhere in sight. Man today is painfully aware of the fact that neither his great religions nor his various philosophies seem to provide him with those powerful ideas that would give him the certainty and security he needs in face of the present condition of the world.

600   I know that the Buddhists would say, as indeed they do: if only people would follow the noble eightfold path of the Dharma (doctrine, law) and had true insight into the Self; or the Christians: if only people had the right faith in the Lord; or

the rationalists: if only people could be intelligent and reasonable—then all problems would be manageable and solvable. The trouble is that none of them manages to solve these problems himself. Christians often ask why God does not speak to them, as he is believed to have done in former days. When I hear such questions, it always makes me think of the Rabbi who was asked how it could be that God often showed himself to people in the olden days but that nowadays one no longer saw him. The Rabbi replied: "Nor is there anyone nowadays who could stoop so low."

601   This answer hits the nail on the head. We are so captivated by and entangled in our subjective consciousness that we have simply forgotten the age-old fact that God speaks chiefly through dreams and visions. The Buddhist discards the world of unconscious fantasies as "distractions" and useless illusions; the Christian puts his Church and his Bible between himself and his unconscious; and the rationalist intellectual does not yet know that his consciousness is not his total psyche, in spite of the fact that for more than seventy years the unconscious has been a basic scientific concept that is indispensable to any serious student of psychology.

602   We can no longer afford to be so God-almighty as to set ourselves up as judges of the merits or demerits of natural phenomena. We do not base our botany on a division into useful and useless plants, or our zoology on a classification into harmless and dangerous animals. But we still go on blithely assuming that consciousness is sense and the unconscious is nonsense—as if you could make out whether any natural phenomenon makes sense or not! Do microbes, for instance, make sense or nonsense? Such evaluations merely demonstrate the lamentable state of our mind, which conceals its ignorance and incompetence under the cloak of megalomania. Certainly microbes are very small and most despicable, but it would be folly to know nothing about them.

603   Whatever else the unconscious may be, it is a natural phenomenon that produces symbols, and these symbols prove to be meaningful. We cannot expect someone who has never looked through a microscope to be an authority on microbes; in the same way, no one who has not made a serious study of natural symbols can be considered a competent judge in this matter. But

the general undervaluation of the human psyche is so great that neither the great religions nor the philosophies nor scientific rationalism have been willing to look at it twice. In spite of the fact that the Catholic Church admits the occurrence of dreams sent by God, most of its thinkers make no attempt to understand them. I also doubt whether there is a Protestant treatise on dogmatics that would "stoop so low" as to consider the possibility that the *vox Dei* might be perceived in a dream. But if somebody really believes in God, by what authority does he suggest that God is unable to speak through dreams?

604   I have spent more than half a century investigating natural symbols, and I have come to the conclusion that dreams and their symbols are not stupid and meaningless. On the contrary, dreams provide you with the most interesting information if only you take the trouble to understand their symbols. The results, it is true, have little to do with such worldly concerns as buying and selling. But the meaning of life is not exhaustively explained by your business activities, nor is the deep desire of the human heart answered by your bank account, even if you have never heard of anything else.

605   At a time when all available energy is spent in the investigation of nature, very little attention is paid to the essence of man, which is his psyche, although many researches are made into its conscious functions. But the really unknown part, which produces symbols, is still virtually unexplored. We receive signals from it every night, yet deciphering these communications seems to be such an odious task that very few people in the whole civilized world can be bothered with it. Man's greatest instrument, his psyche, is little thought of, if not actually mistrusted and despised. "It's only psychological" too often means: It is nothing.

606   Where, exactly, does this immense prejudice come from? We have obviously been so busy with the question of what *we* think that we entirely forget what the unconscious psyche thinks about us. Freud made a serious attempt to show why the unconscious deserves no better judgment, and his teachings have inadvertently increased and confirmed the existing contempt for the psyche. Before him it had been merely overlooked and neglected; now it has become a dump for moral refuse and a source of fear.

607   This modern standpoint is surely onesided and unjust. It does not even accord with the known facts. Our actual knowledge of the unconscious shows it to be a natural phenomenon, and that, like nature herself, it is at least *neutral*. It contains all aspects of human nature—light and dark, beautiful and ugly, good and evil, profound and silly. The study of individual as well as collective symbolism is an enormous task, and one that has not yet been mastered. But at last a beginning has been made. The results so far gained are encouraging, and they seem to indicate an answer to many of the questions perplexing present-day mankind.

III

THE SYMBOLIC LIFE

[A seminar talk given on 5 April 1939 to the Guild of Pastoral Psychology, London. Issued privately, as a transcript from shorthand notes by Derek Kitchin, as Guild Lecture No. 80 (London, 1954). Jung had approved the transcript. Subsequently published, in abbreviated form, in *Darshana* (Moradabad, India), I:3 (August 1961), 11–22; the issue was dedicated to the memory of C. G. Jung, who had died on 6 June of that year. The Guild Lecture is reproduced here with stylistic revisions.]

THE SYMBOLIC LIFE

Professor Jung was asked two questions:

First, had he any views on what was likely to be the next step in religious development? Did he, for example, think that there would be a new revelation—as some would phrase it, a new incarnation of the World Teacher, a new collective fantasy? Or was there likely to be a reinterpretation and new appreciation of the esoteric meaning of Christianity—perhaps with the aid of psychology? Or would there be no collective expression, but a period in which each man had to make his own individual contact and live out his own personal expression?

Secondly, would he explain why the believing Catholic was not subject to neurosis, and what could be done by the Protestant churches to counteract the tendency of their members to neurotic conditions?

608   I am not as ambitious as the questions that have been put to me! I should like to start with the second question, about the Roman Catholics, which has not been considered as of primary importance, but which, from a technical point of view, deserves full attention.

609   You have heard that I said Roman Catholics are less threatened by neurosis than members of other religious confessions. Of course there are Catholic neurotics just as well as others, but it is a fact that in my forty years of experience I have had no more than six practising Catholics among my patients. Naturally I do not count all those who *have been* Catholics, or who say that they are Catholics but who do not practise; but of practising Catholics I have had not more than about six. That is also the experience of my colleagues. In Zurich we are surrounded by Catholic cantons; not quite two-thirds of Switzerland is Protestant and the rest is Catholic. And then we have on the frontier Southern Germany, which is Catholic. So we should have a fair number of Catholic patients, but we have not; we have very few.

610   I was once asked by students of divinity a very interesting ques-

tion: whether in my view people in modern times, in case of psychological trouble, would go to the doctor rather than to the parson or the priest? Now, I said I could not answer that question, but I would enquire. So I sent round a questionnaire with detailed questions. I did not do it myself, because if I ask something, of course that is already a prejudice, and every answer would be prejudiced. So I gave the questionnaire to certain people who were not known to be acquainted with me, or in any kind of relation to me, and they sent it around, and we got hundreds of very interesting answers. And there I found the confirmation of what I already knew, namely, a large percentage—by far the majority—of Catholics said that, in case of psychological trouble, they would go to the priest and not to the doctor. The vast majority of Protestants said they would naturally go to the doctor. I had a very large number of answers from members of families of parsons, and they nearly all said that they would not go to the parson, they would rather go to the doctor. (I can talk quite freely about this. I am the son of a parson, and my grandfather was a sort of bishop, and I had five uncles all parsons, so I know something about the job! I have no hostile attitude to the clergy. On the contrary; but this is a fact.) I also had answers from Jews, and not one single Jew said he would go to the Rabbi—he wouldn't even think of it. And I had one Chinese, who gave me a classical answer. He said: "When I am young I go to the doctor, and when I am old I go to the philosopher."

611   I also had answers from representatives of the clergy, and I must mention one answer, which I hope is not in any way representative, but which casts a certain light upon a certain kind of theologian. The writer said, "Theology has nothing to do with the practical man." What has it to do with, then? You could say, "With God"; but you are not going to tell me that theology deals with God in that sense. Theology is really meant for man, if it is meant for anything. God needs no theology, I should say. That [answer] is a symptom of a certain attitude which explains a lot.

612   Now, I have spoken of my own experience in this field, but recently statistical researches have been made in America about the very same question, but from another angle. It is a sort of appreciation of the amount of complexes, or complex manifestations, you find in people. You find the least or the smallest number of complex manifestations in practising Catholics, far more in Protestants, and the most in Jews. That is absolutely independent of

my own researches; a colleague of mine in the United States made these researches,[1] and that bears out what I have told you.

613 So there must be something in the Catholic Church which accounts for this peculiar fact. Of course, we think in the first place of confession. That is only the outer aspect. I happen to know a great deal about confession, because I have often had to do with the Catholic clergy, particularly with Jesuits, who were busy in psychotherapy. For many years the Catholic clergy have studied psychotherapy; they have followed it up very closely. In the first place it was, of course, the Jesuits who studied it, and now recently I have heard that the Benedictines have done so too. There is an old tradition in the Catholic Church of the *directeur de conscience*—a sort of leader of souls. These directors have an extraordinary amount of experience and training in that work, and I have often been amazed at the wisdom with which Jesuits and other Catholic priests advised their patients.

614 Just recently it happened that a patient of mine, a woman of the nobility, who had a Jesuit father-confessor, discussed with him all the critical points of the analysis she made under my care. Of course, a number of things were not quite orthodox, and I was fully aware that there was a great conflict in her mind, and I advised her to discuss these matters with her father-confessor. (He was a famous Jesuit—he is now dead.) And then, after she had had that very frank talk, she told me all he said to her, and he had confirmed every word I had told her—a thing that was rather amazing to me, particularly from the mouth of a Jesuit. That opened my eyes to the extraordinary wisdom and culture of the Catholic *directeur de conscience*. And it explains to a certain extent why the practising Catholic would rather go to the priest.

615 The fact is that there are relatively few neurotic Catholics, and yet they are living under the same conditions as we do. They are presumably suffering from the same social conditions and so on, and so one would expect a similar amount of neurosis. There must be something in the cult, in the actual religious practice, which explains that peculiar fact that there are fewer complexes, or that these complexes manifest themselves much less in Catholics than in other people. That something, besides confession, is really the

[1] [Henry A. Murray, in his "Conclusions" to *Explorations in Personality: A Clinical and Experimental Study of Fifty Men of College Age,* by the Workers at the Harvard Psychological Clinic, under Murray's direction (1938), p. 739, sec. 17. Cited also in "Psychotherapy Today" (1941), C.W., vol. 16, par. 218.]

cult itself. It is the Mass, for instance. The heart of the Mass contains a living mystery, and that is the thing that works. When I say "a living mystery," I mean nothing mysterious; I mean mystery in that sense which the word has always had—a *mysterium tremendum.*[2] And the Mass is by no means the only mystery in the Catholic Church. There are other mysteries too. They begin with the very preparations, the simple things, in the Church. Take, for instance, the preparation of the baptismal water—the rite of the *benedictio fontis major,* or *minor,* on the night of the Sabbath before Easter. There you can see that a part of the Eleusinian Mysteries is still performed.

616   If you ask the average priest, he is unable to give you any account of these things. He does not know them. I once asked the Bishop of Fribourg, in Switzerland, to send us a man who could give a good account of the mystery of the Mass. It was a sad failure; he could tell us nothing. He could only confess to the wonderful impressicn, the marvellous mystical feeling, but he could say nothing at all as to why he had that feeling. It was only sentiments, and we could do nothing with it. But if you go into the history of the rite, if you try to understand the whole structure of that rite, including all the other rites round it, then you see it is a mystery that reaches down into the history of the human mind; it goes back very far—far beyond the beginnings of Christianity. You know that very important parts of the Mass—for instance, the Host—belonged to the cult of Mithras. In the cult of Mithras they used bread stamped with the cross, or divided into four; they used the little bells; and they used baptismal water—that is quite certainly pre-Christian. We even have texts that bear this out. The rite of the divine water, or the *aqua permanens*—the "eternal water"—is an alchemical conception, older than its Christian use; and when you study the *benedictio fontis,* the actual making of the water, you see that it is an alchemical procedure; and we have a text from the first century, a text of Pseudo-Democritus, which says what the blessing was done for.

617   These are absolute facts which are quite surely established. They point back into prehistory, into a continuity of tradition perhaps hundreds of years before Christianity. Now these mysteries have always been the expression of a fundamental psychological condition. Man expresses his most fundamental and most important psychological conditions in this ritual, this magic, or whatever you

[2] ["tremendous mystery."]

call it. And the ritual is the cult performance of these basic psychological facts. That explains why we should not change anything in a ritual. A ritual must be done according to tradition, and if you change one little point in it, you make a mistake. You must not allow your reason to play with it. For instance, take that most difficult dogma, the dogma of the Virgin Birth: it is absolutely wrong to rationalize it. If you leave it as it is, as it has been handed down, then it is true; but if you rationalize it, it is all wrong, because then you shift it over to the plane of our playful intellect, which does not understand the secret. It is the secret of virginity and the virginal conception, and that is a most important psychological fact. The sad truth is that we do not understand it any more. But, you know, in former centuries man did not need that kind of intellectual understanding. We are very proud of it; but it is nothing to be proud of. Our intellect is absolutely incapable of understanding these things. We are not far enough advanced psychologically to understand the truth, the extraordinary truth, of ritual and dogma. Therefore such dogmas should never be submitted to any kind of criticism.

618   So, you see, if I treat a real Christian, a real Catholic, I always keep him down to the dogma, and say, "You stick to it! And if you begin to criticize it in any way intellectually, then I am going to analyse you, and then you are in the frying-pan!" When a practising Catholic comes to me, I say, "Did you confess this to your father-confessor?" Naturally he says, "No, he does not understand." "What in hell, then," I say, "did you confess?" "Oh, lousy little things of no importance"—but the main sins he never talked of. As I said, I have had quite a number of these Catholics—six. I was quite proud to have so many, and I said to them, "Now, you see, what you tell me here, this is really serious. You go now to your father-confessor and you confess, whether he understands or does not understand. That is of no concern. It must be told before God, and if you don't do it, you are out of the Church, and then analysis begins, and then things will get hot, so you are much better off in the lap of the Church." So, you see, I brought these people back into the Church, with the result that the Pope himself gave me a private blessing for having taught certain important Catholics the right way of confessing.

619   For instance, there was a lady who played a very great role in the war. She was very Catholic, and always in the summer she used to come to Switzerland to pass her summer holiday. There is a famous monastery there with many monks, and she used to

go to it for confession and spiritual advice. Now, being an interesting person, she got a bit too interested in her father-confessor, and he got a bit too interested in her, and there was some conflict. He was then removed to the Clausura,[3] and she naturally collapsed, and she was advised to go to me. So she came to me in full resistance against the authorities who had interfered, and I made her go back to her spiritual authorities and confess the whole situation. And when she went back to Rome, where she lived, and where she had a confessor, he asked her, "Well, I know you from many years ago: how is it that you now confess so freely?" And she said she had learnt it from a doctor. That is the story of how I got the Pope's private blessing.

620 My attitude to these matters is that, as long as a patient is really a member of a church, he ought to be serious. He ought to be really and sincerely a member of that church, and he should not go to a doctor to get his conflicts settled when he believes that he should do it with God. For instance, when a member of the Oxford Group comes to me in order to get treatment, I say, "You are in the Oxford Group; so long as you are there, you settle your affair with the Oxford Group. I can't do it better than Jesus."

621 I will tell you a story of such a case. A hysterical alcoholic was cured by this Group movement, and they used him as a sort of model and sent him all round Europe, where he confessed so nicely and said that he had done wrong and how he had got cured through the Group movement. And when he had repeated his story twenty, or it may have been fifty, times, he got sick of it and took to drink again. The spiritual sensation had simply faded away. Now what are they going to do with him? They say, now he is pathological, he must go to a doctor. See, in the first stage he has been cured by Jesus, in the second by a doctor! I should and did refuse such a case. I sent that man back to these people and said, "If you believe that Jesus has cured this man, he will do it a second time. And if he can't do it, you don't suppose that I can do it better than Jesus?" But that is just exactly what they do expect: when a man is pathological, Jesus won't help him but the doctor will.

622 As long as a fellow believes in the Oxford Group movement, he stays there; and as long as a man is in the Catholic Church, he is in the Catholic Church for better or worse and he should

3 [The part of the religious house from which those of the opposite sex are excluded.]

be cured by those means. And mind you, I have seen that they can be cured by those means—that is a fact! Absolution, the Holy Communion, can cure them, even in very serious cases. If the experience of the Holy Communion is real, if the ritual and the dogma fully express the psychological situation of that individual, he can be cured. If the ritual and dogma do not fully express the psychological situation of that individual, he can't be cured. That is the reason why you have Protestantism, and that is why Protestantism is so uncertain, why it splits and splits. That is no objection to Protestantism; it is exactly the same as the story about the Code Napoléon.

623   After the Code Napoléon had been in use a year, the man entrusted with the execution of Napoleon's orders came back with a portfolio of immense size. Napoleon looked at it and asked, "Mais comment? Est-ce que le Code est mort?"—because the man had so many propositions to make. But the man answered, "Au contraire, Sire; il vit!"

624   The splitting up of Protestantism into new denominations—four hundred or more we have—is a sign of life. But, alas! It is not a very nice sign of life, in the sense of a church, because there is no dogma and there is no ritual. There is not the typical symbolic life.

625   You see, man is in need of a symbolic life—badly in need. We only live banal, ordinary, rational, or irrational things—which are naturally also within the scope of rationalism, otherwise you could not call them irrational. But we have no symbolic life. Where do we live symbolically? Nowhere, except where we participate in the ritual of life. But who, among the many, are really participating in the ritual of life? Very few. And when you look at the ritual life of the Protestant Church, it is almost nil. Even the Holy Communion has been rationalized. I say that from the Swiss point of view: in the Swiss Zwinglian Church the Holy Communion is not a communion at all; it is a meal of memory. There is no Mass either; there is no confession; there is no ritual, symbolic life.

626   Have you got a corner somewhere in your house where you perform the rites, as you can see in India? Even the very simple houses there have at least a curtained corner where the members of the household can lead the symbolic life, where they can make their new vows or meditation. We don't have it; we have no such corner. We have our own room, of course—but there is a telephone which can ring us up at any time, and we always must be ready. We

have no time, no place. Where have we got these dogmatic or these mysterious images? Nowhere! We have art galleries, yes—where we kill the gods by thousands. We have robbed the churches of their mysterious images, of their magical images, and we put them into art galleries. That is worse than the killing of the three hundred children in Bethlehem; it is a blasphemy.

627 Now, we have no symbolic life, and we are all badly in need of the symbolic life. Only the symbolic life can express the need of the soul—the daily need of the soul, mind you! And because people have no such thing, they can never step out of this mill—this awful, grinding, banal life in which they are "nothing but." In the ritual they are near the Godhead; they are even divine. Think of the priest in the Catholic Church, who is in the Godhead: he carries himself to the sacrifice on the altar; he offers himself as the sacrifice. Do we do it? Where do we know that we do it? Nowhere! Everything is banal, everything is "nothing but"; and that is the reason why people are neurotic. They are simply sick of the whole thing, sick of that banal life, and therefore they want sensation. They even want a war; they all want a war. They are all glad when there is a war: they say, "Thank heaven, now something is going to happen—something bigger than ourselves!"

628 These things go pretty deep, and no wonder people get neurotic. Life is too rational, there is no symbolic existence in which I am something else, in which I am fulfilling my role, my role as one of the actors in the divine drama of life.

629 I once had a talk with the master of ceremonies of a tribe of Pueblo Indians, and he told me something very interesting. He said, "Yes, we are a small tribe, and these Americans, they want to interfere with our religion. They should not do it," he said, "because we are the sons of the Father, the Sun. He who goes there" (pointing to the sun)—"that is our Father. We must help him daily to rise over the horizon and to walk over Heaven. And we don't do it for ourselves only: we do it for America, we do it for the whole world. And if these Americans interfere with our religion through their missions, they will see something. In ten years Father Sun won't rise any more, because we can't help him any more."

630 Now, you may say, that is just a sort of mild madness. Not at all! These people have no problems. They have their daily life, their symbolic life. They get up in the morning with a feeling of their great and divine responsibility: they are the sons of the Sun, the Father, and their daily duty is to help the Father over the

horizon—not for themselves alone, but for the whole world. You should see these fellows: they have a natural fulfilled dignity. And I quite understood when he said to me, "Now look at these Americans: they are always seeking something. They are always full of unrest, always looking for something. What are they looking for? There is nothing to be looked for!" That is perfectly true. You can see them, these travelling tourists, always looking for something, always in the vain hope of finding something. On my many travels I have found people who were on their third trip round the world—uninterruptedly. Just travelling, travelling; seeking, seeking. I met a woman in Central Africa who had come up alone in a car from Cape Town and wanted to go to Cairo. "What for?" I asked. "What are you trying to do that for?" And I was amazed when I looked into her eyes—the eyes of a hunted, a cornered animal—seeking, seeking, always in the hope of something. I said, "What in the world are you seeking? What are you waiting for, what are you hunting after?" She is nearly possessed; she is possessed by so many devils that chase her around. And why is she possessed? Because she does not live the life that makes sense. Hers is a life utterly, grotesquely banal, utterly poor, meaningless, with no point in it at all. If she is killed today, nothing has happened, nothing has vanished—because she was nothing! But if she could say, "I am the daughter of the Moon. Every night I must help the Moon, my Mother, over the horizon"—ah, that is something else! Then she lives, then her life makes sense, and makes sense in all continuity, and for the whole of humanity. That gives peace, when people feel that they are living the symbolic life, that they are actors in the divine drama. That gives the only meaning to human life; everything else is banal and you can dismiss it. A career, producing of children, are all *maya* compared with that one thing, that your life is meaningful.

631   That is the secret of the Catholic Church: that they still, to a certain extent, can live the meaningful life. For instance, if you can watch daily the sacrifice of the Lord, if you can partake of his substance, then you are filled with the Deity, and you daily repeat the eternal sacrifice of Christ. Of course, what I say is just so many words, but to the man who really lives it, it means the whole world. It means more than the whole world, because it makes sense to him. It expresses the desire of the soul; it expresses the actual facts of our unconscious life. When the wise man said, "Nature demands death," he meant just that.

275

632   So I think we can go on now to the next question. What I
have spoken of is, alas, to a great extent the past. We cannot turn
the wheel backwards; we cannot go back to the symbolism that
is gone. No sooner do you know that this thing is symbolic than
you say, "Oh, well, it presumably means something else." Doubt
has killed it, has devoured it. So you cannot go back. I cannot
go back to the Catholic Church, I cannot experience the miracle
of the Mass; I know too much about it. I know it is the truth,
but it is the truth in a form in which I cannot accept it any more.
I cannot say "This is the sacrifice of Christ," and see him any
more. I cannot. It is no more true to me; it does not express my
psychological condition. My psychological condition wants something else. I must have a situation in which that thing becomes
true once more. I need a new form. When one has had the misfortune to be fired out of a church, or to say "This is all nonsense,"
and to quit it—that has no merit at all. But to be in it and to
be forced, say, by God, to leave it—well, then you are legitimately
extra ecclesiam. But *extra ecclesiam nulla salus;* then things really
become terrible, because you are no more protected, you are no
more in the *consensus gentium,* you are no more in the lap of the
All-compassionate Mother. You are alone and you are confronted
with all the demons of hell. That is what people don't know. Then
they say you have an anxiety neurosis, nocturnal fears, compul-
sions—I don't know what. Your soul has become lonely; it is *extra
ecclesiam* and in a state of no-salvation. And people don't know
it. They think your condition is pathological, and every doctor helps
them to believe it. And, of course, when they say, and when everybody holds, that this is neurotic and pathological, then we have
to talk that language. I talk the language of my patients. When
I talk with lunatics, I talk the lunatic language, otherwise they
don't understand me. And when I talk with neurotics, I talk neurotic with them. But it is neurotic talk when one says that this
is a neurosis. As a matter of fact it is something quite different:
it is the terrific fear of loneliness. It is the hallucination of loneliness,
and it is a loneliness that cannot be quenched by anything else.
You can be a member of a society with a thousand members, and
you are still alone. That thing in you which should live is alone;
nobody touches it, nobody knows it, you yourself don't know it;
but it keeps on stirring, it disturbs you, it makes you restless, and
it gives you no peace.

633   So, you see, I was forced simply through my patients to try

to find out what we could do about such a condition. I am not going to found a religion, and I know nothing about a future religion. I only know that in certain cases such and such things develop. For instance, take any case you want: if I go far enough, if the case demands it, or if certain conditions are favourable, then I shall observe certain unmistakable things, namely, that the unconscious facts are coming up and becoming threateningly clear. That is very disagreeable. And therefore Freud had to invent a system to protect people, and himself, against the reality of the unconscious, by putting a most depreciatory explanation upon these things, an explanation that always begins with "nothing but." The explanation of every neurotic symptom was known long ago. We have a theory about it: it is all due to a father fixation, or to a mother fixation; it is all nonsense, so you can dismiss it. And so we dismiss our souls—"Oh, I am bound by a fixation to my mother, and if I see that I have all kinds of impossible fancies about my mother, I am liberated from that fixation." If the patient succeeds, he has lost his soul. Every time you accept that explanation you lose your soul. You have not helped your soul; you have replaced your soul by an explanation, a theory.

634   I remember a very simple case.[4] There was a student of philosophy, a very intelligent woman. That was quite at the beginning of my career. I was a young doctor then, and I did not know anything beyond Freud. It was not a very important case of neurosis, and I was absolutely certain that it could be cured; but the case had not been cured. That girl had developed a terrific father-transference to me—projected the image of the father on me. I said, "But, you see, I'm not your father!" "I know," she said, "that you're not my father, but it always seems as if you were." She behaved accordingly and fell in love with me, and I was her father, brother, son, lover, husband—and, of course, also her hero and saviour—every thinkable thing! "But," I said, "you see, that is absolute nonsense!" "But I can't live without it," she answered. What could I do with that? No depreciatory explanation would help. She said, "You can say what you like; it is so." She was in the grip of an unconscious image. Then I had the idea: "Now, if anybody knows anything about it, it must be the unconscious, that has produced such an awkward situation." So I began to watch the dreams seriously, not just in order to catch certain fantasies, but because I really wanted to understand how her psychic system

[4] [Cf. *Two Essays on Analytical Psychology* (C.W., vol. 7), pars. 206ff.]

reacted to such an abnormal situation—or to such a very normal situation, if you like to say so, because that situation is usual. She produced dreams in which I appeared as the father. That we dealt with. Then I appeared as the lover, and I appeared as the husband—that was all in the same vein. Then I began to change my size: I was much bigger than an ordinary human being; sometimes I had even divine attributes. I thought "Oh, well, that is the old saviour idea." And then I took on the most amazing forms. I appeared, for instance, the size of a god, standing in the fields and holding her in my arms as if she were a baby, and the wind was blowing over the corn and the fields were waving like waves of water, and in the same way I rocked her in my arms. And then, when I saw that picture, I thought, "Now I see what the unconscious really is after: the unconscious wants to make a god of me: that girl needs a god—at least, her unconscious needs a god. Her unconscious wants to find a god, and because it cannot find a god, it says 'Dr. Jung is a god." And so I said to her what I thought: "I surely am not a god, but your unconscious needs a god. That is a serious and a genuine need. No time before us has fulfilled that need; you are just an intellectual fool, just as much as I am, but we don't know it." That changed the situation completely; it made all the difference in the world. I cured that case, because I fulfilled the need of the unconscious.

635   I can tell you another case.[5] The patient was a Jewish girl. She was a funny little character, a very pretty, elegant little thing—and I thought "What a useless beast!" She had a frightful neurosis, a terrible anxiety neurosis, with awful attacks of fear, and she had suffered from these things for years. She had been with another analyst and had turned his head altogether; he fell in love with her, and she found no help in him. Then she came to me. The night before she came—before I had seen her at all—I had a dream, and I dreamed of a young girl, a pretty girl, that came to me, and I did not understand her case at all. Suddenly I thought, "By Jove! Hasn't she an extraordinary father complex!" And I felt it as a sort of revelation. I was much impressed by that dream; I did not know to what it referred. Then, when that girl came in next day, instantly I thought of my dream: "Perhaps she is the one!" First she told me her story. At first I couldn't see what it was all about, and then I thought, "Isn't it a father complex?"

5 [Cf. *Memories, Dreams, Reflections*, pp. 138f./137f.]

I saw nothing of a father complex, but it gave me the idea of asking more about the history of her family. Then I found out that she came from a Hasidic family—you know, those great mystics. Her grandfather had been a sort of wonder-rabbi—he had second sight—and her father had broken away from that mystic community, and she was completely sceptical and completely scientific in her outlook on life. She was highly intelligent, with that murderous kind of intellect that you very often find in Jews. So I thought, "Aha! What does that mean with reference to her neurosis? Why does she suffer from such an abysmal fear?" And I said to her, "Look here, I'm going to tell you something, and you will probably think it is all foolishness, but you have been untrue to your God. Your grandfather led the right life, but you are worse than a heretic; you have forsaken the mystery of your race. You belong to holy people, and what do you live? No wonder that you fear God, that you suffer from the fear of God."

636   Within one week I had cured that anxiety neurosis, and that is no lie (I am too old to lie!)—that is a fact. Before she had had months, many months, of analysis, but all too rational. With that remark she turned the corner, as if she suddenly began to understand, and her whole neurosis collapsed. It had no point in it any more: it had been based upon the mistake that she could live with her miserable intellect alone in a perfectly banal world, when in fact she was a child of God and should have lived the symbolic life, where she would have fulfilled the secret will in herself that was also in her family. She had forgotten all that, and was living, of course, in full contradiction to her whole natural system. Suddenly her life had a meaning, and she could live again; her whole neurosis went by the board.

637   In other cases, of course, it is not so—should I say—simple (it was not quite simple, you know!). I do not want to tell you further details of that case. It was a most instructive one, but I would rather tell you of other cases where things are not so simple, where you have to guide people quite slowly and wait for a long time until the unconscious produces the symbols that bring them back into the original symbolic life. Then you have to know a great deal about the language of the unconscious, the language of dreams. Then you see how the dreams begin to produce extraordinary figures. These are all found in history under different names. They are unknown quantities, but you find these figures in a literature which is itself completely obsolete. If you happen to know these

279

symbols, you can explain to your patients what the unconscious is after.

638   Of course, I can't give you a full description of these things, I can only mention them. From my observations I learned that the modern unconscious has a tendency to produce a psychological condition which we find, for instance, in medieval mysticism. You find certain things in Meister Eckhart; you find many things in Gnosticism; that is a sort of esoteric Christianity. You find the idea of the Adam Kadmon in every man—the Christ within. Christ is the second Adam, which is also, in exotic religions, the idea of the Atman or the complete man, the original man, the "all-round" man of Plato, symbolized by a circle or a drawing with circular motifs. You find all these ideas in medieval mysticism; you find them all through alchemical literature, beginning with the first century after Christ. You find them in Gnosticism, you find many of them in the New Testament, of course, in Paul. But it is an absolutely consistent development of the idea of Christ within—not the historical Christ without, but the Christ within; and the argument is that it is immoral to allow Christ to suffer for us, that he has suffered enough, and that we should carry our own sins for once and not shift them off on to Christ—that we should carry them all. Christ expresses the same idea when he says, "I appear in the least of your brethren";[6] and what about it, my dear son, if the least of your brethren should be yourself—what about it then? Then you get the intimation that Christ is not to be the least in your life, that we have a brother in ourselves who is really the least of our brethren, much worse than the poor beggar whom you feed. That is, in ourselves we have a shadow; we have a very bad fellow in ourselves, a very poor man, and he has to be accepted. What has Christ done—let us be quite banal about it—what has Christ done when we consider him as an entirely human creature? Christ was disobedient to his mother; Christ was disobedient to his tradition; Christ falsified himself, and played it out to the bitter end: he carried through his hypothesis to the bitter end. How was Christ born? In the greatest misery. Who was his father? He was an illegitimate child—humanly the most miserable situation: a poor girl having a little son. That is our symbol, that is ourselves; we are all that. And if anyone lives his own hypothesis to the bitter end (and pays with his death, perhaps), he knows that Christ is his brother.

[6] [Cf. Matthew 25:40.]

639   That is modern psychology, and that is the future. That is the true future, that is the future of which I know—but, of course, the historical future might be quite different. We do not know whether it is not the Catholic Church that will reap the harvest that is now going to be cut down. We do not know that. We do not know whether Hitler is going to found a new Islam. (He is already on the way; he is like Mohammed. The emotion in Germany is Islamic; warlike and Islamic. They are all drunk with a wild god.) That can be the historic future. But I do not care for a historic future at all, not at all; I am not concerned with it. I am only concerned with the fulfilment of that will which is in every individual. My history is only the history of those individuals who are going to fulfil their hypotheses. That is the whole problem; that is the problem of the true Pueblo: that I do today everything that is necessary so that my Father can rise over the horizon. That is my standpoint. Now I think I have talked enough!

Discussion

Canon H. England:

640   In the Church of England ritual we have, after the Holy Communion: "Here we offer and present unto Thee, O Lord, ourselves, our souls and bodies, to be a reasonable, holy, and lively sacrifice." That is the sacrifice and that is the ritual which should satisfy the conditions you demand, is it not?

Professor Jung:

641   Absolutely. Yes, the Church of England has a great asset in that. The Church of England, of course, is not the whole Protestant world, and it is not quite Protestant in England.

The Bishop of Southwark:

642   The question is whether it is quite a Protestant world.

Professor Jung:

643   But I should call the Church of England a real church. Protestantism in itself is no church at all.

The Bishop of Southwark:

644   But there are other parts of the Protestant world which have churches. There are, for instance, the Lutherans in Sweden; take them as an example of a reformed church. Their conditions are more like our own. Have your ever come across the Orthodox ritual? Does the Russian ritual have the same effect?

Professor Jung:

645   I am afraid that, owing to historical events, the whole thing has been interrupted. I have seen a few Orthodox people, and I am afraid they were no longer very orthodox.

The Bishop of Southwark:

646   I meet a good number of Russian exiles in Paris, in a colony there, who are very deliberately trying to keep alive the old Russian religious life with as little change as possible.

Professor Jung:

647   I have never seen a real member of the Orthodox Church, but I am quite convinced that as they live the symbolic life in that church they are all right.

The Bishop of Southwark:

648   We Anglicans are in much closer touch with the Orthodox Church than with the Catholics, and they seem to us rather too symbolic—not quite to be facing up to the straight path, the facts they ought to be dealing with. They have rather the exile psychology—a world of their own—and I am rather frightened of that psychology for some of our own people, who seem to want to take refuge in symbolism from the responsibilities of life.

Professor Jung:

649   With the best truth you can cheat; you can cheat with anything, so there are people who take illegitimate refuge in symbolism. For instance, monasteries are full of people who run away from life and its obligations and live the symbolic life—the symbolic life of their past. Such cheats are always punished, but it is a peculiar fact that they can stand it somehow without getting too neurotic. There is a peculiar value in the symbolic life. It is a fact that the primitive Australians sacrifice to it two-thirds of their available time—of their lifetime in which they are conscious.

The Bishop of Southwark:

650   King Alfred the Great did something very much like that.

Professor Jung:

651   Yes, that is the secret of primitive civilizations.

The Bishop of Southwark:

652   He was a very practical civilizing man.

Professor Jung:

653   Yes, because the very fact that you live the symbolic life has an extraordinarily civilizing influence. Those people are far more

civilized and creative on account of the symbolic life. People who are only rational have very little influence; it is all talk, and with talk you get nowhere.

Canon England:

654   But symbols may appeal to reason, for all that; to an enlightened reason.

Professor Jung:

655   They may, yes! Symbols often cause an extraordinary intensity of mental life, even of intellectual life. If you look through the Patristic literature you find mountains of emotion, all couched in symbolism.

The Reverend D. Glan Morgan:

656   But what are the Protestants to do now, especially we of the left—the Free Churches—the Nonconformists? We have no symbols at all, we have rejected them, lock, stock, and barrel. Our chapels are dead, our pulpits are platforms.

Professor Jung:

657   Excuse me! You have a lot of symbolism still. You speak of God or of Jesus? There you are! What could be more symbolic? God is a symbol of symbols!

Mr. Morgan:

658   Even that symbol becomes a contradiction. And there are crowds of people in our churches who can believe in Jesus Christ, but who cannot believe in God.

Professor Jung:

659   Yes, and in the Catholic Church there are plenty who believe in the Church, but don't believe in God—nor in anything else!

The Bishop of Southwark:

660   How far has this something to do with it? Not only has the Roman Catholic Church a very full symbolic system, but it is combined with the profession of absolute certitude—the dogma of infallibility. That must have a direct bearing on the value of symbols.

Professor Jung:

661   Very important. The Church is absolutely right, wholly right, in insisting on that absolute validity, otherwise she opens the door to doubt.

Dr. Ann Harling:

662   To conflict or neurosis?

Professor Jung:

663   Absolutely. Therefore "extra ecclesiam nulla salus."

The Bishop of Southwark:

664   Are all forms of conflict neurosis?

Professor Jung:

665   Only when the intellect breaks away from that symbolic obser-
vance. When the intellect does not serve the symbolic life it is the
devil; it makes you neurotic.

Mr. Morgan:

666   May there be a transition, a moving over from one system to
another, and may not that be neurotic?

Professor Jung:

667   Neurosis is a transitory phase, it is the unrest between two
positions.

Mr. Morgan:

668   I am asking because I myself feel at the moment that there
is a good deal of neurosis among Protestants on account of the
price that has to be paid for moving over from one state to the
other.

Professor Jung:

669   That is what I say: "extra ecclesiam nulla salus." You get into
a terrible frying-pan when you get out of the Church; therefore
I don't wish it on people. I point out the validity of the primary
Church.

The Bishop of Southwark:

670   What are we to do with the great majority of people we have
to deal with who are not in any church? They say they are in
the Church of England, but they don't belong in any sense.

Professor Jung:

671   I am afraid you can't do anything with such people. The
Church is there and is valid for those who are inside. Those who
are outside the walls of the Church cannot be brought back into
the Church by the ordinary means. But I wish the clergy would
understand the language of the soul, and that the clergyman would
be a *directeur de conscience!* Why should I be a *directeur de conscience?* I am a doctor; I have no preparation for that. It is the
natural calling of the clergyman; he should do it. Therefore I wish
that a new generation of clergymen would come in and do the
same as they do in the Catholic Church: that they would try to

translate the language of the unconscious, even the language of dreams, into proper language. For instance, I know that there is now in Germany the Berneuchener Circle,[7] a liturgical movement; and one of the main representatives is a man who has a great knowledge of symbolism. He has given me quite a number of instances, which I am able to check, where he translated the figures in dreams into dogmatic language with the greatest success, and these people quietly slipped back into the order of the Church. They have no right to be neurotic. They belong to a church, and if you can help them to slip back to the Church you have helped them. Several of my patients became Catholics, others went back into the Church organization. But it must be something that has substance and form. It is by no means true that when one analyses somebody he necessarily jumps into the future. He is perhaps meant for a church, and if he can go back into a church, perhaps that is the best thing that can happen.

Mr. Morgan:

672   What if he can't?

Professor Jung:

673   Then there is trouble; then he has to go on the Quest; then he has to find out what his soul says; then he has to go through the solitude of a land that is not created. I have published such an example in my lectures[8]—that of a great scientist, a very famous man, who lives today.[9] He set out to see what the unconscious said to him, and it gave him a wonderful lead. That man got into order again because he gradually accepted the symbolic data, and now he leads the religious life, the life of the careful observer. Religion is careful observation of the data. He now observes all the things that are brought him by his dreams; that is his only guidance.

674   We are in a new world with that; we are exactly like primitives. When I went to East Africa, I went to a small tribe in Mount Elgon and I asked the medicine-man about dreams. He said, "I know what you mean; my father still had dreams." I said, "You have no dreams?" And then he wept and answered, "No, I have no dreams any more." I asked, "Why?" He answered, "Since the British came into the country." "Now, how is that?" He said, "The

---

[7] [A German Protestant movement (founded at Berneuchen, Neumark) aiming at a deepening of religious life. See *Letters,* ed. G. Adler, vol. 1, p. 215, n. 1.]
[8] [Cf. "Traumsymbole des Individuationsprozesses," *Eranos Jahrbuch 1935.* The material was subsequently incorporated in *Psychology and Alchemy,* Part II.]
[9] Wolfgang Pauli (1900–1958), Swiss physicist and Nobel Prize winner.]

District Commissioner knows when there shall be war; he knows when there are diseases; he knows where we must live—he does not allow us to move." The political guidance is now represented by the D.C., by the superior intelligence of the white man; therefore, why should they need dreams? Dreams were the original guidance of man in the great darkness. Read that book of Rasmussen's about the Polar Eskimos.[10] There he describes how a medicine-man became the leader of his tribe on account of a vision. When a man is in the wilderness, the darkness brings the dreams—*somnia a Deo missa*—that guide him. It has always been so. I have not been led by any kind of wisdom; I have been led by dreams, like any primitive. I am ashamed to say so, but I am as primitive as any nigger,[11] because I do not know! When you are in the darkness you take the next thing, and that is a dream. And you can be sure that the dream is your nearest friend; the dream is the friend of those who are not guided any more by the traditional truth and in consequence are isolated. That was the case with the old alchemical philosophers, and you read in the *Tractatus Aureus* of Hermes Trismegistus a passage that bears out what I said about isolation. There you read: "(Deus) in quo est adiuvatio cuiuslibet sequestrati" (God, in whom is the help of all who are lonely). Hermes, at the same time, was a real leader of souls and the very incarnation of inspiration, thus representing the unconscious manifest in dreams. So, you see, the one who is going alone and has no guidance, he has the *somnia a Deo missa;* he has no D.C. Of course, when we have a D.C. we do not need a dream, but when we are alone, that is something else.

The Bishop of Southwark:

675   A practising parson, a Roman Catholic, has a D.C., an authority, and does not need dreams.

Professor Jung:

676   Agreed! Nevertheless, there are people in the Church who have *somnia a Deo missa,* and the Church is very careful to appreciate the importance of such dreams. They don't deny the fact that there are *somnia a Deo missa;* the Church reserves the right of judgment, but they do consider it.

---

10 [Cf. Knud Rasmussen, *Across Arctic America,* ch. III: "A Wizard and His Household."]

11 [This offensive term was not invariably derogatory in earlier British and Continental usage, and definitely not in this case.]

Lt.-Colonel H. M. Edwards:

677   Are Roman Catholic priests being trained as psychotherapists?

Professor Jung:

678   Yes.

Colonel Edwards:

679   Not in this country?

Professor Jung:

680   No, the Jesuits are. For example, the main father-confessor of Jena is a Jesuit trained in psychotherapy.

Dr. A. D. Belilios:

681   Of the Jungian school?

Professor Jung:

682   Of all schools. I am afraid he doesn't go as far as I go. I asked him about his position as to dreams, and he said, "Well, there we have to be careful, and we are already a bit suspect. We have the means of grace of the Church." "Right you are," I said, "you don't need dreams. I can give no absolution, I have no means of grace; therefore I must listen to dreams. I am a primitive; you are a civilized man." In a way that man is much more wonderful than I am. He can be a saint; I cannot be a saint—I can only be a nigger, very primitive, going by the next thing—quite superstitious.

Wing-Commander T. S. Rippon:

683   How do you feel with the question of life after death?

Professor Jung:

684   I have not been there consciously yet. When I die, I shall say "Now, let us see!" For the time being I am in this form, and I say, "Now, what is here? Let us do everything we can here." If, when we die, we find there is a new life, I shall say, "Now let us live once more—*encore une fois!*" I don't know, but I can tell you this: the unconscious has no time. There is no trouble about time in the unconscious. Part of our psyche is not in time and not in space. They are only an illusion, time and space, and so in a certain part of our psyche time does not exist at all.

Mr. Derek Kitchin:

685   You wrote somewhere, Professor, that for many persons a belief in a future life was a necessity to psychological health.

Professor Jung:

686   Yes. You would be out of tune if you did not consider immortality when your dreams put you up against that problem; then you should decide. If they don't you can leave it. But if they put you up against it, then you have to say, "I must try how I feel. Let us assume that there is no such thing as immortality, no life after death: how do I feel about that? How do I function with such a conviction?" Then, perhaps, your stomach goes wrong. So you say, "Let us assume that I am immortal," and then you function. So you must say, "That must be right." How do we know? How does an animal know that the particular bit of grass it has eaten is not poisonous, and how do animals know that something is poisonous? They go wrong. That is how we know the truth: the truth is that which helps us to live—to live properly.

The Reverend Francis Boyd:

687   That which works; the pragmatic test.

Professor Jung:

688   That which really works. I have no assumptions about these things. How can I? I only know that if I live in a certain way I live wrongly; I am unhealthy. And if I live in another way I am right. For instance, if the Pueblos believe that they are the sons of the Father Sun, they are in order. So I say, "I wish I could be a son of the Sun." Alas! I can't do it; I can't afford it; my intellect doesn't allow it. So I am bound to find another form. But they are all right. It would be the greatest mistake to tell those people that they are not the sons of the Sun. I tried, for instance, the argument of St. Augustine:[12] "Non est Dominus Sol factus, sed per quem Sol factus est" (God is not the sun but the one who made the sun). But my Pueblo got into a frightful state; he thought that was the most awful blasphemy. He said, "This *is* the Father; there is no Father behind it. How can we think of a Father we cannot see?" And in so far as they live in that belief, it is true. Anything that *lives* on earth, is true. So the Christian dogma is true, much truer than we have ever thought. We think we are much cleverer. As long as we don't understand it, as long as we don't see where it could lead beyond, there is no reason why we should give it up. If we see we are out of it, then we have what we call a superior point of view. That is another thing. Analysis

---

[12] [*In Johannis Evang.*, XXXIV, 2.]

is merely a means of making us more conscious of our perplexity; we are all on the Quest.

The Bishop of Southwark:

689   Would you say the same of the Nazi or the Mohammedan, that they are right to go on in their faith?

Professor Jung:

690   God is terrible; the living God is a living fear. I think it is an instrument, as Mohammed was for that people. All people, for instance, who are filled with that uncanny power, are always most disagreeable for others. I am quite convinced that some of the people in the Old Testament were very disagreeable people.

The Reverend W. Hopkins:

691   There is obviously, and always has been, a conflict between science and religion. It is not so acute now as it has been. How do you bring about a reconciliation, which obviously is the sort of thing that is needed?

Professor Jung:

692   There is no conflict between religion and science. That is a very old-fashioned idea. Science has to consider what there is. There is religion, and it is one of the most essential manifestations of the human mind. It is a fact, and science has nothing to say about it; it simply has to confirm that there is that fact. Science always runs after these things; it does not try to explain the phenomena. Science cannot establish a religious truth. A religious truth is essentially an experience, it is not an opinion. Religion is an absolute experience. A religious experience is absolute, it cannot be discussed. For instance, when somebody has had a religious experience, he just has such an experience, and nothing can take it away from him.

Mr. Hopkins:

693   In the nineteenth century the scientists were apt to be much more dogmatic than they are now. They dismissed all religion as an illusion. But now they admit it, and they experience it themselves.

Professor Jung:

694   Our science is phenomenology. In the nineteenth century science was labouring under the illusion that science could establish a truth. No science can establish a truth.

Mr. Hopkins:

695   But it is the science of the nineteenth century that the ordinary people have today. That is our problem.

Professor Jung:

696   Yes, you are up against it. It has filtered down into the lower strata of the population, and has worked no end of evil. When the asses catch hold of science, that is awful. Those are the great mental epidemics of our time; they are all insane, the whole crowd!

IV

ON OCCULTISM

(related to Volume 1 of the Collected Works)

ON SPIRITUALISTIC PHENOMENA[1]

697   It is impossible, within the short space of a lecture, to say anything fundamental about such a complicated historical and psychological problem as spiritualism[1a] appears to be. One must content
oneself with shedding a little light on one or the other aspect of
this intricate question. This kind of approach will at least give the
hearer an approximate idea of the many facets of spiritualism. Spiritualism, as well as being a theory (its advocates call it "scientific"),
is a religious belief which, like every religious belief, forms the spiritual core of a religious movement. This sect believes in the actual
and tangible intervention of a spiritual world in our world, and
consequently makes a religious practice of communicating with the
spirits. The dual nature of spiritualism gives it an advantage over
other religious movements: not only does it believe in certain articles
of faith that are not susceptible of proof, but it bases its belief on
a body of allegedly scientific, physical phenomena which are supposed to be of such a nature that they cannot be explained except
by the activity of spirits. Because of its dual nature—on the one
side a religious sect, on the other a scientific hypothesis—spiritualism
touches upon widely differing areas of life that would seem to have
nothing in common.

698   Spiritualism as a sect originated in America in the year 1848.
The story of its origin is a strange one.[2] Two girls of the Methodist
family Fox, in Hydesville, near Rochester (New York), were frightened every night by sounds of knocking. At first a great scandal
arose, because the neighbours suspected that the devil was up to
his usual tricks. Gradually, however, communication was established with the knocking sounds when it was discovered that questions were answered with a definite number of knocks. With the
help of a knocking alphabet, it was learned that a man had been

---

[1] [Lecture delivered at the Bernoullianum, Basel, 5 Feb. 1905. Published
serially as "Ueber spiritistische Erscheinungen" in the *Basler Nachrichten,* nos.
311–316 (12–17 Nov. 1905). Jung's original footnotes are given in full.]

[1a] [While "spiritism" (for *Spiritismus*) is the form now preferred by specialists,
"spiritualism," the form in general currency, has been used in this paper and
those that follow.]

[2] Detailed report in Capron, *Modern Spiritualism, Its Facts and Fanaticisms*
(Boston, 1885); résumé in Aksakow, *Animismus und Spiritismus* (1894).

murdered in the Foxes' house, and his body buried in the cellar. Investigations were said to have confirmed this.

699 Thus far the report. The public performances given by the Foxes with the poltergeists were quickly followed by the founding of other sects. Tableturning, much practised earlier, was taken up again. Numerous mediums were sought and found, that is, persons in whose presence such phenomena as knocking noises occurred. The movement spread rapidly to England and the continent. In Europe, spiritualism took the form chiefly of an epidemic of table-turning. There was hardly an evening party or dance where the guests did not steal away at a late hour to question the table. This particular symptom of spiritualism was rampant everywhere. The religious sects made less headway, but they continued to grow steadily. In every big city today there is a fairly large community of practising spiritualists.

700 In America, which swarms with local religious movements, the rise of spiritualism is understandable enough. With us, its favourable reception can be explained only by the fact that the ground had been historically prepared. The beginning of the nineteenth century had brought us the Romantic Movement in literature, a symptom of a widespread, deep-seated longing for anything extraordinary and abnormal. People adored wallowing in Ossianic emotions, they went crazy over novels set in old castles and ruined cloisters. Everywhere prominence was given to the mystical, the hysterical; lectures about life after death, about sleepwalkers and visionaries, about animal magnetism and mesmerism, were the order of the day. Schopenhauer devoted a long chapter to all these things in his *Parerga und Paralipomena,* and he also spoke of them at various places in his *chef d'œuvre.*[3] Even his important concept of "sanctity" is a far-fetched, mystico-aesthetic ideal. Similar movements made themselves felt in the Catholic church, clustering round the strange figure of Johan Joseph von Görres (1776–1848). Especially significant in this respect is his four-volume work *Die christliche Mystik* (Regensburg, 1836–42). The same trends appear in his earlier book, *Emanuel Swedenborg, seine Visionen und sein Verhältnis zur Kirche* (Speyer, 1827). The Protestant public raved about the soulful poetry of Justinus Kerner and his clairvoyante, Frau Friederike Hauffe, while certain theologians gave vent to their catholicizing tendencies by excommunicating spirits. From this period, too,

---

[3] [*The World as Will and Idea.*]

come a large number of remarkable psychological descriptions of abnormal people—ecstatics, somnambulists, sensitives. They were much in demand and were cultivated assiduously. A good example was Frau Hauffe herself, the clairvoyante of Prevorst, and the circle of admirers who gathered round her. Her Catholic counterpart was Katharina Emmerich, the ecstatic nun of Dulmen. Reports of similar personalities were collected together in a weighty tome by an anonymous savant, entitled "The Ecstatic Virgins of the Tyrol. Guiding Stars in the Dark Firmament of Mysticism."[4]

701   When these strange personages were investigated, the following suprasensible processes were observed:

    1. "Magnetic" phenomena.
    2. Clairvoyance and prophecy.
    3. Visions.

702   1. *Animal magnetism,* as understood at the beginning of the nineteenth century, covered a vaguely defined area of physiological and psychological phenomena which, it was thought, could all be explained as "magnetic." "Animal magnetism" had been in the air ever since the brilliant experiments of Franz Anton Mesmer. It was Mesmer who discovered the art of putting people to sleep by light passes of the hand. In some people this sleep was like the natural one, in others it was a "waking sleep"; that is, they were like sleepwalkers, only part of them was asleep, while some senses remained awake. This half-sleep was also called "magnetic sleep" or somnambulism. People in these states were wholly under the will of the magnetist, they were "magnetized" by him. Today, as we know, there is nothing wonderful about these states; they are known as hypnosis and we use the mesmeric passes as a valuable adjunct to other methods of suggestion. The significance attributed to the passes quickly led to their being grossly overestimated. People thought that some vitalistic force had been discovered; they spoke of a "magnetic fluid" that streamed from the magnetist into the patient and destroyed the diseased tissue. They also used it to explain the movements of the table in tableturning, imagining that the table was vitalized by the laying on of hands and could therefore move about like a living thing. The phenomena of the divining rod and the automatically swinging pendulum were explained in the same way. Even completely crazy phenomena of this sort were

[4] *Die Tyroler ekstatischen Jungfrauen. Leitsterne in die dunklen Gebiete der Mystik* (Regensburg, 1843).

widely reported and believed. Thus the *Neue Preussische Zeitung* reported from Barmen, in Pomerania, that a party of seven persons sat themselves round a table in a boat, and magnetized it. "In the first 20 minutes the boat drifted 50 feet downstream. Then it began to turn, with steadily increasing speed, until the rotary movement had carried it through an arc of 180 degrees in 3 minutes. Eventually, by skilful manipulation of the rudder, the boat moved forwards, and the party travelled half a mile upstream in 40 minutes, but on the return journey covered the same distance in 26 minutes. A crowd of spectators, watching the experiment from the banks of the river, received the 'table travellers' with jubilation." In very truth, a mystical motorboat! According to the report, the experiment had been suggested by a Professor Nägeli, of Freiburg im Breisgau.

703　　Experiments in divination are known from the grey dawn of history. Thus Ammianus Marcellinus reports from A.D. 371 that a certain Patricius and Hilarius, living in the reign (364–78) of the Emperor Valens, had discovered by the "abominable arts of soothsaying" who would succeed to the throne. For this purpose they used a metal bowl, with the alphabet engraved round the rim. Over it, amid fearful oaths, they suspended a ring on a thread. This began to swing, and spelt out the name Theodorus. When their magic was divulged, they were arrested and put to death.

704　　Ordinarily, experiments with the automatic movements of the table, the divining rod, and the pendulum are not as bizarre as the first example or as dangerous as the second. The various phenomena that may occur in tableturning have been described in a treatise by Justinus Kerner, bearing the significant title: "The Somnambulant Tables. A History and Explanation of these Phenomena"[5] (1853). They have also been described by the late Professor Thury, of Geneva, in *Les Tables parlantes au point de vue de la physique générale* (1855).

705　　2. *Clairvoyance and prophecy* are further characteristics of somnambulists. Clairvoyance in time and space plays a large role in the biographies and descriptions of these cases. The literature abounds in more or less credible reports, most of which have been collected by Gurney, Myers, and Podmore in their book, *Phantasms of the Living* (1886).

706　　An excellent example of clairvoyance is preserved for us in phil-

[5] *Die somnambulen Tische. Zur Geschichte und Erklärung dieser Erscheinungen.*

osophical literature and is especially interesting because it was personally commented on by Kant. In an undated letter to Charlotte von Knobloch, he wrote as follows about the spirit-seer Swedenborg:[6]

707   The following occurrence appears to me to have the greatest weight of proof, and to place the assertion respecting Swedenborg's extraordinary gift beyond all possibility of doubt.

708   In the year 1759, towards the end of September, on Saturday at four o'clock p.m., Swedenborg arrived at Gottenburg from England, when Mr. William Castel invited him to his house, together with a party of fifteen persons. About six o'clock Swedenborg went out, and returned to the company quite pale and alarmed. He said that a dangerous fire had just broken out in Stockholm, at the Södermalm (Gottenburg is about fifty German miles from Stockholm), and that it was spreading very fast. He was restless, and went out often. He said that the house of one of his friends, whom he named, was already in ashes, and that his own was in danger. At eight o'clock, after he had been out again, he joyfully exclaimed, 'Thank God! the fire is extinguished; the third door from my house.' This news occasioned great commotion throughout the whole city, but particularly amongst the company in which he was. It was announced to the Governor the same evening. On Sunday morning Swedenborg was summoned to the Governor who questioned him concerning the disaster. Swedenborg described the fire precisely, how it had begun and in what manner it had ceased, and how long it had continued. On the same day the news spread through the city, and as the Governor thought it worthy of attention, the consternation was considerably increased; because many were in trouble on account of their friends and property, which might have been involved in the disaster. On Monday evening a messenger arrived at Gottenburg, who was despatched by the Board of Trade during the time of the fire. In the letters brought by him, the fire was described precisely in the manner stated by Swedenborg. On Tuesday morning the Royal Courier arrived at the Governor's with the melancholy intelligence of the fire, of the loss which it had occasioned, and of the houses it had damaged and ruined, not in the least differing from that which Swedenborg had given at the very time when it happened; for the fire was extinguished at eight o'clock.

709   What can be brought forward against the authenticity of this occurrence (the conflagration in Stockholm)? My friend who wrote this to me has examined all, not only in Stockholm, but also, about two months ago, in Gottenburg, where he is well acquainted with the most

[6] [*Dreams of a Spirit-Seer*, trans. by E. F. Goerwitz, pp. 158ff. The unidentified text quoted by Jung gives the date 1756 for Swedenborg's experience. In the Goerwitz edn. the date 1759 is justified in Appendix III, pp. 160–61.]

respectable houses, and where he could obtain the most authentic and complete information, for as only a very short time had elapsed since 1759, most of the inhabitants are still alive who were eyewitnesses of this occurrence.

710   *Prophecy* is a phenomenon so well known from the teachings of religion that there is no need to give any examples.

711   3. *Visions* have always figured largely in miraculous tales, whether in the form of a ghostly apparition or an ecstatic vision. Science regards visions as delusions of the senses, or hallucinations. Hallucinations are very common among the insane. Let me cite an example from the literature of psychiatry:

712   A twenty-four-year-old servant girl, with an alcoholic father and a neurotic mother, suddenly begins falling into peculiar states. From time to time she falls into a state of consciousness in which she sees everything that comes into her mind vividly before her, as though it were there in reality. All the time the images keep changing with breathtaking speed and lifelikeness. The patient, who in actual life is nothing but a simple country girl, then resembles an inspired seer. Her features become transfigured, her movements flow with grace. Famous figures pass before her mind's eye. Schiller appears to her in person and plays with her. He recites his poems to her. Then she herself begins to recite, improvising in verse the things she has read, experienced, and thought. Finally she comes back to consciousness tired and exhausted, with a headache and a feeling of oppression, and with only an indistinct memory of what has happened. At other times her second consciousness has a sombre character. She sees ghostly figures prophesying disaster, processions of spirits, caravans of strange and terrifying beastlike forms, her own body being buried, etc.[7]

713   Visionary ecstasies are usually of this type. Numerous visionaries are known to us from history, among them many of the Old Testament prophets. There is the report of St. Paul's vision on the road to Damascus, followed by a blindness that ceased at the psychological moment. This blindness reminds us on the one hand of the blindness which can be produced by suggestion, and on the other hand of the blindness which occurs spontaneously with certain hysterical patients and again disappears at a suitable psychological moment. The best visions, and the ones that are psychologically the most transparent, are found in the legends of the saints, the visions being most colourful in the case of female saints experiencing

[7] Krafft-Ebing, *Lehrbuch der Psychiatrie* [Buch III, Teil III, cap. 3, Beob. 68; cf. trans. by C. G. Chaddock, *Text-book of Insanity*, p. 495, case 52].

the heavenly marriage. An outstanding visionary type was the Maid of Orleans, who was unconsciously imitated by the devout dreamer Thomas Ignaz Martin at the time of Louis XVIII.[8]

714 Swedenborg, a learned and highly intelligent man, was a visionary of unexampled fertility. His importance is attested by the fact that he had a considerable influence on Kant.[9]

715 These remarks are not meant to be conclusive, they are only intended to sketch in broad outline the state of knowledge at that time and its mystical tendency. They give some idea of the psychological premises which explain the rapid spread of American spiritualism in Europe. The tableturning epidemic of the fifties has already been mentioned. It reached a climax in the sixties and seventies. In Paris, spiritualistic séances were held at the court of Napoleon III. Famous and sometimes infamous mediums appeared —Cumberland, the Davenport brothers, Home, Slade, Miss Cook. This was the real heyday of spiritualism, for these mediums produced marvellous phenomena, quite extraordinary things which went so far beyond the bounds of credibility that a thinking person who was not himself an eyewitness could only treat them with scepticism. The impossible happened: human bodies, and parts of bodies, materialized out of thin air, bodies that had an intelligence of their own and declared themselves to be the spirits of the dead. They complied with the doubting requests of the worldlings and even submitted to experimental conditions; on vanishing from this world, they left behind pieces of their white gauzy robes, prints of their hands and feet, handwriting on the inner side of two slates sealed together, and, finally, even let themselves be photographed.

716 But the full impact of these tidings, impressive as they were, was not felt until the famous English physicist, William Crookes, in his *Quarterly Journal of Science,* presented to the world a report on the observations he had made during the past eight years, which had convinced him of the reality of the phenomena in question. Since the report is concerned with observations at which none of us was present, under conditions which it is no longer possible to check, we have no alternative but to let the observer himself inform us how these observations were mirrored in his brain. The tone

[8] Cf. Kerner, *Die Geschichte des Thomas Ignaz Martin, Landsmanns zu Gallardon, über Frankreich und dessen Zukunft im Jahre 1816 geschaut* (Heilbronn, 1835).

[9] Cf. Gilbert Ballet, *Swedenborg: Histoire d'un visionnaire au XVIII siècle* (Paris, 1899).

of the report at least allows us to surmise the state of his feelings at the time of writing. I shall therefore cite verbatim a passage from his investigations during the years 1870–73:[10]

CLASS VI

The Levitation of Human Beings

717   This has occurred in my presence on four occasions in darkness. The test conditions under which they took place were quite satisfactory, so far as the judgment was concerned; but ocular demonstration of such a fact is so necessary to disturb our preformed opinions as to "the naturally possible and impossible," that I will here only mention cases in which the deductions of reason were confirmed by the sense of sight.

718   On one occasion I witnessed a chair, with a lady sitting on it, rise several inches from the ground. On another occasion, to avoid the suspicion of this being in some way performed by herself, the lady knelt on the chair in such manner that its four feet were visible to us. It then rose about three inches, remained suspended for about ten seconds, and then slowly descended. At another time two children, on separate occasions, rose from the floor with their chairs, in full daylight, under (to me) most satisfactory conditions; for I was kneeling and keeping close watch upon the feet of the chair, and observing that no one might touch them.

719   The most striking cases of levitation which I have witnessed have been with Mr. Home. On three separate occasions have I seen him raised completely from the floor of the room. Once sitting in an easy chair, once kneeling on his chair, and once standing up. On each occasion I had full opportunity of watching the occurrence as it was taking place.

720   There are at least a hundred recorded instances of Mr. Home's rising from the ground, in the presence of as many separate persons, and I have heard from the lips of the three witnesses to the most striking occurrence of this kind—the Earl of Dunraven, Lord Lindsay, and Captain C. Wynne—their own most minute accounts of what took place. To reject the recorded evidence on this subject is to reject all human testimony whatever; for no fact in sacred or profane history is supported by a stronger array of proofs.

721   The accumulated testimony establishing Mr. Home's levitations is overwhelming. It is greatly to be desired that some person, whose evidence would be accepted as conclusive by the scientific world—if indeed there lives a person whose testimony *in favour* of such phenomena

10 ["Notes of an Enquiry into the Phenomena called Spiritual, during the years 1870–73," *Quarterly Journal of Science* (London), XI (n.s., IV) (1874), 85–86.]

would be taken—would seriously and patiently examine these alleged facts. Most of the eye-witnesses to these levitations are now living, and would, doubtless, be willing to give their evidence. But, in a few years, such *direct* evidence will be difficult, if not impossible, to be obtained.

722   It is obvious from the tone of this passage that Crookes was completely convinced of the reality of his observations. I refrain from further quotations because they would not tell us anything new. It is sufficient to remark that Crookes saw pretty well everything that occurred with these great mediums. It is hardly necessary to stress that if this unprecedented happening is an actual fact, the world and science have been enriched by an experience of the most tremendous importance. For a variety of reasons, it is not possible to criticize Crookes's powers of apprehension and retention during those years from the psychiatric point of view. We only know that at that time Crookes was not manifestly insane. Crookes and his observations must remain for the present an unsolved psychological enigma. The same is true of a number of other observers whose intelligence and honesty one does not wish to disparage without good reason. Of numerous other observers, noted for their prejudices, lack of criticism, and exuberant imagination, I shall say nothing: they are ruled out from the start.

723   One does not have to be particularly beset by doubts as to whether our knowledge of the world in the twentieth century has really attained the highest possible peak to feel humanly touched by this forthright testimony of an eminent scholar. But, in spite of our sympathy, we may leave out of account the question of the physical reality of such phenomena, and instead turn our attention to the psychological question: how does a thinking person, who has shown his sober-mindedness and gift for scientific observation to good advantage in other fields, come to assert that something inconceivable is a reality?

724   This psychological interest of mine has prompted me to keep track of persons who are gifted as mediums. My profession as a psychiatrist gave me ample opportunities for this, particularly in a city like Zurich. So many remarkable elements converging in so small a space can perhaps be found nowhere else in Europe. In the last few years I have investigated eight mediums, six of them women and two of them men. The total impression made by these investigations can be summed up by saying that one must approach a medium with a minimum of expectations if one does not want to be disappointed. The results are of purely psychological interest,

and no physical or physiological novelties came to light. Everything that may be considered a scientifically established fact belongs to the domain of the mental and cerebral processes and is fully explicable in terms of the laws already known to science.

725   All phenomena which the spiritualists claim as evidence of the activity of spirits are connected with the presence of certain persons, the mediums themselves. I was never able to observe happenings alleged to be "spiritual" in places or on occasions when no medium was present. Mediums are as a rule slightly abnormal mentally. Frau Rothe, for example, although she could not be declared *non compos mentis* by forensic psychiatrists, nevertheless exhibited a number of hysterical symptoms. Seven of my mediums showed slight symptoms of hysteria (which, incidentally, are extraordinarily common in other walks of life too). One medium was an American swindler whose abnormality consisted chiefly in his impudence. The other seven acted in good faith. Only one of them, a woman of middle age, was born with her gifts; she had suffered since earliest childhood from alterations of consciousness (frequent and slightly hysterical twilight states). She made a virtue of necessity, induced the change of consciousness herself by auto-suggestion, and in this state of auto-hypnosis was able to prophesy. The other mediums discovered their gift only through social contacts and then cultivated it at spiritualistic séances, which is not particularly difficult. One can, with a few skillful suggestions, teach a remarkably high percentage of people, especially women, the simple spiritualistic manipulations, table-turning for instance, and, less commonly, automatic writing.

726   The ordinary phenomena met with in mediums are table-turning, automatic writing, and speaking in a trance.

727   Table-turning consists in one or more persons laying their hands on a table that can move easily. After a time (a couple of minutes to an hour) the table begins to move, making turning or rocking movements. This phenomenon can be observed in the case of all objects that are touched. The automatically swinging pendulum and the divining rod are based on the same principle. It was, then, a very childish hypothesis to assume, as in earlier decades, that the objects touched moved of themselves, like living things. If a fairly heavy object is chosen, and one feels the arm muscles of the medium while the object is moving, the muscular tension is immediately apparent, and hence also the effort of the medium to move the object. The only remarkable thing is that the mediums assert

they feel nothing of this effort, but, on the contrary, have a definite feeling that the object is moving of its own accord, or else that their arm or hand is moved for them. This psychological phenomenon is strange only to people who know nothing of hypnosis. A hypnotized person can be told that, on waking, he will forget everything that happened under the hypnosis, but that at a certain sign he will, without knowing why, suddenly raise his right arm. Sure enough, on waking, he has forgotten everything; at the sign he raises his right arm, without knowing why—his arm "simply rose up in the air of its own accord."

728   Spontaneous phenomena can occasionally be observed in hysterics, for instance the paralysis or peculiar automatic movements of an arm. Either the patients cannot give the reasons for these sudden symptoms, or they give the wrong reasons; for instance, the symptom came from their having caught cold, or from overstrain. One has only to hypnotize the patient in order to discover the real reason and the significance of the symptom. For instance, a young girl wakes up in the morning to find that her right arm is paralysed. She rushes in terror to the doctor and tells him she doesn't know how it happened, she must obviously have overstrained herself doing the housework the day before. That is the only reason she can think of. Under hypnosis it turns out that the day before she had a violent quarrel with her parents, and that her father grabbed her by the right arm and pushed her out of the door. The paralysis of the arm is now clear; it is connected with the unconscious memory of yesterday's scene, which was not present in her waking consciousness. (The existence of "unconscious ideas" is discussed in my paper "The Reaction-time Ratio in the Association Experiment."[11])

729   It is evident from these facts that our bodies can easily execute automatic movements whose cause and origin are not known to us. And if science had not drawn our attention to it, we would not know, either, that our arms and hands are constantly making slight movements, called "intended tremors," which accompany our thoughts. If, for instance, one vividly imagines a simple geometrical figure, a triangle, say, the tremors of the outstretched hand will also describe a triangle, as can be demonstrated very easily by means of a suitable apparatus. Hence, if we sit down at the table with a lively expectation of automatic movements, the intended tremors will reflect this expectation and gradually cause the table to move.

[11] [C.W., vol. 2.]

But once we have felt the apparently automatic movement, we are immediately convinced that "the thing works." The conviction (suggestion) clouds our judgment and observation, so that we do not notice how the tremors, very slight at first, gradually build up into muscular contractions which then naturally produce stronger and stronger and still more convincing effects.

730   Now if an ordinary table, whose simple construction we know, can execute movements apparently of its own accord and behave as if it were alive, then human fantasy is quite ready to believe that the cause of the movement is some mystic fluid or even the spirits of the air. And if, as usually happens, the table composes sentences with an intelligible content out of the letters of the alphabet, then it seems proved beyond a doubt that an "alien intelligence" is at work. We know, however, that the initial, automatic tremors are in large measure dependent on our ideas. If they are capable of moving the table, they can equally well guide its movements in such a way that they construct words and sentences out of the alphabet. Nor is it necessary to visualize the sentence beforehand. The unconscious part of the psyche which controls the automatic movements very soon causes an intellectual content to flow into them.[12] As might be expected, the intellectual content is as a rule on a very low level and only in exceptional cases exceeds the intelligence of the medium. A good example of the poverty of "table-talking" is given in Allan Kardec's *Buch der Medien*.

731   "Automatic writing" follows the same principles as table-turning. The content of the writing is in no way superior to that of "table-talking." The same considerations apply to talking in a trance or ecstasy. Instead of the muscles of the arm and hand, it is the muscles of the speech apparatus that start functioning independently. The content of trance communications is naturally on the same level as the products of the other automatisms.

732   These phenomena are statistically the ones most commonly observed in mediums. Clairvoyance is much rarer. Only two of my mediums had the reputation of being clairvoyant. One of them is a well-known professional, who has already made a fool of herself in various cities in Switzerland. In order to assess her mental state as fairly as possible, I had nearly thirty sittings with her over a period of six months. The results of the investigation, so far as clairvoyance is concerned, can be put very briefly: nothing that

---

[12] For a detailed account of these phenomena, see my "On the Psychology and Pathology of So-Called Occult Phenomena" (C.W., vol. 1, pars. 79ff.).

quite unquestionably exceeded the normal psychological capacities was observed. On the other hand, she did in some instances display a remarkably fine gift for unconscious combination. She could combine "petites perceptions" and guesses and evaluate them in a very skilful way, mostly in a state of slight clouding of consciousness. There is nothing supernatural about this state; on the contrary, it is a well-known subject of psychological research.

733   How delicate is the capacity for unconscious apprehension could be demonstrated experimentally with my second medium. The experiments were conducted as follows. The medium sat opposite me at a small table that stood on a thick soft carpet (to assist greater mobility). Both of us laid our hands on the table. While the medium's mind was occupied by her engaging in conversation with a third person, I thought intensively of a number between 0 and 10— for instance, 3. The arrangement was that the table had to indicate the number thought of by the same number of tilts. The fact that the number was indicated correctly each time when I kept my hands on the table throughout the experiment is not remarkable. What is remarkable is that in 77 per cent of the cases the correct number was also given when I removed my hands immediately after the first tilt. If my hands did not touch the table at all, there were no correct scores. The results of numerous experiments showed that by means of intended tremors it is possible to communicate a number between 0 and 10 to another person, in such a way that though this person could not recognize the number, he could nevertheless reproduce it by automatic movements. I was able to establish to my satisfaction that the conscious mind of the medium never had any inkling of the number I had communicated. Numbers above 10 were reproduced very uncertainly, sometimes only one of the numerals being given. If I thought of the numbers in Roman instead of Arabic numerals, the results were considerably worse. The aforesaid 77 per cent correct scores applies only to experiments with Arabic numerals. From this one can conclude that my unconscious movements must have communicated a pictorial image of the numbers. The more complicated and less customary images of Roman numerals fared worse, as was also the case with numbers above 10.

734   I cannot report these experiments without recalling a curious and instructive observation I made one day when all the psychological experiments with the medium went wrong. Even the experiments with numbers failed to come off, until I finally hit on the

following expedient: In an experiment conducted along much the same lines, I told the medium that the number I was thinking of (3) was between 2 and 5. I then got the table to answer me a dozen times. The numbers it reproduced with iron consistency were 2, 4, and 5, but never 3; thus indicating, negatively but quite clearly, that the table, or rather the unconscious of the medium, was well aware of the number I was thinking of and avoided it out of mere caprice. The capriciousness of the unconscious is something the spiritualists could tell us a good deal about, only in their language it would be said that the good spirits had been supplanted by mischievous mocking spirits who had ruined the experiment.

735 The sensitive apprehension of the unconscious, shown by its capacity to translate another person's tremors into numbers, is a striking but by no means unprecedented fact. There are numerous corroborative examples in the scientific literature. But if the unconscious, as my experiments prove, is capable of registering and reproducing something without the conscious mind knowing anything about it, then the greatest caution is necessary in evaluating clairvoyant performances. Before we jump to the conclusion that thought flies through time and space detached from the brain, we should seek to discover by meticulous psychological investigation the hidden sources of the apparently supernatural knowledge.

736 On the other hand, any unprejudiced investigator will readily admit that we do not stand today on the pinnacle of all wisdom, and that nature still has infinite possibilities up her sleeve which may be revealed in happier days to come. I shall therefore confine myself to pointing out that the cases I observed of supposed clairvoyance might easily be explained in another and more intelligible way than by the assumption of mystic powers of cognition. The apparently inexplicable cases of clairvoyance I know only by hearsay, or have read of in books.

737 The same is true of that other great class of spiritualistic manifestations, the *physical* phenomena. Those I saw were reputed to be such, but in fact were not. Generally speaking, among the countless believers in miracles of our days very few will be found who have ever seen anything manifestly supernatural. And among these few there will be still fewer who do not suffer from an overheated imagination and do not replace critical observation by faith. Nevertheless, we are left with a residue of witnesses who ought not to be cavilled at. Among these I would include Crookes.

738   All human beings are bad observers of things that are unfamiliar to them. Crookes, too, is a human being. There is no universal gift for observation that could claim a high degree of certainty without special training. Human observation achieves something only when trained in a definite field. Take a sensitive observer away from his microscope and turn his attention to wind and weather, and he is more helpless than any hunter or peasant. If we plump a good physicist down in the deceptive, magical darkness of a spiritualistic séance, with hysterical mediums plying their trade with all the incredible refinement many of them have at their command, his observation will be no more acute than a layman's. Everything will then depend on the strength of his prejudice for or against. In this respect the psychic disposition of a man like Crookes would be worth investigating. If as a result of environmental influence and education, or his innate temperament, he is not disinclined to believe in miracles, he will be convinced by the apparition. But if he is disinclined from the start to believe in miracles, he will remain unconvinced in spite of the apparition, just as did many other people who witnessed similar things with the same medium.

739   Human observation and reporting are subject to disturbance by countless sources of error, many of which are still quite unknown. For instance, a whole school of experimental psychology is now studying the "psychology of evidence," that is, the problem of observation and reporting. Professor William Stern,[13] the founder of this school, has published experiments which show man's powers of observation in a bad light. And yet Stern's experiments were conducted on educated people! It seems to me that we must go on working patiently for a few more years in the direction of the Stern school before we tackle the difficult question of the reality of spiritualistic phenomena.

740   So far as the miraculous reports in the literature are concerned, we should, for all our criticism, never lose sight of the limitations of our knowledge, otherwise something embarrassingly human might happen, making us feel as foolish as the academicians felt over Chladni's meteors,[14] or the highly respected Bavarian Board

[13] [(1871–1938), professor of applied psychology, Breslau U.; at Duke U., in the U.S.A., 1934–38. See *The Freud/Jung Letters*, index, s.v., and "The Psychological Diagnosis of Evidence" (C.W., vol. 2), par. 728.]

[14] [Correctly, meteorites, which even into the 19th cent. astronomers believed of terrestrial origin. The German physicist E.F.F. Chladni (1756–1827) advocated the theory of extra-terrestrial origin.]

of Physicians over the railway.[15] Nevertheless I believe that the present state of affairs gives us reason enough to wait quietly until more impressive physical phenomena put in an appearance. If, after making allowance for conscious and unconscious falsification, self-deception, prejudice, etc., we should still find something positive behind them, then the exact sciences will surely conquer this field by experiment and verification, as has happened in every other realm of human experience. That many spiritualists brag about their "science" and "scientific knowledge" is, of course, irritating nonsense. These people are lacking not only in criticism but in the most elementary knowledge of psychology. At bottom they do not want to be taught any better, but merely to go on believing—surely the naïvest of presumptions in view of our human failings.

[15] [When the first German railway was opened, in 1835, from Nuremberg to Fürth, the Board of Physicians held that the speed of the trains would cause dizziness in travellers and onlookers and would sour the milk of cows grazing near the tracks.]

FOREWORD TO JUNG: "PHÉNOMÈNES OCCULTES"[1]

741   The essays collected together in this little volume were written over a period of thirty years, the first in 1902 and the last in 1932. The reason why I am bringing them out together is that all three are concerned with certain borderline problems of the human psyche, the question of the soul's existence after death. The first essay gives an account of a young somnambulistic girl who claimed to be in communication with the spirits of the departed. The second essay deals with the problem of dissociation and "part-souls" (or splinter-personalities). The third discusses the psychology of the belief in immortality and the possibility of the continued existence of the soul after death.

742   The point of view I have adopted is that of modern empirical psychology and the scientific method. Although these essays deal with subjects which usually fall within the province of philosophy or theology, it would be a mistake to suppose that psychology is concerned with the *metaphysical* nature of the problem of immortality. Psychology cannot establish any metaphysical "truths," nor does it try to. It is concerned solely with the *phenomenology of the psyche*. The idea of immortality is a psychic phenomenon that is disseminated over the whole earth. Every "idea" is, from the psychological point of view, a phenomenon, just as is "philosophy" or "theology." For modern psychology, ideas are *entities*, like animals and plants. The scientific method consists in the description of nature. All mythological ideas are *essentially real,* and far older than any philosophy. Like our knowledge of physical nature, they were originally perceptions and experiences. In so far as such ideas are universal, they are symptoms or characteristics or normal exponents of psychic life, which are *naturally* present and need no proof of their "truth." The only question we can profitably discuss is whether they are universal or not. If they are universal, they belong

<hr>

[1] [Paris, 1939. The book is a trans., by E. Godet and Y. Le Lay, of "On the Psychology and Pathology of So-Called Occult Phenomena" (C.W., vol. 1), "The Soul and Death," and "The Psychological Foundations of Belief in Spirits" (both in C.W., vol. 8). The present trans. of the foreword is from the original German MS.]

to the natural constituents and normal structure of the psyche. And if by any chance they are not encountered in the conscious mind of a given individual, then they are present in the unconscious and the case is an abnormal one. The fewer of these universal ideas are found in consciousness, the more of them there will be in the unconscious, and the greater will be their influence on the conscious mind. This state of things already bears some resemblance to a neurotic disturbance.

743   It is normal to think about immortality, and abnormal not to do so or not to bother about it. If everybody eats salt, then that is the normal thing to do, and it is abnormal not to. But this tells us nothing about the "rightness" of eating salt or of the idea of immortality. That is a question which strictly speaking has nothing to do with psychology. Immortality cannot be proved any more than can the existence of God, either philosophically or empirically. We know that salt is indispensable for our physiological health. We do not eat salt for this reason, however, but because food with salt in it tastes better. We can easily imagine that long before there was any philosophy human beings had instinctively found out what ideas were necessary for the normal functioning of the psyche. Only a rather stupid mind will try to go beyond that, and to venture an opinion on whether immortality does or does not exist. This question cannot be asked for the simple reason that it cannot be discussed. More important, it misses the essential point, which is the functional value of the idea as such.

744   If a person does not "believe" in salt, it is up to the doctor to tell him that salt is necessary for physiological health. Equally, it seems to me that the doctor of the soul should not go along with the fashionable stupidities but should remind his patient what the normal structural elements of the psyche are. For reasons of psychic hygiene, it would be better not to forget these original and universal ideas; and wherever they have disappeared, from neglect or intellectual bigotry, we should reconstruct them as quickly as we can regardless of "philosophical" proofs for or against (which are impossible anyway). In general, the heart seems to have a more reliable memory for what benefits the psyche than does the head, which has a rather unhealthy tendency to lead an "abstract" existence, and easily forgets that its consciousness is snuffed out the moment the heart fails in its duty.

745   Ideas are not just counters used by the calculating mind; they are also golden vessels full of living feeling. "Freedom" is not a

mere abstraction, it is also an emotion. Reason becomes unreason when separated from the heart, and a psychic life void of universal ideas sickens from undernourishment. The Buddha said: "These four are the foodstuffs, ye bhikkus, which sustain the creatures that are born, and benefit the creatures that seek rebirth. The first is edible food, coarse or fine; touch is the second; the thinking capacity of the mind is the third; and the fourth is consciousness."[2]

[2] *Samyutta-Nikaya,* 12. 11.

1938

PSYCHOLOGY AND SPIRITUALISM[1]

746   The reader should not casually lay this book aside on discovering that it is about "Invisibles," that is to say about spirits, on the assumption that it belongs to the literature of spiritualism. One can very well read the book without resorting to any such hypothesis or theory, and take it simply as a report of psychological facts or a continuous series of communications from the unconscious— which is, indeed, what it is really about. Even spirits appear to be psychic phenomena whose origins lie in the unconscious. At all events, the "Invisibles" who are the source of information in this book are shadowy personifications of unconscious contents, conforming to the rule that activated portions of the unconscious assume the character of *personalities* when they are perceived by the conscious mind. For this reason, the voices heard by the insane seem to belong to definite personalities who can often be identified, and personal intentions are attributed to them. And in fact, if the observer is able—though this is not always easy—to collect together a fair number of these verbal hallucinations, he will discover in them something very like motives and intentions of a personal character.

747   The same is true to an even greater degree of the "controls" in mediumistic séances who make the "communications." Everything in our psyche has to begin with a personal character, and one must push one's investigations very far before one comes across elements that are no longer personal. The "I" or "we" of these communications has a merely grammatical significance and is never proof of the existence of a spirit, but only of the physical presence

[1] [First published as the foreword to Stewart Edward White, *Uneingeschränktes Weltall* (Zurich, 1948), the German trans. of *The Unobstructed Universe* (New York, 1940), in which a foreword by Jung had not appeared. It was subsequently published as "Psychologie und Spiritismus," *Neue Schweizer Rundschau*, n.s., XVI:7 (Nov., 1948), 430–35. White (1873–1946), American author, chiefly wrote adventure stories with a frontier background; he became involved with spiritualism later in life. Jung was introduced to his books in 1946 by Fritz Künkel, American psychotherapist; see his letter to Künkel, 10 July 1946, discussing *The Unobstructed Universe* at length, in *C. G. Jung: Letters*, ed. G. Adler, vol. 1.]

of the medium or mediums. In dealing with "proofs of identity," such as are offered in this book, one must remember that proofs of this kind would seem to be theoretically impossible considering the enormous number of possible sources of error. We know for a certainty that the unconscious is capable of subliminal perceptions and is a treasure house of lost memories. In addition, it has been proved by experiment that time and space are *relative* for the unconscious, so that unconscious perception, not being impeded by the space-time barrier, can obtain experiences to which the conscious mind has no access. In this connection I would refer to the experiments conducted at Duke University and other places.[2]

748   Considering all this, the proof of identity seems to be a forlorn hope, in theory anyway. In practice, however, things are rather different because cases actually occur which are so overwhelmingly impressive that they are absolutely convincing to those concerned. Even though our critical arguments may cast doubt on every single case, there is not a single argument that could prove that spirits do not exist. In this regard, therefore, we must rest content with a "non liquet." Those who are convinced of the reality of spirits should know that this is a subjective opinion which can be attacked on any number of grounds. Those who are not convinced should beware of naïvely assuming that the whole question of spirits and ghosts has been settled and that all manifestations of this kind are meaningless swindles. This is not so at all. These phenomena exist in their own right, regardless of the way they are interpreted, and it is beyond all doubt that they are genuine manifestations of the unconscious. The communications of "spirits" are *statements about the unconscious psyche,* provided that they are really spontaneous and are not cooked up by the conscious mind. They have this in common with dreams; for dreams, too, are statements about the unconscious, which is why the psychotherapist uses them as a first-class source of information.

749   *The Unobstructed Universe* may therefore be regarded as offering valuable information about the unconscious and its ways. It differs very favourably from the usual run of spiritualistic communications in that it eschews all edifying verbiage and concentrates instead on certain general ideas. This pleasing difference may be attributable to the happy circumstance that the real begetter of the book is the medium Betty, the deceased wife of the author.

[2] J. B. Rhine, *New Frontiers of the Mind* (1937); *The Reach of the Mind* (1948). Also G.N.M. Tyrrell, *The Personality of Man* (1947).

It is her "spirit" that pervades the book. We are familiar with her personality from Mr. White's earlier books,[3] and we know how great an educative influence she had on all those around her, constellating in their unconscious all the things that come to light in these communications.

750   The educative intention behind Betty's activity does not differ essentially from the general tenor of spiritualistic literature. The "spirits" strive to develop man's consciousness and to unite it with the unconscious, and Betty, on her own admission, pursues the same aim. It is interesting to note that the beginnings of American spiritualism coincided with the growth of scientific materialism in the middle of the nineteenth century. Spiritualism in all its forms therefore has a *compensatory* significance. Nor should it be forgotten that a number of highly competent scientists, doctors, and philosophers have vouched for the truth of certain phenomena which demonstrate the very peculiar effect the psyche has upon matter. Among them were Friedrich Zöllner, William Crookes, Alfred Richet, Camille Flammarion, Giovanni Schiaparelli, Sir Oliver Lodge, and our Zurich psychiatrist Eugen Bleuler, not to mention a large number of less well-known names. Although I have not distinguished myself by any original researches in this field, I do not hesitate to declare that I have observed a sufficient number of such phenomena to be completely convinced of their reality. To me they are inexplicable, and I am therefore unable to decide in favour of any of the usual interpretations.

751   Although I do not wish to prejudice the reader of this book, I cannot refrain from drawing attention to some of the issues it raises. What, above all, seems to me worth mentioning—especially in view of the fact that the author has no knowledge of modern psychology—is that the "Invisibles" favour an energic conception of the psyche which has much in common with recent psychological findings. The analogy is to be found in the idea of "frequency." But here we come upon a difference that should not be overlooked. For whereas the psychologist supposes that consciousness has a higher energy than the unconscious, the "Invisibles" attribute to the spirit of the departed (i.e., to a personified unconscious content) a higher "frequency" than to the living psyche. One should not, however, attach too much importance to the fact that the concept

---

[3] [*The Betty Book* (1937); *Across the Unknown* (1939); *The Road I Know* (1942).]

of energy is made use of in both cases, since this is a fundamental category of thought in all the modern sciences.

752   The "Invisibles" further assert that our world of consciousness and the "Beyond" together form a single cosmos, with the result that the dead are not in a different place from the living. There is only a difference in their "frequencies," which might be likened to the revolutions of a propeller: at low speeds the blades are visible, but at high speeds they disappear. In psychological terms this would mean that the conscious and the unconscious psyche are one, but are separated by different amounts of energy. Science can agree with this statement, although it cannot accept the claim that the unconscious possesses a higher energy since this is not borne out by experience.

753   According to the "Invisibles," the "Beyond" is this same cosmos but without the limitations imposed on mortal man by space and time. Hence it is called "the unobstructed universe." Our world is contained in this higher order and owes its existence principally to the fact that the corporeal man has a low "frequency," thanks to which the limiting factors of space and time become operative. The world without limitations is called "Orthos," which means the "right" or "true" world. This tells us clearly enough what kind of significance is imputed to the "Beyond," though it must be emphasized that this does not imply a devaluation of our world. I am reminded of the philosophical riddle which my Arab dragoman asked me when visiting the tombs of the Khalifs in Cairo. "Which man is the cleverer: the one who builds his house where he will be for the longest time, or the one who builds it where he will be only temporarily?" Betty is in no doubt that this limited life should be lived as fully as possible, because the attainment of maximum consciousness while still in this world is an essential condition for the coming life in "Orthos." She is thus in agreement not only with the general trend of spiritualistic philosophy, but also with Plato, who regarded philosophy as a preparation for death.

754   Modern psychology can affirm that for many people this problem arises in the second half of life, when the unconscious often makes itself felt in a very insistent way. The unconscious is the land of dreams, and according to the primitive view the land of dreams is also the land of the dead and of the ancestors. From all we know about it, the unconscious does in fact seem to be relatively independent of space and time, nor is there anything objectionable in the idea that consciousness is surrounded by the sea

of the unconscious, just as this world is contained in "Orthos." The unconscious is of unknown extent and is possibly of greater importance than consciousness. At any rate, the role which consciousness plays in the life of primitives and primates is insignificant compared with that of the unconscious. The events in our modern world, as we see humanity blindly staggering from one catastrophe to the next, are not calculated to strengthen anyone's belief in the value of consciousness and the freedom of the will. Consciousness *should* of course be of supreme importance, for it is the only guarantee of freedom and alone makes it possible for us to avoid disaster. But this, it seems, must remain for the present a pious hope.

755   Betty's aim is to extend consciousness as far as possible by uniting it with "Orthos." To this end it must be trained to listen to the unconscious psyche in order to bring about the collaboration of the "Invisibles." The aims of modern psychotherapy are similar: it too endeavours to compensate the onesidedness and narrowness of the conscious mind by deepening its knowledge of the unconscious.

756   The similarity of aim should not, however, lead us to overlook a profound difference of viewpoint. The psychology of the "Betty Books" differs in no essential respect from the primitive view of the world, where the contents of the unconscious are all projected into external objects. What appears to the primitive to be a "spirit" may on a more conscious level be an abstract thought, just as the gods of antiquity turned into philosophical ideas at the beginning of our era. This primitive projection of psychological factors is common to both spiritualism and theosophy. The advantage of projection is obvious: the projected content is visibly "there" in the object and calls for no further reflection. But since the projection does bring the unconscious a bit nearer to consciousness, it is at least better than nothing. Mr. White's book certainly makes us think, but the kind of thinking it caters to is not psychological; it is mechanistic, and this is of little help when we are faced with the task of integrating projections. Mechanistic thinking is one of the many Americanisms that stamp the book as a typical product and leave one in no doubt as to its origin. But it is well worth while getting to know this side of the American psyche, for the world will hear a great deal more of it in times to come.

July 1948

316

FOREWORD TO MOSER:
"SPUK: IRRGLAUBE ODER WAHRGLAUBE?"[1]

757   The author has asked me for a few introductory words to her book. It gives me all the more pleasure to comply with her request as her previous book on occultism,[2] written with great care and knowledge of the subject, is still fresh in my memory. I welcome the appearance of this new book, a copiously documented collection of parapsychological experiences, as a valuable contribution to psychological literature in general. Extraordinary and mysterious stories are not necessarily always lies and fantasies. Many "ingenious, curious, and edifying tales" were known to previous centuries, among them observations whose scientific validity has since been confirmed. The modern psychological description of man as a totality had its precursors in the numerous biographical accounts of unusual people such as somnambulists and the like at the beginning of the nineteenth century. Indeed, though we owe the discovery of the unconscious to these old pre-scientific observations, our investigation of parapsychological phenomena is still in its infancy. We do not yet know the full range of the territory under discussion. Hence a collection of observations and of reliable material performs a very valuable service. The collector must certainly have courage and an unshakable purpose if he is not to be intimidated by the difficulties, handicaps, and possibilities of error that beset such an undertaking, and the reader, too, must summon up sufficient interest and patience to allow this sometimes disconcerting material to work upon him objectively, regardless of his prejudices. In this vast and shadowy region, where everything seems possible and nothing believable, one must oneself have observed many strange happenings and in addition heard, read, and if possible tested many stories by examining their witnesses in order to form an even moderately sure judgment.

758   In spite of such advances as the founding of the British and American Society for Psychical Research and the existence of a

[1] [Baden, 1950. By Fanny Moser. ("Ghost: False Belief or True?")]
[2] [*Okkultismus: Täuschungen und Tatsachen* (1935).]

considerable and in part well-documented literature, a prejudice is still rampant even in the best informed circles, and reports of this kind meet with a mistrust which is only partially justified. It looks as though Kant will be proved right for a long time to come when he wrote nearly two hundred years ago: "Stories of this kind will have at any time only secret believers, while publicly they are rejected by the prevalent fashion of disbelief."[3] He himself reserved judgment in the following words: "The same ignorance makes me so bold as to absolutely deny the truth of the various ghost stories, and yet with the common, although queer, reservation that while I doubt any one of them, still I have a certain faith in the whole of them taken together."[4] One could wish that very many of our bigots would take note of this wise position adopted by a great thinker.

759   I am afraid this will not come about so easily, for our rationalistic prejudice is grounded—*lucus a non lucendo*—not on reason but on something far deeper and more archaic, namely on a primitive instinct to which Goethe referred when he said in *Faust:* "Summon not the well-known throng . . ." I once had a valuable opportunity to observe this instinct at work. It was while I was with a tribe on Mount Elgon, in East Africa, most of whom had never come into contact with the white man. Once, during a palaver, I incautiously uttered the word *seleteni,* which means "ghosts." Suddenly a deathly silence fell on the assembly. The men glanced away, looked in all directions, and some of them made off. My Somali headman and the chief confabulated together, and then the headman whispered in my ear: "What did you say that for? Now you'll have to break up the palaver." This taught me that one must never mention ghosts on any account. The same primitive fear of ghosts is still deep in our bones, but it is unconscious. Rationalism and superstition are complementary. It is a psychological rule that the brighter the light, the blacker the shadow; in other words, the more rationalistic we are in our conscious minds, the more alive becomes the spectral world of the unconscious. And it is indeed obvious that rationality is in large measure an apotropaic defence against superstition, which is everpresent and unavoidable. The daemonic world of primitives is only a few generations away from us, and the things that have happened and still go on happening in the dictator states teach us how terrifyingly close it is. I must constantly

[3] [*Dreams of a Spirit-Seer,* trans. by Goerwitz, p. 92.]
[4] [Ibid., p. 88.]

remind myself that the last witch was burned in Europe in the year my grandfather was born.

760   The widespread prejudice against the factual reports discussed in this book shows all the symptoms of the primitive fear of ghosts. Even educated people who should know better often advance the most nonsensical arguments, tie themselves in knots and deny the evidence of their own eyes. They will put their names to reports of séances and then—as has actually happened more than once—withdraw their signatures afterwards, because what they have witnessed and corroborated is nevertheless impossible—as though anyone knew exactly what is impossible and what is not!

761   Ghost stories and spiritualistic phenomena practically never prove what they seem to. They offer no proof of the immortality of the soul, which for obvious reasons is incapable of proof. But they are of interest to the psychologist from several points of view. They provide information about things the layman knows nothing of, such as the exteriorization of unconscious processes, about their content, and about the possible sources of parapsychological phenomena. They are of particular importance in investigating the localization of the unconscious and the phenomenon of synchronicity, which points to a relativation of space and time and hence also of matter. It is true that with the help of the statistical method existence of such effects can be proved, as Rhine and other investigators have done. But the individual nature of the more complex phenomena of this kind forbids the use of the statistical method, since this stands in a complementary relation to synchronicity and necessarily destroys the latter phenomenon, which the statistician is bound to discount as due to chance. We are thus entirely dependent on well observed and well authenticated individual cases. The psychologist can only bid a hearty welcome to any new crop of objective reports.

762   The author has put together an impressive collection of factual material in this book. It differs from other collections of the kind by its careful and detailed documentation, and thus gives the reader a total impression of the situation which he often looks for in vain in other reports of this nature. Although ghosts exhibit certain universal features they nevertheless appear in individual forms and under conditions which are infinitely varied and of especial importance for the investigator. The present collection provides the most valuable information in just this respect.

763   The question discussed here is a weighty one for the future.

Science has only just begun to take a serious interest in the human psyche and, more particularly, in the unconscious. The wide realm of psychic phenomena also includes parapsychology, which is opening undreamt-of vistas before our eyes. It is high time humanity took cognizance of the nature of the psyche, for it is becoming more and more evident that the greatest danger which threatens man comes from his own psyche and hence from that part of the empirical world we know the least about. Psychology needs a tremendous widening of its horizon. The present book is a milestone on the long road to knowledge of the psychic nature of man.

April 1950

Jung's Contribution[5]

764   In the summer of 1920 I went to London, at the invitation of Dr. X, to give some lectures. My colleague told me that, in expectation of my visit, he had found a suitable weekend place for the summer. This, he said, had not been so easy, because every thing had already been let for the summer holidays, or else was so exorbitantly expensive or unattractive that he had almost given up hope. But finally, by a lucky change, he had found a charming cottage that was just right for us, and at a ridiculously low price. In actual fact it turned out to be a most attractive old farmhouse in Buckinghamshire, as we saw when we went there at the end of our first week of work, on a Friday evening. Dr. X had engaged a girl from the neighbouring village to cook for us, and a friend of hers would come in the afternoons as a voluntary help. The house was roomy, two-storeyed, and built in the shape of a right angle. One of these wings was quite sufficient for us. On the ground floor there was a conservatory leading into the garden; then a kitchen, dining-room, and drawing-room. On the top floor a corridor ran from the conservatory steps through the middle of the house to a large bedroom, which took up the whole front of the wing. This was my room. It had windows facing east and west, and a fireplace in the front wall (north). To the left of the door stood a bed, opposite the fireplace a big old-fashioned chest of drawers, and to the right a wardrobe and a table. This, together with a few chairs, was all the furniture. On either side of the corridor

[5] [Pp. 253ff.]

was a row of bedrooms, which were used by Dr. X and occasional guests.

765   The first night, tired from the strenuous work of the week, I slept well. We spent the next day walking and talking. That evening, feeling rather tired, I went to bed at 11 o'clock, but did not get beyond the point of drowsing. I only fell into a kind of torpor, which was unpleasant because I felt I was unable to move. Also it seemed to me that the air had become stuffy, and that there was an indefinable, nasty smell in the room. I thought I had forgotten to open the windows. Finally, in spite of my torpor, I was driven to light a candle: both windows were open, and a night wind blew softly through the room, filling it with the flowery scents of high summer. There was no trace of the bad smell. I remained half awake in my peculiar condition, until I glimpsed the first pale light of dawn through the east window. At this moment the torpor dropped away from me like magic, and I fell into a deep sleep from which I awoke only towards nine o'clock.

766   On Sunday evening I mentioned in passing to Dr. X that I had slept remarkably badly the night before. He recommended me to drink a bottle of beer, which I did. But when I went to bed the same thing happened: I could not get beyond the point of drowsing. Both windows were open. The air was fresh to begin with, but after about half an hour it seemed to turn bad; it became stale and fuggy, and finally somehow repulsive. It was hard to identify the smell, despite my efforts to establish its nature. The only thing that came into my head was that there was something sickly about it. I pursued this clue through all the memories of smells that a man can collect in eight years of work at a psychiatric clinic. Suddenly I hit on the memory of an old woman who was suffering from an open carcinoma. This was quite unmistakably the same sickly smell I had so often noticed in her room.

767   As a psychologist, I wondered what might be the cause of this peculiar olfactory hallucination. But I was unable to discover any convincing connection between it and my present state of consciousness. I only felt very uncomfortable because my torpor seemed to paralyze me. In the end I could not think any more, and fell into a torpid doze. Suddenly I heard the noise of water dripping. "Didn't I turn off the tap properly?" I thought. "But of course, there's no running water in the room—so it's obviously raining—yet today was so fine." Meanwhile the dripping went on regularly, one drop every two seconds. I imagined a little pool of water to the

left of my bed, near the chest of drawers. "Then the roof must leak," I thought. Finally, with a heroic effort, so it seemed to me, I lit the candle and went over to the chest of drawers. There was no water on the floor, and no damp spot on the plaster ceiling. Only then did I look out of the window: it was a clear, starry night. The dripping still continued. I could make out a place on the floor, about eighteen inches from the chest of drawers, where the sound came from. I could have touched it with my hand. All at once the dripping stopped and did not come back. Towards three o'clock, at the first light of dawn, I fell into a deep sleep. No—I have heard death-watch beetles. The ticking noise they make is sharper. This was a duller sound, exactly what would be made by drops of water falling from the ceiling.

768   I was annoyed with myself, and not exactly refreshed by this weekend. But I said nothing to Dr. X. The next weekend, after a busy and eventful week, I did not think at all about my previous experience. Yet hardly had I been in bed for half an hour than everything was there as before: the torpor, the repulsive smell, the dripping. And this time there was something else: something brushed along the walls, the furniture creaked now here and now there, there were rustlings in the corners. A strange restlessness was in the air. I thought it was the wind, lit the candle and went to shut the windows. But the night was still, there was no breath of wind. So long as the light was on, the air was fresh and no noise could be heard. But the moment I blew out the candle, the torpor slowly returned, the air became fuggy, and the creakings and rustlings began again. I thought I must have noises in my ear, but at three o'clock in the morning they stopped as promptly as before.

769   The next evening I tried my luck again with a bottle of beer. I had always slept well in London and could not imagine what could give me insomnia in this quiet and peaceful spot. During the night the same phenomena were repeated, but in intensified form. The thought now occurred to me that they must be parapsychological. I knew that problems of which people are unconscious can give rise to exteriorization phenomena, because constellated unconscious contents often have a tendency to manifest themselves outwardly somehow or other. But I knew the problems of the present occupants of the house very well, and could discover nothing that would account for the exteriorizations. The next day I asked the others how they had slept. They all said they had slept wonderfully.

770   The third night it was even worse. There were loud knocking noises, and I had the impression that an animal, about the size of a dog, was rushing round the room in a panic. As usual, the hubbub stopped abruptly with the first streak of light in the east.

771   The phenomena grew still more intense during the following weekend. The rustling became a fearful racket, like the roaring of a storm. Sounds of knocking came also from outside in the form of dull blows, as though somebody were banging on the brick walls with a muffled hammer. Several times I had to assure myself that there was no storm, and that nobody was banging on the walls from outside.

772   The next weekend, the fourth, I cautiously suggested to my host that the house might be haunted, and that this would explain the surprisingly low rent. Naturally he laughed at me, although he was as much at a loss as I about my insomnia. It had also struck me how quickly the two girls cleared away after dinner every evening, and always left the house long before sundown. By eight o'clock there was no girl to be seen. I jokingly remarked to the girl who did the cooking that she must be afraid of us if she had herself fetched every evening by her friend and was then in such a hurry to get home. She laughed and said that she wasn't at all afraid of the gentlemen, but that nothing would induce her to stay a moment in this house alone, and certainly not after sunset. "What's the matter with it?" I asked. "Why, it's haunted, didn't you know? That's the reason why it was going so cheap. Nobody's ever stuck it here." It had been like that as long as she could remember. But I could get nothing out of her about the origin of the rumour. Her friend emphatically confirmed everything she had said.

773   As I was a guest, I naturally couldn't make further inquiries in the village. My host was sceptical, but he was willing to give the house a thorough looking over. We found nothing remarkable until we came to the attic. There, between the two wings of the house, we discovered a dividing wall, and in it a comparatively new door, about half an inch thick, with a heavy lock and two huge bolts, that shut off our wing from the unoccupied part. The girls did not know of the existence of this door. It presented something of a puzzle because the two wings communicated with one another both on the ground floor and on the first floor. There were no rooms in the attic to be shut off, and no signs of use. The purpose of the door seemed inexplicable.

774   The fifth weekend was so unbearable that I asked my host to

give me another room. This is what had happened: it was a beautiful moonlight night, with no wind; in the room there were rustlings, creakings, and bangings; from outside, blows rained on the walls. I had the feeling there was something near me, and opened my eyes. There, beside me on the pillow, I saw the head of an old woman, and the right eye, wide open, glared at me. The left half of the face was missing below the eye. The sight of it was so sudden and unexpected that I leapt out of bed with one bound, lit the candle, and spent the rest of the night in an armchair. The next day I moved into the adjoining room, where I slept splendidly and was no longer disturbed during this or the following weekend.

775   I told my host that I was convinced the house was haunted, but he dismissed this explanation with smiling scepticism. His attitude, understandable though it was, annoyed me somewhat, for I had to admit that my health had suffered under these experiences. I felt unnaturally fatigued, as I had never felt before. I therefore challenged Dr. X to try sleeping in the haunted room himself. He agreed to this, and gave me his word that he would send me an honest report of his observations. He would go to the house alone and spend the weekend there so as to give me a "fair chance."

776   Next morning I left. Ten days later I had a letter from Dr. X. He had spent the weekend alone in the cottage. In the evening it was very quiet, and he thought it was not absolutely necessary to go up to the first floor. The ghost, after all, could manifest itself anywhere in the house, if there was one. So he set up his camp bed in the conservatory, and as the cottage really was rather lonely, he took a loaded shotgun to bed with him. Everything was deathly still. He did not feel altogether at ease, but nevertheless almost succeeded in falling asleep after a time. Suddenly it seemed to him that he heard footsteps in the corridor. He immediately struck a light and flung open the door, but there was nothing to be seen. He went back grumpily to bed, thinking I had been a fool. But it was not long before he again heard footsteps, and to his discomfiture he discovered that the door lacked a key. He rammed a chair against the door, with its back under the lock, and returned to bed. Soon afterwards he again heard footsteps, which stopped just in front of the door; the chair creaked, as though somebody was pushing against the door from the other side. He then set up his bed in the garden, and there he slept very well. The next night he again put his bed in the garden, but at one o'clock it started to rain, so he shoved the head of the bed under the eaves of the conservatory

and covered the foot with a waterproof blanket. In this way he slept peacefully. But nothing in the world would induce him to sleep again in the conservatory. He had now given up the cottage.

777   A little later I heard from Dr. X that the owner had had the cottage pulled down, since it was unsaleable and scared away all tenants. Unfortunately I no longer have the original report, but its contents are stamped indelibly on my mind. It gave me considerable satisfaction after my colleague had laughed so loudly at my fear of ghosts.

*

778   I would like to make the following remarks by way of summing up. I can find no explanation of the dripping noise. I was fully awake and examined the floor carefully. I consider it out of the question that it was a delusion of the senses. As to the rustling and creaking, I think they were probably not objective noises, but noises in the ear which seemed to me to be occurring objectively in the room. In my peculiar hypnoid state they appeared exaggeratedly loud. I am not at all sure that the knocking noises, either, were objective. They could just as well have been heartbeats that seemed to me to come from outside. My torpor was associated with an inner excitation probably corresponding to fear. Of this fear I was unconscious until the moment of the vision—only then did it break through into consciousness. The vision had the character of a hypnagogic hallucination and was probably a reconstruction of the memory of the old woman with carcinoma.

779   Coming now to the olfactory hallucination, I had the impression that my presence in the room gradually activated something that was somehow connected with the walls. It seemed to me that the dog rushing round in a panic represented my intuition. Common speech links intuition with the nose: I had "smelt" something. If the olfactory organ in man were not so hopelessly degenerate, but as highly developed as a dog's, I would have undoubtedly have had a clearer idea of the persons who had lived in the room earlier. Primitive medicine-men can not only smell out a thief, they also "smell" spirits and ghosts.

780   The hypnoid catalepsy that each time was associated with these phenomena was the equivalent of intense concentration, the object of which was a subliminal and therefore "fascinating" olfactory perception. The two things together bear some resemblance to the

325

physical and psychic state of a pointer that has picked up the scent. The source of the fascination, however, seems to me to have been of a peculiar nature, which is not sufficiently explained by any substance emitting a smell. The smell may have "embodied" a psychic situation of an excitatory nature and carried it across to the percipient. This is by no means impossible when we consider the extraordinary importance of the sense of smell in animals. It is also conceivable that intuition in man has taken the place of the world of smells that were lost to him with the degeneration of the olfactory organ. The effect of intuition on man is indeed very similar to the instant fascination which smells have for animals. I myself have had a number of experiences in which "psychic smells," or olfactory hallucinations, turned out to be subliminal intuitions which I was able to verify afterwards.

781   This hypothesis naturally does not pretend to explain all ghost phenomena, but at most a certain category of them. I have heard and read a great many ghost stories, and among them are a few that could very well be explained in this way. For instance, there are all those stories of ghosts haunting rooms where a murder was committed. In one case, bloodstains were still visible under the carpet. A dog would surely have smelt the blood and perhaps recognized it as human, and if he possessed a human imagination he would also have been able to reconstruct the essential features of the crime. Our unconscious, which possesses very much more subtle powers of perception and reconstruction than our conscious minds, could do the same thing and project a visionary picture of the psychic situation that excited it. For example, a relative once told me that, when stopping at a hotel on a journey abroad, he had a fearful nightmare of a woman being murdered in his room. The next morning he discovered that on the night before his arrival a woman had in fact been murdered there. These remarks are only meant to show that parapsychology would do well to take account of the modern psychology of the unconscious.

FOREWORD TO JAFFÉ:
"APPARITIONS AND PRECOGNITION"[1]

782   The author of this book has already made a name for herself by her valuable contributions to the literature of analytical psychology. Here she tells of strange tales which incur the odium of superstition and are therefore exchanged only in secret. They were lured into the light of day by a questionnaire sent out by the *Schweizerischer Beobachter,* which can thereby claim to have rendered no small service to the public. The mass of material that came in arrived first at my address. Since my age and my evergrowing preoccupation with other matters did not allow me to burden myself with further work, the task of sorting out such a collection and submitting it to psychological evaluation could not have been placed in worthier hands than those of the author. She had displayed so much psychological tact, understanding and insight in her approach to a related theme—an interpretation of E.T.A. Hoffmann's story "The Golden Pot"[2]—that I never hesitated in my choice.

783   Curiously enough, the problem of wonder tales as they are currently told—enlightenment or no enlightenment—has never been approached from the psychological side. I naturally don't count mythology, although people are generally of the opinion that mythology is essentially history and no longer happens nowadays. As a psychic phenomenon of the present, it is considered merely a hunting-ground for economics. Nevertheless, ghost stories, warning visions, and other strange happenings are constantly being reported, and the number of people to whom something once "happened" is surprisingly large. Moreover, despite the disapproving silence of the "enlightened," it has not remained hidden from the wider public that for some time now there has been a serious science which goes by the name of "parapsychology." This fact may have helped to encourage the popular response to the questionnaire.

[1] [Aniela Jaffé, *Geistererscheinungen und Vorzeichen* (Zurich, 1958). Trans., New Hyde Park, New York, 1963, with the present trans. of the foreword, here somewhat revised.]
[2] "Bilder und Symbole aus E.T.A. Hoffmanns Märchen 'Der goldne Topf,' " in Jung, *Gestaltungen des Unbewussten* (1950).

784   One of the most notable things that came to light is the fact
that among the Swiss, who are commonly regarded as stolid, unimaginative, rationalistic and materialistic, there are just as many
ghost stories and suchlike as, say, in England or Ireland. Indeed,
as I know from my own experience and that of other investigators,
magic as practised in the Middle Ages and harking back to much
remoter times has by no means died out, but still flourishes today
as rampantly as it did centuries ago. One doesn't speak of these
things, however, They simply happen, and the intellectuals know
nothing of them—for intellectuals know neither themselves nor
people as they really are. In the world of the latter, without their
being conscious of it, the life of the centuries lives on, and things
are continually happening that have accompanied human life from
time immemorial: premonitions, foreknowledge, second sight,
hauntings, ghosts, return of the dead, bewitchings, sorcery, magic
spells, etc.

785   Naturally enough our scientific age wants to know whether such
things are "true," without taking into account what the nature
of any such proof would have to be and how it could be furnished.
For this purpose the events in question must be looked at squarely
and soberly, and it generally turns out that the most exciting stories
vanish into thin air and what is left over is "not worth talking
about." Nobody thinks of asking the fundamental question: what
is the real reason why the same old stories are experienced and
repeated over and over again, without losing any of their prestige?
On the contrary, they return with their youthful vitality constantly
renewed, fresh as on the first day.

786   The author has made it her task to take these tales for what
they are, that is, as *psychic facts,* and not to pooh-pooh them because they do not fit into our scheme of things. She has therefore
logically left aside the question of truth, as has long since been
done in mythology, and instead has tried to inquire into the psychological questions: Exactly *who* is it that sees a ghost? Under what
psychic conditions does he see it? What does a ghost signify when
examined for its content, i.e., as a symbol?

787   She understands the art of leaving the story just as it is, with
all the trimmings that are so offensive to the rationalist. In this way
the *twilight atmosphere* that is so essential to the story is preserved.
An integral component of any nocturnal, numinous experience is
the dimming of consciousness, the feeling that one is in the grip
of something greater than oneself, the impossibility of exercising

criticism, and the paralysis of the will. Under the impact of the experience reason evaporates and another power spontaneously takes control—a most singular feeling which one willy-nilly hoards up as a secret treasure no matter how much one's reason may protest. That, indeed, is the uncomprehended purpose of the experience—to make us feel the overpowering presence of a mystery.

788   The author has succeeded in preserving the total character of such experiences, despite the refractory nature of the reports, and in making it an object of investigation. Anyone who expects an answer to the question of parapsychological truth will be disappointed. The psychologist is little concerned here with what kind of facts can be established in the conventional sense; all that matters to him is whether a person will vouch for the authenticity of his experience regardless of all interpretations. The reports leave no doubt about this; moreover, in most cases their authenticity is confirmed by independent parallel stories. It cannot be doubted that such reports are found at all times and places. Hence there is no sufficient reason for doubting the veracity of individual reports. Doubt is justified only when it is a question of a deliberate lie. The number of such cases is increasingly small, for the authors of such falsifications are too ignorant to be able to lie properly.

789   The psychology of the unconscious has thrown so many beams of light into other dark corners that we would expect it to elucidate also the obscure world of wonder tales eternally young. From the copious material assembled in this book those conversant with depth psychology will surely gain new and significant insights which merit the greatest attention. I can recommend it to all those who know how to value things that break through the monotony of daily life with salutary effects, (sometimes!) shaking our certitudes and lending wings to the imagination.

August 1957

V

THE PSYCHOGENESIS OF
MENTAL DISEASE

(related to Volume 3 of the Collected Works)

THE PRESENT STATUS OF APPLIED PSYCHOLOGY[1]

In German Switzerland

790   Though psychology is not taught in either Basel or Fribourg, a psychological institute has just been opened in Bern, under the direction of Professor Dürr. In the winter semester 1907 he has given a course on general psychology and another on paedagogics based on psychology, as well as an introduction to experimental psychology.

791   As to Zurich: Professor Schumann is giving a course on Special Psychology and conducting a seminar for advanced students at the University laboratory for experimental psychology. — Privatdocent Wreschner[2] is lecturing this winter on physiology and psychology of the voice and language and conducting an introductory course (with demonstrations) on experimental psychology at the psychological laboratory. — At the psychological laboratory of the University's psychiatric clinic, established 1906, I am holding a seminar for advanced students. The programme includes normal and pathological psychology.

792   As to associations concerned with psychology, there is nothing in Bern or Basel. (Fribourg need not be mentioned at all.)

793   In Zurich the following have existed for some years:

1. An association for legal psychiatry, whose chairman I have been since early 1907.[3]

2. There also has existed for many years a psychological-neurological society where an occasional psychological lecture may be heard. The chairman is Professor von Monakow.[4]

---

[1] [(Translated by W. S.) "Der gegenwärtige Stand der angewandten Psychologie in den einzelnen Kulturländern," under "Nachrichten" in *Zeitschrift für angewandte Psychologie und psychologische Sammelforschung* (Leipzig), I (1907–8), 466ff. There were contributions from France, French Switzerland, and the United States, as well as Jung's (pp. 469–70).]

[2] [Arthur Wreschner, German experimental psychologist and physician, practising in Zurich. See *The Freud/Jung Letters*, 124J, n. 9.]

[3] [See *The Freud/Jung Letters*, 198J, n. 2a.]

[4] [Constantin von Monakow, Swiss neurologist. See *The Freud/Jung Letters*, index, s.v. Monakow.]

3. In addition, in the autumn of 1907 a Society for Freudian Researches was founded (with ca. 20 members). The chairman is Professor Bleuler.[5]

C. G. Jung (Burghölzli-Zurich)

[5] [See *The Freud/Jung Letters*, 46J, 47J.]

ON DEMENTIA PRAECOX[1]

794　　The depotentiation of the association process or *abaissement du niveau mental,* which consequently has a downright dreamlike quality, seems to indicate that a pathogenic agent [*Noxe*] contributes to dementia praecox which is absent in, say, hysteria. The characteristics of the *abaissement* were assigned to the pathogenic agent, which was construed as organically conditioned and likened to a symptom of poisoning (e.g., paranoid states in chronic poisoning).

[1] [Jung's abstract contributed to Otto Rank's report of the First International Psychoanalytic Congress (Salzburg, 27 Apr. 1908), in *Zentralblatt für Psychoanalyse* (Wiesbaden), I:3 (Dec. 1910), 128. The original paper is lost. Cf. *The Freud/Jung Letters,* 85J, n. 4.]

REVIEW OF SADGER: "KONRAD FERDINAND MEYER. EINE PATHOGRAPHISCH-PSYCHOLOGISCHE STUDIE"[1]

795   The new art of writing biographies from the psychological point of view has already produced a number of moderately successful studies. One has only to think of Möbius[2] on Goethe, Schopenhauer, Schumann, and Nietzsche, and Lange on Hölderlin.[3] Among these "pathographies," Sadger's book occupies an exceptional position. It does not stand out because of a meticulous unearthing of the diagnosis, nor does it try to squeeze the poet's pathology into a particular clinical frame of reference, as Möbius did in an objectionable manner in the case of Goethe. Sadger's aim is rather to understand the development of the whole personality as a psychological process, and to grasp it from within. It is no matter for regret that the psychiatric pigeon-holing of the "case" receives scant attention. Our understanding is in no way advanced when we know for certain the medical designation of the subject's state of mind. The recognition that Schumann suffered from dementia praecox and K. F. Meyer from periodic melancholia contributes nothing whatever to an understanding of their psyches. People are only too ready to stop at the diagnosis, thinking that any further understanding can be dispensed with. But this is just where the real task of the pathographer begins, if he wants, as he should, to understand more than the ordinary biographer. The biographer would rather not penetrate too deeply into certain areas, and because he does not understand what is going on there and can discover nothing understandable, he calls those areas mad or "pathological." Möbius sticks psychiatric labels on them and reports something of their geography. The proper task of the pathographer,

---

[1] [*Basler Nachrichten,* Nov. 1909. Isidor Sadger, *Konrad Ferdinand Meyer: Eine pathographisch-psychologische Studie* (Grenzfragen des Nerven- und Seelenlebens, 59; Wiesbaden, 1908). For the Viennese psychoanalyst Sadger, see *The Freud/Jung Letters,* 75J, n. 1. In his study he discussed the influence of the mother and sister on the sexual life of the Zurich poet Meyer (1825–98).]

[2] [Paul Julius Möbius (1854–1907), Leipzig neurologist, published on the psychopathology of these and other writers.]

[3] [Wilhelm Lange (1875–1950), *Hölderlin: eine Pathographie* (1909).]

however, is to describe in intelligible language what is actually happening in these locked regions of the psyche, and what powerful influences pass to and fro between the world of the understandable and the world of the not-understood. Up to now psychography has failed miserably, believing that its task is complete once insanity has been established; and there is some justification for this since not a few of the most prominent modern psychiatrists are firmly convinced that insanity is beyond further understanding. The validity of this statement is purely subjective, however: anything we do not understand we are likely to call insane. In view of this limitation, we should not venture so far, let alone assert that what we do not understand is not understandable at all. It *is* understandable, only we are intellectually still so dense and lethargic that our ears cannot hear and our minds cannot grasp the mysteries of which the insane speak. Here and there we do understand something, and occasionally we glimpse inner connections which link up what appears to be wildly fortuitous and utterly incoherent into regular causal chains. We owe this insight to the genius of Sigmund Freud and his psychology, which is now undergoing all the punishments of hell that the scientific Philistines hold in reserve for every new discovery.[4]

796   Anyone who wishes to read Sadger's book with real understanding should first familiarize himself with Freud's psychology, otherwise he will get a curious impression of the special prominence the author gives to the significance of the mother in the life of the poet. Lacking the requisite knowledge the reader will also find it difficult to understand many of the parenthetical remarks concerning the father-son and mother-son relationship and to appreciate their general validity. It will be evident from these hints that Sadger's book can claim a special place among the pathographies because, unlike the others, it digs down far deeper to the very roots of the pathological and annexes wide areas of that dark world of the non-understood to the world of intelligible things. Anyone who has been able to profit by Freud's writings will read with great

[4] A well-known sage writes: "If you have a fresh view or an original idea, if you present men and things from an unexpected point of view, you will surprise the reader. And the reader does not like being surprised. He never looks in a history for anything but the stupidities that he knows already. If you try to instruct him you only humiliate him and make him angry. Do not try to enlighten him; he will only cry out that you insult his beliefs." [Anatole France, preface to *Penguin Island* (1908; trans. by A. W. Evans, 1909), preface, p. vii.]

interest how the sensitive soul of the poet gradually freed itself from the crushing weight of mother-love and its attendant emotional conflicts, and how as a result the hidden source of poetic creativity began to flow. We owe the author a debt of gratitude for this glimpse into the life of an artist whose development presents so many baffling problems. Readers who bring no preliminary knowledge with them may be prompted by this book to acquire some.

REVIEW OF WALDSTEIN: "DAS UNBEWUSSTE ICH"[1]

797   For a variety of reasons it is welcome news that Waldstein's book *The Subconscious Self* has been rescued from oblivion and made accessible to a wider public in an excellent translation. The content of the book is equally good and, in places, very important. In his preface to the German edition, Dr. Veraguth[2] (Zurich) remarks that the book, first published more than a decade ago, is to be valued primarily as an historical document. This, unfortunately, is only too true, for nowhere does the present end sooner and the past begin earlier than in medical literature. The English edition was published at a time when another turn of the ascending spiral of scientific knowledge had just been completed in Germany. The scientists had once again reached the point that had been reached eighty years earlier. Those were the days of that remarkable man Franz Anton Mesmer,[3] perhaps the first in the German-speaking world to observe that, armed with the necessary self-assurance, practically anyone could imitate the miraculous cures wrought at places of pilgrimage, by priests, French kings, and thaumaturges in sheep's clothing (witness Ast the Shepherd, who relieved his milieu of several million marks). This art was named "Mesmerism." It was not a swindle, and much good was accomplished by it. Mesmer offered his art to science, and even founded a school, but he took too little account of the fact that ever since science has existed there has also existed an undying élite enthroned at the top, that knows everything far better than anybody else, and from time to time guards mankind against various pernicious aberrations. It protected us from the erroneous belief that Jupiter had moons, that

---

[1] [*Basler Nachrichten*, 9 Dec. 1909. Louis Waldstein, *Das unbewusste Ich und sein Verhältnis zur Gesundheit und Erziehung* (Wiesbaden, 1908); trans. from the English (*The Subconscious Self and Its Relation to Education and Health*, New York, 1897) by Gertrud Veraguth. Waldstein (1853–1915) was an American neurologist.]

[2] [Otto Veraguth (1870–1944), Zurich neurologist, husband of the translator. For Jung's comments on him and on the book ("abysmally insignificant"), see *The Freud/Jung Letters*, 115J, par. 2.]

[3] [(1734–1815), Austrian physician, experimenter with animal magnetism.]

339

such things as meteors could fall from the air, that puerperal fever was caused by dirty hands, and that the brain possessed a fibrous structure. For eighty years the élite protected psychology from the discovery of hypnotism by pooh-poohing Mesmer's "animal magnetism." Nevertheless a few German crackpots and obscurantists of the Romantic Age kept Mesmer's teachings alive, quietly collecting observations and experiences that were ridiculed by their contemporaries and successors because they smacked of superstition. Notwithstanding the persistent mocking laughter, the numerous books from the pen of Justinus Kerner, Eschenmayer, Ennemoser, Horst, etc.,[4] to name but a few who reported "curious tales of somnambulists," contain, along with obvious nonsense, glaring truths which were put to sleep for the next sixty years. The French country doctor Liébeault,[5] who made a timid attempt in the sixties to publish a little book on this subject, was stuck with his whole edition unsold at the publisher's for twenty years. Thirty years later there existed a literature of hundreds of books and a number of technical periodicals. The spiral had once again entered this domain. All of a sudden it was discovered that an enormous amount could be done, both in theory and practice, with the earlier "Mesmerism"; that apparently dangerous symptoms of nervous ailments, such as paresis, contractures, paraesthesias, etc., could be produced at will by suggestion and then blown away again—in short, that the whole army of the neuroses, accounting for at least eighty per cent of the neurologist's clientele, were disturbances of a psychic nature. (A realization that is so modern today that its rediscoverers are hailed as incalculably great benefactors of mankind.)

798   In its unfathomable wisdom the élite instantly recognized that mankind was in dire peril, and declared (1) that suggestion therapy was fraudulent and ineffective; (2) that it was exceedingly dangerous; (3) that the insights gained by hypnotic methods were sheer fabrication, imagination, and suggestion; and (4) that the neuroses were organic diseases of the brain. It had, however, also been rediscovered that our consciousness obviously does not cover the full range of the psyche, that the psychic factor exists and is effective in regions beyond the reach of consciousness. This psychic factor

[4] [For Kerner (1786–1862), German poet and student of occultism, see "On the Psychology and Pathology of So-Called Occult Phenomena" (C. W., vol. 1), par. 140. Joseph Ennemoser (1787–1854), Karl August Eschenmayer (1768–1852), and Georg Conrad Horst (1767–1838) wrote on magic, mesmerism, etc.]
[5] [Auguste Ambroise Liébeault (1823–1904), French physician and hypnotist.].

beyond consciousness was named the subconscious or the second ego or the unconscious personality, etc. In Germany the heretics were Dessoir, Forel, Moll, Vogt, and Schrenck-Notzing,[6] among others, and in France, Binet, Janet, and their schools. Waldstein's book on the "subconscious" ego came out just when the movement in Germany had reached its climax. All honest researchers greeted this resurgence with enthusiasm, but the élite rightly regarded it as deleterious to the development of logical thought. The leading authorities therefore asserted that the subconscious was (1) non-existent; (2) not psychic but physiological, and hence impenetrable; (3) only feebly conscious, so feeble, in fact, that one is no longer conscious of being conscious of it. Since then the investigators cf the "unconscious" have been branded as unscientific; the "unconscious" has no existence at all and is merely a feeble flicker of consciousness. Or else it is physiological, which is the opposite of psychological, and therefore not the concern of the psychologist or of anybody else. In this way it is barricaded against investigation.

799   But this time, in spite of everything, the seed did not die. Work went ahead steadily, and today we are much further advanced than we were a decade ago. Even so, this advance holds only for the few who have not allowed themselves to become embittered, and who are working indefatigably to open up the abysses of the human psyche to consciousness. For these few, Waldstein's book is, to be sure, no novelty and will add little to their knowledge, but for all others it contains much that is new and much that is good. It has shrewd things to say about aesthetics and the origin of works of art. Still better is its psychological conception of the neuroses, a conception which one hopes will be widely disseminated, seeing that the élite still clings firmly to the notion that hysteria and nervous disorders originate in alterations within the brain. Unfortunately many run-of-the-mill doctors still swear by this gospel to the detriment of their neurotic patients, whom our age produces in swarms. Nearly all these patients have been convinced by the medical dogma that their sickness is of a physical nature. Again and again the doctors back up this nonsense, and the treatment goes muddling on with its medicaments and magic nostrums. It is hardly surprising that nowadays Christian Science has better results to show than many neurologists. This little book performs a valuable service by

[6] [Max Dessoir (author of *Das Doppel-Ich,* 1890), August Forel (infra, par. 921, n. 20), Albert Moll (infra, par. 893), Oskar Vogt, Albert von Schrenck-Notzing: all psychiatrists.]

at least throwing a ray of light on those dark regions of the psyche from which all human achievements ultimately spring, whether they be artistic creations or nervous disorders. It is to be hoped that books of this kind will find favour with the educated public, so as gradually to prepare the ground for a deeper understanding of the human psyche, and to free the minds of the sound and sick alike from the crass materialism of the cerebro-organic dogma. The sensitive psychological note which Waldstein strikes gives his book a particularly attractive character, even though his analysis does not probe nearly as deeply as Freud's researches.

CRIME AND THE SOUL[1]

800   The dual personality of the criminal is frequently apparent at first glance. One need not follow the tortuous path of his psychological experiences, disguises, and eventual unmasking as the story of his dual existence is dramatically told in the film. Generally speaking, every criminal, in his outward show of acting honourably, wears a quite simple disguise which is easily recognizable. Of course, this does not apply to the lowest dregs of the criminal fraternity—to the men and women who have become outcasts from all ordinary human society. Generally, however, criminals, men and women alike, betray a certain ambition to be respectable, and repeatedly emphasize their respectability. The "romance" of a criminal existence is only rarely romantic. A very large number of criminals lead a thoroughly middle-class existence and commit their crimes, as it were, through their second selves. Few criminals succeed in attaining a complete severance between their liking for middle-class respectability, on the one hand, and their instinct for crime on the other.

801   It is a terrible fact that crime seems to creep up on the criminal as something foreign that gradually gains a hold on him so that eventually he has no knowledge from one moment to another of what he is about to do. Let me illustrate this with a striking example from my own experience.

802   A nine-year-old boy stabbed his little sister above the eye with a pair of scissors, which penetrated as far as the cerebral membrane. Had it gone half a millimetre deeper the child would have died instantly. Two years earlier, when the boy was seven, his mother told me that there was something wrong with him. The boy was doing some peculiar things. At school, during lessons, he would suddenly rise from his seat and cling to his teacher with every sign of extreme terror. At home he would often run away from play and hide in the loft. When asked to explain the reason he

1 [Published in the *Sunday Referee* (London), 11 Dec. 1932. A German version, "Blick in die Verbrecherseele," which may have been the original of the English, appeared in the *Wiener Journal*, 15 Jan. 1933. The present text contains some minor changes taken over from the German.]

made no reply. When I spoke to the boy he told me that he had frequent attacks of cramp. Then the following conversation took place:

803 "Why are you always afraid?"

804 The child did not reply. I realized that he was reluctant to speak, so I tried persuasion. Finally he said:

805 "I must not tell you."

806 "Why not?"

807 I pressed him further, but all I was able to get out of him was that he must not say why he was afraid. At last he blurted it out.

808 "I am afraid of the man," he said.

809 "What man?"

810 No reply. Then, after much wheedling, I succeeded in winning his confidence. He told me that at the age of seven a little man appeared to him. The little man had a beard. The boy also gave other details of the little man's appearance. This little man had winked at him, and that had frightened him. That was why he clung to his teacher at school and ran away from play at home to hide in the loft.

811 "What did this little man want of you?" I asked.

812 "He wanted to put the blame on me."

813 "What do you mean by 'blame'?"

814 The boy could not answer. He merely repeated the word "blame." He said that each time the little man came nearer and nearer to him, and last time he had come quite close, and that was why he, the boy, stabbed his sister. The appearance of the little man was none other than the personification of the criminal instinct, and what the boy described as "blame" was a symbol of the second self that was driving him to destruction.

815 After the crime the boy had epileptic fits. Since then he has committed no further crimes. In this case as in many others, epilepsy represented an evasion of the crime, a repression of the criminal instinct. Unconsciously people try to escape the inner urge to crime by taking refuge in illness.

816 In other cases it happens that people who are apparently normal transmit the evil instincts concealed under this appearance of normality to other people, and frequently lead them, quite unconsciously, to carry out the deeds which they themselves would never commit although they would like to.

817 Here is an example: Some time ago there was a murder in

the Rhineland which created a great sensation. A man of up-to-then blameless character killed his entire family, and even his dog. No one knew the reason; no one had ever noticed anything abnormal about the man. This man told me that he had bought a knife without having any particular object in mind. One night he fell asleep in the living-room, where there was a clock with a pendulum. He heard the ticking of the clock, and this tick-tock was like the sound of a battalion of marching soldiers. The sound of marching gradually died away, as though the battalion had passed. When it ceased completely he suddenly felt, "Now I must do it." Then he committed the murders. He stabbed his wife eleven times.

818   According to my subsequent investigations it was the woman who was chiefly to blame for what happened. She belonged to a religious sect, whose members regarded all who do not pray with them as outsiders, children of the devil, and themselves as saints. This woman transmitted the evil that was in her, unconsciously perhaps, but quite certainly, to her husband. She persuaded him that he was evil, whereas she herself was good, and instilled the criminal instinct into his subconscious mind. It was characteristic that the husband recited a saying from the Bible at each stab, which best indicates the origin of his hostility.

819   Far more crime, cruelty, and horror occur in the human soul than in the external world. The soul of the criminal, as manifested in his deeds, often affords an insight into the deepest psychological processes of humanity in general. Sometimes it is quite remarkable what a background such murders have, and how people are driven to perpetrate acts which at any other time and of their own accord they would never commit.

820   Once a baker went for his Sunday walk. The next thing he knew was that on waking up he found himself in a police cell, with his hands and feet manacled. He was amazed. He thought he was dreaming. He had no idea why he was locked up. But in the meantime the man had murdered three people and seriously injured two. Undoubtedly he committed these crimes in a cataleptic state. The baker's Sunday walk turned out quite differently from what he had intended on leaving home. The wife of this baker was a member of the same sect as the other woman, and therefore a "saint," so that the motive of this crime is analogous to that described above.

821   The more evil a person is, the more he tries to force upon others the wickedness he does not want to show to the outside world.

The baker and the Rhinelander were respectable men. Before they committed their crimes they would have been amazed had anyone thought them capable of such things. They certainly never intended to commit murder. This idea was unconsciously instilled into them as a means of abreacting the evil instincts of their wives. Man is a very complicated being, and though he knows a great deal about all sorts of things, he knows very little about himself.

THE QUESTION OF MEDICAL INTERVENTION[1]

The medical journal *Psyche* published answers[2] to a questionnaire sent to twenty-eight doctors concerning a report by Dr. Medard Boss, delivered at the 66th Congress of South-west German Psychiatrists and Neurologists in Badenweiler, in which he presented the case of a transvestite "under its existential-analytical aspect." The treatment ended with the total castration of the patient by Dr. Boss, including amputation of the penis with implantation of artificial labiae. The report provoked critical comments from some of his colleagues[3] followed by a rejoinder from Dr. Boss.[4] In view of the significance of the case for the doctor-patient relationship, the editors of *Psyche* circulated the following questionnaire to the colleagues whom Dr. Boss had named:

1. Do you consider an intervention like that performed by Dr. Boss permissible from the general medical standpoint or not?

2. Do you consider such an intervention permissible from the standpoint of the psychotherapist?

822   I had first of all to plough my way through the report of this case. The totally superfluous existentialist jargon complicates the situation unnecessarily and does not make for enjoyable reading. The patient was obviously bent upon getting himself transformed into a woman as far as possible and equally set against any other kind of influence. It is quite clear that nothing could be done about it psychotherapeutically. That settles Question 2. An operation like this has nothing to do with psychotherapy, because anyone, the patient included, could have advised himself to ask a surgeon to castrate him. If Dr. Boss gave him this advice, that is his own private affair, and something that one does not make a song and dance about in public.

823   Question 1 is not so easy to answer. On the principle *nulla poena sine lege* an intervention of this kind is "justified" if the law either permits it or does not forbid it. There is no law against cosmetic operations, and if I succeed in persuading a surgeon to

---

[1] [*Psyche* (Heidelberg), IV:8 (1950–51), 464–65.]
[2] [Ibid., 448ff.]
[3] [Ibid., IV:4, 229ff.]
[4] [Ibid., IV:7, 394ff.]

347

amputate a finger for me that is his and my private affair, a problem of individual ethics. If anyone who is *compos mentis* wishes to be castrated and feels happier for it afterwards than he did before, there is not much in his action that one can fairly object to. If the doctor is convinced that such an operation really does help his patient, and nobody is injured by it, his ethical disposition to help and ameliorate might very well prompt him to perform the operation without anyone being in a position to object to it on principle. Only, he should realize that he is offending the collective professional ethics of doctors in a hazardous way by his somewhat unusual and unconventional procedure. Moreover, the operation affects an organ that is the object of a collective taboo; that is to say, castration is a *numinous mutilation* which makes a powerful impression on everyone and is consequently hedged about with all sorts of emotional considerations. A doctor who risks this intervention should not be surprised if there is a collective reaction against it. He may be justified before his own conscience, but he risks his reputation by violating collective feeling. (The hangman is in much the same situation.) Insults of this nature are not in the interests of the medical profession and are therefore, quite rightly, abhorred.

824   Dr. Boss would have done better to preserve a decent silence about this painful affair instead of proclaiming it *urbi et orbi* with "existential-analytical" *éclat,* however concerned he was to justify himself in the eyes of his profession. Evidently he has only the dimmest notion of how much his action offends professional medical feeling.

825   So I can answer Question 1 by saying that, for the above reasons, I consider the intervention, from the medical standpoint, hazardous if not impermissible. From the individual standpoint I would prefer to give Dr. Boss the benefit of the doubt.

FOREWORD TO CUSTANCE:
"WISDOM, MADNESS AND FOLLY"[1]

826   When I was working in 1906 on my book *The Psychology of Dementia Praecox*[2] (as schizophrenia was then called), I never dreamt that in the succeeding half-century psychological investigation of the psychoses and their contents would make virtually no progress whatever. The dogma, or intellectual superstition, that only physical causes are valid still bars the psychiatrist's way to the psyche of his patient and impels him to take the most reckless and incalculable liberties with this most delicate of all organs rather than allow himself even to think about the possibility of genuinely psychic causes and effects, although these are perfectly obvious to an unprejudiced mind. All that is necessary is to pay attention to them, but this is just what the materialistic prejudice prevents people from doing, even when they have seen through the futility of metaphysical assumptions. The organic, despite the fact that its nature is largely unknown and purely hypothetical, seems much more convincing than psychic reality, since this still does not exist in its own right and is regarded as a miserable vapour exhaled, as it were, from the albuminous scheme of things. How in the world do people know that the only reality is the physical atom, when this cannot even be proved to exist at all except by means of the psyche? If there is anything that can be described as primary, it must surely be the psyche and not the atom, which, like everything else in our experience, is presented to us directly only as a psychic model or image.

827   I still remember vividly the great impression it made upon me when I succeeded for the first time in deciphering the apparently complete nonsense of schizophrenic neologisms, which must have been infinitely easier than deciphering hieroglyphs or cuneiform

[1] [New York, 1952. By John Custance. The foreword (not included in the British edition, 1951) was translated by an unknown hand from a German MS written in 1951 and is given here in revised form. The German original was published in Custance, *Weisheit und Wahn* (Zurich, 1954).]
[2] [C.W., vol. 3.]

inscriptions. While these give us authentic insight into the intellectual culture of ancient man—an achievement certainly not to be underestimated—deciphering of the products of insanity and of other manifestations of the unconscious unlocks the meaning of far older and more fundamental psychic processes, and opens the way to a psychic underworld or hinterland which is the matrix not only of the mental products of the past but of consciousness itself. This, however, seems quite uninteresting to the psychiatrist and to concern him least of all—just as if it were tremendously important to know exactly where the stones were quarried to build our medieval cathedrals, but of no importance whatever to know what the meaning and purpose of these edifices might be.

828   Half a century has not sufficed to give the psychiatrist, the "doctor of the soul," the smallest acquaintance with the structure and contents of the psyche. Nobody need write an apology for the meaning of the brain since it can actually be put under the microscope. The psyche, however, is nothing, because it is not sufficiently physical to be stained and mounted on a slide. People still go on despising what they don't know, and what they know least of all they claim to know best. The very attempt to bring some kind of order into the chaos of psychological experience is considered "unscientific," because the criteria of physical reality cannot be applied directly to psychic reality. Documentary evidence, though fully recognized in the study of history and in jurisprudence, still seems to be unknown in the realm of psychiatry.

829   For this reason a book like the present one should be particularly welcome to psychologists. It is a *document humain,* unfortunately one of few. I know no more than half a dozen such autochthonous descriptions of psychosis, and of these this is the only one derived from the domain of manic-depressive insanity, all the others being derived from that of schizophrenia. In my experience at any rate it is quite unique. Certainly there are, in numerous clinical histories, comparable descriptions given by the patients themselves, but they never reach the light of day in the form of a printed publication; and besides, few of them could equal the autobiography of our author in point of articulateness, general education, wide reading, deep thought, and self-criticism. The value of this book is all the greater because, uninfluenced by any outside literature, it describes the discovery, or rather the rediscovery, of certain fundamental and typical psychic structures. Although I myself have been studying the very same phenomena for years, and have repeatedly described

them, it still came to me as a surprise and a novelty to see how the delirious flight of ideas and uninhibitedness of the manic state lower the threshold of consciousness to such an extent that, as with the *abaissement du niveau mental* in schizophrenia, the unconscious is laid bare and rendered intelligible. What the author has discovered in the manic state is in exact agreement with my own discoveries. By this I mean more particularly the structure of opposites and their symbolism, the anima archetype, and lastly the unavoidable encounter with the reality of the psyche. As is generally known, these three main points play an essential role in my psychology, with which, however, the author did not become acquainted until afterwards.

830   It is of particular interest, more especially for the expert in this field, to see what kind of total picture emerges when the inhibitions exerted by the conscious mind on the unconscious are removed in mania. The result is a crude and unmitigated system of opposites, of every conceivable colour and form, extending from the heights to the depths. The symbolism is predominantly collective and archetypal in character, and thus decidedly mythological or religious. Clear indications of an individuation process are absent, since the dialectical drama unfolds in the spontaneous, inner confrontation of opposites before the eyes of a perceiving and reflecting subject. He does not stand in any dialectical relationship to a human partner; in other words, there is no dialogue. The values delineate themselves in an undifferentiated system of black and white, and the problem of the differentiated functions is not posed. Hence the absence of any clear signs of individuation; as is well known, the prerequisite for this is an intense relationship with another individual and a coming to terms with him. The question of relationship, or Eros, nowhere appears as a problem in this book. Instead, psychic reality, which the author very rightly calls "actuality," receives all the more attention, and the value of this cannot be denied.

831   As might be expected from the impressive contents of his psychosis, the author was profoundly affected by them. This runs like a leit-motiv through his book from the beginning to the end, making it a confessional monologue addressed to an anonymous circle of listeners, as well as an encounter with the equally anonymous spirit of the age. Its intellectual horizon is wide and does honour to the "logos" of its author. I do not know what sort of impression it will make on the "normal" layman, who has never had anything thrust upon him from the other side of the barrier. I can only

say that psychiatrists and practising psychologists owe the author the greatest possible thanks for the illumination his unaided efforts have given them. As a contribution to our knowledge of those highly significant psychic contents that manifest themselves in pathological conditions or underlie them, his book is as valuable as it is unique.

FOREWORD TO PERRY:
"THE SELF IN PSYCHOTIC PROCESS"[1]

832   As I studied Dr. Perry's manuscript, I could not help recalling the time when I was a young alienist searching vainly for a point of view which would enable me to understand the workings of the diseased mind. Merely clinical observations—and the subsequent post mortem when one used to stare at a brain which ought to have been out of order yet showed no sign of abnormality—were not particularly enlightening. "Mental diseases are diseases of the brain" was the *axiom,* and told one just nothing at all. Within my first months at the Clinic,[2] I realized that the thing I lacked was a *real psychopathology,* a science which showed what was happening in the mind during a psychosis. I could never be satisfied with the idea that all that the patients produced, especially the schizophrenics, was nonsense and chaotic gibberish. On the contrary, I soon convinced myself that their productions meant something which could be understood, if only one were able to find out what it was. In 1901, I started my association experiments with normal test persons in order to create a normal basis for comparison. I found then that the experiments were almost regularly disturbed by psychic factors beyond the control of consciousness. I called them *complexes.* No sooner had I established this fact than I applied my discovery to cases of hysteria and schizophrenia. In both I found an inordinate amount of disturbance, which meant that the unconscious in these conditions is not only opposed to consciousness but also has an extraordinary energic charge. While with neurotics the complexes consist of split-off contents, which are systematically arranged, and for this reason are easily understandable, with schizophrenics the unconscious proves to be not only unmanageable and autonomous, but highly unsystematic, disordered, and even chaotic. Moreover, it has a peculiar dreamlike

---

[1] [Berkeley and Los Angeles: University of California Press; London: Cambridge University Press, 1953. By John Weir Perry. The foreword appears to have been written in English.]
[2] The Burghölzli, Zurich.]

353

quality, with associations and bizarre ideas such as are found in dreams. In my attempts to understand the contents of schizophrenic psychoses, I was considerably helped by Freud's book on dream interpretation, which had just appeared (1900). By 1905, I had acquired so much reliable knowledge about the psychology of schizophrenia (then called "dementia praecox") that I was able to write two papers[3] about it. *The Psychology of Dementia Praecox* (1906) had practically no influence at all, since nobody was interested in pathological psychology except Freud, with whom I had the honour of collaborating for the next seven years.

833   Dr. Perry, in this book, gives an excellent picture of the psychic contents with which I found myself confronted. At the beginning, I felt completely at a loss in understanding the association of ideas which I could observe daily with my patients. I did not know then that all the time I had the key to the mystery in my pocket, inasmuch as I could not help seeing the often striking parallelism between the patients' delusions and mythological motifs. But for a long time I did not dare to assume any relationship between mythological formations and individual morbid delusions. Moreover, my knowledge of folklore, mythology, and primitive psychology was regrettably deficient, so that I was slow in discovering how common these parallels were. Our clinical approach to the human mind was only medical, which was about as helpful as the approach of the mineralogist to Chartres Cathedral. Our training as alienists was much concerned with the anatomy of the brain but not at all with the human psyche. One could not expect very much more in those days, when even neuroses, with their overflow of psychological material, were a psychological *terra incognita*. The main art the students of psychiatry had to learn in those days was how not to listen to their patients.

834   Well, I had begun to listen, and so had Freud. He was impressed with certain facts of neurotic psychology, which he even named after a famous mythological model, but I was overwhelmed with "historical" material while studying the psychotic mind. From 1906 until 1912 I acquired as much knowledge of mythology, primitive psychology, and comparative religion as possible. This study gave me the key to an understanding of the deeper layers of the psyche and I was thus enabled to write my book[4] with the English

[3] [The second paper is probably "The Content of the Psychoses" (C.W., vol. 3). Cf. below, par. 982.]

[4] [*Wandlungen und Symbole der Libido* (1911–12).]

title *Psychology of the Unconscious*. This title is slightly misleading, for the book represents the analysis of a prodromal schizophrenic condition. It appeared forty years ago, and last year I published a fourth, revised edition under the title *Symbols of Transformation*. One could not say that it had any noticeable influence on psychiatry. The alienist's lack of psychological interest is by no means peculiar to him. He shares it with a number of other schools of thought, such as theology, philosophy, political economy, history, and medicine, which all stand in need of psychological understanding and yet allow themselves to be prejudiced against it and remain ignorant of it. It is only within the last years, for instance, that medicine has recognized "psychosomatics."

835   Psychiatry has entirely neglected the study of the psychotic mind, in spite of the fact that an investigation of this kind is important not only from a scientific and theoretical standpoint but also from that of practical therapy.

836   Therefore I welcome Dr. Perry's book as a messenger of a time when the psyche of the mental patient will receive the interest it deserves. The author gives a fair representation of an average case of schizophrenia, with its peculiar mental structure, and, at the same time, he shows the reader what he should know about general human psychology if he wishes to understand the apparently chaotic distortions and the grotesque "bizarrerie" of the diseased mind. An adequate understanding often has a remarkable therapeutic effect in milder cases which, of course, do not appear in mental hospitals, but all the more in the consultation hours of the private specialist. One should not underrate the disastrous shock which patients undergo when they find themselves assailed by the intrusion of strange contents which they are unable to integrate. The mere fact that they have such ideas isolates them from their fellow men and exposes them to an irresistible panic, which often marks the outbreak of the manifest psychosis. If, on the other hand, they meet with adequate understanding from their physician, they do not fall into a panic, because they are still understood by a human being and thus preserved from the disastrous shock of complete isolation.

837   The strange contents which invade consciousness are rarely met with in neurotic cases, least not directly, which is the reason why so many psychotherapists are unfamiliar with the deeper strata of the human psyche. The alienist, on the other hand, rarely has the time or the necessary scientific equipment to deal with, or even to bother with, his patients' psychology. In this respect, the author's

355

book fills a yawning gap. The reader should not be misled by the current prejudice that I produce nothing but theories. My so-called theories are not figments but facts that can be verified, if one only takes the trouble, as the author has done with so much success, to listen to the patient, to give him the credit—that is humanly so important—of meaning something by what he says, and to encourage him to express himself as much as he possibly can. As the author has shown, drawing, painting and other methods are sometimes of inestimable value, inasmuch as they complement and amplify verbal expression. It is of paramount importance that the investigator should be sufficiently acquainted with the history and phenomenology of the mind. Without such knowledge, he could not understand the symbolic language of the unconscious and so would be unable to help his patient assimilate the irrational ideas that bewilder and confuse his consciousness. It is not a "peculiar historical interest," a sort of hobby of mine to collect historical curiosities, as has been suggested, but an earnest endeavour to help the understanding of the diseased mind. *The psyche, like the body, is an extremely historical structure.*

838   I hope that Dr. Perry's book will arouse the psychiatrist's interest in the psychological aspect of his cases. Psychology belongs as much to his training as anatomy and physiology to that of the surgeon.

FOREWORD TO SCHMALTZ:
"KOMPLEXE PSYCHOLOGIE UND KÖRPERLICHES SYMPTOM"[1]

839   Having read his book with lively interest and undivided agreement, I am all the more ready to comply with the author's request that I say a few words by way of introduction. He has successfully undertaken to treat a case from the field of psychosomatic medicine psychologically, in collaboration with an internal specialist, and to describe the whole course of the treatment up to the cure in all its details. The clinical description of the case is impeccable and thorough, and it seems to me that its psychological elucidation and interpretation is equally satisfactory. Nowhere does the author betray any theoretical bias; all his conclusions are amply documented with noteworthy care and circumspection. The clinical history concerns one of those frequent cases of cardiac disorder, a disease that is associated with the lesion of feeling so characteristic of our tme. The author deserves particular credit for fearlessly pointing out the deeper reasons for a neurosis and for setting it in a broader context. A neurosis is an expression of the "affections" of the whole man, and it is impossible to treat the whole man solely within the framework of a medical specialism. Psychogenic causes have to do with the psyche, and this, by its very nature, not only extends beyond the medical horizon but also, as the matrix of all psychic events, transcends the bounds of scientific understanding. Certainly the aetiological details have to be worked out within the limits of a specialist method, but the psychology and therapy of the neurosis demand an Archimedean point outside, without which they merely turn in a circle. Indeed, medicine itself is a science that has been able to make such great progress only because it borrowed lavishly from the other sciences. It necessarily had to draw physics, chemistry, and biology into its orbit, and if this was true of somatic medicine, then the psychology of the neuroses will not be able to get along without borrowing from the humanities.

---

[1] [Stuttgart, 1955. By Gustav Schmaltz. ("Complex Psychology and Somatic Symptom.")]

840   Of decisive importance for the aetiology and therapy of the neuroses is the individual's own attitude. If this is subjected to careful analysis, one finds that it rests on personal and collective premises which can be pathogenic as well as curative in their effects. Just as modern medicine is no longer content to establish that a patient has infected himself with typhoid fever, but must also worry about the water supply responsible for the infection, so the psychology of the neuroses cannot possibly be content with an aetiology that makes do with traumata and infantile fantasies. We have known for a long time that children's neuroses depend on the psychic situation of the parents. We also know to our cost how much these "psychic situations" are due not merely to personal defects but to collective psychic conditions. That would be reason enough for the specialist to take heed of these general conditions— one cannot combat an epidemic of typhoid even with the most careful diagnosis and treatment of individual cases. The older medicine had to be satisfied with handing out any philtre provided only that it helped. Thanks to the auxiliary sciences, modern medicine is in a position to find out the true nature of its nostrums. But what cures a neurosis? In order to find the real answer to this question, the psychology of the neuroses must go far beyond its purely medical confines. There are a few doctors who already have inklings of this. In this respect, too, the author has dared to fling open one or two windows.

VI

FREUD AND PSYCHOANALYSIS

(related to Volume 4 of the Collected Works)

SIGMUND FREUD: "ON DREAMS"[1]
25 January 1901

841   Freud begins by giving a short exposition of his work. He first distinguishes the various interpretations which the problem of dreams has undergone in the course of history:

1. The old "mythological" or, rather, mystical hypothesis that dreams are meaningful utterances of a soul freed from the fetters of sense. The soul is conceived as a transcendent entity which either produces dreams independently, as [Gotthilf Heinrich von] Schubert still supposed, or else represents the medium of communication between the conscious mind and divine revelation.

2. The more recent hypothesis of [K. A.] Scherner and [J.] Volkelt, according to which dreams owe their existence to the operation of psychic forces that are held in check during the day.

3. The critical modern view that dreams can be traced back to peripheral stimuli which partially affect the cerebral cortex and thereby induce dream-activity.

4. The common opinion that dreams have a deeper meaning, and may even foretell the future. Freud, with reservations, inclines to this view. He does not deny the dream a deeper meaning and admits the rightness of the common method of dream interpretation, in so far as it takes the dream-image as a symbol for a hidden content that has a meaning.

842   In his opening observations Freud compares dreams with obsessional ideas, which, like them, are strange and inexplicable to the conscious mind.

---

[1] [Trans. from a typescript discovered in Jung's posthumous papers; apparently a report given to his colleagues on the staff of the Burghölzli Mental Hospital, where Jung had taken up his first professional post, as assistant physician, on 10 Dec. 1900. (Cf. *Memories, Dreams, Reflections,* end of Ch. III, "Student Years.") The subject was Freud's *Über den Traum* (trans., "On Dreams," Standard Edn., V), published as part (pp. 307–344) of a serial publication, *Grenzfragen des Nerven- und Seelenlebens,* ed. L. Löwenfeld and H. Kurella (Wiesbaden, 1901); it was a summary of *Die Traumdeutung* (1900; trans., *The Interpretation of Dreams,* Standard Edn., IV–V). The present trans. was published in *Spring,* 1973.]

843   The psychotherapy of obsessional ideas offers the key to unravelling the ideas in dreams. Just as we get a patient who suffers from an obsession to take note of all the ideas that associate themselves with the dominating idea, we can make upon ourselves the experiment of observing everything that becomes associated with the ideas in the dream if, without criticism, we allow all those things to appear which we are in the habit of suppressing as worthless and disturbing. We take note, therefore, of all psychically valueless ideas, the momentary perceptions and thoughts which are not accompanied by any deeper feeling of value, and which are produced every day in unending quantities.

844   Example, p. 310:[2] On the basis of the results of this method, Freud conjectures that the dream is a kind of substitute, that is, a symbolic representation of trains of thought that have a meaning, and are often bound up with lively affects. The mechanism of this substitution is still not very clear at present, but at any rate we may accord it the status of an extremely important psychological process once we have established its beginning and end by the method just described. Freud calls the content of the dream as it appears in consciousness the *manifest content of the dream*. The material of the dream, the psychological premises, that is to say all the trains of thought that are hidden from the dreaming consciousness and can be discovered only by analysis, he calls the *latent content of the dream*. The synthetic process, which elaborates the disconnected or only superficially connected ideas into a relatively unified dream-image, is called the *dream-work*.

845   We are now faced with two cardinal questions:

1. What is the psychic process that changes the latent dream-content into the manifest dream-content?

2. What is the motive for this change?

846   There are dreams whose latent content is not hidden at all, or barely so, and which in themselves are logical and understandable because the latent content is practically identical with the manifest content. Children's dreams are frequently of this kind, because the thought-world of children is chiefly filled with sensuous, concrete imagery. The more complicated and abstract the thoughts of an adult become, the more confused are most of his dreams. We seldom meet with a completely transparent and coherent dream in an adult. Frequently the dreams of adults belong to the class of dreams which, though meaningful and logical in themselves, are

[2] [Standard Edn., V, p. 641.]

unintelligible because their meaning does not in any way fit the thought-processes of the waking consciousness. The great majority of dreams, however, are confused, incoherent dreams that surprise us by their absurd or impossible features. These are the dreams, also, that are furthest removed from their premise, the latent dream-material, that bear the least resemblance to it and are therefore difficult to analyse, and have required for their synthesis the greatest expenditure of transformative psychic energy.

847   Children's dreams, with their clarity and transparent meaning, are the least subject to the transformative activity of the dream-work. Their nature is therefore fairly clear; most of them are wish-dreams.

848   A child that is hungry dreams of food, a pleasure forbidden the day before is enacted in the dream, etc. Children are concerned with simple sensuous objects and simple wishes, and for this reason their dreams are very simple too. When adults are concerned with similar objects, their dreams as well are very simple. To this class belong the so-called dreams of convenience, most of which take place shortly before waking. For example, it is time to get up, and one dreams that one is up already, washing, dressing, and already at work. Or if any kind of examination is impending, one finds oneself in the middle of it, etc. With adults, however, very simple-looking dreams are often fairly complicated because several wishes come into conflict and influence the formation of the dream-image.

849   For children's dreams and dreams of convenience in adults the author lays down the following formula: A thought expressed in the optative has been replaced by a representation in the present tense.[3]

850   The second of the questions we asked, concerning the motive for the conversion of the latent content into the concrete dream-image, can be answered most easily in these simple cases. Evidently the enacted fulfilment of the wish mitigates its affectivity; in consequence, the wish does not succeed in breaking through the inhibition and waking the sleeping organism. In this case, therefore, the dream performs the function of a guardian of sleep.

851   Our first question, concerning the process of the dream-work, can best be answered by examining the confused dreams.

852   In examining a confused dream, the first thing that strikes us is how very much richer the latent dream-material is than the dream-image constructed from it. Every idea in the manifest dream

[3] [Ibid., p. 647.]

proves, on analysis, to be associated with at least three or four other ideas which all have something in common. The corresponding dream-image frequently combines all the different characteristics of the individual underlying ideas. Freud compares such an image with Galton's family photographs, in which several exposures are superimposed. This combination of different ideas Freud calls *condensation*. To this process is due the indefinite, blurred quality of many dream-images. The dream knows no "either-or" but only the copulative "and."

853   Often, on a superficial examination of two ideas united in a single image, no common factor can be found. But, on penetrating more deeply, we discover that whenever no *tertium comparationis* is present, the dream creates one, and generally does so by manipulating the linguistic expression of the ideas in question. Sometimes dissimilar ideas are homophonous; sometimes they rhyme, or could be confused with one another if attention is poor. The dream uses these possibilities as a *quid pro quo* and thus combines the dissimilar elements. In other cases it works not only wittily but positively poetically, speaking in tropes and metaphors, creating symbols and allegories, all for the purpose of concealment under deceptive veils. The process of condensation begets monstrous figures that far surpass the fabulous beings in Oriental fairytales. A modern philosopher holds that the reason why we are so prosaic in our daily lives is that we squander too much poetic fantasy in our dreams. The figures in a confused dream are thus, in the main, composite structures. (Example on p. 321.)[4]

854   In the manifest dream, the latent dream-material is represented by these composite structures, which Freud calls the dream-elements. These elements are not incoherent, but are connected together by a common dream-thought, i.e., they often represent different ways of expressing the same dominating idea.

855   This rather complicated situation explains a good deal of the confusion and unintelligibility of the dream, but not all of it. So far we have considered only the ideational side of the dream. The feelings and affects, which play a very large part, have still to be discussed.

856   If we analyse one of our own dreams, we finally arrive by free association at trains of thought which at one time or another were of importance to us, and which are charged with a feeling of value. During the process of condensation and reinterpretation, certain

---

[4] [Ibid., p. 651.]

thoughts are pushed onto the stage of the dream, and their peculiar character might easily invite the dreamer to criticize and suppress them, as actually happens in the waking state. The affective side of the dream, however, prevents this, since it imbues the dream elements with feelings that act as a powerful counterweight to all criticism. Obsessional ideas function in the same way. For example, agoraphobia manifests itself with an overwhelming feeling of fear, and so maintains the position it has usurped in consciousness.

857 Freud supposes that the affects attached to the components of the latent dream-material are transferred to the elements of the manifest dream, thus helping to complete the dissimilarity between the latent and the manifest content. He calls this process *displacement,* or, in modern terms, a transvaluation of psychic values.

858 By means of these two principles, the author believes he can offer an adequate explanation of the obscurity and confusion of a dream constructed out of simple, concrete thought-material. These two hypotheses shed a new light on the question of the instigator of a dream, and the connection between the dream and waking life. There are dreams whose connection with waking life is quite evident, and whose instigator is a significant impression received during the day. But far more frequently the dream-instigator is an incident which, although trivial enough in itself, and often positively silly, in spite of its complete valuelessness, introduces a long and intensely affective dream. In these cases, analysis leads us back to complexes of ideas which, though unimportant in themselves, are associated with highly significant impressions of the day by incidental relationships of one kind or another. In the dream the incidental elements occupy a large and imposing place, while the significant ones are completely occluded from the dreaming consciousness. The real instigator of the dream, therefore, is not the trivial, incidental element, but the powerful affect in the background. Why, then, does the affect detach itself from the ideas that are associated with it, and in their place push the nugatory and valueless elements into consciousness? Why does the dreaming intellect trouble to rout out the forgotten, incidental, and unimportant things from every corner of our memory, and to build them up into elaborate and ingenious images?

859 Before turning to the solution of this question, Freud tries to point out further effects of the dream-work in order to shed a clear light on the purposiveness of the dream-functions.

860 In adults, besides visual and auditory memory-images, the mate-

rial underlying the dream includes numerous abstract elements which it is not so easy to represent in concrete form. In considering the *representability of the dream-content,* a new difficulty arises which influences the dream's performance. At this point the author digresses a bit and describes how the dream represents logical relations in sensuous imagery. His observations in this respect are of no further importance for his theory; they merely serve to increase the stock of the discredited dream in the estimation of the public.

861   One extremely remarkable effect of the dream-work is what Freud calls the *dream-composition.* This, according to his definition, is a kind of revision which the disordered mass of dream-elements undergo at the moment of their inception—a regular dramatization frequently conforming to all the rules of art exposition, development, and solution. In this way the dream acquires, as the author says, a façade, which does not of course cover it up at all points. This façade is in Freud's view the crux of the misunderstanding about dreams, since it systematizes the deceptive play of the dream-elements and brings them into a plausible relationship. Freud thinks that the reason for this final shaping of the dream-content is the regard for intelligibility. He imagines the dream producer as a kind of jocular daimon who wants to make his plans plausible to the sleeper.

862   Apart from this last effect of the dream-work, what is created by the dream is nothing in any way new or intellectually superior. Anything of value in the dream-image can be shown by analysis to be already present in the latent material. And it may very well be doubted whether the dream-composition is anything but a direct effect of reduced consciousness, a fleeting attempt to explain the hallucinations of the dream.

863   We now come to the final question: Why does the dream do this work? In analysing his own dreams, the author usually came upon quickly forgotten and unexpected thoughts of a distinctly unpleasant nature, which had entered his waking consciousness only to be suppressed again immediately. He designates the state of these thoughts by the name *repression.*

864   In order to elucidate the concept of repression, the author postulates two thought-producing systems, one of which has free access to consciousness, while the other can reach consciousness only through the medium of the first. To put it more clearly, there is on the borderline between conscious and unconscious a *censorship* which is continually active throughout waking life, regulating the

flow of thoughts to consciousness in such a way that it keeps back all incidental thoughts which for some reason are prohibited, and admits to consciousness only those of which it approves. During sleep there is a momentary predominance of what was repressed by day; the censorship must relax and produces a compromise—the dream. The author does not conceal the somewhat too schematic and anthropomorphic features of this conception, but solaces himself with the hope that its objective correlate may one day be found in some organic or functional form.

865   There are thoughts, often of a preeminently egoistic nature, which are able to slip past the censorship imposed by ethical feelings and criticism when this is relaxed in sleep. The censorship, however, is not entirely abrogated, but only reduced in effectiveness, so that it can still exert some influence on the shaping of the dream-thoughts. The dream represents the reaction of the personality to the intrusion of unruly thoughts. Its contents are repressed thoughts portrayed in distorted or disguised form.

866   From the example of dreams that are comprehensible and have a meaning, it is evident that their content is generally a fulfilled wish. It is the same with confused dreams that are difficult to understand. They, too, contain the fulfilment of repressed wishes.

867   Dreams, therefore, can be divided into three classes:

1. Those that represent an *unrepressed wish in undisguised form*. Such dreams are of the infantile type.

2. Those that represent the fulfilment of a *repressed wish in disguised form*. According to Freud, most dreams belong to this class.

3. Those that represent a *repressed wish in undisguised form*. Such dreams are said to be accompanied by fear, the fear taking the place of dream-distortion.

868   Through the conception of the dream as a compromise we arrive at an explanation of dreams in general. When the waking consciousness sinks into sleep, the energy needed to maintain the inhibition against the sphere of repressed material abates. But just as the sleeper still has some attention at his disposal for sensory stimuli coming from outside, and, by means of this attention, can eliminate sleep-disturbing influences by weaving around them a disguising veil of dreams, so stimuli arising from within, from the unconscious psychic sphere, are neutralized by the periphrasis of a dream. The purpose in both cases is the same, namely, the preservation of sleep, and for this reason Freud calls the dream the "guardian of sleep."

Excellent examples of this are waking dreams, which abound in periphrastic inventions designed to make the continuation of the reverie plausible.

869   Confused dreams are not so clear in this respect, but Freud maintains that, with application and goodwill, repressed wishes can be discovered in them too. On this point he adopts a rather one-sided attitude, since, instead of a wish, the cause of a dream may easily prove to be just the opposite, a repressed fear, which, mani-festing itself in undisguised and often exaggerated form, makes the teleological explanation of dreams appear doubtful.

Freud: Dreams

CONTENTS

REVIEW OF HELLPACH: "GRUNDLINIEN EINER PSYCHOLOGIE DER HYSTERIE" [1]

⁸⁷¹ All those professional colleagues who are interested in the great problem of hysteria will surely welcome with joy and eager expectation a work that, judging by its bulk, promises a thorough-going treatment of the psychology of hysteria on the broadest possible basis. Anyone acquainted with the present position of the hysteria theory, and especially the psychology of hysteria, is aware that our knowledge of this obscure field is unfortunately a minimal one. Freud's researches, which have received but scant recognition though they have not yet been superseded, have prepared the ground for thinking that future research into hysteria will be psychological. Hellpach's book appears to meet this expectation. Casting the most cursory glance at the index of names appended to the end of the book, we find the following cited: Archimedes, Behring, Billroth, Büchner, Buddha, Cuvier, Darwin, Euler, Fichte, Galileo, Gall, Goethe, Herbart, Hume, Kepler, Laplace, de la Mettrie, Newton, Rousseau, Schelling, and many others, all illustrious names among which we now and then light on that of a psychiatrist or neurologist. There can be no doubt at all that a future theory of hysteria will go far beyond the narrow confines of psychiatry and neurology. The deeper we penetrate into the riddle of hysteria, the more its boundaries expand. Hellpach thus starts from a basis of great scope, assuredly not without reason. But when we recall the limitless range of knowledge indicated by the names in the index, Hellpach's basis for a psychology of hysteria would seem to have undergone a dangerous expansion.

⁸⁷² From various hints thrown out by the author we gather that he is inclined to suspect adverse critics of being ill-intentioned. I would therefore like to say at once that I have no prejudices against Hellpach. On the contrary, I have read his book *sine ira* and with

---

[1] [*Zentralblatt für Nervenheilkunde und Psychiatrie* (Berlin), XXVIII (1905), 318–21. Willy Hellpach, *Grundlinien einer Psychologie der Hysterie* (Leipzig, 1904). ("Basics of a Psychology of Hysteria.") See *The Freud/Jung Letters,* 230J, n. 7.]

attention, in the honest endeavour to understand it and be fair to it. The text up to p. 146 can be considered an introduction. There are disquisitions on the concepts, theories, and history of science, ranging over every conceivable field of knowledge, which at first blush have nothing to do with hysteria. A mere handful of aphorisms culled from the history of the hysteria theory, chiefly appreciations of the achievements of Charcot and other investigators, have a tenuous connection with the theme. I do not feel competent to criticize the highly generalized discussions on the theories of scientific research. The sidelights from the history of hysteria research are neither exhaustive as a presentation of the subject nor do they offer the researcher anything new. They make practically no contribution to psychology.

873   The actual treatment of the theme begins on p. 147. First we have a discussion on *suggestibility*. Here Hellpach's thinking and his sure touch must be applauded: he is tackling one of the most difficult points in the hysteria theory. It is immediately obvious that the current concept of suggestibility is rather vague and hence unsatisfactory. Hellpach tries to probe the problem of volition and motivation by analysing "command" and "suggestion." The analysis leads on to a discussion of mechanization and *demotivation:* emancipation of the act of will from the motive. By various convoluted trains of thought we then get to the problem of apperception (as understood by Wundt), which is intimately connected with the problem of volition. Hellpach attaches particular importance to one quality of apperception, and that is the *extinction of sensation*. Stimuli which are only just perceptible on the periphery of the visible field may under certain circumstances be extinguished, but the source of the stimulus (small stars, etc.) disappears as the result of focussing. This observation is extended by analogy to apperception, so-called active apperception taking over the role of focussing. A sensation-extinguishing effect is thus attributed to apperception. Hellpach expatiates at length on this notion, unfortunately in a hardly intelligible manner and without adducing sufficient reasons in support. Extinction of sensation seems to him to be something common and regular. But actually it is an exception, for apperception does not extinguish sensation—on the contrary. The discussion on apperception culminates in the passage: "The control that in the more passive state of apperception extends over the whole field of consciousness disappears with the increasing tension of active apperception. This gives rise to distracted actions."

874   A further "state of apperception" Hellpach finds in "emptiness of consciousness." Here he undertakes, among other things, a little excursion into the uncultivated deserts of dementia praecox and carries off, as a trophy, negativism as a manifestation of suggestibility in the empty consciousness of the catatonic—as though anyone had the slightest idea of what the consciousness of a catatonic looks like!

875   The following sentence may be taken as the final result of his analyisis of suggestibility: "I regard complete senselessness or complete lack of moderation as the criteria for all psychic effects that can be called suggestions." Unfortunately I can make neither head nor tail of this. In the course of a fifty-page analysis the concept of suggestibility has, to be sure, rambled off into nebulosity, one doesn't quite know how, nor does one know what has become of it. Instead we are offered two peculiar criteria for suggestion, whose beginning and end both lie in the realm of unintelligibles.

876   There now follows a chapter on one of the thousand hysterical symptoms: ataxia-abasia. The essence of this chapter is its emphasis on the meaning of hysterical paralysis. Another chapter deals with the meaning of hysterical disturbance of sensation. Hellpach treats hysterical pain-apraxia as an illness on its own, but offers no proof of this. Equally, he treats hysterical hyperaesthesias as a physiological and not a psychological problem. Here again conclusive reasons are lacking. Particularly in hysteria, however, "explanatory principles should not be multiplied beyond the necessary."[2] To explain anaesthesia, Hellpach uses the apperceptive extinction of sensation, that aforementioned paradoxical phenomenon which is anything but a simple, certain, clear-cut fact. The proposition that hysterics cease to feel when they ought to feel must be applauded. But this singular fact should not be explained by an even more obscure and ill-founded observation.

877   Hellpach finds the hysterical intellect characterized by *fantastic apperception* and *tractability*. Fantastic apperception is a psychological state in which "fantasy activity is linked with a tendency towards passivization of apperception." One can dimly guess what Hellpach is getting at with this turgid pronouncement, but I must own I am incapable of forming any clear conception of it. And I do not think that Hellpach had any clear conception of it either, or he would have been able to communicate it to an attentive reader.

[2] [Occam's Razor: "Entia praeter necessitatem non sunt multiplicanda."]

371

878   Hellpach defines tractability as follows: "The tractable person is one who meets the demands made upon him willingly or with psychic indifference, or at least without actively fighting down inner resistances." Suggestibility, which in an earlier chapter vanished beneath a flood of psychological and conceptual verbiage, unexpectedly surfaces here in the innocuous guise of "tractability."

879   In the chapter entitled "The Psychological Bar to a Psychology of Hysteria," we get to the "root phenomenon of hysteria." The "disproportion between the insignificance of the affective cause and the intensity of the expressive phenomenon" is supposed to be the core of hysterical mental abnormity.

880   The last section of the book deals with the further elaboration and application of the principles previously laid down, and partly with a discussion of Freud's teachings in regard to the genesis of hysteria. It is to Hellpach's credit that he understands Freud and is able to keep in check and counterbalance certain biases and exaggerations of the Freudian school. But as regards the genesis of hysteria he nowhere advances beyond Freud, and in point of clarity he lags far behind.

881   Now and then Hellpach makes sorties against the "unconscious." He set out to explain various expressive movements in hysteria without reference to this hypothesis. This attempt deserves to be read in the original (pp. 401ff.). To me it seems neither clear nor convincing. Moreover, expressive movements are, *par excellence,* not unconscious phenomena. It is known that the hypothesis of the psychological unconscious is based on quite other facts, which Hellpach does not touch on. Even so, he makes use of the concept of the unconscious several times, probably because he knows of no better one to put in its place.

882   His attempts in the concluding chapters to elucidate the sociological and historical aspects of the hysteria problem deserve to be greeted as a general tendency; they show that the author has an unusual, indeed splendid over-all view of his material. Unfortunately he remains stuck at all points in the most general and uncertain of concepts. The net result of all this effort is disproportionately small. The psychological gain reduces itself to the announcement of a grand design and to a few astute observations and interpretations. For this failure the blame lies not least with the extreme infelicities of Hellpach's style. If the reader has at last managed to grasp a sentence or a question, and then hopes to find its continuation or answer in the next sentence, he is again and again pulled

up by explanations of how the author arrived at the first sentence and all that can or could be said about this first sentence. In this way the argument proceeds by fits and starts, and the effect of this in the long run is insufferably fatiguing. The number of wrong turns Hellpach takes is astonishing, but he enumerates still more circumstantially how many others he could have taken. The result is that he often has to explain why he is coming back to his theme again. Because of this, the book suffers from a peculiar opacity which makes orientation extraordinarily difficult.

883   The author has, furthermore, committed a grave sin of omission in that he cites next to no examples. This omission is especially painful when pathological phenomena are being discussed. Anyone who wants to teach something new must first teach his public how to see, but without examples this is impossible. Maybe Hellpach could still come out with a few good and new things if he deigned to descend into the nether regions of case material and experimental research. If he wishes to address himself to the empiricist at all, he will find this advice assuredly justified.

884   L. Bruns: *Die Hysterie im Kindesalter*. 2nd revised edn., Halle,
1906. — The author, known for his researches into the symptomatology and therapy of hysteria, has now published a second edition
of his book on hysteria in childhood, a work familiar to most medical men. After a short historical introduction he gives a concise
survey of the symptomatology, keeping to the empirical essentials
and leaving aside all rarities and curiosities with commendable self-
restraint. With the help of clear-cut cases he gives a brief description
of the various forms and localizations of the paralyses and spasms,
tics and choreic affections; somnambulism, lethargies, and states
of possession are treated more cursorily, being less common. The
painful symptoms (neuralgias, etc.) and bladder disturbances, and
particularly the *psychic* symptoms that are so extraordinarily important in hysteria, come off rather poorly. In his discussion of the
aetiology, the author holds, as against Charcot, that too much significance should not be attached to heredity. More important, it
seems to him, and I think rightly, are the psychic causes in the
individual concerned, particularly imitation of bad examples, the
influence of bad upbringing, fright, fear, etc. In many cases the
influence of the parents is directly psychogenic.

885   In view of the admitted frequency of infantile hysteria, diagnosis
is of great importance, for many cases are not only retarded by
a false diagnosis but are completely wrecked by it. The author takes
a firm stand on psychogenesis: the unmistakable psychic element
in hysterical symptoms is of the utmost significance in differential
diagnosis. Often one has to rely on one's own impressions; the

[1] [Twenty-five reviews published in the *Correspondenz-Blatt für Schweizer Ärzte* (Basel), XXVI–XL (1906–10), rediscovered by Henri F. Ellenberger in the course of research for his book *The Discovery of the Unconscious*. The Editors are grateful to Professor Ellenberger for informing them of these articles, which Jung wrote for the *Correspondenz-Blatt* ("Bulletin for Swiss Physicians") during his association with the psychoanalytic movement, and which often express his partiality for Freud's work.]

author quotes the classic words of Möbius:[2] "According to the view I have formed of the nature of hysteria, many symptoms can be hysterical, many others not." In many cases, therefore, the diagnosis of hysteria is less a science than an art. Commendably, the author urges the greatest caution against assuming *simulation*.

886   Treatment is fundamentally *always a psychic one;* water, electricity, etc. work only by suggestion. This excellently written chapter is an invaluable guide for the practitioner, but the details of it cannot be gone into here.

887   The book is written by a practitioner for practitioners; it is no handicap, therefore, that the theoretical side is represented somewhat aphoristically and takes no account of the latest analytical views of Freud.

888   E. Bleuler: *Affektivität, Suggestibilität, Paranoia.*[3] Halle, 1906. — This work, addressed chiefly to psychologists and psychiatrists, is distinguished, like all Bleuler's publications, by its lucidity; its theme is one that is coming more and more into the forefront of psychological interest: namely, affects and their influence on the psyche. This field of research, like some other domains of psychology, suffers greatly from a confusion of concepts. Bleuler therefore proposes, first of all, a clean division between affects proper and intellectual feelings, a conceptual distinction of the greatest value in scientific discussion. *Affectivity,* comprising all affects and quasi-affective processes, is an inclusive concept which covers all non-intellectual psychic processes such as volition, feeling, suggestibility, attention, etc. It is a psychic factor that exerts as much influence on the psyche as on the body.

889   In the first and second parts of his book Bleuler applies this conception in the realm of normal psychology. In the third part he discusses the *pathological alterations of affectivity.* Affectivity is of the greatest imaginable importance in psychopathology. Quite apart from the affective psychoses proper (manic-depressive insanity), it plays a significant role in psychoses which one was wont to regard as predominantly intellectual. Bleuler demonstrates this with the help of careful clinical histories of *paranoia originaria.*[4] He found that the content of the paranoid picture developed from

[2] [See above, par. 795, n. 2.]
[3] [Eugen Bleuler (1857–1939), director of the Burghölzli. See *The Freud/Jung Letters,* 2J, no. 8; 40F, n. 6; 41J; and infra, par. 938.]
[4] [Originating in childhood, a term later rejected by Bleuler.]

a *feeling-toned complex,* that is, from ideas accompanied by intensive affect which therefore have an abnormally strong influence on the psyche. This is the keynote of the book.

890 It is impossible, in a short review, to do justice to the numerous perspectives which Bleuler's book opens out and to the wealth of empirical material it contains. It is urgently recommended first of all to professionals; but non-psychiatrists also, who are interested in the general problems of psychopathology, will not be able to lay it aside without reaping a rich harvest of psychological insights.

891 Carl Wernicke:[5] *Grundriss der Psychiatrie in klinischen Vorlesungen.* 2nd revised edn., Leipzig, 1906. — Following Wernicke's sudden death, Liepmann and Knapp have seen to the publication of the second edition of this important book, which has acted as a ferment in modern psychiatry like no other. Wernicke incarnated, so to speak, that school of psychopathology which believed it could base itself exclusively on anatomical data. His book is an impressive exponent of this thinking; besides a huge mass of empirical material we find many brilliant speculations whose starting point is always anatomical. The book is the work of an entirely original mind that tried, on the basis of clinical data combined with brain anatomy, to introduce new viewpoints into psychotherapy, hoping to effect a final synthesis of those two mutually repellent disciplines, brain anatomy and psychology. Wernicke is always the master where psychopathological events come closest to the anatomical, above all, therefore, in the treatment of problems clustering round the question of aphasia. His "Psychophysiological Introduction," where he tries to answer questions concerning the connection between cerebral and psychophysiological data, is, even for the non-psychiatrist, one of the most interesting in recent medical literature.

892 The section that follows, "Paranoid States," introduces Wernicke's famous sejunction theory,[6] which is the cornerstone of his system. The third and longest section treats of "acute psychoses and defective states." Here, with the help of numerous examples, Wernicke develops his revolutionary clinical approach, which has met with only the limited approbation of fellow professionals and has so far not produced a school. Wernicke's ideas, for all their brilliance, are too narrow: brain anatomy and psychiatric clinics are certainly important for psychopathology, but *psychology* is more

[5] [See *The Freud/Jung Letters,* 33J, n. 8.]
[6] [See "The Psychology of Dementia Praecox" (C.W., vol. 3), par. 55.]

important still and this is what is lacking in Wernicke. The danger of dogmatic schematism for anyone who follows in Wernicke's footsteps, but with less brilliance, is very great. It is devoutly to be hoped, therefore, that this admirable book will produce as few schools as possible.

1907

893   Albert Moll:[7] *Der Hypnotismus, mit Einschluss der Hauptpunkte der Psychotherapie und des Occultismus.* 4th enlarged edn., Berlin, 1907. — Moll's well-known book has now attained nearly twice the size of the first edition. The first, historical section is very full and covers the whole range of the hypnosis movement. The second is a lucid and, didactically speaking, very good introduction to the various forms and techniques of hypnotism, followed by a discussion of the hypnotist's work and the nature of suggestion. Moll defines it thus: "Suggestion is a process whereby, under inadequate conditions, an effect is obtained by evoking the idea that such an effect will be obtained." The third part, treating of symptomatology, is very thorough and contains some good criticism. It also covers the very latest phenomena in the domain of hypnotism, including Mme. Madeleine and "Clever Hans."[8] It is incomprehensible to me why Moll, in the section on dreams, does not consider Freud's pioneering researches. Freud is accorded only a few meagre quotations. In his discussion on the relations between certain mental disturbances (catatonia especially) and similar hypnotic states, Moll has overlooked the work of Ragnar Vogt,[9] which is of significance in this respect. Altogether, the examination of the connection of pathological mental states with hypnosis and related functional phenomena is neither exhaustive nor productive of tangible results, as is the case, incidently, in all textbooks of hypnotism to date. The case of echolalia described on p. 200 may well be a simple catatonia, and this is true also of a large number of so-called "imitative illnesses" which are generally observed by doctors who have no knowledge of the symptomatology of catatonia. If Moll can blithely speak of great suggestibility during sleep, then the whole concept of suggestibility needs very drastic revision. In the discussion on the subconscious one again misses the highly important re-

[7] [See *The Freud/Jung Letters,* 94F, n. 1.]
[8] [A talking dog. Cf. C.W., vol. 8, par. 364, n. 27.]
[9] [See the *Freud/Jung Letters,* 102F, n.3]

searches of Freud. Section VIII, "Medicine," gives a very valuable and useful account of the influence of "authorities" on the question of hypnosis and its alleged dangers. Discussing hypnotic methods of treatment, Moll also touches on the cathartic method. He bases himself here on the original publications of Breuer and Freud,[10] which Freud meanwhile has long since superseded. His present technique differs somewhat from the way Moll describes it. Recently Löwenfeld[11] has given up his negative attitude towards Freud, at least as regards anxiety neurosis. The remaining chapters give a comprehensive account of various psychotherapeutic methods. The forensic significance of hypnotism is also discussed at some length. The final chapter, "The Occult," is a critical survey of the most important "occult" phenomena.

894   Apart from Löwenfeld's book,[12] Moll's is the best and fullest introduction to hypnotic psychotherapy. It is warmly recommended to all doctors, nerve specialists in particular.

895   Albert Knapp: *Die polyneuritischen Psychosen.* Weisbaden, 1906. — The first 85 pages are taken up with detailed clinical histories and their epicrises. The following 50 contain a general description of the relevant symptoms, in clear language which makes a rapid orientation possible. The nomenclature is strongly influenced by Wernicke, which will hardly meet with general approval. The preference given to the term "akinetic motility psychosis" for catatonia etc., is hardly intelligible, especially when one considers that it only describes a condition that can take on a totally different appearance the next moment. The book should be especially welcome to psychiatrists.

896   M. Reichhardt: *Leitfaden zur psychiatrischen Klinik.* Jena, date not given. — This book is a valuable introduction to the elements of psychiatry. The author discusses them under three main heads:

897   General symptomatology, with clear and precise definitions.

898   Exploratory methods, with a detailed description of the numerous methods for testing intelligence and apprehension.

899   Special psychiatry. Here the author confines himself to essentials. On the controversial subject of dementia praecox, the empha-

---

[10] [*Studies on Hysteria.*]
[11] [See *The Freud/Jung Letters,* 11F, n. 3.]
[12] [*Der Hypnotismus: Handbuch der Lehre von der Hypnose und der Suggestion.*]

sis falls on dementia simplex, catatonia and paranoia, the latter being treated *in globo,* without reference to the special diagnoses of the Kraepelin school, which in practice are irrelevant anyhow. A good index adds to the book's handiness. Apart from the clear exposition, one of its main advantages is the noteworthy restriction to what is essential. The legal definitions of insanity are taken exclusively from German law-books. On the question of intelligence tests, no mention is made of the not unimportant method of reading a fable with free reproduction afterwards. The statement that in country areas an institution with 1000–1500 beds is enough for a million inhabitants is certainly not true of Switzerland. Besides private institutions, we have in Canton Zurich about 1300 public beds, not nearly enough to meet the demand. For the rest, the book is warmly recommended not only to students, but especially to all doctors called upon to give a judicial opinion on any kind of mental abnormality.

1908

900   Franz C. R. Eschle: *Grundzüge der Psychiatrie.* Vienna, 1907. — The author—director of the sanatorium at Sinsheim in Baden—has tried to present the fundamentals of psychiatry in the form of a manual, drawing upon his many years of experience as an alienist. Part I treats of the nature and development of insanity. He distinguishes, as general forms of psychic abnormality, a distinctive, an affective, and an appetitive insufficiency, corresponding roughly to the old psychology of Kant. This chapter is rather heavy going. The arrangement is far from clear and the style is often tortuous, for instance p. 37: "In hypnotic sleep, which represents the most intense and persistent form of the artificial suggestive insufficiency of the psychosomatic mechanism, Rosenbach holds that the psychic organ is unable to build up the differentiating unity which stands in antithetical relation to the other parts of the body (and to the external world) as the 'ego,' although it nevertheless represents this unity," etc. This but one example among many!

901   In Part II, "Clinical Pictures of Insanity," the author gives a description of the specific diseases with a great deal of interesting case material and original views which one cannot always endorse, as for instance when he asserts with Rosenbach that a widespread use of hypnosis would lead to a general stultification of the public. His classification of the psychoses is a mixture of old and modern

points of view; he groups acute hallucinatory confusion and acute dementia (curable stupidity) with dementia praecox while distinguishing paranoia and paranoid dementia.

902   Part III is a forensic evaluation of doubtful mental conditions. There is a good index of authors and subjects. The book is essentially eclectic and tries to select the best from the old psychiatry and the new and combine them into a unity with a dash of philosophy thrown in. It should therefore prove stimulating reading for doctors in sanatoria who have not kept abreast of the latest developments in psychiatry.

903   P. Dubois:[13] *Die Einbildung als Krankheitsursache.* Wiesbaden, 1907. — Dubois presents in generally understandable outline his view of the nature and the treatment of the psychoneuroses. He begins with a clear and illuminating definition of "imagination" and then proceeds to show the pathological effects of imagination with the help of numerous instructive examples. His therapy, likewise derived from this view and clearly expounded, consists essentially in enlightening the patients on the nature of their symptoms and in re-educating their thinking. Let us hope that this distinguished book will contribute to a general breakthrough of the conception of the psychogenic nature of most neuroses! Like all Dubois' other writings, it is urgently recommended to the practising doctor. Even though the Dubois method may not be successful with every neurosis, it is eminently suited to have a prophylactic effect, so that cases where the symptoms are due to imprudent suggestions on the part of the doctor may gradually become less common. In conclusion Dubois hints at a possible extension of his therapy to the psychoses—but in this matter the alienist is not so optimistic.

904   Georg Lomer: *Liebe und Psychose.* Wiesbaden, 1907.— Lomer's book is more an example of *belles-lettres* than a scientific evaluation of sexuality and its psychological derivates. By far the greater part of it is concerned with normal psychosexual processes which it seeks to present to an intelligent lay public. Readers who would like to penetrate deeper must have recourse to Havelock Ellis and Freud. The pathology of sex is discussed in an appendix, with—in comparison with similar productions—a wholesome reserve in the communication of piquant case histories. One could have wished for a rather deeper grasp of the problems of psycho-

13 [See *The Freud/Jung Letters,* 115J, n. 8, and infra, following par. 1050.]

sexual pathology, where such excellent preparatory work has been done, as witness the researches of Freud.

905   E. Meyer: *Die Ursachen der Geisteskrankheiten.* Jena, 1907. — Meyer's book comes at the right time and will be welcomed not only by every psychiatrist but by all those who are interested in the causes of mental illnesses in the widest sense. It also remedies the palpable lack of any comprehensive account of the aetiology of the psychoses. The author discusses in great detail the numerous factors that have to be taken into account in their causation. The chapter on poisonings is written with especial care. In discussing the psychic causes, which are at present the subject of violent controversy, the author displays a calm impartiality, allowing the psychic elements more freedom of play than do certain other views which would like to reduce the whole aetiology to non-psychic causes. One small error needs correcting: Freud and the Zurich school see in the psychological disposition only the material determinants of the later symptoms, but not the sole cause of psychosis. The author has made a singularly good selection from the extensive literature dealing with the question of aetiology. An excellent index assists easy reference.

906   Sigmund Freud: *Zur Psychopathologie des Alltagslebens.* 2nd enlarged edn., Berlin, 1907.[14] — It is a heartening sign that this important book has now gone into a second edition. It is practically the only major work of Freud's that introduces his ideas into the world with little or no effort, so simply and fluently is it written. Thus it is well suited to initiate the layman (and there are few who are *not* laymen in this field) into the problems of Freudian psychology. It is concerned not with the speculations of theoretical psychology but with psychological case material taken from everyday life. It is just the apparently insignificant incidents of everyday life that Freud has made the theme of his researches, showing with the help of numerous examples how the unconscious influences our thoughts and actions at every turn in an unexpected way. Many of his examples have an implausible look, but one should not be put off by that, because all unconscious trains of thought in an individual look anything but plausible on paper. The profound truth of Freud's ideas will carry conviction only when one tests them for oneself. Even for those who are not especially interested

14 [See *The Freud/Jung Letters,* 27F, n. 11.]

381

in psychological matters Freud's book makes stimulating reading; for those who think more deeply, who by inclination or profession are interested in the psychic processes, it is a rich mine of far-sighted ideas which have a significance that can scarcely be estimated at present for the whole range of mental and nervous diseases. In this respect the book is an easy guide to Freud's latest works on hysteria,[15] which despite the deep truth of their subject-matter, or because of it, have hitherto met only with fanatical opposition and intractable misunderstanding. The book is therefore recommended with all urgency to alienists and to nerve specialists in particular.

1909

907   L. Löwenfeld:[16] *Homosexualität und Strafgesetz.* Wiesbaden, 1908. — This book is the product of the current struggle that has been touched off in Germany by section 175 of the penal code. This section, as is generally known, concerns unnatural vice between men, and also with animals. The author gives a concise history of the clinical concept of homosexuality. He sums up the present state of opinion as follows: "Though homosexuality is an anomaly that may appear in the physical sphere in association with disease and degeneration, in the majority of cases it is an isolated psychic deviation from the norm, which cannot be regarded as pathological or degenerative and is not likely to reduce the value of the individual as a member of society." Section 175, which became law only under the pressure of orthodoxy despite opposition by influential authorities, has so far proved to be not only useless and inhuman, but directly harmful as it offers opportunities for professional blackmail with all its tragic and repulsive consequences. The book gives a very good survey of the whole question of homosexuality.

908   Karl Kleist: *Untersuchungen zur Kenntnis der psychomotorischen Bewegungsstörungen bei Geisteskranken.* Leipzig, 1908 — The book presents the clinical history of a motility psychosis alias catatonia with a detailed epicritical discussion. The author leans heavily on the views of Wernicke, with the result that the book is concerned chiefly with cerebral localizations. The conclusion

---

[15] [This probably refers to "Fragment of an Analysis of a Case of Hysteria," and "Three Essays on the Theory of Sexuality," both in Standard Edn., vol. 7.]
[16] [See n. 11, supra.]

reached is that psychomotor disturbances in catatonics are conditioned by two factors, innervatory and psychic. The seat of disease is supposed to be the terminal point of the cerebellar-cortical tracts, i.e., the frontal cerebral cortex. As the patients occasionally have sensations of strain and fatigue in the performance of the tasks assigned them, and as the psychomotor symptoms are due to a disturbance of the motor reactions coordinated with these sensations, the psychic conditioning factor likewise points to the cerebellar-frontal system. This conclusion is logical if one regards the psychic functional complexes as an appendix of their executive organs from the start. The book is recommended to specialists because of its acute differential-diagnostic analysis of apraxia and related motility disturbances.

909   Oswald Bumke:[17] *Landläufige Irrtümer in der Beurteilung von Geisteskranken.* Wiesbaden, 1908. — This little book contains more than its title indicates. It is a short and clearly written outline of psychiatry, and while it does not give an altogether elementary description of the psychoses it presupposes some knowledge of the main types—knowledge which almost every practitioner possesses today. On this basis the author discusses questions which are wont to present difficulties to doctors with no psychiatric training in their assessment of mental disturbances. Aetiology, diagnosis, prognosis, and therapy are discussed from this standpoint, the author giving valuable advice and hints from his own practical experience. At the end there is a chapter on the forensic view of the insane.

910   A comprehensive and handy little book, highly recommended.

911   Christian von Ehrenfels: *Grundbegriffe der Ethik.* Wiesbaden, 1907. — The author—professor of philosophy in Prague—gives a philosophical but easily understandable account of his basic ethical concepts. His argument culminates in the confrontation between social and individual morality, once more a subject of violent controversy. The conclusion reached, though typical of the general tenor of the book, can hardly be called positive: "Normative morality is identical with correct social morality, the sole proviso being that every individual must be free to modify social morality, not in accordance with his own caprice but in a manner he can defend before the tribunal of the eternal and inscrutable."

[17] [See *The Freud/Jung Letters*, 196J, n. 2.]

1910

912   Christian von Ehrenfels: *Sexualethik*. Wiesbaden, 1907. —
While the author's *Grundbegriffe der Ethik* is mainly of theoretical
interest, this work is of great practical importance. It is the clearest
and best account I know of sexual ethics and its postulates. The
author begins with a deeply thought out and lucid presentation
of natural and cultural sexual morality. The following chapter,
"Contemporary Sexual Morality in the West," discusses the tremendous conflict between the postulates of natural and cultural
sexuality, the socially useful effects of monogamy on the one hand
and its shadow-side on the other, prostitution, the double sexual
morality of society and its pernicious influence on culture. In his
discussion of reform movements the author takes a cautious and
reserved stand, as far from Philistine approval of the *status quo*
as from certain modern tendencies that would like to pull down
all barriers. Although he has no definite programme of reform
(which shows he is no dreamer!), he expresses many liberal views
which will surely help to solve our greatest social problem, beginning with the individual. His book, which unlike others of the kind
is not a parade of garish nudities veiled in scientific garb, deserves
the widest acclaim for its unpretentious and reasonable attempt
to find *possible* solutions.

913   Max Dost: *Kurzer Abriss der Psychologie, Psychiatrie und
gerichtlichen Psychiatrie*. Leipzig, 1908. — This little book is a new
kind of compendium of psychiatry with special reference to intelligence testing. Psychology comes off rather too lightly. The chapters
on psychiatry, however, really offer everything one could expect
from a short outline. For the psychiatrist the enumeration of various
psychic exploratory methods will be particularly welcome. It will
be hard to find so handy an account anywhere in the literature.

914   Alexander Pilcz: *Lehrbuch der speziellen Psychiatrie für
Studierende und Aerzte*. 2nd revised edn., Leipzig and Vienna,
1909. — Not every branch of medicine is in such an infantile state
of development as psychiatry, where a textbook, which ought to
have general validity, is only of local significance. When one considers that dementia praecox is a disease which in Zurich accounts
for half the admissions, in Munich is steadily decreasing (as a result
of new theories), is not common in Vienna, is rare in Berlin and

in Paris hardly occurs at all, the reviewer of a psychiatric textbook must disregard the Babylonian confusion of tongues and concepts and simply accept the standpoint of the textbook in question. Pilcz's book, now in its 2nd edition, is an admirable work which fulfils its purpose. It is excellently written, and contains everything essential. The material is clearly arranged, the exposition terse and precise. Highly recommended.

915   W. von Bechterew: *Psyche und Leben*. 2nd edn., Wiesbaden, 1908. — This book does not treat of psychological problems on the basis of a wide knowledge of the literature, as the title might suggest, but deals with psychophysiological relations in general from the theoretical philosophical side, and then goes on to discuss the relation of energy to the psyche and of the psyche to physiology and biology. The style is aphoristic; the chapters, thirty-one in number, are only loosely connected. The chief value of the book lies in its numerous reports of the views of a great variety of specialist researchers and in its literary references. Readers who want a synthetic or critical clarification of the psychophysiological problems will seek for it in vain. But for anyone who seeks orientation in this interesting field and its complicated, widely dispersed literature this stimulating book is highly recommended.

916   M. Urstein: *Die Dementia praecox und ihre Stellung zum manisch-depressiven Irresein*. Vienna, 1909. — As the title indicates, this is a clinical examination of dementia praecox diagnosis, a topic that has come once more to the forefront because of the recent swing towards the Kraepelin school. Not everyone will be able to imitate the ease with which manic-depressive insanity is now distinguished from dementia praecox, and Urstein is one of them. He sharply criticizes the work of Wilmann and Dreyfus, who would like to restrict dementia praecox diagnosis in favour of manic-depressive insanity. His book can count on the decided sympathy of all who doubt the thoroughness of Kraepelin's diagnostics, and who cannot go along with the idea that a catatonic is from now on a manic-depressive. Pages 125 to 372 are padded out with case histories, an unnecessary appendage in view of the specialist readership for which the book is intended.

917   Albert Reibmayer: *Die Entwicklungsgeschichte des Talentes und Genies*. Munich, 1908. — Only the first volume of the book

is available at present, but despite this drawback it is already apparent that it is a broad and comprehensive study. The present volume is essentially a theoretical, constructive survey of the problem, which naturally has extensive ramifications into biology and history. If the second volume provides the necessary biographies and suchlike material, we shall have in Reibmayer's book an important work meriting the widest attention.

918   P. Näcke:[18] *Über Familienmord durch Geisteskranke.* Halle, 1908. — The book is a monograph on family murder. The author presents 161 cases, classified according to their respective peculiarities. He is of the opinion that family murder is now on the increase. He distinguishes between "complete" and "incomplete" family murder. The first is more common in the case of relatively sane individuals; the second more common with the insane. The murderers are usually in the prime of life. The victims of the men are usually their wives, of the women their children. The commonest causes are chronic alcoholism, paranoia, and epilepsy in men; melancholy, paranoia, and dementia praecox in women.

919   Th. Becker: *Einführung in die Psychiatrie.* 4th revised and enlarged edn., Leipzig, 1908. — This handy little book is a clear and concise introduction to psychiatry. With regard to the classification of the psychoses the author is conservative, allowing a good deal of room for paranoia alongside dementia praecox. The book has much to recommend it as an "introduction" if one disregards the chapter on hysteria, which no longer meets with modern requirements.

920   A. Cramer: *Gerichtliche Psychiatrie.* 4th revised and enlarged edn., Jena, 1908. — Cramer's guide to judicial psychiatry, now in its fourth edition, is one of the best of its kind; it is thorough, comprehensive, and, compared with Hoche's manual,[19] has the great advantage of consistent exposition. As everywhere in psychiatry, the lack of a consistent classification is to be regretted; this is not the fault of the author but of the discipline itself. Were it not for this inconvenience Cramer's book could be generally recommended; as it is, the beginner can rely on it completely only if he is disposed

18 [See *The Freud/Jung Letters,* 49J, n. 2.]
19 [Alfred E. Hoche, *Handbuch der gerichtlichen Psychiatrie.*]

to trust its particular approach. For the rest, the book will prove useful in the hands of psychiatric experts.

921   August Forel:[20] *Ethische und rechtliche Konflikte im Sexualleben in- und ausserhalb der Ehe.* Munich, 1909. — The author introduces his book with the following words: "The following pages are for the most part an attack, based on documentary material, on the hypocrisy, the dishonesty and cruelty of our present-day morality and our almost non-existent rights in matters of sexual life." From which it is apparent that this work is another contribution to the great social task to which Forel has already rendered such signal service. Essentially it presents a large number of psychosexual conflicts of a moral or judicial nature, knowledge of which is indispensable not only for the nerve specialist, but for every doctor who has to advise his patients in the difficult situations of life.

[20] [August (or Auguste) Henri Forel (1848–1931), director of the Burghölzli before Bleuler. See *The Freud/Jung Letters,* index, s.v.]

THE SIGNIFICANCE OF FREUD'S
THEORY FOR NEUROLOGY AND PSYCHIATRY[1]

922   In medical terms, Freud's achievements are on the whole limited
to the fields of hysteria and obsessional neurosis. His investigations
begin with the psychogenetic explanation of the hysterical symptom,
an explanation formulated by Möbius and experimentally tested
by Pierre Janet. According to this point of view, every physical
symptom of a hysterical nature is causally connected with a corresponding psychological event. This view can be corroborated by
a critical analysis of the hysterical symptom, which becomes intelligible only when the psychological factor is taken into account,
as exemplified by the many paradoxical phenomena of cutaneous
and sensory anesthesias. But the theory of psychogenesis cannot explain the *individual determinants* of the hysterical symptom. Stimulated by Breuer's discovery of a psychological connection, Freud
bridged this large gap in our knowledge by his method of psychanalysis, and he demonstrated that a determining psychological factor
can be found for every symptom. The determination always proceeds from a *repressed feeling-toned complex of representations*.
(Lecturer illustrates this statement with a few case histories taken
partly from Freud, partly from his own experience.) The same
principle applies to the obsessional neurosis, the individual manifestation of which is determined by very similar mechanisms. (Lecturer adduces a number of examples.) As Freud maintains, sexuality in the widest sense plays a significant role in the genesis of a
neurosis, quite understandably so, since sexuality plays an important
role in the intimate life of the psyche. Psychanalysis, in addition,
has in many cases an unmistakable therapeutic effect, which however does not mean that it is the only way of treating a neurosis.
By dint of his theory of psychological determination, Freud has
become very important for psychiatry, especially for the elucidation

[1] [(Translated by W. S.) "Über die Bedeutung der Lehre Freud's für Neurologie
und Psychiatrie," a lecture to the Zurich Cantonal Medical Society, autumn
meeting, 26 Nov. 1907: Jung's abstract, *Correspondenz-Blatt für Schweizer
Ärzte*, XXXVIII (1908), 218. See *The Freud/Jung Letters*, 54J.]

of the symptoms, so far completely unintelligible, of dementia praecox. Analysis of this disease uncovers the same psychological mechanisms that are at work in the neuroses, and thus makes us understand the individual forms of illusionary ideas, hallucinations,
paraesthesias, and bizarre hebephrenic fantasies. A vast area of
psychiatry, up until now totally dark, is thus suddenly illuminated.
(Lecturer relates two case histories of dementia praecox as
examples.)

REVIEW OF STEKEL: "NERVÖSE ANGSTZUSTÄNDE UND IHRE BEHANDLUNG"[1]

923   The book contains a presentation of states of nervous anxiety, buttressed by an abundance of case material: in Part I, Anxiety Neuroses, in Part II, Anxiety Hysteria. The clinical boundaries for either group are flung far afield, taking in much more than existing clinical methods have accounted for. Anxiety neurosis, especially, is enriched by many new categories of disease, the symptoms of which are taken to be *equivalents of anxiety*. By its very nature anxiety hysteria has fluctuating boundaries and tends to merge with other forms of hysteria. Part III is concerned with the general diagnostics of anxiety states as well as general therapy and, specifically, the technique of psychotherapy. Now, what makes the book especially attractive is the fact that Stekel, a pupil of Freud, very laudably makes the first attempt to enable a larger medical public to gain insight in the psychological structure of the neuroses. In his case histories, Stekel does not confine himself to presenting only the surface (as has hitherto been usual), but, following the most intimate individual reactions of the patient, gives a penetrating picture of the psychogenesis in each case and its further progress during the therapeutic effect of the psychoanalysis. He analyses many cases with great skill and rich experience and in great detail, while others are presented only in psychological outline, which the psychological layman may have difficulty in following. Such outline presentations, unfortunately, cannot be avoided if the book is not to become inordinately long, even though such cases are hard to understand and can easily lead to misconstruction and to the reproach that the author indulges in rash interpretation. On the basis of this method, which specifically considers every individuality on its own

[1] [(Translated by W. S.) *Medizinische Klinik* (Berlin), IV:45 (8 Nov. 1908), 1735–36. Wilhelm Stekel's book, with a preface by Freud (in Standard Edn., vol. IX), was published in Berlin and Vienna, 1908. The preface was omitted after the 2nd edn. (1912) in view of Stekel's defection from orthodox psychoanalysis. Trans., *Conditions of Nervous Anxiety and Their Treatment* (London, 1922). For Jung's relations with Stekel 1907–13, see *The Freud/Jung Letters,* index, s.v. Stekel.]

terms, Stekel can demonstrate that without exception states of nervous anxiety are determined by psychosexual conflicts of the most intimate nature, thereby once more confirming Freud's assertion that neurotic anxiety is nothing but a converted sexual desire.

924   Up to now we suffered from a lack of case material in the light of Freudian analysis. To an extent Stekel's book fills this gap. It is very readable and therefore must be highly recommended to all practising physicians, not merely to specialists, for open and hidden neuroses are legion and every physician has to cope with them.

EDITORIAL PREFACE TO THE "JAHRBUCH"[1]

925   In the spring of 1908 a private meeting was held in Salzburg of all those who are interested in the development of the psychology created by Sigmund Freud and in its application to nervous and mental diseases. At this meeting it was recognized that the working out of the problems in question was already beginning to go beyond the bounds of purely medical interest, and the need was expressed for a periodical which would gather together studies in this field that hitherto have been scattered at random. Such was the impetus that gave rise to our *Jahrbuch*. Its task is to be the progressive publication of all scientific papers that are concerned in a positive way with the deeper understanding and solution of our problems. The *Jahrbuch* will thus provide not only an insight into the steady progress of work in this domain with its great future, but also an orientation on the current state and scope of questions of the utmost importance for all the humane sciences.

DR. C. G. JUNG

[1] [*Jahrbuch für psychoanalytische und psychopathologische Forschungen* (Leipzig and Vienna), I:1 (1909), of which Jung was editor and Freud and Bleuler co-directors. For its founding and history, see *The Freud/Jung Letters*, index, s.v. The *Jahrbuch*, V:2 (1913), contained Jung's and Bleuler's statements of resignation; see *The Freud/Jung Letters*, comment following 357J, 27 Oct. 1913.]

MARGINAL NOTES ON WITTELS:
"DIE SEXUELLE NOT"[1]

926   This book is written with as much passion as intelligence. It discusses such questions as abortion, syphilis, the family, the child, women, and professions for women. Its motto is: "Human beings must live out their sexuality, otherwise their lives will be warped." Accordingly, Wittels lifts up his voice for the liberation of sexuality in the widest sense. He speaks a language one seldom hears, the language of unsparing, almost fanatical truthfulness, that falls unpleasantly on the ear because it tears away all shams and unmasks all cultural lies. It is not my business to pass judgment on the author's morals. Science has only to listen to this voice and tacitly admit that it is not a lone voice crying in the wilderness, that it could be a leader for many who are setting out on this path, that we have here a movement rising from invisible sources and swelling into a mightier current every day. Science has to test and weigh the evidence—and understand it.

927   The book is dedicated to Freud and much of it is based on Freud's psychology, which is in essence the scientific rationalization of this contemporary movement. For the social psychologist the movement is and remains an intellectual problem, while for the social moralist it is a challenge. Wittels meets this challenge in his own way, others do so in theirs. We should listen to them all. Nowhere is the warning more in place that on the one hand we should refrain from enthusiastic applause, and on the other not kick against the pricks in blind rage. We have to realize, quite dispassionately, that whatever we fight about in the outside world is also a battle in our inner selves. In the end we have to admit that mankind is not just an accumulation of individuals utterly different from one another, but possesses such a high degree of psychological collectivity that in comparison the individual appears as merely a slight variant. How shall we judge this matter fairly if we cannot admit

[1] [*Jahrbuch für psychoanalytische und psychopathologische Forschungen*, II:1 (1910), 312–15. Fritz Wittels, *Die sexuelle Not* ("Sexual Privation"), (Vienna and Leipzig, 1909). See *The Freud/Jung Letters*, 209F and n. 1. The present translation was published in *Spring*, 1973.]

that it is also our own problem? Anyone who can admit this will first seek the solution in himself. This, in fact, is the way all great solutions begin.

928   Most people, however, seem to have a secret love of voyeurism; they gaze at the contestants as though they were watching a circus, wanting to decide immediately who is finally right or wrong. But anyone who has learnt to examine the background of his own thoughts and actions, and has acquired a lasting and salutary impression of the way our unconscious biological impulses warp our logic, will soon lose his delight in gladiatorial shows and public disputation, and will perform them in himself and with himself. In that way we preserve a perspective that is particularly needful in an age when Nietzsche arose as a significant portent. Wittels will surely not remain alone; he is only the first of many who will come up with "ethical" conclusions from the mine of Freud's truly biological psychology—conclusions that will shake to the marrow what was previously considered "good." As a French wit once remarked, of all inventors moralists have the hardest lot, since their innovations can only be immoralities. This is absurd and at the same time sad, as it shows how out of date our conception of morality has become. It lacks the very best thing that modern thought has accomplished: a biological and historical consciousness. This lack of adaptation must sooner or later bring about its fall, and nothing can stop this fall. And here I am reminded of the wise words of Anatole France: "And, although the past is there to point out to them ever-changing and shifting rights and duties, they would look upon themselves as dupes were they to foresee that future humanity is to create for itself new rights, duties and gods. Finally, they fear disgracing themselves in the eyes of their contemporaries, in assuming the horrible immorality which future morality stands for. Such are the obstacles to a quest of the future."[2]

929   The danger of our old-fashioned conception of morality is that it blinkers our eyes to innovations which, however fitting they may be, always carry with them the odium of immorality. But it is just here that our eyes should be clear and far-seeing. The movement I spoke of, the urge to reform sexual morality, is not the invention of a few cranky somnambulists but has all the impact of a force of nature. No arguments or quibbles about the *raison d'être* of morality are any use here; we have to accept what is most intelligent and make the best of it. This means tough and dirty work. Wittels'

[2] [*The White Stone* (1905; trans. by C. E. Roche, 1924), p. 133.]

book gives a foretaste of what is to come, and it will shock and frighten many people. The long shadow of this fright will naturally fall on Freudian psychology, which will be accused of being a hotbed of iniquity. To anticipate this I would like to say a word in its defence now. Our psychology is a science that can at most be accused of having discovered the dynamite terrorists work with. What the moralist and general practitioner do with it is none of our business, and we have no intention of interfering. Plenty of unqualified persons are sure to push their way in and commit the greatest follies, but that too does not concern us. Our aim is simply and solely scientific knowledge, and we do not have to bother with the uproar it has provoked. If religion and morality are blown to pieces in the process, so much the worse for them for not having more stamina. Knowledge is a force of nature that goes its way irresistibly from inner necessity. There can be no hushing up and no compromises, only unqualified acceptance.

930   This knowledge is not to be identified with the changing views of the ordinary medical man, for which reason it cannot be judged by moral criteria. This has to be said out loud, because today there are still people claiming to be scientific who extend their moral misgivings even to scientific insights. Like every proper science, psychoanalysis is beyond morality; it rationalizes the unconscious and so fits the previously autonomous and unconscious instinctual forces into the psychic economy. The difference between the position before and afterwards is that the person in question now really *wants* to be what he is and to leave nothing to the blind dispensation of the unconscious. The objection that immediately arises, that the world would then get out of joint, must be answered first and foremost by psychoanalysis; it has the last word, but only in the privacy of the consulting room, because this fear is an individual fear. It is sufficient that the goal of psychoanalysis is a psychic state in which "you ought" and "you must" are replaced by "I will," so that, as Nietzsche says, a man becomes master not only of his vices but also of his virtues. Inasmuch as psychoanalysis is purely rational—and it is so of its very nature—it is neither moral nor antimoral and gives neither prescriptions nor any other "you oughts." Undoubtedly the tremendous need of the masses to be led will force many people to abandon the standpoint of the psychoanalyst and to start "prescribing." One person will prescribe morality, another licentiousness. Both of them cater to the masses and both follow the currents that drive the masses hither and thither. Science stands

above all this and lends the strength of its armour to Christian and anti-Christian alike. It has no confessional axe to grind.

931   I have never yet read a book on the sexual question that demolishes present-day morality so harshly and unmercifully and yet remains in essentials so true. For this reason Wittels' book deserves to be read, but so do many others that deal with the same question, for the important thing is not the individual book but the problem common to them all.

REVIEW OF WULFFEN: "DER SEXUALVERBRECHER"[1]

932   Wulffen's comprehensive account of sexual misdemeanours is not confined merely to criminal case histories but seeks to get at the psychological and social foundations of the offence. Two hundred and fifty pages alone are devoted to sexual biology in general, sexual psychology, characterology, and pathology. In the chapter on sexual psychology the author himself will surely deplore the absence of psychoanalytic viewpoints. The other chapters on criminology, being written by an experienced criminologist, are of great interest and very stimulating to the researcher in this field. The illustrations are uniformly good, some of them of great psychological value.

933   For a future psychoanalytic investigation of this subject Wulffen's book should be a most valuable source alongside the compilations of Pitaval.[2]

[1] [*Jahrbuch für psychoanalytische und psychopathologische Forschungen,* II:2 (1910), 747. Erich Wulffen, *Der Sexualverbrecher* ("The Sexual Offender," subtitled "A Handbook for Jurists, Magistrates, and Doctors, with numerous original criminological photographs") (Berlin, 1910).]
[2] [François Gayot de Pitaval (1673–1743), French jurisconsult, compiler of *Causes célèbres et intéressantes* (1734–43), in 20 vols.]

ABSTRACTS OF THE PSYCHOLOGICAL
WORKS OF SWISS AUTHORS

(to the end of 1909)[1]

934   This compilation contains among other things all works of the Zurich school that are either directly concerned with psychoanalysis or touch upon it in essentials. Works with a clinical or psychological content not concerned with psychoanalysis have been omitted. Abraham's works, including those written in Zurich, are abstracted in *Jahrbuch* 1909. A few works by German authors that come close to the findings in *Diagnostische Assoziationsstudien* are noted in passing. A consideration of the critical and oppositional literature is unfortunately impossible as long as the scientific soundness of our principles of research is called in question.

935   Bezzola (formerly Schloss Hard, Ermatingen): "Zur Analyse psychotraumatischer Symptome," *Journ. f. Psychol. u. Neurol.,* VIII (1907). — The author still bases himself entirely on the trauma theory. His procedure corresponds in detail to the Breuer-Freud method, which was called "cathartic." The author has no real grasp of later methods. He recommends a modification which he calls *psychosynthesis.* "Every psychically effective experience reaches consciousness in the form of dissociated excitations of the senses. In order to become concepts, these excitations have to be associated among themselves and also with consciousness. But in consequence of the narrow range of consciousness, this process can-

[1] ["Referate über psychologische Arbeiten schweizerischen Autoren (bis Ende 1909)," *Jahrbuch für psychoanalytische und psychopathologische Forschungen,* II:1 (1910), 356–88. The authors and many of the publications mentioned are commented on in *The Freud/Jung Letters* (see index), except the following, on whom information is unavailable: Eberschweiler, Hermann, Ladame, H. Müller, Pototsky, Schnyder, and Schwarzwald. For references by Freud and Jung to the abstracts in general, see ibid., 91J and 209F. The *Jahrbuch,* under Jung's editorship, also published abstracts or survey articles on Freud's writings (by Abraham), the Austrian and German psychoanalytic literature (Abraham), English and American literature on clinical psychology and psychopathology (Jones), Freudian psychology in Russia (Neiditsch), and Freud's theories in Italy (Assagioli).]

not be fully completed, certain components remain in the unconscious or become conscious by false association. Psychosynthesis consists in reinforcing these isolated conscious components by empathy until the components subconsciously associated with them are reactivated, whereupon the development of the whole process reaches consciousness and the dissolution of the psychotraumatic symptoms ensues." This theory is supported by a series of cases. Naturally they are presented with total blindness for the actual psychosexual background. The epilogue contains an attack on Freud's sexual theory in the usual nervous tone and with arguments to match.

Binswanger, see Jung: *Diagnost. Assoz. stud.,* XI.

936   Bleuler (Zurich): "Freudsche Mechanismen in der Symptomatologie von Psychosen," *Psychiatr.-neurol. Wochenschrift,* 1906. — Analyses of symptoms and associations in various psychotic states.

937   Bleuler and Jung: "Komplexe und Krankheitsursache bei Dementia praecox," *Zentralbl. f. Nervenheilkunde u. Psychiatrie,* XXXI (1908), 220ff. — The authors seek to clarify their aetiological standpoint in the light of Meyer's critique of Jung's theory of dementia praecox. They first demonstrate that the new conception is not aetiological but symptomatological. Questions of aetiology are complicated and take second place. Bleuler makes a rigorous distinction between the physical process of disease and the psychological determination of the symptoms, and in view of the importance of the former he attaches no aetiological significance to the latter. As against this, Jung leaves the question of the ideogenic aetiology open, since in physical processes of disease the physical correlate of affect can play an aetiologically significant role.

938   Bleuler: *Affektivität, Suggestibilität, Paranoia.* Halle, 1906. — In this book Bleuler makes a broadminded attempt to provide a general psychological description and definition of affective processes, and to correlate them with an outline of Freudian psychology. The conception of attention and suggestibility as special instances or partial manifestations of affectivity is a pleasing simplification of the Babylonian confusion of tongues and concepts prevailing in psychology and psychiatry today. Even though the last word has not been spoken, Bleuler offers us a simple interpretation, based on experience, of complicated psychic processes. Psychiatry is in

urgent need of this since the psychiatrist is *forced* to think and operate with complicated psychic entities. We could easily wait for a hundred years until we got anything of this kind from experimental psychology. With affectivity as a basis, Bleuler devotes an uncommonly important chapter to the inception of paranoid ideas, demonstrating in four cases that a feeling-toned complex lies at the root of the delusion.

939   The reviewer must rest content with this general sketch of the book's scope and tendency. Its wealth of detail does not lend itself to brief summation. We can say that Bleuler's book is the best general description to date of the psychology of affect. It is warmly recommended to everyone, especially the beginner.

940   ——. "Sexuelle Abnormitäten der Kinder," *Jahrbuch der schweiz. Gesellschaft f. Schulgesundheitspflege,* IX (1908), 623ff. — A lucid description of sexual perversions in children. Frequent reference is made to Freud's psychology. The author favours sexual enlightenment, not in the form of mass sex education at school, but at home, the right moment being tactfully chosen by the parents.

——. See Jung: *Diagnost. Assoz. stud.,* V.

941   Bolte (Bremen): "Assoziationsversuche als diagnostisches Hilfsmittel," *Allgemeine Zeitschrift f. Psychiatrie,* LXIV (1907).— The author demonstrates the use of the association experiment for diagnostic purposes. He concurs in essentials with the basic findings of the *Diagnostische Assoziationsstudien.* Some interesting examples bring the ideas in this book vividly to life.

942   Chalewsky (Zurich): "Heilung eines hysterischen Bellens durch Psychoanalyse," *Zentralbl. f. Nervenheilkunde u. Psychiatrie,* XX (1909). [Abstract, by Maeder, omitted.]

943   Claparède (Geneva): "Quelques mots sur la définition de l'hysterie," *Archives de psychologie,* VII (1908), 1969ff. — The author criticizes with great skill the recent conception of hysteria inaugurated by Babinski. In the concluding chapter he develops his own views into a conception which itself consists of a series of question marks. He acknowledges the importance of Freudian repression and endows it with biological significance. Psychoanalytic resistance, of which he has gained first-hand experience, is for him a defence reaction. He takes the same view of globus [hysteri-

cus = lump in the throat], vomiting, spasms in the oesophagus, lying, simulation, etc. He sees bodily symptoms as a revivification of ancestral reactions that were once useful. Thus the hysterogenic mechanism is conceived as a "tendance à la réversion," an atavistic mode of reaction. Its infantile character and the "disposition ludique" (play tendency) seem to him to support this theory. His arguments lack the necessary empirical basis which of course can only be acquired through psychoanalysis.

944   Eberschweiler (Zurich) : "Untersuchungen über die sprachliche Komponente der Assoziation," *Allgemeine Zeitschrift für Psychiatrie,* 1908. — A painstaking and careful investigation prompted by the reviewer. One finding is of particular interest for complex psychology: it has been shown that in the association experiment certain vowel sequences occur, i.e., successive reactions have the same vowel sound. Now if these "perseverations" are correlated with complex-indicators, we find that, given an average percentage of 0.36 complex-indicators per reaction, 0.65 fall on a word in the vowel sequence. If we take the two associations preceding the vowel sequences without clang affinity, we reach the following result:

a) Association without vowel sequence: 0.10 complex-indicators.

b) Association without vowel sequence: 0.58 complex-indicators.

1. Beginning of vowel sequence (association with vowel sound perseverating in the ensuing series) : 0.91 complex-indicators.

2nd term in the vowel sequence : 0.68.

3rd term in the vowel sequence: 0.10.

4th term in the vowel sequence: 0.05.

945   It is evident that after complex-disturbances there is a distinct tendency to clang perseverations, and this is an important finding as regards the mechanism of punning and rhyming.

946   Flournoy (Geneva) : *Das Indes à la Planète Mars. Étude sur un cas de somnambulisme avec glossolalie.* 3rd edn., Paris, 1900. — "Nouvelles observations sur un cas de somnambulisme avec glossolalie," *Archives de psychologie,* I (1901). — Flournoy's comprehensive and extremely important work on a case of hysterical somnambulism contributes valuable material on fantasy systems and merits the attention not only of psychoanalysts but also of the general public. In presenting his case Flournoy comes very close to

certain of Freud's views, though no use could be made of his more recent discoveries.

947   Frank (Zurich): "Zur Psychoanalyse" (Festschrift for Forel), *Journ. f. Psychol. u. Neurol.*, XIII (1908). — After a short historical introduction based on the studies by Breuer and Freud, the author expresses his regret that Freud has abandoned the original method without giving his reasons for so doing. (Attentive reading of Freud's subsequent writings discloses soon enough why he preferred the perfected technique to the originally imperfect one.) The author restricts himself to the use of the original cathartic method in conjunction with hypnosis, and his case material proves that he is working with a valuable, practically useful method which yields rewarding results. The inevitable attack on Freud's theory of sexuality is consequently set forth in more temperate tones. The author poses the question: "Why should just the sexual affects among the many others with which the psyche is endowed give rise to disturbances, or is the sexual affect supposed to be the root of all others?" (The role of sexuality in the neuroses was not invented *a priori,* but was discovered empirically through the use of psychoanalysis, and this is something quite different from the cathartic method.) The author does not use psychoanalysis because "a practising physician should not be obliged, in each case, to carry the psychoanalysis through to its very end for theoretical reasons only." (This obligation exists nowhere, but for *practical* reasons one has to go further than one did in 1895; had the method of that time accomplished everything, there would have been no need for going further.) The author gained the impression that Freud mastered hypnosis and suggestion very well in theory, but by no means perfectly in actual practice. "I can understand his constant change of method only on the supposition that, because of his *insufficiently thorough hypnotic treatments and their unsatisfactory results,* he, as a theoretician, was constantly trying to find new methods." (Reviewer's italics.) A little earlier in his paper, the author says that "Freud has relinquished these methods *in spite of his successes.*" In connection with this contradiction it should be noted that Frank *utterly ignores* Freud's later works, as well as the writings of other authors and the Zurich Clinic, otherwise he could not possibly assert—in 1908!—that the cathartic method and its results remained "unnoticed" and only "isolated verifications" were attempted.

948   (The reviewer cannot refrain from pointing out how simple it is to obtain information on these seemingly difficult problems. If, for instance, an author is faced with the problem why Freud may have given up hypnosis, he need only compose a letter to Professor Freud and inquire about it. On this point the reviewer is insistent because it is the basic sickness of German psychiatry that one is never eager to *understand,* but only to *misunderstand.* In these matters a *personal discussion* is needed in order to eliminate all unnecessary difficulties and misunderstandings. If this principle, which is fully accepted in America, were acknowledged on our continent, we would not see so many otherwise deserving authors making fools of themselves by their criticism, which is frequently couched in a language that renders any reply impossible.)

Fürst, see Jung: *Diagnost. Assoz. stud.,* X.

949   Hermann (Galkhausen): "Gefühlsbetonte Komplexe im Seelenleben des Kindes, im Alltagsleben und im Wahnsinn," *Zeitschrift für Kinderforschung,* XIII, 129–43. — Clearly written introduction to the theory of complexes and its application to various normal and pathological psychic states.

950   Isserlin (Munich): "Die diagnostische Bedeutung der Assoziationversuche," *Münchner medizinische Wochenschrift,* no. 27 (1907). — In this critical account of the association studies in Zurich, the author acknowledges the existence of several important findings. But where Freudian psychology begins, his approval ends.

951   Jung (Zurich): *Zur Psychologie und Pathologie sogenannter okkulter Phänomene.*[2] Leipzig 1902. — Besides clinical and psychological discussions on the nature of hysterical somnambulism, this work contains detailed observations on a case of spiritualistic mediumship. The splitting of the personality derives from its infantile tendencies and the fantasy systems are found to be rooted in sexual wish-deliria. Examples of neurotic automatisms include a case of cryptomnesia which the author discovered in Nietzsche's *Zarathustra.*

[2] [= "On the Psychology and Pathology of So-called Occult Phenomena" (C.W., vol. 1).]

952   ——. "Ein Fall von hysterischem Stupor bei einer Untersuchungsgefangenen,"[3] *Journ. f. Psychol. u. Neurol.,* I (1902). —
Description of the patient's pathological intention, wish to be ill,
Freudian repression of anything unpleasant, and wish-fulfilling
delusions in a case of the Ganser-Raecke twilight state.

953   ——. "Die psychopathologische Bedeutung des Assoziationsex-
perimentes,"[4] *Archiv für Kriminalanthropologie,* XX (1906),
145ff. — General introduction to the association experiment and
the theory of complexes.

954   ——. "Experimentelle Beobachtungen über das Erinnerungsvermögen,"[5] *Zentralbl. f. Nervenheilkunde u. Psychiatrie,* XXVIII
(1905), 653ff. — The author describes the reproduction procedure
he himself inaugurated. If, on completion of an association experiment, the subject is asked whether he can remember his previous
reaction to each of the stimulus words, it is found that the forgetting
usually occurs at or immediately after complex-disturbances. Hence
it is a "Freudian forgetting." The procedure is of practical value
in pin-pointing complex-indicators.

955   ——. "Die Hysterielehre Freuds. Eine Erwiderung auf die
Aschaffenburgsche Kritik,"[6] (*Münchner medizinische Wochenschrift,* LIII:47 (1906). — As the title indicates, this is a piece
of polemic the aim of which is to induce our opponent to get better
acquainted with the psychoanalytic method before judging it.
Today this paper is merely of historical value, marking, we might
say, the starting-point of the now flourishing Freudian movement.

956   ——. "Die Freudsche Hysterietheorie,"[7] *Monatsschrift f. Psychiatrie u. Neurologie,* XXIII:4 (1908), 310ff. — A report written
at the request of the president of the International Congress for
Psychiatry in Amsterdam, 1907. The author confines his remarks
to the most elementary principles in accordance with his knowledge
at that time, which since then has been considerably enlarged with

[3] [= "A Case of Hysterical Stupor in a Prisoner in Detention" (ibid.).]
[4] [= "The Psychopathological Significance of the Association Experiment"
(C.W., vol. 2).]
[5] [= "Experimental Observations on the Faculty of Memory" (ibid.).]
[6] [= "Freud's Theory of Hysteria: A Reply to Aschaffenburg" (C.W. vol.
4).]
[7] [= "The Freudian Theory of Hysteria" (ibid.).]

increasing experience. Historically, Freud's theory may be regarded as a transformation of the cathartic method into psychoanalysis. The psychoanalytic conception of hysteria is illustrated with the help of a case which may serve as a paradigm. Summary (abbreviated) : Certain precocious sexual activities of a more or less perverse nature grow up on a constitutional basis. At puberty, the fantasies tend in a direction constellated by the infantile sexual activity. The fantasies lead to the formation of complexes of ideas that are incompatible with the other contents of consciousness and are therefore repressed. This repression takes with it the transference of libido to a love-object, thus precipitating a great emotional conflict which then provides occasion for the outbreak of actual illness.

957 ———. "Associations d'idées familiales"[8] (avec 5 graphiques), *Archives de psychologie,* VII (1907). — With the help of Fürst's material (see *Diagnostische Assoziationsstudien,* X) the author evaluates the average difference between various types of association. The results are given in percentages, with graphs.

958 ———. "L'analyse des rêves,"[9] *Année psychologique,* published by Alfred Binet, V (1909), 160ff. — Outline of the elements of Freud's interpretation of dreams, based on examples from the author's own experience.

959 ———. *Über die Psychologie der Dementia praecox.*[10] Halle, 1907. — The book consists of five chapters:
I. Critical survey of theoretical views on the psychology of dementia praecox, as found in the literature up to 1909. In general, a central disturbance is assumed, given different names by different authors, some of whom also mention "fixation" and the "splitting-off of sequences of ideas." Freud was the first to demonstrate the psychogenic mechanism of paranoid dementia.
II. The feeling-toned complex and its general effects on the psyche. A distinction is made between the acute and the chronic effects of the complex, i.e., between the immediate and long-lasting assimilation of its contents.
III. The influence of the feeling-toned complex on the valency of associations. This question is discussed in some detail, the main

[8] [Omitted from the Collected Works. See C.W., vol. 2, par. 999, n. 1.]
[9] [= "The Analysis of Dreams" (C.W., vol. 4).]
[10] [= "The Psychology of Dementia Praecox" (C.W., vol. 3).]

accent falling on the biological problem of working through the complex and of psychological adaptation to the environment.

IV. Dementia praecox and hysteria: a parallel. A comprehensive description of the similarities and differences of both diseases. Summary: Hysteria contains as its innermost core a complex that can never be overcome completely, though the possibility of overcoming it is present *in potentia*. Dementia contains a complex that has become permanently fixed and can never be overcome.

V. Analysis of a case of paranoid dementia as a paradigm. An absolutely typical case of an elderly patient, presumed to be imbecilic, who produced masses of neologisms that could be satisfactorily explained under analysis and confirm the content of the preceding chapters.

960   The book has been translated into English by Peterson and Brill, with an introduction by the translators. Title: C. G. Jung: *The Psychology of Dementia Praecox.* Nervous and Mental Diseases Monograph Series No. 3. Authorized translation with an introduction by Frederick Peterson, M.D., and A. A. Brill, Ph.B., M.D. New York, 1909.

961   ———. *Diagnostische Assoziationsstudien.* Beiträge zur experimentellen Psychopathologie. Edited by C. G. Jung. Vol. I. [Leipzig,] 1906.[11] — This volume contains a selection of works from the Zurich Clinic on association and the association experiment which were previously published separately in the *Journal für Psychologie und Neurologie.* Quite apart from their psychological viewpoint, these works are of practical and medical interest because it was from these researches that the diagnostic association experiment was developed, an experiment which furnishes us with a quick and certain clue to the most important of the complexes. The diagnostic use of the experiment is of primary importance; of secondary importance is its use as a clinical aid to differential diagnosis in very many cases where the diagnosis is still uncertain. [Contents as follows.]

962   Preface: by Professor Bleuler: "Über die Bedeutung von Assoziationsversuchen," pp. 1–6. — Verbal association is one of the few psychological products that can be evaluated experimentally. Much

---

[11] [Jung also abstracted Vol. I of the *Diagnostische Assoziationsstudien* in *L'Année psychologique* (Paris), XIV (1908), 453–55, at the invitation of its editor, Alfred Binet. (See *The Freud/Jung Letters,* 59J and n. 2.) As the abstracts are similar to, but briefer than, those translated here, they are omitted.]

may be expected from these experiments because the whole psychic past and present, with all their experiences and aspirations, are reflected in the associative activity. It is an "index of all psychic processes, and we need only decipher it in order to know the whole man."

963   I. C. G. Jung and Franz Riklin (Zurich): "Experimentelle Untersuchungen über Assoziationen Gesunder,"[12] pp. 7–145. — The aim of this paper was to collect and present a large amount of associations of normal subjects. In order to evaluate the material statistically, a system of classification was needed that would represent an extension and improvement of the Kraepelin-Aschaffenburg system. The system adopted by the two authors follows logical linguistic principles and allows a statistical evaluation which, though imperfect, is nevertheless sufficient for present purposes. The first question to be discussed was whether and if so what types of reaction occur in the normal state. It was found that, on average, educated subjects exhibit a shallower type of reaction than do the uneducated; further, that the subjects fall into two main types, which shade off into each other: an objective and an egocentric type. The first reacts with few signs of emotion, the second with many. The second type is of particular interest from the practical standpoint and falls into two further subdivisions: the so-called constellation or *complex-constellation type* and the *predicate type*. The first tries to suppress emotions, the second to display them.

964   Fatigue, somnolence, alcoholic intoxication, and mania produce a shallow type of reaction. The shallowness is due primarily to disturbance of attention in these states. This was proved by conducting a special experiment designed to distract the subject's attention and then continuing the association test under these conditions. The experiments yielded positive results.

965   II. K. Wehrlin (Zurich): "Über die Assoziationen von Imbezillen und Idioten," pp. 146–174. — The author reports the results of his association experiments with 13 imbeciles. The associations of the most feeble-minded exhibit a distinct type known as the *definition type*. Characteristic reactions:

Winter: consists of snow.
Singing: consists of notes and song-books.

[12] [= "The Associations of Normal Subjects" (C.W., vol. 2.]

Father: member beside the mother.
Cherry: a garden thing.

966   Imbeciles thus display an extraordinarily intense attitude to the intellectual meaning of the stimulus word. It is characteristic that this type is found precisely among the feeble-minded.

967   III. C. G. Jung: "Analyse der Assoziationen eines Epileptikers,"[13] pp. 175–92. — The associations of this epileptic clearly belong to the definition type, having an awkward and cumbersome character that confirms and supplements the subject's own reaction:

Fruit: that is a fruit, a fruity fruit.
Strong: am powerful, that's strong.
Jolly: I'm jolly, I'm merry.

968   There are also an extraordinary number of feeling-toned, egocentric associations that are expressed undisguised. Certain indications support the conjecture that the epileptic feeling-tone has a markedly perseverating character.

969   IV. C. G. Jung: "Über das Verhalten der Reaktionszeit beim Assoziationsexperimente,"[14] pp. 193–228. — The hitherto unknown reasons for the abnormal prolongation of certain reaction-times are here investigated, with the following results: Educated subjects react, on average, quicker than the uneducated. Reaction-time of female subjects is, on average, considerably longer than that of male subjects. The grammatical quality of the stimulus word has a definite influence on reaction-time, and so has the logical linguistic quality of the association. *Reaction-times exceeding the probable mean are for the most part caused by the interference of an unconscious (repressed) complex.* Hence they are an important aid in the discovery of repressed complexes. This is documented with numerous examples of analyses of associations that have been constellated in this way.

970   V. E. Bleuler: "Bewusstsein und Assoziation," pp. 229–57. — Drawing upon literary as well as case material, this paper sets out to prove that "so far as has been observed, no sharp distinction can be made between conscious and unconscious," and that the

[13] [= "An Analysis of the Associations of an Epileptic" (ibid.).]
[14] [= "The Reaction-Time Ratio in the Association Experiment" (ibid.).]

same functional structures and mechanisms that we find in our consciousness can be shown to exist outside it and to influence the psyche just as much as the analogous conscious processes. "In this sense there are unconscious sensations, perceptions, conclusions, feelings, fears and hopes, which differ from their conscious counterparts only because the quality of consciousness is absent." B. cites in particular the cases of multiple personality and remarks that we should not speak merely of *an* unconscious, but that an almost infinite number of different unconscious groupings is possible. The grouping of memory elements into different personalities is due without exception to the overriding influence of affects.

971   B. regards the quality of consciousness as something subsidiary, since psychic processes need to become conscious only under certain conditions, that is to say when they enter into association with "those ideas, sensations, strivings which at a given moment constitute our personality."

972   VI. Jung: "Psychoanalyse und Assoziationsexperiment,"[15] pp. 258–81. — This paper still shows the strong influence of the original Breuer-Freud theory of neurosis, namely, the theory of the psychic trauma. Neurotic symptoms are essentially symbols of repressed complexes. Disturbed reactions in the association experiment reveal the words and things that lead directly to the unknown complex. Thus far the experiment can be a valuable aid in analysis. This possibility is discussed by means of a practical example, a case of obsessional neurosis. The building up of disturbed reactions into a legend proves the existence of an extensive erotic complex containing a number of individual determinants. In this way we gain a deep insight into the actual personality. Subsequent psychoanalysis justified the expectations the association experiment had aroused, thus bearing out the conclusion that the experiment renders the complex hidden behind the neurotic symptoms accessible to investigation. Every neurosis harbours a complex that exerts considerable influence on the experiment and, as countless experiences show, it must have a causal significance.

*

Contributions VII to XI have now been published in Vol. II of *Diagnostische Assoziationsstudien:*

[15] [= "Psychoanalysis and Association Experiments" (ibid.).]

973   VII. Riklin: "Kasuistische Beiträge zur Kenntnis hysterischer Assoziationsphänomene," pp. 1–30. — The author examines the association phenomena in eight hysterics and comes to the following conclusions: The hysterical type of reaction is dominated by more or less autonomous complexes of great affective power, the development of which seems to be much more pronounced than with normal subjects. One or the other complex dominates the reaction to the exclusion of everything else, so that the experiment is thickly studded with complex-disturbances. Domination by one complex is the hallmark of hysterical psychology; it is probable that all the symptoms can be derived directly from the complex.

974   VIII. Jung: "Assoziation, Traum und hysterisches Symptom,"[16] pp. 31–66. — This paper undertakes to describe and to determine the various ways in which the erotic complex manifests itself in a case of hysteria. First, analysis of the associations shows how they are constellated by the erotic complex, then follows an analysis of its transformations in a dream-series, and finally the complex is shown to be the root of the neurosis as well. In hysteria the complex possesses an abnormal degree of autonomy and tends to lead an active existence on its own, which progressively diminishes and replaces the power of the ego-complex. In this way a new, pathological personality comes into being, whose inclinations, judgments, and decisions tend only in the direction of the pathological will. The second personality consumes the normal ego-remnant and forces it into the role of a secondary (controlled) complex.

975   IX. Jung: "Über die Reproduktionsstörungen beim Assoziationsexperiment,"[17] pp. 67–76. — The subject of this paper is the reproduction method discussed above (Jung, "Experimentelle Beobachtungen über das Erinnerungsvermögen"). On the basis of extensive pathological material it is shown that a faultily reproduced association has a reaction-time that exceeds the mean for the experiment, and exhibits an average of more than twice as many complex-indicators as a correctly reproduced association. From this it is evident that disturbance of reproduction is another indicator for the interference of a complex.

976   X. Emma Fürst (Schaffhausen): "Statistische Untersuchungen über Wortassoziationen und über familiäre Überstimmung im

[16] [= "Association, Dream, and Hysterical Symptom" (ibid.).]
[17] [= "Disturbances of Reproduction in the Association Experiment" (ibid.).]

Reaktiontypus bei Ungebildeten," pp. 77–112. — Association experiments were made with 24 families totalling 100 subjects; this interim paper presents the results of the evaluation of only 9 of the uneducated families consisting of 37 subjects. Evaluation of the remaining material is not yet complete.

977   It was found that husbands tend to produce rather more outer associations than their wives, and sons rather more than their sisters. 54% of the subjects, predominantly women, were pronounced predicate-types. The tendency to form value-judgments is greater in age than in youth; with women it begins at 40 and with men at 60. Relatives have a tendency to conform in reaction type to concordance of associations. The most striking and most regular conformity occurs between parents and children of the same sex.

978   XI. Ludwig Binswanger (Kreuzlingen): "Über das Verhalten des psychogalvanischen Phänomens beim Assoziationsexperiment," pp. 113–95. [Abstract, by Binswanger, omitted.]

*

The following works of the Zurich Clinic are concerned with the diagnostic use of the association experiment:

979   Jung: *Die psychologische Diagnose des Tatbestandes.*[18] Halle, 1906. — General description and interpretation of the experiment. Practical application to a case of theft.

980   ———. "Le nuove vedute della psicologia criminale. Contributo al metodo della 'Diagnosi della conoscenza del fatto,' "[19] *Rivista di psicologia applicata,* IV (1908), pp. 285–304. — Practical application to an actual case of theft with several suspects.

981   Philipp Stein (Budapest): "Tatbestandsdiagnostische Versuche bei Untersuchungsgefangenen," *Zeitschrift für Psychologie und Physiologie der Sinnesorgane,* 1909. — Investigation of factual evidence presented by guilty, suspected, and innocent persons. The material was collected partly from the Psychiatric Clinic and partly from prisoners held in detention in Zurich, and is of particular interest as stemming from the living reality of criminal practice.

*

[18] [= "The Psychological Diagnosis of Evidence" (ibid.).]
[19] [= "New Aspects of Criminal Psychology" (ibid., appendix).]

982   Jung: *Der Inhalt der Psychose.*[20] (Freuds Schriften zur angewandten Seelenkunde, No. 3, 1908). — This paper, an academic
lecture, discusses the great change which the introduction of Freudian psychology has wrought in our psychological conception of the
psychoses. First a simple account is given of the switch from the
anatomical to the psychological approach; then follows an outline
of the psychological structure of dementia praecox, illustrated by
a number of concrete cases. The paper does not purport to be anything more than an introduction to the modern problems of psychological psychiatry. It was published in Russian and Polish in 1909.

983   Ladame (Geneva): "L'association des idées et son utilisation
comme méthode d'examen dans les maladies mentales," *L'Encé-
phale, journal mensuel de neurologie et de psychiatrie,* No. 8,
(1908). — Extremely objective account of the results of association
studies.

984   ———. Review of Jung's *Psychologie der Dementia praecox.
Archives de psychologie,* IX (1909), 76. — The author summarizes
the content of the book in some detail, but refrains from criticism
and only adds the following passage at the end: "In conclusion,
let us remark how fruitful attempts of this kind . . . are. After reading them it is impossible to go to sleep again mentally and to take
a calm or desultory view of the innumerable dementia praecox
patients who inhabit our asylums. One feels irresistibly compelled
to look for something else behind the banal symptoms of psychosis,
to discover the individual himself and his normal and abnormal
personality."

985   Alphonse Maeder (Zurich): I. "Contributions à la psychopathologie de la vie quotidienne," *Archives de psychologie,* VI. — II.
"Nouvelles contributions à la psychopathologie," *Archives de psychologie,* VII. (I) Simple analyses of Freudian slips of the tongue,
forgetting, *faux pas,* demonstrating the existence of a repressed idea
with negative feeling-tone. (II) The author gives examples of various kinds of forgetting caused by "isolation" and "derivation," discusses abreaction ("décharge émotionnelle") in relation to the concept of the complex, and offers evidence of dissociation in normal
persons, including the mechanisms of displacement, "irradiation"
and identification. Attention is drawn to "automatismes musicaux"

[20] [= "The Content of the Psychoses" (C.W., vol. 3).]

and to the indirect means of expression employed by the unconscious. The author stresses the fruitfulness of this branch of
psychopathology.

986 ———. "Essai d'interprétation de quelques rêves," *Archives de
psychologie,* VI. — A short introductory account of Freud's theory
of dream interpretation and of psychoanalysis, illustrated by four
of the author's dream analyses. He shows that the same symbols
are frequently employed in dreams, legends, and myths in exactly
the same way (notably the snake, dog, bird, garden, house, box).

987 ———. "Die Symbolik in den Legenden, Märchen, Gebräuchen
und Träumen," *Psychiatrisch-neurologische Wochenschrift,*
X. — Thinking in symbols is an inferior stage of association that
equates similarity with identity; it is frequently a process of unconscious activity (hence its role in dreams, hallucinations, delusional
ideas, as well as in poetry). Examples are taken from epileptic twilight states. Author discusses the assimilative tendency of the sexual
complex in relation to symbol formation. Interpretation of the fish
as a sexual symbol provides the clue to numerous customs, folk
beliefs (fish on Friday, April fish = April fool, the game on Ash
Wednesday), legends and fairytales (Grimm: "The Golden Fish").

988 ———. *Une voie nouvelle en psychologie.* Coenobium Lugano-
Milano, 1909. — Informative essay on Freudian psychology (excluding psychopathology). By uncovering unconscious motivations,
psychoanalysis provides a coherent view of the way a person thinks
and acts.

989 Disturbances of unconscious activity are discussed with the help
of the author's own analyses. These disturbances should be regarded
as expressions of the unconscious, as revelations of unadmitted tendencies. The gradual transition to the pathological is stressed
throughout. Dreams are intimately connected with the individual's
actual conflicts; they are solutions offered by the unconscious which
are often accepted later on and become realities. Conflicts are due
partly to the stresses of civilization.

990 Section III treats of symbols in dreams, hallucinations, fairytales, and legends, and in ordinary speech. The symbol is a special
form of thought association characterized by its impreciseness: vague
analogies are taken as identities. This is probably typical of the
unconscious: it has something infantile and primitive about it. Sym-

bolisms in popular speech (Rabelais, folklore), in legends, in the language of primitives show affinities with associations under fatigue, in *abaissement du niveau mental,* in symptomatic actions when attention is distracted, in dreams, psychoses, and neuroses.

991   ———. "À propos des Symboles," *Journal de Psychologie normale et pathologique,* 1909. [Abstract, by Maeder, omitted.]

992   Hermann Müller (Zurich) : "Beiträge zur Kenntnis der Hyperemesis Gravidarum," *Psychiatrische-neurologische Wochenschrift,* X. — On the basis of careful clinical observations on a number of cases of hyperemesis[21] the author comes to the following conclusions:

    1. *Vomitus matutinus gravidarum* is a psychogenic symptom.

    2. Hyperemesis is in the majority of cases psychogenic.

993   Although the author does not put forward any complete analysis, in several of his cases he makes psychological insight possible. Attention is paid throughout to the views of the Freudian school.

994   ———. "Ein Fall von induziertem Irresein nebst anschliessenden Erörterungem," *Psychiatrisch-neurologische Wochenschrift, XI.* — A case of religious exaltation in a female religious fanatic induced a psychosis in a female hysteric who lived with her, by reason of the "same aetiological demand." The presentation of the two cases is elegant and lucid, thanks to the application of Freudian analysis.

995   Oskar Pfister (Zurich) : "Wahnvorstellung und Schülerselbstmord. Auf Grund einer Traumanalyse beleuchtet," *Schweizerische Blätter für Schulgesundheitspflege,* I (1909). — "Psychoanalytische Seelsorge und experimentelle Moralpädogogik," *Protestantische Monatshefte,* I (1909). — "Ein Fall von psychoanalytischer Seelsorge und Seelenheilung," *Evangelische Freiheit. Monatsschrift für die kirchliche Praxis in der gegenwärtigen Kultur,* II–V (1909). [Abstract, by Pfister, covering all three items, omitted.]

996   Pototsky (Berlin) : "Die Verwertbarkeit des Assoziationsversuches für die Beurteilung der traumatischen Neurosen," *Monatsschrift für Psychiatrie und Neurologie,* XXV, pp. 521ff. — The

—————
[21] [Excessive vomiting in pregnancy.]

author applied the association experiment to two patients with neuroses due to an accident. In the first case there was an overwhelming predominance of the compensation complex, in the second a striking absence of the same complex. Prognostic conclusions are drawn from these findings.

997   Frank Riklin (Zurich): "Hebung epileptischer Amnesien durch Hypnose," *Journ. f. Psychol. u. Neurol.,* I:5/6 (1903). — The author's success in clearing up the amnesias of epileptics under hypnosis demonstrates their affinity with hysterical amnesias. Association experiments of clinical, diagnostic interest are also reported.

998   ——. "Zur Anwendung der Hypnose bei epileptischen Amnesien," *Journ. f. Psychol. u. Neurol.,* II (1903). — Report of another case with epileptic twilight states and disappearance of amnesia, though it is to be regretted that no analysis is given of their content. During these states the patient lovingly stroked a cat, and sometimes a goat too. It has since been brought to my knowledge that this scene was a fragment of an infantile erotic experience.

999   ——. "Zur Psychologie hysterischer Dämmerzustände und des Ganserschen Symptoms," *Psychiatrisch-neurologische Wochenschrift,* No. 22 (1904). — Ganser has described the symptom of "irrelevant talk" in hysterical twilight states. Subsequently, the concept of Ganser's symptom has been taken by various authors (Raecke in particular) now in a broader and now in a narrower sense. Further, it was maintained that the symptom is exclusively associated with the outbreak of twilight states among prisoners in detention. The psychological affinity between the irrelevant talk of hysterics and the mechanism of simulation forced itself upon these authors largely because of this fact. Jung ("Ein Fall von hysterischem Stupor bei einer Untersuchungsgefangenen," *Journ. f. Psychol. u. Neurol.,* I, 1902) was the first to place the problem on the footing of Freudian psychology, thus facilitating the correct evaluation and interpretation of Ganser's symptom and the twilight state.[21a]

1000   The paper reports four cases of hysterical twilight states with Ganser's symptom. Only one of them was a prisoner in detention, the others not. The psychic situation of the detainee is exceptional: he is driven into a corner, gives false answers, tells lies, and in an

[21a] [Cf. "A Case of Hysterical Stupor in a Prisoner in Detention," pars. 278ff.]

extremity of distress falls into a twilight state; and only under these conditions will the symptom of "automatized simulation," of not knowing and not understanding, come markedly to the fore. The general situation at the onset of Ganser's twilight state is that a painful event is immediately repressed and thrust into oblivion because it is incompatible with the other contents of consciousness. The motive of not knowing or of not wanting to know produces the symptom of irrelevant talk. Disturbance of orientation proves to be a wish not to be oriented in regard to the existing situation. In twilight states, not knowing can also be replaced by compensatory wish-fantasies. The pronounced "restriction of consciousness" serves to split off the intolerably painful idea and to allow the emergence of censored, wish-fulfilling situations.

1001 ———. "Analytische Untersuchungen der Symptome und Assoziationen eines Falles von Hysterie," *Psychiatrisch-neurologische Wochenschrift,* No. 46 (1905). — For the main part the analysis stems from the year 1902–3 and concerns a typical, severe case of conversion hysteria. At that time the Breuer-Freud *Studien über Hysterie* still served as a theoretical and technical model. The therapeutic results must be rated very good; during the 6–7 years since then, the patient's physical symptoms have come back only occasionally. Her personality, however, shows signs of moral deterioration. Nowadays, perhaps, we would no longer have the courage or the desire to analyse a personality of so little value and so poorly developed, and with so few hopes for the future. The results are therefore to be rated all the more highly. An important contributory factor was the transference to the analyst. While the author found that abreaction was not sufficient to account for the therapeutic result, he was handicapped by insufficient knowledge of the nature of the transference.

1002 At the time of the analysis the author was also not familiar enough with dream interpretation to derive much benefit from it.

1003 The structure of the symptoms was analysed and a number of psychic traumata were discovered. The patient's early childhood received scant attention; on the other hand the mechanism by which hysterical ailments of the body are produced is amply documented.

1004 One section of the book is devoted to association experiments. At that time it was of great importance to show that the same mechanisms are at work in the association experiment as those which produce hysterical phenomena, and that the laws governing the effects of the complex are the same in the experiment as in normal persons, but only emerge with greater clarity.

1005 Another section is concerned with the association mechanism leading to conversion hysteria and with the theory of abreaction. The author was keenly aware of the gap between theory and fact, which has since been filled by introducing the concepts of transference, libido, and infantile sexuality.

1006 ———. *Die diagnostische Bedeutung von Assoziationsversuchen bei Hysterischen.* — Lecture delivered at the 35th meeting of the Society for Swiss Psychiatrists in St. Urban, 1904. Abstract in the annual report of the Society and in the *Psychiatrisch-neurologische Wochenschrift*, No. 29 (1904).

1007 ———. "Über Versetzungsbesserungen," *Psychiatrisch-neurologische Wochenschrift*, Nos. 16/18 (1905). — The opening of the annexes to the Rheinau Sanatorium (Canton Zurich) affords an opportunity to observe the effect of transferring mentally ill patients from one institution to another. The observations relate to 85 patients of whom the author has previous knowledge at the Burghölzli. In more than half the cases an improvement was noted.

1008 Adaptation to reality is helped by greater freedom of movement and, above all, by work therapy. Especially in the commonest disease, dementia praecox, this draws the patient out of his introversion and transfers his interest to reality. In order to show how the patients assimilate their new milieu, the author briefly discusses the psychological significance of the most important symptoms of this disease (negativism, blocking, wish-fulfilment in delusional ideas, servant-girl psychoses, fertility symbols, mistaken identity due to complexes, religious delusions as translation of wish fantasies into paranoid ideas; their elaboration, condensation, stereotypization, cathexis of the motor apparatus by complex-automatisms).

1009 The best results are obtained through the exercise of complexes of ideas and functions that have remained normal. Equally effective are early discharge, replacement whenever possible of bed treatment, which only accentuates introversion and "dreaminess," by work therapy which draws the patients out of themselves.

1010 With the aid of two case histories it is shown how the introversion comes about, where the transference of interest to the outside world fails, and how the process of introversion goes much further than simple wish-fulfilment in fantasy would require. In the second case even the attempt at wish-fulfilment in reality was unable to check the introversion; the unconscious produced ideas of self-destruction to which the patient succumbed by committing suicide.

1011 In about half the cases the transfer had no noticeable influence.

1012 The effects of the transfer are illustrated by a series of excerpts from case histories analytically interpreted.

1013 ———. "Beitrag zur Psychologie der kataleptischen Zustände bei Katatonie," *Psychiatrisch-neurologische Wochenschrift,* Nos. 32/33 (1906). — The author succeeded in making contact with a catatonic while in a severe cataleptic state and in discovering something of what was going on in this state. We learn from the anamnesis that this condition set in after a psychosis lasting for four years. The psychosis first manifested itself in the patient's autoerotic self-aggrandizement from the age of 18. He tried to win the hand of a relative's rich daughter, completely ignoring the impossibility of doing so. Despite being rebuffed he continued to press his suit undeterred. Cataleptic symptoms were already present on his admission to the clinic, along with a persistent tendency to break out and get to his cousin.

1014 The patient's condition can be outlined as follows: underlying the catalepsy is a powerful tendency to sleep, to "be a dead man," as was evident from the patient's own statements. The result of this tendency resembles natural sleep, but actually it is more like hypnotic sleep. It is motivated by the repression of a complex, a wish to forget.

1015 Although the author succeeded in breaking through this sleep tendency, the breakthrough was not complete, so that, side by side with adequate discharge of affect, for instance weeping over the utter hopelessness of ever reaching the beloved, a peculiar compromise between the discharge of affect and the sleep tendency could be observed in the patient's facial expression and demeanour. The two components were sometimes divided into the two halves of the face: one side weeping, one eye open. Keeping the eyes open meant rapport with the investigator; closing the eyes meant breaking off the rapport and the victory of the tendency to sleep or forget.

1016 Throughout the investigation the thought perseverated, "I am going to marry Emma C.," or "I love Emma C.," counterbalanced by another thought which maintains the sleep tendency as a protective factor and which voices the cousin's reply, "Don't expect anything of the future."

1017 The patient readily imagined wish-fulfilling situations in which he believed his beloved was standing before him, went towards her, tried to embrace her, took other persons present (doctor, warder) as substitutes (mistaken identity), but always through the veil of cataleptic sleep.

1018 Through this veil it is possible to perceive quite adequate and profound discharges of affect.

1019 Evaluation of the questions and modes of reaction follows the laws of complex-reactions in the association experiment.

1020 This study suggests that the catatonic phenomena in dementia praecox have in general the significance attributed to them in the present case.

1021 ———. "Über Gefängnispsychosen," *Psychiatrisch-neurologische Wochenschrift,* XI, Nos. 30/37. — An attempt to explain and classify the clinical pictures of prison psychosis along psychoanalytic lines. Prison is a psychological situation which, despite differences of constitution in the diagnostic sense, releases psychological and pathological reactions that are more or less uniform.

1022 ———. "Psychologie und Sexualsymbolik der Märchen," *Psychiatrisch-neurologische Wochenschrift,* IX, Nos. 22/24. — Excerpts from the author's major work: *Wunscherfüllung und Symbolik im Märchen.*

———. *Wunscherfüllung und Symbolik im Märchen.* (Schriften zur angewandten Seelenkunde, edited by Freud, No. 2, 1908.) [Abstract, by Riklin, omitted.]

1023 Schnyder (Bern): *Définition et nature de l'hystérie.* (Congrès des médecins aliénistes et neurologistes de France et des pays de langue française, XVIIième Session.) Geneva, 1907. — The doctrinal tenets of a wide-ranging literature are scrutinized in this volume. Among the reviews there is an objective account of the Breuer-Freud method, as well as of the theory of complexes. Schnyder rejects the modern viewpoints. "The ideas of Freud and his partisans are certainly an important contribution to the solution of the problem of hysteria. However, the sage of Vienna might be reproached for having introduced an arbitrary mechanization into the psychological conception of hysteria, and for relying on hypotheses which, however ingenious, are of too subjective a nature to lay claim to incontestable scientific value."

1024   Schwarzwald (Lausanne): "Beitrag zur Psychopathologie der hysterischen Dämmerzustände und Automatismen," *Journ. f. Psychol. u. Neurol.,* XV (1909). — Investigation of a psychogenic twilight state in which the patient set fire to his house. The material allows glimpses into the psychological mechanism of the deed and of the case itself. The infantile history is unfortunately incomplete, but the author is mistaken in dispensing entirely with infantile development. The patient's childhood is of the greatest importance for the subsequent development of neurosis, at least as great as the situation at the moment, if not greater.

1025   A refining of his psychoanalytic technique would convince the author of the soundness of this view. The dream of "Tom Thumb" which the patient had the day before the incendiarism is very significant and clearly indicates that the act was determined by infantile reminiscences. This has escaped the attention of the author. Analysis of childhood and the correct evaluation of its results is one of the most difficult parts of the psychoanalytical technique, particularly for the beginner.

Editorial Note

[Jung contributed several abstracts to the periodical *Folia neuro-biologica* (Leipzig),[22] for which he was an editorial consultant. As these are summaries without critical comment, they are not translated but merely listed here:

In Vol. I:3 (1908):

(388) Jung, C. G. "Associations d'idées familiales," *Archives de psychologie,* VII:26 (1907).

(389) Metral, M. "Expériences scolaires sur la mémoire de l'orthographe," ibid.

(394) Lombard, Emile. "Essai d'une classification des phénomènes de glossolalie," ibid., VII:25 (1907).

(395) Claparède, Ed. "Quelques mots sur la définition de l'hystérie," ibid., VII:26 (1907). [See above, par. 943.]

(396) Flournoy, Th. "Automatisme téléologique antisuicide. Un cas de suicide empêché par une hallucination," ibid.

[22] [For Freud's disparagement of this journal, see *The Freud/Jung Letters,* 55F and n. 3.]

(397) Leroy, E.-Bernard. "Escroquerie et hypnose. Escroqueries prolongées pendant plusiers mois à l'acide de manoeuvres hypnotiques pratiquées sur une des victimes," ibid.

(398) Lemaître, Aug. "Un nouveau cycle somnambulique de Mlle Smith. Les peintures réligieuses," ibid., VII:25 (1907).

In Vol. II:1 (1908) :

(122) Piéron, H. "La Théorie des émotions et les données actuelles de la physiologie," *Journal de psychologie normal et pathologique,* IV–V (1907–8).

(123) Revault d'Allones, G. "L'Explication physiologique de l'émotion," ibid.

(124) Hartenberg, P. "Principe d'une physiognomie scientifique," ibid.

(130) Dumas, G. "Qu'est-ce que la psychologie pathologique?," ibid.

(131) Dromard, G. "De la dissociation de la mimique chez les aliénés," ibid.

(132) Marie, A. "Sur quelques troubles fonctionnels de l'audition chez certains débiles mentaux," ibid.

(133) Janet, P. "Le renversement de l'orientation ou l'allochirie des représentations."

(134) Pascal, Constanza. "Les Maladies mentales de Robert Schumann," ibid.

(135) Vigouroux, A., and Juquelier, P. "Contribution clinique à l'étude des délires du rêve," ibid.

In Vol. II:3 (1908) :

(348) Varendonck, J. "Les idéals des enfants," *Archives de psychologie,* VII:28 (1908).

(349) Claparède, Ed. "Classification et plan des méthodes psychologiques," ibid.

(350) Katzaroff, Dimitre. (Travail du Laboratoire de psychologie de l'Université de Genève.) "Expériences sur le rôle de la récitation comme facteur de la mémorisation," ibid.

(351) Maeder, Alphonse. "Nouvelles contributions à la psychopathologie de la vie quotidienne," ibid., VII:27 (1908). [See above, par. 985.]

(352) Rouma, Georges. "Un cas de mythomanie, Contribution à l'étude du mensonge et de la fabulation chez l'enfant," ibid.

EDITORS.]

REVIEW OF HITSCHMANN:
"FREUD'S NEUROSENLEHRE"[1]

1026   Hitschmann's book meets a longfelt need. A book that introduces the beginner to the problems of psychoanalysis in a clear and simple way has long been wanted. Hitschmann has fulfilled this task most satisfactorily. It cannot have been easy to present the manifold discoveries and conclusions of psychoanalysis in systematic order, for, contrary to the prejudices of our opponents, it is not at all a question of a preconceived system that puts no difficulties in the way of further theoretical development, but of extraordinarily complicated material that throws into relief the whole laboriousness of patient empirical research (only, of course, if one works in this field oneself.) The content of the book is very diverse but in no way confusing. The author has confined himself to essentials and, where the problems are still fluid, has been satisfied with hints. He has thus succeeded in painting an excellent picture of the present state of psychoanalysis and its far-reaching problems. It is to be hoped that the book will reach the widest possible public, not least because it will dispel numerous prejudices and false opinions which have arisen among medical men through inadequate knowledge of the literature. We must also hope that it will soon be translated into foreign languages, for which purpose it is better suited than many original researches which are so specialized that they are difficult to understand.

[1] [*Jahrbuch für psychoanalytische und psychopathologische Forschungen,* III:1 (1911), 480. Eduard Hitschmann, *Freuds Neurosenlehre; nach ihrem gegenwärtigen Stande zusammenfassend dargestellt* ("Freud's Theory of Neurosis: a Comprehensive Interpretation of Its Present Status") (Leipzig and Vienna, 1911). See *The Freud/Jung Letters,* 194F, n. 3.]

ANNUAL REPORT (1910/11) BY THE PRESIDENT OF THE INTERNATIONAL PSYCHOANALYTIC ASSOCIATION[1]

1027   A year and a half ago at the Congress in Nuremberg it was decided to establish an International Association; the foundation of local branches in Vienna, Berlin, and Zurich followed in quick succession. The Berlin branch, with nine members, was set up in March 1910, with Dr. Abraham[2] as chairman; Vienna followed in April with twenty-four members, under the chairmanship of Dr. Adler.[3] Zurich was established in June with nineteen members, under Dr. Binswanger[4] as chairman. These branches formed the base of our International Psychoanalytic Association, though with its fifty-two members in three countries it was still a tender shoot. With great pleasure and satisfaction I now can announce that in the past year our Association has led a most vigorous life. In February the seed planted in America sprouted. A local branch was established in New York with twenty-one members under the chairmanship of Dr. Brill.[5] And at long last South Germany joined in: the Munich branch was established in March with six members under Dr. Seif[6] as chairman.

1028   During 1911 the respective memberships grew as follows: Berlin, from 9 to 12; Vienna, from 24 to 38; Zurich, from 19 to

[1] [(Translated by W. S.) Part of the Report on the Third Psychoanalytic Congress, Weimar, 21–22 Sept. 1911, in the *Bulletin,* or *Korrespondenzblatt der internationalen psychoanalytischen Vereinigung,* in *Zentralblatt für Psychoanalyse* (Wiesbaden), II:3 (Dec. 1911), 233–34. Jung had been elected president of the International Psychoanalytic Association upon its founding at the Second Psychoanalytic Congress at Nuremberg, 30–31 Mar. 1910. For the Congress programmes, see *The Freud/Jung Letters,* appendix 4, pp. 473–76.]

[2] [Karl Abraham: see *The Freud/Jung Letters,* 35J, n. 7.]

[3] [Alfred Adler: see ibid., 20F, n. 5, and 260F, n. 3. Adler had resigned from the Vienna Society the previous June, but his resignation was not officially announced until 11 Oct. 1911.]

[4] [Ludwig Binswanger: see ibid., 16J, n. 1.]

[5] [Abraham A. Brill: see ibid., 69J, n. 2, and 238F, n. 4.]

[6] [Leonhard Seif: see ibid., 137J, n. 1.]

29. Thus the total membership rose from 52 to 106. In other words, we have slightly more than doubled.

1029   The Zurich group is deeply grateful to the stimulus provided by Freud's scientific theories. It may to some extent lessen our debt of gratitude if we may be allowed to point out that the founders of the branches in Berlin, Munich, and New York have come out of the Zurich school.

1030   This encouraging proliferation in the outside world is matched by the teeming scientific activity within the sections. I refer to the variety of topics on which lectures were given in the individual groups. Positive contributions to our scientific problems, however, can be expected only when an individual member's rich experience is brought to bear on the solution of the problem adduced. In general, such an ideal condition is difficult to bring about; specifically, groups with comparatively recent local traditions will consider it their foremost goal to instruct and educate their members. At this time psychoanalysis demands of anybody who wants to master it an uncommon amount of industry and scientific concentration, if it is to be more than the free-wheeling exercise of highly individualized talents. The temptation to eschew empirical evidence is very strong in psychoanalytic work, especially since scientific *pseudo-exactitude,* like all cultural absurdities, collapses before the gaze of the analysand into its own nothingness. Yet, this does not do away with the need for systematic planning of scientific research and exposition, which must be well conceived and immediately convincing. We who are favoured with taking possession of these newly discovered territories are obliged to use self-discipline so as to prevent these goods from being jeopardized by an unbridled imagination. Let us never forget that everything we conceive and create is well conceived and well created only when it is addressed to mankind in a humanly intelligible language. What fate expects of us is that we faithfully husband the enormous store of knowledge provided by Freud's discoveries and pass it on to our fellow men, rather than pervert it for the gratification of our own ambitions. This task requires from each of us not only a high degree of self-criticism, but also a thorough psychoanalytic training. We know well that this training is hard to come by in isolation; it is easier to obtain it when many different heads work together. This task of teaching and training is one of the main purposes of the branches of our Association, and I should like to recommend it to the local chairmen with special emphasis. Next to the results of new research, discussions of elementary questions should be on the agenda of local meetings; they would enable younger members to acquire knowledge of fundamental ideas and principles with which a thorough familiarity is the *sine qua non* of the scientific method. Such basic discussions would make it possible to dispose of many theoretical and practical misconceptions. And it seems to me of great importance to expose deviations of opinion to immediate and thorough discussion in order to forestall any squandering of our strength on pointless side-issues. This possibility, as the events in Vienna[7] have shown, lies not so far afield, inasmuch as the present unbridled ways of psychoanalytic investigation and the multitude of problems that are touched upon encourage changes, as revolutionary as they are unjustified, in the principles of neurosis theory that Freud discovered and elaborated in decades of hard work. I believe, vis-à-vis such temptations, that we must never forget that our Association also has the important purpose of discrediting "wild" psychoanalysis and not admitting it to its own ranks. We need not fear that dogmatism—long desired by our opponents—would surely invade psychoanalysis; but it rather means that we are holding tightly to the principles we have gained and to which we will adhere until they have been either entirely confirmed or else recognized as wholly false.

1031 After these remarks and wishes concerning the cultivation of our science in the local branches, I must also call your attention to the publishing activities in the psychoanalytic field. The past year has seen the *Zentralblatt für Psychoanalyse*[8] added to the *Jahrbuch;* under its alert editorship the new journal has already published a great deal of material and by its variety rendered a good account of the variety of psychoanalysis. Next year a further organ will be added,[9] of a more general rather than strictly medical character.

1032 This year I have witnessed with my own eyes the tremendous

---

[7] [The allusion is to the secession of Adler and several of his followers from the Vienna Society in June.]

[8] [The first issue appeared in Oct. 1910 under the direction of Freud and the joint editorship of Adler and Stekel.]

[9] [*Imago: Zeitschrift für Anwendung der Psychoanalyse auf die Geisteswissenschaften* ("Journal for the Application of Psychoanalysis to the Humanities"), directed by Freud, edited by Otto Rank and Hanns Sachs; its first issue appeared in March 1912.]

impression that the efforts on behalf of our cause have created in the world. Knowledge and appreciation of psychoanalysis are more widespread than is generally assumed.

1033   This past year has brought us in Zurich a loss, a loss of special poignancy for the hopes for our scientific future. It is the death of our friend Honegger,[10] who had recommended himself to the membership by his ingenious paper read at Nuremberg.

[10] [Johann Jakob Honegger, Jr., who committed suicide on 28 Mar. 1911. See *The Freud/Jung Letters*, 148J, n. 2, and 247J; and H. H. Walser, "An Early Psychoanalytical Tragedy," *Spring*, 1974. The "paper read at Nuremberg" has not survived.]

TWO LETTERS ON PSYCHOANALYSIS[1]

10 January 1912

1034   In the communication from Dr. Kesselring and Dr. B. of the Keplerbund, which appeared in this column, exception was taken to the following remark of the reporter: "Dr. Kesselring, as he himself observed, spoke as an opponent of Freud's psychoanalytic method and at the request of the Keplerbund. This Society is opposed to a tendentiously materialistic pursuit of the natural sciences and wishes to combat the erroneous view that scientific knowledge stands in the way of religious belief. Hence the impression which the speaker intended to make upon his audience is perfectly understandable."

1035   In saying this the reporter did not "discredit" Dr. Kesselring's willingness to speak on Freud in the Keplerbund, nor did he discredit the general activity of that Society—he merely stated something that was self-evident. The Keplerbund has the following article in its programme, which it claims is based on a "scientifically and ethically unassailable foundation": "The Keplerbund holds the conviction that the truth contains within itself the harmony of scientific facts with philosophical knowledge and with religious experience." Further: "The Keplerbund differs quite consciously from the materialistic dogma of monism and combats the atheistic propaganda resulting therefrom, which wrongly seeks support in the findings of natural science."

[1] [*Neue Zürcher Zeitung,* on the dates given. Jung's article "Neue Bahnen der Psychologie" ("New Paths in Psychology," C.W., vol. 7, appendix), in *Raschers Jahrbuch für Schweizer Art und Kunst,* 1912 (issued in Dec. 1911), precipitated controversy which led to a public lecture attacking psychoanalysis by Max Kesselring, M.D., a neurologist of Zurich, on 15 Dec. 1911 in the Schwurgerichtssaal, sponsored by the Zurich branch of the Keplerbund. During Jan. 1912 articles in the *Zeitung* by Kesselring and others carried the polemic on; Jung contributed these two. He published an article designed to close the discussion, in *Wissen und Leben* (Zurich), 15 Feb. 1912: "Concerning Psychoanalysis," C.W., vol. 4. The entire controversy is summarized in H. F. Ellenberger, *The Discovery of the Unconscious,* pp. 810–14; see also *The Freud/Jung Letters,* 287J, n. 7; 293F, n. 7; 294J; 295J.]

1036   According to this programme, therefore, the Keplerbund is not merely a champion of enlightenment and popular education, but also a militant organization. Since Freud's teachings likewise stand in sharpest contrast to the "harmony" sought for by the Keplerbund, every thinking person will know that the society must, on its own admission, fight against them. When an organization arranges a lecture, it usually makes sure beforehand of the point of view of the lecturer, no matter whether its interest in the theme is religious, political, artistic, or scientific. Anyone who knows that Dr. Kesselring was a pupil of Freud's must also know—so at least one must assume—that he is Freud's opponent in theory and in practice. Equally, a reporter engaged by the Keplerbund knows that he cannot defend Freud's "pan-sexualism" within its precincts. The reporter, who incidentally is neither a Freudian nor against the Keplerbund, did not credulously rely on the opinions of others, but to the best of his ability oriented himself beforehand on the theme of the lecture, the principles of the Keplerbund, and the views of Dr. Kesselring.

1037   In this same connection a correspondent wrote: "To the amazement of professional people Dr. Kesselring's lecture 'On Psychoanalysis' brought before the public at the Schwurgerichtssaal a recent line of medical research which, among other things, has to include within the scope of its analytical work the most intimate and repulsive of all human fantasies. Disputes over the results of this research are taking a violent form in professional circles, and opinions are very much divided. But however violent the scientific discussion may be, opponents and friends of psychoanalysis are alike agreed that such things, even if only for the sake of good taste, should not be paraded before the public at the Schwurgerichtssaal, quite apart from the fact that even the best educated public can exercise no competent judgment in these matters. One could, with as much right, hold gynaecological examinations at the Schwurgerichtssaal in order to arouse public feeling against some of the findings of medical research."

1038   For the rest, the lecture, whose lack of objectivity must have struck even the layman, contained so many distortions that it seemed designed to spread confusion and error. Those who wish to find out what psychoanalysis is really about are recommended to read Freud's *Über Psychoanalyse*[2] (publ. Deuticke, Vienna and

[2] [Freud's Clark University lectures, pub. by Deuticke 1910; trans. as "Five Lectures on Psychoanalysis" (Standard Edn., XI).]

Leipzig), in which he gives an account of his views and methods in more or less popular language. Reference should also be made to the invaluable work *Die Psychoanalyse Freuds*[3] (Deuticke) by Eugen Bleuler, professor of psychiatry at Zurich, who discusses in an objective and critical way the pros and cons of psychoanalysis. The authority and continental reputation of this excellent scholar should guarantee the educated public a more competent view of psychoanalysis than the statements of Dr. Kesselring.

Dr. J.

17 January 1912

1039   In connection with the article on "Psychoanalysis" that was published in your columns last Saturday, I would like to remark that the concept of sexuality used by Freud and me has a far wider range of meaning than it has in common usage. As I have often pointed out, we understand by "sexuality" all those instinctual forces which extend beyond the domain of the instinct of self-preservation. The scientific justification for this conception cannot be discussed here. It can be read about in Freud's and my writings. Confusion between the common conception and our biological conception of sexuality naturally leads to the greatest misunderstandings.

1040   I further allow myself to remark that it is not permissible to lay at our door all the immature researches that have been undertaken by less qualified persons. We can accept responsibility only for what we ourselves have written, and not for the manifold sins of other writers. One could just as well hold Christianity responsible for the abominations of the Inquisition, if one wished to adopt so summary a procedure. Naturally, I am not thinking of the invaluable researches of Dr. Riklin, with which I am in full agreement, but of the book by Michelsen,[4] mentioned by my critic F. M.,[5] and a number of other writings whose standpoints and method of exposition I must repudiate.

Dr. Jung

---

[3] [Originally in the *Jahrbuch für psychoanalytische und psychopathologische Forschungen*, II:2 (1910). Trans. by C. R. Payne, *Freud's Theories of the Neuroses* (1913).]

[4] [Johann Michelsen, *Ein Wort an geistigen Adel deutscher Nation* (Munich, 1911) (from Ellenberger, p. 877, n. 270).]

[5] [Fritz Marti, literary editor of the *Neue Zürcher Zeitung*, who signed ("F.M.") some of the articles.]

ON THE PSYCHOANALYTIC TREATMENT
OF NERVOUS DISORDERS[1]

1041   Psychoanalysis differs from other psychotherapeutic methods in that, by preference, it takes as its starting point those products of the human psyche which originate outside the selective effect of attention—parapraxes, the seemingly pointless fantasies of daydreaming, nocturnal dreams. The founder of the method, Professor Freud of Vienna, has succeeded in demonstrating from this material the existence of a principle which governs psychic events, the principle of *determination*. These inferior products, accordingly, are not fortuitous, but clearly and demonstrably are causally conditioned, or in psychological terms determined. They are formed under the influence of feeling-toned, unconscious ideas.

1042   The application of the method to the pathological formations of psychoneurotics has shown that these are built up in a similar way, only they are much more complicated. The first formulation of the newly won insights was the trauma theory, as propounded by Breuer and Freud in their *Studies on Hysteria,* published in 1895.

1043   Further investigations showed, however, that the trauma is of less pathological significance than the *conflict,* or rather, that most experiences acquire traumatic force only when they release a conflict within the patient. These conflicts are in the overwhelming majority of cases between sexual wishes (in the widest sense) and opposing tendencies of a moral and aesthetic nature. The result of such conflicts, which affect the emotional life, is a series of pathological processes, mechanisms altogether comparable to the defensive measures which the body puts up against a noxious agent.

1044   To trace these mechanisms is now the task of the therapy, the ultimate aim of which is to free the psyche from the conflict.

1045   In the case of a 35-year-old female hysteric, married, mother

---

[1] [Jung's abstract of a report to the Medical-Pharmaceutical Society of Bern at a meeting on 4 June 1912. The abstract, including the discussion, was published in the *Correspondenzblatt für Schweizer Ärzte,* XLII (1 Oct. 1912), 1079–84. Cf. *The Freud/Jung Letters,* 318J, last par., and 319F, for the "Kreuzlingen episode," which occurred shortly before this occasion.]

of several children, who since her 20th year had exhibited a number of hysterical physical symptoms, psychoanalysis was carried out after numerous other treatments had failed. Three of her symptoms, which all affected the respiratory activity, could be traced back to a trauma at the age of puberty, an attempted rape, when the full impact of the man's body had compressed the thorax. But the ultimate determinant was to be found in the experiences of earliest childhood, when the patient had listened with sexual excitement to the nightly intercourse of her parents. Thus the symptom which seemed like a sudden involuntary expiration with simultaneous closure of the glottis was a repetition of the following scene: her mother once came to her bed, whereupon she started violently and wanted to let out a scream, which she was just able to suppress. These two opposed innervations persisted in the form of the aforesaid symptom.

1046 Now when, as a result of unfavourable experiences, the individual does not obtain sufficient sexual gratification in later life, a process occurs which Freud calls regression: as a substitute for the failure of gratification, the patient reverts to an earlier, infantile one.

1047 This infantile gratification, however, is not re-experienced in its original form, but only in the form of its somatic, physiological concomitant. There is a *conversion* of sexual excitation into somatic-motor excitation.

1048 So with this patient the respiratory disturbance induced by the two opposed innervations became fixated not because of the fright she had received, but because of the sexual excitement that had accompanied her listening.

1049 The onset of the disorder was directly connected with her marriage, which had brought the patient disappointments, so that in intercourse she remained frigid. The libido that was nevertheless present consequently chose the way of regression and led to the reactivation of those past and forgotten experiences of gratification, or rather to their physiological concomitants.

1050 The result of the treatment was that all symptoms disappeared but for a few traces.

[The discussion that followed did not deal specifically with Jung's case. The speakers, including Paul-Charles Dubois, of Bern,[2] recounted cases of their own that had been cured by nonpsychoanalytic means and made various hostile remarks. Jung concluded:]

2 [See ibid., 116F, n. 8.]

1051   It is regrettable that the discussion failed to deal more specifically with the analysis presented here. The method of psychoanalytic research and treatment cannot be rejected as a whole unless
on examination it turns out to be defective, but this was not done
here. Psychoanalysis represents a radical theory which should be
used together with other methods.

1052   The view that it should not be used because its usefulness has
not been proved or theoretically established cannot be supported
by the facts [of the case], and it would disregard the principle of
scientific research that practical experimentation is to be given preference over theoretical considerations.

1053   Failures, naturally, do occur, but just as in other fields they
do not permit us to draw conclusions of a general validity.

1054   The discussion of sexual matters is admittedly not easy and not
to everyone's taste; tactfully employed, however, it is an essential
ingredient of any psychotherapy. — Dreams are often inexactly reported or added to; these additions are, however, as Freud has
shown, not fortuitous coincidences, but governed by the same unconscious ideas that informed the dream itself. That childhood impressions persist throughout one's life, even if they seemingly are
insignificant, is a certainty. The explanation for this is that such
impressions have been repressed because of a certain significant conjunction of ideas, and for this very reason could survive in the unconscious until they were uncovered by analysis.

A COMMENT ON TAUSK'S CRITICISM OF NELKEN[1]

1055   In the first issue of this periodical there was a review by Tausk
of Nelken's "Analytische Beobachtungen über Phantasien eines
Schizophrenen."[2] In this review I came upon the following passage:

In the first catatonic attack the patient produced the fantasy that
mice and rats were gnawing at his genitals. Nelken derives the symbolic
significance of these animals from a suggestion of Jung's, who sees them
as symbolizing nocturnal fear. There is no doubt that this interpretation is correct, but it comes from a later elaboration of this symbol and
bars the way to deeper insight. Analysis of dreams and neuroses has
taught me beyond question—and I find my view supported by other
psychoanalysts—that mice and rats are cloacal animals and that they
represent, in symbolic form, the defecation complex (anal complex).

1056   I would like to defend Nelken's view against Tausk's. I do not
doubt in the least that Tausk's view is also right. We have known
this for a long time, and it has been completely confirmed once
more by Freud's rat-man.[3] Further, we know very well that catatonic
introversion and regression reactivate all the infantile impulses, as
is evident from numerous observations in Nelken's analysis. So there
is no question of this aspect of the case having escaped us; it merely
seemed unimportant because by now it is self-evident. It is no longer
of vital importance to know that the anal complex can act as a
substitute for normal modes of transference or adaptation, since
we know already that the pathological regression of libido reactivates every variety of infantile sexualism and produces infantile
fantasies of every conceivable kind. Anyone who still thinks that
a definite group of fantasies, or a "complex" has been singled out

[1] ["Eine Bemerkung zur Tauskschen Kritik der Nelkenschen Arbeit," *Internationale Zeitschrift für ärztliche Psychoanalyse* (Vienna and Leipzig), I:3
(1913), 285–88. For Victor Tausk, of Vienna, see *The Freud/Jung Letters*,
348J, n. 4. For Jan Nelken, a psychiatrist of the Zurich School, see ibid., 305J,
n. 3. The present trans. was published in *Spring*, 1973.]
[2] [In the *Jahrbuch für psychoanalytische und psychopathologische Forschungen*,
IV:1 (1912). ("Analytical Observations on the Fantasies of a Schizophrenic.")]
[3] [Freud, "Notes upon a Case of Obsessional Neurosis" (orig., 1909), Standard
Edn., X.]

just hasn't seen enough cases. We therefore consider it irrelevant that the castration is performed by cloacal animals. Incidentally, mice are not "cloacal animals" but animals that live in holes, and this is a more comprehensive concept than "cloacal animals."

1057   The only thing we learn from this interpretation is that an infantile complex or infantile interest takes the place of the normal interest. It may be of some value for the specialist to know that in this particular case it was the anal fantasy that contributed a bit of symbolism for the purpose of expressing the introversion and regression of libido. But this interpretation does not supply a generally applicable principle of explanation when we come to the far more important task of discovering the real functional significance of the castration motif. We cannot content ourselves with a simple reduction to infantile mechanisms and leave it at that.

1058   I was once given a very impressive example of this kind of interpretation. In a discussion on the historical fish-symbol, one of those present remarked that the fish vanishing in the sea was simply the father's penis vanishing in his wife's vagina. This kind of interpretation, which I consider sterile, is what I call sexual concretism. It seems to me that psychoanalysts are confronted with the much greater and more important task of understanding what these analogies are trying to say. What did men of many different races and epochs mean by the symbol of the fish? Why—in the present case too, for that matter—were these infantile channels of interest reactivated? What does this fetching up of infantile material signify? For this obviously is the problem. The statement: "Infantile reminiscences are coming to the surface again" is vapid and self-evident. It also leads us away from the real meaning. In Nelken's case the problem is not the derivation of part of the rat-symbol from the anal complex, but the castration motif to which the fantasy obviously belongs. The rats and mice are the instrument of the castration. But there are many other kinds of castrating instrument which are by no means anally determined. Tausk's reduction of the rats is merely of value to the specialist and has no real significance as regards the problem of sacrifice, which is at issue here.

1059   The Zurich school naturally recognizes that the material is reducible to simpler infantile patterns, but it is not content to let it go at that. It takes these patterns for what they are, that is, images through which the unconscious mind is expressing itself. Thus, with reference to the fish-symbol, we would argue as follows: We do not deny the Viennese school the possibility that the fish-symbol can ultimately be reduced to parental intercourse. We are ready to assume this provided there are fairly cogent reasons for doing so. But, because we are not satisfied with this relatively unimportant reduction, we ask ourselves what the evocation of parental intercourse or something similar means to the patient. We thus carry the assumption a stage further, because with the reduction to the infantile pattern we have not gained an understanding of the real significance of the fact that the reminiscence was regressively reactivated. Were we to remain satisfied with the reduction, we would come back again and again to the long-since-accepted truth that the infantile lies at the root of the mental world, and that adult mental life is built upon the foundations of the infantile psyche.

1060   Even in the backwaters of the psychoanalytic school one should have got beyond marvelling over the fact that, for instance, the artist makes use of images relating to the incest complex. Naturally every wish has these infantile patterns which it makes use of in every conceivable variation in order to express itself. But if the pattern, the infantile element, were still absolutely operative (i.e., not just regressively reactivated), all mental products would turn out to be unbelievably trivial and deadly monotonous. It would always be the same old infantile story that formed the essential core of all mental products. Fortunately, the infantile motifs are not the essential; that is to say, for the most part they are regressively reactivated, and are fittingly employed for the purpose of expressing currents and trends in the actual present—and most clearly of all when the things to be expressed are as far-off and intangible as the most distant childhood. Nor should it be forgotten that there is also a future. The reduction to infantile material makes the inessential in art—the limited human expression—the essence of art, which consists precisely in striving for the greatest variety of form and the greatest freedom from the limitations of the conventional and the given.

1061   Herbert Silberer[4] once made the very good observation that there is a mythological stage of cognition which *apprehends symbolically*. This saying holds good for the employment of infantile reminiscences: they aid cognition or apprehension and are expressive symbols. No doubt the infantile reminiscence or tendency is still partly operative and thus has an extraordinarily disturbing and obstructive

---

[4] [Cf. Herbert Silberer, "Über die Symbolbildung," *Jahrbuch*, III:1 (1911) and "Von den Kategorien der Symbolik," *Zentralblatt für Psychoanalyse*, II:4 (1912).]

effect in actual life. That is also the reason why it is so easy to find. But we would be wrong to regard it as a *source of energy* on that account; it is much more a limitation and an obstacle. But because of its undeniable existence it is at the same time a necessary means of expression by analogy, for the furthest reaches of fantasy cannot offer any other material for analogical purposes. Accordingly, even if we do approach the primitive images analytically, we are not content with reduction and with establishing their self-evident existence, but, by comparing them with similar material, we try rather to reconstruct the actual problem that led to the employment of these primitive patterns and seeks expression through them. In this sense we take incest primarily as a symbol, as a means of expression, as Adler too has suggested.

1062   Hence I cannot agree with Tausk when he says that comparison with analogous material "bars the way to deeper insight." We do not regard the discovery of the anal fantasy as an insight that could be compared in importance with an understanding of the castration motif. I must therefore defend Nelken's attempt to establish general connections in a wider context. We can hardly expect proof of the self-evident existence of infantile fantasies to furnish any insight into the general problem of sacrifice, which makes use of the castration motif among others. That Nelken has this question in mind is clear from his footnote, in which he refers to the snake and scorpion as historical castration animals.

1063   I have taken the liberty of dwelling at some length on Tausk's comment because it seemed to offer a favourable opportunity to sketch out our different approach to these matters. We do not by any means deny the possibility of Tausk's reduction, as should be obvious. But in this and all similar reductions we find nothing that seems to us to offer a satisfactory explanation. We believe, on the contrary, that a satisfactory explanation must make clear the teleological significance of the castration motif. In psychology, as is generally known, you cannot get very far with purely causal explanations, since a very large number of psychic phenomena can be satisfactorily explained only in teleological terms. This does nothing to alter or to detract from the exceedingly valuable discoveries of the Freudian school. We merely add the factor of teleological observation to what already exists. I have devoted a special study to this question, which will shortly appear in the *Jahrbuch*.[5]

---

[5] ["Versuch einer Darstellung der psychoanalytischen Theorie," *Jahrbuch*, V:1 (1913); trans., "The Theory of Psychoanalysis" (C.W., vol. 4).]

1064   Our attempts to develop and broaden the previous insights have given rise to absurd talk of a schism. Anything of that sort can only be the invention of people who take their working hypotheses as articles of faith. This rather childish standpoint is one which I do not share. My scientific views change with my experience and insight, as has always been the case in science generally. It would be a matter for suspicion if this were not so.

ANSWERS TO QUESTIONS ON FREUD[1]

On 24 July 1953, the representative of the *New York Times* in Geneva, Michael L. Hoffman, sent Jung the following questionnaire in connection with a projected article on Freud:

1. What part of Freud's work do you accept?
2. What was the role of Freud's work and views in the development of your own analytical psychology?
3. In your opinion does Freudian sexuality play any part in the aetiology of neuroses?
4. Would you care to make an estimate of Freud's contribution to our knowledge of the psyche?
5. Would you care to comment on the value of Freud's procedure as a therapeutic procedure?

1065   As it is impossible to deal with a critique of Freud's work in a short article I have to restrict myself to concise answers.

1066   1. I accept the facts Freud has discovered, but accept his theory only partially.

1067   2. The facts of repression, substitution, symbolization, and systematic amnesia described by Freud coincided with the results of my association experiments (1902–4). Later on (1906) I discovered similar phenomena in schizophrenia. I accepted in those years all of Freud's views, but I could not make up my mind to accept the sexual theory of neurosis and still less of psychosis, no matter how much I tried. I came to the conclusion (1910) that Freud's one-sided emphasis on sex must be a subjective prejudice.

1068   3. It is obvious that the sexual instinct plays a considerable role everywhere in life, and thus also in neurosis, and it is equally obvious that the power-drive, the many forms of fear, and the individual necessities are of equal importance. I object only to the uniqueness of sexuality as suggested by Freud.

1069   4. Freud's contribution to our knowledge of the psyche is without doubt of the greatest importance. It yields an insight into the

---

[1] [Jung wrote this reply (in English) to Hoffman's questions on 7 Aug. 1953. So far as is known, Jung's answers were not published by the *New York Times*. First published in *Spring*, 1968.]

438

dark recesses of the human mind and character which can be compared only to Nietzsche's *Genealogy of Morals*. In this respect Freud was one of the great cultural critics of the nineteenth century. His specific resentment explains the one-sidedness of his explanatory principle.

1070   One could not say that Freud is the discoverer of the unconscious—C. G. Carus and Eduard von Hartmann were before him and Pierre Janet was his contemporary—but he certainly showed a way to the unconscious and a definite possibility of investigating its contents. In this respect his book on dream interpretation proved to be most helpful, although from a scientific standpoint it is most objectionable.

1071   5. The question of psychological therapy is exceedingly complex. We know for certain that just any method or any procedure or any theory, seriously believed, conscientiously applied and supported by a humanly congenial understanding, can have a most remarkable therapeutic effect. Therapeutic efficacy is by no means the prerogative of any particular system; what counts is the character and the attitude of the therapist. For this reason I tell my pupils: you must know the best you can about the psychology of neurotic individuals as well as of yourself. If it is the best, you are likely to believe it, and then you can be serious enough to apply what you know with devotion and responsibility. If it is the best *you* know, then you will always entertain a reasonable doubt whether somebody else might not know better than yourself, and out of sheer compassion with your patient you will make sure that you don't lead him astray. Therefore you will never forget to inquire how far he agrees or disagrees with you. When he disagrees you are stuck, and if this fact is overlooked both doctor and patient are fooled.

1072   Theory is important in the first place for science. In practice you can apply as many theories as there are individuals. If you are honest you will preach your individual gospel, even if you don't know it. If you are right, it will be good enough. If you are wrong, even the best theory will be equally wrong. Nothing is worse than the right means in the hands of the wrong man. Never forget that the analysis of a patient analyses yourself, as you are just as much in it as he is.

1073   I am afraid psychotherapy is a very responsible business and anything but an impersonal application of a convenient medical method. There was a time when the surgeon did not even think

439

of washing his hands before an operation, and the time is still with us when doctors believe they are not personally concerned when they apply psychotherapeutic methods.

1074   For this reason I object to any kind of prejudice in the thera-peutical approach. In Freud's case I disagree with his materialism, his credulity (trauma theory), his fanciful assumptions (totem and taboo theory), and his asocial, merely biological point of view (theory of neurosis).

1075   This is a mere outline of critical viewpoints. I myself regard such statements as futile, since it is much more important to put forward facts that demand an altogether different conception of the psyche, i.e., new facts unknown to Freud and his school.

1076   It has never been my purpose to criticize Freud, to whom I owe so much. I have been far more interested in the continuation of the road he tried to build, namely the further investigation of the unconscious so sadly neglected by his own school.

VII

ON SYMBOLISM

(related to Volume 5 of the Collected Works)

[Though not recorded by Jung himself, these brief abstracts are included as evidence of Jung's preparatory work for *Wandlungen und Symbole der Libido* (1911–12), revised as *Symbols of Transformation* (1952). *The Freud/Jung Letters* contains references to preliminary drafts, e.g., the unrecovered "Herisau lecture," in 193J, par. 3, which Freud subjected to detailed criticism in 199aF.]

THE CONCEPT OF AMBIVALENCE[1]

Discussion.[2] C. G. Jung: The concept of ambivalence is probably a valuable addition to our terminology. In one and the same thing the opposite may be contained. *Altus* = high and deep. Pleasure may derive from pain. This implies not a sequence of one after the other, but a simultaneous one-in-the-other: a uniform given. He [Jung] objects to the statement "Ambivalence is the driving force." Ambivalence probably is not the driving force, but rather a formal aspect as we find it everywhere. Freud has adduced many examples from the history of language. Modern words too show ambivalence, e.g., *sacré,*[3] *luge* (Irish) = contract;[4] *bad* (English) = *bat* = *bass* (Middle High German) = good. Through the migration of language the meaning of a word is transformed into its historical opposite. Dreams make use of similarities as well as of opposites. Among the possibilities of similarity, contrast is closest at hand. He, Jung, had this dream: *He is a small man with a beard, wears no glasses and is no longer young.* Hence, everything the opposite. If we want to demonstrate our psychoanalytic view, we too, just like the anatomists, command an unambiguous kind of material that we find in the monuments of antiquity and in the field of mythology. For example, the fertility god is at the same time the destroyer (Indra). The sun means fertility and destruction. Therefore we have the lion as a zodiac sign standing for the intense heat of the sun. Ambivalence is evident in the mythological successions. Odin becomes the wild hunter who molests lonely girls on

[1] [(Translated by W. S.) Abstract of remarks by Jung at the Winter Meeting of Swiss Psychiatrists, Bern, 27 Nov. 1910, reported in the *Zentralblatt für Psychoanalyse,* I:5/6 (Feb./Mar. 1911), 267–68. The report, more or less abbreviated, appeared also in the *Psychiatrisch-neurologische Wochenschrift* (Halle), XII:43 (21 Jan. 1911), and the *Correspondenzblatt für Schweizer Ärzte,* XLI:6 (20 Feb. 1911). See *The Freud/Jung Letters,* 222J (29 Nov. 1910), n. 1.]

[2] [Of a paper by Eugen Bleuler, "Über Ambivalenz" ("On Ambivalence"); its publication, if any, could not be traced.]

[3] [In French, *sacré* can mean both "blessed" and "cursed."]

[4] [The word intended is probably *luige,* "oath," but the point of this example is obscure.]

the highways. Freia has turned into a she-devil. Venus, as the philologists teach us, acquired a good aspect and turned into St. Verena (St. Verena, the patron saint of Baden, Ct. Aargau; watering places, as we know from history, were consecrated and subject to Venus). St. Verena, Venus, however, also lends her name to dangerous mountains (Verenelisgärtli near the Glärnisch; St. Verenakehle is the name of the great avalanche chute on the Schafburg in the Säntis mountains). *Devas* (Sanskrit, = angel) becomes the devil in Persian. The snake on the pole corresponds to the ambivalence of the concept of Christ.

1078   The representation of libido oscillates between the symbols of the lion and the snake, the principle of dry and wet: both are opposite sexual or phallic symbols. Jung saw a stele of Priapus in Verona. The god smilingly holds a basket full of phalli on his arm and points with the other hand to a snake which bites off his erect penis.[5]

1079   Nice examples of ambivalence are shown by the language of erotic jokes, such as occur in the *Golden Ass* of Apuleius;[6] also in the language of mysticism; Mechtild of Magdeburg says: "By Christ's love I have been wounded unto death." Through the killing of the bull (in the Mithras mythologies) creation is brought about. "The bull is the father of the snake and the snake is the father of the bull."[7] Our Christian religious ideas are likewise based on this principle. Through Christ's death, man is redeemed for life eternal. We encounter the same idea in the cult of Mithras, which was of great importance in antiquity and helped spread the concepts of Christianity.

. . .

1080   *Discussion.*[8] C. G. Jung: The expression "taken off my chest"[9] in reference to the discussion of the tormenting complex is very apt and characteristic of analytic therapy. An officer, whenever his complex was about to get the better of him, commanded: "At-

---

[5] [Cf. *Symbols of Transformation* (C.W., vol 5), par. 680 and pl. LXIb; also in 1911/12 edn. See also *The Freud/Jung Letters*, 215J, par. 1.]

[6] [Cf. *Symbols of Transformation,* par. 439, n. 43.]

[7] [Cf. ibid., par. 671.]

[8] [Of a lecture by Prof. von Speyr, "Zwei Fälle von eigentümlicher Affektverschiebung" ("Two Cases of the Displacement of Affect"); its publication could not be traced.]

[9] ["vom Leibe gerückt," lit., "removed from my body."]

tention—halt! Six paces to the rear—march!" and every time felt very much relieved by this objectivation of his disease.

. . .

1081   *Discussion.*[10] As a contribution from child psychology to the significance of sacrifice, C. G. Jung tells about the "Tantalus Club" which was founded by some youngsters for the celebration of sexual mysteries. Their emblem depicted a man who hung from a gallows by a rope tied to his penis and his nose. The sacrificed and tormented were the youngsters themselves, just like Tantalus whose torment consists in constantly being denied satisfaction of his most ardent desires.

[10] [Of a lecture by Franz Riklin, "Die 'Allmacht der Gedanken' bei der Zwangs-neurose" ("The 'Omnipotence of Thoughts' in Compulsion Neurosis"); its publication could not be traced.]

CONTRIBUTIONS TO SYMBOLISM[1]

1082   Starting from the contrast that exists between hysterical fantasies and those of dementia praecox, the lecturer points out that in order to understand the latter, historical parallels must be adduced, because in dementia praecox the patient suffers from the reminiscences of mankind. In contrast to hysteria, his language uses ancient images of universal validity, even though at first glance they seem incomprehensible to us.

1083   The case of a 34-year-old female neurotic serves to illustrate how a recent fantasy can be documented and elucidated by historical material. The patient's fantasy deals with a man she loves unrequitedly who is suspended by the genitals, a fantasy which was also found in a 9-year-old boy as a symbolic expression of his unfulfilled libido ("Hanging and fearing, suspended in pain").[2] This fantasy, when taken together with corresponding ethnological traditions and mythological parallels of the sacrifice of the god of spring by hanging or flaying, signifies a sacrifice of sexuality which one hangs on to and cannot get rid of and which in ancient cults was offered to the Great Mother as a sacrifice of the phallus.[3]

---

[1] [(Translated by W. S.) An abstract, recorded by Otto Rank, of Jung's lecture, entitled "Beiträge zur Symbolik," at the Third Psychoanalytic Congress in Weimar, 21–22 Sept. 1911. Abstracts of the twelve papers read at the Congress were published in the *Zentralblatt für Psychoanalyse,* II:2 (Nov. 1911), 100–104. A MS of Jung's lecture has not been found.]

[2] [Goethe, *Egmont,* Klärchen's song, Act III.]

[3] [For the parallels, see *Symbols of Transformation,* index, s.v. "Attis" and "castration." (also in 1911/12 edn.)]

VIII

TWO ESSAYS ON ANALYTICAL PSYCHOLOGY

(related to Volume 7 of the Collected Works)

ADAPTATION, INDIVIDUATION, COLLECTIVITY[1]

1. Adaptation

1084　　A. *Psychological adaptation* consists of two processes:
　　　　1. Adaptation to outer conditions.
　　　　2. Adaptation to inner conditions.

1085　　By outer conditions are meant not only the conditions of the surrounding world, but also my conscious judgments, which I have formed of objective things.

1086　　By inner conditions are meant those facts or data which force themselves upon my inner perception from the unconscious, independently of my conscious judgment and sometimes even in opposition to it. Adaptation to inner conditions would thus be adaptation to the unconscious.

1087　　B. In *neurosis* the adaptation process is disturbed, or rather we might say that the neurosis is itself a disturbed or diminished process of adaptation that takes two basic forms:
　　　　1. Disturbance of adaptation to outer conditions.
　　　　2. Disturbance of adaptation to inner conditions.

1088　　In the first case we must again distinguish two different and fundamental situations:
　　　　1. Adaptation to outer conditions is disturbed because the subject tries to adapt entirely and exclusively to the outside, while entirely neglecting the inside, thereby upsetting the balance of the act of adaptation.
　　　　2. The disturbance arises from a preferential adaptation to the inside.

[1] [Translated from typescripts discovered 1964 in the archives of the Psychological Club, Zurich. The papers are signed and dated "Oct. 1916" in Jung's handwriting, and would thus have been written about the same time as "The Transcendent Function" (C.W., vol. 8) and "The Structure of the Unconscious" (C.W., vol. 7, 2nd edn., Appendix 2). Their content appears to be, in part, a further elaboration of the Addendum to the latter, pars. 503ff. The present trans., with a prefatory note and postscript by R.F.C. Hull, was published in *Spring*, 1970.]

1089   Equally, adaptation to inner conditions can be disturbed in two ways:

   1. By exclusive adaptation to the outside.

   2. By neglect of the outside in favour of adaptation to the inside.

1090   C. *The Energetics of Adaptation:* These considerations lead to the energetics of the adaptation process. When the libido invested in a particular function cannot be equilibrated by the exercise of the function, it accumulates until it attains a value which exceeds that of the neighbouring functional system. Then a process of equilibration begins, because a potential is present. The energy flows over, as it were, into another system. When, therefore, adaptation to the inside is not achieved, the libido intended for that purpose accumulates until it begins to flow out of the system of inner adaptation into the system of outer adaptation, with the result that characteristics belonging to inner adaptation are carried over into outer— that is to say, fantasies intervene in the relation to the real world. Conversely, when the system of outer adaptation overflows into the system of inner adaptation, characteristics belonging to the former are carried over into the latter, namely, qualities belonging to the reality-function.

1091   D. *Adaptation in Analysis:* Adaptation in analysis is a special question. During the analysis, experience shows that, barring quite exceptional circumstances, the analysis is the main thing. There is no categorical imperative, "The analysis *must* be the main thing"; it is simply that, judging by the average run of experience, the analysis *is* the main thing. Hence the main achievement is in the first place adaptation to the analysis, which for one patient is represented by the person of the analyst, and for another by the "analytical idea." The purpose in either case is to secure trust: the one who starts off with an unconscious mistrust of his fellow seeks above everything to make sure of the personality of the analyst; the other, whose main desire is to be instructed about the reliability of methods of thinking, seeks above everything to understand the basic ideas.

1092   As the analysis proceeds, the former must naturally catch up in understanding the idea, the latter in learning to trust the analyst's personality.

   When adaptation has been carried thus far, the analysis is generally held to have come to an end for all practical purposes, in so far as it is assumed that this personal balance is the essential aim and demand. There is, on the fact of it, nothing to be said against this view.

1094   Experience shows, however, that in certain and not too uncommon cases a demand is raised by the unconscious, which expresses itself to begin with in the extraordinary intensity of the transference, and in the influence thus exerted on the patient's lifeline. This heightened transference seems, at first, to contain the demand for a particularly intensive adaptation to the analyst, and for the time being it should be accepted as such, though it is at bottom an over-compensation for a resistance to the analyst that is felt to be irrational. This resistance arises from the demand for individuation, which is *against* all adaptation to others. But since the breaking of the patient's previous personal conformity would mean the destruction of an aesthetic and moral ideal, the first step in individuation is a tragic *guilt*. The accumulation of guilt demands *expiation*. This expiation cannot be offered to the analyst, for that would only restore the patient's personal conformity. The guilt and its expiation call for a *new collective function:* just as before the object of faith and love, namely the image of the analyst, was a *representative* of humanity, so now humanity itself takes the place of the analyst and to it is offered the expiation for the guilt of individuation.

1095   Individuation cuts one off from personal conformity and hence from collectivity. That is the guilt which the individuant leaves behind him for the world, that is the guilt he must endeavour to redeem. He must offer a ransom in place of himself, that is, he must bring forth values which are an equivalent substitute for his absence in the collective personal sphere. Without this production of values, final individuation is immoral and—more than that—suicidal. The man who cannot create values should sacrifice himself consciously to the spirit of collective conformity. In so doing, he is free to choose the collectivity to which he will sacrifice himself. Only to the extent that a man creates objective values can he and may he individuate. Every further step in individuation creates new guilt and necessitates new expiation. Hence individuation is possible only so long as substitute values are produced. Individuation is exclusive adaptation to inner reality and hence an allegedly "mystical" process. The expiation is adaptation to the outer world. It has to be offered to the outer world, with the petition that the outer world accept it.

1096   The individuant has no *a priori* claim to any kind of esteem.

He has to be content with whatever esteem flows to him from outside by virtue of the values he creates. Not only has society a right, it also has a duty to condemn the individuant if he fails to create equivalent values, for he is a deserter.

1097   When, therefore, the demand for individuation appears in analysis under the guise of an exceptionally strong transference, it means farewell to personal conformity with the collective, and stepping over into solitude, into the cloister of the inner self. Only the shadow of the personality remains in the outer world. Hence the contempt and hate that come from society. But inner adaptation leads to the conquest of inner realities, from which values are won for the reparation of the collective.

1098   Individuation remains a pose so long as no positive values are created. Whoever is not creative enough must re-establish collective conformity with a group of his own choice, otherwise he remains an empty waster and windbag. Whoever creates *unacknowledged* values belongs to the contemned, and he has himself to blame for this, because society has a right to expect *realizable* values. For the existing society is always of absolute importance as the point of transition through which all world development passes, and it demands the highest collaborative achievement from every individual.

2. *Individuation and Collectivity*

1099   Individuation and collectivity are a pair of opposites, two divergent destinies.[2] They are related to one another by guilt. The individual is obliged by the collective demands to purchase his individuation at the cost of an equivalent work for the benefit of society. So far as this is possible, individuation is possible. Anyone who cannot do this must submit directly to the collective demands, to the demands of society, or rather, he will be caught by them automatically. What society demands is *imitation* or conscious identification, a treading of accepted, authorized paths. Only by accomplishing an equivalent is one exempted from this. There are *very many people* who *at first* are altogether incapable of accomplishing this equivalent. They are therefore bound to the well-trodden path. If they are pushed off it, they are seized by helpless anxiety, from which only another of the prescribed paths can deliver them. Such people can achieve self-reliance only after imitating for a very long

2 [*Bestimmungen;* could also mean "destinations."]

time one of the models they have chosen. A person who by reason of special capacities is entitled to individuate must accept the contempt of society until such time as he has accomplished his equivalent. Only a few are capable of individuating, because individuation rules out any renunciation of collective conformity until an equivalent has been accomplished whose objective value is acknowledged. Human relationship establishes itself automatically on the basis of an acknowledged equivalent, because the libido of society goes directly towards it. Without the equivalent, all attempts at conformity are foredoomed to failure.

1100 Through imitation, one's own values become *reactivated*. If the way to imitation is cut off, they are nipped in the bud. The result is helpless anxiety. If the imitation is a demand made by the analyst, i.e., if it is a demand for the sake of adaptation, this again leads to a destruction of the patient's values, because imitation is an automatic process that follows its own laws, and lasts as long and goes as far as is necessary. It has quite definite limits which the analyst can never know. Through imitation the patient learns individuation, because it reactivates his own values.

1101 The collective function may be divided into two functions, which from the "mystical" or metapsychological point of view are identical:

1. The collective function in relation to society.

2. The collective function in relation to the unconscious.

1102 The unconscious is, as the collective psyche, the psychological representative of society. The persona can have no relation to the unconscious since it is collectively identical with it, being itself collective. Hence the persona must be extinguished or, in other words, restored to the unconscious. From this arises individuality as one pole that polarizes the unconscious, which in turn produces the counterpole, the God-concept.

1103 The individual must now consolidate himself by cutting himself off from God and becoming wholly himself. Thereby and at the same time he also separates himself from society. Outwardly he plunges into solitude, but inwardly into hell, distance from God. In consequence, he loads himself with guilt. In order to expiate this guilt, he gives his good to the soul, the soul brings it before God (the polarized unconscious), and God returns a gift (productive reaction of the unconscious) which the soul offers to man, and which man gives to mankind. Or it may go another way: in order to expiate the guilt, he gives his supreme good, his love, not to the soul but to a human being who stands for his soul, and from this human being it goes to God and through this human being it comes back to the lover, but only so long as this human being stands for his soul. Thus enriched, the lover begins to give to his soul the good he has received, and he will receive it again from God, in so far as he is destined to climb so high that he can stand in solitude before God and before mankind.

1104   Thus I, as an individual, can discharge my collective function either by giving my love to the soul and so procuring the ransom I owe to society, or, as a lover, by loving the human being through whom I receive the gift of God.

1105   But here as well there is a discord between collectivity and individuation: if a man's libido goes to the unconscious, the less it goes to a human being; if it goes to a human being, the less it goes to the unconscious. But if it goes to a human being, and it is a true love, then it is the same as if the libido went direct to the unconscious, so very much is the other person a representative of the unconscious, though only if this other person is truly loved.

1106   Only then does love give him the quality of a mediator, which otherwise and in himself he would not possess.

FOREWORD TO THE HUNGARIAN EDITION OF JUNG: "ON THE PSYCHOLOGY OF THE UNCONSCIOUS"[1]

1107   The Hungarian translation of my book *On the Psychology of the Unconscious*,[2] by Dr. Peter Nagy, carefully collated and checked by Dr. Jolande Jacobi, deserves to be greeted as a novum since this is the first Hungarian publication of any of my writings. Except for a few translations into Russian, one of my earliest books now appears in a language of Eastern Europe for the first time. I am indebted to Dr. Jacobi not only for making this possible, but more particularly because she was closely associated with the revision of this book and its publication, and was ready with helpful suggestions and useful advice. It is also due to her conscientious collaboration that the Hungarian edition is equipped with an index, lacking in the Swiss edition, as well as with a short glossary to elucidate the terminology, which is often difficult and new, attaching to the theme.

1108   For it is a particular pleasure that my book is now available in Hungary, a country from which signs of the liveliest interest have again and again come my way. I hope to pay off a little of my debt of gratitude, at least indirectly, with this foreword. Of my many pupils, who all come from the Western half of the world, Dr. Jacobi is the first Hungarian; she has worked for years under my personal direction in Zurich, and in so doing has acquired a profound knowledge of that very extensive and difficult territory, the psychology of the unconscious. In her book *The Psychology of C. G. Jung*,[3] an excellent introduction to my work in general, she has given evidence of this. Her knowledge also guarantees the accuracy and fidelity of the translation, so very necessary in dealing with such tricky and delicate material as the psychology of the unconscious.

1109   This essay makes no claim to be a comprehensive exposition; its aim is to acquaint the reader with the main problems of the

[1] [*Bevezetés a Tudattalan Pszichologiájába,* trans. by Peter Nagy (Budapest: Bibliotheca, 1948).]
[2] [C.W., vol. 7.]
[3] [See infra, par. 1121, n. 1.]

psychology of the unconscious, and this only within the limits pre-scribed by direct medical experience. As it does not pretend to be more than an introduction, the manifold relations with the history of human thought, mythology, religion, philosophy, the psychology of primitives, and so on are only hinted at.

Küsnacht-Zurich, January 1944

IX

THE STRUCTURE AND DYNAMICS
OF THE PSYCHE

(related to Volume 8 of the Collected Works)

FOREWORDS TO JUNG: "ÜBER PSYCHISCHE ENERGETIK UND DAS WESEN DER TRÄUME"[1]

First Edition (1928)

1110   In this volume, the second of the *Psychologische Abhandlungen,*[2] I am publishing four papers of which three have so far appeared only in English.[3] One of the papers deals with the still unsolved problem of dream interpretation, while the others are concerned with—in my view—a question of central importance: the fundamental psychic factors, the *dynamic images,* which it seems to me express the nature of psychic energy. My concept of psychic energy, first put forward in *Wandlungen und Symbole der Libido* (1912),[4] has met with so much opposition and misunderstanding that it seemed to me worth working over the problems of psychic energetics once again, this time not from the practical but from the theoretical side. The reader, therefore, need fear no repetitions.

Küsnacht-Zurich 1928

Second Edition (1948)

1111   The papers in this volume are attempts to introduce some order into the chaotic profusion of psychic phenomena by means of concepts that are current in other fields of research besides psychology. Since our psychological knowledge is still in its infancy, our primary

---

[1] [Originally titled *Über die Energetik der Seele.*]

[2] [A series of psychological publications edited by Jung. See addenda, par. 1825.]

[3] ["General Aspects of Dream Psychology," first published as "The Psychology of Dreams," in *Collected Papers on Analytical Psychology* (1916); "Instinct and the Unconscious," first published in the *British Journal of Psychology,* X:1 (1919); "The Psychological Foundations of Belief in Spirits," first published in *Proceedings of the Society for Psychical Research,* XXXI:79 (May, 1920). The latter two papers were reprinted in *Contributions to Analytical Psychology* (1928), together with the fourth paper, "On Psychic Energy." All four papers are in C.W., vol. 8.]

[4] [Trans. as *Psychology of the Unconscious* (1916); revised edn., *Symbols of Transformation,* C.W., vol. 5.]

459

concern must be with elementary concepts and groups of facts, and not with the individual complications in which our case histories abound, and which can never be completely elucidated. The Freudian "model" of neurosis and dreams gives only a partial explanation of the empirical material. As medical psychologists, we must seek to refine our methods as well as our psychological concepts, more particularly because the "academic" psychologists have abandoned the attempt to investigate the unconscious empirically. It falls to the lot of the medical psychologist to probe more deeply into the compensatory relationship between conscious and unconscious which is so vital for an understanding of the psyche as a whole.

1112   Except for some improvements I have made no drastic alterations to the text. The number of papers has been increased to six, as I have added a short "Review of the Complex Theory" and some recent aperçus on dream research, "On the Nature of Dreams."[1]

Küsnacht-Zurich, May 1947

[1] [Both in C.W., vol. 8.]

ON HALLUCINATION[1]

¹ [Contribution to a discussion at a meeting of the Schweizerische Gesellschaft für Psychiatrie, Prangins (near Geneva), 1933. Trans. from the Proceedings in *Schweizer Archiv für Neurologie und Psychiatrie*, XXXII (1933): 2, 382.]

13   Hallucination is not merely a pathological phenomenon but one that also occurs in the sphere of the normal. The history of prophecy as well as experiences among primitives show that psychic contents not infrequently come to consciousness in hallucinatory form. In this respect only the form is worthy of note, not the function, which is nothing other than what is commonly called a "brain wave" [*Einfall*]. As the word itself indicates, a certain spontaneity attaches to the phenomenon; it is as though the psychic content had a life of its own and forced its way into consciousness by its own strength. This peculiarity probably explains the ease with which the brain wave assumes an hallucinatory character. Common speech is familiar with these transitions from brain wave to hallucination. In the mildest cases we say: "I thought"; "it occurred to me" is a little stronger; stronger still is "it was as though an inner voice said," and finally "it was as though someone were calling to me," or "I heard a voice quite distinctly."

14   Hallucinations of this kind usually derive from the still subliminal, maturer personality which is not yet capable of direct consciousness, as observations of somnambulists show. In the case of primitive medicine-men they come from a subliminal thinking or intuiting which at that level is not yet capable of becoming conscious.

FOREWORD TO SCHLEICH:
"DIE WUNDER DER SEELE"[1]

1115   When, after many years, I again took up the works of Carl
Ludwig Schleich and tried to capture the mental world of this remarkable thinker in a telling image, what persistently came into
my mind was the indelible impression which another powerful
thinker—very unlike Schleich and yet so very like him—had made
upon me: Paracelsus. Odd bedfellows indeed—the contemporary
of the humanists and the modern, forward-looking Schleich, separated by four centuries of spiritual growth and change, not to speak
of differences of personality. The very idea would have struck me
as preposterous had I not been strangely moved just by the affinity
of opposites. Above all, it seemed to me significant that Paracelsus
stood at the beginning of an epoch in the history of medicine and
Schleich at its end. Both were typical representatives of a period
of transition, and both of them revolutionaries. Paracelsus cleared
the way for scientific medicine, benighted at times by age-old animistic beliefs yet filled with the liveliest apprehension of an age
in which the intangibles of the soul would be replaced by a massive
materialism. Schleich was a revolutionary in the opposite sense.
Although steeped in anatomical and physiological concepts, he
boldly reached out towards the very same psychic realm upon which
Paracelsus, obeying the dictates of his age, had half-reluctantly
turned his back. Both were enthusiasts, uplifted and fortified by
the certitudes of their vision, optimistically credulous, rejoicing in
their hopes, pioneers of a new spiritual outlook who went their
head-spinning way sure-footed and undismayed. Both gazed fearlessly into suprahuman, metaphysical abysses and both avowed their
faith in the eternal images deeply engraved in the human psyche.
Paracelsus' way took him down to the divine but essentially pre-
Christian *prima materia*, the "Hyliaster."[2] Schleich, starting from

---

[1] [Berlin, 1934. A collection of essays. Schleich (1859–1922), German surgeon
and writer, discovered local anaesthesia. Cf. his autobiographical *Those Were
Good Days!* trans. by B. Miall (1936).]

[2] ["Paracelsus as a Spiritual Phenomenon" (C.W., vol. 13), pars. 170f.
("Iliaster").]

the darkness of the blood vessels, ducts, and the labyrinth of the nerve-endings, mounted the ganglionic ladder of the sympathetic nervous system to a transcendental soul which appeared to him in all its Platonic glory in the "supracelestial place." Both were inspired by the effervescence of an age of decay and change. Both were born out of their time, eccentric figures eyed askance by their contemporaries. One's contemporaries are always dense and never understand that enthusiasm, and what appears to them to be unseemly ebullience come less from personal temperament than from the still unknown well-springs of a new age. How people looked askance at Nietzsche's volcanic emotion, and how long he will be spoken of in times to come! Even Paracelsus has now been gratefully disinterred after four hundred years in an attempt to resuscitate him in modern dress. What will happen with Schleich? We know that he was aiming at that unitary vision of psychic and physical processes which has given the strongest impetus to medical and biological research today. Though hampered by a terminology inherited from an age of scientific materialism, he broke through the narrow confines of a de-psychized materiality and crossed the threshold, barricaded with thorny prejudices, which separated the soul from the body. And though he had no knowledge of my own efforts, which for a long time remained unknown to the scientific public in Germany, in his own way he fought shoulder to shoulder with me for the recognition of the soul as a factor *sui generis,* and thus broke a new path for psychology, which till then had been condemned to get along without a psyche.

116   The breakthrough initiated by Paracelsus led the way out of medieval scholasticism into the then unknown world of matter. This is the great and essential service which has placed medicine forever in his debt. And it is not isolated facts, methods, or laws which make Schleich important for us, but his pushing forward into a new field of vision where the mass of known facts appears in a new and different light. By syncretizing all our previous knowledge and seeking a standpoint from which to gain a view of the whole, he succeeded in escaping from the charmed circle of pure empiricism and touched upon the very foundation of the empirical method itself, though most people are quite unaware of it. This fundamental thing is the relation of the body's chemistry to psychic life. Paracelsus ultimately decided in favour of "chemism," despite his allegiance to a view of the world dominated by the spirit as the highest authority. Schleich, four hundred years later, decided in favour

of psychic animation, and thus raised the psyche from its undignified position as a subsidiary product to that of the *auctor rerum.* With a bold stroke he put the mechanisms and chemisms of the body in a new hierarchy. The "vestigial" sympathetic nervous system, an apparently fortuitous tangle of ganglionic nodes that regulate the vegetative functions of the body in an astoundingly purposive way, becomes the matrix of the cerebrospinal system, whose crowning miracle, the brain, seems to our fascinated gaze the controller of all bodily processes. Nay more: the sympathetic system is, for Schleich, the mysterious "cosmic nerve," the true "ideoplast," the original and most immediate realization of a body-building and body-sustaining World Soul, which was there before mind and body came into existence. The Hyliaster of Paracelsus is thus stripped of its unfathomable creative secret. Once again the solidity and tangibility of matter, so fervently believed in and so convincing to the senses, dissolve into Maya, into a mere emanation of primordial thought and will, and all hierarchies and all values are reversed. The intangible, the psyche, becomes the ground and substrate, and the "merely vegetative" sympathetic system the possessor and realizer of unthinkable creative secrets, the vehicle of the life-giving World Soul, and, ultimately, the architect of the brain, this newest achievement of the pre-existent creative will. What lay modestly hidden beneath the overwhelming grandeur of the cerebrospinal system, which, as the vehicle of consciousness, seems to be identical with the psyche as such—this same sympathetic system is "psyche" in a deeper and more embracing sense than is the interplay of the cortical fields of the cerebrum. Notwithstanding its quantitative and qualitative insignificance, it is the exponent of a psyche far excelling consciousness both in depth and scope, and is not, like this, defencelessly exposed to the potions of the endocrine system, but itself creates these magical secretions with single-minded purposiveness.

1117   Just as Paracelsus laboured to concoct sylphids and succubi out of mandrakes, hangman's amulets, and the blackest folk-medicine in his alchemical retort while yet having intimations of the truth, so Schleich spoke the language of the best "brain mythology" of the pre-war era and yet penetrated into the deepest problems and symbols of the human psyche, following his inner intuition and without knowing what he was doing. His soaring imagination transmuted figures of speech into forms which, unbeknownst to him, are actually archetypes of the collective unconscious that manifest themselves wherever introspection seeks to plumb the depths of the psyche, as for instance in Indian and Chinese yoga.

8   Schleich was thus a pioneer not only in somatic medicine but also in the remoter reaches of psychology, where it coalesces with the vegetative processes of the body. This is without doubt the darkest area of all, which scientific research has long sought to elucidate in vain. It is just this darkness which fascinated Schleich's mind and let loose a spate of imaginative ideas. Though they were not based on any new facts, they will certainly stimulate new interpretations and new modes of observation. As the history of science shows, the progress of knowledge does not always consist in the discovery of facts but, just as often, in opening up new lines of inquiry and in formulating hypothetical points of view. One of Schleich's favourite ideas was that of a psyche spread through the whole of the body, and dependent more on the blood than on grey matter. This is a brilliant notion of incalculable import. It enabled him to reach certain conclusions as to the way in which the psychic processes are determined, and these conclusions have independently confirmed my own research work. I am thinking chiefly of the historical factors determining the psychic background, as formulated in my theory of the collective unconscious. The same might be said of the mysterious connections between the psyche and the geographical locality, which Schleich linked up with dietetic differences—a possibility that should not be dismissed out of hand. When one considers the remarkable psychic and biological changes to which European immigrants are subject in America,[3] one cannot help feeling that in this matter science has still a number of important problems to solve.

1119   Although Schleich's thought and language were wholly dependent on the data of the body, he was nevertheless impressed by the incorporeal nature of the psyche. What struck him about dreams was their spacelessness and timelessness, and for him hysteria was a "metaphysical problem"—metaphysical because the "ideoplastic" capacities of the unconscious psyche were nowhere more palpably in evidence than in the neuroses. Marvelling he gazed at the bodily changes wrought by the unconscious in hysteria. One can see from this almost childlike amazement how new and unexpected such

---

[3] ["The Role of the Unconscious," par. 18; "Mind and Earth," pars. 94f; "The Complications of American Psychology," pars. 947ff, 970f. (all in C.W., vol. 10).]

observations were for him, although for the psychopathologist they have long been truisms. But one also sees from what generation of medical men he came—a generation blinded by prejudice, that passed unheedingly by the workings of the psyche upon the body, and even with its first, groping steps in psychology believed that the psyche could be dispensed with. Considering this lack of psychological knowledge, it is all the more astonishing and greatly to Schleich's credit that he was able to break through to a recognition of the psyche and to a complete reversal of biological causality. His conclusions seem almost too radical to the psychologist, or at any rate over-audacious, since they trespass upon regions which philosophical criticism must put beyond the bounds of human understanding.

1120   Schleich's limited knowledge of psychology and his enthusiasm for intuitive speculation are responsible for a certain lack of reflection and for the occasional shallow patches in his work, for instance, his blindness to the psychic processes in dreams, which he sees through the spectacles of materialistic prejudice. Again, there is no inkling of the philosophical and moral problems that are conjured up by his identification of conscience with the function of hormones. Schleich thus paid tribute to the scientific past and to the spirit of the Wilhelmine era, when the authority of science swelled into blind presumption and the intellect turned into a ravening beast. But he saw very clearly that if medicine considered only the body and had no eyes for the living man, it was doomed to stultification. For this reason he turned away from the investigation of mere facts and used his knowledge of biology for wider purposes, to construct a bold synoptic view which would eradicate the grave errors of an obsolete materialism. The nineteenth century did everything it could to bring the psyche into disrepute, and it is Schleich's great achievement to have thrust the psychic meaning of vital processes into the light of day. His works may serve as an introduction to the revolution that has taken place in our general outlook and extricated us from the straitjacket of academic specialism.

FOREWORD TO JACOBI:
"THE PSYCHOLOGY OF C. G. JUNG"[1]

1121   The present work, I believe, meets a generally felt need which I myself up to now have not been in a position to satisfy—the wish for a concise presentation of the elements of my psychological theories. My endeavours in psychology have been essentially pioneer work, leaving me neither time nor opportunity to present them systematically. Dr. Jacobi has taken this difficult task upon herself with a happy result, having succeeded in giving an account free from the ballast of technical particulars. It is a synopsis that includes or at least touches upon all essential points, so that it is possible for the reader—with the aid of the references and the bibliography of my writings—to orient himself readily wherever needful. An additional merit is that the text has been supplemented with a number of diagrams, which are a help in understanding certain functional relations.

1122   It is a particular satisfaction to me that the author has been able to avoid furnishing any support to the opinion that my researches constitute a doctrinal system. Expositions of this kind slip all too easily into a dogmatic style which is wholly inappropriate to my views. Since it is my firm conviction that the time for an all-inclusive theory, taking in and describing all the contents, processes, and phenomena of the psyche from one central viewpoint, has not yet arrived, I regard my concepts as tentative attempts to formulate a scientific psychology based in the first place upon immediate experience with human beings. This is not a kind of psychopathology, but a general psychology which also takes cognizance of the empirical material of pathology.

---

[1] [Jolan (or Jolande) Jacobi, *Die Psychologie von C. G. Jung* (Zurich: Rascher, 1940). Concerning the author (1890–1973), see infra, par. 1134. The foreword was trans. by K. W. Bash in *The Psychology of C. G. Jung* (New Haven: Yale University Press, 1942); an edition published the same year by Routledge & Kegan Paul, London, omits the foreword. A revised edn. of the entire book, including the foreword, was retrans. by Ralph Manheim and published by both houses, 1962; 8th edn., revised, 1973. The version published here has been revised by R.F.C. Hull.]

1123   I hope that it may be the lot of this book not only to give the general reader an insight into my researches, but also to save him much laborious searching in his study of them.

August 1939

Foreword to the Spanish Edition[1]

1124   It gives me particular pleasure to know that this book is now appearing in a Spanish translation. It will acquaint the Spanish public with the most recent developments of a psychology that has grown out of the experiences of the physician's art. This psychology is concerned with complex psychic phenomena that are continually encountered in daily life. It is not an abstract academic science, but a formulation of practical experiences which remains faithful to the scientific method. As a result, this psychology includes within its scope wide areas of other sciences and of life in general. My very best wishes accompany this book on its journey through the world.

[1] [Jolan Jacobi, *La Psicología de C. G. Jung,* trans. by José M. Sacristan (Madrid, 1947). The present trans. is from the German MS.]

FOREWORD TO HARDING: "PSYCHIC ENERGY"[1]

1125   This book presents a comprehensive survey of the experiences of analytical practice, a survey such as anyone who has spent many years in the conscientious pursuit of professional duties may well feel the need of making. In the course of time, insights and recognitions, disappointments and satisfactions, recollections and conclusions mount to such proportions that one would gladly rid oneself of the burden of them in the hope not merely of throwing out worthless ballast but also of presenting a summation which will be useful to the world of today and of the future.

1126   The pioneer in a new field rarely has the good fortune to be able to draw valid conclusions from his total experience. The efforts and struggles, the doubts and uncertainties of his voyage of discovery have penetrated his marrow too deeply to allow him the perspective and clarity of vision needed for a comprehensive survey. Those of the second generation, who base their work on the groping experiments, the lucky hits, the circuitous approaches, the half truths and mistakes of the pioneer, are less burdened and can take more direct roads, envisage more distant goals. They can cast off many doubts and hesitations, concentrate on essentials, and, in this way, map out a simpler and clearer picture of the newly discovered territory. This simplification and clarification redound to the benefit of those of the third generation, who are thus equipped from the outset with an over-all chart. With this chart they are enabled to formulate new problems and mark out the boundary lines more sharply than ever before.

1127   We can congratulate the author on the success of her attempt to provide a general orientation on the problems of medical psychotherapy in its most modern aspects. Her many years of practical

---

[1] [M. Esther Harding, *Psychic Energy: Its Source and Goal* (New York, Bollingen Series X, and London, 1947). The author (1889–1971), originally English, practiced in New York. The foreword was trans. for the 1947 edn. by Hildegard Nagel; republished in 2nd edn., 1963, with subtitle of the book changed to "Its Source and Its Transformation." The Nagel trans. is published here with minor revisions. For forewords to other works of Harding's, see infra, pars. 1228ff. and 1795ff.]

experience have stood her in good stead; without them her undertaking would not have been possible at all. For it is not a question, as many believe, of a "philosophy," but rather of facts and their formulation, which in turn must be tested in practice. Concepts like "shadow" and "anima" are in no sense intellectual inventions. They are designations for psychic facts of a complex nature which are empirically verifiable. These facts can be observed by anyone who takes the trouble to do so and who is able to lay aside his preconceived ideas. Experience shows how difficult this is. For instance, how many people still labour under the delusion that the term archetype denotes an inherited idea! Such completely unwarranted assumptions naturally make any understanding impossible.

1128   It is to be hoped that Dr. Harding's book, with its simple and lucid exposition, will be especially suited to dispel such absurd misunderstandings. In this respect it can be of the greatest service not only to the doctor but also to the patient. I should like to emphasize this point particularly. It is obviously necessary for a doctor to have an adequate understanding of the material laid before him; but if he is the only one who understands, it is of no great help to the patient, since he is actually suffering from lack of consciousness and should therefore become more conscious. To this end, he needs knowledge; and the more of it he acquires, the greater is his chance of overcoming his difficulties. For those of my patients who have reached the point where greater spiritual independence is necessary, Dr. Harding's book is one that I should unhesitatingly recommend.

Küsnacht-Zurich, July 8, 1947

ADDRESS ON THE OCCASION OF THE FOUNDING OF THE C. G. JUNG INSTITUTE, ZURICH, 24 APRIL 1948[1]

1129 It is a particular pleasure and satisfaction for me to have the privilege of speaking to you on this memorable day of the founding of an Institute for Complex Psychology. I am honoured that you have come here for the purpose of establishing this institute of research which is designed to carry on the work begun by me. I hope, therefore, I may be allowed to say a few words about what has been achieved up to the present, as well as about our aims for the future.

1130 As you know, it is nearly fifty years since I began my work as a psychiatrist. At that time, the broad fields of psychopathology and psychotherapy were so much wasteland. Freud and Janet had just begun to lay the foundations of methodology and clinical observation, and Flournoy in Geneva had made his contribution to the art of psychological biography, which is still far from being appreciated at its true value. With the help of Wundt's association experiments, I was trying to evaluate the peculiarities of neurotic states of mind as exactly as possible. In the face of the layman's prejudice that the psyche was something immeasurably subjective and boundlessly capricious, my purpose was to investigate what appeared to be the most subjective and most complicated psychic process of all, namely, the associative reaction, and to describe its nature in numerically expressible quantities. This work led directly to the discovery of the *feeling-toned complex*, and indirectly to a new question, namely, the problem of *attitude*, which exerts a decisive influence upon the associative reaction. The answer to this question was found by clinical observation of patients and by analysis of their behaviour. From these researches there emerged a *psychological typology*, which distinguished two attitude-types, the extravert and the introvert, and four function-types corresponding to the four orienting functions of consciousness.

[1] [Trans. from the unpublished German MS. A translation by Hildegard Nagel appeared in the *Bulletin* of the Analytical Psychology Club of New York, 10:7 (Oct. 1948), Supplement. The present trans. is new.]

1131   The existence of complexes and of typical attitudes could not be adequately explained without the hypothesis of the unconscious. From the beginning, therefore, the above-mentioned experiments and researches went hand in hand with an investigation of unconscious processes. This led, about 1912, to the actual discovery of the *collective unconscious*. The term itself is of a later date. If the theory of complexes and type psychology had already overstepped the bounds of psychiatry proper, with the hypothesis of the collective unconscious the scope of our researches was extended without limit. Not only the domain of normal psychology, but also those of racial psychology, folklore, and mythology in the widest sense became the subject-matter of complex psychology. This expansion found expression in the collaboration with the sinologist Richard Wilhelm and the indologist Heinrich Zimmer. Both are now dead, but our science has not forgotten the inestimable contribution they made. Wilhelm above all introduced me to medieval Chinese alchemy and thus prepared the ground for an understanding of the rudiments of modern psychology that are to be found in the medieval texts. Into the painful gap left by the death of these two fellow workers there stepped, a few years ago, Karl Kerényi, one of the most brilliant philologists of our time. Thus a wish I personally had long cherished saw fulfillment, and our science was granted a new helper.[1a]

1132   The insights gained originally in the domains of psychopathology and normal psychology proved to be keys to the most difficult Taoist texts and to abstruse Indian myths, and Kerényi has now supplied such a wealth of connections with Greek mythology that the cross-fertilization of the two branches of science can no longer be doubted. In the same way that Wilhelm aroused an interest in alchemy and made possible a true interpretation of this little understood philosophy, Kerényi's work has stimulated a large number of psychological researches, in particular the investigation and elucidation of one of the most important problems in psychotherapy, namely, the *phenomenon of the transference*.[2]

1133   Recently an unexpected and most promising connection has been forged between complex psychology and physics, or to be more accurate, *microphysics*. On the psychological side, it was first of all C. A. Meier who pointed out the common conception of comple-

---

[1a] [The work of Richard Wilhelm (1873–1930), Heinrich Zimmer (1890–1943), and Karl Kerényi (1897–1973) has been widely translated.]

[2] [Cf. *Mysterium Coniunctionis*, pp. xiii and xv.]

mentarity. Pascual Jordan approached psychology from the physicist's side by drawing attention to the phenomenon of spatial relativity which applies equally to the phenomena of the unconscious. W. Pauli has taken up the new "psychophysical" problem on a much broader basis, examining it from the standpoint of the formation of scientific theories and their archetypal foundations.[3] Recently, in two impressive lectures, he showed on the one hand how the archetypal triad or trinity formed the point of departure for Kepler's astronomy, and on the other how Fludd's polemics with Kepler were based on the alchemical thesis of the quaternity. The object at issue, the *proportio sesquitertia* or ratio of 3 : 1, is likewise a fundamental problem in the psychology of the unconscious. Thirty years ago, the problem first presented itself in psychology as a typological phenomenon, i.e., as the relation of three more or less differentiated functions to one inferior function which was contaminated with the unconscious. Since then it has been considerably widened and deepened by the study of Gnostic and alchemical texts. It appears there partly in the form of the social or folkloristic *marriage quaternio,* derived originally from the primitive cross-cousin-marriage, and partly in the form of a differentiation in the sequence of elements, in which one or the other element, usually fire or earth, is distinguished from the other three. The same problem appears in the controversy between the trinitarian and the quaternarian standpoint in alchemy. In complex psychology the quaternity symbol has been shown to be an expression of psychic totality, and in the same way it could be established that the *proportio sesquitertia* commonly occurs in the symbolism produced by the unconscious. If, as conjectured, the quaternity or above-named proportion is not only fundamental to all concepts of totality but is also inherent in the nature of observed microphysical processes, we are driven to the conclusion that the space-time continuum, including mass, is psychically relative—in other words, that it forms a unity with the unconscious psyche. Accordingly, there must be phenomena which can be explained only in terms of a psychic relativity of space, time, and mass. Besides numerous individual observations the experiments conducted at Duke University by Rhine and elsewhere by other investigators have furnished sufficient proof of this. You will forgive me if I have dwelt on the latest connections of

[3] ["The Influence of Archetypal Ideas on the Scientific Theories of Kepler," in Jung and Pauli, *The Interpretation of Nature and the Psyche* (trans., 1955).]

our psychology with physics at some length. It did not seem to me superfluous in view of the incalculable importance of this question.

1134   To round out the position of complex psychology as it is at present, I would like to mention some major works by pupils. These include the "Einführung in die Grundlagen der komplexen Psychologie," by Toni Wolff,[4] a work distinguished for its philosophical clarity; the books of Esther Harding on feminine psychology;[5] the analysis of the *Hypnerotomachia* of Francesco Colonna, by Linda Fierz-David,[6] a showpiece of medieval psychology; the valuable introduction to our psychology by Jolande Jacobi:[7] the books on child psychology by Frances Wickes,[8] notable for their interesting material; the great book by H. G. Baynes, *Mythology of the Soul;*[9] a synoptic study by Gerhard Adler;[10] a large-scale work in several volumes by Hedwig von Roques and Marie-Louise von Franz;[11] and finally, a work of significant content and scope on the evolution of consciousness by Erich Neumann.[12]

1135   Of particular interest are the repercussions of complex psychology in the psychology of religion. The authors here are not my personal pupils. I would draw attention to the excellent book by Hans Schaer[13] on the Protestant side, and to the writings of W. P. Witcutt[14] and Father Victor White[15] concerning the relations

---

[4] [In *Die kulturelle Bedeutung der Komplexen Psychologie* (1935); reprinted posthumously in *Studien zu C. G. Jungs Psychologie* (1959), with introduction by Jung (in C.W., vol. 10).]

[5] [*Woman's Mysteries* and *The Way of All Women*. Cf. infra, pars. 1228ff. and 1795ff.]

[6] [*The Dream of Poliphilo*. Cf. infra, pars. 1749ff.]

[7] [*The Psychology of C. G. Jung*. Cf. supra, pars. 1121ff. Also *Complex/Archetype/Symbol,* infra, pars. 1256ff.]

[8] [*The Inner World of Childhood*. Cf. C.W., vol. 17.]

[9] [London, 1940. Cf. infra, pars. 1421ff.]

[10] [*Studies in Analytical Psychology*. Cf. infra, pars. 1238ff.]

[11] [*Symbolik des Märchens* and *Gegensatz und Erneuerung im Märchen* (Bern, 1959), by Hedwig von Beit, maiden name of Frau von Roques; the publications are based on the work of Dr. von Franz.]

[12] [*The Origins and History of Consciousness*. Cf. infra, pars. 1234ff.]

[13] [(1910–1968), professor of philosophy and the psychology of religion, Bern U. The reference is to his *Religion and the Cure of Souls in Jung's Psychology* (trans. by R.F.C. Hull, 1950). Cf. his *Erlösungsvorstellungen und ihre psychologischen Aspekte* (1950).]

[14] [English priest, at that time a Roman Catholic convert; after 1949, Anglican. Cf. his *Catholic Thought and Modern Psychology* (1943), and his account of his reconversion, *Return to Reality* (1954).]

[15] [*God and the Unconscious*. Cf. Jung's foreword, C.W., vol. 11.]

of our psychology to Thomist philosophy, and finally to the excellent account of the basic concepts by Gebhard Frei,[16] whose unusual erudition facilitates an understanding from all sides.

1136   To the picture of the past and present I must now try to sketch out one for the future. This can naturally take the form only of programmatic hints.

1137   The manifold possibilities for the further development of complex psychology correspond to the various developmental stages it has already passed through. So far as the experimental aspect is concerned, there are still numerous questions which need to be worked out by experimental and statistical methods. I have had to leave many beginnings unfinished because of more pressing tasks that claimed my time and energies. The potentialities of the association experiment are by no means exhausted yet. For instance, the question of the periodic renewal of the emotional tone of complex-stimulators is still unanswered; the problem of familial patterns of association has remained stuck in its beginnings, promising though these were; and so has the investigation of the physiological concomitants of the complex.

1138   In the medical and clinical field there is a dearth of fully elaborated case histories. This is understandable, because the enormous complexity of the material puts almost insurmountable difficulties in the way of exposition and makes the highest demands not only on the knowledge and therapeutic skill of the investigator but also on his descriptive capacity. In the field of psychiatry, analyses of paranoid patients coupled with research into comparative symbolism would be of the utmost value. Special consideration might be given to the collection and evaluation of dreams in early childhood and pre-catastrophal dreams, i.e., dreams occurring before accidents, illness, and death, as well as dreams during severe illnesses and under narcosis. The investigation of pre- and post-mortal psychic phenomena also comes into this category. These are particularly important because of the relativation of space and time that accompanies them. A difficult but interesting task would be research into the processes of compensation in psychotics and in criminals, and in general into the goal of compensation and the nature of its directedness.

1139   In normal psychology, the most important subjects for research

16 [(1905–68), professor of philosophy and comparative religion, Theological Seminary of Schöneck (Cant. Nidwalden). Cf. his *Probleme der Parapsychologie: Gesammelte Aufsätze*, ed. A. Resch (1969).]

would be the psychic structure of the family in relation to heredity, the compensatory character of marriage and of emotional relationships in general. A particularly pressing problem is the behaviour of the individual in the mass and the unconscious compensation to which this gives rise.

1140   A rich harvest is to be reaped in the field of the humanities. Here a tremendous prospect opens out, and at present we are standing only on its extreme periphery. Most of it is still virgin territory. The same applies to biographical studies, which are especially important for the history of literature. But above all, analytical work remains to be done on questions concerned with the psychology of religion. The study of religious myths would throw light not only on racial psychology but also on certain borderline problems such as the one I mentioned earlier. In this respect, particular attention would have to be paid to the quaternity symbol and the *proportio sesquitertia,* as exemplified in the alchemical axiom of Maria, both from the side of the psychologist and from that of the physicist. The physicist may have to consider revising his concept of space-time, and for the psychologist there is need of a more thorough investigation and description of triadic and tetradic symbols and their historical development, to which Frobenius has contributed valuable material. Comprehensive studies are also needed of symbols of the goal or of unity.

1141   This list, put together more or less at random, makes no claim to completeness. What I have said may suffice to give you a rough idea of what has already been achieved in complex psychology and of the direction which future researches conducted by the Institute might be expected to take. Much will remain a mere desideratum. Not all of it will be fulfilled; the individual differences of our workers on the one hand, and the irrationality and unpredictability of all scientific development on the other, will see to that. Happily, it is the prerogative of any institution with limited means, and not run by the State, to produce work of high quality in order to survive.

DEPTH PSYCHOLOGY[1]

¹¹⁴² "Depth psychology" is a term deriving from medical psychology, coined by Eugen Bleuler to denote that branch of psychological science which is concerned with the phenomenon of the unconscious.

¹¹⁴³ As a philosophical and metaphysical concept, the unconscious occurs fairly early, for instance as "petites perceptions" in Leibniz,[2] "eternal unconscious" in Schelling, "unconscious Will" in Schopenhauer, and as the "divine Absolute" in von Hartmann.

¹¹⁴⁴ In the academic psychology of the nineteenth century, the unconscious occurs as a basic theoretical concept in Theodor Lipps, who defines it as the "psychic reality which must necessarily be thought to underlie the existence of a conscious content"; and in F. H.W. Myers and William James, who stress the importance of an unconscious psyche. With Theodor Fechner, the unconscious becomes an empirical concept. Nevertheless, the empirical approach to the unconscious may properly be said to date from quite recent times, since up to the turn of the century the psyche was usually identified with consciousness, and this made the idea of the unconscious appear untenable (Wundt).

¹¹⁴⁵ The real pioneers of experimental research into the unconscious were Pierre Janet and Sigmund Freud, two medical psychologists whose investigations of pathological psychic life laid the foundations of the modern science of the unconscious. Great credit is due to Janet for his investigation of hysterical states, which he developed in his theory of "partial psychic dissociation," drawing a distinction between the "partie supérieure" and "partie inférieure" of a function. Equally fruitful was his experimental proof of "idées fixes" and "obsessions," and of their autonomous effects upon consciousness.

---

[1] [Article written (in 1948) for the *Lexicon der Paedogogik* (Bern, 1951), vol. II, pp. 768–73: "Tiefenpsychologie."]

[2] [That is, subliminal perceptions which are not apperceived. Cf. "Synchronicity" (C.W., vol. 8), pars. 931, 937. For the references in this and the following par., cf. L. L. Whyte, *The Unconscious before Freud*, index, ss.vv.]

1146   The prominence given to the unconscious as a fundamental concept of empirical psychology, however, goes back to Freud, the true founder of the depth psychology which bears the name of psychoanalysis. This is a special method of treating psychic illnesses, and consists essentially in uncovering what is "hidden, forgotten, and repressed" in psychic life. Freud was a nerve specialist. His theory was evolved in the consulting room and always preserved its stamp. His fundamental premise was the pathological, neurotically degenerate psyche.

1147   The development of Freud's thought can be traced as follows. He began by investigating neurotic symptoms, more particularly hysterical symptom-formation, whose psychic origin Breuer, employing a method borrowed from hypnotism, had previously discovered in the existence of a causal connection between the symptoms and certain experiences of which the patient was unconscious. In these experiences Freud recognized affects which had somehow got "blocked," and from which the patient had to be freed. He found there was a meaningful connection between the symptom and the affective experience, so much so that conscious experiences which later became unconscious were essential components of neurotic symptoms. The affects remained unconscious because of their painful nature. In consequence, Freud made no further use of hypnosis in "abreacting" the blocked affects, but developed instead his technique of "free association" for bringing the repressed processes back to consciousness. He thus laid the foundations of a causal-reductive method, of which special use was to be made in his interpretation of dreams.

1148   In order to explain the origin of hysteria, Freud established the theory of the sexual trauma. He found that traumatic experiences were especially painful because most of them were caused by instinctual impulses coming from the sexual sphere. He assumed to begin with that hysteria in general was due to a sexual trauma in childhood. Later he stressed the aetiological significance of infantile-sexual fantasies that proved to be incompatible with the moral values of consciousness and were therefore repressed. The theory of repression forms the core of Freud's teaching. According to this theory, the unconscious is essentially a phenomenon of repression, and its contents are elements of the personal psyche that although once conscious are now lost to consciousness. The unconscious would thus owe its existence to a moral conflict.

1149   The existence of these unconscious factors can be demonstrated,

478

as Freud showed, with the help of parapraxes (slips of the tongue, forgetting, misreading) and above all with the help of dreams, which are an important source of information regarding unconscious contents. It is Freud's particular merit to have made dreams once more a problem for psychologists and to have attempted a new method of interpretation. He explained them by means of the repression theory, and maintained that they consisted of morally incompatible elements which, though capable of becoming conscious, were suppressed by an unconscious moral factor, the "censor," and could therefore appear only in the form of disguised wish-fulfillments.

1150   The instinctual conflict underlying this phenomenon Freud described initially as the conflict between the pleasure principle and the reality principle, the latter playing the part of an inhibiting factor. Later he described it as the conflict between the sexual instinct and the ego-instinct (or between the life-instinct and the death-instinct). The obtaining of pleasure was correlated with the pleasure principle, and the culture-creating impulse with the reality principle. Culture required the sacrifice of instinctual gratification by the whole of mankind and the individual alike. Resistance to this sacrifice led to secret wish-fulfillments distorted by the "censor." The danger inherent in this theory was that it made culture appear a substitute for unsatisfied natural instincts, so that complex psychic phenomena like art, philosophy, and religion became "suspect," as though they were "nothing but" the outcome of sexual repression. It would seem that Freud's negative and reductive attitude towards cultural values was historically conditioned. His attitude towards myth and religion was that of the scientific materialism of the nineteenth century. As his psychology was mainly concerned with the neuroses, the pathological aspect of the transformation of instinct claims a disproportionately large place in his theory of the unconscious and of the neuroses themselves. The unconscious appears to be essentially an appendix of consciousness; its contents are repressed wishes, affects, and memories that owe their pathogenic significance to infantile sexuality. The most important of the repressed contents is the so-called Oedipus complex, which represents the fixation of infantile sexual wishes on the mother and the resistance to the father arising from feelings of envy and fear. This complex forms the core of a neurosis.

1151   The question of the dynamics of unconscious fantasy-formations led Freud to a concept of great importance for the further develop-

479

ment of depth psychology, namely, the concept of libido. At first he regarded this as the sexual instinct, but later broadened it by assuming the existence of "libidinal affluxes" due to the displacement and dissociability of the libido. Through the investigation of libido-fixations Freud discovered the "transference," a fundamental phenomenon in the treatment of neurosis. Instead of recollecting the repressed elements, the patient "transfers" them to the analyst in the form of some current experience; that is, he projects them and thereby involves the analyst in his "family romance." In this way his illness is converted into the "transference neurosis" and is then acted out between them.

1152 Freud later expanded the concept of the unconscious by calling it the "id" in contradistinction to the conscious ego. (The term derives from Groddeck.) The id represents the natural unconscious dynamism of man, while the ego forms that part of the id which is modified under the influence of the environment or is replaced by the reality principle. In working out the relations between the ego and the id, Freud discovered that the ego contains not only conscious but also unconscious contents, and he was therefore compelled to frame a concept to characterize the unconscious portion of the ego, which he called the "super-ego" or "ego-ideal." He regarded this as the representative of the parental authority, as the successor of the Oedipus complex, that impels the ego to restrain the id. It manifests itself as conscience, which, invested with the authority of collective morality, continues to display the character of the father. The super-ego accounts for the activity of the censor in dreams.

1153 Although Alfred Adler is usually included among the founders of depth psychology, his school of *individual psychology* represents only a partial continuation of the line of research initiated by his teacher Freud. Confronted with the same empirical material, Adler considered it from an entirely different point of view. For him, the primary aetiological factor was not sexuality but the power-drive. The neurotic individual appeared to him to be in conflict with society, with the result that his spontaneous development was blocked. On this view the individual never exists for himself alone; he maintains his psychic existence only within the community. In contrast to the emphasis Freud laid on instinctual strivings, Adler stressed the importance of environmental factors as possible causes of neurosis. Neurotic symptoms and disturbances of personality were the result of a morbidly intensified valuation of the ego, which, instead of adapting to reality, develops a system of "guiding fictions." This hypothesis gives expression to a finalistic viewpoint diametrically opposed to the causal-reductive method of Freud, in that it emphasizes the direction towards a goal. Each individual chooses a guiding line as a basic pattern for the organization of all psychic contents. Among the possible guiding fictions, Adler attached special importance to the winning of superiority and power over others, the urge "to be on top." The original source of this misguided ambition lies in a deep-rooted feeling of inferiority, necessitating an over-compensation in the form of security. A primary organ-inferiority, or inferiority of the constitution as a whole, often proves to be an aetiological factor. Environmental influences in early childhood play their part in building up this psychic mechanism, since it is then that the foundations are laid for the development of the guiding fiction. The fiction of future superiority is maintained by tendentiously distorting all valuations and giving undue importance to being "on top" as opposed to "underneath," "masculine" as opposed to "feminine," a tendency which finds its clearest expression in the so-called "masculine protest."

1154　　In Adler's individual psychology, Freud's basic concepts undergo a process of recasting. The Oedipus complex, for example, loses its importance in view of the increasing drive for security; illness becomes a neurotic "arrangement" for the purpose of consolidating the life-plan. Repression loses its aetiological significance when understood as an instrument for the better realization of the guiding fiction. Even the unconscious appears as an "artifice of the psyche," so that it may very well be asked whether Adler can be included among the founders of depth psychology. Dreams, too, he regarded as distortions aiming at the fictive security of the ego and the strengthening of the power drive. Nevertheless, the services rendered by Adler and his school to the phenomenology of personality disturbances in children should not be overlooked. Above all, it must be emphasized that a whole class of neuroses can in fact be explained primarily in terms of the power drive.

1155　　Whereas Freud started out as a neurologist, and Adler later became his pupil, C. G. Jung was a pupil of Eugen Bleuler and began his career as a psychiatrist. Before he came into contact with Freud's ideas, he had, in treating a case of somnambulism in a fifteen-year-old girl (1899), observed that her unconscious contained the beginnings of a future personality development, which took the form of a split (or "double") personality. Through experimental researches on association (1903) he found that in normal individuals as well as in neurotics the reactions to word-tests were disturbed by split-off ("repressed") emotional *complexes* ("feeling-toned complexes of ideas"), which manifested themselves by means of definite symptoms ("complex-indicators"). These experiments confirmed the existence of the repressions described by Freud and their characteristic consequences. In 1906 Jung gave polemical support to Freud's discovery. The theory of complexes maintains that neurosis is caused by the splitting-off of a vitally important complex. Similar splinter-complexes can be observed in schizophrenia. In this disease the personality is, as it were, broken up into its complexes, with the result that the normal ego-complex almost disappears. The splinter-complexes are relatively autonomous, are not subject to the conscious will, and cannot be corrected so long as they remain unconscious. They lend themselves to personification (in dreams, for instance), and, with increasing dissociation and autonomy, assume the character of partial personalities (hence the old view of neuroses and psychoses as states of possession).

1156   In 1907 Jung became personally acquainted with Freud, and derived from him a wealth of insights, particularly in regard to dream psychology and the treatment of neurosis. But in certain respects he arrived at views which differed from those of Freud. Experience did not seem to him to justify Freud's sexual theory of neurosis, and still less that of schizophrenia. The conception of the unconscious needed to be broadened, inasmuch as the unconscious was not just a product of repression but was the creative matrix of consciousness. Equally, he was of the opinion that the unconscious could not be explained in personalistic terms, as a merely personal phenomenon, but that it was also in part collective. Accordingly, he rejected the view that it possessed a merely instinctual nature, as well as rejecting the wish-fulfillment theory of dreams. Instead, he emphasized the compensatory function of the unconscious processes and their teleological character. For the wish-fulfillment theory he substituted the concept of development of personality and development of consciousness, holding that the unconscious does not consist only of morally incompatible wishes but is largely composed of hitherto undeveloped, unconscious portions of the personality which strive for integration in the wholeness of the individual. In the neurotic, this process of realization is manifested in the conflict between the relatively mature side of the personality and the side which Freud rightly described as infantile. The conflict

has at first a purely personal character and can be explained per-
sonalistically, as the patients themselves do, and moreover in a manner which agrees both in principle and in detail with the Freudian
explanation. Their standpoint is a purely personal and egoistic one,
and takes no account of the collective factors, this being the very
reason why they are ill. In schizophrenics, on the other hand, the
collective contents of the unconscious predominate strongly in the
form of mythological motifs. Freud could not subscribe to these
modifications of his views, so Jung and he parted company.

1157   Such differences of viewpoint, further increased by the contradiction between Freud's and Adler's explanation of neurosis,
prompted Jung to investigate more closely the important question
of the conscious attitude, on which the compensatory function of
the unconscious depends. Already in his association experiments
he had found indications of an *attitude-type,* and this was now
confirmed by clinical observations. As a general and habitual disposition in every individual, there proved to be a more or less pronounced tendency towards either *extraversion* or *introversion,* the
focus of interest falling in the first case on the object, and in the
second on the subject. These attitudes of consciousness determine
the corresponding modes of compensation by the unconscious: the
emergence in the first case of unconscious demands upon the subject, and in the second of unconscious ties to the object. These
relationships, in part complementary, in part compensatory, are
complicated by the simultaneous participation of the variously
differentiated *orienting functions* of consciousness, namely, *thinking,
feeling, sensation,* and *intuition,* which are needed for a whole judgment. The most differentiated ("superior") function is comple-
mented or compensated by the least differentiated ("inferior")
function, but at first only in the form of a conflict.

1158   Further investigation of the collective material of the unconscious, presented by schizophrenics and by the dreams of neurotics
and normal people, elicited typical figures or motifs which have
their counterparts in myth and may therefore be called *archetypes.*
These are not to be thought of as inherited ideas; rather, they are
the equivalent of the "pattern of behaviour" in biology. The archetype represents a mode of psychic behaviour. As such, it is an
"irrepresentable" factor which unconsciously arranges the psychic
elements so that they fall into typical configurations, much as a
crystalline grid arranges the molecules in a saturated solution. The
specific associations and memory images forming these configurations

vary endlessly from individual to individual; only the basic pattern remains the same. One of the clearest of these archetypal figures is the *anima,* the personification of the unconscious in feminine form. This archetype is peculiar to masculine psychology, since the unconscious of a man is by nature feminine, probably owing to the fact that sex is determined merely by a preponderance of masculine genes, the feminine genes retreating into the background. The corresponding role in a woman is played by the *animus.* A figure common to both sexes is the *shadow,* a personification of the inferior side of the personality. These three figures appear very frequently in the dreams and fantasies of normal people, neurotics and schizophrenics. Less frequent is the archetype of the *wise old man* and of the *earth mother.* Besides these there are a number of functional and situational motifs, such as ascent and descent, the crossing (ford or strait), tension and suspension between opposites, the world of darkness, the breakthrough (or invasion), the creation of fire, helpful or dangerous animals, etc. Most important of all is the supposedly central archetype or *self,* which seems to be the point of reference for the unconscious psyche, just as the ego is the point of reference for consciousness. The symbolism associated with this archetype expresses itself on the one hand in circular, spherical, and quaternary forms, in the "squaring of the circle," and in mandala symbolism; on the other hand in the imagery of the supraordinate personality (God-image, Anthropos symbolism).

1159   These empirical findings show that the unconscious consists of two layers: a superficial layer, representing the *personal unconscious,* and a deeper layer, representing the *collective unconscious.* The former is made up of personal contents, i.e., things forgotten and repressed, subliminal or "extrasensory" perceptions and anticipations of future developments, as well as other psychic processes that never reach the threshold of consciousness. A neurosis originates in a conflict between consciousness and the personal unconscious, whereas a psychosis has deeper roots and consists in a conflict involving the collective unconscious. The great majority of dreams contain mainly personal material, and their protagonists are the ego and the shadow. Normally, the dream material serves only to compensate the conscious attitude. There are, however, comparatively rare dreams (the "big" dreams of primitives) which contain clearly recognizable mythological motifs. Dreams of this sort are of especial importance for the development of personality. Their psychotherapeutic value was recognized even in ancient times.

1160   Since the personal unconscious contains the still active residues of the past as well as the seeds of the future, it exerts a direct and very considerable influence on the conscious behaviour of the individual. All cases of unusual behaviour in children should be investigated for their psychic antecedents through rigorous interrogation of both child and parents. The behaviour of the parents, whether they have open or hidden conflicts, etc., has an incalculable effect on the unconscious of the child. The causes of infantile neurosis are to be sought less in the children than in the parents or teachers. The teacher should be more conscious of his shadow than the average person, otherwise the work of one hand can easily be undone by the other. It is for this reason that medical psychotherapists are required to undergo a training analysis, in order to gain insight into their own unconscious psyche.

1160a   Thanks to the parallelism between mythological motifs and the archetypes of the unconscious, depth psychology has been applied in widely differing fields of research, especially by students of mythology, folklore, comparative religion, and the psychology of primitives (Richard Wilhelm, Heinrich Zimmer, Karl Kerényi, Hugo Rahner, Erich Neumann), as was also the case with the Freudian school earlier (Karl Abraham, Otto Rank, Ernest Jones). As the archetypes have a "numinous" quality and underlie all religious and dogmatic ideas, depth psychology is also of importance for theology.

1161   The activity of the collective unconscious manifests itself not only in compensatory effects in the lives of individuals, but also in the mutation of dominant ideas in the course of the centuries. This can be seen most clearly in religion, and, to a lesser extent, in the various philosophical, social, and political ideologies. It appears in most dangerous form in the sudden rise and spread of psychic epidemics, as for instance in the witch hunts in Germany at the end of the fourteenth century, or in the social and political utopias of the twentieth century. How far the collective unconscious may be considered the efficient cause of such movements, or merely their material cause, is a question for ethnologists and psychologists to decide; but certain experiences in the field of individual psychology indicate the possibility of a spontaneous activity of archetypes. These experiences usually concern individuals in the second half of life, when it not infrequently happens that drastic changes of outlook are thrust upon them by the unconscious as a result of some defect in their conscious attitude. While the activity

485

of the personal unconscious is confined to compensatory changes in the personal sphere, the changes effected by the collective unconscious have a collective aspect: they alter our view of the world, and, like a contagion, infect our fellow men. (Hence the astonishing effects of certain psychopaths on society!)

1162   The regulating influence of the collective unconscious can be seen at work in the psychic development of the individual, or *individuation process*. Its main phases are expressed by the classic archetypes that are found in the ancient initiation mysteries and in Hermetic philosophy. These archetypal figures appear in projected form during the transference. Freud recognized only the personal aspect of this psychotherapeutically very important phenomenon. Despite appearances to the contrary, its real psychotherapeutic value does not lie in the sphere of personal problems (a misunderstanding for which the neurotic patient has to pay dearly), but in the projection of archetypal figures (anima, animus, etc.). The archetypal relationships thus produced during the transference serve to compensate the unlimited exogamy of our culture by a realization of the unconscious endogamous tendency. The goal of the psychotherapeutic process, the self-regulation of the psyche by means of the natural drive towards individuation, is expressed by the above-mentioned mandala and Anthropos symbolism.

FOREWORD TO THE FIRST VOLUME OF STUDIES FROM THE C. G. JUNG INSTITUTE[1]

1163   The works which the Institute proposes to publish in this series derive from many different spheres of knowledge. This is understandable since they are predominantly psychological in character. Psychology, of its very nature, is the intermediary between the disciplines, for the psyche is the mother of all the sciences and arts. Anyone who wishes to paint her portrait must mingle many colours on his palette. In order to do justice to its subject, psychology has to rely on any number of auxiliary sciences, on whose findings its own growth and prosperity depend. The psychologist gratefully acknowledges his borrowings from other sciences, though he has neither the intention nor the ambition to usurp their domains or to "know better." He has no wish to intrude into other fields but restricts himself to using their findings for his own purposes. Thus, for example, he will not use historical material in order to write history but rather to demonstrate the nature of the psyche—a concern which is foreign to the historian.

1164   The forthcoming publications in this series will show the great diversity of psychological interests and needs. Recent developments in psychological research, in particular the psychology of the collective unconscious, have confronted us with problems which require the collaboration of other sciences. The facts and relationships unearthed by the analysis of the unconscious offer so many parallels to the phenomenology of myths, for example, that their psychological elucidation may also shed light on the mythological figures and their symbols. At all events, we must gratefully acknowledge the invaluable support psychology has received from students of myths and fairy-tales, as well as from comparative religion, even if they

[1] [Vol. I of Studien aus dem C. G. Jung Institut, Zurich, 1949: C. A. Meier, *Antike Inkubation und moderne Psychotherapie*. The foreword was published in a trans. by Ralph Manheim, in the first vol. of Studies in Jungian Thought, James Hillman, General Editor: *Evil: Essays by Carl Kerényi* [and others] (Evanston, Ill., 1967), and (same series, same year), in a trans. of Meier's book: *Ancient Incubation and Modern Psychotherapy*. The present trans. is by R.F.C. Hull.]

on their part have not yet learnt how to make use of its insights. The psychology of the unconscious is still a very young science which must first justify its existence before a critical public. This is the end which the publications of the Institute are designed to serve.

September 1948

FOREWORD TO FRIEDA FORDHAM:
"INTRODUCTION TO JUNG'S PSYCHOLOGY"[1]

1165   Mrs. Frieda Fordham has undertaken the by no means easy task of producing a readable résumé of all my various attempts at a better and more comprehensive understanding of the human psyche. As I cannot claim to have reached any definite theory explaining all or even the main part of the psyche's complexities, my work consists of a series of different approaches, or one might call it a circumambulation of unknown factors. This makes it rather difficult to give a clear-cut and simple account of my ideas. Moreover, I always felt a particular responsibility not to overlook the fact that the psyche does not reveal itself only in the doctor's consulting-room, but above all in the wide world, as well as in the depths of history. What the doctor observes of its manifestations is an infinitesimal part of the psychic world, and moreover often distorted by pathological conditions. I was always convinced that a fair picture of the psyche could be obtained only by a comparative method. But the great disadvantage of such a method is that one cannot avoid the accumulation of comparative material, with the result that the layman becomes bewildered and loses his tracks in the maze of parallels.

1166   The author's task would have been much simpler if she had been in possession of a neat theory for a *point de départ,* and of well-defined case material without digressions into the immense field of general psychology. The latter, however, seems to me to form the only safe basis and criterion for the evaluation of pathological phenomena, even as normal anatomy and physiology are an indispensable precondition for a study of their pathological aspects. Just as human anatomy has a long evolution behind it, the psychology of modern man depends upon its historical roots and can only be judged by its ethnological variants. My works offer innumerable possibilities of side-tracking the reader's attention with considerations of this sort.

---

[1] [Penguin Books, 1953. The foreword was written in English.]

1167   Under those somewhat trying conditions the author has nevertheless succeeded in extricating herself from all the opportunities to make mis-statements. She has presented a fair and simple account of the main aspects of my psychological work. I am indebted to her for this admirable piece of work.

September 1952

FOREWORD TO MICHAEL FORDHAM: "NEW DEVELOPMENTS IN ANALYTICAL PSYCHOLOGY"[1]

1168   It is not easy to write a foreword to a book consisting of a collection of essays, especially when each essay requires one to take up an attitude or stimulates the reader into discursive comments. But this is just what Dr. Fordham's papers do: every single one of them is so carefully thought out that the reader can hardly avoid holding a conversation with it. I do not mean in a polemical sense, but rather in the sense of affirmation and in the desire to carry the objective discussion a stage further and collaborate on the solution of the problems involved. Opportunities for such enjoyable dialogues are unfortunately rather rare, so that one feels it as a distinct loss when one has to forgo them. A foreword ought not to make remarks to the author and, so to speak, buttonhole him for a private conversation. It ought, rather, to convey to the reader something of the impressions which the writer of the foreword received when reading the manuscript. If I may be forgiven a somewhat frivolous expression, the foreword should be content with the role of an intellectual aperitif.

1169   Thus I can confess myself grateful for the stimulation the book has brought me, and salute the author's collaboration in the field of psychotherapy and analytical psychology. For in this territory questions arise of a practical and theoretical kind, which are so difficult to answer that they will continue to exercise our minds for a long time to come. Above all I would like to draw attention to Dr. Fordham's discussion of the problem of synchronicity, first mooted by me and now dealt with by him in a masterly manner. I must rate his achievement all the higher because it demands not only understanding, but courage too, not to let oneself be prevented from going more deeply into this problem by the prejudices of our intellectual compeers. Also I must acknowledge that the author has in no wise succumbed to the very understandable temptation to underestimate the problem, to pass off one's own lack of comprehension as the stupidity of others, to substitute other terms for the

---

1 [London, 1957. The foreword was written in English.]

concepts I have proposed and to think that something new has been said. Here Dr. Fordham's feeling for essentials is confirmed in the finest way.

1170 The paper on the transference merits attentive reading. Dr. Fordham guides his reader through the multifarious aspects of this "problem with horns"—to use an expression of Nietzsche's—with circumspection, insight, and caution, as befits this in every respect delicate theme. The problem of the transference occupies a central position in the dialectical process of analytical psychology and therefore merits quite special interest. It makes the highest demands not only on the doctor's knowledge and skill but also on his moral responsibility. Here the truth of the old alchemical dictum is proved yet again: "ars totum requirit hominem" (the art requires the total man). The author takes full account of the overriding importance of this phenomenon and accordingly devotes to it a particularly attentive and careful exposition. The practising psychologist would be very wrong if he thought he could dismiss general considerations of this kind based on broader principles, and dispense with all deeper reflection. Even if psychotherapy admits of numerous provisional and superficial solutions in practice, the practising analyst will nevertheless come up against cases from time to time that challenge him as a man and a personality in a way that may be decisive. The usual interim solutions and other banal expedients, such as appeals to collective precepts, which are invariably constructed with "must" or "ought," then have a habit of breaking down, and the question of ultimate principles, or of the ultimate meaning of the individual, arises. This is the moment when dogmatic tenets and pragmatic rules of thumb must make way for a creative solution issuing from the total man, if his therapeutic endeavours are not to get miserably silted up and stuck. In such cases he will need reflection and will be thankful to those who have been farsighted enough to struggle for an all-round understanding.

1171 For it is not only a routine performance that is expected of the analyst, but also a readiness and ability to master unusual situations. This is particularly true of psychotherapy, where in the last analysis we are concerned with the whole of the human personality and not merely with life in its partial aspects. Routine cases can be disposed of in a variety of ways—with good advice, with suggestion, with a bit of training, with confession of sin, with any more or less plausible system of views and methods. It is the uncommon cases that set us the master test, by forcing us into fundamental reflections and demanding decisions of principle. From this vantage point we shall then discover that even in ordinary cases there is adumbrated a line that leads to the central theme, namely, the individuation process with its problem of opposites.

1172   This level of insight cannot be reached without the dialectical discussion between two individuals. Here the phenomenon of the transference forcibly brings about a dialogue that can only be continued if both patient and analyst acknowledge themselves as partners in a common process of approximation and differentiation. For, in so far as the patient frees himself from his infantile state of unconsciousness and its restrictive handicaps, or from its opposite, namely unbounded egocentricity, the analyst will see himself obliged to diminish the distance between them (hitherto necessary for reasons of professional authority), to a degree that does not prevent him from displaying that measure of humanity which the patient needs in order to assure himself of his right to exist as an individual. Just as it is the duty of parents and educators not to keep children on the infantile level but to lead them beyond it, so it is incumbent on the analyst not to treat patients as chronic invalids but to recognize them, in accordance with their spiritual development and insight, as more or less equal partners in the dialogue, with the same rights as himself. An authority that deems itself superior, or a personality that remains *hors concours,* only increases the patient's feelings of inferiority and of being excluded. An analyst who cannot risk his authority will be sure to lose it. In order to maintain his prestige he will be in danger of wrapping himself in the protective mantle of a doctrine. But life cannot be mastered with theories, and just as the cure of neurosis is not, ultimately, a mere question of therapeutic skill, but is a moral achievement, so too is the solution of problems thrown up by the transference. No theory can give us any information about the ultimate requirements of individuation, nor are there any recipes that can be applied in a routine manner. The treatment of the transference reveals in a pitiless light what the healing agent really is: it is the degree to which the analyst himself can cope with his own psychic problems. The higher levels of therapy involve his own reality and are the acid test of his superiority.

1173   I hope Dr. Fordham's book, which is distinguished for its farsightedness, carefulness, and clarity of style, will meet with the interest it so much deserves.

June 1957

AN ASTROLOGICAL EXPERIMENT[1]

1174   In the Swiss edition[2] I purposely set out the results of the astrological statistics in tabular form in this chapter, so that the reader could gain some insight into the behaviour of the figures—in other words, see for himself how fortuitous these results were. Subsequently, I wanted to suppress that account of the experiment in the English edition and for a very peculiar reason indeed. That is, it has been forcibly borne in on me that practically nobody has understood it the right way, despite—or perhaps because—of the fact that I took the trouble to describe the experiment in great detail and in all its vicissitudes. Since it involved the use of statistics and comparative frequencies, I had the (as it now seems) unlucky idea that it would be helpful to present the resultant figures in tabular form. But evidently the suggestive effect emanating from statistical tables is so strong that nobody can rid himself of the notion that such an array of figures is somehow connected with the tendentious desire to *prove* something. Nothing could have been further from my mind, because all I intended to do was to describe a certain sequence of events in all its aspects. This altogether too unassuming intention was misunderstood all round, with the consequence that the meaning of the whole exposition went by the board.

1175   I am not going to commit this mistake again, but shall make my point at once by anticipating the result: the experiment shows how synchronicity plays havoc with statistical material. Even the choice of my material seems to have thrown my readers into confusion, since it is concerned with *astrological* statistics. One can easily imagine how obnoxious such a choice must be to a prudish intellectualism. Astrology, we are told, is unscientific, absolute nonsense, and everything to do with it is branded as rank superstition. In

---

[1] [A condensed version of ch. II of "Synchronicity: An Acausal Connecting Principle" (C.W., vol. 8). Published as "Ein astrologisches Experiment," *Zeitschrift für Parapsychologie und Grenzgebiete der Psychologie* (Bern), I:2/3 (May 1958), 81–92. A long prefatory note by the editor, Hans Bender, quoted a letter to him from Jung, 12 Feb. 1958, in further clarification; it is in *Letters*, ed. G. Adler, vol. 2.]

[2] [Jung and Pauli, *Naturerklärung und Psyche,* 1952.]

such a dubious context, how could columns of figures mean anything except an attempt to furnish proofs in favour of astrology,
proofs whose invalidity is a foregone conclusion? I have already
said that there was never any question of that—but what can words
do against numerical tables?

1176   We hear so much of astrology nowadays that I determined to
inquire a little more closely into the empirical foundations of this
intuitive method. For this reason I picked on the following question:
*How do the conjunctions and oppositions of the sun, moon, Mars,
Venus, ascendant, and descendant behave in the horoscopes of married people?* The sum of all these aspects amount to fifty.

1177   The material to be examined, namely, marriage horoscopes, was
obtained from friendly donors in Zurich, London, Rome, and
Vienna. The horoscopes, or rather the birth data, were piled up
in chronological order just as the post brought them in. The misunderstanding already began here, as several astrological authorities
informed me that my procedure was quite unsuited to evaluating
the marriage relationship. I thank these amiable counsellors, but
on my side there was never any intention of evaluating marriage
astrologically but only of investigating the question raised above.
As the material only trickled in very slowly I was unable to restrain
my curiosity any longer, and I also wanted to test out the methods
to be employed. I therefore took the 360 horoscopes (i.e., 180 pairs)
that had so far accumulated and gave the material to my co-
worker, Dr. Liliane Frey-Rohn, to be analysed. I called these 180
pairs the "first batch."

1178   Examination of this batch showed that the conjunction of sun
(masculine) and moon (feminine) was the most frequent of all
the 50 aspects, occurring in 10% of all cases. The second batch,
evaluated later, consisted of 440 additional horoscopes (220 pairs)
and showed as the most frequent aspect a moon-moon conjunction
(10.9%). A third batch, consisting of 166 horoscopes (83 pairs),
showed as the most frequent aspect the ascendant-moon conjunction (9.6%).

1179   What interested me most to begin with was, of course, the question of probability: were the maximum results obtained "significant" figures or not; that is, were they improbable or not? Calcula-
tions undertaken by a mathematician showed unmistakably that
the average frequency of 10% in all three batches is far from representing a significant figure. Its probability is much too great; in
other words, there is no ground for assuming that our maximum

frequencies are more than mere dispersions due to chance. Thus far the result of our statistics (which nevertheless cover nearly one thousand horoscopes) is disappointing for astrology. The material is, however, much too scanty for us to be able to draw from it any conclusions either for or against.

1180 But if we look at the results qualitatively, we are immediately struck by the fact that in all three batches it is a *moon conjunction,* and what is more—a point which the astrologer will doubtless appreciate—a conjunction of moon and sun, moon and moon, moon and ascendant, respectively. The sun indicates the month, the moon the day, and the ascendant the "moment" of birth. The positions of sun, moon, and ascendant form the three main pillars of the horoscope. It is altogether probable that a moon conjunction should occur once, but that it should occur three times is extremely improbable (the improbability increases by the square each time), and that it should single out precisely the three main positions of the horoscope from among 47 other possibilities is something supranormal and looks like the most gorgeous falsification in favour of astrology.

1181 These results, as simple as they are unexpected, were consistently misunderstood by the statisticians. They thought I wanted to prove something with my set of figures, whereas I only wished to give an ocular demonstration of their "chance" nature. It is naturally a little unexpected that a set of figures, meaningless in themselves, should "arrange" a result which everybody agrees to be improbable. It seems in fact to be an instance of that possibility which Spencer-Brown has in mind when he says that "the results of the best-designed and most rigorously observed experiments in psychical research are chance results after all," and that "the concept of chance can cover a wider natural field than we previously suspected."[3] In other words what the previous statistical view obliged us to regard as "significant," that is, as a quasi-intentional grouping or arrangement, must be regarded equally as belonging to the realm of chance, which means nothing less than that the whole concept of probability must be revised. One can also interpret Spencer-Brown's view as meaning that under certain circumstances the quality of "pseudo-intention" attaches to chance, or—if we wish to avoid a negative formulation—that chance can "create" meaningful arrangements that look as if a causal intention had been

[3] [G. Spencer-Brown, "Statistical Significance in Psychical Research," *Nature,* vol. 172, 25 July 1953, p. 154.]

at work. But that is precisely what I mean by "synchronicity," and what I wanted to demonstrate in the report on my astrological experiment. Naturally I did not embark on the experiment for the purpose of achieving, or in anticipation of, this unexpected result, which no one could have foreseen; I was only curious to find out what sort of numbers would turn up in an investigation of this kind. This wish seemed suspicious not only to certain astrologers but also to my friendly mathematical adviser, who saw fit to warn me against thinking that my maximal figures would be a proof of the astrological thesis. Neither before nor afterwards was there any thought of such proof, besides which my experiment was arranged in a way most unsuited to that purpose, as my astrological critics had already pointed out.

1182   Since most people believe that numbers have been *invented* or thought out by man, and are therefore nothing but concepts of quantities, containing nothing that was not previously put into them by the human intellect, it was naturally very difficult for me to put my question in any other form. But it is equally possible that numbers were *found* or discovered. In that case they are not only concepts but something more—autonomous entities which somehow contain more than just quantities. Unlike concepts they are based not on any psychic assumption but on the quality of being themselves, on a "so-ness" that cannot be expressed by an intellectual concept. Under these circumstances they might easily be endowed with qualities that have still to be discovered. Also one could, as with all autonomous beings, raise the question of their behaviour; for instance one could ask what numbers do when they are intended to express something as archetypal as astrology. For astrology is the last remnant, now applied to the stars, of that fateful assemblage of gods whose numinosity can still be felt despite the critical procedures of our scientific age. In no previous age, however "superstitious," was astrology so widespread and so highly esteemed as it is today.

1183   I must confess that I incline to the view that numbers were as much found as invented, and that in consequence they possess a relative autonomy analogous to that of the archetypes. They would then have, in common with the latter, the quality of being pre-existent to consciousness, and hence, on occasion, of conditioning it rather than being conditioned by it. The archetypes too, as *a priori* forms of representation, are as much found as invented: they are *discovered* inasmuch as one did not know of their unconscious autonomous existence, and *invented* by the mind inasmuch as their presence was inferred from analogous representational structures. Accordingly it would seem that natural numbers must possess an archetypal character. If that is so, then not only would certain numbers have a relation to and an effect on certain archetypes, but the reverse would also be true. The first case is equivalent to number magic, but the second is equivalent to my question whether numbers, in conjunction with the numinous assemblage of gods which the horoscope represents, would show a tendency to behave in a special way.

1184   All reasonable people, especially mathematicians, are acutely concerned with the question of what we can do by means of numbers. Only a few devote any attention to the question of what, in so far as they are autonomous, numbers do in themselves. The question sounds so absurd that one hardly dares to utter it in decent intellectual society. I could not predict what result my scandalous statistics would show. I had to wait and see. And as a matter of fact my figures behaved in so obliging a fashion that an astrologer can probably appreciate them far better than a mathematician. Owing to their excessively strict adherence to reason, mathematicians seem unable to see beyond the fact that in each separate case my result has too great a probability to prove anything about astrology. Of course it doesn't, because it was never intended to do any such thing, and I never for a moment believed that the maximum, falling each time on a moon conjunction, represented a so-called significant figure. Yet in spite of this critical attitude a number of mistakes were made in working out and computing the statistics, which all without exception contrived to bring about the most favourable possible result for astrology. As though to punish him for his well-meaning warning, the worst mistake of all fell to the lot of my mathematician, who at first calculated far too small a probability for the individual maxima, and was thus unwittingly deceived by the unconscious in the interests of astrological prestige.

1185   Such lapses can easily be explained by a secret support for astrology in face of the violently prejudiced attitude of the conscious mind. But this explanation does not suffice in the case of the extremely significant over-all result, which with the help of quite fortuitous numbers produced the picture of the classical marriage tradition in astrology, namely the conjunction of the moon with the three principal positions of the horoscope, when there were 47 other possibilities to choose from. Tradition since the time of

Ptolemy predicts that the moon conjunction with the sun or moon of the partner is the marriage characteristic. Because of its position in the horoscope, the ascendant has just as much importance as the sun and moon. In view of this tradition one could not have wished for a better result. The figure giving the probability of this predicted concurrence, unlike the first-obtained maximum of 10%, is indeed highly significant and deserves emphasizing, although we are no more able to account for its occurrence and for its apparent meaningfulness than we can account for the results of Rhine's experiments, which prove the existence of a perception independent of the space-time barrier.

1186   Naturally I do not think that this experiment or any other report on happenings of this kind proves anything; it merely points to something that even science can no longer overlook—namely, that its truths are in essence statistical and are therefore not absolute. Hence there is in nature a background of acausality, freedom, and meaningfulness which behaves complementarily to determinism, mechanism, and meaninglessness; and it is to be assumed that such phenomena are observable. Owing to their peculiar nature, however, they will hardly be prevailed upon to lay aside the chance character that makes them so questionable. If they did this they would no longer be what they are—acausal, undetermined, meaningful.[4]

1187   [Pure causality is only meaningful when used for the creation and functioning of an efficient instrument or machine by an intelligence standing outside this process and independent of it. A self-running process that operates entirely by its own causality, i.e., by absolute necessity, is meaningless. One of my critics accuses me of having too rigid a conception of causality. He has obviously not considered that if cause and effect were not necessarily[5] connected there would hardly be any meaning in speaking of causality at all. My critic makes the same mistake as the famous scientist[6] who refuses to believe that God played dice when he created the world. He fails to see that if God did not play dice he had no choice but to create a (from the human point of view) meaningless machine. Since this question involves a transcendental judgment

---

[4] [The following two paragraphs, not represented in the *Zeitschrift* version, were added by Jung respectively to the German MS and to a letter containing queries sent to him by the translator, 23 April 1954.]

[5] With all due respect to their statistical nature! (C.G.J.)

[6] [Albert Einstein.]

there can be no final answer to it, only a paradoxical one. *Meaning arises not from causality but from freedom, i.e., from acausality.*

1188 [Modern physics has deprived causality of its axiomatic character. Thus, when we explain natural events we do so by means of an instrument which is not quite reliable. Hence an element of uncertainty always attaches to our judgment, because—theoretically, at least—we might always be dealing with an exception to the rule which can only be registered negatively by the statistical method. No matter how small this chance is, it nevertheless exists. Since causality is our only means of explanation and since it is only relatively valid, we explain the world by applying causality in a paradoxical way, both positively and negatively: A is the cause of B and possibly not. The negation can be omitted in the great majority of cases. But it is my contention that it cannot be omitted in the case of phenomena which are relatively independent of space and time. As the time-factor is indispensable to the concept of causality, one cannot speak of causality in a case where the time-factor is eliminated (as in precognition). *Statistical truth leaves a gap open for acausal phenomena.* And since our causalistic explanation of nature contains the possibility of its own negation, it belongs to the category of *transcendental judgments,* which are paradoxical or antinomian. That is so because nature is still beyond us and because science gives us only an average picture of the world, but not a true one. If human society consisted of average individuals only, it would be a sad sight indeed.]

1189 From a rational point of view an experiment like the one I conducted is completely valueless, for the oftener it is repeated the more probable becomes its lack of results. But that this is also *not* so is proved by the very old tradition, which would hardly have come about had not these "lucky hits" often happened in the past. They behave like Rhine's results: they are exceedingly improbable, and yet they happen so persistently that they even compel us to criticize the foundations of our probability calculus, or at least its applicability to certain kinds of material.

1190 When analysing unconscious processes I often had occasion to observe synchronistic or ESP phenomena, and I therefore turned my attention to the psychic conditions underlying them. I believe I have found that they nearly always occur in the region of archetypal constellations, that is, in situations which have either activated an archetype or were evoked by the autonomous activity of an archetype. It is these observations which led me to the idea of getting the combination of archetypes found in astrology to give a quantitatively measurable answer. In this I succeeded, as the result shows; indeed one could say that the organizing factor responded with enthusiasm to my prompting. The reader must pardon this anthropomorphism, which I know positively invites misinterpretation; it fits in excellently well with the psychological facts and aptly describes the emotional background from which synchronistic phenomena emerge.

1191   I am aware that I ought at this point to discuss the psychology of the archetype, but this has been done so often and in such detail elsewhere[7] that I do not wish to repeat myself now.

1192   I am also aware of the enormous impression of improbability made by events of this kind, and that their comparative rarity does not make them any more probable. The statistical method therefore excludes them, as they do not belong to the average run of events.

[7] [Cf. "On the Nature of the Psyche" (C.W., vol. 8), pars. 397ff.]

LETTERS ON SYNCHRONICITY

To Markus Fierz[1]

21 February 1950

Dear Professor Fierz,

1193   You were kind enough to read through my MS on synchronicity, for which I have never thanked you sufficiently. I have been too engrossed in working out this idea.

1194   Today I take the liberty of burdening you with yet another portion of this manuscript, my excuse being that I am in great perplexity as regards the mathematical evaluation of the results worked out. I enclose the Tables, together with the commentary. For your general orientation I would only remark that the peculiar nature of the material has necessitated a somewhat peculiar arrangement of the Tables. The basis of the experiment consists of 180 married pairs, whose horoscopes were compared for the frequency of the so-called classical marriage aspects, namely, the conjunction and opposition of sun and moon, Mars and Venus, ascendant and descendant. These yield 50 aspects. The results obtained for married pairs were compared with $180 \times 180 - 1 = 32,220$ combinations of unmarried pairs. To the original material of 180 married pairs another 145 were added later, which were also included in the statistics. They were examined in part separately, in part together with the 180, as you can see from the Tables.

1195   The most interesting seems to me to be Table VI,[2] which shows the dispersions in the frequency values of the aspects. I would now be most grateful if you would give me your criticism and view of the Tables as a whole, and, in particular, answer a question arising out of Table VI. We have here some aspects which considerably exceed the probable mean value of the combinations. I would now like to know what is the probability of these deviations from the probable mean. I know that for this purpose a calculation is

---

[1] [Cf. "Synchronicity: An Acausal Connecting Principle" (C.W., vol. 8). See other letters to Fierz in *Jung: Letters,* ed. G. Adler.]
[2] [Table II in the English edn.]

used which is based on the so-called "deviation standard."[3] But this method is beyond my mathematical capacity and here I am wholly dependent on your help. I would be very glad if you would concentrate mainly on this question. For outside reasons there is some urgency with these Tables, as the book is soon to go to press. Failing all else it would be enough for me if you could simply confirm that the Tables as a whole are in order, and if you could give me the probability at least for the two highest values in Table VI, column 1. All the rest, I devoutly hope, you will be able to see from the Tables themselves. After brooding on them for a long time they have become clear to me, and I must confess I would not know how to make them any clearer.

1196   Should you be interested in the whole of the manuscript, or think it desirable to read it for the present purpose, it is naturally at your disposal. But I wouldn't like to send such an avalanche crashing down on you without warning.

Thanking you in advance for the trouble you are taking,

Yours sincerely, C. G. JUNG

2 March 1950

Dear Professor Fierz,

1197   My best thanks for all the trouble you have taken. You have given me just what I hoped for from you—an objective opinion as to the significance of the statistical figures obtained from my material of now 400 marriages. Only I am amazed that my statistics have amply confirmed the traditional view that the sun-moon aspects are marriage characteristics, which is further underlined by the value you give for the moon-moon conjunction, namely 0.125%.

For myself I regard the result as very unsatisfactory and have therefore stopped collecting further material, as the approximation to the probable mean with increasing material seems to me suspicious.

1198   Although the figure of 0.125% is still entirely within the bounds of possibility, I would nevertheless like to ask you, for the sake of clarity, whether one may regard this value as "significant" in so far as its represents a relatively low probability that coincides with the historical tradition? May one at least *conjecture* that it argues for rather than against the tradition (since Ptolemy)? I fully share your view of divinatory methods as *catalysts* of intuition. But the result of these statistics has made me somewhat sceptical, espe-

[3] [English in the original.]

cially in connection with the latest ESP experiments which have obtained probabilities of 10^{-31}. These experiments and the whole experience of ESP are sufficient proof that meaningful coincidences do exist. There is thus some probability that the divinatory methods actually produce synchronistic phenomena. These seem to me most clearly discernible in astrology. The statistical findings undoubtedly show that the astrological correspondences are nothing more than chance. The statistical method is based on the assumption of a continuum of uniform objects. But synchronicity is a qualified individual event which is ruined by the statistical method; conversely, synchronicity abolishes the assumption of [a continuum of] uniform objects and so ruins the statistical method. It seems, therefore, that a *complementarity relationship* exists between synchronicity and causality. Rhine's statistics have proved the existence of synchronicity *in spite of unsuitable methods*. This aroused false hopes in me as regards astrology. In Rhine's experiments the phenomenon of synchronicity is an extremely simple matter. The situation in astrology is incomparably more complicated and is therefore more sensitive to the statistical method, which emphasizes just what is least characteristic of synchronicity, that is, uniformity. Now my results, mischievously enough, exactly confirm the old tradition although they are as much due to chance as were the results in the old days. So again something has happened that shows all the signs of synchronicity, namely a "meaningful coincidence" or "Just So" story. Obviously the ancients must have experienced the same thing quite by chance, otherwise no such tradition could ever have arisen. I don't believe any ancient astrologer statistically examined 800 horoscopes for marriage characteristics. He always had only small batches at his disposal, which did not ruin the synchronistic phenomenon and could therefore, as in my case, establish the prevalence of moon-moon and moon-sun conjunctions, although these are bound to diminish with a higher range of numbers. All synchronistic phenomena, which are more highly qualified than ESP, are as such unprovable, that is to say a single authenticated instance is sufficient proof in principle, just as one does not need to produce ten thousand duckbilled platypi in order to prove they exist. It seems to me synchronicity represents a *direct act of creation* which manifests itself as chance. The statistical proof of natural conformity to law is therefore only a very limited way of describing nature, since it grasps only uniform events. But nature is essentially discontinuous, i.e., subject to chance. To describe it we need a principle of discontinuity. In psychology this is the drive to individuation, in biology it is differentiation, but in nature it is the "meaningful coincidence," that is to say synchronicity.

1199   Forgive me for putting forward these somewhat abstruse-looking reflections. They are new to me too and for that reason are still rather chaotic like everything *in statu nascendi.*

Thanks again for your trouble! I should be glad to have your impressions.

Best regards, C. G. JUNG

20 October 1954

Dear Professor Fierz,

1200   Just now an English version of my book on synchronicity is being prepared. I would like to take this opportunity to make the necessary corrections for the probabilities of the maximal figures which you have so kindly calculated for me. My publishers now want to see the details of your calculation, as they don't understand what method you have employed. If it would be possible for you to let me have this report fairly soon I should be most grateful. Unfortunately I must still add a special request, namely the answer to the question: What is the probability of the total result that the 3 conjunctions, moon-sun, moon-moon, moon asc., all come out together?[4] This result (though consisting of chance figures) corresponds to the traditional astrological prediction and at least *imitates* that picture, and if it consisted of "significant figures" would prove the rightness of astrological expectations.

1201   I hope I have succeeded in expressing myself clearly. I am indeed extremely sorry to bother you with this question and take up your valuable time. Perhaps you can assign the task to a student. Naturally in this matter I am helpless and am therefore quite prepared to recompense you or the student for the expenses involved. Please do not be offended at this practical suggestion.

Best thanks in advance!

Yours sincerely, C. G. JUNG

28 October 1954

Dear Professor Fierz,

1202   Let me thank you most cordially for your kind and prompt fulfilment of my request. There is, of course no need for you to

---

[4] [The report is summarized in "Synchronicity," pp. 483f.]

repeat your exposition; I will send it direct to Dr. Michael Fordham.

1203   A misunderstanding seems to have arisen over my question about the moon-sun, moon-moon, moon-asc. triad:

1. The fact that my figures are due to chance was something I myself had noticed when putting my tables together. That is why I had the Tables printed in full; they express the chance nature of the figures quite clearly and so enable the non-mathematical reader to take it in at a glance. For the sake of accuracy I then asked you to give me the probability of my maxima. Your answer is more or less in line with what I expected. It was never my intention to prove that the astrological prediction is correct—I know the unreliability of astrology much too well for that. I only wanted to find out the exact degree of probability of my figures. You have already warned me twice about the impossibility of proving anything. That, if you will permit me to say so, is carrying coals to Newcastle. It doesn't matter to me at all whether astrology is right or not, but only (as said) what degree of probability those figures ("maxima") have, which *simulate* an apparent proof of the rightness of the astrological prediction.

2. The astrological prediction consists in the *traditional* assertion that my three moon conjunctions are specifically characteristic of marriage. (Sun, moon, asc. are the main pillars of the horoscope.) So this triad is not arbitrarily selected at all, for which reason I consider the analogy of the three white ants[5] entirely to the point. With all due respect, you seem to me to go very wide of the mark if you imagine that I regard my results as other than statistically determined. Naturally they fall within the limits of mathematical probability, but that does not stop my maxima from occurring at the very places the astrologer would expect. The only thing that interests me is the degree of probability to be attributed to this coincidence, merely for the sake of accuracy! I don't want to *prove* anything with my figures but only to *show what has happened* and what I have done. *Quite by chance,* as I have tried to show with all possible clarity, a configuration resulted which, if it consisted of significant figures, would argue in favour of astrology. The whole story is in other words a case like the scarab[6] and simply shows what chance can do—a "Just So" story in fact! That such coincidences are in principle more than merely statistically

5 [Cf. ibid., par. 902.]
6 [Ibid., par. 843.]

determined is proved by Rhine's results, but not by an isolated instance like my statistics.

1204 Naturally I speak in favour of chance in one respect, because I contest the absolute validity of statistical statements in so far as they dismiss all exceptions as unimportant. This gives us an abstract, average picture of reality which is to some extent a falsification of it, and this cannot remain a matter of indifference to the psychologist since he has to cope with the pathological consequences of this abstract substitute for reality.

1205 The exception is actually more real than the average since it is the vehicle of reality *par excellence,* as you yourself point out in your letter of October 24th.

1206 I am sorry to have caused you so much work, and that you now have to read this long letter as well. But I really do not know what could have led you to believe that I wanted to prove the truth of astrology. I only wanted to present a case of "meaningful coincidence" which would illustrate the main idea of my paper on synchronicity. This fact has been generally overlooked. In London they have called in a top statistician[7] to solve the riddle of my Tables. That is rather like a peasant not being able to open his barn door and then sending for an expert on safes, who naturally can't open it either. Regrettably, he too has succumbed to the error that I wanted to prove something in favour of astrology, although I disclaim this at some length in my book.

1207 Unfortunately I am unable to understand how you can consider any other constellations (among my 50) just as "meaningful" as the three moon conjunctions. None of the others are "classical predictions." Nor does just any ant appear, but only the "predicted" white ant. I am interested to know the probability of this meaningful occurrence precisely because it is not very probable that the white ant will be the first to come out of the box three times in succession. If the probability of a single time is $1:50$, wouldn't the probability of three times be $1:50^3$? A quite appreciable figure, it seems to me. This result may surely be taken as complying with my intention to present a case of synchronicity, even though it proves nothing about astrology, which was never my intention anyway.

Hoping that I have succeeded this time in clearing up the misunderstanding,

I remain with best thanks and cordial greetings,

Yours, C. G. JUNG

[7] [M. J. Moroney, Fellow of the Royal Statistical Society.]

To Michael Fordham[8]

1st July 1955

Dear Fordham,

1208   Synchronicity tells us something about the nature of what I call the *psychoid* factor, i.e., the unconscious archetype (not its conscious representation!). As the archetype has the tendency to gather suitable forms of expression round itself, its nature is best understood when one imitates and supports this tendency through amplification. The natural effect of an archetype and its amplification can be certainly understood as an analogy of the synchronistic effect, inasmuch as the latter shows the same tendency of arranging collateral and coincidental facts which represent suitable expressions of the underlying archetype. It is difficult or even impossible, however, to prove that amplificatory associations are *not causal,* whereas amplificatory facts coincide in a way that defies causal explanation. That is the reason why I call spontaneous and artificial amplification a mere analogy of synchronicity. It is true, however, that we cannot prove a causal connection in every case of amplification, and thus it is quite possible that in a number of cases, where we assume causal "association," it is really a matter of synchronicity. What is "association" after all? We don't know. It is not impossible that psychic arrangement in general is based upon synchronicity with the exception of the secondary rational "enchaînement" of psychic events in consciousness. This is analogous to the natural course of events, so different from our scientific and abstract reconstruction of reality based upon the statistical average. The latter produces a picture of nature consisting of mere probabilities, whereas reality is a crisscross of more or less impracticable events. Our psychic life shows the same phenomenological picture. This is the reason why I am rather inclined to think that it would be presumptuous to suppose the psyche is based exclusively upon the synchronistic principle, at least in our present state of knowledge.

1209   I quite agree with your idea of the two complementary attitudes of understanding, viz., rational and irrational or synchronistic. But it remains to be seen whether all irrational events are *meaningful coincidences.* I doubt it.

1210   It is refreshing to see you at work with these interesting problems and to hear something intelligent from you instead of the amazing stupidities dished out by our contemporaries.

[8] [Handwritten, in English.]

1211   I am sorry that I cannot come over to England to celebrate with you. I am writing in hospital, where I am nursing some prostatic trouble. Tomorrow I shall be dismissed for the time being. Old age is not exactly my idea of a joke.

My best wishes, Yours cordially, C. G. JUNG

1212 P.S. As you are going to celebrate my 80th birthday in London and I am unfortunately unable to attend I thought it might be a nice gesture if you could send an invitation to the Swiss Ambassador to Great Britain. I am sure that he would appreciate at least your friendly gesture to one of his countrymen.

THE FUTURE OF PARAPSYCHOLOGY

The *International Journal of Parapsychology* (New York), in its 1963 autumn issue (V:4, pp. 450f.), published Jung's answers to a questionnaire which had been circulated in June 1960 among various authorities in connection with a survey on "The Future of Parapsychology."

How do you define parapsychology?

1213   Parapsychology is the science dealing with those biological or psychological events which show that the categories of matter, space, and time (and thus of causality) are not axiomatic.

Which areas of research, in your opinion, should be classified as belonging within parapsychology?

1214   The psychology of the unconscious.

Do you anticipate that future research would emphasize quantitative or qualitative work?

1215   Future research will have to emphasize both.

Do you believe that a repeatable *experiment is essential to strengthen the position of parapsychological studies within the scientific community?*

1216   The repeatable experiment is desirable but, inasmuch as most of the events are spontaneous and irregular, the experimental method will not be generally applicable.

Have you any comments on recent criticisms with regard to statistical methods employed in parapsychological studies?

1217   The statistical method is most desirable and indispensable to scientific research, where and when it can be applied. But this is only possible when the material shows a certain regularity and comparability.

Do you believe that certain qualitative researches may be quantified in order to gain wider acceptance?

1218   The quantification of qualitative research is surely the best means of conviction.

In the qualitative area, where do you foresee the greatest potential for future research progress—spontaneous phenomena, crisis telepathy, survival studies, out-of-the-body experiences, or any other?

1219   The greatest and most important part of parapsychological research will be the careful exploration and qualitative description of spontaneous events.

Do you feel that during the past decade parapsychology has become more widely accepted among scientists active in other areas?

1220   My impression is that, in Europe, at least, open-mindedness has increased.

Have you any comments regarding the psychological significance of certain psychic phenomena?

1221   The psychological significance of parapsychological events has hardly been explored yet.

Have you any comments regarding the special psychological conditions that seem to favour, or reduce, the likelihood of an occurrence of psychic phenomena?

1222   The factor which favours the occurrence of parapsychological events is the presence of an active archetype, i.e., a situation in which the deeper, instinctual layers of the psyche are called into action. The archetype is a borderline phenomenon, characterized by a relativation of space and time, as already pointed out by Albertus Magnus (*De mirabilibus mundi*),[1] whom I have mentioned in my paper "Synchronicity: An Acausal Connecting Principle."

[1] [Incunabulum, undated, Zentralbibliothek, Zurich. Cf. C.W., vol. 8, par. 859.]

THE ARCHETYPES AND THE COLLECTIVE UNCONSCIOUS

(related to Volume 9 of the Collected Works)

THE HYPOTHESIS OF THE COLLECTIVE
UNCONSCIOUS[1]

1223   Indications of the concept of a collective psyche are to be found in Leibniz's theory of "petites perceptions," also in Kant's anthropology. In Schelling the "eternally unconscious" is the absolute ground of consciousness. Despite different terminology Hegel's view is similar. C. G. Carus was the first to base a developed philosophical system on the concept of the unconscious. Related features may be found in Schopenhauer. Eduard von Hartmann exalted the unconscious to the concept of an absolute, universal Spirit. The scientific investigation of the psychological unconscious began with the discovery of hypnotism and was continued via the Salpêtrière school in the works of Janet and Flournoy. Independently of this, it was the Breuer-Freud discovery of the aetiology of neurosis that led to Freud's sexual theory of the unconscious. Independent, again, of the Freudian school was the discovery of the so-called "complexes" and "autonomous contents" of the unconscious by the author.

1224   Whereas for Freud the unconscious is essentially a function of consciousness, the author holds the unconscious to be an independent psychic function prior to consciousness and opposed to it. According to this view the unconscious may be divided into a *personal* and a *collective* unconscious. The latter is a psychic propensity to a regular functioning, independent of time and race. Its products may be compared with "mythological motifs." Despite the autochthonous origin of the former, the two are analogous in principle, which may be taken as an indication of their conforming to psychological law.

1225   In the further course of the lecture the author, with the help of a special department of symbology, the so-called mandala symbolism, demonstrated the parallelism between the symbol of the circle, as produced by educated patients undergoing treatment, and

[1] [Author's abstract of a lecture delivered at the Federal Polytechnic Institute (ETH), Zurich, 1 Feb. 1932. Published in the *Vierteljahrschrift der Naturforschenden Gesellschaft in Zurich*, LXXVII, Pt. 2 (1932), iv–v. The MS of the original lecture has not been found. Cf. supra, pars. 1143–45.]

the ritual mandalas of lamaism and *kundalini* yoga, as well as the parallels with the views of the Tantrists, of classical Chinese philosophy, and Chinese yoga. Further parallels are children's drawings, the prehistoric mandalas of Rhodesia, the sand-paintings from the healing ceremonies (*yaibichy* dances) of the Navaho (Arizona),[2] the visions of Hildegard of Bingen from the Codex Lucca[3] (12th to 13th cent.), and the eschatological views of Jacob Boehme.[4] The modern pictorial material was derived from people who produced it spontaneously and were not in any way influenced.

[2] [Cf. *Psychology and Alchemy*, C.W., vol. 12, fig. 110.]
[3] [Ibid., fig. 195.]
[4] [Ibid., pars. 214–16.]

FOREWORD TO ADLER: "ENTDECKUNG DER SEELE"[1]

1226   This book is a systematic account of the three different approaches now current in psychotherapy: Freud's, Alfred Adler's, and my own. Drawing on his wide professional knowledge, the author has carefully elaborated the principal viewpoints underlying each approach, and thus gives the reader, who may have neither the time nor the opportunity to study the originals, a complete and rigorously objective survey of this controversial field. The exposition and manner of expression are such that the educated layman can follow the argument without difficulty.

1227   Psychological theories, which at the outset seemed destined for use only in the strictly delimited domain of medical psychotherapy, have long since burst the bounds of a specialized science, and have not only penetrated into the provinces of its sister sciences but become—even if fragmentarily—the common property of all educated persons. This means, however, that informed public opinion has been infected with the same confusion which still prevails today in medical psychology. What distinguishes Dr. Adler's work in particular is his thoroughly reliable and comprehensive account of my own views, which differ in so radical and characteristic a way from those of the other two investigators. His book, sober, lucid, and systematic, is a worthy companion to the earlier works by Kranefeldt[2] and Heyer.[3] It is a milestone in the slow but sure conquest of the crises and confusions that hang over the psychological views of our day.

December 1933

[1] [Zurich, 1934. By Gerhard Adler, at that time in Berlin; after 1936, in England. ("Discovery of the Soul.")]

[2] [See infra, pars. 1727f., and Jung's introduction to W.M. Kranefeldt's *Secret Ways of the Mind* (C.W., vol. 4, pars. 745ff.).]

[3] [See infra, pars. 1774ff.]

FOREWORD TO HARDING:
"WOMAN'S MYSTERIES"[1]

1228   Esther Harding, the author of this book, is a physician and specialist in the treatment of psychogenic illness. She is a former pupil of mine who has endeavoured not only to understand the modern psyche but also, as the present book shows, to explore its historical background. Preoccupation with historical subjects may at first glance seem to be merely a physician's personal hobby, but to the psychotherapist it is a necessary part of his mental equipment. The psychology of primitives, folklore, mythology, and the science of comparative religion open our eyes to the wide horizons of the human psyche and give us that indispensable aid we so urgently need for an understanding of unconscious processes. Only when we see in what shape and what guise dream symbols, which seem to us unique, appear on the historical and ethnic scene, can we really understand what they are pointing at. Also, once equipped with this extensive comparative material, we can comprehend more nearly that factor which is so decisive for psychic life, the archetype. Of course this term is not meant to denote an inherited idea, but rather an inherited mode of psychic functioning, corresponding to the inborn way in which the chick emerges from the egg, the bird builds its nest, a certain kind of wasp stings the motor ganglion of the caterpillar, and eels find their way to the Bermudas. In other words, it is a "pattern of behaviour." This aspect of the archetype, the purely biological one, is the proper concern of scientific psychology.

1229   But the picture changes at once when looked at from the inside, from within the realm of the subjective psyche. Here the archetype appears as a numinous factor, as an experience of fundamental significance. Whenever it clothes itself in suitable symbols (which

[1] [M. Esther Harding, *Woman's Mysteries: Ancient and Modern;* A Psychological Interpretation of the Feminine Principle as Portrayed in Myth, Story, and Dreams. The original edn. (New York, 1935) did not contain this foreword, which was written for the German trans., *Frauen-Mysterien* (Zurich, 1949); trans. by Edward Whitmont for the revised edn. of the book (New York, 1955). The present version is revised. See supra, pars. 1125ff.]

is not always the case), it seizes hold of the individual in a startling way, creating a condition amounting almost to possession, the consequences of which may be incalculable. It is for this reason that the archetype is so important in the psychology of religion. All religious and metaphysical concepts rest upon archetypal foundations, and, to the extent that we are able to explore them, we can cast at least a superficial glance behind the scenes of world history, and lift a little the veil of mystery which hides the meaning of metaphysical ideas. Metaphysics is, as it were, a physics or physiology of the archetypes, and its dogmas formulate the insights that have been gained into the nature of these dominants—the unconscious leitmotifs that characterize the psychic happenings of a given epoch. The archetype is "metaphysical" because it transcends consciousness.

1230   Dr. Harding's book is an attempt to describe some of the archetypal foundations of feminine psychology. In order to understand the author's intention, the reader must overcome the prejudice that psychology consists merely of what Mr. Smith and Mrs. Jones happen to know about it. The psyche consists not only of the contents of consciousness, which derive from sensory impressions, but also of ideas apparently based on perceptions which have been modified in a peculiar way by preexistent and unconscious formative factors, i.e., by the archetypes. The psyche can therefore be said to consist of consciousness plus the unconscious. This leads us to conclude that one part of the psyche is explicable in terms of recent causes, but that another part reaches back into the deepest layers of our racial history.

1231   Now the one certain fact about the nature of neurosis is that it is due to a disturbance of the primary instincts, or at least affects the instincts to a considerable degree. The evolution of human anatomy and of human instincts extends over geological periods of time. Our historical knowledge throws light upon only a few stretches of the way, whose total length would have to be reckoned in millions of miles. However, even that little bit is a help when, as psychotherapists, we are called upon to remedy a disturbance in the sphere of instinct. Here it is the therapeutic myths offered by religion that teach us the most. The religions might indeed be considered as psychotherapeutic systems which assist our understanding of instinctual disturbances, for these are not a recent phenomenon but have existed from time immemorial. Although certain types of disease, notably infectious ones like *typhus antiquorum*, may disappear and others take their place, it is still not very probable that tuberculosis, shall we say, was an entirely different disease five or ten thousand years ago. The same is true of psychic processes. Therefore, in the descriptions of abnormal psychic states left us by antiquity, we are able to recognize certain features that are familiar to us; and when it comes to the fantasies of neurotic and psychotic patients, it is just here, in ancient literature, that we find the most illuminating parallels.

1232   From the empirical evidence, it has now been known for some time that any one-sidedness of the conscious mind, or a disturbance of the psychic equilibrium, elicits a compensation from the unconscious. The compensation is brought about by the constellation and accentuation of complementary material which assumes archetypal forms when the *fonction du réel,* or correct relation to the surrounding world, is disturbed. When, for instance, a woman develops too masculine an attitude—something that may very easily happen owing to the social emancipation of women today—the unconscious compensates this one-sidedness by a symptomatic accentuation of certain feminine traits. This process of compensation takes place within the personal sphere so long as the vital interests of the personality have not been harmed. But if more profound disturbances should occur, as when a women alienates herself from her husband through her insistence on always being in the right, then archetypal figures appear on the scene. Difficulties of this kind are very common, and once they have grown to pathological proportions they can be remedied only by psychotherapeutic methods. For this reason, it has long been the endeavour of analytical psychologists to acquire as wide a knowledge as possible of the network of archetypal images produced by the unconscious, with a view to understanding the nature of the archetypal compensation in each individual case.

1233   Dr. Harding's systematic survey of the archetypal material of feminine compensation comes as a most welcome contribution to these endeavours, and we must be grateful to her for having devoted herself to this task with such self-sacrificing effort in addition to her professional work. Her investigation is valuable and important not only for the specialist but for the educated layman who is interested in a psychology founded on experience of life and a knowledge of human nature. Our times, characterized as they are by an almost total disorientation in regard to the ends of human existence, stand in need, above all else, of a vast amount of psychological knowledge.

August 1948

FOREWORD TO NEUMANN: "THE ORIGINS AND HISTORY OF CONSCIOUSNESS"[1]

1234   The author has requested me to preface his book with a few words of introduction, and to this I accede all the more readily because I found his work more than usually welcome. It begins just where I, too, if I were granted a second lease of life, would start to gather up the *disjecta membra* of my own writings, to sift out all those "beginnings without continuations" and knead them into a whole. As I read through the manuscript of this book it became clear to me how great are the disadvantages of pioneer work: one stumbles through unknown regions; one is led astray by analogies, forever losing the Ariadne thread; one is overwhelmed by new impressions and new possibilities; and the worst disadvantage of all is that the pioneer only knows afterwards what he should have known before. The second generation has the advantage of a clearer, if still incomplete, picture; certain landmarks that at least lie on the frontiers of the essential have grown familiar, and one now knows what must be known if one is to explore the newly discovered territory. Thus forewarned and forearmed, a representative of the second generation can spot the most distant connections; he can unravel problems and give a coherent account of the whole field of study, whose full extent the pioneer can only survey at the end of his life's work.

1235   This difficult and meritorious task the author has performed with outstanding success. He has woven his facts into a pattern and created a unified whole, which no pioneer could have done nor could ever have attempted to do. As though in confirmation of this, the present work opens at the very place where I unwittingly made landfall on the new continent long ago, namely, the realm of *matriarchal symbolism;* and, as a conceptual framework for his discoveries, the author uses a symbol whose significance first dawned on me in my recent writings on the psychology of alchemy: the

[1] [New York (Bollingen Series XLII), 1954; London, 1955. Trans. by R.F.C. Hull (including the foreword) from *Ursprungsgeschichte des Bewusstseins* (Zurich, 1949). Erich Neumann (1905–1960), originally German, later lived in Israel.]

uroboros. Upon this foundation he has succeeded in constructing a unique history of the evolution of consciousness, and at the same time is representing the body of myths as the phenomenology of this same evolution. In this way he arrives at conclusions and insights which are among the most important ever to be reached in this field.

1236   Naturally to me, as a psychologist, the most valuable aspect of the work is the fundamental contribution it makes to a psychology of the unconscious. The author has placed the concepts of analytical psychology—which for many people are so bewildering—on a firm evolutionary basis, and erected upon this a comprehensive structure in which the empirical forms of thought find their rightful place. No system can ever dispense with an over-all hypothesis which in its turn depends upon the temperament and subjective assumptions of the author as well as upon objective data. This factor is of the greatest importance in psychology, for the "personal equation" colours the mode of seeing. Ultimate truth, if there be such a thing, demands the concert of many voices.

1237   I can only congratulate the author on his achievement. May this brief foreword convey to him my heartfelt thanks.

1 March 1949

FOREWORD TO ADLER:
"STUDIES IN ANALYTICAL PSYCHOLOGY"[1]

1238   It gave me particular pleasure to hear that Dr. Gerhard Adler's admirable book *Studies in Analytical Psychology* is now to appear in German. The author is a skilled psychotherapist and therefore in a position to handle his theme on the basis of practical experience. This advantage can hardly be overrated, for therapeutic work means not only the daily application of psychological views and methods to living people and to sick people in particular, but also a daily criticism which success or failure brings to bear upon the therapy and its underlying assumptions. We may therefore expect from the author a well-pondered judgment amply backed by experience. In this expectation we are not disappointed. Everywhere in these essays we come across nicely balanced opinions and never upon prejudices, bigotries, or forced interpretations.

1239   With a happy choice the author has picked out a number of problems which must inevitably engage the attention of every thinking psychotherapist. First and foremost he has been concerned—very understandably—to stress the peculiarity of analytical psychology as compared with the materialistic and rationalistic tendencies of the Freudian school—an undertaking which, in view of the latter's delight in sectarian seclusion, has still lost nothing of its topicality. This is by no means a matter of specialist or merely captious differences that would not interest a wider public; it is more a matter of principle. A psychology that wants to be scientific can no longer afford to base itself on so-called philosophical premises such as materialism or rationalism. If it is not to overstep its competence irresponsibly, it can only proceed phenomenologically and abandon preconceived opinions. But the opinion that we can pass transcendental judgments, even when faced with highly complicated material like that presented by psychological experience, is so ingrown that philosophical statements are still imputed to analyti-

[1] [The foreword, not in the original edn. (London and New York, 1948), was written for the German edition, *Zur analytischen Psychologie* (Zurich, 1952), and is included (trans. by R.F.C. Hull) in the new English edition (London, 1966; New York, 1967).]

cal psychology, although this is completely to misunderstand its phenomenological standpoint.

1240   A major interest of psychotherapy is, for practical reasons, the psychology of dreams, a field where theoretical assumptions have not only suffered the greatest defeats but are applied at their most odious. The dream analysis in the third essay is exemplary.

1241   It is much to be welcomed that the author pays due attention to the important role of the ego. He thus counters the common prejudice that analytical psychology is only interested in the unconscious, and at the same time he gives instructive examples of the relations between the unconscious and the ego in general.

1242   The controversial question of whether, and if so how, the raising to consciousness of unconscious contents is therapeutically effective meets with adequate treatment. Although their conscious realization is a curative factor of prime importance, it is by no means the only one. Besides the initial "confession" and the emotional "abreaction" we have also to consider transference and symbolization. The present volume gives excellent illustrations of the latter two from case histories.

1243   It is much to the credit of the author that he has also turned to the religious aspect of psychic phenomena. This question is not only delicate—it is particularly apt to irritate philosophical susceptibilities. But, provided that people are able to read and to give up their prepossessions, I truly have no idea how anybody could feel himself affronted by the author's remarks—provided, again, that the reader is able to understand the phenomenological viewpoint of science. Unhappily this understanding, as I often had occasion to know, does not appear to be particularly widespread—least of all, it would seem, in professional medical circles. The theory of knowledge does not of course figure in the medical curriculum, but is indispensable to the study of psychology.

1244   Not only on account of the lucidity of its exposition, but also because of its wealth of illustrative case histories, this book fills a gap in psychological literature. It gives both the professional and the psychologically minded layman a welcome set of bearings in territory which—at any rate to begin with—most people find rather hard of access. But the examples drawn direct from life offer an equally direct approach, and this is an aid to understanding. I would therefore like to recommend this book most cordially to the reading public.

May 1949

FOREWORD TO JUNG:
"GESTALTUNGEN DES UNBEWUSSTEN" (1950)[1]

1245   In so far as poetry is one of those psychic activities that give shape to the contents of the unconscious, it seems to me not unfitting to open this volume with an essay which is concerned with a number of fundamental questions affecting the poet and his work.[1a] This discussion is followed by a lecture on the rebirth motif,[2] given on the occasion of a symposium on this theme. Drama, the principal theme of poetic art, had its origin in ceremonial, magically effective rites which, in form and meaning, represented a δρωμένον or δράμα, something "acted" or "done." During this time the tension builds up until it culminates in a περεπέτεια, the dénouement, and is resolved. Menacingly, the span of life narrows down to the fear of death, and out of this *angustiae* (straits, quandary, wretchedness, distress) a new birth emerges, redemptive and opening on to larger horizons. It is evident that drama is a reflection of an eminently psychological situation which, infinitely varied, repeats itself in human life and is both the expression and the cause of a universally disseminated archetype clothed in multitudinous forms.

1246   The third contribution is a case history.[3] It is the description of a process of transformation illustrated by pictures. This study is supplemented by a survey of mandala symbolism drawn from case material.[4] The interpretation of these pictures is in the main formal and, unlike the preceding essay, lays more emphasis on the common denominators in the pictures than on their individual psychology.

1247   The fifth and last contribution is a psychological study of E.T.A. Hoffmann's tale "The Golden Pot," by Aniela Jaffé.[5] This tale of Hoffmann's has long been on my list of literary creations which

---

[1] [("Configurations of the Unconscious.") Psychologische Abhandlungen, VII. For contents, see the following notes.]

[1a] ["Psychology and Literature" (in C.W., vol. 15).]

[2] ["Concerning Rebirth" (in C.W., vol. 9, i).]

[3] ["A Study in the Process of Individuation" (ibid.).]

[4] ["Concerning Mandala Symbolism" (ibid.).]

[5] ["Bilder und Symbole aus E.T.A. Hoffmanns Märchen 'Der goldne Topf.'"]

cry out for interpretation and deeper understanding. I am greatly indebted to Mrs. Jaffé for having undertaken the not inconsiderable labour of investigating the psychological background of "The Golden Pot," thus absolving me from a task which I felt to be an obligation.

January 1949

FOREWORD TO WICKES:
"VON DER INNEREN WELT DES MENSCHEN"[1]

1248   Frances G. Wickes' book, which first appeared in America in 1938,[2] is now available in a German translation. It is the fruit of a long and industrious life, uncommonly rich in experience of people of all classes and ages. Anyone who wishes to form a picture of the inner life of the psyche and broaden his knowledge of psychic phenomena in general is warmly recommended to read this book. The author has taken the greatest pains to express the inner experiences of her patients with the help of the viewpoints I have introduced into psychology. Her collection of case histories is of the greatest value to the skilled psychotherapist and practising psychologist, not to mention the layman, for whom she opens vistas into a world of experience hitherto inaccessible to him.

1249   If, as in this book, fantasy is taken for what it is—a natural expression of life which we can at most seek to understand but cannot correct—it will yield possibilities of psychic development that are of the utmost importance for the cure of psychogenic neuroses and of the milder psychotic disturbances. Fantasies should not be negatively valued by subjecting them to rationalistic prejudices; they also have a positive aspect as creative compensations of the conscious attitude, which is always in danger of incompleteness and one-sidedness. Fantasy is a self-justifying biological function, and the question of its practical use arises only when it has to be channeled into so-called concrete reality. So long as this situation has not arisen, it is completely beside the point to explain fantasy in terms of some preconceived theory and to declare it invalid, or to reduce it to some other biological process. Fantasy is the natural life of the psyche, which at the same time harbours in itself the irrational creative factor. The neurotic's involuntary over- or under-

---

[1] [Zurich, 1953. Frances G. Wickes (1875–1967), American psychotherapist, was influenced by Jung's theories. Cf. Jung's introduction to her *Analyse der Kinderseele* (*The Inner World of Childhood*, 1927), C.W., vol. 17, pars. 8off.]
[2] [*The Inner World of Man* (New York and Toronto), without this foreword (which was also published in E. D. Kirkham's trans. in the *Bulletin of the Analytical Psychology Club of New York*, 16:2, Feb. 1954).]

valuation of fantasy is as injurious to the life of the psyche as its rationalistic condemnation or suppression, for fantasy is not a sickness but a natural and vital activity which helps the seeds of psychic development to grow. Frances Wickes illustrates this in exemplary fashion by describing the typical figures and phases that are encountered in involuntary fantasy processes.

September 1953

FOREWORD TO JUNG:
"VON DEN WURZELN DES BEWUSSTSEINS" (1954)[1]

1250   In this ninth volume of the "Psychologische Abhandlungen" I have put together a number of works which for the most part grew out of Eranos lectures. Some have been revised, some augmented, and some completely reworked. The essay on "The Philosophical Tree" is new, although I have dealt with this theme earlier in a sketchy way. The central theme of this book is the *archetype,* the nature and significance of which are described and elucidated from various angles: history, psychology both practical and theoretical, case material. In spite of the fact that this theme has often been discussed by me as well as by other authors, such as Heinrich Zimmer, Karl Kerényi, Erich Neumann, Mircea Eliade, etc., it has proved to be both inexhaustible and particularly difficult to comprehend, if one may give credence to criticisms vitiated by prejudice and misunderstanding. One is left with the suspicion that the psychological standpoint and its consequences are felt in many quarters to be disagreeable and for this reason are not permitted a hearing. The simplistic approach is instantly assured of the applause of the public because it pretends to make the answering of difficult questions superfluous, but well-founded observations that cast doubt on things which appear simple and settled arouse displeasure. The theory of archetypes seems to come into this category. For some it is self-evident and a welcome aid in understanding symbol-formation, individual as well as historical and collective. For others it seems to epitomize an annoying aberration that has to be extirpated by all possible means, however ridiculous.

1251   Although it is easy to demonstrate the existence and efficacy of the archetypes, their phenomenology leads to really difficult questions of which I have given a few samples in this book. For the present there is still no possibility of simplification and of building highways "that fools may not err."

May 1953

---

1 [("From the Roots of Consciousness.") Contents: "Archetypes of the Collective Unconscious," "Concerning the Archetypes, with Special Reference to the Anima Concept," "Psychological Aspects of the Mother Archetype" (all in C.W., vol. 9, i); "The Visions of Zosimos" (in C.W., vol. 13); "Transformation Symbolism in the Mass" (in C.W., vol. 11); "The Philosophical Tree" (in C.W., vol. 13); "On the Nature of the Psyche" (in C.W., vol. 8).]

FOREWORD TO VAN HELSDINGEN:
"BEELDEN UIT HET ONBEWUSTE"[1]

1252   Dr. R. J. van Helsdingen has asked me to write a foreword
to his book. I am happy to comply with his request for a particular
reason: the case that is discussed and commented on was one that
I treated many years ago, as can now be said publicly with the
kind permission of my former patient. Such liberality is not encountered everywhere, because many one-time patients are understandably shy about exposing their intimate, tormenting, pathogenic
problems to the eye of the public. And indeed one must admit
that their drawings or paintings do not as a rule have anything
that would recommend them to the aesthetic needs of the public
at large. If only for technical reasons the pictures are usually unpleasant to look at and, lacking artistic power, have little expressive
value for outsiders. These shortcomings are happily absent in the
present case: the pictures are artistic compositions in the positive
sense and are uncommonly expressive. They communicate their
frightening, daemonic content to the beholder and convince him
of the terrors of a fantastic underworld.

1253   While it was the patient's own mother country that produced
the great masters of the monstrous, Hieronymus Bosch and others,
who opened the flood-gates of creative fantasy, the pictures in this
book show us imaginative activity unleashed in another form: the
Indomalaysian phantasmagoria of pullulating vegetation and of
fear-haunted, stifling tropical nights. Environment and inner disposition conspired to produce this series of pictures which give expression to an infantile-archaic fear. Partly it is the fear of a child
who, deprived of her parents, is defencelessly exposed to the unconscious and its menacing, phantasmal figures; partly the fear of a
European who can find no other attitude to everything that the East
conjures up in her save that of rejection and repression. Because
the European does not know his own unconscious, he does not
understand the East and projects into it everything he fears and
despises in himself.

[1] [Arnhem (Netherlands), 1957. ("Pictures from the Unconscious.") Foreword
in German.]

530

1254   For a sensitive child it is a veritable catastrophe to be removed from her parents and sent to Europe after the unconscious influence of the Oriental world had moulded her relation to the instincts, and then, at the critical period of puberty, to be transported back to the East, when this development had been interrupted by Western education and crippled by neglect.[2] The pictures not only illustrate the phase of treatment that brought the contents of her neurosis to consciousness, they were also an instrument of treatment, as they reduced the half conscious or unconscious images floating about in her mind to a common denominator and fixated them. Once an expression of this kind has been found, it proves its "magical" efficacy by putting a spell, as it were, on the content so represented and making it relatively innocuous. The more complex this content is, the more pictures are needed to depotentiate it. The therapeutic effect of this technique consists in inducing the conscious mind to collaborate with the unconscious, the latter being integrated in the process. In this way the neurotic dissociation is gradually remedied.

1255   The author is to be congratulated on having edited this valuable and unusual material. Although only the initial stages of the analysis are presented here, some of the pictures indicate possibilities of a further development. Even with these limitations, however, the case offers a considerable enrichment of the literature on the subject, which is still very meagre.

May 1954

[2] [This case is not to be confused with the similar case—the patients were in fact sisters—discussed in "The Realities of Practical Psychotherapy," appendix to *The Practice of Psychotherapy* (C.W., vol. 16, 2nd edn.).]

FOREWORD TO JACOBI:
"COMPLEX/ARCHETYPE/SYMBOL"[1]

1256   The problem this book is concerned with is one in which I, too, have been interested for a long time. It is now exactly fifty years since I learned, thanks to the associaton experiment, the role which complexes play in our conscious life. The thing that most impressed me was the peculiar autonomy the complexes display as compared with the other contents of consciousness. Whereas the latter are under the control of the will, coming or going at its command, complexes either force themselves on our consciousness by breaking through its inhibiting effect, or else, just as suddenly, they obstinately resist our conscious intention to reproduce them. Complexes have not only an obsessive, but very often a possessive, character, behaving like imps and giving rise to all sorts of annoying, ridiculous, and revealing actions, slips of the tongue, and falsifications of memory and judgment. They cut across the adapted performance of consciousness.

1257   It was not difficult to see that while complexes owe their relative autonomy to their emotional nature, their expression is always dependent on a network of associations grouped round a centre charged with affect. The central emotion generally proved to be individually acquired, and therefore an exclusively personal matter. Increasing experience showed, however, that the complexes are not infinitely variable, but mostly belong to definite categories, which soon began to acquire their popular, and by now hackneyed, names—inferiority complex, power complex, father complex, mother complex, anxiety complex, and all the rest. This fact, that there are well-characterized and easily recognizable types of complex, suggests that they rest on equally typical foundations, that is, on emotional aptitudes or *instincts*. In human beings instincts express themselves in the form of unreflected, involuntary fantasy images, attitudes, and actions, which bear an inner resemblance

[1] [Jolande Jacobi, *Komplex/Archetypus/Symbol in der Psychologie C. G. Jungs* (Zurich, 1957), trans. by Ralph Manheim (New York, Bollingen Series LVII, and London, 1959). The foreword was trans. by R.F.C. Hull. For Jacobi, see supra, pars. 1121ff.]

532

to one another and yet are identical with the instinctive reactions specific of *Homo sapiens*. They have a dynamic and a formal aspect. Their formal aspect expresses itself, among other things, in fantasy images that are surprisingly alike and can be found practically everywhere at all epochs, as might have been expected. Like the instincts, these images have a relatively autonomous character; that is to say, they are "numinous" and can be found above all in the realm of numinous or religious ideas.

1258   For reasons that I cannot enter into here, I have chosen the term "archetype" for this formal aspect of the instinct. Dr. Jacobi has made it her task, in this book, to expound the important connection on the one hand between the individual complex and the universal, instinctual archetype, and on the other hand between this and the symbol. The appearance of her study is the more welcome to me in that the concept of the archetype has given rise to the greatest misunderstandings and—if one may judge by the adverse criticisms—must be presumed to be very difficult to comprehend. Anyone, therefore, who has misgivings on this score can seek information in this volume, which also takes account of much of the literature. My critics, with but few exceptions, usually do not take the trouble to read over what I have to say on the subject, but impute to me, among other things, the opinion that the archetype is an inherited idea. Prejudices seem to be more convenient than seeking the truth. In this respect, too, I hope that the author's endeavours, especially the theoretical considerations contained in Part I, illustrated by examples of the archetype's mode of manifestation and operation in Part II, may shed a little illumination. I am grateful to her for having spared me the labour of having constantly to refer my readers to my own writings.

February 1956

FOREWORD TO BERTINE:
"HUMAN RELATIONSHIPS"[1]

1259   The author of this book has undertaken the important task of
investigating the problems of human relationship from the standpoint of analytical psychology, an undertaking which will be welcome not only to the psychotherapist but also to those interested
in the wider field of general psychology. Facts that are of the greatest significance for an understanding of human relationships have
undoubtedly come to light in the course of my own and my colleagues' researches. While the conclusions which Freud and Adler
had drawn from their intensive studies of neurosis were based on
the personal psychology of their neurotic patients, which they tried
to apply to the psychology of society, analytical psychology has
called attention to more general human facts which also play an
important role in neurosis but are not specifically characteristic of
it, being a normal part of the human constitution. I would mention
in particular the existence of differences in type, such as extraversion
and introversion, which are not difficult for a layman to recognize.
It is obvious that these two diametrically opposed attitudes must
have a very decisive influence on the relationship of individuals,
and the psychology of the function types—thinking, feeling, sensation, and intuition—further differentiates the general effects of extraversion and introversion.

1260   These attitude and function types belong mainly to man's conscious psychology. The researches of analytical psychology have
shown, further, that it is not only the data of the senses and unconscious personal repressions which exert an influence of consciousness. It is also profoundly affected by unconscious, instinctive—that
is, innate—patterns of psychic behaviour. These patterns are just
as characteristic of man as are the instincts in the behaviour of
animals. But while we know about the instinctive patterns in ani-

<hr>

[1] [New York and London, 1958. Jung wrote the foreword for the Swiss edn.,
Menschliche Beziehungen (Zurich, 1957), and it was trans. by Barbara Hannah
for the English edn. It appears here in slightly revised form. Eleanor Bertine
(1887–1968) was an American analytical psychologist.]

mals only by observing their outward behaviour, the human psyche offers a great advantage in that—thanks to ideas and language—the instinctive process can be visualized in the form of fantasy images, and this inner perception can be communicated to an outside observer by means of speech. If the animal psyche were capable of such an accomplishment, we would be able to recognize the mythology which the weaver bird is expressing when it builds its nest, and the yucca moth when it deposits its eggs in the yucca flower.[2] That is, we would know what kind of fantasy images trigger off their instinctive actions. This insight, however, is possible only in the case of human beings, where it opens up the boundless world of myth and folklore that spans the globe with analogies and parallel motifs. The images which appear here conform with those in dreams and hallucinations to an astonishing degree, to say the least.

1261   This discovery was actually made by Freud, and he erected a monument to it in his concept of the Oedipus complex. He was gripped by the numinosity of this motif, or archetype, and accordingly gave it a central place in his theory-building. But he failed to draw the further and inescapable conclusion that there must be another, "normal" unconscious beyond the one produced by arbitrary repressions. This "normal" unconscious consists of what Freud described as "archaic remnants." But if the Oedipus complex represents a universal type of instinctive behaviour independent of time, place, and individual conditioning, it follows inevitably that it cannot be the only one. Although the incest complex is undoubtedly one of the most fundamental and best known complexes, it must obviously have its feminine counterpart which will express itself in corresponding forms. (At the time I proposed calling it the Electra complex.)[3] But incest, after all, is not the only complication in human life, though this sometimes seems to be the case according to Freudian psychology. There are also other typical patterns which regulate the relation of father to son, mother to daughter, parents to children, brothers and sisters to each other, and so on. Oedipus is only one of the existing patterns and determines only the behaviour of the son, and this only up to a point. Mythology, folklore, dreams, and psychoses do not fall short in this respect. They offer a veritable plethora of patterns and formulas not only

[2] [Cf. "Instinct and the Unconscious" (C.W., vol. 8), pars. 268, 277.]

[3] ["The Theory of Psychoanalysis" (1912), (C.W., vol. 4), pars. 347ff. Cf. Freud's comment, "An Outline of Psycho-Analysis" (1940), Std. Edn., XXIII, p. 194.]

for family relationships but also for man and woman, individual and society, conscious and unconscious, dangers to body and soul, and so forth.

1262   These archetypes exert a decisive influence on human relationships. Here I would mention only the eminently practical significance of the animus (the archetype of man in woman) and anima (the archetype of woman in man), which are the source of so much fleeting happiness and long-drawn-out suffering in marriage and friendship.

1263   The author has much to say about these things, based on her medical practice and on her arduous but rewarding work with people. She deserves to be heard, and I hope her book will find a large number of attentive readers.

August 1956

PREFACE TO DE LASZLO: "PSYCHE AND SYMBOL"[1]

1264   Dr. de Laszlo has risked shocking the American reader by including some of my most difficult essays in her selection from my writings. In sympathy with the reader I acknowledge how tempting if not unavoidable it is to fall into the trap of appearances as the eye wanders over the pages in a vain attempt to get at the gist of the matter in the shortest possible time. I know of so many who, opening one of my books and, stumbling upon a number of Latin quotations, shut it with a bang, because Latin suggests history and therefore death and unreality. I am afraid my works demand some patience and some thinking. I know: it is very hard on the reader who expects to be fed by informative headlines. It is not the conscientious scientist's way to bluff the public with impressive résumés and bold assertions. He tries to explain, to produce the necessary evidence, and thus to create a basis for understanding. In my case, moreover, understanding is not concerned with generally known facts, but rather with those that are little known or even new. It was therefore incumbent upon me to make these facts known. In so far as such unexpected novelties demand equally unexpected means of explanation I found myself confronted with the task of explaining the very nature of my evidential material.

1265   The facts are experiences gained from a careful and painstaking analysis of certain psychic processes observed in the course of psychic treatment. As these facts could not be satisfactorily explained by themselves, it was necessary to look round for possible comparisons. When, for instance, one comes across a patient who produces symbolic mandalas in his dreams or his waking imagination and proceeds to explain these circular images in terms of certain sexual or other fantasies, this explanation carries no conviction, seeing that another patient develops wholly different motivations. Nor is it permissible to assume that a sexual fantasy is a more likely motivation than, for instance, a power drive, since we know from

[1] [A selection from the writings of C. G. Jung, ed. by Violet S. de Laszlo (Anchor Books, New York, 1958). The foreword appears here in slightly revised form.]

experience that the individual's disposition will of necessity lead him to give preference to the one or the other. Both patients, on the other hand, may have one fact in common—a state of mental and moral confusion. We would surely do better to follow up this clue and try to discover whether the circular images are connected with such a state of mind. Our third case producing mandalas is perhaps a schizophrenic in such a disturbed state that he cannot even be asked for his accompanying fantasies. This patient is obviously completely dissolved in a chaotic condition. Our fourth case is a little boy of seven who has decorated the corner of the room where his bed stands with numerous mandalas without which he cannot go to sleep. He only feels safe when they are around him. His fantasy tells him that they protect him against nameless fears assailing him in the night. What is his confusion? His parents are contemplating divorce.[2] And what shall we say of a hard-boiled scientific rationalist who produced mandalas in his dreams and in his waking fantasies? He had to consult an alienist, as he was about to lose his reason because he had suddenly become assailed by the most amazing dreams and visions. What was *his* confusion? The clash between two *equally real* worlds, one external, the other internal: a fact he could no longer deny.[3]

1266   There is no need to prolong this series since, leaving aside all theoretical prejudices, the underlying reason for producing a mandala seems to be a certain definable mental state. But have we any evidence which might explain why such a state should produce a mandala? Or is this mere chance? Consequently we must ask whether our experiences are the only ones on record and, if not, where we can find comparable occurrences. There is no difficulty in finding them; plenty of parallels exist in the Far East and the Far West, or right here in Europe, several hundred years ago. The books of reference can be found in our university libraries, but for the last two hundred years nobody has read them, and they are—oh horror!—written in Latin and some even in Greek. But are they dead? Are those books not the distant echo of life once lived, of minds and hearts quick with passions, hopes, and visions, as keen as our own? Does it matter so much whether the pages before us tell the story of a patient still alive, or dead for fifty years? Does it really matter whether their confessions, their anguish, their strivings speak the English of today or Latin or Greek? No matter

---

[2] [Cf. "Concerning Mandala Symbolism" (C.W., vol. 9,i), par. 687 and fig. 33.]
[3] [Cf. the dream series in *Psychology and Alchemy*, C.W., vol. 12, Part II.]

how much we are of today, there has been a yesterday, which was just as real, just as human and warm, as the moment we call Now, which—alas—in a few hours will be a yesterday as dead as the first of January anno Domini 1300. A good half of the reasons why things now are what they are lies buried in yesterday. Science in its attempt to establish causal connections has to refer to the past. We teach comparative anatomy, why not comparative psychology? The psyche is not only of today, it reaches right back to prehistoric ages. Has man really changed in ten thousand years? Have stags changed their antlers in this short lapse of time? Of course the hairy man of the Ice Ages has become unrecognizable when you try to discover him among the persons you meet on Fifth Avenue. But you will be amazed when you have talked with them for a hundred hours about their intimate life. You will then read the mouldy parchments as if they were the latest thrillers. You will find the secrets of the modern consulting room curiously expressed in abbreviated mediaeval Latin or in an intricate Byzantine hand.

1267   What the doctor can hear, when he listens attentively, of fantasies, dreams, and intimate experiences is not mentioned in the Encyclopaedia Britannica or in textbooks and scientific journals. These secrets are jealously guarded, anxiously concealed, and greatly feared and esteemed. They are very private possessions, never divulged and talked about, because they are feared as ridiculous and revered as revelations. They are numinous, a doubtful treasure, perhaps comical, perhaps miraculous, at all events a painfully vulnerable spot, yet presiding over all the crossroads of one's individual life. They are officially and by general consent just as unknown and despised as the old parchments with their indecipherable and unaesthetic hieroglyphics, evidence of old obscurantisms and foolishness. We are ignorant of their contents, and we are equally ignorant of what is going on in the deeper layers of our unconscious, because "those who know do not talk, those who talk do not know."[4] As inner experiences of this kind increase, the social nexus between human beings decreases. The individual becomes isolated for no apparent reason. Finally this becomes unbearable and he has to confide in someone. Much will then depend on whether he is properly understood or not. It would be fatal if he were to be misinterpreted. Fortunately, such people are instinctively careful and as a rule do not talk more than necessary.

1268   When one hears a confession of this kind, and the patient wants

4 [Tao-te-ching, ch. 56.]

to understand himself better, some comparative knowledge will be most helpful. When the hard-boiled rationalist mentioned above came to consult me for the first time, he was in such a state of panic that not only he but I myself felt the wind blowing over from the lunatic asylum! As he was telling me of his experiences in detail he mentioned a particularly impressive dream. I got up and fetched an ancient volume from my bookshelf and showed it to him, saying: "You see the date? Just about four hundred years old. Now watch!" I opened the book at the place where there was a curious woodcut, representing his dream almost literally. "You see," I said, "your dream is no secret. You are not the victim of a pathological insult and not separated from mankind by an inexplicable psychosis. You are merely ignorant of certain experiences well within the bounds of human knowledge and understanding." It was worth seeing the relief which came over him. He had seen with his own eyes the documentary evidence of his sanity.

1269 This illustrates why historical comparison is not a mere learned hobby but very practical and useful. It opens the door to life and humanity again, which had seemed inexorably closed. It is of no ultimate advantage to deny or reason away or ridicule such seemingly abnormal or out-of-the-way experiences. They should not get lost, because they contain an intrinsic individual value, the loss of which entails definite damage to one's personality. One should be aware of the high esteem which in past centuries was felt for such experiences, because it explains the extraordinary importance that we ignorant moderns are forced to attribute to them in spite of ourselves.

1270 Understanding an illness does not cure it, but it is a definite help because you can cope with a comprehensible difficulty far more easily than with an incomprehensible darkness. Even if in the end a rational explanation cannot be reached, you know at least that you are not the only one confronted by a "merely imaginary" wall, but one of the many who have vainly tried to climb it. You still share the common human lot and are not cut off from humanity by a subjective defect. Thus you have not suffered the irreparable loss of a personal value and are not forced to continue your way on the crutches of a dry and lifeless rationalism. On the contrary, you find new courage to accept and integrate the irrationality of your own life and of life in general.

1271 Instincts are the most conservative determinants of any kind of life. The mind is not born a *tabula rasa*. Like the body, it has its predetermined individual aptitudes: namely, patterns of behaviour. They become manifest in the ever-recurring patterns of psychic functioning. As the weaver-bird will infallibly build its nest in the accustomed form, so man despite his freedom and superficial changeability will function psychologically according to his original patterns—up to a certain point; that is, until for some reason he collides with his still living and ever-present instinctual roots. The instincts will then protest and engender peculiar thoughts and emotions, which will be all the more alien and incomprehensible the more man's consciousness has deviated from its original conformity to these instincts. As nowadays mankind is threatened with self-destruction through radioactivity, we are experiencing a fundamental reassertion of our instincts in various forms. I have called the psychological manifestations of instinct "archetypes."

1272   The archetypes are by no means useless archaic survivals or relics. They are living entities which cause the preformation of numinous ideas or dominant representations. Insufficient understanding, however, accepts these prefigurations in their archaic form, because they have a numinous fascination for the underdeveloped mind. Thus Communism is an archaic, highly insidious pattern of life which characterizes primitive social groups. It implies lawless chieftainship as a vitally necessary compensation, a fact which can be overlooked only by means of a rationalistic bias, the prerogative of a barbarous mind.

1273   It is important to remember that my concept of the archetypes has been frequently misunderstood as denoting inherited ideas or as a kind of philosophical speculation. In reality they belong to the realm of instinctual activity and in that sense they represent inherited patterns of psychic behaviour. As such they are invested with certain dynamic qualities which, psychologically speaking, are characterized as "autonomy" and "numinosity."

1274   I do not know of any more reliable way back to the instinctual basis than through an understanding of these psychological patterns, which enable us to recognize the nature of an instinctive attitude. The instinct to survive is aroused as a reaction against the tendency to mass suicide represented by the H-bomb and the underlying political schism of the world. The latter is clearly man-made and due to rationalistic distortions. Conversely, if understood by a mature mind, the archetypal preformations can yield numinous ideas ahead of our actual intellectual level. That is just what our time is in need of. This, it seems to me, is an additional incentive to pay attention to the unconscious processes which in many persons today anticipate future developments.

1275   I must warn the reader: this book will not be an easy pastime. Once in a while he will meet with thoughts which demand the effort of concentration and careful reflection—a condition unfortunately rare in modern times. On the other hand, the situation today seems to be serious enough to cause at least uneasy dreams if nothing else.

August 1957

FOREWORD TO BRUNNER:
"DIE ANIMA ALS SCHICKSALSPROBLEM
DES MANNES"[1]

1276   The antecedents of this book are such that it might give rise to misunderstandings unless the reader is acquainted with them beforehand. Let me therefore say at once that its subject-matter is a dialogue extending over a period of eight years. The partners to this dialogue made it a condition from the start that the record they kept of it should be as honest and complete as was humanly possible. In order to fulfil this condition, and not restrict it to the conscious aspects of the situation, they made it their task to take note also of the unconscious reactions that accompanied or followed the dialogue. Obviously, this ambitious project could be completed only if the unconscious reactions of *both* partners were recorded. A "biographical" debate of such a nature would indeed be something unique in our experience, requiring exceptionally favourable circumstances for its realization. In view of the unusual difficulties she was faced with, the author deserves our thanks for having reproduced, scrupulously and in all the necessary detail, at least three-quarters of the dialogue. Her experiment will be acclaimed by all those who are interested in the real life of the psyche, and more particularly because it gives a vivid account of a typical masculine problem which invariably arises in such a situation.

1277   Although every case of this kind follows an archetypal ground plan, its value and significance lie in its uniqueness, and this uniqueness is the criterion of its objectivity. The true carrier of reality is the individual, and not the "statistical average" who is a mere abstraction. So if the author confines her observations to two persons only, this shows her feeling for the psychological facts. The value of the personality, too, lies in its uniqueness, and not in its collective and statistical qualities, which are merely those of human species and, as such, irreducible factors of a suprapersonal nature. Although the limitation to two persons creates an "unscientific" impression

---

[1] [Vol. XIV of *Studien aus dem C. G. Jung Institut* (Zurich, 1963), by Cornelia Brunner. ("The Anima as a Problem in the Man's Fate.")]

of subjectivity, it is actually a guarantee of psychological objectivity: this is how real psychic life behaves, this is what happens in reality. That part of it which can be formulated theoretically belongs to the common foundations of psychic life and can therefore be observed just as easily under other conditions and in other individuals. Scientific insight is essentially a by-product of a psychological process of dialectic. During this process, "true" and "untrue," "right" and "wrong" are valid only in the moral sense and cannot be judged by any general criterion of "truth" or "rightness." "True" and "right" simply tell us whether what is happening is "true" or "right" for the person concerned.

1278   The reader of this book is thus an invisible listener at a serious dialogue between two cultivated persons of our time, who discuss the various questions that come their way. Both of them make their contribution in complete freedom and remain true to their purpose throughout. I lay particular emphasis on this because it is by no means certain at the outset that such a dialogue will be continued. Often these discussions come to an abrupt stop for lack of enthusiasm in one partner or both, or for some other reason, good or bad. Very often, too, they give up at the first difficulty. The circumstances must have been unusually favourable for the dialogue to have continued over such a long period of time. Special credit is due to the author for having recorded the proceedings on two levels at once and successfully communicated them to the outside world. The thoughts and interior happenings she describes form a most instructive *document humain,* but its very uniqueness exposes it to the danger of being misunderstood and contemptuously brushed aside as a "subjective fantasy." For it is concerned mainly with that special relationship which Freud summed up under the term "transference," whose products he regarded as "infantile fantasies." As a result of this devaluation and rationalistic prejudice, their importance as phenomena of psychic transformation was not recognized. This scientific sin of omission is only one link in the long chain of devaluation of the human psyche that has nothing to justify it. It is a symptom of profound unconsciousness that our scientific age has lost sight of the paramount importance of the psyche as a fundamental condition of human existence. What is the use of technological improvements when mankind must still tremble before those infantile tyrants, ridiculous yet terrible, in the style of Hitler? Figures like these owe their power only to the frightening immaturity of the man of today, and to his barbarous unconsciousness. Truly we can no longer afford to underestimate the importance of the psychic factor in world affairs and to go on despising the efforts to understand psychic processes. We are still very far from understanding where we ourselves are at fault, and this book should grant us a deep insight. It is, indeed, only a random sample, but all experience consists of just that. Without individual experience there can be no general insight.

1279 The author has done well to take a well-known case from the history of literature as an introduction to the real *pièce de resistance* of her book. The case is that of Rider Haggard, who was afflicted with a similar problem. (One might also mention Pierre Benoît and Gérard de Nerval.) Rider Haggard is without doubt the classic exponent of the anima motif, though it had already appeared among the humanists of Renaissance, for instance, as the nymph Polia in the *Hypnerotomachia* of Francesco Colonna,[2] or as a psychological concept in the writings of Richard White of Basingstoke,[3] or as a poetic figure among the "fedeli d'amore."[4]

1280 The motif of the anima is developed in its purest and most naïve form in Rider Haggard. True to his name, he remained her faithful knight throughout his literary life and never wearied of his conversation with her. He was a spiritual kinsman of René d'Anjou, a latter-day troubadour or knight of the Grail, who had somehow blundered into the Victorian Age and was himself one of its most typical representatives. What else could he do but spin his strange tale of past centuries, harking back to the figures of Simon Magus and Helena, Zosimos and Theosebeia, in the somewhat sorry form of a popular "yarn?" Psychology, unfortunately, cannot take aesthetic requirements into account. The greatness and importance of a motif like that of the anima bear no relation to the form in which it is presented. If Rider Haggard uses the modest form of a yarn, this does not detract from the psychological value of its content. Those who seek entertainment or the higher art can easily find something better. But anyone who wants to gain insight into his own anima will find food for thought in *She,* precisely because of the simplicity and naïveté of presentation, which is entirely devoid of any "psychological" intent.

---

[2] [Cf. infra, pars, 1749ff.]

[3] [Cf. Jung, *Mysterium Coniunctionis,* C.W., vol. 14, pars. 91ff.]

[4] [Mystical cult in Sufism; its attitudes are compared to those of Dante toward Beatrice. See Corbin, *Creative Imagination in the Ṣūfism of Ibn 'Arabī,* esp. Part II, pp. 136ff.]

1281   Rider Haggard's literary work forms an excellent introduction to the real purpose of this book, since it provides a wealth of material illustrating the symbolism of the anima and its problems. Admittedly, *She* is only a flash in the pan, a beginning without continuation, for at no point does the book come down to earth. Everything remains stuck in the realm of fantasy, a symbolic anticipation. Rider Haggard was unaware of his spiritual predecessors, so did not know that he had been set a task at which the philosophical alchemists had laboured, and which the last of the Magna Opera, Goethe's *Faust,* could bring to fruition not in life but only after death, in the Beyond, and then only wistfully. He followed in the footsteps of the singers and poets who enchanted the age of chivalry. The romantic excursions of his German contemporary, Richard Wagner, did not pass off so harmlessly. A dangerous genius, Friedrich Nietzsche, had a finger in the pie and Zarathustra raised his voice, with no wise woman at his side as partner to the dialogue. This mighty voice emanated from a migraine-ridden bachelor, "six thousand feet beyond good and evil," who met his "Dudu and Suleika"[5] only in the tempests of madness and penned those confessions which so scandalized his sister that traces of them can be found only in his clinical history. This sounds neither good nor beautiful, but it is part of the business of growing up to listen to the fearful discords which real life grinds out and to include them among the images of reality. Truth and reality are assuredly no music of the spheres—they are the beauty and terror of Nature herself.

1282   The richest yield of all is naturally to be found in the primary material itself, that is to say in the dreams, which are not thought up or "spun" like a yarn. They are involuntary products of nature, spontaneously expressing the psychic processes without the interference of the conscious will. But this richness reveals itself, one might say, only to him who understands the language of animals and plants. Although this is a tall order, it is not putting too great a burden on the learning capacity of an intelligent person who has a moderate amount of intuition and a healthy aversion for doctrinal opinions. Following its instinct for truth, intuition goes along with the stream of images, feels its way into them until they begin to speak and yield up their meaning. It rediscovers forgotten or choked-up paths where many have wandered in distant times and places—perhaps even one's partner in the dialogue. Picking up the

---

[5] [In Nietzsche, *Thus Spake Zarathustra,* Part IV.]

trail, he will pursue a parallel path and in this way learn the natural structure of the psyche.

1283   The author has successfully evoked in the dreamer the intuitive attitude he needs in order to follow the unconscious process of development. The "interpretation" does not adhere to any particular theory, but simply takes up the symbolic hints given by the dreams. Even though use is made of psychological concepts such as the anima, this is not a theoretical assumption, because "anima" is merely a name for a special group of typical psychic happenings that anyone can observe. In an extensive dialogue like this, interpretations can only be passing phases and tentative formulations, but they do have to prove themselves correct when taken as a whole. Only at the end of the journey will it be discovered whether they have done so, and whether one was on the right path or not. The dialectical process is always a creative adventure, and at every moment one has to stake one's very best. Only then, and with God's help, can the great work of transformation come to pass.

April 1959

XI

CIVILIZATION IN TRANSITION

(related to Volume 10 of the Collected Works)

REPORT ON AMERICA[1]

1284   Lecturer described a number of impressions he had gained on two journeys in North America.[2] The psychological peculiarities of the Americans exhibit features that would be accessible to psychoanalysis, since they point to intense sexual repression. The reasons for repression are to be sought in the specifically American complex, namely, living together with lower races, more particularly the Negroes. Living together with barbarous races has a suggestive effect on the laboriously subjugated instincts of the white race and drags it down. Hence strongly developed defensive measures are necessary, which manifest themselves in the particular aspects of American culture.

[1] [An abstract, recorded by Otto Rank, of Jung's "Bericht über Amerika," at the Second Psychoanalytic Congress in Nuremberg, 30–31 Mar. 1910. Abstracts of the papers read at the Congress were published in the *Jahrbuch für psychoanalytische und psychopathologische Forschungen*, II:2 (1910). Rank also published a briefer abstract in the *Zentralblatt für Psychoanalyse*, I:3 (Dec. 1910), 130; trans. in *The Freud/Jung Letters*, 223F, n. 6. Also see ibid., index, s.v. Jung: "Report on America," for evidence that a report on the psychoanalytic movement in the U.S.A. had originally been planned. A MS of Jung's report has not been found.]

[2] [In Aug–Sept. 1909, to the Clark Conference, and in Mar. 1910, to Chicago.]

ON THE PSYCHOLOGY OF THE NEGRO[1]

1285   The psychoses of Negroes are the same as those of white men. In milder cases the diagnosis is difficult because one is not sure whether one is dealing with superstition. Investigation is complicated by the fact that the Negro does not understand what one wants of him, and besides that is ignorant [does not know his age, has no idea of time].[2] He shows a great inability to look into his own thoughts, a phenomenon that is analogous to resistance among our patients. Little is said of hallucinations, and equally little of delusional ideas and dreams. — The Negro is extraordinarily religious: his concepts of God and Christ are very concrete. The lecturer has pointed out on an earlier occasion[3] how certain qualities of the Americans (for instance, their self-control) may be explained by their living together with the (uncontrolled) Negroes. In the same way this living together also exerts an influence on the Negro. For him the white man is pictured as an ideal: in his religion Christ is always a white man. He himself would like to be white or to have white children; conversely, he is persecuted by white men. In the dream examples given by the lecturer, the wish or the task of the Negro to adapt himself to the white man appears very frequently. One is struck by the large number of sacrificial symbols that occur in the dreams, just as the lecturer has mentioned in his book *Wandlungen und Symbole der Libido*.[4] This is yet another indication that such symbols are not only Christian but have their origin in a biological necessity.

[1] [Abstract of a lecture to the Zurich Psychoanalytic Society on 22 Nov. 1912, published in the *Internationale Zeitschrift für ärztliche Psychoanalyse,* I:1 (1913), 115 (*Bulletin* section). See *The Freud/Jung Letters,* 323J, n. 3. For Jung's later views on the influence of Negroes and American Indians on American behaviour, see "Mind and Earth" and "The Complications of American Psychology" (C.W., vol. 10). A MS of the present lecture has not been discovered.]

[2] [So bracketed in the abstract.]

[3] [Not traced; perhaps an earlier lecture to the Society, but cf. the preceding "Report on America."]

[4] [Neither this work (trans. by Hinkle, *Psychology of the Unconscious*) nor its revision, C.W., vol. 5, contains reference to sacrificial symbols in the dreams of Negroes. Concerning the dreams of psychotic Negroes otherwise, see C.W., vol. 6, par. 747, and C.W., vol. 5, par. 154.]

A RADIO TALK IN MUNICH[1]

1286   Your question is not so easy to answer. My interest in these matters was not the result of a primary interest in Chinese philosophy, from a study of which, it might be supposed, I had learnt all sorts of valuable things for my psychology. On the contrary, Chinese thought was very alien to me to begin with. I owe my relations to China and to Richard Wilhelm simply and solely to certain psychological discoveries. In the first place, it was the discovery of the collective unconscious, that is to say, of impersonal psychic processes, that aroused my interest in primitive and Oriental psychology. Among these impersonal psychic processes there are quite a number which seem absolutely strange and incomprehensible and cannot be brought into connection with any of the historical symbols known to us, but for which we can find plenty of unquestionable analogies in the psychologies of the Orient. Thus a whole group or layer of impersonal contents can only be understood in terms of the psychology of primitives, while others have their nearest analogies in India or China. It had previously been supposed that mythological symbols were disseminated by migration. But I have found that the occurrence of the same symbols in different countries and continents does not depend on migration, but rather on the spontaneous revival of the same contents.

1287   Years of observing such processes has convinced me that—for the present at least—the unconscious psyche of Europeans shows a distinct tendency to produce contents that have their nearest analogies in the older Chinese philosophy and the later Tantric philosophy. This prompted me to submit my observations to the eminent sinologist Richard Wilhelm, who thereupon confirmed the existence of some astonishing parallels. The fruit of our collaboration is the recently published book called *The Secret of the Golden Flower*.[2] These parallels bear out a conjecture I have long held,

[1] [Unpublished; from a MS in Jung's hand, dated 19 Jan. 1930. The background of Jung's remarks could not be ascertained.]

[2] [*Das Geheimnis der goldenen Blüte* (late 1929); trans. by Cary F. Baynes, *The Secret of the Golden Flower* (1931; revised edn., 1962). See Jung's commentary, C.W., vol. 13, and his memorial address for Wilhelm (who died 1 Mar. 1930), C.W., vol. 15.]

that our psychic situation is now being influenced by an irruption of the Oriental spirit, and that this is a factor to be reckoned with. What is going on is analogous to the psychic change that could be observed in Rome during the first century of our era. As soon as the Romans, beginning with the campaigns of Pompey, made themselves the political masters of Asia Minor, Rome became inundated with Hellenistic-Asiatic syncretism. The cults of Attis, Cybele, Isis, and the Magna Mater spread throughout the Roman Empire. Mithras conquered Roman officialdom and the entire army, until all these cults were overthrown by Christianity. I do not know how much the spiritual and political decline of Spain and Portugal had to do with their conquest of the primitive South American continent, but the fact remains that the two countries which first established their rule in East Asia, namely Holland and England, were also the first to be thoroughly infected with theosophy. It seems to be a psychological law that though the conquerer may conquer a country physically, he will secretly absorb its spirit. Today the old China has succumbed to the West, and my purely empirical findings show that the Chinese spirit is making itself clearly perceptible in the European unconscious. You will understand that this statement is no more for me than a working hypothesis, but one which can claim a considerable degree of probability in view of the historical analogies.

*

1288 My journey to Africa[3] arose from the same need that had taken me to New Mexico[4] the year before. I wanted to get to know the psychic life of primitives at first hand. The reason for this is the aforementioned fact that certain contents of the collective unconscious are very closely connected with primitive psychology. Our civilized consciousness is very different from that of primitives, but deep down in our psyche there is a thick layer of primitive processes which, as I have said, are closely related to processes that can still be found on the surface of the primitive's daily life. Perhaps I can best illustrate this difference by means of an example. When I ask an employee to deliver a letter to a certain address, I simply say to him: "Please take this letter to Mr. X." In Africa I lived for a time with a very primitive tribe, the Elgonyis, who inhabit the primeval forests of Mount Elgon, in East Africa, and are still partly

[3] [In 1925; see *Memories, Dreams, Reflections,* ch. IX, iii.]
[4] [In 1924–25; ibid., ch. IX, ii.]

troglodytes. One day I wanted to send some letters. The nearest white men were some engineers who were working at the terminus of a branch line of the Uganda railway, two and a half days' journey away. In order to reach them, I needed a runner, and at my request the chief put a man at my disposal. I gave him a bundle of letters, telling him in Swahili (which he understood) to take the letters to the white *bwanas*. Naturally, everybody within a radius of a hundred miles would know where to find them, for news travels fast in Africa. But after receiving my order, the man remained standing before me as though struck dumb and did not stir from the spot. I thought he was waiting for baksheesh in the form of cigarettes, and gave him a handful, but he stood there as dumb and stiff as before. I had no idea what this meant, and, looking round me in perplexity, my eye fell on my safari headman Ibrahim, a long thin Somali, who, squatting on the ground, was watching the scene, grinning. In his frightful English he said to me: "You no do it like so, Bwana, but like so—" And he sprang up, seized his rhinoceros whip, cracked it through the air a couple of times in front of the runner, then gripped him by the shoulders, and with shouts and gesticulations delivered himself of the following peroration: "Here, the great bwana M'zee, the wise old man, gives you letters. See, you hold them in your hand. But you must put them in a cleft stick. Ho boys"—this to my servants—"bring a cleft stick, give it to this pagan. Hold it in your hand so—put the letters in the cleft here—bind it tight with grass—so—and now hold it high, so that all will see you are the runner of the great bwana. And now go to the bwanas at the waterfall and seek one till you find him, and then go to him and say to him: 'The great bwana M'zee has given me letters, they are in my stick here, take them!' And the white bwana will say: 'It is well.' Then you can return home. And now run, but so—" and Ibrahim began running with upraised whip—"so must you run and run, until you come to the place where the little houses go on wheels. Run, run, you dog, run like hell!" The runner's face had gradually lit up as though witnessing a great revelation. Grinning all over, he raised his stick and hurtled away from us, as though shot from a cannon, Ibrahim close behind him with cracking whip and a flood of curses. The man ran 74 miles in 36 hours without stopping.

1289   Ibrahim had succeeded, with an enormous expenditure of mime and words, in putting the man into the mood of the runner, hypnotizing him into it, so to speak. This was necessary because a mere order from me could not conjure up a single movement. Here you see the chief difference between primitive and civilized psychology: with us a word is enough to release an accumulation of forces, but with primitives an elaborate pantomime is needed, with all manner of embellishments which are calculated to put the man into the right mood for acting. If these primitive vestiges still exist in us—and they do—you can imagine how much there is in us civilized people that cannot catch up with the accelerated tempo of our daily life, gradually producing a split and a counter-will that sometimes takes a culturally destructive form. That this really is so, is clearly shown by the events of the last few decades.

1290   Naturally, the purpose of my travels was not to investigate only the differences, but also the similarities between the civilized and the primitive mind. Here there are many points of connection. For instance, in dreams we think in very much the same way as the primitive thinks consciously. With primitives, waking life and dream life are less divided than with us—so little, in fact, that it is often difficult to find out whether what a primitive tells you was real or a dream. Everything that we reject as mere fantasy because it comes from the unconscious is of extraordinary importance for the primitive, perhaps more important than the evidence of his senses. He values the products of the unconscious—dreams, visions, fantasies, and so on—quite differently from us. His dreams are an extremely important source of information, and the fact that he has dreamt something is just as significant for him as what happens in reality, and sometimes very much more significant. My Somali boys, those of them that could read, had their Arabic dream books with them as their only reading matter on the journey. Ibrahim assiduously instructed me in what I ought to do if I dreamt of Al Khidr, the Verdant One,[5] for that was the first angel of Allah, who sometimes appeared in dreams.

1291   For primitives, certain dreams are the voice of God. They distinguish two types of dream: ordinary dreams that mean nothing, and the dreams they call the great vision. So far as I was able to judge, the "big dreams" are of a kind that we too would consider significant. The only dream that occurred while I was there—at least, the only one that was reported to me—was the dream of an old chief, in which he learnt that one of his cows had calved, and was now standing with her calf down by the river, in a particular clearing. He was too old to keep track of his many cattle that

[5] [Cf. "Concerning Rebirth" (C.W., vol. 9, i), par. 250.]

pastured in the various open places in the forest, so he naturally didn't know this cow was going to calve, let alone where. But the cow and the calf were found just where he had dreamt they would be. These people are extraordinarily close to nature. Several other things happened which made it quite clear to me why they were so convinced that their dream told the truth. Part of the reason is that their dreams often fulfil the thinking function over which they still do not have full conscious control. They themselves say that the appearance of the white man in their country has had a devastating effect on the dream life of their medicine-men and chiefs. An old medicine-man told me with tears streaming down his face: "We have no dreams any more since the white man is in the land." After many talks on this subject, I finally discovered that the leading men owed their leadership chiefly to dreams that came true. Since everything is now under British control, the political leadership has been taken out of the hands of the chiefs and medicine-men. They have become superfluous, and the guiding voice of their dreams is silenced.

FOREWORDS TO JUNG:
"SEELENPROBLEME DER GEGENWART"

First Edition (1931)

1292 The lectures and essays contained in this volume[1] owe their existence primarily to questions addressed to me by the public. These questions are enough in themselves to sketch a picture of the psychological problems of our time. And, like the questions, the answers have come from my personal and professional experience of the psychic life of our so remarkable era. The fundamental error persists in the public that there are definite answers, "solutions," or views which need only be uttered in order to spread the necessary light. But the most beautiful truth—as history has shown a thousand times over—is of no use at all unless it has become the innermost experience and possession of the individual. Every unequivocal, so-called "clear" answer always remains stuck in the head and seldom penetrates to the heart. The needful thing is not to *know* the truth but to *experience* it. Not to have an intellectual conception of things, but to find our way to the inner, and perhaps wordless, irrational experience—that is the great problem. Nothing is more fruitless than talking of how things must or should be, and nothing is more important than finding the way to these far-off goals. Most people know very well how things should be, but who can point the way to get there?

1293 As the title of this book shows, it is concerned with problems, not solutions. The psychic endeavours of our time are still caught in the realm of the problematical; we are still looking for the essential question which, when found, is already half the solution. These essays may open the reader's eyes to our wearisome struggle with that tremendous problem, the "soul," which perhaps torments

Küsnacht-Zurich, December 1930

[1] [("Contemporary Psychic Problems.") Psychologische Abhandlungen, III. Thirteen articles by Jung, originally published from 1925 on, and assigned to seven C.W. vols.; and one essay, " 'Komplex' und Mythos," by W. M. Kranefeldt.]

modern man in even higher degree than it did his near and distant ancestors.

Second Edition (*1933*)

1294 As only one and a half years have gone by since the appearance of the first edition, there are no reasons for essential alterations in the text. The collection of my essays therefore appears in unaltered form. And as no fundamental objections or misunderstandings that might have provided occasion for an explanatory answer have become known to me, there is no need either of a longer foreword. At any rate, the reproach of psychologism so often levelled at me would be no excuse for a long disquisition, for no fair-minded person will expect me to prefer the attitude of a metaphysician or a theologian in my own field of work. I shall never stop seeing and judging all observable psychic phenomena psychologically. Every reasonable man knows that this does not express any final and ultimate truth. Absolute assertions belong to the realm of faith—or of immodesty.

Küsnacht-Zurich, July 1932

Italian New Edition (*1959*)[2]

1295 This book is a collection of lectures and essays which originated in the 1920's and constitute volume III of my "Psychologische Abhandlungen." They are for the most part popular expositions of certain fundamental questions of practical psychology, which concerns itself not only with the sick but with the healthy. The latter also have "problems," the same in principle as those of the neurotic, but because practically everybody has them and knows them they are counted as "contemporary questions," while in their neurotic form they appear rather as biographical *curiosa*. The treatment of the neuroses has naturally confronted doctors with many questions they could not answer by medical means alone. They had to resort to an academic psychology that had never concerned itself with living human beings, or only under restrictive experimen-

---

[2] [*Il problema dell'inconscio nella psicologia moderna,* trans. by Arrigo Vita and Giovanni Bollea (Turin), originally published 1942; new edn., 1959, with the present foreword, here trans. from the German original.]

tal conditions which were a direct hindrance to the natural expression of the psyche as a whole. Since the doctors received no help from outside (with the exception of a few philosophers like C. G. Carus, Schopenhauer, Eduard von Hartmann, Nietzsche), they saw themselves compelled to build up a medical psychology of real human beings. The essays in this volume bear witness to these efforts.

March 1959

FOREWORD TO ALDRICH: "THE PRIMITIVE MIND AND MODERN CIVILIZATION"[1]

1296   The author of this book, who studied analytical psychology in Zurich a few years ago, has asked me for a few introductory words to his work. I accede to his request with all the more pleasure as I was not bored but decidedly delighted by reading his book. Books of this kind are often of a very dry, though learned and useful, character. There are indeed not a few of them, because, together with the discovery of a new empirical psychology, the modern scientific mind has become interested in what were formerly called "curiosités et superstitions des peuples sauvages," a field formerly left to missionaries, traders, hunters, and geographical and ethnographical explorers. A rich harvest of facts has been gleaned and gathered up in long rows of volumes even more formidable than Sir James Frazer's *Golden Bough* series. As everywhere in the science of the nineteenth century, the collection type of method has prevailed, producing an accumulation of disconnected and undigested facts which in the long run could not fail to make a survey almost impossible. Such an ever increasing accumulation, here as well as in other sciences, has hindered the formation of judgment. It is a truism that there are never facts enough, but, on the other hand, there is only one human brain, which only too easily gets swamped by the boundless flood of material. This happens particularly to the specialist, whose mind is trained to a careful consideration of facts. But when judgment is required the mind must turn away from the impression of the facts and should lift itself to a higher level from which a survey becomes possible. One might almost say: as a rule the higher standpoint is not given by the specialized science but by a convergence of viewpoints from other scientific realms.

[1] [With an introduction by Bronislaw Malinowski (London and New York, 1931). Aldrich's trans. of the foreword is reproduced here with minor changes. The original appears to have been lost. See Jung's letter to the author, 5 Jan. 1931, in *Letters,* ed. G. Adler, vol. 1. Charles Roberts Aldrich, who resided in California, died in 1933.]

561

1297   Thus the understanding of primitive psychology would have remained an almost insoluble task without the assistance of mythology, folklore, history, and comparative religion. Sir James Frazer's work is a splendid example of this composite method. It is rather astonishing that among the co-operating sciences psychology seems to be lacking. It was, however, not completely absent. Among the many who tried to tackle the problems of the primitive mind, no one has done so without psychology. But the psychological point of view employed by each investigator was his own—just as if there were only one psychological standpoint, i.e., the author's own psychology. Seen from Tylor's point of view, animism is quite obviously his individual bias. Lévy-Bruhl measures primitive facts by means of his extremely rational mind. From his standpoint it appears quite logical that the primitive mind should be an "état prélogique." Yet the primitive is far from being illogical and is just as far from being "animistic." He is by no means that strange being from whom the civilized man is separated by a gulf that cannot be bridged. The fundamental difference between them is not a difference in mental functioning, but rather in the premises upon which the functioning is based.

1298   The reason why psychology has hitherto rendered so little assistance to the explorer in the vast field of primitive psychology is not so much the natural disinclination of the specialist to appeal to principles outside his particular domain as the fact that a psychology which would be really helpful simply did not exist. The psychology that is needed must be a psychology of the complex functions, i.e., a psychology that does not reduce the complexities of the mind to their hypothetical elements, which is the method of experimental or physiological psychology. The first attempt at a complex psychology was made by Freud, and his essay *Totem and Taboo* was one of the first direct contributions of the new psychology to the investigation of the primitive mind. It matters little that his attempt is nothing more than an application of his sexual theory, originally gleaned from pathological minds. His essay nevertheless demonstrates the possibility of a *rapprochement* between psychology and the problem of the primitive mind. Sometime before the work above mentioned, I undertook a similar task[2] that eventually led me to the primitive mind, but with a very different method. While Freud's method consisted in the application of an already existing theory, my method was a comparative one. I have reason to believe that

2 [*Wandlungen und Symbole der Libido* (1912).]

the latter yields better results. The main reason is that our new psychology is in no way advanced enough to present a theory of the mind that would have universal application. With modesty we can claim no more than the possession of sound facts and some rules of thumb which might prove useful in the attempt to master the problem of the primitive mind.

1299 Mr. Aldrich, I observe, has made use of his studies in analytical psychology, to the advantage of his research. His sane and balanced opinions, equally distant from the Charybdis of dry empirical enumeration of facts and the Scylla of deduction from arbitrary premises, owe their vitality and colour in no small measure to a consideration of analytical psychology. I am sure that the analytical psychologist will welcome Mr. Aldrich's book as one of the most vivid and clear presentations of the primitive mind in its relation to civilized psychology. I may also express the hope that the co-operation of the psychologist will prove its usefulness to all students of primitive psychology who approach their subject from the ethnological standpoint.

PRESS COMMUNIQUÉ ON VISITING THE
UNITED STATES[1]

September 1936

1300   The reason why I come to the United States is the fact that Harvard University has bestowed upon me the great honour of inviting me to its Tercentenary Celebration. Being a psychopathologist as well as psychologist, I have been asked to participate in a symposium about "Psychological Factors Determining Human Behaviour."[2]

1301   This is not my first visit to the United States, though my last visit dates back as far as 1924. I am eagerly looking forward to observing the changes which the last eventful decade has brought to public as well as to private life over here and to compare them with those of our own profoundly upset Europe. It is my sincere hope to find more common sense, more social peace, and less insanity in the United States than in the old countries. As a psychologist I am deeply interested in mental disturbances, particularly when they infect whole nations. I want to emphasize that I despise politics wholeheartedly: thus I am neither a Bolshevik, nor a National Socialist, nor an Anti-Semite. I am a neutral Swiss and even in my own country I am uninterested in politics, because I am convinced that 99 per cent of politics are mere symptoms and anything but a cure for social evils. About 50 per cent of politics is definitely obnoxious inasmuch as it poisons the utterly incompetent mind of the masses. We are on our guard against contagious diseases of the body, but we are exasperatingly careless when it comes to the even more dangerous collective diseases of the mind.

1302   I make this statement in order to disillusion any attempt to claim me for any particular political party. I have some reason

1 [Unpublished typescript, written in English. While it apparently was intended for the New York press, no instance of its publication or quotation has been discovered. For an interview that Jung gave the *New York Times* (4 Oct. 1936) upon leaving New York, see "The 2,000,000 Year Old Man," in *C. G. Jung Speaking.*]

2 [For Jung's contribution, under this title, see C.W., vol. 8. The symposium at Harvard was actually entitled *Factors Determining Human Behavior.*]

for it, since my name has been repeatedly drawn into the political discussion, which is, as you best know, in a feverish condition actually. It happened chiefly on account of the fact that I am interested in the undeniable differences in national and racial psychology, which chiefly account for a series of most fatal misunderstandings and practical mistakes in international dealings as well as in internal social frictions. In a politically poisoned and overheated atmosphere the sane and dispassionate scientific discussion of such delicate, yet most important problems has become well-nigh impossible. To discuss such matters in public would be about as successful as if the director of a lunatic asylum were to set out to discuss the particular delusions of his patients in the midst of them. You know, the tragicomical thing is that they are all convinced of their normality as much as the doctor himself of his own mental balance.

1303   It will soon be thirty years since my first visit to the United States. During this time I watched the tremendous progress of the country, and I learned to appreciate also the enormous change America has undergone and is still undergoing, namely the transition from a still pioneering mood to the very different attitude of a people confined to a definite area of soil.

1304   I shall spend my time chiefly at Harvard, and after a short visit to the museums of New York I intend to sail again in the first days of October.

PSYCHOLOGY AND NATIONAL PROBLEMS[1]

1305   The question of psychology and national problems with which I have been asked to deal is indeed of some topicality. It is a question, however, that would not have been asked before the World War. People in general were then not aware of any disturbance in the mental or psychic atmosphere of Europe, although the psychological critic or a philosopher of the antique style could have found enough to talk about. It was a prosperous world then and one which believed in what the eye saw and the ear heard and in what rationalism and philosophical positivism had to say. Even the rational possibility of a great war seemed, in spite of historical evidence, a far-fetched and artificial nightmare, nothing more than a theoretical scarecrow occasionally conjured up by politicians and newspapers when they had nothing else to say. One was thoroughly convinced that international, financial, commercial, and industrial relations were so tightly knit together as to exclude the mere possibility of a war. The Agadir incident[2] and similar gestures seemed to be mere pranks of a psychopathic monarch, otherwise safely enmeshed in an international network of financial obligations, whose gigantic proportions were supposed to rule out any attempts of a serious military nature. Moreover the fabulous development of science, the high standard of public education in most European countries, and a public opinion organized as never before in history, allowed European humanity to believe in man's conscious achievements, in his reason, intelligence and will-power. It almost appeared

[1] [A lecture delivered in English at the Institute of Medical Psychology (The Tavistock Clinic), London, 14 Oct. 1936, when Jung had just returned from his visit to the United States (see the preceding article). He had written the lecture during the voyage, according to his daughter Marianne Niehus-Jung. The text, based on a holograph MS, has not been previously published, though similar ideas are found in an interview with Jung in the *Observer* (London, date undetermined), reprinted in *Time,* 9 Nov. 1936, *The Living Age* (New York), Dec. 1936, and as "The Psychology of Dictatorship" in *C. G. Jung Speaking.*]

[2] [Arrival of a German warship at the port of Agadir, Morocco, which precipitated an international crisis in 1911.]

as if man and his ideals were going to possess the earth and rule it wisely for the welfare of all peoples.

1306   The World War has shattered this dream and has crushed most of the ideals of the preceding era. In this postwar mood originated the doubt: Is everything right with the human mind? One began to question its sanity because thinking people grew more and more astonished at all the things humanity could do. The benevolent god of science that had done such marvellous things for the benefit of man had uncovered his dark face. He produced the most diabolical war machinery, including the abomination of poison gases, and human reason got more and more obscured by strange and absurd ideas. International relations turned into the most exaggerated nationalism, and the very God of the earth, the *ultima ratio* of all things worldly—money—developed a more and more fictitious character never dreamt of before. Not only the security of the gold standard but also that of treaties and other international arrangements, already badly shaken by the War, did not recover but became increasingly illusory. Nearly all major attempts at reduction of armaments and at stabilization of international finances went wrong. Slowly it dawned upon mankind that it was caught in one of the worst moral crises the world had ever known.

1307   It is natural enough that in many quarters the doubt arose as to whether the human mind had not changed. It did not appear preposterous any more to assume that possibly there were peculiar psychological reasons for all these disquieting developments which otherwise could hardly be explained. Many people wondered what psychology would have to say about the world situation. Such questions, as a matter of fact, have often been put to me, and I must confess I always felt not only definitely uncomfortable but singularly incompetent to give a satisfactory answer. The subject is really too complicated. The predominant and immediate reasons for the crisis are factors of an economic and political nature. Inasmuch as these are activities of the human mind they should be subject to certain psychological laws. But the economic factors especially are not wholly psychological in character; they depend to a great extent on conditions that can hardly be linked up with psychology. In politics on the other hand psychology seems to prevail, but there is an ultimate factor of numbers, of sheer force and violence, that corresponds to a caveman's or an animal's psychology rather than to anything human. There is no psychology yet of such infinitely complex matters as economics or politics. It is still quite questionable whether there is any hope at all that psychology can be applied to things due to non-psychological factors. I don't consider myself competent to deal with the ultimate meaning of our world crisis. There are certain sides to it, however, that possess a definitely psychological aspect, offering an opportunity for comment. It seems to be within the reach of contemporary psychology to produce a certain point of view at least.

1308   Before entering upon this subject I want to say a few words about psychology in general:

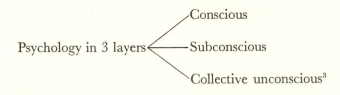

1309   Having given you a short account of what I understand psychology consists of, let me turn now to our subject. First of all a negative statement: I exclude from psychological consideration the strictly economic and political aspect of present-day events. I am doing this because they are, partly at least, non-psychological. Whatever the psychological reasons for the Great War may have been, they transcend my psychological competence. I shall concern myself chiefly with the psychological situation brought about by the War. That there is a so-called psychological situation at all appears to be borne out by a great number of phenomena which we have to call symptoms. You call a certain phenomenon a symptom when it is obvious that it does not function as a logical means to an end but rather stands out as a mere result of chiefly causal conditions without any obvious purposiveness. Thus the yellow colour of the skin in a case of jaundice is a phenomenon with no purposiveness and we therefore call it a symptom, as contrasted with the war-paint of a Red Indian which is a purposive part of the war ceremonial. Or a man drives a nail into the wall and we ask him why he is doing it; if he answers that it is to hang his coat there, then what he does is purposive because it makes sense. But if he answers that it is because he happened to hold a hammer and a nail in his hands, then his action is a symptom, or at least he wants it to appear as such.

³ [Jung evidently elaborated this schema in his lecture.]

1310   Likewise we could imagine mass organizations without the Roman salute, lictor bundles, swastikas, neo-paganism, and other paraphernalia because our political parties as well as Standard Oil or Dutch Shell can do without them. Therefore it appears to us as if such peculiarities were chiefly symptoms of a particular causal condition of the mind. On the other hand we know that symbols and ceremonies mainly occur in religious organizations where it is indeed a matter of a peculiar mental state. Of course if you are in that frame of mind you would not talk of symptomatology. On the contrary, you would call those peculiarities purposive and meaningful, because to you they appear to serve a definite end. As long as one is within a certain phenomenology one is not astonished and nobody wonders what it is all about. Such philosophical doubt only comes to the man who is outside the game.

1311   The countries where the most remarkable symptoms occur are chiefly those that have been actually at war and have therefore found themselves afterwards in a state of appalling misery and disorder. I mean particularly Russia, Germany, Austria, and Italy. No matter what the cause, misery is a definite psychological condition characterized by definite emotions, such as depression, fear, despair, insecurity, unrest, and resentments of every description.

1312   Since our empirical psychology is based entirely on the experience of individual cases, our argument must necessarily start from the individual. This leads us to the question: What will an individual do when under the strain of acute misery? There is a positive and a negative reaction to such a condition:

I. *Positive.* A greater effort is called forth. The individual will show more strength and will-power and will try to overcome the obstacle or the cause of misery through physical, intellectual, and moral effort. It will be an entirely conscious and rational attempt supported by all the means at an individual's disposal. If the strength of *one* individual is not sufficient he will seek the help of others; perhaps a greater number of individuals will form some sort of organization in order to remove the cause of suffering. If such an ultimate attempt fails, or if an individual is too weak from the start to show fight, then a negative reaction takes place.

II. *Negative.* Instead of suitable measures of defence, and instead of a concentration of energy, of efforts of the will, and of all the rational ways and methods applicable to such a condition, an emotional reaction will take place. Emotional reaction always denotes an inferior adjustment. This does not necessarily mean that the adjustment is ineffectual. It merely denotes that, if the individual comes through successfully, the success is due to the fact that he has been passively carried through on the crest of an emotional wave rather than by conscious and deliberate effort of the will. In other words the success has been reached in a primitive and inferior way, in the main through a merely instinctive reaction. But more often the emotional reaction is not successful just because it is too primitive and therefore a maladjustment to a perhaps highly complicated situation. In either case the individual is passive and he is more the object of the emotion than its subject. The emotional reaction as a rule consists of depression, fear, and even panic. Emotional conditions always call up instinctive reactions. The hierarchy of human reason becomes weakened and disintegrated, leaving a door open for the intrusion of primitive instinctive forces. *Emotional reaction always means regression.* The first effect of regression is as a rule the reawakening of infantile methods and attitudes. People under the influence of fear and despair very often become infantile, exaggeratedly helpless and demoralized.[4] Helplessness and panic also lead to group formation, or rather to a clustering together in masses for the sake of gregarious security.

1313   Group formation under the influence of panic cannot be called an organization because it is not an attempt based on reason and will but on a fundamentally emotional movement. It is an accumulation rather than an organization. Such group formations all show unmistakable traces of infantile and archaic psychology, infantile inasmuch as they always look for the father, and archaic inasmuch as the father-image appears in a mythological setting. It seems to be unavoidable that such group formations regress to primitive tribal associations that are held together on the one hand by a chief or medicine-man, and on the other by a sort of mystical doctrine, the tribal teaching.

1314   We turn now to the question: What would a nation do when in a state of psychological misery? Since a multitude of people or a nation is nothing but an accumulation of individuals, its psychology is likewise an accumulation of individual psychologies. The individual psyche, however, is characterized by individual differences, partly congenital, partly acquired. Nearly every individual

---

[4] [As examples of regression, presumably elaborated in the lecture, the holograph itemizes: 1. Father and mother complex. 2. Complex of infantile religion. 3. Regression to infantile criminality. 4. Regression to archetypes: schizophrenia, mystical experience, and analytical experience.]

shows certain specific achievements which add to his relative uniqueness. On the other hand each individual is partly similar to any other, a fact that produces the aspect of human equality. Thus individuals are like each other inasmuch as they have qualities in no way different from those of others, but unlike each other inasmuch as they develop qualities and achievements that cannot be compared with those of other people. Whatever people have in common can accumulate in a group formation, but their individual achievements never accumulate—rather they extinguish each other. Thus a large group, considered as *one* being, exhibits merely the traits common to all people but none of their individual achievements. The traits common to all people consist chiefly of instinctual qualities; these are of a relatively primitive character and indubitably inferior in comparison with the mental level of most of the members of the group. Thus a hundred intelligent people together make one hydrocephalus.

1315   The psychology of masses is always inferior, even in their most idealistic enterprises. The whole of a nation never reacts like a normal modern individual, but always like a primitive group being. Therefore masses are never properly adjusted except on very primitive levels. Their reactions belong to our second category—the negative form. Man in the group is always unreasonable, irresponsible, emotional, erratic, and unreliable. Crimes the individual alone could never stand are freely committed by the group being. A society woman would rather die than appear at a dinner in an obscene dress, but if it were the fashion in the group she would not hesitate for a second to put on the most shocking monstrosity. Think for a moment of the famous *cul de Paris* that embellished the youth of our older generation. And men are no better. The larger an organization the lower its morality. The leader of a great religious movement, when caught out in a lie, said, "Oh! for Christ you may even lie."

1316   Nations being the largest organized groups are from a psychological point of view clumsy, stupid, and amoral monsters like those huge saurians with an incredibly small brain. They are inaccessible to reasonable argument, they are suggestible like hysterical patients, they are childish and moody, helpless victims of their emotions. They are caught in every swindle, called slogans, they are stupid to an amazing degree, they are greedy, reckless, and blindly violent, like a rhino suddenly aroused from sleep. They persevere in every nonsense, in every emotion and resentment, in every prejudice, far beyond the psychological moment, and they get ensnared by the cheapest of all obvious tricks. Most of the time they live in dreams and primitive illusions usually rigged out as "isms." As long as they can feed on open ground in an undisturbed way they are sleepy and harmless. But if their food gets scarce and they begin to migrate and to encroach upon neighbouring territory, they resort to violence. They are not to be convinced that human beings have evolved much better methods in many thousands of years and that these individual men believe in reason and intelligence.

1317   Monster groups have a natural leaning to leaders. But a leader always means a group within the nation, and such a group is more greedy and eats more than the other groups it leads. And as all greedy monsters are jealous they get rid of their leaders and call the new condition a democracy, in which nobody rules and nobody is ruled. The logic of this procedure closely resembles the story of the man who got stranded on an uninhabited island. The first thing he did was an act of statesmanship: he called himself a democracy and consequently felt extraordinarily free and in full possession of all political rights.

1318   Even a group being can't help noticing that in living in a democracy you run your head against remarkably unintelligent restrictions of freedom, imposed upon each free, self-ruling citizen by an invisible, wholly legendary being called the "State." When a monster group first called itself a "democracy" it surely did not think that its former ruler, now dethroned, would turn into a ghost. Yet he did. He became the State.

1319   The State is the psychological mirror-image of the democracy monster. As the nation always rises as *one man,* the State is just as good as one man. As a matter of fact it is quite a person, of unlimited means, more exacting than any tyrant ever was, greedy to the limit and biologically dangerous. It, the State, is not like a Roman Caesar, enslaving prisoners of war on the lower strata of the population; it squeezes its contributions out of the most vital and most gifted individuals of its domain, making slaves of them for its own wasteful devices. It does not know that energy only works when accumulated. Its energy is *money.* It taps all carefully prepared and studied accumulations of this energy and dissipates it so that it becomes ineffectual, thereby causing an artificial entropy.

1320   It seems that "democracy" was a suitable name only in the very youth of the State-ghost. In order to support its boundless

572

ambitions two brand-new "isms" had to be invented: Socialism and Communism. They enhance its ultra-democratic character to an extraordinary degree: the man on the lonely island is now the communistic social democracy. Together with these illusions goes another helpful procedure, the hollowing out of money, which in the near future will make all savings illusory and, along with cultural continuity, guaranteed by individual responsibility. The State takes over responsibility and enslaves every individual for its own ridiculous schemes. All this is done by what one calls inflation, devaluation, and, most recently, "dilution," which you should not mix up with the unpopular term "inflation." Dilution is now the right word and only idiots can't see the striking difference between this concept and inflation. Money value is fast becoming a fiction guaranteed by the State. Money becomes paper and everybody convinces everybody else that the little scraps are worth something because the State says so.

1321   I am by no means sure that what I am saying is not fictitious too. I don't know exactly what has gone wrong, but I have a strong and most uncomfortable feeling that something has gone wrong and that it is even getting worse. I am also certain that I am not the only one to experience such a queer feeling. There must be hundreds of people who have lost their confidence in the direction in which things are apparently moving. As group beings we are all befogged in the same way, but as individuals we might just as well apply as much of our psychiatric knowledge as seems to befit the peculiar symptomatology of our bewildering epoch.

1322   As I mentioned at the beginning, we find the symptoms chiefly in those nations that have been mangled the most by the war beast. There is for instance the German case. As far back as 1918 I published a paper[5] in which I called the attention of my contemporaries to an astounding development in the German edition of the collective unconscious. I had caught hold of certain collective dreams of Germans which convinced me that they portrayed the beginning of a national regression analogous to the regression of a frightened and helpless individual, becoming first infantile and then primitive or archaic. I saw Nietzsche's "blond beast" looming up, with all that it implies. I felt sure that Christianity would be challenged and that the Jews would be taken to account. I therefore tried to start the discussion in order to forestall the inevitable violence of the unconscious outburst of which I was afraid—though not

[5] [Cf. "The Role of the Unconscious" (C.W., vol. 10), pars. 17ff.]

573

enough, as subsequent events have unfortunately shown only too clearly. I don't need to say that I was not heard at all. The fog of war-psychology was just too dense.

1323 Germany was the first country to experience the miracles worked by democracy's ghost, the State. She saw her money becoming elastic and expanding to astronomical proportions and then evaporating altogether. She experienced all in one heap what the ghosts of other democracies are trying to do to us in a sort of slow-motion picture, probably hoping that nobody understands the eye-wash. Germany got it right in the neck and there was no joke about it. The whole educated middle class was utterly ruined, but the State was on top, putting on more and more of the "-istic" rouge as war-paint. The country was in a condition of extreme misery and insecurity, and waves of panic swept over the population. In an individual case these are the symptoms of an oncoming outburst. Any such outburst would bring up archaic material, archetypes that join forces with the individual as well as with the people. There is some teleology about this: it creates strength where there was weakness, conviction instead of doubt, courage instead of fear. But the energy needed to bring about such a transformation is taken away from many old values and the success gained is paid for dearly. Such an outburst is always a regression into history and it always means a lowering of the level of civilization.

1324 Through Communism in Russia, through National Socialism in Germany, through Fascism in Italy, the State became all-powerful and claimed its slaves body and soul. Democracy became its own mirror-image, its own ghost, while the ghost became appallingly real, an all-embracing mystical presence and personality that usurped the throne a pious theocratic Christianity had hoped God would take. The old totalitarian claim of the *Civitas Dei* is now voiced by the State: one sheep as good as another and the whole herd crowded together, guarded by plain-clothed and uniformed wolf-dogs, utterly deprived of all the rights which the man on the island who called himself a democracy had dreamt of. There are no rights left, only duties. Every source of energy, industry, commerce, money, even private enterprise, is sucked up into the new slave-owner, the State.

1325 And a new miracle happened. Out of nowhere certain men came, and each of them said like Louis XIV, "L'état c'est moi." They are the new leaders. The State has proved its personal reality by incarnating itself in men that came from Galilee, inconspicuous nobodies previously, but equipped with the great spirit voice that cowed the people into soundless obedience. They are like Roman Caesars, usurpers of empires and kingdoms, and like those incarnations of a previously invisible deity devoutly invoked and believed in by everybody. They are the State that has superseded the medieval theocracy.

1326 This process of incarnation is particularly drastic in Hitler's case. Hitler himself as an ordinary person is a shy and friendly man with artistic tastes and gifts. As a mere man he is inoffensive and modest, and has nice eyes. But he comes from Braunau, a little town that has already produced two famous mediums—the Schneider brothers. (Harry Price has written a book about one of them.[6]) Hitler is presumably the third and the most efficient medium from Braunau. When the State-spirit speaks through him, he sends forth a voice of thunder and his word is so powerful that it sweeps together crowds of millions like fallen autumn leaves.

1327 There is obviously no power left in the world and particularly no State-loving "-ism" which is capable of resisting this incredible force. Of course you will say, as everybody does, "One must be a German to understand such miracles." Yes, this is just as true as that you must be an Italian to understand the mythology of the Fascio, or a Russian to appreciate the charms of Stalin's paternal regime. Of course you can't understand those funny foreigners, Sir Oswald Mosley and Colonel de la Rocque[7] being still babes in arms. But if you carefully study what President Roosevelt is up to and what the famous N.R.A.[8] meant to the world of American commerce and industry, then you get a certain idea of how near the great State in America is to becoming Roosevelt's incarnation. Roosevelt is the stuff all right, only the circumstances are not bad enough. Great Britain seems to be pretty conservative, yet you have a taxation which makes the great estates uninhabitable. That is

[6] [Cf. Price, *An Account of Some Further Experiments with Willy Schneider* (1925), *The Phenomena of Rudi Schneider* (1926), and other books on these Austrian mediums.]

[7] [Mosley founded the British Union of Fascists ("Blackshirts") in 1932. Col. François de la Rocque was leader of the French reactionary group "Croix de Feu."]

[8] [National Recovery Administration, established to administer the National Industrial Recovery Act (13 June 1933), recognizing a "national emergency" and vesting in the President (F. D. Roosevelt) authority to approve codes of fair competition for various trades and industries, regulate wages, hours of labour, etc.]

exactly how things began in Italy. You have devalued your money, this is the second step. You could not stop the boastful march of Roman legions through the bottleneck of Suez, and Sir Samuel[9] meekly and wisely took all the air out of that magnificent gesture of a proud British fleet adorning the entrance to Italy's triumph. This was the third step. England comes perhaps so late into the paradise of a new age that she arrives there with many old-world values well preserved by sheer lack of interest. Being Swiss I heartily sympathize with this attitude. Knowing of nothing that would be better, we hang on to the rear of events and muddle along as we have been used to do for six hundred years. We can't imagine our dictator yet, but already an unfortunate majority believes in the mighty ghost to whom we have sacrificed all our railways and the gold standard on top of that.

1328   The incarnation of the State-ghost is no mean affair. It competes with famous historical parallels; it even challenges them. Just as Christianity had a cross to symbolize its essential teaching, so Hitler has a swastika, a symbol as old and widespread as the cross. And just as it was a star over Bethlehem that announced the incarnation of God, so Russia has a red star, and instead of the Dove and the Lamb a hammer and sickle, and instead of the sacred body a place of pilgrimage with the mummy of the first witness. Even as Christianity challenged the Roman Imperium, enthroned ambitious Roman bishops as *Pontifices Romani,* and perpetuated the great Empire in the theocracy of the Church and the Holy Roman Empire, so the Duce has produced once more all the stage scenery of the Imperium which will soon reach from Ethiopia to the Pillars of Hercules as of old.

1329   Again it is Germany that gives us some notion of the underlying archetypal symbolism brought up by the eruption of the collective unconscious. Hitler's picture has been erected upon Christian altars. There are people who confess on their tombstones that they died in peace since their eyes had beheld not the Lord but the Führer. The onslaught on Christianity is obvious; it would not even need corroboration through a neo-pagan movement incorporating three million people. This movement can only be compared with the archetypal material exhibited by a case of paranoid schizophrenia. You find in neo-paganism the most beautiful Wotanistic symbolism, Indogermanic speculation, and so on. In North Germany there is

9 [Sir Samuel Hoare, later Viscount Templewood (1880–1959), British foreign secretary in 1935, when he sought to appease Italy in its conquest of Ethiopia.]

a sect that worships Christ in the form of a rider on a white horse.[10] It does not go as far as collective hallucinations, though the waves of enthusiasm and even ecstasy are running high.

1330   Nations in a condition of collective misery behave like neurotic or even psychotic individuals. First they get dissociated or disintegrated, then they pass into a state of confusion and disorientation. As it is not a question of psychotic disintegration in an individual case, the confusion affects mainly the conscious and subconscious layers but does not touch the fundamental instinctual structure of the mind, the collective unconscious. On the contrary, the confusion in the top layers produces a compensatory reaction in the collective unconscious, consisting of a peculiar personality surrogate, an archaic personality equipped with superior instinctive forces. This new constellation is at first completely unconscious, but as it is activated it becomes perceptible in the form of a projection. It is usually the doctor treating a patient who unwittingly assumes the role of the projected figure. The mechanism of this projection is the transference. By transference the doctor appears in the guise of the father, for instance, as that personality who symbolizes superior power and intelligence, a guarantee of security and a protection against overwhelming dangers. So long as the disintegration has not reached the deeper layers, the transference will not produce more than the projection of the father-image. But once the confusion has stirred up these unknown depths, the projection becomes more collective and takes on mythological forms. In this case the doctor appears as a sort of sorcerer or saviour. With actively religious persons the doctor would be superseded by an activated image of Christ or by that of an invisible divine presence.

1331   Mystical literature abounds in descriptions of such experiences. You also find detailed records in William James' *Varieties of Religious Experience*. But if you observe the dreams of such patients you will find peculiar symbolic images, often long before the patients themselves become conscious of any so-called mystical experiences. These images always show a specific pattern: they are circular or square, or like a cross or a star, or are composites of such elements. The technical term I use for such figures is the *mandala,* the Sanskrit word for "circle."[11] The corresponding medieval Latin term is the *circulus quadratus* or *rosa.* In Hindu literature you

[10] [Cf. "Wotan" (C.W., vol. 10), par. 373.]
[11] [Cf. "A Study in the Process of Individuation" and "Concerning Mandala Symbolism" (C.W., vol. 9, i).]

also find the terms *padma* (lotus) and *chakra,* meaning the flower-like centres of different localizations of consciousness.[12]

1332   Because of its circular form the mandala expresses roundness, that is, completeness or integration. In Tantrism and Lamaism it is used as an instrument of concentration and as a means of uniting the individual consciousness, the human ego-personality, with the superior divine personality of the non-ego, i.e., of the unconscious. Mandalas often have the character of *rotating* figures. One such figure is the swastika. We may therefore interpret it as a projection of an unconscious collective attempt at the formation of a compensatory unified personality. This unconscious attempt plays a great role in the general personification of the State. It gives it its ghost-like quality and bestows upon it the faculty of incarnating itself in a human personality. The almost personal authority and apparent efficiency of the State are, in a sense, nothing else than the unconscious constellation of a superior instinctual personality which compensates the obvious inefficiency of the conscious ego-personality.

1333   When Nietzsche wrote his prophetic masterpiece, *Thus Spake Zarathustra,* he certainly had not the faintest notion that the superman he had created out of his personal misery and inefficiency would become a prophetic anticipation of a Führer or Duce. Hitler and Mussolini are more or less ordinary human beings, but ones who, curiously enough, assume that they themselves know what to do in a situation which practically nobody understands. They seem to have the superhuman courage or the equally superhuman recklessness to shoulder a responsibility which apparently nobody else is willing or able to carry. Only a superman could be entrusted with faculties that are equal to the difficulties of the actual situation. But we know that mystical experience as well as identification with an archetypal figure lend almost superhuman force to the ordinary man. Not in vain do the Germans call their Führer "our Joan of Arc." He is very much the character that is open to unconscious influences. I am told that Hitler locked himself in his room for three days and nights when his whole staff beseeched him not to leave the League of Nations. When he appeared again he said without any explantion, "Gentlemen, Germany must leave the League." This story sounds as if German politics were not made but revealed.

1334   Hitler's unconscious seems to be female. Mussolini's Latin and very masculine temperament does not allow a comparison with Hitler. As an Italian he is imbued with Roman history, and indeed

12 [Cf. "The Realities of Practical Psychotherapy" (C.W., vol. 16, 2nd edn., Appendix), par. 560. Also Arthur Avalon, *The Serpent Power.*]

in every gesture he betrays his identity with the Caesar. It is most characteristic what rumour has to say about him. I am told—I don't know whether there is any truth in it or not—that not very long ago he appeared at a reception in the Roman toga and the golden laurel wreath of the Caesar, creating a panic that could only be hushed up by the most drastic measures. Even if this is a mere legend it shows beautifully how rumour interprets the Duce's role. Gossip is surely a bad thing, but I confess I always find it interesting because it is often the only means of getting information about a public figure. Gossip does not need to be true in order to be of value. Even if it gives an entirely twisted picture of a man, it clearly shows the way in which his persona, that is his public appearance, functions. The persona is never the true character; it is a composite of the individual's behaviour and of the role attributed to him by the public.[13] Most of the biography of a public figure consists of the persona's history and often of very little individual truth. Well, this is the penalty the man in the limelight has to pay!

1335   It seems as if in nearly all the countries of Europe the gulf between the right and left wing were widening, in so far as these countries are not already Fascist. It is so in Spain and it soon might be as obvious in France. Since Socialism and Communism merely enhance the attributes of democracy, i.e., of a Constitution where there is a ruler without subjects and subjects without a ruler, they only serve to hollow out the meaning of Parliament, of government, of money, and of the so-called rights of the free citizen. The only possible synthesis seems to be the eventual incarnation of the State-ghost in a superman with all his mythological paraphernalia. Recently Ramsay MacDonald made a very clear statement. Speaking of the Labour Party he literally said: "Its members are a flock without a shepherd and with a plethora of sheep-dogs in disagreement with one another about the fold in which the flock should be penned. Is it not time for Labour policy to be realistic? By its fumbling with the cardinal issues of defence and peace, it is casting doubt on the competence of democracy and playing straight into the hands of Fascism. The problems of modern life are too urgent to remain the playthings of shortsighted partisans."[14]

1336   It is doubtful whether the European nations would remain for any length of time in the chaotic disorder of the childish Commu-

[13] [Concerning the persona, cf. *Two Essays on Analytical Psychology*, C.W., vol. 7, pars. 243ff., 305ff.]

[14] [Source unidentifiable. MacDonald (1886–1937) was Great Britain's first Labour prime minister, 1924, and again 1929–1935.]

nistic doctrine. They rather revert to type, to a state of enforced order which is nothing else than dictatorship and tyrannical oligarchy. At least this form has come to light even in sluggish Russia, where 170 million people are kept in order by a few million members of the Communist Party. In Italy it is the Fascio, and in Germany the S.S. is fast on the way to becoming something like a religious order of knights that is going to rule a colony of sixty million natives. In the history of the world there has never been a case where order was established with sweet reasonableness in a chaos. Chaos yields only to enforced order.

1337   In the dictator and his oligarchical hierarchy the State-ghost appears in the flesh. Yet such statesmen are human beings who assume power over their fellow beings, and instantly the latter feel suppressed, which they did not feel as long as they were called democrats. Of course this State slavery is just as bad as before, but now they remember they might have to say something political and are told to shut up. Then they feel as if something dreadful had happened to them. They don't realize that whatever they talked about in the democracy was just as futile as anything they might talk about now. It is true that democrats talk and socialists talk more and communists beat them all at talk. It is just that sort of thing that has led them to disintegration, and that's why in a condition of enforced order talk comes abruptly to an end.

1338   Disorder is destructive. Order is always a cage. Freedom is the prerogative of a minority and it is always based on the disadvantage of others. Switzerland, the oldest democracy in the world, calls herself a free country because no foreigner ever enjoyed a liberty to her disadvantage until America and Great Britain went off the gold standard. Since then we have felt like victims. Now we play the same trick on the other countries that hold Swiss bonds (mind you, Switzerland is the third biggest banker in Europe!) and we probably feel better for it. But are we really free? We are weak and unimportant and we try to be so; our style of life is narrow and our outlook hampered not only by ordinary hills but by veritable mountains of prejudice against anything and everybody that exceeds our size. We are locked in the cage of order and we enjoy just enough air not to suffocate. We have one virtue yet: we are modest and our ambitions are small. That is why we can stick to order and why we don't believe much in talk. But our freedom is exceedingly limited—fortunately enough. It may save us from a dictator.

1339   In continental Europe today, I am afraid it is hardly a question of whether we are going to enjoy more freedom or less. As a matter of fact things have gone so far that soon even the problem of freedom will be obsolete. The question is rather that of "to be or not to be." The dilemma is now between chaos and enforced order. Will there be civil war or not? — that is what we anxiously ask the dark Fates of Europe. I would like to quote here Miguel de Unamuno, one of those Spanish liberals who undermined the traditional order in the hope of creating greater freedom. Here is his most recent confession: "Times have changed. It is not any more a question of Liberalism and Democracy, Republic or Monarchy, Socialism or Capitalism. It is a question of civilization and barbarity. Civilization is now represented in Spain by General Franco's Army."[15]

1340   Compulsory order seems to be preferable to the terrors of chaos, at all events the lesser of two great evils. Orders, I am afraid, have to be heard in silence.

1341   But there is a majority of people to whom it seems the most serious matter in the world when they can't talk any more. This appears to be the reason why even the most [   ][16] dictatorships are eventually talked out of existence, and why the senseless and lamentable gamble of politics is meandering its way through history—a sad comedy to the thinking mind and to the feeling heart.

1342   If we are stumbling into an era of dictators, Caesars, and incarnated States, we have accomplished a cycle of two thousand years and the serpent has again met with its own tail. Then our era will be a near replica of the first centuries A.D., when Caesar was the State and a god, and divine sacrifices were made to Caesar while the temples of the gods crumbled away. You know that thousands in those days turned their eyes away from this visible world, filled with horror and disgust, and adopted a philosophy which healed their souls. Since history repeats itself and the spiral of evolution seemingly returns to the point where it took off, there is a possibility that mankind is approaching an epoch when enough will be said about things which are never what we wish them to be, and when the question will be raised why we were ever interested in a bad comedy.

15 [*The Observer* (London), 11 Oct. 1936, in an article written from Salamanca 3 Oct. 1936. Unamuno (1964–1936) repudiated the Franco regime in a moving speech at Salamanca on 12 Oct. 1936.]
16 [Illegible in holograph.]

RETURN TO THE SIMPLE LIFE[1]

What are your views on a return of the Swiss people to the simple life?

1343   The return to the simple life can be regarded as an unhoped-for piece of good fortune even though it demands considerable self-sacrifice and is not undertaken voluntarily. Thanks to the mass media and the cheap sensationalism offered by the cinema, radio, and newspapers, and thousands of amusements of all kinds, life in the recent past has rapidly been approaching a condition that was not far removed from the hectic American tempo. Indeed, in the matter of divorces, Zurich has already reached the American record. All time-saving devices, amongst which we must count easier means of communication and other conveniences, do not, paradoxically enough, save time but merely cram our time so full that we have no time for anything. Hence the breathless haste, superficiality, and nervous exhaustion with all the concomitant symptoms—craving for stimulation, impatience, irritability, vacillation, etc. Such a state may lead to all sorts of other things, but never to any increased culture of the mind and heart.

Do you think we should turn more and more to the treasures of our culture?

1344   As the booming book trade in many countries shows, if the worst comes to the worst people will even turn to a good book. Unfortunately, such a decision always needs a compelling external cause. Unless driven by necessity, most people would never dream of "turning to the treasures of our culture." The delusion of steady social improvement has been dinned into them so long that they want to forget the past as quickly as possible so as not to miss the brave new world that is constantly being dangled before their eyes by unreformable world-reformers. Their neurasthenic craving

[1] [Translated from "Rückkehr zum einfachen Leben," *DU: Schweizerische Monatsschrift,* Jhg. I, no. 3 (May 1941). An editorial note in *DU* states that it is a summation of Jung's reply to a questionnaire sent out by the Schweizer Feuilleton-Dienst (features service) to various eminent Swiss, on the effects of wartime conditions in Switzerland.]

for the latest novelty is a sickness and not culture. The essence of culture is continuity and conservation of the past; craving for novelty produces only anti-culture and ends in barbarism. The inevitable outcome is that eventually the whole nation will yearn for the very culture which, owing to the delusion of better conditions in the future (which seldom if ever materialize), has almost (or entirely) disappeared. Unfortunately our world, or perhaps the moral structure of man, is so constituted that no progress and no improvement are consistently good, since sooner or later the corresponding misuse will appear which turns the blessing into a curse. Can anyone seriously maintain that our wars are in any way "better" than those of the Romans?

1345   The craze for mass organization wrenches everyone out of his private world into the deafening tumult of the market-place, making him an unconscious, meaningless particle in the mass and the helpless prey of every kind of suggestion. The never failing bait is the alleged "better future," which prevents him from adapting himself to the actual present and making the best of it. He no longer lives *in* the present and *for* the future, but—in a totally unrealistic way—already *in* the future, defrauded of the present and even more of the past, cut off from his roots, robbed of his continuity, and everlastingly duped by the mocking *fata morgana* of a "better future." A tremendous disillusionment is needed to save people from wishful thinking and bring them back to the sound bases of tradition, and to remind them of the blessings of a spiritual culture which the "age of progress" has destroyed with its nihilistic criticism. One has only to think of the spiritual devastation that has already been wrought by materialism, the invention of would-be intellectuals equipped with truly infantile arguments. It will be difficult to get rid of the kind of thinking whose very stupidity makes it so popular.

Do you believe that happiness is found not in material but in spiritual things?

1346   To remove the ideal from the material to the spiritual world is a tricky business, because material happiness is something tangible (if ever it is attained), and the spirit an invisible thing which it is difficult to find or to demonstrate. It is even supposed that most of what goes by the name of "spirit" is so much empty talk and a clattering of words. An attainable sausage is as a rule more illuminating than a devotional exercise; in other words, to find happiness

583

in the spirit one must be possessed of a "spirit" to find happiness in. A life of ease and security has convinced everyone of all the material joys, and has even compelled the spirit to devise new and better ways to material welfare, but it has never *produced* spirit. Probably only suffering, disillusion, and self-denial do that. Anyone who can live under such stresses and still find life worth while already has spirit, or at least has some inklings of it. But at all times there are only very few who are convinced from the bottom of their hearts that material happiness is a danger to the spirit, and who are able to renounce the world for its sake.

1347   I hope, therefore, that the scourge which is now lashing Europe will bring the nations to realize that this world, which was never the best of all possible worlds in the past, will not be so in the future either. It is, as always, compounded of day and night, light and darkness, brief joys and abiding sorrows, a battleground without respite or peace, because it is nothing but the melting-pot of human desires. But the spirit is another world within this world. If it is not just a refuge for cowards, it comes only to those who *suffer* life in this world and accept even happiness with a gesture of polite doubt. Had the Christian teachings not been so utterly forgotten in the face of all this technological "progress," the avalanches that now threaten to engulf Europe would never have started rolling. Belief in this world leaves room neither for the spirit of Christianity nor for any other good spirit. The spirit is always hidden and safe from the world, an inviolable sanctuary for those who have forsworn, if not the world, at least their belief in it.

Can there be an optimism of austerity?

1348   Instead of "optimism," I would have said an "optimum" of austerity. But if "optimism" is really meant, very much more would be required, for "austerity" is anything but enjoyable. It means real suffering, especially if it assumes acute form. You can be "optimistic" in the face of martyrdom only if you are sure of the bliss to come. But a certain minimal degree of austerity I regard as beneficial. At any rate, it is healthier than affluence, which only a very few people can enjoy without ill effects, whether physical or psychic. Of course one does not wish anything unpleasant for anybody, least of all oneself, but, in comparison with other countries, Switzerland has so much affluence to spare (however honourably earned) that we are in an excellent position to give some of it away. There is an "optimum" of austerity which it is dangerous to exceed, for too much of it does not make you good but hard and bitter. As the Swiss proverb trenchantly puts it: "Behind every rich man stands a devil, and behind every poor man two."

1349   Since "optimism" seems to have been meant, and hence an optimistic attitude towards something unpleasant, I would add that in my view it would be equally instructive to speak of a "pessimism" of austerity. Human temperaments being extremely varied, indeed contradictory, we should never forget that what is good for one man is harmful for another. One man, because of his inner weakness, needs encouragement; another, because of his inner assurance, needs the restraint of austerity. Austerity enforces simplicity, which is true happiness. But to live simply, without regret and bitterness, is a moral task which many people will find very hard.

Will turning away from material things foster the team-spirit?

1350   A common need naturally strengthens the team-spirit, as we can see in England at this moment. But the very existence of many moral weaklings increases the danger of selfishness. All extraordinary conditions bring men's badness as well as their goodness to light. However, since the majority of our people may be regarded as morally healthy, there is ground for hope that a common need will cause their virtues to shine more brightly.

1351   Believing as I do in the virtues and diligence of the Swiss, I am convinced that they have an absolute will to preserve their national independence and are ready to make the heaviest sacrifices. At any rate, the team-spirit in Switzerland is not undeveloped and hardly needs special strengthening. Above all, we do not have those social contrasts between a solid upper crust or party on the one hand and an anonymous mass on the other, which in other countries keep citizens apart. Class conflicts with us are mainly imported from abroad. Instead of pushing the team-spirit artificially to the fore, it seems to me more important to stress the development of the personality, since this is the real vehicle of the team. Faced with the question of *what* a man does, one should never forget *who* is doing it. If a community consists of nothing but trash, then it amounts to nothing, for a hundred imbeciles still do not add up to anything sensible. The noisy and insistent preaching of the team-spirit only causes them to forget that their contribution to society consists of nothing but their own uselessness. If I belong to an organization with 100,000 members it does not prove in the least that I am any good, let alone if there are millions of them.

585

And if I pat myself on the back for being a member, I am merely adding to my non-value the illusion of excessive value. Since, in accordance with the laws of mass psychology, even the best man loses his value and meaning in the mass, it is doubly important for him to be in secure possession of his good qualities in order not to damage the community of which he is a member. Instead of talking so much about the team-spirit it would be more to the point to appeal to the spiritual maturity and responsibility of the individual. If a man is capable of leading a responsible life himself, then he is also conscious of his duties to the community.

1352   We Swiss believe in quality; let us therefore use our national belief for improving the value of the individual, instead of letting him become a mere drop in the ocean of the community. Self-knowledge and self-criticism are perhaps more necessary for us in Switzerland, and more important for the future, than a great herd of social irresponsibles. In Switzerland we could do nothing anyway with masses welded together and controlled by iron discipline; our country is far too small. What counts with us are the virtues, the stoutheartedness and toughness of the individual who is conscious of himself. In the case of extreme necessity everyone has to do his bit in his allotted place. It is nice to hope for a helper in time of need, but self-reliance is better. The community is not anything good in itself, as it gives countless weaklings a wonderful opportunity to hide behind each other and palm off their own incompetence on their fellows. People are only too willing to expect the community to do what they themselves are incapable of doing, and they hold it responsible when they as individuals fail to fulfil their necessary obligations.

1353   Although we Swiss do undoubtedly have a fairly well-developed team-spirit, most of our attempts at community are miserable specimens. They grow on stony ground and are divided by thorny hedges. One and all suffer from the Swiss national vices of obstinacy and mistrustfulness—at least, these national qualities are called vices when people get annoyed about them, as very often happens. But from another point of view they could almost be extolled as virtues. It is quite impossible to say how much of our political, intellectual, and moral independence of the powerful world around us we owe to these unpleasant qualities. Fortunately—I am almost inclined to say—their roots penetrate into the deepest recesses of every Swiss heart. We are not easily fooled. How many poisonous infections, how many fantastic ideas may we not have avoided in the course of the centuries thanks to these qualities! The fact that we are in some respects a hundred years behind the times, and that many reforms are desperately overdue, is the price we have to pay for such useful national failings.

1354   Hence I expect more from the Swiss national character than from an artifically fostered team-spirit, because it has deeper roots in our native soil than an enthusiasm which wanes with the words that conjure it up. It is all very fine to be swept along on a tide of enthusiasm, but one cannot enthuse indefinitely. Enthusiasm is an exceptional state, and human reality is made up of a thousand vulgarities. Just what these are is the decisive thing. If the ordinary Swiss makes very sure that he himself has it good and can summon up no enthusiasm whatever for the joys of having nothing in glorious solidarity with everybody else, that is certainly unromantic—worse, it is selfish, but it is sound instinct. The healthy man does not torture others—generally it is the tortured who turn into torturers. And the healthy man also has a certain amount of goodness which he is the more inclined to expend since he does not enjoy a particularly good conscience on account of his obvious selfishness. We all have a great need to be good ourselves, and occasionally we like to show it by the appropriate actions. If good can come of evil self-interest, then the two sides of human nature have cooperated. But when in a fit of enthusiasm we begin with the good, our deep-rooted selfishness remains in the background, unsatisfied and resentful, only waiting for an opportunity to take its revenge in the most atrocious way. Community at all costs, I fear, produces the flock of sheep that infallibly attracts the wolves. Man's moral endowment is of so dubious a nature that a stable condition seems possible only when every sheep is a bit of a wolf and every wolf a bit of a sheep. The truth is that a society is more secure the more the much maligned instincts can, of their own accord, start off the counterplay of good and evil. "Pure good" and "pure evil" are both superhuman excesses.

1355   Although there is naturally no need to preach self-interest, since it is omnipresent, it should not be needlessly slandered; for when the individual does not prosper neither does the whole. And when he is driven to unnatural altruism, self-interest reappears in monstrous, inhuman form—"changing shape from hour to hour, I employ my savage power"[2]—for the instincts cannot be finally suppressed or eradicated. Excessive sacrifice of the individual for the

2 [*Faust II,* Act 5.]

sake of the community makes no sense in our case anyway, since, our country being so small, we are in no position to assert our self-interest in nationalistic form, that is, by the conquest of foreign countries.

1356   In sober scepticism as opposed to propaganda talk, in sure instinct and closeness to nature, in self-limitation grounded in self knowledge, I see more health for our Fatherland than in fervent speeches about regeneration and hysterical attempts at a reorientation. Sooner or later it will be found that nothing really "new" happens in history. There could be talk of something really novel only if the unimaginable happened: if reason, humanity, and love won a lasting victory.

EPILOGUE TO JUNG:
"L'HOMME À LA DÉCOUVERTE DE SON ÂME"[1]

1357   The fundamental concepts of my psychology have been set forth in the course of this book. Helped by the perceptive translation of M. Cahen-Salabelle, the reader will not have failed to take note that this psychology does not rest on academic postulates, but on my experiences of man, in health and in sickness. That is why it could not be confined to a study of the contents and functions of consciousness: it had to concern itself also with that part of the psyche we call the unconscious. Everything we say about the unconscious should be taken with a grain of salt; we have only indirect evidence for its existence since it is not open to direct observations; whatever conceptions we form of it are but logical deductions from its effects. These deductions possess only a hypothetical validity because it cannot be determined beforehand whether the nature of the unconscious can be adequately grasped by the conscious mind. I have always endeavoured, therefore, to find a formulation which brings together in a logical relationship the greatest possible number of observed facts, or else, on the basis of my knowledge of a given psychic state, to predict its probable future development, which is also a method for proving the correctness of a given hypothesis. Many a medical diagnosis, as we know, can hardly be proved right at the moment the doctor formulates it, and can be confirmed only when the disease takes its predicted course. It is in this way that my views concerning the unconscious have little by little been built up.

1358   It is my conviction that the investigation of the psyche is the science of the future. Psychology is the youngest of the sciences and is only at the beginning of its development. It is, however,

---

[1] [(Translated from the French by A.S.B.G.) The volume for which this was written (in the series Collection Action et Pensée, no. 10, Geneva, 1944) contained five essays by Jung, translated, with a preface, by Roland Cahen-Salabelle, together with extracts from Jung's Basel Seminar (1934) and "Tavistock Lectures" (supra, pars. 1ff.), edited by Dr. Cahen (later form of his name). Only two of the essays are among the eleven that composed *Modern Man in Search of a Soul* (New York and London, 1933).]

the science we need most. Indeed, it is becoming ever more obvious that it is not famine, not earthquakes, not microbes, not cancer but man himself who is man's greatest danger to man, for the simple reason that there is no adequate protection against psychic epidemics, which are infinitely more devastating than the worst of natural catastrophes. The supreme danger which threatens individuals as well as whole nations is a *psychic danger*. Reason has proved itself completely powerless, precisely because its arguments have an effect only on the conscious mind and not on the unconscious. The greatest danger of all comes from the masses, in whom the effects of the unconscious pile up cumulatively and the reasonableness of the conscious mind is stifled. Every mass organization is a latent danger just as much as a heap of dynamite is. It lets loose effects which no man wants and no man can stop. It is therefore in the highest degree desirable that a knowledge of psychology should spread so that men can understand the source of the supreme dangers that threaten them. Not by arming to the teeth, each for itself, can the nations defend themselves in the long run from the frightful catastrophes of modern war. The heaping up of arms is itself a call to war. Rather must they recognize those psychic conditions under which the unconscious bursts the dykes of consciousness and overwhelms it.

1359   It is my hope that this book will help to throw light on this fundamental problem for mankind.

1360   Until a few centuries ago those regions of the world which have since been illuminated by science were shrouded in deepest darkness. Nature was still in her original state, as she had been from time immemorial. Although she had long since been bereft of gods, she had not by any means been *de-psychized*. Demonic spirits still haunted the earth and water, and lingered in the air and fire; witchcraft and prophecies cast their shadows over human relationships, and the mysteries of faith descended deep into the natural world. In certain flowers there could be found images of the martyrs' instruments of torture, and of Christ's blood; the clockwise spiral of the snail's shell was a proof of the existence of God; in alchemy the Virgin birth was figured in the awakening of the *infans mercurialis* in the womb of the earth; Christ's passion was represented by the *separatio, solutio,* and *digestio* of the arcane substance; his death and resurrection were reproduced in the processes of chemical transformation. These depicted the otherwise unimaginable transubstantiation. The secret of the baptismal water was rediscovered in the marvellous properties of the solvent *par excellence,* the ὕδωρ θεῖον or *aqua permanens.* Christ's crucifixion was like a prefiguration of the task of natural science, for the tree of the Cross corresponded to the *arbor philosophica,* which in turn stood for the *opus alchymicum* in general.

1361   Today we can scarcely imagine this state of mind any more, and we can form no proper conception of what it meant to live in a world that was filled from above with the mysteries of God's wonder, down to the very crucible of the smelter, and was corrupted from below by devilish deception, tainted by original sin, and secretly animated by an autochthonous demon or an *anima mundi*—or by those "sparks of the World Soul" which sprang up

[1] [Translated from a typescript, "Randglossen zur Zeitgeschichte," dated 1945, unpublished except for the last nine paragraphs (see below, par. 1374, n. 5). Cf. Jung, *Aufsätze zur Zeitgeschichte* (1946); trans. as *Essays on Contemporary Events* (1947); its contents (in C.W., vols. 10 and 16) were published originally 1936–45.]

as the seeds of life when the Ruach Elohim brooded on the face of the waters.

1362   One can scarcely imagine the unspeakable change that was wrought in man's emotional life when he took farewell from that almost wholly antique world. Nevertheless, anyone whose childhood was filled with fantasy can feel his way back to it to a certain extent. Whether one laments or welcomes the inevitable disappearance of that primordial world is irrelevant. The important thing is the question that nobody ever asks: What happens to those figures and phantoms, those gods, demons, magicians, those messengers from heaven and monsters of the abyss, when we see that there is no mercurial serpent in the caverns of the earth, that there are no dryads in the forest and no undines in the water, and that the mysteries of faith have shrunk to articles in a creed? Even when we have corrected an illusion, it by no means follows that the psychic agency which produces illusions, and actually needs them, has been abolished. It is very doubtful whether our way of rectifying such illusions can be regarded as valid. If, for example, one is content to prove that there is no whale that could or would like to swallow a Jonah, and that, even if it did, a man would rapidly suffocate under those conditions and could not possibly be spewed forth alive again—when we criticize in this way we are not doing justice to the myth. Indeed, such an argument is decidedly ridiculous because it takes the myth literally, and today this seems a little bit too naïve. Already we are beginning to see that enlightened correction of this kind is painfully beside the point. For it is one of the typical qualities of a myth to fabulate, to assert the unusual, the extraordinary, and even the impossible. In the face of this tendency, it is quite inappropriate to trot out one's elementary-school knowledge. This sort of criticism does nothing to abolish the mythologizing factor. Only an inauthentic conception of the myth has been corrected. But its real meaning is not touched, even remotely, and the mythologizing psychic factor not at all. One has merely created a new illusion, which consists in the belief that what the myth says is not true. Any elementary-school child can see that. But no one has any idea of what the myth is really saying. It expresses psychic facts and situations, just as a normal dream does or the delusion of a schizophrenic. It describes, in figurative form, psychic facts whose existence can never be dispelled by mere explanation. We have lost our superstitious fear of evil spirits and things that go bump in the night, but, instead, are seized with terror of people who, possessed by demons, perpetrate the frightful deeds of darkness. That the doers of such deeds think of themselves not as possessed, but as "supermen," does not alter the fact of their possession.

1363   The fantastic, mythological world of the Middle Ages has, thanks to our so-called enlightenment, simply changed its place. It is no longer incubi, succubi, wood-nymphs, melusines, and the rest that terrify and tease mankind; man himself has taken over their role without knowing it and does the devilish work of destruction with far more effective tools than the spirits did. In the olden days men were brutal, now they are dehumanized and possessed to a degree that even the blackest Middle Ages did not know. Then a decent and intelligent person could still—within limits—escape the devil's business, but today his very ideals drag him down into the bloody mire of his national existence.

1364   The development of natural science as a consequence of the schism in the Church continued the work of the de-deification of Nature, drove away the demons and with them the last remnants of the mythological view of the world. The result of this process was the gradual dissolution of projections and the withdrawal of projected contents into the human psyche. Thus the rabble of spooks that were formerly outside have now transported themselves into the psyche of man, and when we admire the "pure," i.e., depsychized, Nature we have created, we willy-nilly give shelter to her demons, so that with the end of the Middle Ages anno 1918 the age of total blood baths, total demonization, and total dehumanization could begin. Since the days of the Children's Crusade, of the Anabaptists and the Pied Piper of Hamelin, no such psychic epidemics have been seen, especially not on a national scale. Even the torture chamber—that staggering achievement of modern times!—has been reintroduced into Europe. Everywhere Christianity has proved incapable[2] of stopping the abomination, although many Christians have set their lives at stake. Finally, the invention of human slaughterhouses—compared with which the Roman circuses of 2,000 years ago were but a piffling prelude—is a scarcely surpassable achievement of the neo-German spirit.

1365   These facts make one think. The demonism of Nature, which man had apparently triumphed over, he has unwittingly swallowed

---

[2] This can be disputed, since it is the Christian *organizations* that have demonstrated their impotence. But if you identify the Church with Christianity, this distinction collapses.

into himself and so become the devil's marionette. This could happen only because he believed he had abolished the demons by declaring them to be superstition. He overlooked the fact that they were, at bottom, the products of certain factors in the human psyche. When these products were unreal and illusory, their sources were in no way blocked up or rendered inoperative. On the contrary, after it became impossible for the demons to inhabit the rocks, woods, mountains, and rivers, they used human beings as much more dangerous dwelling places. In natural objects much narrower limits were drawn to their effectiveness: only occasionally did a rock succeed in hitting a hut, only rarely was it possible for a river to overflow its banks, devastate the fields, and drown people. But a man does not notice it when he is governed by a demon; he puts all his skill and cunning at the service of his unconscious master, thereby heightening its power a thousandfold.

1366   This way of looking at the matter will seem "original," or peculiar, or absurd, only to a person who has never considered where those psychic powers have gone which were embodied in the demons. Much as the achievements of science deserve our admiration, the psychic consequences of this greatest of human triumphs are equally terrible. Unfortunately, there is in this world no good thing that does not have to be paid for by an evil at least equally great. People still do not know that the greatest step forward is balanced by an equally great step back. *They still have no notion of what it means to live in a de-psychized world.* They believe, on the contrary, that it is a tremendous advance, which can only be profitable, for man to have conquered Nature and seized the helm, in order to steer the ship according to his will. All the gods and demons, whose physical nothingness is so easily passed off as the "opium of the people," return to their place of origin, Man, and become an intoxicating poison compared with which all previous dope is child's play. What is National Socialism[3] except a vast intoxication that has plunged Europe into indescribable catastrophe?

1367   What science has once discovered can never be undone. The

[3] All -isms that promise a "better" world are to be distrusted on principle, for this world only becomes different, but not better. Man can, however, to a certain extent adopt a better or worse *attitude,* one that is more reasonable or less. Of the basic evils of existence, inner and outer, he will never be freed. He would do better to realize that this world is a battleground, and at any time only a short span between birth and death.

advance of truth cannot and should not be held up. But the same urge for truth that gave birth to science should realize what progress implies. Science must recognize the as yet incalculable catastrophe which its advances have brought with them. The still infantile man of today has had means of destruction put into his hands which require an immeasurably enhanced sense of responsibility, or an almost pathological anxiety, if the fatally easy abuse of their power is to be avoided. The most dangerous things in the world are immense accumulations of human beings who are manipulated by only a few heads. Already those huge continental blocs are taking shape which, from sheer love of peace and need of defence, are preparing future catastrophes. The greater the equalized masses, the more violent and calamitous their movement!

1368   When mankind passed from an animated Nature into an exanimated Nature, it did so in the most discourteous way: animism was held up to ridicule and reviled as superstition. When Christianity drove away the old gods, it replaced them by one God. But when science de-psychized Nature, it gave her no other soul, merely subordinating her to human reason. Under the dominion of Christianity the old gods continued to be feared for a long time, at least as demons. But science considered Nature's soul not worth a glance. Had it been conscious of the world-shattering novelty of what it was doing, it would have reflected for a moment and asked itself whether the greatest caution might not be indicated in this operation, when the original condition of humanity was abolished. If yes, then a "rite de sortie," a ceremonial proclamation to the gods it was about to dethrone, and a reconciliation with them, would have been necessary. That at least would have been an act of reverence. But science and so-called civilized man never thought that the progress of scientific knowledge would be a "peril of the soul" which needed forestalling by a powerful rite. This was presumed impossible, because such a "rite de sortie" would have been nothing but a polite kowtowing to the demons, and it was the triumph of the Enlightenment that such things as nature-spirits did not exist at all. But it was merely that what one *imagined* such spirits to be did not exist. They themselves exist all right, here in the human psyche, unperturbed by what the ignorant and the enlightened think. So much so that before our very eyes the "most industrious, efficient, and intelligent" nation in Europe could fall into a state of *non compos mentis* and put a poorly gifted housepainter, who was never distinguished by any particular intelligence but only by the use of the right means of mass intoxication, quite literally on the altar of totalitarianism, otherwise reserved for a theocracy, and leave him there. Evidently neither knowledge nor preparation of any kind is needed for the direction of the State, and without any military training one can be a great Field Marshal. Even intelligence blenches at the sight of it and cannot but marvel at the unprecedented "genius." It was indeed something quite out of the ordinary when a person came along and cold-bloodedly stated that *he* would take over the responsibility. It was so stupefying that nobody thought of asking *who* was accepting the responsibility, or of taking the necessary precautions against public mischief. At all events the thing promised far too much for anyone to take serious offence. The psychopathologist is familiar with this particular "genius" of irresponsible promises: it is called *pseudologia phantastica,* and it is considered quite a feat not to be duped by such people, especially when they exhibit in a high degree symptoms of possession, such as divinatory phenomena (hunches, thought-reading, etc.), and fits of pathological affect (the classic frenzy of the prophets). Nothing is so infectious as affect and nothing is so disarming as the promised fulfillment of one's own selfish wishes. I do not dare to think of what might have happened to us Swiss if we had had the misfortune to be a nation of eighty millions. According to all the psychological precedents our stupidity would have been multiplied, and our morality divided, by twenty. The greater the accumulation of masses, the lower the level of intelligence and morality. And if any further proof were needed of this truth, the descent of Germany into the underworld would be an example. We should not delude ourselves that we would not have succumbed too. The presence of traitors in our midst shows how easily we succumb to suggestion, even without the mitigating excuse of being a nation of eighty millions.

1369   What protected us was above all our *smallness* and the inevitable psychological consequences of this. First the *distrust* of the little man, whose one thought day and night is to ensure that the big man shall not bully or cheat him—for this, if one is small, must be expected of the big man. Hence, the more hectoring his words, the more they arouse *defiance* and *obstinacy:* "Now I certainly won't," says the honest citizen. Whether he is accused of being a misoneist or a conservative or a numskull has no effect on his instinctive reaction—at the moment; in the long run, however, the Swiss is so "reasonable" that he is secretly ashamed of his stolidity, his pigheadedness, his being a hundred years behind the times and consequently runs the risk of involving himself after all in the tumult of "world organization," "living space," "economic blocs," or whatever the nostrums today are called. In this respect it is no mistake to be stuck in the past. It is as a rule better to postpone the future, since it is doubtful whether what comes afterwards will be so much better. Usually it is so with reservations, or not at all.

1370   Far be it from me to encourage such nasty things as envy and stinginess, but the fact is they exist and contribute to the heightening of distrust and not wanting to get "with it." Yet, like harmful animals, they have their uses. Naturally I don't want to speak in favour of the bad qualities, but I enjoy studying them just because, in a collectivity, they prove to be so much more effective than the virtues. They have the great advantage of piling up in proportion to the size of the population while the virtues have the disadvantage of extinguishing each other under the same conditions. They suffer from the same drawback as famous galleries, where the accumulated masterpieces kill each other stone dead. Virtue is jealous, but vice seeks companions (and the evil one loves large numbers, small ones he despises, and therefore occasionally overlooks them).

1371   In times of unrest such as these, we are protected by our deep roots, by tradition, which—thank God—is still alive and cherished, by love of country, by a profound conviction that no tree ever reaches up to heaven, and that the higher it grows the closer its roots approach to hell, by a taste that likes the middle, the μηδὲν ἄγαν ("do nothing to excess") of the Greek sages, who knew only their *polis* and presumably never even dreamt of a nation of eighty millions, and lastly by the aforesaid bad qualities, which we certainly don't wish to conceal. We have had enough of this from the other side of the Rhine: "The healthiest, most industrious, most efficient, and staunchest nation"—how the fish rise to this bait! Anyone who is really convinced of his own and his nation's imperfections will not fall for the power of the superlative, the whopping lie. He knows, or should know, that the statesman who toys with unlawful measures is ultimately working for the ruin of the nation. The demand for the probity of the nation's leaders must be the fundamental principle of all politics, however humdrum, undiplomatic, unmodern, and short-sighted that may sound. Success that is obtained by bad means sooner or later ends in ruin. The history of the German Reich since 1871 is an object lesson in this respect. But the danger that one will learn nothing from history is great.

1372   Just as ruinous, it seems to me, as the worship of success and the belief in superlatives is the fashionable tendency to turn man

597

into a mere function of economic factors. Moleschott's celebrated dictum, "Man is what he eats," cannot claim to be even a physiological truth, for although he depends on his food, he is not what this is but how he digests it. All schemes for world improvement, world communications, economic spheres of influence, national alliances, etc., stand or fall by the way man deals with them. And if there is anyone who does not believe that even the best idea will in all probability be sabotaged by man's notorious short-comings, by his stupidity, laziness, unscrupulousness, egotism, etc., he can safely pack up his statistical tables. Even in a system patched together out of countless compromises, and weighed down with all sorts of impractical and seemingly unnecessary historical appendages, the State will prosper tolerably well if the majority of its citizens still possess an unatrophied sense of justice. Nobody can deny the importance of economic conditions, but what is far more important is how the public reacts to their inevitable ups and downs. Over and above all external factors the ultimate decisions always rest with the human psyche. Whether one had a large or a small "living space" matters little in comparison with whether one has a sound or a gullible psyche. In this respect the "leaders," with sure grasp, have understood what is so crucially lacking: an unquestionable spiritual and moral authority. The pope or the Church could say they are such an authority, but how many people believe it? No doubt one *ought* to believe it, but doesn't one always use this little word "ought" when one is forced to admit that one simply doesn't know how the necessary remedy is to be brought about?

1373   I think the appeal to the religious conscience of humanity no longer arouses any response worth mentioning today. The modern peddlers of poisonous intoxicants have replaced this "opium" with far more effective drugs. Nowadays it is science more than anything that is the great power for good or ill. Science has done more than usher in a new age of unbelief: it *is* that age. When anything is labelled "scientific," you can be quite sure that it will be given a welcome hearing by everyone who values his intelligence and his intellectual reputation. Here, then, we would have a quite passable authority which has given proof not only of its iconoclastic but also of its positive powers.

1374   For about half a century now science has been examining under the microscope something that is more invisible than the atom—the human psyche—and what it discovered at first was very far from enjoyable. If one had the necessary imagination one would actually be shattered by these discoveries. But the psychologist today is in the same position as the physicist, who has discovered the elements of a future atomic bomb capable of turning the earth into a nova. He sees it merely as an interesting scientific problem, without realizing that the end of the world has come tangibly closer. In the case of psychology things are not quite as bad as that, but all the same it has discovered where those demons, which in earlier ages dominated nature and man's destiny, are actually domiciled, and, what is more, that they are none the worse for enlightenment. On the contrary, they are as sprightly as ever, and their activity has even extended its scope so much that they can now get their own back on all the achievements of the human mind. We know today that in the unconscious of every individual there are instinctive propensities or psychic systems charged with considerable tension. When they are helped in one way or another to break through into consciousness, and the latter has no opportunity to intercept them in higher forms, they sweep everything before them like a torrent and turn men into creatures for whom the word "beast" is still too good a name. They can then only be called "devils." To evoke such phenomena in the masses all that is needed is a few possessed persons, or only one. Possession, though old-fashioned, has by no means become obsolete; only the name has changed. Formerly they spoke of "evil spirits," now we call them "neuroses" or "unconscious complexes." Here as everywhere the name makes no difference. The fact remains that a small unconscious cause is enough to wreck a man's fate, to shatter a family, and to continue working down the generations like the curse of the Atrides. If this unconscious disposition should happen to be one which is common to the great majority of the nation, then a single one of these complex-ridden individuals, who at the same time sets himself up as a megaphone, is enough to precipitate a catastrophe. The good people, in their innocence and unconsciousness, do not know what is happening to them when they are changed overnight into a "master race" (a work of the devil, who has so often changed horse-apples into gold), and an amazed Europe is hard put to accommodate itself to the "new order" where anything so monstrous (one thinks of Maidenek[4] in relation to Eckhart, Luther, Goethe, and Kant!) is not merely a possibility but a *fait accompli*.[5]

[4] [Nazi concentration camp of World War II, near Lublin, Poland.]

[5] [Pars. 1375–83 were published in the *Basler Nachrichten*, no. 486 (16 Nov. 1946), under the title "Zur Umerziehung des deutschen Volkes" ("On the Re-education of the German People").]

1375   Countless people have asked themselves how it was possible for a civilized nation like Germany to fall into this hellish morass. I once wrote that Germany is the land of spiritual catastrophes.[6] If the neo-German madness proclaims that the Germans are the chosen people, and if they then, out of envious rivalry, persecute the Jews with whom they have certain psychological peculiarities in common (behind every persecution there lurks a secret love, as doubt behind every fanaticism), we are indeed confronted with something quite apart, a state of being "elect." For nobody can fall so low unless he has a great depth. If such a thing can happen to a man, it challenges his best and highest on the other side; that is to say, this depth corresponds to a potential height, and the blackest darkness to a hidden light. This light is certainly invisible today, because it is blocked up in the depths of the psyche. Indeed everything has gone so desperately awry in Germany, and what has happened is an infernal caricature of the answer the German spirit should have given to the question put to Europe by a new age. Instead of reflecting on this question, it was taken in by that fake figure of the Superman, which the neurotically degenerate mind of Nietzsche invented as a compensation for his own weakness. (Not without some excuse, however, since the Faust that made the pact with the devil was his godfather.) Germany has soiled her name and her honour with the blood of the innocent and brought upon her own head the curse of election. She has aroused such hatred in the world that it is difficult to make the scales of justice balance. And yet the first to enter with the Saviour into paradise was the thief. And what does Meister Eckhart say? "For this reason God is willing to bear the brunt of sins and often winks at them, mostly sending them to people for whom he has prepared some high destiny. See! Who was dearer to our Lord or more intimate with him than his apostles? Not one of them but fell into mortal sin, and all were mortal sinners."[7]

1376   Nowhere are the opposites wrenched further apart than in the German. He is like a sick man who has fallen a victim to his unconscious and no longer knows himself.

1377   The psychiatrist knows that certain dangerous unconscious forces can be rendered harmless, or at least held in check, if they are made conscious, that is, if the patient can assimilate them and integrate them with his personality. In so far as psychiatrists are

[6] ["Wotan" (C. W., vol. 10), par. 391.]

[7] [*Works,* trans, by C. de B. Evans, II, pp. 18f.]

concerned with the psychic treatment of such complexes, they have to do every day with "demons," i.e., with psychic factors that display demonic features when they appear as a mass phenomenon. To be sure, a bloodless operation of this kind is successful only when a single individual is involved. If it is a whole family, the chances are ten to one against, and only a miracle can provide the remedy. But when it is a whole nation the artillery speaks the final word. If this is to be avoided one must begin with the individual—and a lamentably long-drawn-out and hopeless labour of Sisyphus this may seem. At any rate people are so impressed by the suggestive power of megaphone oratory that they are inclined to believe that this bad means—mass hypnotism—could be put to a good purpose by "inflammatory" speeches, "pungent" words, and soul-stirring sermons. Though I don't want to dismiss altogether the saying about the end justifying the means, I must emphasize that mass persuasion for the sake of the good compromises its end and aim, because at bottom it is simply a whipped-up mood whose effect peters out at the earliest opportunity. The innumerable speeches and articles on the "renewal" are futile, so much chatter that hurts nobody and bores everyone.

1378   *If the whole is to change, the individual must change himself.* Goodness is an individual gift and an individual acquisition. In the form of mass suggestion it is mere intoxication, which has never yet been counted a virtue. Goodness is acquired only by the individual as his own achievement. No masses can do it for him. But evil needs masses for its genesis and continued existence. The mastermen of the S.S. are all, when segregated each by himself, indescribably small and ugly. But the good man shines like a jewel that was lost in the Sahara. The scientist knows that no epidemic can be sealed off by a *cordon sanitaire* unless the individual is prevented from breaking it. Nor can one hope for the cleanliness of a people unless the individual is induced to wash himself daily. Perhaps in a more enlightened era a candidate for governmental office will have to have it certified by a psychiatric commission that he is not a bearer of psychic bacilli. How much this would have spared the world had it been done before 1933!

1379   The disinfection of the upper echelons would certainly be merely a palliative, for a real cure would consist in the immunization of individuals. The snag here is that the alteration of the individual seems to be such an infinitely long and discouraging way round. It should be remembered, however, that only two other possibilities exist. First, the undoubtedly successful method of mass suggestion, which unfortunately works best only when you want to make something slide downhill or collapse. All that can be built with it are houses of cards or concentration camps or death pits. This method, therefore, is not to be recommended. Second, you can fold your hands in your lap, stick your head in the sand, and let things run on in God's or the devil's name. But it is extremely difficult and irritating to let a thing run on. If anything sensible came of it in the end, it would be like a *lèse-majesté* of man. So this way, too, is out.

1380   What then remains? *Only with the individual can anything be done.* The rise and spread of Christianity show that something of the kind is not altogether impossible. Even a sceptic will have to admit that Christianity has brought about a psychic change of sorts, even if only a superficial one.[8] It expelled many demons (and piled them up somewhere else), and it actually effected the de-deification of nature. If we disregard the mass conversions, its spread was due mainly to the work of one individual upon another. The individual was directly appealed to in early Christian times, and this appeal has continued down through the centuries in the ecclesiastical cure of souls. (In the case of Protestantism one has to ask oneself where, for sheer kerygmatics, the cure of souls has got to!) Without a personal appeal there is no personal influence, which alone can change the attitude of the individual for the better. This requires the personal commitment not only of the one to be changed, but above all of the one who wants to do the changing. Words and gestures influence only the man who is ready to go downhill and is merely waiting for the final push.

1381   What we need are a few illuminating truths, but no articles of faith. Where an intelligible truth works, it finds in faith a willing ally; for faith has always helped when thinking and understanding could not quite make the grade. Understanding is never the hand-maiden of faith—on the contrary, faith completes understanding. To educate men to a faith they do not understand is doubtless a well-meant undertaking, but one runs the risk of creating an attitude that believes everything it does not understand. This—it seems to me—unwittingly prepared the ground for the "genius of the Führer." It is so convenient to be able to believe when one fears the effort of understanding.

[8] In view of the most recent events in Europe one must guard against the assumption that a Christian education has penetrated to the marrow.

1382   The medical name for make-believe and preaching faith is suggestion therapy. It has the disadvantage of adding something to a person, or taking it away from him, without his insight and decision. Childlike faith, when it occurs naturally, is certainly a charisma. But when "joyful faith" and "childlike trust" are instilled by religious education, they are no charisma but a gift of the ambiguous gods, because they can be manipulated only too easily and with greater effect by other "saviours" as well. Hence the lament of many Germans about the shameful misuse that was made of the best qualities of the German people, their faith, their loyalty, and their idealism.

1383   Since the Church is still the greatest institution for mass education, with nothing of comparable value to set beside it, it will probably have to consider refining its methods if it wants to appeal to the educated person. The latter is by no means a *quantité négligeable,* as statistics show that what he thinks and writes percolates down to the broad masses within rather less than a generation. Thus, for example, that outstandingly stupid book by Herr Büchner, *Kraft und Stoff,*[9] became in the course of twenty years the most-read book in the public libraries of Germany. The educated man is and remains a leader of the people, whether he knows it or not and whether he wants it or not. The people seek, despite everything, to understand. Although it was not clearly provided for in the original plan of creation that our first parents would eat of the tree of knowledge, it seems nevertheless to have happened, and since then the wheel of history cannot be turned back. The people want still more of those fruits. This is a hopeful sign, for besides stratospheric bombs and the alluring possibilities of uranium there are also, perhaps, salutary truths which instruct man on his true nature and demonstrate its dangerousness as incontestably as modern hygiene demonstrates the aetiology of typhus and virulent smallpox. At the same time, they lend renewed plausibility to an attitude which it has been the constant endeavour of all the higher religions to inculcate into humanity.

[9] [Ludwig Büchner (1824–99), German physician and philosopher, apostle of extreme materialism.]

ANSWERS TO "MISHMAR" ON ADOLF HITLER[1]

Eugen Kolb, Geneva correspondent of *Mishmar* (*The Daily Guardian*) of Tel Aviv, wrote to Jung on 4 September 1945 for his answers to the following questions. Jung replied on 14 September.

How do you, as a psychiatrist, judge Hitler as a "patient"?

1384　　Hitler was in my view primarily an *hysteric*. (Already in the first World War he had been officially diagnosed as such.) More particularly he was characterized by a subform of hysteria: *pseudologia phantastica*. In other words he was a "pathological liar." If these people do not start out directly as deceivers, they are the sort of idealists who are always in love with their own ideas and who anticipate their aims by presenting their wish-fantasies partly as easily attainable and partly as having been attained, and who believe these obvious lies themselves. (Quisling, as his trial showed, was a similar case.) In order to realize their wish-fantasies *no means is too bad* for them, just because they believe they can thereby attain their beloved aim. They "believe" they are doing it for the benefit of humanity, or at least of the nation or their party, and cannot under any circumstances see that their aim is invariably egoistic. Since this is a common failing, it is difficult for the layman to recognize such cases as psychopathic. Because only a convinced person is immediately convincing (by psychic contagion), he exercises as a rule a devastating influence on his contemporaries. Almost everybody is taken in by him.

How could this "psychopath" influence whole nations to such an extent?

1385　　If his maniacal wish-system is a socio-political one, and if it corresponds to the pet ideas of a majority, it produces a psychic epidemic that swells like an avalanche. The majority of the German

[1] [Not published until 15 Nov. 1974, when Kolb's and Jung's letters were printed in *Mishmar* (in Hebrew), with editorial comments, under the heading, "What Did Jung Say to Mishmar's Correspondent in Switzerland 29 Years Ago?" The publication was the consequence of an inquiry sent to *Mishmar* by the editors of the C.W., attempting to learn whether the late Eugen Kolb had published Jung's letter.]

people were discontented and hugged feelings of revenge and resentment born of their national inferiority complex and identified themselves with the underdogs. (Hence their special hatred and envy of the Jews, who had anticipated them in their idea of a "chosen people"!)

Do you consider his contemporaries, who executed his plans, equally "psychopathic"?

1386   Suggestion works only when there is a secret wish to fulfil it. Thus Hitler was able to work on all those who compensated their inferiority complex with social aspirations and secret dreams of power. As a result he collected an army of social misfits, psychopaths, and criminals around him, to which he also belonged. But at the same time he gripped the unconscious of normal people, who are always naïve and fancy themselves utterly innocent and right. The majority of normal people (quite apart from the 10 per cent or so who are inferior) are ridiculously unconscious and naïve and are open to any passing suggestion. So far as lack of adaptation is a disease, one can call a whole nation diseased. But this is normal mass psychology; it is a herd phenomenon, like panic. The more people live together in heaps, the stupider and more suggestible the individual becomes.

If that is so, how can they be cured?

1387   Education for fuller consciousness! Prevention of social herd-formations, of proletarianization and mass-mindedness! No one-party system! No dictatorship! Communal autonomy!

TECHNIQUES OF ATTITUDE CHANGE CONDUCIVE TO WORLD PEACE[1]

Memorandum to Unesco

I

1388   Psychotherapy as it is taught and practised at the C. G. Jung Institute for Analytical Psychology, Zurich, can be described as a technique for changing the mental attitude. It is a method by which not only neuroses and functional psychoses can be treated, but also all sorts of mental and moral conflicts in normal people. It consists chiefly in the integration of unconscious contents into consciousness. As the unconscious mind complements or—more accurately—compensates the conscious attitude, it becomes of considerable practical importance when the attitude of consciousness deviates to one side to such a degree that the mental balance is upset. This is the case in neuroses and psychoses. The mental and moral conflicts of nor-

[1] [From a holograph, with typescript passages, written (in English) in 1948 in response to a request from the United Nations Educational, Scientific and Cultural Organization (Unesco). The Second General Conference of Unesco, in Nov.–Dec. 1947, had adopted a resolution instructing the Director General to promote "enquiries into modern methods which have been developed in education, political science, philosophy and psychology for changing mental attitudes and into the social and political circumstances which favour the employment of particular techniques." Accordingly, memoranda were commissioned from individuals at specialized institutes, including the International Psychoanalytic Association, the Tavistock Institute of Human Relations, and the C. G. Jung Institute for Analytical Psychology. Mr. P. W. Martin, an official of Unesco, conducted the arrangements with the Jung Institute. Jung's memorandum, published here (with minor stylistic revisions), was later partially incorporated in a text prepared by Dr. Jolande Jacobi on behalf of the Jung Institute, which was sent to Unesco on 23 June 1948 for discussion at the Conference on Methods of Attitude Change Conducive to International Understanding in October 1948, at Royaumont (near Paris). The Jung Institute's memorandum was not, however, included in the agenda of the Royaumont Conference. Acknowledgment is made to the Unesco Press for permission to publish this memorandum and to Mr. J. Havet, Director of the Unesco Department of Social Sciences, for his advice and assistance in 1974.]

mal people show a disturbance of balance of a somewhat different kind: the conflicting opposites are both conscious, whereas in the neuroses the opposing half is mostly unconscious. But even with normal people the mental attitude is only partially based upon conscious and rational motives. Quite a number of—often decisive—motives remain unconscious.

1389   The unconscious mind consists of:

a. Previously conscious but forgotten or repressed contents.

b. Subliminal elements and combinations of elements not yet conscious.

c. Inherited instinctual patterns, so-called archetypes determining human behaviour.

All these contents and elements form together a matrix of the conscious mind, which would not be able to function without their continuous collaboration. A dissociation between conscious and unconscious immediately causes pathological disturbances. The unconscious, therefore, is a factor of the greatest biological importance. Its physiological aspect consists of the functioning of all the subcortical centres, which cannot be influenced by the will, and its psychological aspect of those dominant emotional tendencies in human nature which cannot be ruled by reason. These tendencies are exceedingly dynamic and of an ambivalent nature. If properly understood, they form a most welcome and useful support and *vis a tergo* to conscious convictions and decisions. If misunderstood or misdirected they paralyse and blindfold people, pushing them into a mass-psychosis. It is, therefore, of vital importance in medical psychology to gain access to this reservoir of energy, and no attempt to change mental attitudes can be permanently successful without first establishing a new contact with the unconscious. Hitler's enormous psychological effect was based upon his highly ingenious method of playing on the well-known national inferiority complex of the Germans, of which he himself was the most outstanding example. A similar yet positive release of unconscious dynamism was the overwhelming expansion of Christianity in the second and third centuries, and the explosive spread of Islam in the seventh century. An instructive example of epidemic insanity was the witch-hunting mania in Germanic countries in the fifteenth century. This was the cause of a veritable campaign of enlightenment initiated by the Papal Bull *Summis desiderantes* in 1484.

1390   It must be emphasized that "mental attitude" is a concept which does not describe or define accurately enough what we understand by this term. The attitude our method is concerned with is not only a mental but a *moral* phenomenon. An attitude is governed and sustained by a dominant conscious idea accompanied by a so-called "feeling-tone," i.e., an *emotional value,* which accounts for the efficacy of the idea. The mere idea has no practical or moral effect whatever if it is not supported by an emotional quality having as a rule an *ethical value.* More often than not a neurotic dissociation is due to the effect of an intellectual or moral idea that forms an ideal incompatible with human nature. The contrary is also true, since a dominant immoral idea suppresses the better nature of an individual. In either case the attitude is determined by mental as well as moral factors. This explains why a change of attitude is by no means an easy task, since it always involves considerable moral effort. Should this be lacking, the attitude would not really be changed and the old ways would persist under the disguise of new slogans.

1391 The *method* can be described only in its general outlines:

a. The patient gives an honest account of his biography.

b. He collects his dreams and other products of the unconscious and submits them to analysis.

c. The analytical procedure tries to establish the *context* surrounding each item of the dream, etc. This is done by collecting the associations to a given item. This part of the work is carried out chiefly by the patient.

d. The context elucidates the incomprehensible dream-text in the same way as corrupt or mutilated texts become readable with the help of philological parallels.

e. In this way it is possible to establish a *reading of the dream-text.* This, however, does not imply an understanding of the *dream's meaning.* Determination of its meaning is a matter of practice, i.e., the apparent meaning has to be related to and compared with the conscious attitude. Without such a comparison it is impossible to understand the functional meaning of the dream.

f. As a rule the meaning of a dream is compensatory to the conscious attitude, i.e., it adds to the latter what was lacking in it. The dream is a *natural attempt to redress a lack of balance,* and it changes the conscious attitude to such an extent that a state of equilibrium is restored.

g. The method can be applied only in individual cases and only if the individual voluntarily submits to it.

h. A change of attitude can be brought about only when there is a motive strong enough to enforce a serious submission to the method. In pathological cases it is, as a rule, the illness itself and its intolerable consequences that provide the necessary motivation. In normal cases of conflict it is strong depression, despair, or a religious problem which enables an individual to make a sustained effort to achieve an ultimate change of attitude. A provisional or experimental application of the method rarely produces the desired effect, i.e., a complete change of attitude.

i. It is, however, possible that an earnest and conscientious person with a trained mind and a scientific education can acquire sufficient knowledge through a careful study of the existing literature to apply the method to himself to a certain extent. By this means he can at least obtain some understanding of its possibilities. But as the method is in essence a *dialectical procedure,* he will not be able to progress beyond a certain point without the help of an experienced teacher. Since the method does not involve intellectual factors only, but also feeling values and above all the important question of *human relationship,* the principle of collaboration becomes imperative.

II

1392 The applicability and efficacy of the method described above are severely restricted to the individual. A change of attitude can be brought about this way only in the individual and through individual treatment. Moreover, one can apply this method with reasonable hope of success only to individuals endowed with a certain degree of intelligence and sound sense of morality. A marked lack of education, a low degree of intelligence and a moral defect are prohibitive. As 50 per cent of the population are below normal in one or other of these respects, the method could not have any effect on them even under ideal circumstances. Since the most intimate and delicate problems have to be confronted the moment one begins to delve into the meaning of dreams, a man's attitude cannot be changed unless he takes account of the most questionable and painful aspects of his own character. One cannot, therefore, expect much from the application of such a method to a *group.* A change of attitude never starts with a group but only with an individual.

1393 If a number of individuals were to undergo such treatment separately, and—provided their motive was strong enough—were to experience a change of attitude, they could subsequently form a group, a *leading minority,* which might become the nucleus of a larger body of people. Their numbers could be increased

    a. by individual treatment,
    b. by suggestion through authority.

The great mass of the people is led by its suggestibility. It cannot be changed in its *attitude,* only in its *behaviour.* The latter depends upon the *authority of leaders* whose attitude has been really changed.

1394   In this way the ideas of modern psychology have spread and in a similar way religious and all sorts of intellectual, moral, and immoral movements have gained ground. Such a development seems to be theoretically possible as long as we can be sure that the causes of human attitude are of a psychological nature and can be reached by psychological means. On the other hand we have to remember that psychology in our days is still a very young science and might be still in its cradle. We have to admit, therefore, the possibility of causal factors beyond our rational expectations.

1395   Within the above-mentioned limits a change of attitude is something that can be taken for granted. Success is not easily attainable and the method is neither infallible nor foolproof. It requires a considerable amount of education and training of physician and teacher and a very strong motive on the part of the patient or pupil. But it is also a fact that the interest of the general public in psychology had rapidly increased in spite of the marked resistance of academic authority. Psychological ideas and concepts have spread far and wide, which is irrefutable proof of real need to know more about psychology. Under these circumstances it would not be unreasonable to consider the possibility of a wider application of the said method.

1396   The first thing needed would be *teachers.* But here we come up against the inevitable question of motive. The motive must be a vital one and stronger than any prejudice. This is a very serious obstacle. It needs more than mere idealism—the teacher has to be absolutely convinced that his personal attitude is in need of revision, even of actual change. Nobody will condescend to this unless he feels that there really is something wrong. In view of the actual condition of the world every intelligent person is ready to admit that there is something utterly wrong with our attitude. Yet this inclusive statement rarely ever includes the individual in question, namely, the would-be teacher. His attitude is surely right and only needs confirmation and support, but no change. It is a very long step from this conviction to the conclusion: the world is wrong and therefore I am wrong too. To pronounce such words is easy, but to feel their truth in the marrow of one's bones is a very different proposition, yet it is the *sine qua non* of the true teacher. In other words, it is a question of personalities, without which no method and no organization make sense. *A man whose heart is not changed will not change any other's.* Unfortunately the world of today is inclined to belittle and to ridicule such a simple and evident truth as this and thereby proves its own psychological immaturity, which is one of the prime causes of the present state of affairs as well as of numberless neuroses and individual conflicts.

1397   Since the Middle Ages our mental horizon has been immensely enlarged, but unfortunately in a one-sided way. The object without prevails over the condition within. We know very little of ourselves, we even hate to know more. Yet it is man that experiences the world and any experience is determined by the subject as well as by the object. Logically the subject should be just as important as the object. But actually we know infinitely less of our psyche than of external objects. This fact cannot fail to impress anybody who tries to understand the motivation of human attitudes. The unconscious of highly educated people is often well-nigh incredible in certain respects, not to mention their prejudices and their irresponsible ways of dealing—or rather not dealing—with them. Naturally they set a suggestive example to the masses with disastrous results, but they are little concerned with the *trahison des clercs*. Our insight and our self-education have not kept pace with the ever-expanding external horizon. On the contrary, we know in some ways less of the psyche than in the Middle Ages.

1398   It is evident that a better knowledge of man's psyche begins with a better understanding of oneself. If the method is successful it often integrates a vast amount of hitherto unconscious material into consciousness, enlarging both its range of vision and its moral responsibility. When parents know which of their unconscious tendencies and habits are injurious to their children's psyches, they will feel a moral obligation to do something about it, provided their sense of duty and their love are normally developed. The same law will operate in groups and, last but not least, in nations, that is, in the leading minorities, in so far as these consist of individuals who are conscious of certain tendencies which could seriously endanger human relationships. The main danger is *direct and indirect egotism,* i.e., unconsciousness of the ultimate equality of our fellow men. Indirect egotism manifests itself chiefly in an abnormal altruism, which is even capable of forcing something that seems right or good to us upon our neighbour under the disguise of Christian love, humanity and mutual help. Egotism always has the character of *greed,* which shows itself chiefly in three ways: the power-drive, lust, and moral laziness. These three moral evils are supplemented by a fourth which is the most powerful of all—*stupidity.* Real intelligence is very rare and forms statistically an infinitesimal part of the average mind. Viewed from the level of a more highly qualified mind, the average intelligence is very low. Unfortunately unusual intelligence is often—as an uncommon individual quality—dearly paid for by a corresponding moral weakness or even defect, and is thus a doubtful gift of the gods.

1399   Greed is uncontrollable except when counteracted by an equally violent morality. Morality, however, if it exceeds the norm, becomes a real danger to human relationship, because it is the direct instigator of compensatory immoral behaviour and thus reveals its secret root, greed.

1400   A nation consists of the sum of its individuals, and its character corresponds to the moral average. Nobody is immune to a nation-wide evil unless he is unshakably convinced of the danger of his own character being tainted by the same evil. But the immunity of the nation depends entirely upon the existence of a leading minority immune to the evil and capable of combatting the powerful suggestive effect of seemingly possible wish-fulfilments. If the leader is not absolutely immune, he will inevitably fall a victim to his own will-to-power.

1401   The accumulated greed of a nation becomes utterly uncontrollable unless counteracted by all the forces (civil and military) a government is equipped with. No suggestion works unless one is convinced of its power. Arguments are ineffectual.

III

1402   As to the next step for further development of the aforesaid method we propose:

a. Giving publicity to the ideas mentioned above in circles likely to influence the few who are capable of drawing their own conclusions.

b. If there are some who share the conviction that their own attitude is really in need of revision, they should be given the opportunity to submit to individual treatment.

c. Since a great deal of self-deception is to be expected as to the seriousness of one's motivations, some would soon drop out while others would need more time than was foreseen. In this case the financial allowance granted to the former would go to the latter, so that they could continue their work for as long as from six months to a year.

d. As "a change of attitude" is a rather indefinite term, we must emphasize that we understand by this the change brought about through the integration of formerly unconscious contents into consciousness. Such an addition inevitably involves a change that is felt as such. The change is never neutral. It is essentially an increase of consciousness and it depends entirely upon the individual's character what form it will ultimately take. It is, when it comes to the worst, an inoculation with one's own virtue. It is a challenge to the whole man, and it must be considered a risk—the risk involved in the further development of man's consciousness.[2]

---

[2] Here a list of "books of reference" was appended: (1) Attitude: *Psychological Types*. (2) Method: *The Relations between the Ego and the Unconscious; L'Homme à la découverte de son âme;* Baynes, *Mythology of the Soul;* Wickes, *Inner World of Childhood* and *Inner World of Man; Psychologie und Erziehung.* (3) Psychology: *Über die Psychologie des Unbewussten; Psychology and Religion; Über psychische Energetik und das Wesen der Träume; Psychologie der Übertragung;* Jacobi, *The Psychology of C. G. Jung.*

THE EFFECT OF TECHNOLOGY
ON THE HUMAN PSYCHE[1]

1403   The question you ask me, concerning the effect of technology on the human psyche, is not at all easy to answer, as you may well imagine. The problem is a very complicated one.

1404   Since technology consists of certain procedures invented by man, it is not something that somehow lies outside the human sphere. One may therefore conjecture that certain modes of human adaptation also exist which would meet the requirements of technology. Technological activities mostly consist in the identical repetition of rhythmical procedures. This corresponds to the basic pattern of primitive labour, which is never performed without rhythm and an accompanying chant. The primitive, that is, the man who is relatively instinctive, can put up with an extraordinary amount of monotony. There is even something fascinating about it for him. When the work is accompanied by drumming, he is able to heat himself up into an ecstasy, or else the monotony of the action makes him fall into a semi-unconscious condition, which is not so unpleasant either. The question naturally is: What is the effect of these primitive techniques on modern man, who no longer has the capacity to transport himself into semi-unconscious or ecstatic states for any length of time?

1405   In general it can be said that for modern man technology is an imbalance that begets dissatisfaction with work or with life. It estranges man from his natural versatility of action and thus allows many of his instincts to lie fallow. The result is an increased resistance to work in general. The remedy would presumably be to move industry out of the towns, a four-hour day, and the rest of the time spent in agricultural work on one's own property—if such a thing could be realized. In Switzerland it might be, given time. Naturally it is different with the slum mentality of huge worker-populations, but that is a problem in itself.

[1] [Letter, of 14 Sept. 1949, to the editors of the *Zürcher Student* (Eidgenossische Technische Hochschule = Federal Polytechnic Institute), published in the Nov. 1949 issue, Jhg. 27.]

1406   Considered on its own merits, as a legitimate human activity, technology is neither good nor bad, neither harmful nor harmless. Whether it be used for good or ill depends entirely on man's own attitude, which in turn depends on technology. The technologist has something of the same problem as the factory worker. Since he has to do mainly with mechanical factors, there is a danger of his other mental capacities atrophying. Just as an unbalanced diet is injurious to the body, any psychic imbalances have injurious effects in the long run and need compensating. In my practice I have observed how engineers, in particular, very often developed philosophical interests, and this is an uncommonly sound reaction and mode of compensation. For this reason I have always recommended the institution of Humanistic Faculties at the Federal Polytechnic, to remind students that at least such things exist, so that they can come back to them if ever they should feel a need for them in later life.

1407   Technology harbours no more dangers than any other trend in the development of human consciousness. The danger lies not in technology but in the possibilities awaiting discovery. Undoubtedly a new discovery will never be used only for the good, but will certainly be used for ill as well. Man, therefore, always runs the risk of discovering something that will destroy him if evilly used. We have come very close to this with the atom bomb. Faced with such menacing developments, one must ask oneself whether man is sufficiently equipped with reason to be able to resist the temptation to use them for destructive purposes, or whether his constitution will allow him to be swept into catastrophe. This is a question which experience alone can answer.

FOREWORD TO NEUMANN:
"DEPTH PSYCHOLOGY AND A NEW ETHIC"[1]

1408   The author has asked me if I would write a foreword to the present book. I am happy to comply with this request, although it is only as an empiricist, and never as a philosopher, that I have been concerned with depth psychology, and cannot boast of ever having tried my hand at formulating ethical principles. My professional work has certainly given me plenty of opportunities to do this, since the chief causes of a neurosis are conflicts of conscience and difficult moral problems that require an answer. The psychotherapist thus finds himself in an extremely awkward situation. Having learnt by long and often painful experience the relative ineffectiveness of trying to inculcate moral precepts, he has to abandon all admonitions and exhortations that begin with "ought" and "must." In addition, with increasing experience and knowledge of psychic relationships, the conviction dwindles away that he knows exactly what is good and bad in every individual case. His *vis-à-vis*, the other person, is indeed "another," a profound stranger, if ever the discussion should penetrate to the core of the problem, namely, the unique individuality of the patient. What is then meant by "good"? Good for him? Good for me? Good for his relatives? Good for society? Our judgment becomes so hopelessly caught in a tangle of subsidiary considerations and relationships that, unless circumstances compel us to cut through the Gordian knot, we would do better to leave it alone, or content ourselves with offering the sufferer what modest help we can in unravelling the threads.

1409   For these reasons it is particularly difficult for the medical psychologist to formulate any ethical principles. I do not mean that such a task does not exist, or that its solution is absolutely impossible. I fully recognize that there is an urgent need today to formulate

---

[1] [Written in 1949 for a proposed English edition of Erich Neumann, *Tiefenpsychologie und neue Ethik* (Zurich, 1949). An English edition was published only in 1969 (New York and London), trans. by Eugene Rolfe, with the present trans. of the foreword by R.F.C. Hull (here slightly revised). For Jung's appraisal of the book when it was published in German, see *Letters*, ed. G. Adler, vol. 1, to Neumann, Dec. 1948, and to J. Fierz, 13 Jan. 49.]

the ethical problem anew, for, as the author aptly points out, an entirely new situation has arisen since modern psychology broadened its scope by the study of unconscious processes. Concurrently with this, things have happened in Europe, and still go on happening, that far surpass the horrors of imperial Rome or the French reign of terror; things that have ruthlessly revealed the weakness of our whole system of ethics.

1410   Moral principles that seem clear and unequivocal from the standpoint of ego-consciousness lose their power of conviction, and hence their applicability, when we consider the *compensatory significance of the shadow* in the light of ethical responsibility. No man endowed with any ethical sense can avoid doing this. Only a man who is repressed or morally stupid will be able to neglect this task, though he will not be able to get rid of the evil consequences of such behaviour. (In this respect the author utters some heartening truths.)

1411   The tremendous revolution of values that has been brought about by the discovery of the unconscious, with repercussions still to come, is scarcely understood today or even noticed. The psychological foundation of all philosophical assertions, for example, is still assiduously overlooked or deliberately obscured, so much so that certain modern philosophies unconsciously lay themselves open to psychological attack. The same is true of ethics.

1412   It is, understandably enough, the medical psychologist who is the first to be impressed by the shortcomings or evils of the epoch, for he is the first to have to deal with its casualities. The treatment of neurosis is not, in the last resort, a technical problem, but a moral one. There are, admittedly, interim solutions that are technical, but they never result in the kind of ethical attitude that could be described as a real cure. Although every act of conscious realization is at least a step forward on the road to individuation, to the "making whole" of the individual, the integration of the personality is unthinkable without the responsible, and that means moral, relation of the parts to one another, just as the constitution of a state is impossible without mutual relations between its members. The ethical problem thus poses itself, and it is primarily the task of the psychologist to provide an answer or to help his patient find one. Often this work is wearisome and difficult, because it cannot be accomplished by intellectual shortcuts or moral recipes, but only by careful observation of the inner and outer conditions. Patience and time are needed for the gradual crystallization of a goal and a direction for which the patient can take responsibility. The analyst learns that ethical problems are always intensely individual and can convince himself again and again that the collective rules of conduct offer at most provisional solutions, but never lead to those crucial decisions which are the turning-points in a man's life. As the author rightly says: "The diversity and complexity of the situation make it impossible for us to lay down any theoretical rule of ethical behaviour."

1413   The formulation of ethical rules is not only difficult but actually impossible because one can hardly think of a single rule that would not have to be reversed under certain conditions. Even the simple proposition "Conscious realization is good" is only of limited validity, since we not infrequently meet with situations in which conscious realization would have the worst possible consequences. I have therefore made it a rule to take the "old ethic" as binding only so long as there is no evidence of its injurious effects. But if dangerous consequences threaten, one is then faced with a problem of the first order,[2] the solution of which challenges the personality to the limit and demands the maximum of attention, patience and time. The solution, in my experience, is always individual and is only subjectively valid. In such a situation, all those reflections which the author passes under review have to be considered very seriously. Despite their subjective nature, they cannot very well be formulated except as collective concepts. But since these reflections constantly recur in practice—for the integration of unconscious contents continually poses such questions—it necessarily follows that, in spite of individual variation, they will exhibit certain regular features which make it seem possible to abstract a limited number of rules. I do not, myself, think that any of these rules are absolutely valid, for on occasion the opposite may be equally true. That is what makes the integration of the unconscious so difficult: we have to learn to think in antinomies, constantly bearing in mind that every ultimate truth turns into an antinomy if it is thought out to the end. All our statements about the unconscious are "eschatological" truths, that is, borderline concepts which formulate a partially apprehended fact or situation, and are therefore only conditionally valid.

1414   The ethical problems that cannot be solved in the light of collective morality or the "old ethic" are *conflicts of duty,* otherwise they

---

[2] "The most wretched of inventors are those who invent a new morality: they are always immoralists," says a French aphorist. [Untraceable.]

would not be ethical. Although I do not share Friedrich Theodor Vischer's optimistic view that morality is always self-evident, I am nevertheless of the opinion that in working out a difficult problem the moral aspect of it has to be considered if one is to avoid a repression or a deception. He who deceives others deceives himself, and vice versa. Nothing is gained by that, least of all the integration of the shadow. Indeed, its integration makes the highest demands on an individual's morality, for the "acceptance of evil" means nothing less than that his whole moral existence is put in question. Decisions of the most momentous kind are called for. The alchemical dictum "The art requires the whole man" is particularly true of the integration of the unconscious, and this process was in fact symbolically anticipated by the alchemists. It is evident, therefore, that the solution will be satisfactory only if it expresses the whole of the psyche. This is not possible unless the conscious mind takes account of the unconscious, unless desire is confronted with its possible consequences, and unless action is subjected to moral criticism.

1415   Nor should it be forgotten that moral law is not just something imposed upon man from outside (for instance, by a crabbed grandfather). On the contrary, it expresses a psychic fact. As the regulator of action, it corresponds to a preformed image, a pattern of behaviour which is archetypical and deeply embedded in human nature. This has no fixed content; it represents the specific form which any number of different contents may take. For one person it is "good" to kill those who think differently from him; for another the supreme law is tolerance; for a third it is a sin to skin an animal with an iron knife; for a fourth it is disrespectful to step on the shadow of a chief. Fundamental to all these rules is "religious observation" or "careful consideration," and this involves a moral effort which is indispensable for the development of consciousness. A saying of Jesus in the Codex Bezae (referring to Luke 6:4) expresses it in lapidary form: "Man, if thou knowest what thou doest, thou art blessed. But if thou knowest not, thou art accursed and a transgressor of the law."

1416   We might therefore define the "new ethic" as a development and differentiation within the old ethic, confined at present to those uncommon individuals who, driven by unavoidable conflicts of duty, endeavour to bring the conscious and the unconscious into responsible relationship.

1417   In so far as ethics represent a system of moral demands, it follows that any innovations within or outside this system would also possess a "deontological" character. But the psychic situation to which the new admonition "you ought" would be applicable is so complicated, delicate and difficult that one wonders who would be in a position to make such a demand. Nor would it be needed at all since the ethically minded person who gets into a situation of this sort has already been confronted with this same demand, from within, and knows only too well that there is no collective morality that could extricate him from his dilemma. If the values of the old ethic were not seated in the very marrow of his bones, he would never have got into this situation in the first place. Let us take as an example the universally valid commandment: Thou shalt not lie. What is one to do if, as frequently happens to a doctor, one finds oneself in a situation where it would be a catastrophe to tell the truth or to suppress it? If one does not want to precipitate the catastrophe directly, one cannot avoid telling a convincing lie, prompted by psychological common sense, readiness to help, Christian charity, consideration for the fate of the other people concerned—in short, by ethical motives just as strong as if not stronger than those which compel one to tell the truth. One comforts oneself with the excuse that it was done in a good cause and was therefore moral. But anyone who has insight will know that on the one hand he was too cowardly to precipitate a catastrophe, and on the other hand that he has lied shamelessly. He has done evil but at the same time good. No one stands beyond good and evil, otherwise he would be out of this world. Life is a continual balancing of opposites, like every other energic process. The abolition of opposites would be equivalent to death. Nietzsche escaped the collision of opposites by going into the madhouse. The yogi attains the state of *nirdvandva* (freedom from opposites) in the rigid lotus position of non-conscious, non-acting *samadhi*. But the ordinary man stands between the opposites and knows that he can never abolish them. There is no good without evil, and no evil without good. The one conditions the other, but it does not become the other or abolish the other. If a man is endowed with an ethical sense and is convinced of the sanctity of ethical values, he is on the surest road to a conflict of duty. And although this looks desperately like a moral catastrophe, it alone makes possible a higher differentiation of ethics and a broadening of consciousness. A conflict of duty forces us to examine our conscience and thereby to discover the shadow. This, in turn, forces us to come to terms with the unconscious. The ethical aspect of this process of integration is described with praise-worthy clarity by the author.

1418   Those who are unfamiliar with the psychology of the uncon-scious will have some difficulty in envisaging the role which the unconscious plays in the analytical process. The unconscious is a living psychic entity which, it seems, is relatively autonomous, be-having as if it were a personality with intentions of its own. At any rate it would be quite wrong to think of the unconscious as mere "material," or as a passive object to be used or exploited. Equally, its biological function is not just a mechanical one, in the sense that it is merely *complementary* to consciousness. It has far more the character of *compensation,* that is, an intelligent choice of means aiming not only at the restoration of the psychic equi-librium but at an advance towards wholeness. The reaction of the unconscious is far from being merely passive; it takes the initiative in a creative way, and sometimes its purposive activity predominates over its customary reactivity. As a partner in the process of conscious differentiation, it does not act as a mere opponent, for the revelation of its contents enriches consciousness and assists differentiation. A hostile opposition takes place only when consciousness obstinately clings to its one-sidedness and insists on its arbitrary standpoint, as always happens when there is a repression and, in consequence, a partial dissociation of consciousness.

1419   Such being the behaviour of the unconscious, the process of coming to terms with it, in the ethical sense, acquires a special character. The process does not consist in dealing with a given "ma-terial," but in negotiating with a psychic minority (or majority, as the case may be) that has equal rights. For this reason the author compares the relation to the unconscious with a parliamentary de-mocracy, whereas the old ethic unconsciously imitates, or actually prefers, the procedure of an absolute monarchy or a tyrannical one-party system. Through the new ethic, the ego-consciousness is ousted from its central position in a psyche organized on the lines of a monarchy or totalitarian state, its place being taken by *wholeness* or the *self,* which is now recognized as central. The self was of course always at the centre, and always acted as the hidden director. Gnosticism long ago projected this state of affairs into the heavens, in the form of a metaphysical drama: ego-consciousness appearing as the vain demiurge, who fancies himself the sole creator of the world, and the self as the highest, unknowable God, whose emanation the demiurge is. The union of conscious and unconscious in the individuation process, the real core of the ethical problem, was projected in the form of a drama of redemption and, in some Gnostic systems, consisted in the demiurge's discovery and recognition of the highest God.

1420   This parallel may serve to indicate the magnitude of the problem we are concerned with, and to throw into relief the special character of the confrontation with the unconscious on an ethic plane. The problem is indeed a vital one. This may explain why the question of a new ethic is of such serious and urgent concern to the author, who argues his case with a boldness and passion well matched by his penetrating insight and thoughtfulness. I welcome this book as the first notable attempt to formulate the ethical problems raised by the discovery of the unconscious and to make them a subject for discussion.

March 1949

FOREWORD TO BAYNES: "ANALYTICAL PSYCHOLOGY AND THE ENGLISH MIND"[1]

1421   I write these few introductory words to this collection of essays and lectures in affectionate memory of their author. The late H. G. Baynes was my assistant for several years, my travelling companion on our African expedition, and my faithful friend till his all too early death, which has left a painful gap in the circle of his friends and colleagues.

1422   His first published work was his most excellent translation of my book *Psychological Types*.[2] Later he became well known as the author of two important works, *Mythology of the Soul*[3] and *Germany Possessed*.[4] The first of these deals with the daily reality of the psychotherapist, and the second with contemporary events.

1423   In *Mythology of the Soul* the author uses raw material—such as the psychotherapist meets with daily in his consulting hours—as a clue to guide the reader through the maze of individual reflections, opinions, interpretations, and attempts at explanation which a psychologist gathers in the course of his experience. The empirical material stimulates such considerations, and they are also indispensable in order to integrate it in consciousness.

1424   *Germany Possessed* is concerned with the great contemporary problems which form a direct challenge to the psychologically minded doctor. This book made the author known to a very wide public.

1425   His shorter writings, which have been collected in this present volume, deal with the complex psychic conditions characteristic of medical psychology. Psychology is thus a discipline which obliges

---

[1] [London, 1950. The foreword was written in English. Helton Godwin Baynes (1882–1943), English analytical psychologist, accompanied Jung on his expedition to East Africa in 1925–26.]

[2] [London and New York, 1923. The version in C.W., vol. 6, is the Baynes trans. revised by R.F.C. Hull. Baynes also translated, in collaboration with his then wife Cary F. Baynes, Jung's *Contributions to Analytical Psychology* (London and New York, 1928) and *Two Essays on Analytical Psychology* (London and New York, 1928).]

[3] [London, 1940.]

[4] [London, 1941.]

the medical psychologist to deal with complex psychic factors, for the psychotherapeutic process can only take place on this level. Therefore analytical psychology is also rightly called "complex psychology."

1426   A simplifying theory is naturally exceedingly popular in this highly complicated field, but the author has wisely resisted any such temptation. In its place he has drawn from a really remarkable wealth of theoretical and practical points of view and has opened up possibilities and connections worthy of further discussion.

1427   H. G. Baynes left us too soon. May this volume, which he has left to us, become a milestone on the road of psychological research.

THE RULES OF LIFE[1]

1428   In reply to your kind enquiry about "rules of life," I would like to remark that I have had so much to do with people that I have alway endeavoured to live by no rules as far as possible. Non-observance of rules requires, of course, far less effort, for usually one makes a rule in order to repress the tendency in oneself not to follow it. In psychology, above all, rules are valid only when they can be reversed. Also, they are not without their dangers, since they consist of words and our civilization is largely founded on a superstitious belief in words. One of the supreme religious assumptions is actually the "Word." Words can take the place of men and things. This has its advantages but it is also a menace. One can then spare oneself the trouble of thinking for oneself or making any effort, to one's own advantage or disadvantage and that of one's fellows.

1429   I have, for instance, a tendency to make a principle of doing what I want to do or should do as soon as possible. This can be very unwise and even stupid. The same applies to practically all adages and "rules of life." Take, for example, the saying, "Quidquid id est, prudenter agas et respice finem" (Whatever it be, act prudently and consider the end). But in this way, however praiseworthy the principle is, you can let a vitally important decision of the moment slip through your fingers.

1430   No rules can cope with the paradoxes of life. Moral law, like natural law, represents only one aspect of reality. It does not prevent one from following certain "regular" habits *unconsciously*—habits which one does not notice oneself but can only discover by making careful inquiries among one's fellows. But people seldom enjoy having what they don't know about themselves pointed out to them by others, and so they prefer to lay down rules which are the exact opposite of what they are doing in reality.

---

[1] [*Weltwoche* (Zurich), Jhg. 22, no. 1100 (10 Dec. 1954). Jung was one of several prominent persons asked to comment on this subject.]

ON FLYING SAUCERS[1]

1431   Your wish to bring up the "Flying Saucers" for discussion is certainly a timely one. But though you may not have overshot the mark in questioning me, I must tell you that in spite of the interest I have taken in the subject since about 1946, I have still not been able to establish an empirical basis sufficient to permit any conclusions to be drawn. In the course of years I have accumulated a voluminous dossier on the sightings, including the statements of two eyewitnesses well-known to me personally (I myself have never seen anything!) and have read all the available books, but I have found it impossible to determine even approximately the nature of these observations. So far only one thing is certain: it is not just a rumour, *something is seen*. What is seen may in individual cases be a subjective vision (or hallucination), or, in the case of several observers seeing it simultaneously, a collective one. A psychic phenomenon of this kind would, like a rumour, have a compensatory significance, since it would be a spontaneous answer of the unconscious to the present conscious situation, i.e., to fears created by an apparently insoluble political situation which might at any moment lead to a universal catastrophe. At such times men's eyes turn to heaven for help, and marvellous signs appear from on high, of a threatening or reassuring nature. (The "round" symbols are

---

[1] [Letter to *Weltwoche* (Zurich), Jhg. 22, no. 1078 (9 July 1954), in reply to the editor's request for an interview by Georg Gerster. It was followed by further questions and answers, printed in the same issue. Extracts subsequently appeared as an article (not submitted to Jung before publication) in the *Flying Saucer Review* (London), May–June 1955, which was reprinted by the Aerial Phenomena Research Organization in the *APRO Bulletin* (Alamogordo, New Mexico), July 1958. The extracted version of the *Weltwoche* letters resulted in misunderstandings which were given much publicity, and on 13 August Jung released a statement to the United Press International (UPI) and to the National Investigations Committee on Aerial Phenomena (NICAP), of which an English version was published in the Sept. issue of the *APRO Bulletin*. A further statement, in the form of a letter to the director of NICAP, Major Donald E. Keyhoe (infra, pars. 1447f.), was published by NICAP in the *UFO Investigator*, I:5 (Aug.–Sept. 1958). All these documents were republished in *CSI of New York,* Publication No. 27 (July 1959).]

particularly suggestive, appearing nowadays in many spontaneous fantasies directly associated with the threatening world situation.)

1432   The possibility of a purely psychological explanation is illusory, for a large number of observations point to a natural phenomenon, or even a physical one—for instance, those explicable by reflections from "temperature inversions" in the atmosphere. Despite its contradictory statements, the American Air Force, as well as the Canadian, consider the sightings to be "real," and have set up special bureaux to collect the reports. The "disks," however, that is, the objects themselves, do not behave in accordance with physical laws but as though they were weightless, and they show signs of *intelligent guidance* such as would suggest quasi-human pilots. Yet the accelerations are so tremendous that no human being could survive them.

1433   The view that the disks are real is so widespread (in America) that reports of landings were not long in coming. Recently I read accounts of this kind from two different sources. In both of them the mystical element in the vision or fantasy was very much in evidence: they described half-human, idealized human beings like angels who delivered the appropriate edifying messages.[2] Unfortunately, there is a total lack of any useful information. And in both cases the photographs failed to come out. Reports of landings, therefore, must for the time being be taken with considerable caution.

1434   What astonishes me most of all is that the American Air Force, despite all the information it must possess, and despite its alleged fear of creating a panic similar to the one which broke out in New Jersey on the occasion of Welles's radio play,[3] is systematically working towards that very thing by refusing to release an authentic and reliable account of the facts.[4] All we have to go on is the occasional information squeezed out by journalists. It is therefore impossible for the uninitiated to form an adequate picture of what is happening. Although for eight years I have been collecting everything that came within my reach, I must admit I am no further forward today than I was at the beginning. I still do not know what we

[2] George Adamski's book (with Desmond Leslie), *Flying Saucers Have Landed,* appeared in 1953 (London). In it he tells the story of how he met a saucer-man in the California desert.

[3] [*The War of the Worlds,* adapted by Orson Welles (1938) from H. G. Wells's novel. It is about Martians invading the United States.]

[4] The report by Major Donald E. Keyhoe concerning his struggle with the Pentagon for recognition of the interplanetary origin of the Ufos was published in 1953 under the title *Flying Saucers from Outer Space.*

are up against with these "flying saucers." The reports are so weird that, granted the reality of these phenomena, one feels tempted to compare them with parapsychological happenings.

1435   Because we lack any sure foundation, all speculation is worthless. We must wait and see what the future brings. So-called "scientific" explanations, such as Menzel's reflection theory, are possible only if all the reports that fail to fit the theory are conveniently overlooked.

1436   That is all I have to say on the subject of Flying Saucers. An interview would therefore not be worthwhile.

[Supplementary Questions Addressed to Jung by Letter]

Supposing it should turn out that we are being spied upon by non-human, intelligent beings, do you think that this could be assimilated into the existing world-picture without harmful results? Or do you think it would necessarily lead to a kind of Copernican revolution, and that consequently the panic you fear would be a legitimate counteraction?

Further, should the responsible authorities take steps to prevent a panic, and what psychohygienic measures seem suitable to you for this purpose?

1437   These questions are entirely legitimate today, since there are responsible persons—better informed than I—who are of the opinion that the phenomena we are discussing are of extraterrestrial origin. As I have said, I cannot, or cannot yet, share this view, because I have not been able to obtain the necessary confirmation. If these "objects" are, as claimed, of extraterrestrial or possibly planetary origin (Mars, Venus), we still have to consider the reports of Saucers rising out of the sea or the earth. We must also take account of numerous reports of phenomena resembling ball lightning, or strange, stationary will-o'-the-wisps (not to be confused with St. Elmo's fire). In rare cases ball lightning can attain considerable dimensions, appearing as a dazzling ball of light, half as big as the moon, moving slowly from cloud to cloud, or ripping a path about five yards wide and 200 yards long through a forest, smashing all the trees in its way. It is either soundless, like the Saucers, or it can vanish with a clap of thunder. It is possible that ball lightning in the form of isolated charges of electricity (so-called "bead-lightning") is the origin of those Saucers arranged in a row which have been photographed on several occasions. Other electrical phenomena have frequently been reported in connection with the Saucers.

1438   If, despite this still unclarified possibility, the extraterrestrial origin of the Saucers should be confirmed, this would prove the existence of intelligent interplanetary communication. What such a fact might mean for humanity cannot be imagined. But there is no doubt we would find ourselves in the same critical situation as primitive societies confronted with the superior culture of the white man. The reins of power would be wrenched from our hands, and, as an old witch doctor once told me with tears in his eyes, we would have "no dreams any more"—the lofty flights of our spirit would have been checked and crippled forever.

1439   Naturally, the first thing to be consigned to the rubbish heap would be our science and technology. What the moral effects of such a catastrophe would be can be seen from the pitiful decay of primitive cultures taking place before our eyes. That the construction of such machines would be evidence of a scientific technology immensely superior to ours admits of no two opinions. Just as the Pax Britannica put an end to tribal warfare in Africa, so our world could roll up its Iron Curtain and use it as so much scrap along with all the billions of tons of armaments, warships, and munitions. That wouldn't be such a bad thing, but we would have been "discovered" and colonized—reason enough for universal panic!

1440   If we wish to avoid such a catastrophe, the officials in possession of authoritative information should not hesitate to enlighten the public as speedily and thoroughly as possible, and above all stop this stupid game of mystification and suggestive allusion. Instead, they have allowed a lot of fantastic and mendacious publicity to run riot—the best possible preparation for panic and psychic epidemics.

[Further Supplementary Questions]

The idea of a possible parallel with parapsychological processes is extremely interesting. Presumably you are thinking of apparitions?

You write that in times like these men's eyes turn to heaven for help. Are you thinking of some period of upheaval in the past, which produced comparable phenomena? Is there evidence of other collective visions or hallucinations with a similar content?

How do you explain the fact that with few exceptions Saucers have so far been observed only over the North American continent?

Does this, in your view, suggest that they are more likely to be psychic—specifically American "apparitions," as it were—or, on the contrary, that they are of an objective nature?

1441   It is hardly possible to answer your question about the analogy of the Saucers with parapsychological phenomena, since a basis for comparison is totally lacking. If we wished to take such a possibility seriously, it would first have to be shown that the "apparitions" are causally connected with psychic states; in other words, that under the influence of certain emotional conditions a major population group experiences the same psychic dissociation and the same exteriorization of psychic energy as does a single medium. All we know at present is that collective visions do exist. But whether collective *physical* phenomena, such as levitations, apparitions of light, materializations, etc., can also be produced is a moot question. At present any reference to the parapsychological aspect only demonstrates the boundless perplexity in which we find ourselves today.

1442   I cannot refrain from remarking, however, that the whole collective psychological problem that has been opened up by the Saucer epidemic stands in compensatory antithesis to our scientific picture of the world. In the United States this picture has if possible an even greater dominance than with us. It consists, as you know, very largely of statistical or "average" truths. These exclude all rare borderline cases, which scientists fight shy of anyway because they cannot understand them. The consequence is a view of the world composed entirely of normal cases. Like the "normal" man, they are essentially *fictions,* and particularly in psychology fictions can lead to disastrous errors. Since it can be said with a little exaggeration that reality consists mainly of exceptions to the rule, which the intellect then reduces to the norm, instead of a brightly coloured picture of the real world we have a bleak, shallow rationalism that offers stones instead of bread to the emotional and spiritual hungers of the world. The logical result is an insatiable hunger for anything extraordinary. If we add to this the great defeat of human reason, daily demonstrated in the newspapers and rendered even more menacing by the incalculable dangers of the hydrogen bomb, the picture that unfolds before us is one of universal spiritual distress, comparable to the situation at the beginning of our era or to chaos that followed A.D. 1000, or the upheavals at the turn of the fifteenth century. It is therefore not surprising if, as the old chroniclers report, all sorts of signs and wonders appear in the sky, or if miraculous intervention, where human efforts have failed, is expected from heaven. Our Saucer sightings can be found—*mutatis mutandis*—in many reports that go back to antiquity, though not, it would seem, with the same overwhelming frequency. But then, the possibility of destruction on a global scale, which has been given into the hands of our so-called politicians, did not exist in those days.

1443   McCarthyism and the influence it has exerted are evidence of the deep and anxious apprehensions of the American public. Therefore most of the signs in the skies will be seen in North America.

1444   At the beginning of this century I was firmly convinced that nothing heavier than air could fly and that the atom was really "a-tomic" (indivisible). Since then I have become very cautious and will only repeat what I said at the beginning of our correspondence: Despite a fairly thorough knowledge of the available literature (six books and countless reports and articles, including two eyewitness reports), I still do not know what kind of reality the Flying Saucers may have. So I am not in a position to draw conclusions and to form any reliable judgment. I just don't know what one should make of this phenomenon.

Statement to the United Press International[5]

1445   As a result of an article published in the *APRO Bulletin,* the report has been spread by the press that in my opinion the Ufos are physically real. This report is altogether false. In a recently published book (*Ein Moderner Mythus,* Zurich, 1958),[6] I expressly state that I cannot commit myself on the question to the physical reality or unreality of the Ufos since I do not possess sufficient evidence either for or against. I therefore concern myself solely with the psychological aspect of the phenomenon, about which a great deal of material is available. I have formulated the position I take on the question of the reality of Ufos in the following sentence: "Something is seen, but it isn't known what." This formulation leaves the question of "seeing" open. Something material could be seen, or something psychic could be seen. Both are realities, but of different kinds.

[5] [See above, n. 1. This text is translated from the *Badener Tageblatt,* 29 Aug. 1958, and differs in some respects from the translation in the *APRO Bulletin.*]
[6] [Trans. by R.F.C. Hull as *Flying Saucers: A Modern Myth of Things Seen in the Skies* (New York and London, 1959); in C.W., vol. 10.]

1446   My relations with APRO are confined to the following: while I was collecting material for the above-mentioned book, the *APRO Bulletin* approached me in a friendly manner. When this organization recently asked me if they might consider me to be an honorary member, I consented. I have sent my book to APRO to inform them of my position in regard to the Ufo question. APRO advocates the physical reality of the Ufo with much zeal and idealism. I therefore regard its misleading article as a regrettable accident.

Letter to Keyhoe[7]

16 August 1958

Major Donald E. Keyhoe
National Investigation Committee on Aerial Phenomena
1536 Connecticut Avenue
Washington 6, D. C.

Dear Major Keyhoe,

1447   Thank you very much for your kind letter! I have read all you have written concerning Ufos and I am a subscriber to the *NICAP Bulletin*. I am grateful for all the courageous things you have done in elucidating the thorny problem of Ufo-reality.

1448   The article in *APRO Bulletin* July 1958, which caused all that stir in the press, is unfortunately inaccurate. As you know I am an alienist and medical psychologist. I have never seen a Ufo and I have no first-hand information either about them or about the dubious attitude of the AAF [American Air Force]. On account of this regrettable lack I am unable to form a definite opinion concerning the physical nature of the Ufo-phenomenon. As I am a scientist, I only say what I can prove and reserve my judgment in any case where I doubt my competence. Thus I said: "Things are seen, but one does not know what." I neither affirm, nor deny. But it is certain beyond all possible doubt that plenty of statements about Ufos are made and they are of all sorts. I am chiefly concerned with this aspect of the phenomenon. It yields a rich harvest of insight into its universal significance. My special preoccupation precludes neither the physical reality of the Ufos nor their extraterrestrial origin, nor the purposefulness of their behaviour, etc. But I do not possess sufficient evidence which would enable me to draw

[7] [Original in English. See above, n. 1.]

definite conclusions. The evidence available to me however is convincing enough to arouse a continuous and fervent interest. I follow with my greatest sympathy your exploits and your endeavours to establish the truth about the Ufos.

1449   In spite of the fact that I hold my judgment concerning the nature of the Ufos—temporarily let us hope—in abeyance, I thought it worth while to throw a light upon the rich fantasy material which has accumulated round the peculiar observations in the skies. Any new experience has two aspects: (1) the pure fact and (2) the way one conceives of it. It is the latter I am concerned with. If it is true that the AAF or the Government withholds telltale facts, then one can only say that this is the most unpsychological and stupid policy one could invent. Nothing helps rumours and panics more than ignorance. It is self-evident that the public ought to be told the truth, because ultimately it will nevertheless come to the light of day. There can be hardly any greater shock than the H-bomb and yet everyone knows of it without fainting.

1450   As to your question about the possible hostility of the Ufos, I must emphasize that I have no other knowledge about them than that which everybody can get out of printed reports. That is the reason why I am still far from certain about the Ufos' physical reality.

1451   Thank you for your kind offer to send me clippings. I have got enough of them. It is a curious fact that whenever I make a statement it is at once twisted and falsified. The press seems to enjoy lies more than the truth.

I remain, dear Major,

Yours, C. G. JUNG

HUMAN NATURE DOES NOT YIELD EASILY
TO IDEALISTIC ADVICE[1]

1452   There is little to criticize in Mr. Roberts' article since its author is obviously a man of good will and optimistic enthusiasm. Moreover, he points in the right direction, and he gives proper value to man's mental and moral attitude. He hopes and believes, it seems to me, that saying the right and good thing will be enough to produce the desired effect. Unfortunately, human nature is a bit more complicated and does not yield to a well-meaning hint or to idealistic advice.

1453   It always has been and still is the great question how to get the ordinary human to the point where he can make up his mind to draw the right conclusion and to do the right thing, or how to make him listen at all. His moral and mental inertia and his notorious prejudices are the most serious obstacle to any moral or spiritual renaissance. If he had been inclined to resist the overwhelming impact of his emotional entanglements, passions, and desires, and to put a stop to the haste and rush of his daily activities, and to try at least to get out of his lamentable yet cherished unconsciousness about himself, the world and its sad history of intrigue, violence, and cruelty would have reached a state of peace and humanity long before Christ—in the time of Buddha or Socrates. But to get him there, that's just the trouble.

1454   It is perhaps a good idea to liberate man from all inhibitions and prejudices that hamper, torment, and disfigure him. But the question is less to liberate from something, than rather, as Nietzsche asked, to which end? In certain cases it looks as if in getting rid of one's inhibitions and burdens, one had "thrown away one's best." Liberation can be a good or a very bad solution. It largely depends

---

[1] [Written in English as an invited comment on an article, "Analysis and Faith," by William H. Roberts, which together with comments by Jung and others—including Gregory Zilboorg, Erich Fromm, and Karl Menninger—was published in *The New Republic* (Washington), 132:20 (16 May 1955). The article was subtitled: "How close are religion and psychiatry in their approaches to sin and salvation?" Roberts was professor of philosophy and religion at Philander Smith College, a Black college in Little Rock, Arkansas.]

upon the choice of one's further goal whether the liberation has been a boon or a fatal mistake.

1455   I don't want to go further into the complexities of this problem, and moreover it would be unfair to criticize the author for something he obviously is not aware of, viz., the fact that this formulation of the problem dates from about forty years ago. Since that time, a voluminous literature thoroughly dealing with the point in question has come into existence. I don't know which circumstances have prevented the author from informing himself about the more modern developments in the discussion between religion and psychology. In view of Freud's notorious inability to understand religion, the reader would have welcomed, if not expected, a summary at least of the main work done along this line during the past four decades. Goodwill and enthusiasm are not to be underrated, but ignorance is regrettable.

ON THE HUNGARIAN UPRISING[1]

I

1456   1. The bloody suppression of the Hungarian people by the Russian army is a vile and abominable crime, to be condemned forthwith.

2. The Egyptian dictator has by unlawful measures provoked Great Britain and France to a warlike act. This is to be deplored as a relapse into obsolete and barbarous methods of politics.

II

1457   The crushing of Hungary is one more link in the chain of iniquitous events which make the middle of the twentieth century one of the blackest chapters in history, rich in infamies as it is. Western Europe had to endure the spectacle of a civilized European country being throttled and, conscious of its own miserable impotence, be content to play the Good Samaritan. Though the great storm of indignation unleashed by outraged public feeling was unable to blow away the Russian tanks, it at least brought with it the relief everyone feels when guilt can be laid beyond all doubt at somebody else's door. In the worldwide moral outcry we scarcely heard the voice of our own conscience, reminding the West of those wicked deeds of Machiavellianism, short-sightedness, and stupidity without which the events in Hungary would not have been possible. The focus of the deadly disease lies in Europe.

---

[1] [Contributions to symposia: (I) "Das geistige Europa und die ungarische Revolution," *Die Kultur* (Munich), Jhg. 5, no. 73 (1 Dec. 1956); (II) *Aufstand der Freiheit: Dokumente zur Erhebung des ungarischen Volkes* (Zurich, 1957).]

ON PSYCHODIAGNOSTICS[1]

Can one, with today's psychodiagnostic methods, determine the suitability of a candidate for a job, in a matter of hours or days, more efficiently than the employer could with the help of his general knowledge of human nature?

1458   The employer may have a very good knowledge of human nature, able to size up the total situation intuitively in a few seconds. Naturally you can't acquire a knack like this from any method. There are, however, employers who are anything but good judges of men. In this case a careful and conscientious psychodiagnosis is the only right thing. Anyway, it is better than nothing, and certainly better than the employer's illusions and projections.

Are we right to oppose the use of psychodiagnostics in the selection of candidates, or is it simply another futile attempt to turn back the wheel of history?

1459   It would be plain stupid to oppose the use of psychodiagnostics, for these tests are so widely used today that nobody can fight against them. By refusing them one puts oneself in a false position from the start, as in certain cases of refusal to testify in court. But if you are faced with a good judge of men, he will extract your painful secrets from your trouser pocket with the greatest skill without your knowing it, and do it much better than was ever done by a psychodiagnostic method.

We would like to ask you for a short prognosis concerning the further development of these methods and their influence on society.

1460   I am no prophet, and I cannot predict the future of our society. I can only tell you that I hope for a further improvement in psychodiagnostic methods and in the understanding of man in general, as contrasted with the other possibility that any man may be pushed into any kind of job anywhere. Anything that promotes the understanding of one's fellow men is welcome to me.

[1] [Letter of 27 June 1958, answering questions from the editors of the *Zürcher Student* (see above, par. 1403, n. 1) and published in the July 1958 issue, Jhg. 36.]

IF CHRIST WALKED THE EARTH TODAY[1]

1461   It is absolutely certain that if a Christ should reappear in the world he would be interviewed and photographed by the press and would not live longer than one month. He would die being fed up with himself, as he would see himself banalized beyond all endurance. He would be killed by his own success, morally and physically.

[1] [Contribution, written in English, to a symposium published in *Cosmopolitan* (New York), CXLV:6 (Dec. 1958), and consisting of "ten highly individual opinions from noted thinkers who have devoted their lives to problems of the spirit." These also included Norman Vincent Peale, Aldous Huxley, Pitirim A. Sorokin, and Billy Graham.]

FOREWORD TO "HUGH CRICHTON-MILLER, 1877–1959"[1]

1462 It is more than thirty years ago—on the occasion of a short stay in England—that I became acquainted with Dr. Hugh Crichton-Miller. Being a stranger and, on account of my unorthodox views, a psychiatric outsider, I was deeply impressed by the friendly, open, and unprejudiced manner of his welcome. Not only did he introduce me to the staff of his clinic, he also invited me to give them a short address—much to my embarrassment, since I never felt particularly certain of myself when called upon to talk to an entirely unknown audience. But I soon felt the presence of an atmosphere of mutual trust and confidence between chief and staff, so that I could talk to them in a more or less natural way—at least I hope so. Talking to Crichton-Miller was easy. I felt we were speaking the same language, though our views were not always the same. But they were reasonably different, so that a satisfactory discussion was possible. Whenever I had a chance in the course of many years, I very much enjoyed discussing controversial points with him. He was for I don't know how many years the only man of my age with whom I could talk as man to man, without constantly fearing that my partner would suddenly throw a fit or become otherwise impolite. We took each other at our face value and in the course of years we grew slowly into the conviction that we had a good relationship. Such a silent conviction can be, in spite of everything, an illusion as long as it has not come to an actual showdown. The proof of this came in the last years before the second World War.

1463 We then had an international Society for Psychotherapy on the continent consisting of a Dutch, Danish, Swiss, and a very large German group. The president of the Society had been Professor Kretschmer up to 1933, when he resigned in the fatal year of Hitler's usurpation of power. I had been up to then in the inactive

[1] [The book (Dorchester, 1961) had the subtitle "A Personal Memoir by His Friends and Family." The foreword, written in English, is published here with minor stylistic changes.]

role of an honorary vice-president. The German group, afraid of getting amalgamated with, i.e., overshadowed by, the far more influential "Society for Psychiatry" with its well-known anti-psychological prejudice, asked me to take over the function of president, just because I was non-German and would therefore emphasize the international character of the organization. They hoped in that way to escape complete annihilation, even if they had to survive in a society of herb addicts and believers in "natural healing." I knew it would be a very difficult task if I were to accept this proposition. But having been vice-president for a number of years, I did not consider it particularly honourable conduct to get cold feet, and so I stepped in.

1464.   The first task confronting me was to increase the non-German membership in order to form an adequate counterweight. We added a Swedish group, and I opened negotiations with French representatives, but I looked most toward England and America. The first person I approached was Crichton-Miller, and I did not find him wanting. He understood the situation and my motives. The Germans became more and more difficult and tried to overwhelm us with a large Italian and even a Japanese membership. Since nothing was known of modern medical psychology in either of those contries, the long lists of new members were composed by order and consisted of people who were absolutely innocent of the slightest professional knowledge of modern psychotherapy. Shortly before the outbreak of the war, it came to a decisive showdown with the Germans in Zurich. Being the British representative, Crichton-Miller lent me personally his invaluable help to ward off the German intrigue. I am forever grateful to him for his sturdy co-operation and his truly loyal friendship. That was the man I shall never forget.

1465   During the war we naturally saw nothing of each other, and it was only afterwards that I received the shocking news of his fatal disease. I wanted very much to see him again but was overburdened with urgent work and hampered by the consequences of an injury to my heart. I found no occasion to go to England. Fortunately enough, in 1949 he could manage to come out to Switzerland, to the Bernese Oberland, where I went to meet him and his wife. I found him in an advanced stage of his illness. As he had expressed the urgent wish to talk to me, I was eager to hear from him what it was. After lunch we withdrew. He took out a sheet of paper with a closely written text. As our talks hitherto had never been intimate or personal, I was surprised when he plunged straight *in medias res* and asked me to answer a number of questions on religion. It was a complete survey of the *religio medici,* of all the religious conclusions an old doctor might draw from his innumerable experiences of suffering and death and from the inexorable reality of life's reverses. I knew we were talking *in conspectu mortis* of ultimate things, at the end of days. Then we took leave of each other, shook hands amiably and politely, as if after a delightful lunch with a distant yet friendly acquaintance. *Vale amice!*

January 1960

XII

PSYCHOLOGY AND RELIGION

(related to Volume 11 of the Collected Works)

WHY I AM NOT A CATHOLIC[1]

1466   *Firstly:* Because I am a practical Christian to whom love and justice to his brother mean more than dogmatic speculations about whose ultimate truth or untruth no human being can ever have certain knowledge. The relation to my brother and the unity of the true "catholic" Christendom is to me infinitely more important than "justification by *fide sola.*" As a Christian I have to share the burden of my brother's wrongness, and that is most heavy when I do not know whether in the end he is not more right than I. I hold it to be immoral, in any case entirely unchristian, to put my brother in the wrong (i.e., to call him fool, ass, spiteful, obdurate, etc.) simply because I suppose myself to be in possession of the absolute truth. Every totalitarian claim gradually isolates itself because it excludes so many people as "defectors, lost, fallen, apostate, heretic," and so forth. The totalitarian maneuvers himself into a corner, no matter how large his original following. I hold all confessionalism to be completely unchristian.

1467   *Secondly:* Because I am a doctor. If I possessed the absolute truth I could do nothing further than to press into my patient's hand a book of devotion or confessional guidance, just what is no longer of any help to him. When, on the other hand, I discover in his untruth a truth, in his confusion an order, in his lostness something that has been found, then I have helped him. This requires an incomparably greater self-abnegation and self-surrender for my brother's sake than if I assessed, correctly from the standpoint of one confession, the motivations of another.

1468   You underestimate the immense number of those of goodwill, but to whom confessionalism blocks the doors. A Christian has to concern himself, especially if he is a physician of souls, with the spirituality of the reputedly unspiritual (spirit = confessionalism!) and he can do this only if he speaks their language and certainly not if, in the deterrent way of confessionalism, he sounds the kerygmatic

[1] [(Translated by H. N.) Written as part of a letter to H. Irminger of Zurich, 22 Sept. 1944, but not sent; instead, Jung retained it in his literary papers. For the letter to Irminger, see *Jung: Letters,* ed. G. Adler, vol. 1.]

trumpet, hoarse with age. Whoever talks in today's world of an absolute and single truth is speaking in an obsolete dialect and not in any way in the language of mankind. Christianity possesses a εὐαγγέλιον, good tidings from God, but no textbook of a dogma with claim to totality. Therefore it is hard to understand why God should never have sent more than one message. Christian modesty in any case strictly forbids assuming that God did not send εὐαγγέλια in other languages, not just in Greek, to other nations. If we think otherwise our thinking is in the deepest sense unchristian. The Christian—my idea of Christian—knows no curse formulas; indeed he does not even sanction the curse put on the innocent fig-tree by the rabbi Jesus, nor does he lend his ear to the missionary Paul of Tarsus when he forbids cursing to the Christian and then he himself curses the next moment.

1469   *Thirdly:* Because I am a man of science.

1470   The Catholic doctrine, as you present it to me so splendidly, is familiar to me to that extent. I am convinced of its "truth" in so far as it formulates determinable psychological facts, and thus far I accept this truth without further ado. But where I lack such empirical psychological foundations it does not help me in the least to believe in anything beyond them, for that would not compensate for my missing knowledge; nor could I ever surrender to the self-delusion of knowing something where I merely believe. I am now nearly seventy years old, but the charisma of belief has never arisen in me. Perhaps I am too overweening, too conceited; perhaps you are right in thinking that the cosmos circles around the God Jung. But in any case I have never succeeded in thinking that what I believe, feel, think, and understand is the only and final truth and that I enjoy the unspeakable privilege of God-likeness by being the possessor of the sole truth. You see that, although I can estimate the charisma of faith and its blessedness, the acceptance of "faith" is impossible for me because it says nothing to me.

1471   You will naturally remonstrate that, after all, I talk about "God." I do this with the same right as humanity has from the beginning equated the numinous effects of certain psychological facts with an unknown primal cause called God. This cause is beyond my understanding, and therefore I can say nothing further about it except that I am convinced of the existence of such a cause, and indeed with the same logic by which one may conclude from the disturbance of a planet's course the existence of a yet unknown heavenly body. To be sure, I do not believe in the absolute validity of the law of causality, which is why I guard against "positing" God as cause, for by this I would have given him a precise definition.

1472   Such restraint is surely an offense to confessors of the Faith. But according to the fundamental Christian commandment I must not only bear with and understand my schismatic Protestant brother, but also my brothers in Arabia and India. They, too, have received strange but no less notable tidings which it is my obligation to understand. As a European, I am burdened most heavily by my unexpectedly dark brother, who confronts me with his antichristian Neo-Paganism. This extends far beyond the borders of Germany as the most pernicious schism that has ever beset Christianity. And though I deny it a thousand times, *it is also in me*. One cannot come to terms with this conflict by imputing wrong to someone else and the undoubted right to onself. This conflict I can solve first of all only within myself and not in another.

THE DEFINITION OF DEMONISM[1]

1473   Demonism (synonymous with daemonomania = possession) denotes a peculiar state of mind characterized by the fact that certain psychic contents, the so-called complexes, take over the control of the total personality in place of the ego, at least temporarily, to such a degree that the free will of the ego is suspended. In certain of these states ego-consciousness is present, in others it is eclipsed. Demonism is a primordial psychic phenomenon and frequently occurs under primitive conditions. (Good descriptions in the New Testament, Luke 4:34, Mark 1:23, 5:2, etc.) The phenomenon of demonism is not always spontaneous, but can also be deliberately induced as a "trance," for instance in shamanism, spiritualism, etc. (Cf. J. Hastings, *Encyclopaedia of Religion and Ethics;* Schürer. "Zur Vorstellung von der Besessenheit im Neuen Testament," *Jahrbuch für protestantische Theologie,* 1892.)

1474   Medically, demonism belongs partly to the sphere of the psychogenic neuroses, partly to that of schizophrenia. Demonism can also be epidemic. One of the most celebrated epidemics of the Middle Ages was the possession of the Ursulines of London, 1632. The epidemic form includes the induced collective psychoses of a religious or political nature, such as those of the twentieth century. (Cf. G. le Bon, *The Crowd, a Study of the Popular Mind,* 1896; Otto Stoll, *Suggestion und Hypnotismus in der Völkerpsychologie,* 2nd edn., 1904.)

[1] [Written July 1945, at the request of Encyclios-Verlag, Zurich, publishers of the *Schweizer Lexikon*. The first sentence and the references at the end of the article were published (without attribution) as the definition of "Dämonie" in the *Lexikon* (1949), vol. I.]

FOREWORD TO JUNG: "SYMBOLIK DES GEISTES"
(1948)

1475   The present volume, the sixth of the *Psychologische Abhandlungen,* contains five essays which are concerned with the symbolism of the spirit: a study of Satan in the Old Testament by Dr. Riwkah Schärf,[1] and four essays from my pen. The first essay in the book, "The Phenomenology of the Spirit in Fairytales,"[2] gives an account of the "spirit archetype," or rather, of a dream and fairytale motif whose behaviour is such that one has to conceive of it as "spirit." Examples are also given of the dramatic entanglements to which the appearance of this motif leads. The second essay describes how, in the medieval natural philosophy of the alchemists, the primitive "nature-spirit" developed into the "Spirit Mercurius."[3] As the original texts show, a spirit-figure came into being that was directly opposed to the Christian view of the spirit. The third contribution, by Dr. Schärf, describes the historical development of the ungodly spirit, Satan, as depicted in the texts of the Old Testament. The fourth essay, "A Psychological Approach to the Dogma of the Trinity,"[4] gives a brief sketch of the historical development of the trinitarian concept before and after Christ, followed by a synopsis of psychological viewpoints that need to be taken into account for a rational comprehension of the idea of the Trinity. It goes without saying that in any such discussion, metaphysical views cannot be considered, because, within the confines of a scientific psychology and its tasks, an idea characterized as "metaphysical" can claim the significance only of a psychic phenomenon. Equally the psychologist does not presume to say anything "metaphysical," i.e., transcending his proper province, about his subject-matter— that lies outside his competence. In so far—and only so far—as the Trinity is not merely an object of belief but, over and above that, a human concept falling within the purview of psychology,

---

[1] ["Die Gestalt Satans im Alten Testament"; trans., *Satan in the Old Testament* (Evanston, 1967).]

[2] [In *The Archetypes and the Collective Unconscious,* C.W., vol. 9, i.]

[3] [In *Alchemical Studies,* C.W., vol. 13.]

[4] [In *Psychology and Religion: West and East,* C.W., vol. 11.]

can it be subjected to scientific observation. This does not affect the object of belief in any way. The reader will do well to keep this limitation of the theme constantly in mind.

1476   The final contribution[5] is a description and analysis of a Chinese, but originally Indian, text which describes a way of meditation for the attainment of Buddhahood. I have added this essay for the purpose of rounding out the picture for my reader, showing him an Eastern aspect of it.

1477   It now remains for me to correct an error. In my book *The Psychology of the Transference*[6] I promised to publish my new work, *Mysterium Coniunctionis*,[7] as volume 6 of the "Psychologische Abhandlungen." Owing to illness and other causes I had to alter plans and am therefore publishing *Symbolik des Geistes* in its stead. The above-mentioned work will not go to press until later.

June 1947

5 ["The Psychology of Eastern Mediation," ibid.]
6 [*Die Psychologie der Übertragung*, p. xi. Cf. foreword to "The Psychology of the Transference" (C.W., vol. 16).]
7 [C.W., vol. 14.]

FOREWORD TO QUISPEL: "TRAGIC CHRISTIANITY"[1]

1478   The author of this essay has asked me to start off his book with a few introductory words. Although I am not a philologist, I gladly accede to this request because Dr. Quispel has devoted particular attention to a field of work which is familiar also to me from the psychological standpoint. Gnosticism is still an obscure affair and in need of explanation, despite the fact that sundry personages have already approached it from the most diverse angles and tried their hands at explanations with doubtful success. One even has the impression that the ban on heresy still hangs over this wide domain, or at least the disparagement which specialists are accustomed to feel for annoying incomprehensibilities. We have an equivalent of this situation in psychiatry, which has ostentatiously neglected the psychology of the psychoses and shows pronounced resistances to all attempts in this direction. This fact, though astonishing in itself, is, however, comprehensible when one considers the difficulties to be overcome once one tries to fathom the psychology of delusional ideas. We can understand mental illness only if we have some understanding of the mind in general. Delusional ideas cannot be explained in terms of themselves, but only in terms of our knowledge of the normal mind. Here the only phenomenological method that promises success, as opposed to philosophical and religious prejudice, has made next to no headway, indeed it has still not even been understood. The fundamental reason for this is that the doctor, to whom alone psychopathological experiences are accessible, seldom or never has the necessary epistemological premises at his command. Instead of which, if he reflects at all and does not merely observe and register, he has usually succumbed to a philosophical or religious conviction and fills out the gaps in his knowledge with professions of faith.

---

[1] [According to information from Gilles Quispel (professor of ancient church history, Utrecht University, Netherlands), in 1949 he planned to publish in Bollingen Series a volume of his lectures given at the Eranos conferences. The projected title was *Tragic Christianity,* and Jung consented to write this foreword. The book was never published.]

1479   What is true of psychopathology can—*mutatis mutandis*—be applied directly to the treatment which Gnosticism has undergone. Its peculiar mental products demand the same psychological understanding as do psychotic delusional formations. But the philologist or theologian who concerns himself with Gnosticism generally possesses not a shred of psychiatric knowledge, which must always be called upon in explaining extraordinary mental phenomena. The explanation of Gnostic ideas "in terms of themselves," i.e., in terms of their historical foundations, is futile, for in that way they are reduced only to their less developed forestages but not understood in their actual significance.

1480   We find a similar state of affairs in the psychopathology of the neuroses, where, for instance, Freud's psychoanalysis reduces the neurotic symptomatology only to its infantile forestages and completely overlooks its functional, that is, its *symbolic* value. So long as we know only the causality or the historical development of a normal biological or psychic phenomenon, but not its functional development, i.e., its purposive significance, it is not really understood. The same is true of Gnostic ideas: they are not mere symptoms of a certain historical development, but creative new configurations which were of the utmost significance for the further development of Western consciousness. One has only to think of the Jewish-Gnostic presuppositions in Paul's writings and of the immense influence of the "gnostic" gospel of John. Apart also from these important witnesses, and in spite of being persecuted, branded as heresy, and pronounced dead within the realm of the Church, Gnosticism did not die out at once by any means. Its philosophical and psychological aspects went on developing in alchemy up to the time of Goethe, and the Jewish syncretism of the age of Philo[2] found its continuation within orthodox Judaism in the Kabbala. Both these trends, if not exactly forestages of the modern psychology of the unconscious, are at all events well-nigh inexhaustible sources of knowledge for the psychologist. This is no accident inasmuch as parallel phenomena to the empirically established contents of the collective unconscious underlie the earliest Gnostic systems. The archetypal motifs of the unconscious are the psychic source of Gnostic ideas, of delusional ideas (especially of the paranoid

---

[2] [Philo Judaeus (fl. A.D. 39), Graeco-Judaic philosopher of Alexandria. His works include commentaries on the Old Testament, which he interpreted allegorically, finding in it the source of the main doctrines of Plato, Aristotle, and other Greek philosophers.]

schizophrenic forms), of symbol-formation in dreams, and of active imagination in the course of an analytical treatment of neurosis.

1481   In the light of these reflections, I regret Dr. Quispel's quotations from the Gnostics, that the "Autopator contained in himself all things, in [a state of] unconsciousness (ἐν ἀγνωσίᾳ)"[3] and that "The Father was devoid of consciousness (ἀνεννόητος),"[4] as a fundamental discovery for the psychology of Gnosticism. It means nothing less than that the Gnostics in question derived the knowable ὑπερκόσμα from the unconscious, i.e., that these represented unconscious contents. This discovery results not only in the possibility but also in the necessity of supplementing the historical method of explanation by one that is based on a scientific psychology.

1482   Psychology is indebted to the author for his endeavours to facilitate the understanding of Gnosticism, not merely because we psychologists have made it our task to explain Gnosticism, but because we see in it a *tertium comparationis* which affords us the most valuable help in the practical understanding of modern individual symbol-formation.

May 1949

[3] Epiphanius, *Panarium,* XXXI, cap V. [The quotation is here abbreviated; for Jung's fuller version of the Greek text see *Aion* (C.W., vol. 9, ii), par. 298 and n. 16.]

[4] Hippolytus, *Elenchos,* VI, 42, 4. [This quotation, also abbreviated here, comes immediately after the one from Epiphanius in *Aion,* par. 298, where Jung cites Quispel's French trans. of the Greek text.]

FOREWORD TO ABEGG:
"OSTASIEN DENKT ANDERS"[1]

1483 The author of this book, the entire text of which unfortunately I have not seen, has talked to me about her project and about her ideas with regard to the difference between Eastern and Western psychology. Thus I was able to note many points of agreement between us, and also a competence on her part to make judgments which is possible only to one who is a European and at the same time possesses the invaluable advantage of having spent more than half a lifetime in the Far East, in close contact with the mind of Asia. Without such first-hand experience it would be a hopeless task to approach the problem of Eastern psychology. One must be deeply and directly moved by the strangeness, one might almost say by the incomprehensibility, of the Eastern psyche. Decisive experiences of this kind cannot be transmitted through books; they come only from living in immediate, daily relationship with the people. Having had unusual advantages in this respect, the author is in a position to discuss what is perhaps the basic, and is in any case an extremely important, question of the difference between Eastern and Western psychology. I have often found myself in situations where I had to take account of this difference, as in the study of Chinese and East Indian literary texts and in the psychological treatment of Asiatics. Among my patients, I am sorry to say, I have never had a Chinese or a Japanese, nor have I had the privilege of visiting either China or Japan. But at least I have had the opportunity to experience with painful clarity the insufficiency of my knowledge. In this field we still have everything to learn, and whatever we learn will be to our immense advantage. Knowledge of Eastern psychology provides the indispensable basis for a

[1] [Zurich, 1950. ("East Asia Thinks Otherwise.") The foreword was not included in the English-language edition of the book, by Lily Abegg, *The Mind of East Asia* (London and New York, 1952). It is reproduced here, in a translation by Hildegard Nagel and Ellen Thayer, titled "The Mind of East and West," from the *Inward Light* (Washington, D.C.), no. 49, (autumn 1955), having previously appeared in the *Bulletin of the Analytical Psychology Club of New York* vol. 15, no. 3 (Mar. 1953).]

critique of Western psychology, as indeed for any objective understanding of it. And in view of the truly lamentable psychic situation of the West, the importance of a deeper understanding of our Occidental prejudices can hardly be overestimated.

1484   Long experience with the products of the unconscious has taught me that there is a very remarkable parallelism between the specific character of the Western unconscious psyche and the "manifest" psyche of the East. Since our experience shows that the biological role which the unconscious plays in the psychic economy is compensatory to consciousness, one can venture the hypothesis that the mind of the Far East is related to our Western consciousness as the unconscious is, that is, as the left hand to the right.

1485   Our unconscious has, fundamentally, a tendency toward wholeness, as I believe I have been able to prove. One would be quite justified in saying the same thing about the Eastern psyche, but with this difference: that in the East it is consciousness that is characterized by an apperception of totality, while the West has developed a differentiated and therefore necessarily one-sided attention or awareness. With it goes the Western concept of causality, a principle of cognition irreconcilably opposed to the principle of synchronicity which forms the basis and the source of Eastern "incomprehensibility," and explains as well the "strangeness" of the unconscious with which we in the West are confronted. The understanding of synchronicity is the key which unlocks the door to the Eastern apperception of totality that we find so mysterious. The author seems to have devoted particular attention to just this point. I do not hesitate to say that I look forward to the publication of her book with the greatest interest.

March 1949

FOREWORD TO ALLENBY: "A PSYCHOLOGICAL STUDY OF THE ORIGINS OF MONOTHEISM"[1]

1486   It can no longer be doubted today that meaningful connections are discoverable in dreams and other spontaneous manifestations of the unconscious. This raises the question of the origin of unconscious contents. Are they genuine creations of the unconscious psyche, or thoughts that were originally conscious but subsequently became unconscious for one reason or another?

1487   The individual dream-thoughts, or at least their elements, are always of conscious origin, otherwise they could not be represented or recognized. Also, a whole sequence of images connected together in a meaningful way, or an entire scene, frequently derives from the conscious memory. But when we consider the meaning of the dream as a whole, the question of derivation becomes much more difficult to answer. So far as can be established empirically, the function of dreams is to compensate the conscious situation, as though there were a natural drive to restore the balance. The more one-sided the conscious situation is, the more the compensation takes on a *complementary* character. Obvious examples of this can be found in people who naïvely deceive themselves or who hold to some fanatical belief. As we know, the most lurid scenes of temptation are depicted in the dreams of ascetics. In such cases it would be very difficult to prove that the meaning of the dream derives from a conscious thought that subsequently became unconscious, for obviously no such reflection or self-criticism ever took place and for that very reason had to be performed by the dream. The hypothesis becomes completely untenable when the dreams produce meaningful connections which are absolutely unknown to the dreamer or which *cannot* be known to him. The clearest phenomena of this kind, convincing even to the layman, are telepathic dreams which give information concerning events at a distance or in the future, beyond the range of sense-perception.

1488   These phenomena offer striking proof that there are meaningful

1 [Written for Amy I. Allenby's book (Ph.D. dissertation, Oxford U.), which was not published. Dr. Allenby is an analytical psychologist in Oxford.]

656

connections in the unconscious which are not derived from conscious reflection. The same is true of dream motifs found otherwise only in myths and fairytales, and exhibiting characteristic forms of which the dreamer has no conscious knowledge. Here we are not dealing in any sense with ideas, but with instinctual factors, the fundamental forms that underlie all imaginative representation; in short, with a pattern of mental behaviour which is ingrained in human nature. This accounts for the universal occurrence of these archetypes of the imagination. Their *a priori* presence is due to the fact that they, like the instincts, are inherited, and therefore constantly produce mythological motifs in every individual as soon as his imagination is given free play, or whenever the unconscious gains the upper hand.

1489   Modern psychological experience has shown that not only the meaning of the dream, but also certain dream-contents, must derive entirely from the unconscious, for the simple reason that they could not have been known to consciousness and therefore cannot be derived from it.

1490   However slight the effect of a particular dream may be, the unconscious compensation is of great importance for a man's conscious life and for what one calls his "fate." The archetypes naturally play a considerable role here, and it is no accident that these determining factors have always been personified in the form of gods and demons.

1491   Since the relation of the unconscious to consciousness is not a mechanical one and not purely complementary, but performs a meaningful and compensatory function, the question arises as to who might be the "author" of the effects produced. In our ordinary experience, phenomena of this kind occur only in the realm of the thinking and willing ego-consciousness. There are, however, very similar "intelligent" acts of compensation in nature, especially in the instinctual activities of animals. For us, at least, they do not have the character of conscious decisions, but appear to be just like human activities that are exclusively controlled by the unconscious. The great difference between them is that the instinctual behaviour of animals is predictable and repetitive, whereas the compensatory acts of the unconscious are individual and creative.

1492   The "author" in both cases seems to be the pattern of behaviour, the archetype. Although in human beings the archetype represents a collective and almost universal mode of action and reaction, its activity cannot as a rule be predicted; one never knows when an archetype will react, and which archetype it will be. But once it is constellated, it produces "numinous" effects of a determining character. Thus Freud not only stumbled on the Oedipus complex but also discovered the dual-mother motif of the hero myth in Leonardo da Vinci. But he made the mistake of deriving this motif from the fact that Leonardo had two mothers in reality, namely, his real mother and a stepmother. Actually, the dual-mother motif occurs not only in myths but also in the dreams and fantasies of individuals who neither have two mothers nor know anything about the archetypal motifs in mythology. So there is no need of two mothers in reality to evoke the dual-mother motif. On the contrary, the motif shows the tendency of the unconscious to reproduce the dual-mother situation, or the story of double descent or child-substitution, usually for the purpose of compensating the subject's feelings of inferiority.

1493   As the archetypes are instinctive, inborn forms of psychic behaviour, they exert a powerful influence on the psychic processes. Unless the conscious mind intervenes critically and with an effort of will, things go on happening as they have always happened, whether to the advantage or disadvantage of the individual. The advantages seem to preponderate, for otherwise the development of consciousness could hardly have come about. The advantage of "free" will is indeed so obvious that civilized man is easily persuaded to leave his whole life to the guidance of consciousness, and to fight against the unconscious as something hostile, or else dismiss it as a negligible factor. Because of this, he is in danger of losing all contact with the world of instinct—a danger that is still further increased by his living an urban existence in what seems to be a purely man-made environment.

1494   This loss of instinct is largely responsible for the pathological condition of our contemporary culture. The great psychotherapeutic systems embodied in religion still struggle to keep the way open to the archetypal world of the psyche, but religion is increasingly losing its grip with the result that much of Europe today has become dechristianized or actually anti-Christian. Seen in this light, the efforts of modern psychology to investigate the unconscious seem like salutary reactions of the European psyche, as if it were seeking to re-establish the connection with its lost roots. It is not simply a matter of rescuing the natural instincts (this seems to have been Freud's particular preoccupation), but of making contact again with the archetypal functions that set bounds to the instincts and give them form and meaning. For this purpose a knowledge of the archetypes is indispensable.

1495 The question of the existence of an archetypal *God-image* is naturally of prime importance as a factor determining human behaviour. From the history of symbols as well as from the case histories of patients it can be demonstrated empirically that such a God-image actually exists, an image of wholeness which I have called the symbol of the *self*. It occurs most frequently in the form of *mandala* symbols. The author of this book has made it her task to investigate the psychological aspect of the God-image on the one hand and the theological aspect of the self on the other—a task which in my view is as necessary as it is timely. At a time when our most valuable spiritual possessions are being squandered, we would do well to consider very carefully the meaning and purpose of the things we so heedlessly seek to cast overboard. And before raising the cry that modern psychology destroys religious ideas by "psychologizing" them, we should reflect that it is just this psychology which is trying to renew the connection with the realities of the psyche, lest consciousness should flutter about rootlessly and helplessly in the void, a prey to every imaginable intellectualism. Atrophy of instinct is equivalent to pathological suggestibility, the devastating effects of which may be witnessed in the recurrent psychic epidemics of totalitarian madness.

1496 I can only hope this book finds a wide circle of serious readers.

May 1950

THE MIRACULOUS FAST OF BROTHER KLAUS[1]

1497   The fact that Brother Klaus, on his own admission and according to the reports of reliable witnesses, lived without material sustenance for twenty years is something that cannot be brushed aside however uncomfortable it may be. In the case of Therese of Konnersreuth[2] there are also reports, whose reliability of course I can neither confirm nor contest, that for a long period of time she lived simply and solely on holy wafers. Such things naturally cannot be understood with our present knowledge of physiology. One would be well advised, however, not to dismiss them as utterly impossible on that account. There are very many things that earlier were held to be impossible which nevertheless we know and can prove to be possible today.

1498   Naturally I have no explanation to offer concerning such phenomena as the fast of Brother Klaus, but I am inclined to think it should be sought in the realm of parapsychology. I myself was present at the investigation of a medium who manifested physical phenomena. An electrical engineer measured the degree of ionization of the atmosphere in the immediate vicinity of the medium. The figures were everywhere normal except at one point on the right side of the thorax, where the ionization was about sixty times the normal. At this point, when the (parapsychological) phenomena were in progress, there was an emission of ectoplasm capable of acting at a distance. If such things can occur, then it is also conceivable that persons in the vicinity of the medium might act as a source of ions—in other words, nourishment might be effected

---

[1] [Translated from "Das Fastenwunder des Bruder Klaus," *Neue Wissenschaft* (Baden, Switzerland), 1950/51, no. 7; revised from a letter to Fritz Blanke, 10 Nov. 1948, thanking him for his book *Bruder Klaus von Flüe* (Zurich, 1948). Cf. *Letters,* ed. G. Adler, vol. 1. A prefatory note by the editor of *Neue Wissenschaft* states: "The period of Brother Klaus's fast lasted from 1467 to 1487. All contemporary witnesses, even those in the immediate neighbourhood of the saint, agree that during this time he took no nourishment."]

[2] [Therese Neumann (1889–1962), generally known as Therese of Konnersreuth, Switzerland, stigmatized since 1926, when she claimed to have re-experienced Christ's Passion.]

by the passage of living molecules of albumen from one body to another. In this connection it should be mentioned that in parapsychological experiments decreases of weight up to several kilograms have been observed during the (physical) phenomena, in the case both of the medium and of some of the participants, who were all sitting on scales. This seems to me to offer a possible approach to an explanation. Unfortunately these things have been far too little investigated at present. This is a task for the future.

CONCERNING "ANSWER TO JOB"[1]

1498a   This is not a "scientific" book but a personal confrontation with the traditional Christian world view, occasioned by the impact of the new dogma of the Assumption. It echoes the reflections of a physician and theological layman, who had to find the answers to many questions on religious matters and was thus compelled to wrestle with the meaning of religious ideas from his particular, non-confessional standpoint. In addition, the questions were motivated by contemporary events: falsehood, injustice, slavery, and mass murder engulfed not only major parts of Europe but continue to prevail in vast areas of the world. What has a benevolent and almighty God to say to these problems? This desperate question, asked a thousand times, is the concern of this book.

[1] [(Translated by R. H.) Author's description, printed on the dust jacket of the original edn. of *Antwort auf Hiob,* which was published in Zurich around 1 Apr. 1952. It was reprinted in the appendix to *Gesam. Werke,* XI, p. 687, but not in C.W., vol. 11 (which contains "Answer to Job").]

RELIGION AND PSYCHOLOGY:
A REPLY TO MARTIN BUBER[1]

1499   Some while ago the readers of your magazine were given the opportunity to read a posthumous article by Count Keyserling,[2] in which I was characterized as "unspiritual." Now, in your last issue, I find an article by Martin Buber[3] which is likewise concerned with my classification. I am indebted to his pronouncements at least in so far as they raise me out of the condition of unspirituality, in which Count Keyserling saw fit to present me to the German public, into the sphere of spirituality, even though it be the spirituality of early Christian Gnosticism, which has always been looked at askance by theologians. Funnily enough this opinion of Buber's coincides with another utterance from an authoritative theological source accusing me of agnosticism—the exact opposite of Gnosticism.

1500   Now when opinions about the same subject differ so widely, there is in my view ground for the suspicion that none of them is correct, and that there has been a misunderstanding. Why is so much attention devoted to the question of whether I am a Gnostic or an agnostic? Why is it not simply stated that I am a psychiatrist whose prime concern is to record and interpret his empirical material? I try to investigate facts and make them more generally comprehensible. My critics have no right to slur over this in order to attack individual statements taken out of context.

1501   To support his diagnosis Buber even resorts to a sin of my youth, committed nearly forty years ago, which consists in my once having perpetrated a poem.[4] In this poem I expressed a number of psycho-

---

[1] [Written 22 Feb. 1952 as a letter to the editor, published as "Religion und Psychologie" in *Merkur* (Stuttgart), VI:5 (May 1952), 467–73, and reprinted as "Antwort an Martin Buber" in *Gesam. Werke*, XI, Anhang. The present translation was published in *Spring*, 1973.]

[2] [Hermann Keyserling (1880–1946), "Begegnungen mit der Psychoanalyse," *Merkur*, IV:11 (Nov. 1950), 1151–68.]

[3] ["Religion und modernes Denken," *Merkur* VI:2 (Feb. 1952). Trans., "Religion and Modern Thinking," together with Buber's reply to Jung (in the same issue with Jung's reply, *Merkur*, VI:5), in *Eclipse of God* (1953).]

[4] [*VII Sermones ad Mortuos*, by Basilides of Alexandria (n.d. [1916]), privately printed. English trans. by H. G. Baynes, privately printed 1925; reprinted in the 2nd edn. of *Memories, Dreams, Reflections*, appendix.]

logical *aperçus* in "Gnostic" style, because I was then studying the Gnostics with enthusiasm. My enthusiasm arose from the discovery that they were apparently the first thinkers to concern themselves (after their fashion) with the contents of the collective unconscious. I had the poem printed under a pseudonym and gave a few copies to friends, little dreaming that it would one day bear witness against me as a heretic.

1502   I would like to point out to my critic that I have in my time been regarded not only as a Gnostic and its opposite, but also as a theist and an atheist, a mystic and a materialist. In this concert of contending opinions I do not wish to lay too much stress on what I consider myself to be, but will quote a judgment from a leading article in the *British Medical Journal* (9 February 1952), a source that would seem to be above suspicion. "Facts first and theories later is the keynote of Jung's work. He is an empiricist first and last." This view meets with my approval.

1503   Anyone who does not know my work will certainly ask himself how it is that so many contrary opinions can be held about one and the same subject. The answer to this is that they are all thought up by "metaphysicians," that is, by people who for one reason or another think they know about unknowable things in the Beyond. I have never ventured to declare that such things do *not* exist; but neither have I ventured to suppose that any statement of mine could in any way touch them or even represent them correctly. I very much doubt whether our conception of a thing is identical with the nature of the thing itself, and this for very obvious scientific reasons.

1504   But since views and opinions about metaphysical or religious subjects play a very great role in empirical psychology,[5] I am obliged for practical reasons to work with concepts corresponding to them. In so doing I am aware that I am dealing with anthropomorphic ideas and not with actual gods and angels, although, thanks to their specific energy, such (archetypal) images behave so autonomously that one could describe them metaphorically as "psychic daimonia." The fact that they are autonomous should be taken very seriously; first, from the theoretical standpoint, because it explains the dissociability of the psyche as well as actual dissociation, and second, from the practical one, because it forms the basis for a dialectical discussion between the ego and the unconscious, which is one of the mainstays of the psychotherapeutic

[5] Cf. G. Schmaltz, *Östliche Weisheit und westliche Psychotherapie* (1951).

method. Anyone who has any knowledge of the structure of a neurosis will be aware that the pathogenic conflict arises from the counterposition of the unconscious relative to consciousness. The so-called "forces of the unconscious" are not intellectual concepts that can be arbitrarily manipulated, but dangerous antagonists which can, among other things, work frightful devastation in the economy of the personality. They are everything one could wish for or fear in a psychic "Thou." The layman naturally thinks he is the victim of some obscure organic disease; but the theologian, who suspects it is the devil's work, is appreciably nearer to the psychological truth.

1505 I am afraid that Buber, having no psychiatric experience, fails to understand what I mean by the "reality of the psyche" and by the dialectical process of individuation. The fact is that the ego is confronted with psychic powers which from ancient times have borne sacred names, and because of these they have always been identified with metaphysical beings. Analysis of the unconscious has long since demonstrated the existence of these powers in the form of archetypal images which, be it noted, *are not identical with the corresponding intellectual concepts.* One can, of course, believe that the concepts of the conscious mind are, through the inspiration of the Holy Ghost, direct and correct representations of their metaphysical referent. But this conviction is possible only for one who already possesses the gift of faith. Unfortunately I cannot boast of this possession, for which reason I do not imagine that when I say something about an archangel I have thereby confirmed that a metaphysical fact. I have merely expressed an opinion about something that can be experienced, that is, about one of the very palpable "powers of the unconscious". These powers are numinous "types"—unconscious contents, processes, and dynamisms—and such types are, if one may so express it, immanent-transcendent. Since my sole means of cognition is experience I may not overstep its boundaries, and cannot therefore pretend to myself that my description coincides with the portrait of a real metaphysical archangel. What I have described is a psychic factor only, but one which exerts a considerable influence on the conscious mind. Thanks to its autonomy, it forms the counterposition to the subjective ego because it is a piece of the *objective psyche*. It can therefore be designated as a "Thou." For me its reality is amply attested by the truly diabolical deeds of our time: the six million murdered Jews, the uncounted victims of the slave labour camps in Russia, as well as the invention of the atom bomb, to name but a few examples of the darker side. But I have also seen the other side which can be expressed by the words beauty, goodness, wisdom, grace. These experiences of the depths and heights of human nature justify the metaphorical use of the term "daimon."

1506 It should not be overlooked that what I am concerned with are psychic phenomena which can be proved empirically to be the bases of metaphysical concepts, and that when, for example, I speak of "God" I am unable to refer to anything beyond these demonstrable psychic models which, we have to admit, have shown themselves to be devastatingly real. To anyone who finds their reality incredible I would recommend a reflective tour through a lunatic asylum.

1507 The "reality of the psyche" is my working hypothesis, and my principal activity consists in collecting factual material to describe and explain it. I have set up neither a system nor a general theory, but have merely formulated auxiliary concepts to serve me as tools, as is customary in every branch of science. If Buber misunderstands my empiricism as Gnosticism, it is up to him to prove that the facts I describe are nothing but inventions. If he should succeed in proving this with empirical material, then indeed I am a Gnostic. But in that case he will find himself in the uncomfortable position of having to dismiss all religious experiences as self-deception. Meanwhile I am of the opinion that Buber's judgment has been led astray. This seems especially evident in his apparent inability to understand how an "autonomous psychic content" like the God-image can burst upon the ego, and that such a confrontation is a living experience. It is certainly not the task of an empirical science to establish how far such a psychic content is dependent on and determined by the existence of a metaphysical deity. That is the concern of theology, revelation, and faith. My critic does not seem to realize that when he himself talks about God, his statements are dependent firstly on his conscious and then on his unconscious assumptions. Of *which* metaphysical deity he is speaking I do not know. If he is an orthodox Jew he is speaking of a God to whom the incarnation in the year 1 has not yet been revealed. If he is a Christian, then his deity knows about the incarnation of which Yahweh still shows no sign. I do not doubt his conviction that he stands in a living relationship to a divine Thou, but now as before I am of the opinion that this relationship is primarily to an autonomous psychic content which is defined in one way by him and in another by the Pope. Consequently I do not permit myself the least judgment as to whether and to what extent it has pleased a metaphysical deity to reveal himself to the devout Jew as he was before the incarnation, to the Church Fathers as the Trinity, to the Protestants as the one and only Saviour without co-redemptrix, and to the present Pope as a Saviour with co-re-demptrix. Nor should one doubt that the devotees of other faiths, including Islam, Buddhism, Hinduism, and so on, have the same living relationship to "God," or to Nirvana and Tao, as Buber has to the God-concept peculiar to himself.

1508   It is remarkable that he takes exception to my statement that God cannot exist apart from man and regards it as a transcendental assertion. Yet I say expressly that everything asserted about "God" is a human statement, in other words a psychological one. For surely the image we have or make for ourselves of God is never detached from man? Can Buber show me where, apart from man, God has made an image of himself? How can such a thing be substantiated and by whom? Here, just for once, and as an exception, I shall indulge in transcendental speculation and even in "poetry": God has indeed made an inconceivably sublime and mysteriously contradictory image of himself, without the help of man, and implanted it in man's unconscious as an archetype, an ἀρχέτυπον φῶς, archetypal light: not in order that theologians of all times and places should be at one another's throats, but in order that the unpresumptuous man might glimpse an image, in the stillness of his soul, that is akin to him and is wrought of his own psychic substance. This image contains everything he will ever imagine concerning his gods or concerning the ground of his psyche.

1509   This archetype, whose existence is attested not only by ethnology but by the psychic experience of individuals, satisfies me completely. It is so humanly close and yet so strange and "other"; also, like all archetypes, it possesses the utmost determinative power with which it is absolutely necessary that we come to terms. The dialectical relationship to the autonomous contents of the collective unconscious is therefore, as I have said, an essential part of therapy.

1510   Buber is mistaken in thinking that I start with a "fundamentally Gnostic viewpoint" and then proceed to "elaborate" metaphysical assertions. One should not misconstrue the findings of empiricism as philosophical premises, for they are not obtained by deduction but from clinical and factual material. I would recommend him to read some autobiographies of the mentally ill, such as John Custance's *Wisdom, Madness and Folly* (1951), or D. P. Schreber's

Memoirs of My Nervous Illness (first published 1903), which certainly do not proceed from Gnostic hypotheses any more than I do; or he might try an analysis of mythological material, such as the excellent work of Dr. Erich Neumann, his neighbour in Tel Aviv: *Amor and Psyche* (1952). My contention that the products of the unconscious are analogous and related to certain metaphysical ideas is founded on my professional experience. In this connection I would point out that I know quite a number of influential theologians, Catholics as well as Protestants, who have no difficulty in grasping my empirical standpoint. I therefore see no reason why I should take my method of exposition to be quite so misleading as Buber would have us believe.

1511   There is one misunderstanding which I would like to mention here because it comes up so often. This is the curious assumption that when a projection is withdrawn nothing more of the object remains. When I correct my mistaken opinion of a man I have not negated him and caused him to vanish; on the contrary, I see him more nearly as he is, and this can only benefit the relationship. So if I hold the view that all statements about God have their origin in the psyche and must therefore be distinguished from God as a metaphysical being, this is neither to deny God nor to put man in God's place. I frankly confess that it goes against the grain with me to think that the metaphysical God himself is speaking through everyone who quotes the Bible or ventilates his religious opinions. Faith is certainly a splendid thing if one has it, and knowledge by faith is perhaps more perfect than anything we can produce with our laboured and wheezing empiricism. The edifice of Christian dogma, for instance, undoubtedly stands on a much higher level than the somewhat wild "philosophoumena" of the Gnostics. Dogmas are spiritual structures of supreme beauty, and they possess a wonderful meaning which I have sought to fathom in my fashion. Compared with them our scientific endeavors to devise models of the objective psyche are unsightly in the extreme. They are bound to earth and reality, full of contradictions, incomplete, logically and aesthetically unsatisfying. The empirical concepts of science and particularly of medical psychology do not proceed from neat and seemly principles of thought, but are the outcome of our daily labours in the sloughs of ordinary human existence and human pain. They are essentially irrational, and the philosopher who criticizes them as though they were philosophical concepts tilts against windmills and gets into the greatest difficulties, as Buber does with the concept of the self. Empirical concepts are names for existing complexes of facts. Considering the fearful paradoxicality of human existence, it is quite understandable that the unconscious contains an equally paradoxical God-image which will not square at all with the beauty, sublimity, and purity of the dogmatic concept of God. The God of Job and of the 89th Psalm is clearly a bit closer to reality, and his behaviour does not fit in badly with the God-image in the unconscious. Of course this image, with its Anthropos symbolism, lends support to the idea of the incarnation. I do not feel responsible for the fact that the history of dogma has made some progress since the days of the Old Testament. This is not to preach a new religion, for to do that I would have to follow the old-established custom of appealing to a divine revelation. I am essentially a physician, whose business is with the sickness of man and his times, and with remedies that are as real as the suffering. Not only Buber, but every theologian who baulks at my odious psychology is at liberty to heal my patients with the word of God. I would welcome this experiment with open arms. But since the ecclesiastical cure of souls does not always produce the desired results, we doctors must do what we can, and at present we have no better standby than that modest "gnosis" which the empirical method gives us. Or have any of my critics better advice to offer?

1512   As a doctor one finds oneself in an awkward position, because unfortunately one can accomplish nothing with that little word "ought." We cannot demand of our patients a faith which they reject because they do not understand it, or which does not suit them even though we may hold it ourselves. We have to rely on the curative powers inherent in the patient's own nature, regardless of whether the ideas that emerge agree with any known creed or philosophy. My empirical material seems to include a bit of everything—it is an assortment of primitive, Western, and Oriental ideas. There is scarcely any myth whose echoes are not heard, nor any heresy that has not contributed an occasional oddity. The deeper, collective layers of the human psyche must surely be of a like nature. Intellectuals and rationalists, happy in their established beliefs, will no doubt be horrified by this and will accuse me of reckless eclecticism, as though I had somehow invented the facts of man's nature and mental history and had compounded out of them a repulsive theosophical brew. Those who possess faith or prefer to talk like philosophers do not, of course, need to wrestle with the facts, but a doctor is not at liberty to dodge the grim realities of human nature.

1513   It is inevitable that the adherents of traditional religious systems should find my formulations hard to understand. A Gnostic would not be at all pleased with me, but would reproach me for having no cosmogony and for the cluelessness of my gnosis in regard to the happenings in the Pleroma. A Buddhist would complain that I was deluded by Maya, and a Taoist that I was too complicated. As for an orthodox Christian, he can hardly do otherwise than deplore the nonchalance and lack of respect with which I navigate through the empyrean of dogmatic ideas. I must, however, once more beg my unmerciful critics to remember that I start from *facts* for which I seek an interpretation.

ADDRESS AT THE PRESENTATION OF THE
JUNG CODEX[1]

Mr. President, viri magnifici, Ladies and Gentlemen!

1514   It gives me much pleasure to accept this precious gift in the name of our Institute. For this I thank you, and also for the surprising and undeserved honour you have done me in baptising the Codex with my name. I would like to thank Dr. Meier personally for his persistent and successful efforts to acquire the Codex, and for organizing this celebration. He has asked me to say something about the psychological significance of Gnostic texts.

1515   At present, unfortunately, I know only three of the treatises contained in the Codex. One of these is an important, so it seems, early Valentinian text that affords us some insight into the mentality of the second century A.D. It is called "The Gospel of Truth,"[2] but it is less a gospel than a treatise explaining the Christian message, its purpose being to assimilate this strange and hardly understandable message to the Hellenistic-Egyptian world of thought. It is evident that the author was appealing to the intellectual understanding of his reader, as if in remembrance of the words: "We preach Christ crucified, unto the Jews a stumbling-block, and unto the Greeks foolishness" (I Cor. 1:23). For him Christ was primarily a light-bringer, who went forth from the Father in order to illuminate the stupidity, darkness, and unconsciousness of mankind. This deliverance from *agnosia* relates the text to the accounts which Hippolytus has left of the Gnostics, and of the Naassenes and Peratics in particular, in his *Elenchos*.[3] There we also find most of what I call the "phenomena of assimilation." They consisted partly of allegories and partly of genuine symbols, and their purpose was to shed light on the essentially metaphysical figure of Christ and make it more comprehensible to the mentality of that epoch. For the modern mind this accumulation of symbols, parables, and syno-

---

[1] [Draft written for a convocation at the Gesellschaftshaus zum Rüden, Zurich, 15 Nov. 1953. For Jung's final version, see the Addenda. The Jung Codex is a Gnostic papyrus in Coptic found in 1945 near the village of Nag Hamadi in Upper Egypt and acquired in 1952 for the C. G. Jung Institute.]

[2] [Published under the editorship of M. Malinine, H. C. Puech, and G. Quispel, *Evangelium Veritatis* (Zurich, 1956).]

[3] [Otherwise known as *Philosophoumena, or The Refutation of All Heresies*, trans. by F. Legge (1921).]

nyms has just the opposite effect, since it only deepens the darkness and entangles the light-bringer in a network of barely intelligible analogies. It is not likely that the Gnostic attempts at elucidation met with much success in the pagan world, especially as the Church very soon opposed them and whenever possible suppressed them. Luckily during this process some of the best pieces (to judge by their content) were preserved for posterity, so that today we are in a position to see in what way the Christian message was taken up by the unconscious of that age.

1516   These phenomena are naturally of especial significance for psychologists and psychiatrists, who are professionally concerned with the psychic background, and this is the reason why our Institute is so interested in acquiring and translating Gnostic texts. Although suppressed and forgotten, the process of assimilation that began with Gnosticism continued all through the Middle Ages, and it can still be observed in modern times whenever the individual consciousness is confronted with its own shadow, or the inferior part of the personality. This happens spontaneously in certain cases, whether they be normal or pathological. The general rule, however, is that modern man needs expert help to become conscious of his darkness, because in most cases he has long since forgotten this basic problem of Christianity: the moral and intellectual *agnosia* of the merely natural man. Christianity, considered as a psychological phenomenon, contributed a great deal to the development of consciousness, and wherever this dialectical process has not come to a standstill we find new evidence of assimilation. Even in medieval Judaism a parallel process took place over the centuries, independently of the Christian one, in the Kabbala. Its nearest analogy in the Christian sphere was philosophical alchemy, whose psychological affinities with Gnosticism can easily be demonstrated.

1517   The urgent therapeutic necessity of confronting the patient with his own dark side is a continuation of the Christian development of consciousness and leads to phenomena of assimilation similar to those found in Gnosticism, the Kabbala, and Hermetic philosophy. Since comparison with these earlier historical stages is of the greatest importance in interpreting the modern phenomena, the discovery of authentic Gnostic texts is of the utmost practical value to us in our researches. These few hints must suffice to explain our interest in a Gnostic codex. A detailed account of these relationships may be found in a number of studies that have already been published.

LETTER TO PÈRE BRUNO[1]

5 November 1953

Dear Fr. Bruno,

1518   Your questions interested me extremely. You ask for information about the method to be followed in order to establish the existence of an archetype. Instead of a theoretical discourse, I propose to give you a practical demonstration of my method by trying to tell you what I think about that probably historical personage, Elijah.

1519   If the tradition were concerned with a person characterized rather by individual and more or less unique traits, to whom few or no legends, miraculous deeds, and exploits or relations or parallels with mythological figures were attached, there would be no reason to suppose the presence of an archetype. If on the other hand the biography of the person concerned contains mythical motifs and parallels, and if posterity has added elements that are clearly mythological, then there is no longer any doubt that we are dealing with an archetype.

1520   *The prophet Elijah is a highly mythical person,* though that does not prevent his being a historical one at the same time, like for example St. John the Baptist or even Jesus, the rabbi of Nazareth. I call the mythical attributes "phenomena of assimilation." (I have just published a study on the astrological assimilation of Christ as fish in my book *Aion,* 1951.)

1521   There is no need to repeat to you the well-known Old Testament traditions. Let us rather glance at the Christian tradition in the New Testament and later. As a "hairy" man [2 Kings 1:8] Elijah is analogous to St. John the Baptist [Mark 1:6]. His calling of an apostle (Elisha), walking on the water, the discouragement (I Kings 19: 4ff.) prefigure analogous incidents in the life of Christ, who is also interpreted as a reappearance of Elijah, and his saying

[1] [(Translated from the French by A.S.B.G. and J.A.P.) Published in *Élie le prophète,* ed. by Père Bruno de Jésus-Marie, O.C.D., vol. II (Les Études Carmélitaines, Paris, 1956), pp. 13–18. Comments were supplied by Charles Baudouin, René Laforgue, and Father Bruno to form a chapter entitled "Puissance de l'archétype," signed by the four. See also Jung's letter of 20 Nov. 1956 to Père Bruno in *Letters,* ed. G. Adler, vol. 2.]

on the cross: "Eli, Eli . . ." as an invocation of Elijah. The name derives from El (= God). Chrysostom derives the name Elias [= Elijah] from Helios: "quod sicut sol ex oceano emergens versus supremum coelus tendit."[2] At his birth he was hailed by angels. He was wrapped in fiery swaddling clothes and nourished by flames. He had *two souls* (!). (See J. Fr. Mieg, *De raptu Eliae*, 1660, and Schulinus, *De Elia corvorum alumno*, 1718.) In Roman days, there was a pagan sanctuary on Carmel, which seems to have consisted only of an altar (Tacitus, *Hist.* II, 78, "tantum ara et reverentia").[3] Vespasian is said to have obtained an oracle in this sanctuary. Iamblichus (*Vita Pythagorica* III, 15) says that the mountain is sacred and represents a taboo area and that Pythagoras often stayed in the sacred solitude of Carmel. It is possible that the Druses have preserved in their sanctuary on the mountain the place of the altar of Elijah.

1522   In *Pirkê Eliezer* 31, Elijah is the incarnation of an eternal soul-substance and is of the same nature as the angels. It was his spirit that called up the ram which was substituted for Isaac. He wears the ram's skin as a girdle or apron. He is present at the circumcision as the "Angel of the Covenant" (*Pirkê Eliezer* 29). Even in our own day, a special chair is reserved for Elijah at the rite of circumcision, and at the feast of the Passover a goblet of wine is placed on the table and the head of the family opens the door to invite Elijah to enter and share the feast.

1523   Legend calls him "violent," "quarrelsome," and "merciless." It was because of these unfavourable qualities that he had to yield up his office of prophet to Elisha. He caused the sun to stand still during the sacrifice of Carmel. In the time to come he will awaken the dead. The boy he raised to life was Jonah (later swallowed by the monster). Since his ascension to heaven he is among the angels, and he hovers over the earth like an eagle spying out the secrets of men.

1524   He is also considered to be a parallel of Moses. They have in common the murder of a man, their flight, being nourished by a woman, the vision of God, the calling together of the people by a mountain. Elijah and Moses were present at the transfiguration on Tabor.

1525   Elijah helped Rabbi Meir by transforming himself into a hetaira. He is generally a helper in all sorts of human difficulties (healing even the toothache, enriching the poor, bringing leaves from

2 ["which extends toward the highest heaven as the sun rising from the ocean."]
3 ["only an altar and the worship (of the god)"]

paradise, building magic palaces, etc.) He also plays tricks by making people lose their purses. He slays on the spot a man who does not pray properly. Thus Elijah is identical with the figure of Khadir or Khidr in Islamic tradition.[4] When, yielding to the prayer of Rabbi Hiyya, he reveals the secret of resurrecting the dead, the angels intercede, carry the rabbi off, and give him a good hiding with fiery whips. The village dogs bark joyously when Elijah appears (in disguise). Three days before the appearing of the Messiah, Elijah will manifest himself on the *mountains* of Israel.

1526   According to Moses ben Leon, Elijah belongs to the category of angels who recommended the creation of man. Moses Cordovero compares him to Enoch, but whereas the latter's body is consumed by fire, Elijah retains his earthly form so as to be ready to appear again. His body descends from the Tree of Life. Since he was not dead, he was supposed to dwell invisibly on Mount Carmel; for example, the Shunamite went to look for him and found him at Carmel (II Kings 4:25). (For the Jewish tradition, see Strack and Billerbeck, *Kommentar zum N.T.*, vol. IV, part 2, pp. 764ff. Also *Encyclopedia Judaica*, 1930, vol. 6.) In Hasidic tradition, Elijah was endowed with the *collective soul* of Israel. Every male child, when presented for the covenant with God, receives a part of the soul of Elijah and after attaining adult age and developing this soul, Elijah appears to him. Abraham ibn Ezra of Toledo is said to have been unable to develop this soul completely. (It is evident that Elijah represents both the collective unconscious and the "self," atman, purusha, of man. It is a question of the *individuation process*. See M. Buber, *Die Erzählungen der Chassidim* (1949), p. 402.[5] M. Buber is one of my relentless adversaries. He has not understood even what he wrote himself!).[6]

1527   Islamic tradition depends in the first place on the Jewish commentaries. Ilyās (Elijah) has received from God power to control the rain. He causes a great drought. He ascends to heaven on a fiery horse and God transforms him into a half-human angel (according to al-Tabarī). In the Koran, Sura 18, 64ff., he is replaced by al-Khadir. (In a Jewish legend it is Elijah who travels with Joshua ben Levi, in the Koran it is al-Khadir with Joshua ben Nun.) Ordinarily, Ilyās and al-Khadir are immortal twins. They spend Ramadan at Jerusalem every year and afterwards they take

---

[4] [Cf. "Concerning Rebirth" (C.W., vol. 9, i), pars. 240ff.]

[5] [Buber, *Tales of the Hasidim*, vol. I: "Elijah," by Elimelekh of Lizhensk, p. 257.]

[6] [Cf. supra, "Reply to Buber," pars. 1499ff.]

part in the pilgrimage to Mecca without being recognized. Ilyās is identified with Enoch and Idrīs (= Hermes Trismegistus). Later Ilyas and al-Khadir are identified with St. George (see *Encyclopedia of Islam,* Leiden and Leipzig, 1913).

1528　　In medieval Christian tradition, Elijah continues to haunt the imagination. For example, it is specially fascinated by his ascent to heaven, which is frequently represented. In illuminated MSS, the model is followed of the Mithraic representation of the ascent of Sol inviting Mithras to join him in the fiery chariot. (See Bousset, "Die Himmelsreise der Seele," *Arch. f. Relig. wiss.,* 1901, IV, p. 160ff., Cumont, *Textes et monuments,* I, p. 178, fig. 11.) Tertullian (*De praescriptione hereticorum* 40) says of Mithras: "imaginem resurrectionis inducit."[7] The Mandaean hero-saviour Saoshyant, the next to come in the series of millenniary saviours or prophets, is fused with Mithras, as is the latter with Idrīs (Hermes, Mercurius; see Dussaud, "Notes de myth. syrienne," pp. 23ff.).[8] In these circumstances, it is not very surprising that Elijah should become "Helyas Artista" in medieval alchemy (e.g., Dorn, "De transmut. met.," *Theatr. chem.,* 1602, I, p. 610: "usque in adventum Heliae Artistae quo tempore nihil tam occultum quod non revelabitur").[9] This passage has its origin in the treatise "De tinctura physicorum" of Paracelsus. (See also Helvetius, *Vitulus aureus,* 1667; Glauber, *De Elia Artista,* 1668, and Kopp, *Die Alchemie,* 1886, I, pp. 250ff.)[10]

---

[7] ["he offers an image of the resurrection."]

[8] [René Dussaud, *Notes du mythologie syrienne* (Paris, 1903–5).]

[9] ["until the coming of Helyas Artista, in whose time all that is hidden will be revealed"]

[10] [Following this letter, Bruno quoted another letter from Jung of 22 Dec. 1954(misdated by Bruno 1953; here trans. by J.A.P.):

"So far as concerns the Helias of the alchemists, let me remind you of the text by Gerardus Dorneus [quoted as above]. Instead of saying 'usque ad adventum Christi,' the alchemist prefers an earlier form of the anthropos, Elijah, who is one of the four persons raised to heaven with their bodies: Enoch, Elijah, Christ, and Mary.

"The reason why the alchemist preferred Elijah, a figure or condition prior to Christ, is probably because in Paracelsus Elijah, like Enoch, belongs among the 'Enochdiani and Heliezati,' that is, among those whose bodies are capable of longevity (up to a thousand years) or else incorruptible, like the bodies of Enoch and Elijah. The prolongation of life was a very special interest of the master's, whereas the premature death of Christ did not seem interesting to him. (Certainly Paracelsus verged on the scientific materialism of the eighteenth century! Cf. *Theophrasti Paracelsi Tract. De Vita Longa,* edit. by Adam v. Bodenstein, 1562.)

"Jewish tradition says that Elijah remained in the corporeal state so as

¹⁵²⁹   It is unnecessary to continue this long list of *phenomena of
assimilation* which follow without interruption, so to speak, from
the remotest times to our own day. This proves irrefutably that
Elijah is a *living archetype*. In psychology, we call it a *constellated
archetype,* that is to say one that is more or less generally active,
giving birth to new forms of assimilation. One of these phenomena
was the choice of Carmel for the foundation of the first convent in
the twelfth century. The mountain had long been a numinous place
as the seat of the Canaanite deities Baal and Astarte. (Cf. the duality
of Elijah, the transformation into a hetaira.) YHWH supplants
them as inhabitant of the sacred place (Eli-yah like Khadir a kind
of personification of YHWH or Allah. Cf. the temperament and the
fire of the prophet!). The numinous inhabitant of Carmel is chosen
as the patron of the order. The choice is curious and unprecedented.
According to the empirical rule, an archetype becomes active and
chooses itself when a certain lack in the conscious sphere calls for a
compensation on the part of the unconscious. What is lacking on the
conscious side is the immediate relation with God: in so far as
Elijah is an angelic being fortified with divine power, having the
magic name of Eli-YHWH, delivered from corruptibility, omniscient
and omnipresent, he represents the ideal compensation not only for
Christians but for Jews and Moslems also. He is the typical θεός
ανθρωπος, more human than Christ inasmuch as he is begotten and
born in *peccatum originale,* and more universal in that he included
even the pre-Yahwist pagan deities like Baal, El-Elyon, Mithras,
Mercurius, and the personification of Allah, al-Khadir.

to be visible to mortal eyes during his peregrinations on earth. After reading
a little book I had just written (which had to do among other things with
the archetypal nature of Yahweh as revealed in the Book of Job), an intellectual and agnostic (or materialistic) Jew had a dream which was sent to me.
In his dream he was back in a concentration camp (where he had actually
been during the war). Suddenly he perceived an extraordinarily large eagle
circling over the camp. He felt spied upon and watched by the menacing
bird and, in a highly emotional state, wanted to defend himself by attacking
it. To this end, he was looking for a combat plane with which to bring
the animal down.
    "Thanks to my book, he had realized that in reality it is possible to
abolish the idea of a god by means of reason, yet not possible to free oneself
from it when one is dealing with an archetype innate in the structure of
the psyche itself. (This dream is discussed in "The Philosophical Tree" [C.W.
13], pars. 466ff.) Elijah in the shape of an eagle represents the eye of Yahweh
which sees all—'oculi Dei qui discurrent in universam terram' (Zach. 4:10).
The fear of God had seized him. Thus the theriomorphic attribute of the
ancient prophet still plays its part in our time."]

677

1530   I have already said that the archetype "gets itself chosen" rather than is deliberately chosen. I prefer this way of putting it because it is almost the rule that one follows unconsciously the attraction and suggestion of the archetype. I think that the legend of Elijah and the unique atmosphere of Mount Carmel exercised an influence from which the founder of the order could no more withdraw himself than could the Druses, the Romans, Jews, Canaanites, or Phoenicians. It was not only the *place* which favoured the choice for the adoption of a compensatory figure but the *time*. The twelfth century and the beginning of the thirteenth were just the period which activated the spiritual movements brought into being by the new aeon which began with the eleventh century.[11] These were the days of Joachim of Flora and the Brethren of the Free Spirit, of Albertus Magnus and Roger Bacon, of the beginning of Latin alchemy and of the natural sciences and also of a feminine religious symbol, the Holy Grail. (For the significance of the year 1000, see my *Aion,* chs. VI and X, 3.)

1531   To complete the establishment of a living archetype, the historical proofs do not wholly suffice, since one can explain the historical documentation by tradition (whose beginnings, however, always remain unexplained). That the archetype also manifests itself spontaneously outside tradition needs to be added to the evidence. God as collective soul, as spirit of nature, eternally renewed, incorruptible, archetype of the spirit even in the form of the "Trickster," pagan divinity, is encountered in ancient and medieval alchemy having nothing to do with the local tradition of Carmel. The *Deus absconditus* of alchemy has the same compensating function as the figure of Elijah. Lastly—as is little known—the psychology of alchemy has become comprehensible to us thanks to the fact that we observe analogous compensations in pathological and normal individuals in modern times. In calling themselves "atheists" or "agnostics," people dissatisfied with the Christian tradition are not being merely negative. In many cases it is easy to observe the phenomenon of the "compensating God," as I have demonstrated in my most recent works.

I hope, dear Fr. Bruno, that I have shown you the way an archetype is established and have answered your question concerning the choice of the archetype.

Yours sincerely, C. G. JUNG

[11] [Cf. *Aion,* pars. 137ff.]

Küsnacht, 27 March 1954

Dear Sir,

1532   It was very kind of you to send me your booklet[2] on the reception and action of the Holy Spirit. I have read it with special interest since the subject of the Holy Spirit seems to me one of current importance. I remember that the former Archbishop of York, Dr. Temple, admitted, in conversation with me, that the Church has not done all that it might to develop the idea of the Holy Spirit. It is not difficult to see why this is so, for τὸ πνεῦμα πνεῖ ὅπου θέλει[3]—a fact which an institution may find very inconvenient! In the course of reading your little book a number of questions and thoughts have occurred to me, which I set out below, since my reactions may perhaps be of some interest to you.

1533   I quite agree with your view that one pauses before entrusting oneself to the "unforeseeable action" of the Holy Spirit. One feels afraid of it, not, I think, without good reason. Since there is a marked difference between the God of the Old Testament and the God of the New, a definition is desirable. You nowhere explain your idea of God. Which God have you in mind: The New Testament God, or the Old? The latter is a paradox; good and demon-like, just and unjust at the same time, while the God of the New Testament is by definition perfect, good, the Summum Bonum even, without any element of the dark or the demon in him. But if you identify these two Gods, different as they are, the fear and resistance one feels in entrusting oneself unconditionally to the Holy Spirit are easy to understand. The divine action is so unforeseeable that it may well be really disastrous. That being so, the prudence of the serpent counsels us not to approach the Holy Spirit too closely.

1534   If, on the other hand, it is the New Testament God you have in mind, one can be absolutely certain that the risk is more apparent

---

[1] [(Translated from the French by A.S.B.G.) See Jung's letters of 18 Jan. and 29 June 1955 to Père William Lachat in Letters, ed. G. Adler, vol. 2.]

[2] [La Réception et l'action du Saint-Esprit dans la vie personnelle et communautaire (Neuchâtel, 1953).]

[3] ["The spirit bloweth where it listeth." John 3:8.]

than real since the end will always be good. In that event the experiment loses its venturesome character; it is not really dangerous. It is then merely foolish not to give oneself up entirely to the action of the Holy Spirit. Rather one should seek him day by day, and one will easily lay hold of him, as Mr. Horton[4] assures us. In the absence of a formal statement on your part, I assume that you identify the two Gods. In that case the Holy Spirit would not be easy to apprehend; it would even be highly dangerous to attract the divine attention by specially pious behaviour (as in the case of Job and some others). In the Old Testament Satan still has the Father's ear, and can influence him even against the righteous. The Old Testament furnishes us with quite a number of instances of this kind, and they warn us to be very careful when we are dealing with the Holy Spirit. The man who is not particularly bold and adventurous will do well to bear these examples in mind and to thank God that the Holy Spirit does not concern himself with us overmuch. One feels much safer under the shadow of the Church, which serves as a fortress to protect us against God and his Spirit. It is very comforting to be assured by the Catholic Church that it "possesses" the Spirit, who assists regularly at its rites. Then one knows that he is well chained up. Protestantism is no less reassuring in that it represents the Spirit to us as something to be sought for, to be easily "drunk," even to be possessed. We get the impression that he is something passive, which cannot budge without us. He has lost his dangerous qualities, his fire, his autonomy, his power. He is represented as an innocuous, passive, and purely beneficent element, so that to be afraid of him would seem just stupid.

1535   This characterization of the Holy Spirit leaves out of account the terrors of YHWH. It does not tell us what the Holy Spirit is, since it has failed to explain to us clearly what it has done with the *Deus absconditus.* Albert Schweitzer naïvely informs us that he takes the side of the ethical God and avoids the *absconditus,* as if a mortal man had the ability to hide himself when faced with an almighty God or to take the other, less risky side. God can implicate him in unrighteousness whenever he chooses.

1536   I also fail to find a definition of Christ; one does not know whether he is identical with the Holy Spirit, or different from him. Everyone talks about Christ; but who is this Christ? When talking to a Catholic or Anglican priest, I am in no doubt. But when I

4 [Unidentified.]

680

am talking to a pastor of the Reformed Church, it may be that Christ is the Second Person of the Trinity and God in his entirety, or a divine man (the "supreme authority," as Schweitzer has it, which doesn't go too well with the error of the parousia), or one of those great founders of ethical systems like Pythagoras, Confucius, and so on. It is the same with the idea of God. What is Martin Buber talking about when he discloses to us his intimate relations with "God"? YHWH? The olden Trinity, or the modern Trinity, which has become something more like a Quaternity since the Sponsa has been received into the Thalamus?[5] Or the rather misty God of Protestantism? Do you think that everyone who says that he is surrendering himself to Christ has really surrendered himself to Christ? Isn't it more likely that he has surrendered himself to the image of Christ which he has made for himself, or to that of God the Father or the Holy Spirit? Are they all the same Christ— the Christ of the Synoptics, of the *Exercitia Spiritualia,* of a mystic of Mount Athos, of Count Zinzendorf,[6] of the hundred sects, of Caux[7] and Rudolf Steiner, and—last but not least—of St. Paul? Do you really believe that anyone, be he who he may, can bring about the real presence of one of the Sacred Persons by an earnest utterance of their name? I can be certain only that someone has called up a psychic image, but it is impossible for me to confirm the real presence of the Being evoked. It is neither for us nor for others to decide *who* has been invoked by the holy name and to whom one has surrendered oneself. Has it not happened that the invocation of the Holy Spirit has brought the devil on the scene? What are invoked are in the first place images, and that is why images have a special importance. I do not for a moment deny that the deep emotion of a true prayer may reach transcendence, but it is above our heads. There would not even be any transcendence if our images and metaphors were more than anthropomorphism and the words themselves had a magical effect. The Catholic Church protects itself against this insinuation *expressis verbis,* insisting on its teaching that God cannot go back on his own institutions. He is morally obliged to maintain them by his Holy Spirit or his

[5] [*Apostolic Constitution ("Munificentissimus Deus") of Pius XII* (1950), sec. 33: ". . . on this day the Virgin Mother was taken up to her heavenly bridal-chamber." Cf. "Answer to Job" (C.W., vol. 11), par. 743, n. 4.]
[6] [Count Nikolaus Ludwig von Zinzendorf (1700-60), founder of the Herrnhuter Brüdergemeinde, a community of Moravian Brethren.]
[7] [Caux-sur-Montreux, Switzerland, a conference centre of the Moral Re-Armament movement. A World Assembly was held there in 1949.]

grace. All theological preaching is a mythologem, a series of archetypal images intended to give a more or less exact description of
the unimaginable transcendence. It is a paradox, but it is justified.
The totality of these archetypes corresponds to what I have called
the *collective unconscious*. *We are concerned here with empirical
facts, as I have proved.* (Incidentally, you don't seem to be well
informed about either the nature of the unconscious or my psychology. The idea that the unconscious is the abyss of all the horrors
is a bit out of date. The collective unconscious is neutral; it is only
nature, both spiritual and chthonic. To impute to my psychology
the idea that the Holy Spirit is "only a projection of the human
soul" is false. He is a transcendental fact which presents itself to
us under the guise of an archetypal image (e.g, [   ][8], or are
we to believe that he is really "breathed forth" by the Father and
the Son?). There is no guarantee that this image corresponds exactly to the transcendental entity.

1537   The unconscious is ambivalent; it can produce both good and
evil effects. So the image of God also has two sides, like YHWH
or the God of Clement of Rome with two hands; the right is Christ,
the left Satan, and it is with these two hands that he rules the
world.[9] Nicholas of Cusa calls God a *complexio oppositorum* (naturally under the apotropaic condition of the *privatio boni*!).
YHWH's paradoxical qualities are continued in the New Testament. In these circumstances it becomes very difficult to know what
to make of *prayer*. Can we address our prayer to the good God
to the exclusion of the demon, as Schweitzer recommends? Have
we the power of dissociating God like the countrywoman who said
to the child Jesus, when he interrupted her prayer to the Virgin:
"Shhh, child, I'm talking to your mother"? Can we really put on
one side the God who is dangerous to us? Do we believe that God
is so powerless that we can say to him: "Get out, I'm talking to
your better half?" Or can we ignore the *absconditus?* Schweitzer
invites us to do just this; we're going to have our bathe in the
river, and never mind the crocodiles. One can, it seems, brush them
aside. Who is there who can produce this "simple faith"?

1538   Like God, then, the unconscious has two aspects; one good,
favourable, beneficent, the other evil, malevolent, disastrous. The
unconscious is the immediate source of our religious experiences.
This psychic nature of all experience does not mean that the tran-

8 [Lacuna in the file copy of the letter.]
9 [Cf. *Aion*, C.W., vol. 9, ii, pars. 99ff.]

scendental realities are also psychic; the physicist does not believe that the transcendental reality represented by his psychic model is also psychic. He calls it *matter,* and in the same way the psychologist in no wise attributes a psychic nature to his images or archetypes. He calls them "psychoids"[10] and is convinced that they represent transcendental realities. He even knows of "simple faith" as that *conviction which one cannot avoid.* It is vain to seek for it; it comes when it wills, for it is the gift of the Holy Spirit. There is only one divine spirit—an immediate presence, often terrifying and in no degree subject to our choice. There is no guarantee that it may not just as well be the devil, as happened to St. Ignatius Loyola in his vision of the *serpens oculatus,* interpreted at first as Christ or God and later as the devil.[11] Nicholas of Flüe had his terrifying vision of the *absconditus,* and transformed it later into the kindly Trinity of the parish church of Sachseln.[12]

1539   Surrender to God is a formidable adventure, and as "simple" as any situation over which man has no control. He who can risk himself wholly to it finds himself directly in the hands of God, and is there confronted with a situation which makes "simple faith" a vital necessity; in other words, the situation becomes so full of risk or overtly dangerous that the deepest instincts are aroused. An experience of this kind is always numinous, for it unites all aspects of totality. All this is wonderfully expressed in Christian religious symbolism: the divine will incarnate in Christ urges towards the fatal issue, the catastrophe followed by the fact or hope of resurrection, while Christian faith insists on the deadly danger of the adventure; but the Churches assure us that God protects us against all danger and especially against the fatality of our character. Instead of taking up our cross, we are told to cast it on Christ. He will take on the burden of our anguish and we can enjoy our "simple faith" at Caux. We take flight into the Christian collectivity where we can forget even the will of God, for in society we lose the feeling of personal responsibility and can swim with the current. One feels safe in the multitude, and the Church does everything to reassure us against the fear of God, as if it did not believe that He could bring about a serious situation. On the other hand psychology is painted as black as possible, because it teaches, in full agreement

[10] [Cf. *Mysterium Coniunctionis,* C.W., vol. 14, pars. 786f.]
[11] [Cf. "On the Nature of the Psyche" (C.W., vol. 8), par. 395.]
[12] [Cf. "Brother Klaus" (C.W., vol. 11) and "Archetypes of the Collective Unconscious" (C.W., vol. 9, i), pars. 12ff.]

with the Christian creed, that no man can ascend unless he has first descended. A professor of theology once accused me publicly that "in flagrant contradiction to the words of Christ" I had criticized as *childish* the man who remains an infant retaining his early beliefs. I had to remind him of the fact that Christ never said "remain children" but "become like children." This is one small example of the way in which Christian experience is falsified; it is prettied up, its sombre aspects are denied, its dangers are hidden. But the action of the Holy Spirit does not meet us in the atmosphere of a normal, bourgeois (or proletarian!), sheltered, regular life, but only in the insecurity outside the human economy, in the infinite spaces where one is alone with the *providentia Dei*. We must never forget that Christ was an innovator and revolutionary, *executed with criminals*. The reformers and great religious geniuses were *heretics*. It is there that you find the footprints of the Holy Spirit, and no one asks for him or receives him *without having to pay a high price*. The price is so high that no one today would dare to suggest that he possesses or is possessed by the Holy Spirit, or he would be too close to the psychiatric clinic. The danger of making oneself ridiculous is too real, not to mention the risk of offending our real god: *respectability*. There one even becomes very strict, and it would not be at all allowable for God and his Spirit to permit themselves to give advice or orders as in the Old Testament. Certainly everyone would lay his irregularities to the account of the unconscious. One would say: God is faithful, he does not forsake us, God does not lie, he will keep his word, and so on. We know it isn't true, but we go on repeating these lies ad infinitum. It is quite understandable that we should seek to hold the truth at arm's length, because it seems impossible to give oneself up to a God who doesn't even respect his own laws when he falls victim to one of his fits of rage or forgets his solemn oath. When I allow myself to mention these well-attested facts the theologians accuse me of blasphemy, unwilling as they are to admit the ambivalence of the divine nature, the demonic character of the God of the Bible and even of the Christian God. Why was that cruel immolation of the Son necessary if the anger of the "deus ultionum" is not hard to appease? One doesn't notice much of the Father's goodness and love during the tragic end of his Son.

1540   True, we ought to abandon ourselves to the divine will as much as we can, but admit that to do so is difficult and dangerous, so dangerous indeed that I would not dare to advise one of my clients to "take" the Holy Spirit or to abandon himself to him until I had first made him realize the risks of such an enterprise.

1541   Permit me here to make a few comments. On pp. 11f.: The Holy Spirit is to be feared. He is revolutionary *especially* in religious matters (not at all "perhaps even religious," p. 11 bottom). Ah, yes, one does well to refuse the Holy Spirit, because people would like to palm him off on us without telling us what this sacred fire is which killeth and maketh to live. One may get through a battle without being wounded, but there are some unfortunates who do not know how to avoid either mutilation or death. Perhaps one is among their number. One can hardly take the risk of that without the most convincing necessity. It is quite normal and reasonable to refuse oneself to the Holy Spirit. Has M. Boegner's[13] life been turned upside down? Has he taken the risk of breaking with convention (e.g., eating with Gentiles when one is an orthodox Jew, or even better with women of doubtful reputation), or been immersed in darkness like Hosea, making himself ridiculous, overturning the traditional order, etc.? It is deeds that are needed, not words.

1542   p. 13. It is very civil to say that the Holy Spirit is "uncomfortable and sometimes upsetting," but very characteristic.

1543   p. 16. It is clear that the Holy Spirit is concerned in the long run with the collectivity (*ecclesia*), but in the first place with the individual, and to create him he isolates him from his environment, just as Christ himself was thought mad by his own family.

1544   p. 19. The Holy Spirit, "the accredited bearer of the holiness of God." But who will recognize him as such? Everyone will certainly say that he is drunk or a heretic or mad. To the description "bearer of the holiness" needs to be added the holiness which God himself sometimes sets on one side (Ps. 89).

1545   p. 21. It is no use for Mr. Horton to believe that receiving the Holy Spirit is quite a simple business. It is so to the degree that we do not realize what is at issue. We are surrendering ourselves to a Spirit with two aspects. That is why we are not particularly ready to "drink" of him, or to "thirst" for him. We hope rather that God is going to pass us by, that we are protected against his injustice and his violence. Granted, the New Testament speaks otherwise, but when we get to the Apocalypse the style changes remarkably and approximates to that of older times. Christ's kingdom has been provisional; the world is left thereafter for another aeon to Antichrist and to all the horrors that can be envisaged by a pitiless

[13] [Unidentified.]

and loveless imagination. This witness in favour of the god with two faces represents the last and tragic chapter of the New Testament which would like to have set up a god exclusively good and made only of love. This Apocalypse—was it a frightful gaffe on the part of those Fathers who drew up the canon? I don't think so. They were still too close to the hard reality of things and of religious traditions to share our mawkish interpretations and prettily falsified opinions.

1546   p. 23. "Surrender without the least reserve." Would Mr. Horton advise us to cross the Avenue de l'Opéra blindfold? His belief in the good God is so strong that he has forgotten the fear of God. For Mr. Horton God is dangerous no longer. But in that case— what is the Apocalypse all about? He asks nevertheless, "To what interior dynamism is one surrendering oneself, natural or supernatural?" When he says, "I surrender myself wholly to God," how does he know what is "whole"? Our wholeness is an unconscious fact, whose extent we cannot establish. God alone can judge of human wholeness. We can only say humbly: "As wholly as possible."

1547   There is no guarantee that it is really *God* when we say "god." It is perhaps a word concealing a demon or a void, or it is an act of grace coincident with our prayer.

1548   This total surrender is disturbing. Nearly twenty years ago I gave a course at the Ecole Polytechnique Suisse for two semesters on the *Exercitia Spiritualia* of St. Ignatius.[14] On that occasion I received a profound impression of this total surrender, in relation to which one never knows whether one is dealing with sanctity or with spiritual pride. One sees too that the god to whom one surrenders oneself is a clear and well-defined prescription given by the director of the Exercises. This is particularly evident in the part called the "colloquium," where there is only one who speaks, and that is the initiand. One asks oneself what God or Christ would say if it were a real dialogue, but no one expects God to reply.

1549   p. 26. The identity of Christ with the Holy Spirit seems to me to be questionable, since Christ made a very clear distinction between himself and the paraclete, even if the latter's function resembles Christ's. The near-identity of the Holy Spirit with Christ in St. John's Gospel is characteristic of the evangelist's Gnosticism.

[14] [Lectures at the Federal Polytechnic Institute (ETH), Zurich, June 1939 to March 1940. Privately issued.]

It seems to me important to insist on the chronological sequence of the Three Persons, for there is an evolution in three stages:

1. The Father. The opposites not yet differentiated; Satan is still numbered among the "sons of God." Christ then is only hinted at.

2. God is incarnated as the "Son of Man." Satan has fallen from heaven. He is the other "son." The opposites are differentiated.

3. The Holy Spirit is One, his prototype is the Ruach Elohim, an emanation, an active principle, which proceeds (as quintessence) *a Patre Filioque.* Inasmuch as he proceeds also from the Son he is different from the Ruach Elohim, who represents the active principle of Yahweh (not incarnate, with only angels in place of a son). The angels are called "sons," they are not begotten and there is no mother of the angels. Christ on the other hand shares in human nature, he is even man by definition. In this case it is evident that the Holy Spirit proceeding from the Son does not arise from the divine nature only, that is, from the second Person, but also from the human nature. Thanks to this fact, human nature is included in the mystery of the Trinity. Man forms part of it.

¹⁵⁵⁰   This "human nature" is only figuratively human, for it is exempt from original sin. This makes the "human" element definitely doubtful inasmuch as man without exception, save for Christ and his mother, is begotten and born bearing the stamp of the *macula peccati.* That is why Christ and his mother enjoy a nature divine rather than human. For the Protestant there is no reason to think of Mary as a goddess. Thus he can easily admit that on his mother's side Christ was contaminated by original sin; this makes him all the more human, at least so far as the *filioque* of the Protestant confession does not exclude the true man from the "human" nature of Christ. On the other hand it becomes evident that the Holy Spirit necessarily proceeds *from the two natures* of Christ, not only from the God in him, but also from the man in him.

¹⁵⁵¹   There were very good reasons why the Catholic Church has carefully purified Christ and his mother from all contamination by the *peccatum originale.* Protestantism was more courageous, even daring or—perhaps?—more oblivious of the consequences, in not denying—*expressis verbis*—the human nature (in part) of Christ and (wholly) of his mother. *Thus the ordinary man became a source of the Holy Spirit,* though certainly not the only one. It is like lightning, which issues not only from the clouds but also

from the peaks of the mountains. This fact signifies the continued and progressive divine incarnation. Thus man is received and integrated into the divine drama. He seems destined to play a decisive part in it; that is why he must receive the Holy Spirit. I look upon the receiving of the Holy Spirit as a highly revolutionary fact which cannot take place until the ambivalent nature of the Father is recognized. If God is the *summum bonum*, the incarnation makes no sense, for a good god could never produce such hate and anger that his only son had to be sacrificed to appease it. A Midrash says that the Shofar is still sounded on the Day of Atonement to remind YHWH of his act of injustice towards Abraham (by compelling him to slay Isaac) and to prevent him from repeating it. A conscientious clarification of the idea of God would have consequences as upsetting as they are necessary. They would be indispensable for an interior development of the trinitarian drama and of the role of the Holy Spirit. The Spirit is destined to be incarnate in man or to choose him as a transitory dwelling-place. "Non habet nomen proprium," says St. Thomas;[15] because he will receive the name of man. That is why he must not be identified with Christ. We cannot receive the Holy Spirit unless we have accepted our own individual life as Christ accepted his. Thus we become the "sons of god" fated to experience the conflict of the divine opposites, represented by the crucifixion.

1552   Man seems indispensable to the divine drama. We shall understand this role of man's better if we consider the paradoxical nature of the Father. As the Apocalypse has alluded to it (*evangelium aeternum*) and Joachim of Flora[16] has expressed it, the Son would seem to be the intermediary between the Father and the Holy Spirit. We could repeat what Origen said of the Three Persons, that the Father is the greatest and the Holy Spirit the least. This is true inasmuch as the Father by descending from the cosmic immensity became the least by incarnating himself within the narrow bounds of the human soul (cult of the child-god, Angelus Silesius). Doubtless the presence of the Holy Spirit enlarges human nature by divine attributes. Human nature is the divine vessel and as such the union of the Three. This results in a kind of quaternity which always signifies *totality*, while the triad is rather a process, but never the natural division of the *circle*, the natural symbol of wholeness. The quaternity as union of the Three seems to be aimed at by the

15 ["He has no proper name." *Summa theologica*, I, xxvi, art. 1.]
16 [The "everlasting gospel" in Rev. 14:7 is "Fear God." For Joachim's view, see *Aion*, pars. 137ff.]

Assumption of Mary. This dogma adds the feminine element to the masculine Trinity, the terrestrial element (*virgo terra!*) to the spiritual, and thus sinful man to the Godhead. For Mary in her character of *omnium gratiarum mediatrix* intercedes for the sinner before the judge of the world. (She is his "paraclete.") She is φιλάνθρωπος like her prefiguration, the Sophia of the Old Testament.[17] Protestant critics have completely overlooked the symbolic aspect of the new dogma and its emotional value, which is a capital fault.

1553   The "littleness" of the Holy Spirit stems from the fact that God's pneuma dissolves into the form of little flames, remaining none the less intact and whole. His dwelling in a certain number of human individuals and their transformation into υἱῷ τοῦ θεοῦ signifies a very important step forward beyond "Christocentrism." Anyone who takes up the question of the Holy Spirit seriously is faced with the question whether Christ is identical with the Holy Spirit or different from him. With dogma, I prefer the independence of the Holy Spirit. The Holy Spirit is *one,* a *complexio oppositorum,* in contrast to YHWH after the separation of the divine opposites symbolized by God's two sons, Christ and Satan. On the level of the Son there is no answer to the question of good and evil; there is only an incurable separation of the opposites. The annulling of evil by the *privatio boni* (declaring to be μὴ ὄν) is a *petitio principii* of the most flagrant kind and no solution whatever.[18] It seems to me to be the Holy Spirit's task and charge to reconcile and reunite the opposites in the human individual through a special development of the human soul. The soul is paradoxical like the Father; it is black and white, divine and demon-like, in its primitive and natural state. By the discriminative function of its conscious side it separates opposites of every kind, and especially those of the moral order personified in Christ and Devil. Thereby the soul's spiritual development creates an enormous tension, from which man can only suffer. Christ promised him redemption. But in what exactly does this consist? The *imitatio Christi* leads us to Calvary and to the annihilation of the "body," that is, of biological life, and if we take this death as symbolic it is a state of suspension between the opposites, that is to say, an unresolved conflict. That is exactly what Przywara has named the "rift,"[19] the gulf separating good from evil, the latent and apparently incurable dualism of

[17] [Cf. "Answer to Job," pars. 613ff.]
[18] [Cf. *Aion,* pars. 89ff.]
[19] [Erich Przywara, *Deus semper maior,* I, pp. 71f.]

Christianity, the eternity of the devil and of damnation. (Inasmuch as good is real so also is evil.)

1554   To find the answer to this question we can but trust to our mental powers on the one hand and on the other to the functioning of the unconscious, that spirit which we cannot control. It can only be hoped that it is a "holy" spirit. The cooperation of conscious reasoning with the data of the unconscious is called the "transcendent function" (cf. *Psychological Types,* par. 828).[20] This function progressively unites the opposites. Psychotherapy makes use of it to heal neurotic dissociations, but this function had already served as the basis of Hermetic philosophy for seventeen centuries. Besides this, it is a natural and spontaneous phenomenon, part of the process of individuation. Psychology has no proof that this process does not unfold itself at the instigation of God's will.

1555   The Holy Spirit will manifest himself in any case in the psychic sphere of man and will be presented as a psychic experience. He thus becomes the object of empirical psychology, which he will need in order to translate his symbolism into the possibilities of this world. Since his intention is the incarnation, that is, the realization of the divine being in human life, he cannot be a light which the darkness comprehendeth not. On the contrary, he needs the support of man and his understanding to comprehend the *mysterium iniquitatis* which began in paradise before man existed. (The serpent owes his existence to God and by no means to man. The idea: *omne bonum a Deo, omne malum ab homine* is an entirely false one.) YHWH is inclined to find the cause of evil in men, but he evidently represents a moral antinomy accompanied by an almost complete lack of reflection. For example, he seems to have forgotten that he created his son Satan and kept him among the other "sons of God" until the coming of Christ—a strange oversight!

1556   The data of the collective unconscious favour the hypothesis of a paradoxical creator such as YHWH. An entirely good Father seems to have very little probability; such a character is difficult to admit, seeing that Christ himself endeavoured to reform his Father. He didn't completely succeed, even in his own logia. Our unconscious resembles this paradoxical God. That is why man is faced with a psychological condition which does not let him differentiate himself from the image of God (YHWH). Naturally we can believe that God is different from the image of him that we possess, but it must be admitted on the other side that the Lord

20 [Cf. also "The Transcendent Function" (C.W., vol. 8).]

himself, while insisting on the Father's perfect goodness, has given a picture of him which fits in badly with the idea of a perfectly moral being. (A father who tempts his children, who did not prevent the error of the immediate parousia, who is so full of wrath that the blood of his only son is necessary to appease him, who left the crucified one to despair, who proposes to devastate his own creation and slay the millions of mankind to save a very few of them, and who before the end of the world is going to replace his Son's covenant by another gospel and complement the love by the fear of God.) It is interesting, or rather tragic, that God undergoes a complete relapse in the last book of the New Testament. But in the case of an antinomian being we could expect no other development. The opposites are kept in balance, and so the kingdom of Christ is followed by that of Antichrist. In the circumstances the Holy Spirit, the third form of God, becomes of extreme importance, for it is thanks to him that the man of good will is drawn towards the divine drama and mingled in it, and the Spirit is *one*. In him the opposites are separated no longer.

1557   Begging you to excuse the somewhat heretical character of my thoughts as well as their imperfect presentation, I remain, dear monsieur, yours sincerely,

C. G. JUNG

ON RESURRECTION[1]

1558   You are quite right: I have never dealt with all aspects of the Christ-figure for the simple reason that it would have been too much. I am not a theologian and I have had no time to acquire all the knowledge that is wanted in order to attempt the solution of such problems as that of the Resurrection.

1559   Indubitably resurrection is one of the most—if not the most—important item in the myth or the biography of Christ and in the history of the primitive church.

1. Resurrection as a historical fact in the biography of Jesus

1560   Three Gospels have a complete report about the postmortal events after the Crucifixion. Mark, however, mentions only the open and empty tomb and the presence of the angel, while the apparition of the visible body of Christ has been reported by a later hand in an obvious addendum. The first report about the resurrected Christ is made by Mary Magdalene, from whom Christ had driven out seven devils. This annotation has a peculiarly cursory character (cf. in particular Mark 11:19),[2] as if somebody had realized that Mark's report was altogether too meagre and that the usual things told about Christ's death ought to be added for the sake of completeness.

1561   The earliest source about the Resurrection is St. Paul, and he is no eyewitness, but he strongly emphasizes the absolute and vital importance of resurrection as well as the authenticity of the reports. (Cf. I Cor. 15:14ff and 15:5ff.) He mentions Cephas (Peter) as the first witness, then the twelve, then the five hundred, then James,

---

[1] [Written in English, 19 Feb. 1954, in reply to an inquiry from Martha Dana, Peggy Gerry, and Marian Reith, members of a seminar on Jung's *Aion* led by Dr. James Kirsch, Los Angeles, 1953–54, during which (Dr. Kirsch has stated) "every line of the book was read and commented upon. While the seminar was in progress Mrs. Dana, Mrs. Gerry, and Mrs. Reith became curious about the fact that in all of the writings of Jung they had not found any commentary on the idea of Resurrection . . . [which] seemed to be the central event in the Christ story, and they therefore wondered why Jung had not said anything about it."]

[2] [Evidently an error for 16:9ff.]

then the apostles, and finally himself. This is interesting, since his experience was quite clearly an understandable vision, while the later reports insist upon the material concreteness of Christ's body (particularly Luke 24:42 and John 20:24ff.). The evangelical testimonies agree with each other only about the emptiness of the tomb, but not at all about the chronology of the eyewitnesses. There the tradition becomes utterly unreliable. If one adds the story about the end of Judas, who must have been a very interesting object to the hatred of the Christians, our doubts of the Resurrection story are intensified: there are two absolutely different versions of the way of his death.

1562   *The fact of the Resurrection is historically doubtful.* If we extend the *beneficium dubii* to those contradictory statements we could consider the possibility of an individual as well as collective vision (less likely of a materialization).

1563   The conclusion drawn by the ancient Christians—since Christ has risen from the dead so shall we rise in a new and incorruptible body—is of course just what St. Paul has feared most,[3] viz., invalid and as vain as the expectation of the immediate parousia, which has come to naught.

1564   As the many shocking miracle-stories in the Gospels show, spiritual reality could not be demonstrated to the uneducated and rather primitive population in any other way but by crude and tangible "miracles" or stories of such kind. Concretism was unavoidable with all its grotesque implications—for example, the believers in Christ were by the grace of God to be equipped with a glorified body at their resurrection, and the unbelievers and unredeemed sinners were too, so that they could be plagued in hell or purgatory for any length of time. An incorruptible body was necessary for the latter performance, otherwise damnation would have come to an end in no time.

1565   Under those conditions, resurrection as a historical and concrete fact cannot be maintained, whereas the vanishing of the corpse could be a real fact.

2. *Resurrection as a psychological event*

1566   The facts here are perfectly clear and well documented: The life of the God-man on earth comes to an end with his resurrection and transition to heaven. This is firm belief since the beginning

---

[3] "If Christ be not risen, then is our preaching vain, and your faith is also vain" (I Cor. 15:14).

of Christianity. In mythology it belongs to the hero that he conquers death and brings back to life his parents, tribal ancestors, etc. He has a more perfect, richer, and stronger personality than the ordinary mortal. Although he is also mortal himself, death does not annihilate his existence: he continues living in a somewhat modified form. On a higher level of civilization he approaches the type of the dying and resurrected god, like Osiris, who becomes the greater personality in every individual (like the Johannine Christ), viz., his τέλειος ἄνθρωπος, the complete (or perfect) man, the self.

1567   The self as an archetype represents a numinous wholeness, which can be expressed only by symbols (e.g., mandala, tree, etc.). As a collective image it reaches beyond the individual in time and space[4] and is therefore not subjected to the corruptibility of *one* body: the realization of the self is nearly always connected with the feeling of timelessness, "eternity," or immortality. (Cf. the personal and superpersonal ātman.) We do not know what an archetype is (i.e., consists of), since the nature of the psyche is inaccessible to us, but we know that archetypes exist and work.

1568   From this point of view it is no longer difficult to see to what degree the story of the Resurrection represents the projection of an indirect realization of the self that had appeared in the figure of a certain man, Jesus of Nazareth, of whom many rumors were circulating.[5] In those days the old gods had ceased to be significant. Their power had already been replaced by the concrete one of the visible god, the Caesar, whose sacrifices were the only obligatory ones. But this substitution was as unsatisfactory as that of God by the communistic state. It was a frantic and desperate attempt to create—out of no matter how doubtful material—a spiritual monarch, a *pantokrator,* in opposition to the concretized divinity in Rome. (What a joke of the *esprit d'escalier* of history—the substitution for the Caesar of the pontifical office of St. Peter!)

1569   Their need of a spiritual authority then became so particularly urgent, because there was only one divine individual, the Caesar, while all the others were anonymous and hadn't even private gods listening to their prayers.[6] They took therefore to magic of all kinds.

---

[4] Cf. the so-called parapsychological phenomena.

[5] Cf. the passage about Christ in the Church Slavonic text of Josephus, *The Jewish War,* in G.R.S. Mead, *The Gnostic John the Baptizer,* pp. 97ff. [= ch. III: "The Slavonic Josephus' Account of the Baptist and Jesus," pp. 106ff.]

[6] Their condition was worse than that of the Egyptians in the last pre-Christian centuries: these had already acquired an individual Osiris. As a matter of fact, Egypt turned Christian at once with no hesitation.

Our actual situation is pretty much the same: we are rapidly becoming the slaves of an anonymous state as the highest authority ruling our lives. Communism has realized this ideal in the most perfect way. Unfortunately our democracy has nothing to offer in the way of different ideals; it also believes in the concrete power of the state. There is no spiritual authority comparable to that of the state anywhere. We are badly in need of a spiritual counterbalance to the ultimately bolshevistic concretism. It is again the case of the "witnesses" against the Caesar.

1570   The gospel writers were as eager as St. Paul to heap miraculous qualities and spiritual significances upon that almost unknown young rabbi, who after a career lasting perhaps only one year had met with an untimely end. What they made of him we know, but we don't know to what extent this picture has anything to do with the truly historical man, smothered under an avalanche of projections. Whether he was the eternally living Christ and Logos, we don't know. It makes no difference anyhow, since the image of the God-man lives in everybody and has been incarnated (i.e., projected) in the man Jesus, to make itself visible, so that people could realize him as their own interior *homo,* their self.

1571   Thus they had regained their human dignity: everybody had divine nature. Christ had told them: *Dii estis:* "ye are gods"; and as such they were his brethren, of his nature, and had overcome annihilation either through the power of the Caesar or through physical death. They were "resurrected with Christ."

1572   Since we are psychic beings and not entirely dependent upon space and time, we can easily understand the central importance of the resurrection idea: we are not completely subjected to the powers of annihilation because our psychic totality reaches beyond the barrier of space and time. Through the progressive integration of the unconscious we have a reasonable chance to make experiences of an archetypal nature providing us with the feeling of continuity before and after our existence. The better we understand the archetype, the more we participate in its life and the more we realize its eternity or timelessness.

1573   As roundness signifies completeness or perfection, it also expresses rotation (the rolling movement) or progress on an endless circular way, an identity with the sun and the stars (hence the beautiful confession in the "Mithraic Liturgy"; ἐγώ εἰμι σύμπλανος ὑμῖν ἀστήρ ("I am a Star following his way like you"). The realization of the self also means a re-establishment of Man as the microcosm, i.e., man's cosmic relatedness. Such realizations are frequently accompanied by synchronistic events. (The prophetic experience of vocation belongs to this category.)

1574   To the primitive Christians as to all primitives, the Resurrection had to be a concrete, materialistic event to be seen by the eyes and touched by the hands, as if the spirit had no existence of its own. Even in modern times people cannot easily grasp the reality of a psychic event, unless it is concrete at the same time. Resurrection as a psychic event is certainly not concrete, it is just a psychic experience. It is funny that the Christians are still so pagan that they understand spiritual existence only as a body and as a physical event. I am afraid our Christian churches cannot maintain this shocking anachronism any longer, if they don't want to get into intolerable contradictions. As a concession to this criticism, certain theologians have explained St. Paul's glorified (subtle) body given back to the dead on the day of judgment as the authentic individual "form," viz., a spiritual idea sufficiently characteristic of the individual that the material body could be skipped. It was the evidence for man's survival after death and the hope to escape eternal damnation that made resurrection in the body the mainstay of Christian faith. We know positively only of the fact that space and time are relative to the psyche.

ON THE DISCOURSES OF THE BUDDHA[1]

¹575   It was neither the history of religion nor the study of philosophy that first drew me to the world of Buddhist thought, but my professional interests as a doctor. My task was the treatment of psychic suffering, and it was this that impelled me to become acquainted with the views and methods of that great teacher of humanity whose principal theme was the "chain of suffering, old age, sickness, and death." For although the healing of the sick naturally lies closest to the doctor's heart, he is bound to recognize that there are many diseases and states of suffering which, not being susceptible of a direct cure, demand from both patient and doctor some kind of attitude to their irremediable nature. Even though it may not amount to actual incurability, in all such cases there are inevitably phases of stagnation and hopelessness which seem unendurable and require treatment just as much as a direct symptom of illness. They call for a kind of moral attitude such as is provided by religious faith or a philosophical belief. In this respect the study of Buddhist literature was of great help to me, since it trains one to observe suffering objectively and to take a universal view of its causes. According to tradition, it was by objectively observing the chain of causes that the Buddha was able to extricate his consciousness from the snares of the ten thousand things, and to rescue his feelings from the entanglements of emotion and illusion. So also in our sphere of culture the suffering and the sick can derive considerable benefit from this prototype of the Buddhist mentality, however strange it may appear.

¹576   The discourses of the Buddha, here presented in K. E. Neumann's new translation, have an importance that should not be

---

[1] [Statement in the publisher's prospectus for *Die Reden Gotamo Buddhos*, translated from the Pali Canon by Karl Eugen Neumann, 3 vols. Zurich, Stuttgart, Vienna, 1956). Statements were also contributed to the prospectus by Thomas Mann and Albert Schweitzer. Neumann (1865–1915) had published an earlier version of his translation in 1911, which Jung cited in *Wandlungen und Symbole der Libido* (1911–12); cf. *Psychology of the Unconscious* (New York, 1916), p. 538, n. 25. The present statement was published as "Zu *Die Reden Gotamo Buddhos*" in *Gesam. Werke*, XI, Anhang.]

underestimated. Quite apart from their profound meaning, their solemn, almost ritual form emits a penetrating radiance which has an exhilarating and exalting effect and cannot fail to work directly upon one's feelings. Against this use of the spiritual treasures of the East it might be—and indeed, often has been—objected from the Christian point of view that the faith of the West offers consolations that are at least as significant, and that there is no need to invoke the spirit of Buddhism with its markedly rational attitude. Aside from the fact that in most cases the Christian faith of which people speak simply isn't there, and no one can tell how it might be obtained (except by the special providence of God), it is a truism that anything known becomes so familiar and hackneyed by frequent use that it gradually loses its meaning and hence its effect; whereas anything strange and unknown, and so completely different in its nature, can open doors hitherto locked and new possibilities of understanding. If a Christian insists so much on his faith when it does not even help him to ward off a neurosis, then his faith is vain, and it is better to accept humbly what he needs no matter where he finds it, if only it helps. There is no need for him to deny his religion convictions if he acknowledges his debt to Buddhism, for he is only following the Pauline injunction: "Prove all things; hold fast that which is good" (I Thess. 5:21).

1577   To this good which should be held fast one must reckon the discourses of the Buddha, which have much to offer even to those who cannot boast of any Christian convictions. They offer Western man ways and means of disciplining his inner psychic life, thus remedying an often regrettable defect in the various brands of Christianity. The teachings of the Buddha can give him a helpful training when either the Christian ritual has lost its meaning or the authority of religious ideas has collapsed, as all too frequently happens in psychogenic disorders.

1578   People have often accused me of regarding religion as "mental hygiene." Perhaps one may pardon a doctor his professional humility in not undertaking to prove the truth of metaphysical assertions and in shunning confessions of faith. I am content to emphasize the importance of having a *Weltanschauung* and the therapeutic necessity of adopting some kind of attitude to the problem of psychic suffering. Suffering that is not understood is hard to bear, while on the other hand it is often astounding to see how much a person can endure when he understands the why and the wherefore. A philosophical or religious view of the world enables him to do this, and such views prove to be, at the very least, psychic methods of healing if not of salvation. Even Christ and his disciples did not scorn to heal the sick, thereby demonstrating the therapeutic power of their mission. The doctor has to cope with actual suffering for better or worse, and ultimately has nothing to rely on except the mystery of divine Providence. It is no wonder, then, that he values religious ideas and attitudes, so far as they prove helpful, as therapeutic systems, and singles out the Buddha in particular, the essence of whose teaching is deliverance from suffering through the maximum development of consciousness, as one of the supreme helpers on the road to salvation. From ancient times physicians have sought a panacea, a *medicina catholica,* and their persistent efforts have unconsciously brought them nearer to the central ideas of the religion and philosophy of the East.

1579   Anyone who is familiar with methods of suggestion under hypnosis knows that plausible suggestions work better than those which run counter to the patient's own nature. Consequently, whether he liked it or not, the doctor was obliged to develop conceptions which corresponded as closely as possible with the actual psychological conditions. Thus, there grew up a realm of theory which not only drew upon traditional thought but took account of the unconscious products that compensated its inevitable one-sidedness—that is to say, all those psychic factors which Christian philosophy left unsatisfied. Among these were not a few aspects which, unknown to the West, had been developed in Eastern philosophy from very early times.

1580   So if, as a doctor, I acknowledge the immense help and stimulation I have received from the Buddhist teachings, I am following a line which can be traced back some two thousand years in the history of human thought.

FOREWORD TO FROBOESE-THIELE:
"TRÄUME — EINE QUELLE RELIGIÖSER ERFAHRUNG?"[1]

1581   This book has the merit of being the first to investigate how the unconscious of Protestants behaves when it has to compensate an intensely religious attitude. The author examines this question with the help of case material she has collected in her practical work. She has evidently had the good fortune to come upon some very instructive cases who, moreover, did not object to the publication of their material. Since we owe our knowledge of unconscious processes primarily to dreams, the author is mainly concerned with the dreams of her patients. Even for one familiar with this material, the dreams and symbols reported here are remarkable. As a therapist, she handles the dreams in a very felicitous manner, from the practical side chiefly, so that a reciprocal understanding of the meaning of the dream is gradually built up between her and the patient. This puts the reader in the advantageous position of listening in on a dialogue, so to speak. The method is as instructive as it is satisfying, since it is possible to present in this way several fairly long sequences of dreams. A detailed scientific commentary would take up a disproportionate amount of space without making the dream interpretation any more impressive. If the interpretation is at times uncertain, or disregards various details, this in no way affects the therapeutic intention to bring the meaning of the dream nearer to consciousness. In actual practice, one can often do full justice to a dream if one simply puts its general tendency, its emotional atmosphere, and its approximate meaning in the right light, having first, of course, assured oneself of the spontaneous approval of the dreamer. With intelligent persons, this thoughtful feeling of one's way into the meaning of the dream can soon be left to the patient himself.

1582   The author has been entirely successful in bringing out the religious meaning of the dreams and so demonstrating her thesis. A

---

[1] [Göttingen, 1957. By Felicia Froboese-Thiele. ("Dreams—a Source of Religious Experience?")]

religious attitude does in fact offer a direct challenge to the unconscious, and the more inimical the conscious attitude is to life, the more forceful and drastic will be this unconscious reaction. It serves the purpose, firstly, of compensating the extremism of the conscious attitude and, secondly, of individuation, since it re-establishes the approximate wholeness of the personality.

1583   The material which Dr. Froboese-Thiele has made available in her book is of considerable importance for doctors and theologians alike, since both of them have here an opportunity to assure themselves that the unconscious possesses a religious aspect against which no cogent arguments can be mustered. One is left with a feeling of shame that so little of the empirical case material which would give the layman an adequate idea of these religious processes has been published. The author deserves our special thanks for having taken the trouble to write up these exacting cases *in extenso*. I hope her book will come into the hands of many thoughtful persons whose minds are not stopped up with needless prejudices, and who would be in a position to find a satisfactory answer to religious questions, or at least to come by those experiences which ought to underlie any authentic religious convictions.

JUNG AND RELIGIOUS BELIEF[1]

1. Questions to Jung and His Answers[2]

QUESTION 1. *You say that religion is psychically healthy and often for the latter part of life essential, but is it not psychically healthy only if the religious person believes that his religion is true?*

Do you think that in your natural wish to keep to the realm of psychology you have tended to underestimate man's search for truth and the ways in which he might reach this as, for example, by inference?

1584   Nobody is more convinced of the importance of the search for truth than I am. But when I say: something transcendental is true, my critique begins. If I call something true, it does not mean that it is absolutely true. It merely seems to be true to myself and/or to other people. If I were not doubtful in this respect it would mean that I implicitly assume that I am able to state an absolute truth. This is an obvious hybris. When Mr. Erich Fromm[3] criticizes

---

[1] [Extracts from H. L. Philp, *Jung and the Problem of Evil* (London, 1958). The book consists of correspondence between the author and Jung in the form of questions and answers (in English), and an extended critical attack of 175 pages on Jung's writings on religion, with particular reference to *Answer to Job*. It concludes with Jung's answers to questions sent by another correspondent, the Rev. David Cox (author of *Jung and St. Paul,* 1959). In both cases the answers are reproduced here with minor stylistic revisions and additional footnotes. The bibliographical references to Jung's works have been brought up to date. For other letters from Jung to Philp, see *Letters,* ed. G. Adler, vol. 2.]

[2] [Philp, pp. 8–21. (9 Nov. 1956.)]

[3] [In his question, Philp quoted the following passage from Fromm, *Psychoanalysis and Religion*, pp. 23f.: "Before I present Jung's analysis of religion a critical examination of these methodological premises seems warranted. Jung's use of the concept of truth is not tenable. He states that 'truth is a fact and not a judgment,' that 'an elephant is true because it exists.' But he forgets that truth always and necessarily refers to a judgment and not to a description of a phenomenon which we perceive with our senses and which we denote with a word symbol. Jung then states that an idea is 'psychologically true inasmuch as it exists.' But an idea 'exists' regardless of whether it is a delusion or whether it corresponds to fact. The existence of an idea does

702

me for having a wrong idea and quotes Judaism, Christianity, and Buddhism he demonstrates how illogical his standpoint is, as are the views of those religions themselves, i.e., their truths contradict each other. Judaism has a morally ambivalent God; Christianity a Trinity and Summum Bonum; Buddhism has no God but has interior gods. Their truth is relative and not an absolute truth—if you put them on the same level, as Mr. Fromm does. I naturally admit, and I even strongly believe, that it is of the highest importance to state a "truth." I should be prepared to make transcendental statements, but on one condition: that I state at the same time the possibility of their being untrue. For instance "God is," i.e., is as I think he is. But as I know that I could not possibly form an adequate idea of an all-embracing eternal being, my idea of him is pitifully incomplete; thus the statement "God is not" (so) is equally true and necessary. To make absolute statements is beyond man's reach, although it is ethically indispensable that he give all the credit to his subjective truth, which means that he admits being bound by his conviction to apply it as a principle of his actions. Any human judgment, no matter how great its subjective conviction, is liable to error, particularly judgments concerning transcendental subjects. Mr. Fromm's philosophy has not transcended yet—I am afraid—the level of the twentieth century; but the power-drive of man and his hybris are so great that he believes in an absolutely valid judgment. No scientifically minded person with a sense of intellectual responsibility can allow himself such arrogance. These are the reasons why I insist upon the criterion of *existence*, both in the realm of science and in the realm of religion, and upon immediate and primordial *experience*. Facts are facts and contain no falsity. It is our judgment that introduces the element of deception. To my mind it is more important that an idea exists than that it is true. This despite the fact that it makes a great deal of difference subjectively whether an idea seems to

not make it 'true' in any sense. Even the practising psychiatrist could not work were he not concerned with the truth of an idea, that is, with its relation to the phenomena it tends to portray. Otherwise, he could not speak of a delusion or a paranoid system. But Jung's approach is not only untenable from a psychiatric standpoint; he advocates a standpoint of relativism which though on the surface more friendly to religion than Freud's, is in its spirit fundamentally opposed to religions like Judaism, Christianity, and Buddhism. These consider the striving for truth as one of man's cardinal virtues and obligations and insist that their doctrines whether arrived at by revelation or only by the power of reason are subject to the criterion of truth."]

me to be true or not, though this is a secondary consideration since there is no way of establishing the truth or untruth of a transcendental statement other than by a subjective belief.

QUESTION 2. *Is it possible that you depreciate consciousness through an overvaluation of the unconscious?*

1585   I have never had any tendency to depreciate consciousness by insisting upon the importance of the unconscious. If such a tendency is attributed to me it is due to a sort of optical illusion. Consciousness is the "known," but the unconscious is very little known and my chief efforts are devoted to the elucidation of our unconscious psyche. The result of this is, naturally, that I talk more about the unconscious than about the conscious. Since everybody believes or, at least, tries to believe in the unequivocal superiority of rational consciousness, I have to emphasize the importance of the unconscious irrational forces, to establish a sort of balance. Thus to superficial readers of my writings it looks as if I were giving the unconscious a supreme significance, disregarding consciousness. As a matter of fact the emphasis lies on consciousness as the *conditio sine qua non* of apperception of unconscious contents, and the supreme arbiter in the chaos of unconscious possibilities. My book about *Types* is a careful study of the empirical structure of consciousness. If we had an inferior consciousness, we should all be crazy. The ego and ego-consciousness are of paramount importance. It would be superfluous to emphasize consciousness if it were not in a peculiar compensatory relationship with the unconscious.

1586   People like Demant[4] start from the prejudiced idea that the unconscious is something more or less nasty and archaic that one should get rid of. This is not vouched for by experience. The unconscious is neutral, rather like nature. If it is destructive on the one side, it is as constructive on the other side. It is the source of all sorts of evils and also the matrix of all divine experience and—paradoxical as it may sound—it has brought forth and brings forth consciousness. Such a statement does not mean that the source *originates,* i.e., that the water is created just at the spot where you see the source of a river; it comes from deep down in the mountain and runs along its secret ways before it reaches daylight. When I say, "Here is the source," I only mean the spot where the water becomes visible. The water-simile expresses rather aptly the nature and importance of the unconscious. Where there is no water nothing

---

[4] [Cf. *The Religious Prospect,* pp. 188ff., quoted by Philp in his question.]

lives; where there is too much of it everything drowns. It is the task of consciousness to select the right place where you are not too near and not too far from water; but the water is indispensable. An unfavourable opinion about the unconscious does not enable proper Christians, like Demant, to realize that religious experience, so far as the human mind can grasp it, cannot be distinguished from the experience of so-called unconscious phenomena. A metaphysical being does not as a rule speak through the telephone to you; it usually communicates with man through the medium of the soul, in other words, our unconscious, or rather through its transcendental "psychoid" basis.[5] If one depreciates the unconscious one blocks the channels through which the *aqua gratiae* flows, but one certainly does not incapacitate the devil by this method. Creating obstacles is just his métier.

1587   When St. Paul had the vision of Christ, that vision was a psychic phenomenon—if it was anything. I don't presume to know what the psyche is; I only know that there is a psychic realm in which and from which such manifestations start. It is the place where the *aqua gratiae* springs forth, but it comes, as I know quite well, from the immeasurable depths of the mountain and I don't pretend to know about the secret ways and places the water flows through before it reaches the surface.

1588   As the general manifestations of the unconscious are ambivalent or even ambiguous ("It is a fearful thing to fall into the hands of the living God," Heb. 10:31), decision and discriminating judgment are all-important. We see that particularly clearly in the development of the individuation process, when we have to prevent the patient from either rejecting blindly the data of the unconscious or submitting to them without criticism. (Why has Jacob to fight the angel of the Lord? Because he would be killed if he did not defend his life.) There is no development at all but only a miserable death in a thirsty desert if one thinks one can rule the unconscious by our arbitrary rationalism. That is exactly what the German principle, "Where there is a will, there is a way," tried to do, and you know with what results.

QUESTION 3. *In your "Answer to Job" you state, page 463 (Collected Works, Vol. 11): "I have been asked so often whether I believe in the existence of God or not that I am somewhat concerned lest I be taken for an adherent of 'psychologism' far more*

---

[5] [Cf. "On the Nature of the Psyche" (C.W., vol. 8), par. 368.]

commonly than I suspect." You go on to say, "God is an obvious psychic and non-physical fact," but I feel in the end you do not actually answer the question as to whether or not you believe in the existence of God other than as an archetype. Do you?

This question is important because I should like to answer the kind of objection raised by Glover in his Freud or Jung, *page 163: "Jung's system is fundamentally irreligious. Nobody is to care whether God exists, Jung least of all. All that is necessary is to 'experience' an "attitude' because it 'helps one to live.' "*

1589   An archetype—so far as we can establish it empirically—is an *image*. An image, as the very term denotes, is a picture of something. An archetypal image is like the portrait of an unknown man in a gallery. His name, his biography, his existence in general are unknown, but we assume nevertheless that the picture portrays a once living subject, a man who was real. We find numberless images of God, but we cannot produce the original. There is no doubt in my mind that there is an original behind our images, but it is inaccessible. We could not even be aware of the original since its translation into psychic terms is necessary in order to make it perceptible at all. How would Kant's *Critique of Pure Reason* look when translated into the psychic imagery of a cockroach? And I assume that the difference between man and the creator of all things is immeasurably greater than between a cockroach and man. Why should we be so immodest as to suppose that we could catch a universal being in the narrow confines of our language? We know that God-images play a great role in psychology, but we cannot prove the physical existence of God. As a responsible scientist I am not going to preach my personal and subjective convictions which I cannot prove. I add nothing to cognition or to a further improvement and extension of consciousness when I confess my personal prejudices. I simply go as far as my mind can reach, but to venture opinions beyond my mental reach would be immoral from the standpoint of my intellectual ethics. If I should say, "I believe in such and such a God," it would be just as futile as when a Negro states his firm belief that the tin-box he found on the shore contains a powerful fetish. If I keep to a statement which I think I can prove, this does not mean that I deny the existence of anything else that might exist beyond it. It is sheer malevolence to accuse me of an atheistic attitude simply because I try to be honest and disciplined. Speaking for myself, the question whether God exists or not is futile. I am sufficiently convinced of the effects man has always attributed to a divine being. If I should express a belief beyond that or should assert the existence of God, it would not only be superfluous and inefficient, it would show that I am not basing my opinion on facts. When people say that they believe in the existence of God, it has never impressed me in the least. Either I know a thing and then I don't need to believe it; or I believe it because I am not sure that I know it. I am well satisfied with the fact that I know experiences which I cannot avoid calling numinous or divine.

QUESTION 4. *Do you ignore the importance of other disciplines for the psyche?*

Goldbrunner in his Individuation, *page 161, says that your treatment of "what God is in Himself" is a question which you regard as beyond the scope of psychology, and adds: "This implies a positivistic, agnostic renunciation of all metaphysics." Do you agree that your treatment amounts to that? Would you not agree that such subjects as metaphysics and history have their place in the experience of the psyche?*

1590 I do not ignore the importance of other disciplines for the psyche. When I was professor at the E.T.H. in Zurich I lectured for a whole year about Tantrism[6] and for another year about the *Spiritual Exercises* of St. Ignatius of Loyola.[7] Moreover, I have written a number of books about the peculiar spiritual discipline of the alchemists.

1591 What Goldbrunner says is quite correct. I don't know what God is in himself. I don't suffer from megalomania. Psychology to me is an honest science that recognizes its own boundaries, and I am not a philosopher or a theologian who believes in his ability to step beyond the epistemological barrier. Science is made by man, which does not mean that there are not occasionally acts of grace permitting transgression into realms beyond. I don't depreciate or deny such facts, but to me they are beyond the scope of science as pointed out above. I believe firmly in the intrinsic value of the human attempt to gain understanding, but I also recognize that the human mind cannot step beyond itself, although divine grace may and probably does allow at least glimpses into a transcendental

[6] [Seminar on Buddhism and Tantric Yoga (Oct. 1938 to June 1939), in *The Process of Individuation*. Notes on Lectures at the ETH, Zurich, trans. and ed. by Barbara Hannah. Privately issued.]
[7] [Exercitia Spiritualia of St. Ignatius of Loyola (June 1939 to Mar. 1940), in ibid.]

order of things. But I am neither able to give a rational account of such divine interventions nor can I prove them. Many of the analytical hours with my patients are filled with discussions of "metaphysical" intrusions, and I am in dire need of historical knowledge to meet all the problems I am asked to deal with. For the patient's mental health it is all-important that he gets some proper understanding of the numina the collective unconscious produces, and that he assigns the proper place to them. It is, however, either a distortion of the truth or lack of information when Goldbrunner calls my attitude "positivistic," which means a one-sided recognition of scientific truth. I know too well how transitory and sometimes even futile our hypotheses are, to assume their validity as durable truths and as trustworthy foundations of a *Weltanschauung* capable of giving man sure guidance in the chaos of this world. On the contrary, I rely very much on the continuous influx of the numina from the unconscious and from whatever lies behind it. Goldbrunner therefore is also wrong to speak of an "agnostic renunciation of all metaphysics." I merely hold that metaphysics cannot be an object of science, which does not mean that numinous experiences do not happen frequently, particularly in the course of an analysis or in the life of a truly religious individual.

QUESTION 5. *If my reading of your views is correct, I should judge that you think evil to be a far more active force than traditional theological views have allowed for. You appear unable to interpret the condition of the world today unless this is so. Am I correct in this? If so, is it really necessary to expect to find the dark side in the Deity? And if you believe that Satan completes the quaternity does this not mean that the Deity would be amoral?*

Victor White in his God and the Unconscious *writes at the end of his footnote on page 76: "On the other hand, we are unable to find any intelligible, let alone desirable, meaning in such fundamental Jungian conceptions as the 'assimilation of the shadow' if they are not to be understood as the supplying of some absent good (e.g., consciousness) to what is essentially valuable and of itself 'good.' "*

1592   I am indeed convinced that evil is as positive a factor as good. Quite apart from everyday experience it would be extremely illogical to assume that one can state a quality without its opposite. If something is good, then there must needs be something that is evil or bad. The statement that something is good would not be possible if one could not discriminate it from something else. Even if one says that something exists, such a statement is only possible alongside the other statement that something does not exist. Thus when the Church doctrine declares that evil is not (μὴ ὄν) or is a mere shadow, then the good is equally illusory, as its statement would make no sense.

1593   Suppose one has something 100-per-cent good, and if anything evil comes in it is diminished, say by 5 per cent. Then one possesses 95 per cent of goodness and 5 per cent is just absent. If the original good diminished by 99 per cent, one has 1 per cent good and 99 per cent is gone. If that 1 per cent also disappears, the whole possession is gone and one has nothing at all. To the very last moment one had only good and oneself was good, but on the other side there is simply nothing and nothing has happened. Evil deeds simply do not *exist*. The identification of good with *ousia* is a fallacy, because a man who is thoroughly evil does not disappear at all when he has lost his last good. But even if he has 1 per cent of good, his body and soul and his whole existence are still *thoroughly good;* for, according to the doctrine, evil is simply identical with non-existence. This is such a horrible syllogism that there must be a very strong motive for its construction. The reason is obvious: it is a desperate attempt to save the Christian faith from dualism. According to this theory [of the *privatio boni*] even the devil, the incarnate evil, must be good, because he exists, but inasmuch as he is thoroughly bad, he does not exist. This is a clear attempt to annihilate dualism in flagrant contradiction to the dogma that the devil is eternal and damnation a very real thing. I don't pretend to be able to explain the actual condition of the world, but it is plain to any unprejudiced mind that the forces of evil are dangerously near to a victory over the powers of good. Here Basil the Great would say, "Of course that is so, but all evil comes from man and not from God," forgetting altogether that the serpent in Paradise was not made by man, and that Satan is one of the sons of God, prior to man. If man were positively the origin of all evil, he would possess a power equal or almost equal to that of the good, which is God. But we don't need to inquire into the origin of Satan. We have plenty of evidence in the Old Testament that Yahweh is moral and immoral at the same time, and Rabbinic theology is fully aware of this fact. Yahweh behaves very much like an immoral being, though he is a guardian of law and order. He is unjust and unreliable according to the Old Testament. Even the God of the New Testament is still irascible and vengeful to such a degree that he needs the self-sacrifice of his son to quench his wrath. Christian theology has never denied the identity of the God of the Old Testament with that of the New Testament. Now I ask you: what would you call a judge that is a guardian of the Law and is himself unjust? One would be inclined to call such a man immoral. I would call him both immoral and moral, and I think I express the truth with this formula. Certainly the God of the Old Testament is good and evil. He is the Father or Creator of Satan as well as of Christ. Certainly if God the Father were nothing else than a loving Father, Christ's cruel sacrificial death would be thoroughly superfluous. I would not allow my son to be slaughtered in order to be reconciled to my disobedient children.

1594 What Victor White writes about the assimilation of the shadow is not to be taken seriously. Being a Catholic priest he is bound hand and foot to the doctrine of his Church and has to defend every syllogism. The Church knows all about the assimilation of the shadow, i.e., how it is to be repressed and what is evil. Being a doctor I am never too certain about my moral judgments. Too often I find that something that is a virtue in one individual is a vice in another, and something that is good for the one is poison for another. On the other hand, pious feeling has invented the term of *felix culpa* and Christ preferred the sinner. Even God does not seem particularly pleased with mere righteousness.

1595 Nowhere else is it more important to emphasize that we are speaking of our traditional image of God (which is not the same as the original) than in the discussion of the *privatio boni*. We don't produce God by the magic word or by representing his image. The word for us is still a fetish, and we assume that it produces the thing of which it is only an image. What God is in himself nobody knows; at least I don't. Thus it is beyond the reach of man to make valid statements about the divine nature. If we disregard the short-comings of the human mind in assuming a knowledge about God, which we cannot have, we simply get ourselves into most appalling contradictions and in trying to extricate ourselves from them we use awful syllogisms, like the *privatio boni*. Moreover our superstitious belief in the power of the word is a serious obstacle to our thinking. That is the historical reason why quite a number of shocking contradictions have been heaped up, offering facile opportunities to the enemy of religion. I strongly advocate, therefore, a revision of our religious formulas with the

aid of psychological insight. It is the great advantage of Protestantism that an intelligent discussion is possible. Protestantism should
make use of this freedom. Only a thing that changes and evolves,
lives, but static things mean spiritual death.[8]

2. *Final Questions and Answers*[9]

QUESTION 1. *If Christ, in His Incarnation, concentrated, as you
contend, on goodness ("Answer to Job," pp. 414, 429f.) what do
you mean by "Christ preferred the sinner" and "Even God does
not seem particularly pleased with mere righteousness"? Is there
not an inconsistency here?*

1596   Of course there is. I am just pointing it out.

QUESTION 2. *You stress the principle of the opposites and the importance of their union. You also write of enantiodromia in relation
to the opposites but this (in the sense in which Heraclitus used
the term) would never produce a condition of stability which could
lead to the union of the opposites. So is there not a contradiction
in what you say about the opposites?*

1597   "Enantiodromia" describes a certain psychological fact, i.e., I
use it as a psychological concept. Of course it does not lead to
a union of opposites, has—as a matter of fact—nothing to do with
it. I see no contradiction anywhere.

QUESTION 3. *If the principle of enantiodromia, a perpetual swinging of the pendulum, is always present would we not have a condition in which there would be no sense of responsibility, but one
of amorality and meaninglessness?*

1598   Naturally life would be quite meaningless if the enantiodromia
of psychological states kept on for ever. But such an assumption
would be both arbitrary and foolish.

QUESTION 4. *When we come into close contact with pharisaism,
theft or murder, involving uncharitableness, ruthless and selfish
treatment of others, we know that they are evil and very ugly. In*

---

[8] For the comprehension of the problems here mentioned, I recommend:
"Answer to Job"; "A Psychological Approach to the Dogma of the Trinity"
(ch. 5, "The Problem of the Fourth"); *Aion* (ch. 5, "Christ, A Symbol
of the Self"); *Psychology and Alchemy* (Introduction, especially par. 36).
For the biography of Satan, see R. Schärf-Kluger, *Satan in the Old Testament.*
[9] [Philp, pp. 214–25. (8 Oct. 1957.) Page references for "Answer to Job"
are to C.W., vol. 11.]

actual life what we call goodness—loyalty, integrity, charitableness—does not appear as one of a pair of opposites but as the kind of behavior we want for ourselves and others. The difficulty is that we cannot judge all the motives involved in any action with certainty. We are unable to see the complete picture and so we should be cautious and charitable in our judgments. But this does not mean that what is good is not good, or what is evil is not evil. Do you not think that what you have to say about the quaternity and enantiodromia ultimately blurs the distinction between good and evil? Is not what is blurred only our capacity always to see the real moral issues clearly?

1599   It only means that moral judgment is human, limited, and under no condition metaphysically valid. Within these confines good is good, and evil is evil. One must have the courage to stand up for one's convictions. We cannot imagine a state of wholeness (quaternity) which is good and evil. It is beyond our moral judgment.

QUESTION 5. *Theologians who believe in Satan have maintained that he was created good but that through the use of his free will he became evil. What necessity is there to assume that he is the inevitable principle of evil in the Godhead—the fourth member of the quaternity?*

1600   Because the Three are the Summum Bonum, and the devil is the principle and personification of evil. In a Catholic quaternity the fourth would be the Mother, 99-per-cent divine. The devil would not count, being μὴ ὄν, an empty shadow owing to the *privatio boni,* in which the Bonum is equal to οὐσία.

QUESTION 6. *You build much on the existence of four functions, thinking, feeling, sensation, and intuition. Is this a final or satisfactory typology? If feeling is included, why not conation?*

1601   The four functions are a mere model for envisaging the qualities of *consciousness.* Conation is a term applicable to the creative process starting in the unconscious and ending in a conscious result, in other words a dynamic aspect of psychic life.

QUESTION 7. *By different approaches in your later writings you add Satan and the Blessed Virgin Mary to the Trinity, but this would make a quinary. Who compose the quaternity?*

1602   The quaternity can be a hypothetical structure, depicting a wholeness. It is also not a logical concept, but an empirical fact. The *quinarius* or *quinio* (in the form of 4 + 1, i.e., quincunx) does occur as a symbol of wholeness (in China and occasionally in alchemy) but relatively rarely. Otherwise the *quinio* is not a symbol of wholeness, quite the contrary (e.g., the five-rayed star of the Soviets or of U.S.A.). Rather, it is a chaotic *prima materia.*

QUESTION 8. *Would not the quaternity involve not only a revision of doctrine but of moral issues as well, for it would appear inevitably to mean complete moral relativity and so amorality having its source in the Godhead Itself?*

1603   Man cannot live without moral judgment. From the fact of the empirical quaternary structure of $3 + 1$ ($3 =$ good, $1 =$ evil) we can conclude that the unconscious characterizes itself as an unequal mixture of good and evil.

1604   There are also not a few cases where the structure is reversed: $1 + 3$ ($1 =$ good, $3 =$ evil). 3 in this case would form the so-called "lower triad." Since the quaternity as a rule appears as a unity, the opposites annul each other, which simply means that our anthropomorphic judgment is no more applicable, i.e., the divinity is beyond good and evil, or else metaphysical assertion is not valid. In so far as the human mind and its necessities issue from the hands of the Creator, we must assume that moral judgment was provided by the same source.

QUESTION 9. *What exactly are you referring to when you use the word "quaternity" in relation to religion? Are you using "quaternity" purely for images which men form of the Godhead? You sometimes give the impression that you are referring to God-images alone. At other times you write as if you have in mind the Godhead itself. This is especially so when you stress the necessity of including Satan and also the Blessed Virgin Mary in the Godhead. If you do not refer to the Godhead itself, there seems to me to be no explanation of the urgency of your words about recognizing the evil principle in God and your welcome of the promulgation of the Assumption.*

1605   I use the term "quaternity" for the mandala and similar structures that appear *spontaneously* in dreams and visions, or are "invented" (from *invenire* = to find), to express a totality (like four winds and seasons or four sons, seraphim, evangelists, gospels, fourfold path, etc.). The quaternity is of course an image or picture, which does not mean that there is no original!

1606   If the opposites were not contained in the image, it would not be an image of totality. But it is meant to be a picture of ineffable wholeness, in other words, its symbol. It has an importance for the theologian only in so far as the latter attributes significance to it. If he assumes that his images or formulations are not contents of his consciousness (which is a *contradictio in adiecto*), he can only state that they are exact replicas of the original. But who could suggest such a thing? In spite of the fact that the Church long ago discouraged the idea of a quaternity, the fact remains that Church symbolism abounds in quaternity allusions. As Three (Trinity) is only one (albeit the main) aspect of the Deity, the remaining fourth principle is wiped out of existence by the *privatio boni* syllogism. But the Catholic Church was aware that the picture without opposites is not complete. It therefore admitted (at least tentatively) the existence of a feminine factor within the precincts of the masculine Trinity (*Assumptio Beatae Virginis*). For good reasons the devil is still excluded, and even annihilated, by the *privatio boni*.

1607 The admission of the *Beata Virgo* is a daring attempt, in so far as she belongs to *lubricum illud genus*[10] (St. Epiphanius), so suspect to the moralistic propensities of the said Church. However, she has been spiritually "disinfected" by the dogma of *Conceptio immaculata*. I consider the Assumption as a cautious approach to the solution of the problem of opposites, namely, to the integration of the fourth metaphysical figure into the divine totality. The Catholic Church has almost succeeded in creating a *quaternity without shadow,* but the devil is still outside. The Assumption is at least an important step forward in Christian (?) symbolism. This evolution will be completed when the dogma of the Co-Redemptrix is reached. But the main problem will not be solved, although one pair of opposites (♂ and ♀) has been smuggled into the divine wholeness. Thus the Catholic Church (in the person of the Pope) has at least seen fit to take the Marianic movement in the masses, i.e., a *psychological fact,* so seriously that he did not hesitate to give up the time-hallowed principle of apostolic authority.

1608 Protestanism is free to ignore the spiritual problems raised by our time, but it will remove itself from the battlefield and thereby lose its contact with life.

1609 Being a natural and spontaneous symbol, the quaternity has everything to do with human psychology, while the trinitarian symbol (though equally spontaneous) has become cold, a remote abstraction. Curiously enough, among my collection of mandalas I have only a small number of trinities and triads. They stem one

10 ["that slippery sex."]

and all from Germans![11] (Unconscious of their shadows, therefore unaware of collective guilt!)

1610   I do not know at all to what extent human formulas, whether invented or spontaneous, correspond with the original. I only know that we are profoundly concerned with them, whether people know it or not, just as you can be with an illness of which you are unaware. It makes an enormous practical difference whether your dominant idea of totality is three or four. In the former case all good comes from God, all evil from man. Then man is the devil. In the latter case man has a chance to be saved from devilish possession, in so far as he is not inflated with evil. What happened under National Socialism in Germany? What is happening under Bolshevism? With the quaternity the powers of evil, so much greater than man's, are restored to the divine wholeness, whence they originated, even according to Genesis. The serpent was not created by man.

1611   The quaternity symbol has as much to do with the Godhead as the Trinity has. As soon as I begin to think at all about the experience of "God," I have to choose from my store of images between [concepts representing him as a] monad, dyad, triad, tetrad or an indistinct multiplicity. In any serious case the choice is limited by the kind of revealed image one has received. Yahweh and Allah are monads, the Christian God a triad (historically), the modern experience presumably a tetrad, the early Persian deity a dyad. In the East you have the dyadic monad Tao and the monadic Anthropos (*purusha*), Buddha, etc.

1612   In my humble opinion all this has very much to do with psychology. We have nothing to go by but these images. Without images you could not even speak of divine experiences. You would be completely inarticulate. You only could stammer "mana" and even that would be an image. Since it is a matter of an ineffable experience the image is indispensable. I would completely agree if you should say: God approaches man in the form of symbols. But we are far from knowing whether the symbol is correct or not.

1613   The *privatio boni* cannot be compared to the quaternity, because it is not a revelation. On the contrary, it has all the earmarks of a "doctrine," a philosophical invention.

1614   It makes no difference at all whether I say "God" or "Godhead." Both are in themselves far beyond man's reach. To us they are revealed as psychic images, i.e., symbols.

1615   I am far from making any statements about God himself. I

11 [Cf. "Flying Saucers: A Modern Myth" (C.W., vol. 10), par. 775.]

am talking about images, which it is very important to think and talk about, and to criticize, because so much depends upon the nature of our dominant ideas. It makes all the difference in the world whether I think that the source of evil or good is myself, my neighbour, the devil, or the supreme being.

1616 Of course I am pleading the cause of the *thinking* man, and, inasmuch as most people do not think, of a small minority. Yet it has its place in creation and presumably it makes sense. Its contribution to the development of consciousness is considerable and since Nature has bestowed the highest premium of success on the *conscious* being, consciousness must be more precious to Nature than unconsciousness. Therefore I think that I am not too far astray in trying to understand the symbol of the Deity. My opinion is that such an attempt—whether successful or not—could be of great interest to theology which is built on the same primordial images, whether one likes it or not. At all events you will find it increasingly difficult to convince the educated layman that theology has nothing to do with psychology, when the latter acknowledges its indebtedness to the theological approach.

1617 My discussion with theology starts from the fact that the naturally revealed central symbols, such as the quaternity, are not in harmony with trinitarian symbols. While the former includes the darkness in the divine totality, the Christian symbol excludes it. The Yahwistic symbol of the star of David is a *complexio oppositorum:* △, fire ▽ and water ⚥, a mandala built on three, an unconscious acknowledgment of the Trinity but including the shadow. Properly so, because Satan is still among the *benê Elohim* [sons of God], though Christ saw him falling out of heaven [Luke 10:18]. This vision points to the Gnostic abscission of the shadow, mentioned by Irenaeus.[12] As I have said, it makes a great and vital difference to man whether or not he considers himself as the source of evil, while maintaining that all good stems from God. Whether he knows it or not, this fills him with satanic pride and hybris on the one side and with an abysmal feeling of inferiority on the other. But when he ascribes the immense power of the opposites to the Deity, he falls into his modest place as a small image of the Deity, not of Yahweh, in whom the opposites are unconscious, but of a quaternity consisting of the main opposites: male and female, good and evil, and reflected in human consciousness as confirmed by psychological experience and by the historical evi-

---

12 [*Adversus haereses*, II, 5, 1. Cf. *Aion*, C.W., vol. 9,ii, par. 75 and n. 23.]

dence. Or have I invented the idea of Tao, the living spiritual symbol of ancient China? Or the four sons of Horus in ancient Egypt? Or the alchemical quaternity that lived for almost a thousand years? Or the Mahayana mandala which is still alive?

QUESTION 10. *One of your objections to the* privatio boni *doctrine is that it minimizes evil, but does not your view of the quaternity, which includes both good and evil, minimize evil much more surely and assume its existence for ever?*

1618   The quaternity symbol relativizes good and evil, but it does not minimize them in the least.

QUESTION 11. *You argue in "Answer to Job" (pp. 399, 430) that, because of his virgin birth, Christ was not truly man and so could not be a full incarnation in terms of human nature. Do you believe that Christ was born of a virgin? If not, the argument in "Answer to Job" falls to pieces. If you believe in the Virgin Birth, would it not be logical to accept the whole emphasis of the Christian Creeds, for they would not appear to be more difficult to believe in than the Virgin Birth?*

1619   The dogma of the Virgin Birth does not abolish the fact that "God" in the form of the Holy Ghost is Christ's father. If Yahweh is his father, then it is a matter of an *a priori* union of opposites. If the Summum Bonum is his father, then the powers of darkness are missing and the term "good" has lost its meaning and Christ has not become man, because man is afflicted with darkness.

QUESTION 12. *Christ, so the Gospel narratives assert, was born in a manger because there was no room for Him in the inn at Bethlehem; His early life included the Slaughter of the Innocents and His family lived for a time exiled in Egypt; He faced temptation in the wilderness; His ministry was carried on under such hard conditions that He "had not where to lay His head" (Matt. 8:20). He met and ministered to numerous sufferers; sinners received His sympathy and understanding; He endured an agony of suffering in the Garden of Gethsemane and this was followed by His trials, and finally the cruellest of deaths by crucifixion. On what grounds then can you argue that Christ was an incarnation of the light side of God and that He did not enter fully into the dark aspects of existence? ("Answer to Job," pp. 398f., 414, 430.) On the contrary, traditionally He has often been thought of as "a man of sorrows, and acquainted with grief."*

1620   All that has nothing to do with the dark side of man. Christ is on the contrary the innocent and blameless victim without the *macula peccati,* therefore not really a human being who has to live without the benefit of the Virgin Birth and is crucified in a thousand forms.

QUESTION 13. *What do you mean when in "Answer to Job" you refer to Antichrist and his reign, and state that this was astrologically foretold?*

1621   It is potentially foretold by the aeon of the Fishes (⟩—⟨) then beginning, and in fact by the Apocalypse. Cf. my argument in *Aion,* ch. VI.; also Rev. 20:7: "And when the thousand years are expired, Satan shall be loosed out of his prison."

QUESTION 14. *What do you mean by "divine unconsciousness" in "Answer to Job" (footnote on page 383)? Is God more limited than man?*

1622   This is just the trouble. From Job it is quite obvious that Yahweh behaves like a man with inferior consciousness and an absolute lack of moral self-reflection. In this respect God-image is more limited than man. Therefore God must incarnate.

QUESTION 15. *One of Job's greatest problems was: Can I believe in a just God? Individuation, "the Christification of many," the solution given in "Answer to Job" [p. 470], does not do justice to Job's question. Did not Job want meaning, a good God and not simply individuation? He was concerned with metaphysical and theological issues, and the modern Job is too, and just as man cannot live by bread alone, so is he unlikely to feel that he can live by individuation alone which, at its most successful, would appear to be little more than a preparatory process enabling him to face these issues more objectively.*

1623   Job wanted justice. He saw that he could not obtain it. Yahweh cannot be argued with. He is unreflecting power. What else is left to Job but to shut his mouth? He does not dream of individuation, but he knows what kind of God he is dealing with. It is certainly not Job drawing further conclusions but God. He sees that incarnation is unavoidable because man's insight is a step ahead of him. He must "empty himself of his Godhead and assume the shape of the δοῦλος,"[13] i.e., man is his lowest form of existence, in order to obtain the jewel which man possesses in his self-reflection.

13 [Cf. Philippians 2:6.]

Why is Yahweh, the omnipotent creator, so keen to have his "slave," body and soul, even to the point of admitted jealousy?

1624 Why do you say "by individuation alone"? *Individuation is the life in God,* as mandala psychology clearly shows. Have you not read my later books? You can see it in every one of them. The symbols of the self coincide with those of the Deity. The self is not the ego, it symbolizes the totality of man and he is obviously not whole without God. That seems to be what is meant by incarnation and incidentally by individuation.

3. Answers to Questions from the Rev. David Cox[14]

I

This question concerned Jung's statement in Two Essays on Analytical Psychology (*par. 327*) *that Western culture has no name or concept for the "union of opposites by the middle path" which could be compared to the concept of Tao. It was suggested that the Christian doctrine of justification by faith is such a concept.*

1625 Not being a theologian I cannot see a connection between the doctrine of justification and Tao. Tao is the cooperation of opposites, bright-dark, dry-humid, hot-cold, south-north, dragon-tiger, etc., and has nothing to do with moral opposites or with a reconciliation between the Summum Bonum and the devil. Christian doctrine—so far as I know—does not recognize dualism as the constitution of Tao, but Chinese philosophy does.

1626 It is certainly true that natural man always tries to increase what seems "good" to him and to abolish "evil." He depends upon his consciousness, which, however, may be crossed by "conscience" or by some unconscious intention. This factor can occasionally be stronger than consciousness, so that it cannot be fought. We are very much concerned in psychotherapy with such cases.

1627 The "Will of God" often contradicts conscious principles however good they may seem. Penitence or remorse follows the deviation from the superior will. The result is—if not a chronic conflict—a *coniunctio oppositorum* in the form of the symbol (*symbolum* = the two halves of a broken coin), the expression of totality.

1628 I did not know that you understand Christ as the new centre

14 [Philp, pp. 226–39. (Aug. 1957.) The questions were not directly quoted because of the personal way in which some of them were framed.]

of the individual. Since this centre of the individual appears empirically as a union of opposites (usually a quaternity), Christ must be beyond moral conflict, thus representing ultimate decision. This conception coincides absolutely with my view of the self (= Tao, *nirdvandva*). But since the self includes my consciousness as well as my unconscious, my ego is an integral part of it. Is this also your view of Christ? If this should be so, I could completely agree with you. Life then becomes a dangerous adventure, because I surrender to a power beyond the opposites, to a superior or divine factor, without argument. His supreme decision may be what I call good or what I call bad, as it is unlimited. What is the difference between my behaviour and that of an animal fulfilling the will of God unreservedly? The only difference I can see is that I am conscious of, and reflect on, what I am doing. "If thou knowest what thou art doing, thou art blessed."[15] You have acted.

1629 (*Unjust steward.*) This is Gnostic morality but not that of the decalogue. The true servant of God runs risks of no mean order. *Entendu!* Thus, at God's command, Hosea marries a whore. It is not beyond the bounds of possibility that such orders could be issued even in modern times. Who is ready to obey? And what about the fact that anything coming from the unconscious is expressed in a peculiar language (words, thoughts, feelings, impulses) that might be misinterpreted? These questions are not meant as arguments against the validity of your view. They merely illustrate the enormity of the risk. I ventilate them only to make sure we really believe in a Christ beyond good and evil. I am afraid of unreflecting optimism and of secret loopholes, as for instance, "Oh, you can trust in the end that everything will be all right." *Id est:* "God is good" (and not beyond good and evil). Why has God created consciousness and reason and doubt, if complete surrender and obedience to his will is the *ultima ratio?* He was obviously not content with animals only. He wants reflecting beings who are at the same time capable of surrendering themselves to the primordial creative darkness of his will, unafraid of the consequences.

1630 I cannot help seeing that there is much evidence in primitive Christianity for your conception of Christ, but none in the later development of the Church. Nevertheless there are the seemingly unshakable scriptural testimonies to the essential goodness of God and Christ and there is—to my knowledge—no positive statement in favour of a beyond-good-and-evil conception, not even an implied

---

[51] [Codex Bezae to Luke 6:4.]

one. This seems to me to be a wholly modern and new interpretation of a revolutionary kind, at least in view of the Summum Bonum, as you add the Malum and transcend both. In this I completely agree with you. I only want to make sure that we understand each other when we reach the conclusion that man's true relation to God must include both love and fear to make it complete. If both are true, we can be sure that our relation to him is adequate. The one relativizes the other: in fear we may hope, in love we may distrust. Both conditions appeal to our consciousness, reflection, and reason. Both our gifts come into their own. But is this not a relativization of complete surrender? Or at least an acceptance after an internal struggle? Or a fight against God that can be won only if he himself is his advocate against himself, as Job understood it? And is this not a tearing asunder of God's original unity by man's stubborness? A disruption sought by God himself, or by the self itself? As I know from my professional experience, the self does indeed seek such issues because it seeks *consciousness,* which cannot exist without discrimination (differentiation, separation, opposition, contradiction, discussion). The self is empirically in a condition we call unconscious in our three-dimensional world. What it is in its transcendental condition, we do not know. So far as it becomes an object of cognition, it undergoes a process of discrimination and so does everything emanating from it. The discrimination is intellectual, emotional, ethical, etc. That means: the self is subject to our free decision thus far. But as it transcends our cognition, we are its objects or slaves or children or sheep that cannot but obey the shepherd. Are we to emphasize consciousness and freedom of judgment or lay more stress on obedience? In the former case can we fulfil the divine will to consciousness, and in the latter the primordial instinct of obedience? Thus we represent the intrinsic Yea and Nay of the *opus divinum* of *creatio continua.* We ourselves are in a certain respect "beyond good and evil." This is very dangerous indeed (cf. Nietzsche), but no argument against the truth. Yet our inadequacy, dullness, inertia, stupidity, etc. are equally true. Both are aspects of one and the same being.

1631   Accordingly the alchemists thought of their opus as a continuation and perfection of creation, whereas the modern psychological attempt confronts the opposites and submits to the tension of the conflict: "Expectans naturae operationem, quae lentissima est, aequo animo,"[16] to quote an old master. We know that a

[16] ["Patiently awaiting a work of nature, which is very slow."]

tertium quid develops out of an opposition, partly aided by our conscious effort, partly by the co-operation of the unconscious effort, partly by the co-operation of the unconscious (the alchemists add: *Deo concedente*). The result of this opus is the *symbol,* in the last resort the self. The alchemists understood it to be as much physical as spiritual, being the *filius macrocosmi,* a parallel to Christ, the υἱὸς τοῦ ἀνθρώπου. The Gnostics understood the serpent in paradise to be the λόγος, and in the same way the alchemists believed that their *filius philosophorum* was the chthonic *serpens mercurialis* transformed (taking the serpent on the σταυρός [cross] as an *allegoria ad Christum spectans*).[17] Their naïveté shows a hesitation (which I feel too) to identify the self with Christ. Their symbol is the *lapis.* It is incorruptible, *semel factus* (from the *increatum,* the primordial chaos), everlasting, our tool and master at the same time ("artifex non est magister lapidis, sed potius eius minister"),[18] the redeemer of creation in general, of minerals, plants, animals, and of man's physical imperfection. Hence its synonyms: panacea, *alexipharmacum, medicina catholica,* etc. (and hellebore, because it heals insanity).

1632   Of course if you understand Christ by definition as a *complexio oppositorum,* the equation is solved. But you are confronted with a terrific historical counter-position. As it concerns a point of supreme importance, I wanted to clarify the problem beyond all doubt. This may explain and excuse my long-winded argument.

II

In "Answer to Job" Jung claims that Jesus "incarnates only the light" side of God. This may represent the way in which Jesus is thought of by the majority of Western men and women today, but is it not false to the New Testament and to Christian thought over the centuries?

1633   You must consider that I am an alienist and practical psychologist, who has to take things as they *are* understood, not as they *could* or *should* be understood. Thus the Gnostics thought that Christ had cut off his shadow, and I have never heard that he embodies evil as Yahweh explicitly does. Catholic as well as Protestant teaching insists that Christ is without sin. As a scientist I am chiefly concerned with what is generally believed, although I can't help being impressed by the fact that the ecclesiastical doctrines

---

[17] [Cf. *Psychology and Alchemy,* C.W., vol. 12, fig. 217.]
[18] ["The artifex is not the master of the stone, but rather its minister."]

do not do justice to certain facts in the New Testament. I have however to consider the *consensus omnium* that Christ is without the *macula peccati.* If I should say that Christ contains some evil I am sure to have the Churches against me. As a psychologist I cannot deal with the theological conception of truth. My field is people's common beliefs.

1634   Since I am not chiefly concerned with theology but rather with the layman's picture of theological concepts (a fact you must constantly bear in mind), I am liable to make many apparent contradictions (like the medieval mind acquainted with funny stories about Jesus, as you rightly point out). The Gospels do indeed give many hints pointing to the dark side, but this has not affected the picture of the *lumen de lumine,* which is the general view. I am thinking—as a psychologist—about all sorts of erroneous notions which do exist in spite of higher criticism and accurate exegesis and all the achievements of theological research. My object is the general condition of the Christian mind, and not theology, where I am wholly incompetent. Because the *lumen de lumine* idea is paramount in the layman's mind, I dare to point to certain scriptural evidence (accessible to the layman) showing another picture of Christ. I am certain that your conception of Christ would have a hard time getting through certain thick skulls. It is the same with the idea of evil contained in God. I am concerned with dogmas, prejudices, illusions, and errors and every kind of doubt in the layman's mind, and I try to get a certain order into that chaos by the means accessible to a layman, i.e., to myself as a representative of the humble "ignoramus."

III

This question deals with the relationship between faith and projection. Has Jung, in his writing, treated faith as being connected with an outward form of religion?

1635   This I do not properly understand. Of course "faith" is a relationship to projected contents. But I cannot see how that "corresponds for all practical purposes to a withdrawal of the projection." Faith on the contrary—as it seems to me—maintains the conviction that the projection is a reality. For instance, I project saintly qualities on to somebody. My faith maintains and enhances this projection and creates a worshipful attitude on my part. But it is quite possible that the bearer of the projection is nothing of the kind, perhaps he is even an unpleasant hypocrite. Or I may project, i.e., hypostatize, a religious conviction of a certain kind which I maintain with faith and fervour. Where is the "withdrawal of the projection"?

1636   In case of doubt you had better refer to *Symbols of Transformation*. Once I was at the beginning of things, at the time when I separated from Freud in 1912. I found myself in great inner difficulties, as I had no notion of the collective unconscious or of archetypes. My education was based chiefly on science, with a modest amount of the humanities. It was a time of *Sturm und Drang*. The so-called *Psychology of the Unconscious*[19] was an intuitive leap into the dark and contains no end of inadequate formulations and unfinished thoughts.

1637   I make a general distinction between "religion" and a "creed" for the sake of the layman, since it is chiefly he who reads my books and not the academic scholar. He (the scholar) is not interested in the layman's mind. As a rule he nurses resentments against psychology. I must repeat again: I am a psychologist and thus people's minds interest me in the first place, although I am keen to learn the truth the specialist produces. The layman identifies religion with a creed, that is, with the "things done in the church." Thus Islam, Judaism, Buddhism, etc. are simply religions like Christianity. That there is a genuine inner life, a communion with transcendental powers, a possibility of religious *experience* is mere hearsay. Nor are the churches over-sympathetic to the view that the alpha and omega of religion is the subjective individual experience, but put community in the first place, without paying attention to the fact that the more people there are the less individuality there is. To be alone with God is highly suspect, and, mind you, it is, because the will of God can be terrible and can isolate you from your family and your friends and, if you are courageous or foolish enough, you may end up in the lunatic asylum. And yet how can there be religion without the experience of the divine will? Things are comparatively easy as long as God wants nothing but the fulfilment of his laws, but what if he wants you to break them, as he may do equally well? Poor Hosea could believe in the symbolic nature of his awkward marriage, but what about the equally poor little doctor who has to swear his soul away to save a human life? He cannot even begin to point out what an affliction his act of lying is, although in his solitude with God he may feel justified.

[19] [The translation (1916) of the original (1912) version of *Symbols of Transformation*.]

But in case of discovery he has to face the ignominious consequences of his deed and nobody will believe him to be a witness for the divine will. To be God's voice is not a social function anymore. *Si parva licet componere magnis*—what did I get for my serious struggle over *Job,* which I had postponed for as long as possible? I am regarded as blasphemous, contemptible, a fiend, whose name is mud. It fell to my lot to collect the victims of the Summum Bonum and use my own poor means to help them. But I could not say that a church of any denomination has encouraged my endeavours. You are one of the *very few* who admit the *complexio oppositorum* in the Deity. (Cusanus does not seem to have really known what he was talking about, nor anybody else in those days, otherwise he would have been roasted long ago.) That is the reason why I don't identify religion with a creed. I can have a real communion only with those who have the same or similar religious experience, but not with the believers in the Word, who have never even taken the trouble to understand its implications and expose themselves to the divine will unreservedly. They use the Word to protect themselves against the will of God. Nothing shields you better against the solitude and forlornness of the divine experience than community. It is the best and safest substitute for individual responsibility.

1638 The self or Christ is present in everybody *a priori,* but as a rule in an *unconscious condition* to begin with. But it is a definite *experience* of later life, when this fact becomes *conscious.* It is not really understood by teaching or suggestion. It is only real when it *happens,* and it can happen only when you withdraw your projections from an *outward* historical or metaphysical Christ and thus *wake up* Christ within. This does not mean that the unconscious self is inactive, only that we do not understand it. The self (or Christ) cannot become conscious and real without the withdrawal of external projections. An act of *introjection* is needed, i.e., the realization that the self lives in you and not in an external figure separated and different from yourself. The self has always been, and will be, your innermost centre and periphery, your *scintilla* and *punctum solis.* It is even biologically the archetype of order and—dynamically—the source of life.

IV

Here the question is concerned with Jung's objections to the view that God is the Summum Bonum and sin is a privatio boni.

725

1639   Well, I have noticed that it seems to be a major difficulty for
the theological mind to accept the fact that (1) "good" and "evil"
are man-made judgments. Somebody's "good" may be bad or evil
for another *et vice versa*. (2) One cannot speak of "good" if one
does not equally speak of "evil," any more than there can be an
"above" without a "below," or "day" without "night." (3) The
privatio boni appears to me a syllogism. If "good" and οὐσία are
one without an equally valid counterpart, then "good" is also a
μὴ ὄν because the term "good" has lost its meaning; it is just "being" and evil is just "not-being" and the term means "nothing."
Of course you are free to call "nothing" evil, but nothing is just
nothing and cannot bear another name, making it into "something."
Something non-existing has no name and no quality. The *privatio
boni* suggests that evil is μὴ ὄν, not-being or nothing. It is not even
a shadow. There remains only the ὄν, but it is not good, since there
is no "bad." Thus the epithet "good" is redundant. You can call
God the Summum, but not the Bonum, since there is nothing else
different from "being," from the Summum qua being! Although
the *privatio boni* is not the invention of the Church Fathers, the
syllogism was most welcome to them on account of the Manichaean
danger of dualism. Yet without dualism there is no cognition at all,
because discrimination is impossible.

1640   I have never [as you state] understood from my study of the
Fathers that God is the highest good *with reference to man,* no matter what he is in himself. This is certainly new to me. Obviously
my critique of the Summum Bonum does not apply in this case.
The Bonum then would be an anthropomorphic judgment, "God is
good for me," leaving it an open question whether he is the same
for other people. If one assumes him to be a *complexio oppositorum,*
i.e., beyond good and evil, it is possible that he may appear equally
well as the source of evil which you believe to be ultimately good
for man. I am convinced, as I have seen it too often to doubt
it, that an apparent evil is really no evil at all if you accept and
obediently live it as far as possible, but I am equally convinced
that an apparent good is in reality not always good at all but wholly
destructive. If this were not the case, then everything would be
ultimately good, i.e., good in its essence, and evil would not really
exist, as it would be a merely transitory appearance. In other words:
the term "good" has lost its meaning, and the only safe basis of
cognition is our world of experience, in which the power of evil
is very real and not at all a mere appearance. One can and does

cherish an optimistic hope that ultimately, in spite of grave doubts, "all will be well." As I am not making a metaphysical judgment, I cannot help remarking that at least in our empirical world the opposites are inexorably at work and that, without them, this world would not exist. We cannot even conceive of a thing that is not a form of energy, and energy is inevitably based upon opposites.

1641   I must however pay attention to the psychological fact that, so far as we can make out, *individuation* is a natural phenomenon, and in a way an inescapable goal, which we have reason to call *good for us,* because it liberates us from the otherwise insoluble conflict of opposites (at least to a noticeable degree). It is not invented by man, but Nature herself produces its archetypal image. Thus the credo "in the end all will be well" is not without its psychic foundation. But it is more than questionable whether this phenomenon is of any importance to the world in general, or only to the individual who has reached a more complete state of consciousness, to the "redeemed" man in accordance with our Christian tenet of eternal damnation. "Many are called, but few are chosen" is an authentic logion and not characteristic of Gnosticism alone.

V

Jung has been given the title "Gnostic" which he has rejected. This term has probably been used about him [and his system] because he appears to believe that salvation is for the few and that the many cannot and ought not to attempt individuation. Is it possible that he is a "Gnostic" in this sense?

1642   The designation of my "system" as "Gnostic" is an invention of my theological critics. Moreover I have no "system." I am not a philosopher, merely an empiricist. The Gnostics have the merit of having raised the problem of πόθεν τὸ κακόν; [whence evil?]. Valentinus as well as Basilides are in my view great theologians, who tried to cope with the problems raised by the inevitable influx of the collective unconscious, a fact clearly portrayed by the "gnostic" gospel of St. John and by St. Paul, not to mention the Book of Revelation, and even by Christ himself (unjust steward and Codex Bezae to Luke 6:4). In the style of their time they hypostatized their ideas as metaphysical entities. Psychology does not hypostatize, but considers such ideas as psychological statements about, or models of, essential unconscious factors inaccessible to immediate experience. This is about as far as scientific understanding can go. In our days there are plenty of people who are unable to believe a statement they cannot understand, and they appreciate the help psychology can give them by showing them that human behaviour is deeply influenced by numinous archetypes. That gives them some understanding of why and how the religious factor plays an important role. It also gives them ways and means of recognizing the operation of religious ideas in their own psyche.

1643   I must confess that I myself could find access to religion only through the psychological understanding of inner experiences, whereas traditional religious interpretations left me high and dry. It was only psychology that helped me to overcome the fatal impressions of my youth that everything untrue, even immoral, in our ordinary empirical world *must* be believed to be the eternal truth in religion. Above all, the killing of a human victim to placate the senseless wrath of a God who had created imperfect beings unable to fulfil his expectations poisoned my whole religion. Nobody knew an answer. "With God all things are possible." Just so! As the perpetrator of incredible things he is himself incredible, and yet I was supposed to believe what every fibre of my body refused to admit! There are a great many questions which I could elucidate only by psychological understanding. I loved the Gnostics in spite of everything, because they recognized the necessity of some further *raisonnement*, entirely absent in the Christian cosmos. They were at least human and therefore understandable. But I have no γνῶσις τοῦ θεοῦ. I know the reality of religious experience and of psychological models which permit a limited understanding. I have Gnosis so far as I have immediate experience, and my models are greatly helped by the *représentations collectives* of all religions. But I cannot see why one creed should possess the unique and perfect truth. Each creed claims this prerogative, hence the general disagreement! This is not very helpful. Something must be wrong. I think it is the immodesty of the claim to god-almightiness of the believers, which compensates their inner doubt. Instead of basing themselves upon immediate experience they believe in words for want of something better. The *sacrificium intellectus* is a sweet drug for man's all-embracing spiritual laziness and inertia.

1644   I owe you quite a number of apologies for the fact that my layman's mental attitude must be excruciatingly irritating to your point of view. But you know, as a psychologist I am not concerned with theology directly, but rather with the incompetent general public and its erroneous and faulty convictions, which are however just as real to it as their competent views are to the theologians. I am continually asked "theological" questions by my patients, and when I say that I am only a doctor and they should ask the theologian, then the regular answer is, "Oh, yes, we have done so," or "we do not ask a priest because we get an answer we already know, which explains nothing."

1645　Well this is the reason why I have to try for better or worse to help my patients to some kind of understanding at least. It gives them a certain satisfaction as it has done to me, although it is admittedly inadequate. But to them it sounds as if somebody were speaking their language and understanding their questions which they take very seriously indeed. Once, for instance, it was a very important question to me to discover how far modern Protestantism considers that the God of the Old Testament is identical with the God of the New Testament. I asked two university professors. They did not answer my letter. The third (also a professor) said he didn't know. The fourth said, "Oh, that is quite easy. Yahweh is a somewhat more archaic conception contrasted with the more differentiated view of the New Testament." I said to him, "That is exactly the kind of psychologism you accuse me of." My question must have been singularly inadequate or foolish. But I do not know why. I am speaking for the layman's psychology. The layman is a reality and his questions do exist. My "Answer to Job" voices the questions of thousands, but the theologians don't answer, contenting themselves with dark allusions to my layman's ignorance of Hebrew, higher criticism, Old Testament exegesis, etc., but there is not a single answer. A Jesuit professor of theology asked me rather indignantly how I could suggest that the Incarnation has remained incomplete. I said, "The human being is born under the *macula peccati*. Neither Christ nor his mother suffers from original sin. They are therefore not human, but superhuman, a sort of God." What did he answer? Nothing.

1646　Why is that so? My layman's reasoning is certainly imperfect, and my theological knowledge regrettably meagre, but not as bad as all that, at least I hope not. But I do know something about the psychology of man now and in the past, and as a psychologist I raise the questions I have been asked a hundred times by my patients and other laymen. Theology would certainly not suffer by paying attention. I know you are too busy to do it. I am all the more anxious to prevent avoidable mistakes and I shall feel deeply obliged to you if you take the trouble of showing me where I am wrong.

1647   Gnosis is characterized by the hypostatizing of psychological apperceptions, i.e., by the integration of archetypal contents beyond the revealed "truth" of the Gospels. Hippolytus still considered classical Greek philosophy along with Gnostic philosophies as perfectly possible views. Christian Gnosis to him was merely the best and superior to all of them. The people who call me a Gnostic cannot understand that I am a psychologist, describing modes of psychic behaviour precisely like a biologist studying the instinctual activities of insects. He does not *believe* in the tenets of the bee's philosophy. When I show the parallels between dreams and Gnostic fantasies I *believe* in neither. They are just facts one does not need to believe or to hypostatize. An alienist is not necessarily crazy because he describes and analyses the delusions of lunatics, nor is a scholar studying the *Tripitaka* necessarily a Buddhist.

4. Reply to a Letter
from the Rev. David Cox[20]

1648   The crux of this question is: 'Within your own personality." "Christ" can be an external reality (historical and metaphysical) or an archetypal image or idea in the collective unconscious pointing to an unknown background. I would understand the former mainly as a projection, but not the latter, because it is immediately evident. It is not projected upon anything, therefore there is no projection. Only, "faith" in Christ is different from faith in anyone else, since in this case, "Christ" being immediately evident, the word "faith," including or alluding to the possibility of doubt, seems too feeble a word to characterize that powerful presence from which there is no escape. A general can say to his soldiers, "You must have faith in me," because one might doubt him. But you cannot say to a man lying wounded on the battlefield, "You ought to *believe* that this a real battle," or "Be sure that you are up against the enemy." It is just too obvious. Even the historical Jesus began to speak of "faith" because he saw that his disciples had no immediate evidence. Instead they had to believe, while he himself being identical with God had no need to "have faith in God."

1649   As one habitually identifies the "psyche" with what one knows of it, it is assumed that one can call certain (supposed or believed)

20 [Philp, pp. 239–50. (25 Sept. 1957.)]

metaphysical entities non-psychic. Being a responsible scientist I am unable to pass such a judgment, for all I know of regular religious phenomena seems to indicate that they are psychic events. Moreover I do not know the full reach of the psyche, because there is the limitless extent of the unconscious. "Christ" is definitely an archetypal image (I don't add "only") and that is all I actually know of him. As such he belongs to the (collective) foundations of the psyche. I identify him therefore with what I call the self. The self rules the whole of the psyche. I think our opinions do not differ essentially. You seem to have trouble only with the theological (and self-inflicted) devaluation of the psyche, which you apparently believe to be ultimately definable.

1650   If my identification of Christ with the archetype of the self is valid, he is, or ought to be, a *complexio oppositorum*. Historically this is not so. Therefore I was profoundly surprised by your statement that Christ contains the opposites. Between my contention and historical Christianity there stretches that deep abyss of Christian dualism—Christ and the Devil, good and evil, God and Creation.

1651   "Beyond good and evil" simply means: we pass no moral judgment. But in fact nothing is changed. The same is true when we state that whatever God is or does is *good*. Since God does everything (even man created by him is his instrument) everything is good, and the term "good" has lost its meaning. "Good" is a relative term. There is no good without bad.

1652   I am afraid that even revealed truth has to evolve. Everything living changes. We should not be satisfied with unchangeable traditions. The great battle that began with the dawn of consciousness has not reached its climax with any particular interpretation, apostolic, Catholic, Protestant, or otherwise. Even the highly conservative Catholic Church has overstepped its ancient rule of apostolic authenticity with the *Assumptio Beatae Virginis*. According to what I hear from Catholic theologians, the next step would be the Co-redemptrix. This obvious recognition of the female element is a very important step foward. It means psychologically the recognition of the unconscious, since the representative of the collective unconscious is the *anima,* the archetype of all divine mothers (at least in the masculine psyche)·

1653   The equivalent on the Protestant side would be a confrontation with the unconscious as the counterpart or consort of the masculine Logos. The hitherto valid symbol of the supreme spiritual structure

731

was Trinity + Satan, the so-called 3 + 1 structure, corresponding to three conscious functions versus the one unconscious, so-called inferior function; or 1 + 3 if the conscious side is understood as one versus the co-called inferior or chthonic triad, mythologically characterized as three mother figures.[21] I suppose that the negative evaluation of the unconscious has something to do with the fact that it has been hitherto represented by Satan, while in reality it is the female aspect of man's psyche and thus not wholly evil in spite of the old saying: *Vir a Deo creatus, mulier a simia Dei.*

1654   It seems to me of paramount importance that Protestantism should integrate psychological experience, as for instance Jacob Boehme did. With him God does not only contain love, but, on the other side and in the same measure, the fire of wrath, in which Lucifer himself dwells. Christ is a revelation of his love, but he can manifest his wrath in an Old Testament way just as well, i.e., in the form of evil. Inasmuch as out of evil good may come, and out of good evil, we do not know whether creation is ultimately good or a regrettable mistake and God's suffering. It is an ineffable mystery. At any rate we are not doing justice either to nature in general or to our own human nature when we deny the immensity of evil and suffering and turn our eyes from the cruel aspect of creation. Evil should be recognized and one should not attribute the existence of evil to man's sinfulness. Yahweh is not offended by being feared.

1655   It is quite understandable why it was an Εὐάγγελον [evangel, "good tidings"] to learn of the *bonitas Dei* and of his son. It was known to the ancients that the *cognito sui·ipsius* [self-knowledge][22] was a prerequisite for this, not only in the Graeco-Roman world but also in the Far East. It is to the individual aptitude that the man Jesus owes his apotheosis: he became the symbol of the self under the aspect of the infinite goodness, which was certainly the symbol most needed in ancient civilization (as it is still needed today).

1656   It can be considered a fact that the dogmatic figure of Christ is the result of a condensation process from various sources. One of the main origins is the age-old god-man of Egypt: Osiris-Horus and his four sons. It was a remodeling of the unconscious archetype

---

[21] [Cf. "The Phenomenology of the Spirit in Fairytales" (C.W., vol. 9, i), pars. 425f., 436ff.; *Aion,* par. 351; and "The Spirit Mercurius" (C.W., vol. 13), pars. 270ff.]

[22] [Cf. "The Spirit Mercurius," par. 301.]

hitherto projected upon a divine non-human being. By embodying itself in a historical man it came nearer to consciousness, but in keeping with the mental capacity of the time it remained as if suspended between God and man, between the need for good and the fear of evil. Any doubt about the absolute *bonitas Dei* would have led to an immediate regression to the former pagan state, i.e., to the amorality of the metaphysical principle.

1657   Since then two thousand years have passed. In this time we have learned that good and evil are categories of our moral judgment, therefore relative to man. Thus the way was opened for a new model of the self. Moral judgment is a necessity of the human mind. The Christ (ὁ Χριστός) is the Christian model that expresses the self, as the Ἄνθρωπος is the corresponding Egypto-Judaic formula. Moral qualification is withdrawn from the deity. The Catholic Church has almost succeeded in adding femininity to the masculine Trinity. Protestantism is confronted with the psychological problem of the unconscious.

1658   It is, as far as I can see, a peculiar process extending over at least four thousand years of mental evolution. It can be contemplated in a "euhemeristic" way as a development of man's understanding of the supreme powers beyond his control. [The process consists of the following stages:] (1) Gods. (2) A supreme Deity ruling the gods and demons. (3) God shares our human fate, is betrayed, killed or dies, and is resurrected again. There is a feminine counterpart dramatically involved in God's fate. (4) God becomes man in the flesh and thus historical. He is identified with the abstract idea of the Summum Bonum and loses the feminine counterpart. The female deity is degraded to an ancillary position (Church). Consciousness begins to prevail against the unconscious. This is an enormously important step forward in the emancipation of consciousness and in the liberation of thought from its involvement in things. Thus the foundation of science is laid, but on the other hand, that of atheism and materialism. Both are inevitable consequences of the basic split between spirit and matter in Christian philosophy, which proclaimed the redemption of the spirit from the body and its fetters. (5) The whole metaphysical world is understood as a psychic structure projected into the sphere of the unknown.

1659   The danger of this viewpoint is exaggerated scepticism and rationalism, since the original "supreme powers" are reduced to mere representations over which one assumes one has complete control. This leads to a complete negation of the supreme powers (scientific materialism).

1660   The other way of looking at it is from the standpoint of the archetype. The original chaos of multiple gods evolves into a sort of monarchy, and the archetype of the self slowly asserts its central position as the archetype of order in chaos. One God rules supreme but apart from man. It begins to show a tendency to relate itself to consciousness through a process of penetration: the humanizing effect of a feminine intercession, expressed for instance by the Isis intrigue. In the Christian myth the Deity, the self, penetrates consciousness almost completely, without any visible loss of power and prestige. But in time it becomes obvious that the Incarnation has caused a loss among the supreme powers: the indispensable dark side has been left behind or stripped off, and the feminine aspect is missing. Thus a further act of incarnation becomes necessary. Through atheism, materialism, and agnosticism, the powerful yet one-sided aspect of the Summum Bonum is weakened, so that it cannot keep out the dark side, and incidentally the feminine factor, any more. "Antichrist" and "Devil" gain the ascendancy: God asserts his power through the revelation of his darkness and destructiveness. Man is merely instrumental in carrying out the divine plan. Obviously he does not want his own destruction but is forced to it by his own inventions. He is entirely unfree in his actions because he does not yet understand that he is a mere instrument of a destructive superior will. From this paradox he could learn that—*nolens volens*—he serves a supreme power, and that supreme powers exist in spite of his denial. As God lives in everybody in the form of the *scintilla* of the self, man could see his "daemonic," i.e., ambivalent, nature in himself and thus he could understand how he is penetrated by God or how God incarnates in man.

1661   Through his further incarnation God becomes a fearful task for man, who must now find ways and means to unite the divine opposites in himself. He is summoned and can no longer leave his sorrows to somebody else, not even to Christ, because it was Christ that has left him the almost impossible task of his cross. Christ has shown how everybody will be crucified upon his destiny, i.e., upon his self, as he was. He did not carry his cross and suffer crucifixion so that we could escape. The bill of the Christian era is presented to us: we are living in a world rent in two from top to bottom; we are confronted with the H-bomb and we have to face our own shadows. Obviously God does not want us to remain little children looking out for a parent who will do their job for them. We are cornered by the supreme power of the incarnating Will. God really wants to become man, even if he rends him asunder. This is so no matter what we say. One cannot talk the H-bomb or Communism out of the world. We are in the soup that is going to be cooked for us, whether we claim to have invented it or not. Christ said to his disciples "Ye are gods." This word becomes painfully true. If God incarnates in the empirical man, man is confronted with the divine problem. Being and remaining man he has to find an answer. It is the question of the opposites, raised at the moment when God was declared to be good only. Where then is his dark side? Christ is the model for the human answers and his symbol is the *cross*, the union of the opposites. This will be the fate of man, and this he must understand if he is to survive at all. We are threatened with universal genocide if we cannot work out the way of salvation by a symbolic death.

1662   In order to accomplish his task, man is inspired by the Holy Ghost in such a way that he is apt to identify him with his own mind. He even runs the grave risk of believing he has a Messianic mission, and forces tyrannous doctrines upon his fellow-beings. He would do better to dis-identify his mind from the small voice within, from dreams and fantasies through which the divine spirit manifests itself. One should listen to the inner voice attentively, intelligently and critically (*Probate spiritus!*), because the voice one hears is the *influxus divinus* consisting, as the *Acts of John* aptly state, of "right" and "left" streams, i.e., of opposites.[23] They have to be clearly separated so that their positive and negative aspects become visible. Only thus can we take up a middle position and discover a middle way. That is the task left to man, and that is the reason why man is so important to God that he decided to become a man himself.

1663   I must apologize for the length of this exposition. Please do not think that I am stating a truth. I am merely trying to present a hypothesis which might explain the bewildering conclusions resulting from the clash of traditional symbols and psychological experiences. I thought it best to put my cards on the table, so that you get a clear picture of my ideas.

1664   Although all this sounds as if it were a sort of theological speculation, it is in reality modern man's perplexity expressed in symbolic

[23] [James, *The Apocryphal New Testament*, p. 255: "The Acts of Peter." Cf. "Transformation Symbolism in the Mass" (C.W., vol. 11), par. 429.]

terms. It is the problem I so often had to deal with in treating the neuroses of intelligent patients. It can be expressed in a more scientific, psychological language; for instance, instead of using the term God you say "unconscious," instead of Christ "self," instead of incarnation "integration of the unconscious," instead of salvation or redemption "individuation," instead of crucifixion or sacrifice on the Cross "realization of the four functions or of "wholeness." I think it is no disadvantage to religious tradition if we can see how far it coincides with psychological experience. On the contrary it seems to me a most welcome aid in understanding religious traditions.

1665   A myth remains a myth even if certain people believe it to be the literal revelation of an eternal truth, but it becomes moribund if the living truth it contains ceases to be an object of belief. It is therefore necessary to renew its life from time to time through a *new interpretation*. This means re-adapting it to the changing spirit of the times. What the Church calls "prefigurations" refer to the original state of the myth, while the Christian doctrine represents a new interpretation and re-adaptation to a Hellenized world. A most interesting attempt at re-interpretation began in the eleventh century,[24] leading up to the schism in the sixteenth century. The Renaissance was no more a rejuvenation of antiquity than Protestantism was a return to the primitive Christianity: it was a new interpretation necessitated by the devitalization of the Catholic Church.

1666   Today Christianity is devitalized by its remoteness from the spirit of the times. It stands in need of a new union with, or relation to, the atomic age, which is a unique novelty in history. The myth needs to be retold in a new spiritual language, for the new wine can no more be poured into the old bottles than it could in the Hellenistic age. Even conservative Jewry had to produce an entirely new version of the myth in its Cabalistic Gnosis. It is my practical experience that psychological understanding immediately revivifies the essential Christian ideas and fills them with the breath of life. This is because our worldly light, i.e., scientific knowledge and understanding, coincides with the symbolic statement of the myth, whereas previously we were unable to bridge the gulf between knowing and believing.

1667   Coming back to your letter (pp. 2–3, 25 September) I must say that I could accept your definition of the Summum Bonum,

[24] [Cf. *Aion,* pars, 139ff.]

"Whatever God is, that is good," if it did not interfere with or twist our sense of good. In dealing with the moral nature of an act of God, we have either to suspend our moral judgment and blindly follow the dictates of this superior will, or we have to judge in a human fashion and call white white and black black. In spite of the fact that we sometimes obey the superior will blindly and almost heroically, I do not think that this is the usual thing, nor is it commendable on the whole to act blindly, because we are surely expected to act with conscious moral reflection. It is too dangerously easy to avoid responsibility by deluding ourselves that our will is the will of God. We can be forcibly overcome by the latter, but if we are not we must use our judgment, and then we are faced with the inexorable fact that humanly speaking some acts of God are good and some bad, so much so that the assumption of a Summum Bonum becomes almost an act of hubris.

1668   If God can be understood as the perfect *complexio oppositorum,* so can Christ. I can agree with your view about Christ completely, only it is not the traditional but a very modern conception which is on the way to the desired new interpretation. I also agree with your understanding of Tao and its contrast to Christ, who is indeed the paradigm of the reconciliation of the divine opposites in man brought about in the process of individuation. Thus Christ stands for the treasure and the supreme "good." (In German "good" = *gut,* but the noun *Gut* also means "property" and "treasure.")

1669   When theology makes metaphysical assertions the conscience of the scientist cannot back it up. Since Christ never meant more to me than what I could understand of him, and since this understanding coincides with my empirical knowledge of the self, I have to admit that I mean the self in dealing with the idea of Christ. As a matter of fact I have no other access to Christ but the self, and since I do not know anything beyond the self I cling to his archetype. I say, "Here is the living and perceptible archetype which has been projected upon the man Jesus or has historically manifested itself in him." If this collective archetype had not been associated with Jesus he would have remained a nameless Zaddik. I actually prefer the term "self" because I am talking to Hindus as well as Christians, and I do not want to divide but to unite.

1670   Since I am putting my cards on the table, I must confess that I cannot detach a certain feeling of dishonesty from any metaphysical assertion—one may speculate but not assert. One cannot reach beyond oneself, and if somebody assures you he can reach beyond himself and his natural limitations, he overreaches himself and becomes immodest and untrue.

1671   This may be a *deformation professionelle,* the prejudice of a scientific conscience. Science is an honest-to-God attempt to get at the truth and its rule is never to assert more than one can prove within reasonable and defensible limits. This is my attitude in approaching the problem of religious experience.

1672   I am unable to envisage anything beyond the self, since it is—by definition—a borderline concept designating the unknown totality of man: there are no known limits to the unconscious. There is no reason whatsoever why you should or should not call the beyond-self Christ or Buddha or Purusha or Tao or Khidr or Tifereth. All these terms are recognizable formulations of what I call the "self." Moreover I dislike the insistence upon a special name, since my human brethren are as good and as valid as I am. Why should their name-giving be less valid than mine?

1673   It is not easy for a layman to get the desired theological information, because even the Church is not at one with herself in this respect. *Who* represents authentic Christianity? Thus the layman whether he likes it or not has to quote Protestant or Catholic statements *pêle-mêle* as Christian views because they are backed up by some authority. In my case I believe I have been careful in quoting my sources.

1674   You as a theologian are naturally interested in the best possible view or explanation, while the psychologist is interested in all sorts of opinions because he wants to acquire some understanding of mental phenomenology and cares little for even the best possible metaphysical assertion, which is beyond human reach anyhow. The various creeds are just so many phenomena to him, and he has no means of deciding about the truth or the ultimate validity of any metaphysical statement. I cannot select the "best" or the "ultimate" opinions because I do not know which kind of opinion to choose from which Church. Also I do not care particularly where such opinions come from, and it is quite beyond my capacity to find out whether they are erroneous or not. I would be wrong only if I attributed, for instance, the idea of the *conceptio immaculata* to Protestantism or the *sola fide* standpoint to Catholicism. The many misunderstandings attributed to me come into this category. In either case it is plain to see that someone has been careless in his assumptions. But if I attribute Ritschl's christological views to

Protestantism, it is no error in spite of the fact that the Church of England does not subscribe to the opinions of Mr. Ritschl or of Mr. Barth.[24a] I hope I have not inadvertently been guilty of some misquotation.

1675 I can illustrate the problem by a typical instance. My little essay on Eastern Meditation[25] deals with the popular tract *Amitāyur Dhyāna Sūtra,* which is a relatively late and not very valuable Mahāyāna text. A critic objected to my choice: he could not see why I should take such an inconspicuous tract instead of a genuinely Buddhist and classical Pāli text in order to present Buddhist thought. He entirely overlooked the fact that I had no intention whatever of expounding classical Buddhism, but that my aim was to analyse the psychology of this particular text. Why should I not deal with Jacob Boehme or Angelus Silesius as Christian writers, even though they are not classical representatives either of Catholicism or of Protestantism?

1676 A similar misunderstanding appears in your view that I am not doing justice to the *ideal* of community. Whenever possible I avoid *ideals* and much prefer *realities.* I have never found a community which would allow "full expression to the individual within it." Suppose the individual is going to speak the truth regardless of the feelings of everybody else: he would not only be the most abominable enfant terrible but might equally well cause a major catastrophe. Edifying examples of this can be observed at the meetings of Buchman's so-called Oxford Group Movement. At the expense of truth the individual has to "behave," i.e., suppress his reaction merely for the sake of Christian charity. What if I should get up after a sermon about ideals and ask the parson how much he himself is able to live up to his admonitions? In my own case the mere fact that I am seriously interested in psychology has created a peculiar hostility or fear in certain circles. What has happened to those people in the Church, that is in a Christian community, who ventured to have a new idea? No community can escape the laws of mass psychology. I am critical of the community in the same way as I suspect the individual who builds his castles in Spain while anxiously avoiding the expression of his own convictions. I am shy of ideals which one preaches and never lives up to, simply because one cannot. I want to know rather what we

24a [Albrecht Ritschl (1822–1889) and Karl Barth (1886–1968), resp. German and Swiss Protestant theologians.]
25 ["The Psychology of Eastern Meditation" (C.W., vol. 11).]

can live. I want to build up a possible human life which carries through God's experiment and does not invent an ideal scheme knowing that it will *never* be fulfilled.

Later Letter[26]

1677   I am much obliged to you for telling me exactly what you think and for criticizing my blunt ways of thinking and writing (also of talking, I am afraid). It seems, however, to be the style of natural scientists: we simply state our proposition, assuming that nobody will think it to be more than a disputable hypothesis. We are so imbued with doubts concerning our assumptions that scepticism is taken for granted. We are therefore apt to omit the conventional *captatio benevolentiae lectoris* with its "With hesitation I submit . . . ," "I consider it a daring hypothesis . . . ," etc. We even forget the preamble: "This is the way I look at it . . . ."

1678   The case of the Jesuit[27] was that he put the direct question to me: "How on earth can you suggest that Christ was not human?" The discussion was naturally on the *dogmatic* level, as there is no other basis on which this question can be answered. It is not a question of *truth,* because the problem itself is far beyond human judgment. My "Answer to Job" is merely a reconstruction of the psychology discernible in this and other Old Testament texts for the interested layman. He knows very little of Higher Criticism, which is historical and philological in the main, and it is but little concerned with the layman's reactions to the paradoxes and moral horrors of the Old Testament. He knows his Bible and hears the sermons of his parson or priest. As a Catholic he has had a dogmatic education.

1679   When talking of "Job" you must always remember that I am dealing with the psychology of an archetypal and anthropomorphic image of God and not with a metaphysical entity. As far as we can see, the archetype is a psychic structure with a life of its own to a certain extent.

1680   God in the Old Testament is a guardian of law and morality, yet is himself unjust. He is a moral paradox, unreflecting in an ethical sense. We can perceive God in an infinite variety of images, yet all of them are anthropomorphic, otherwise they would not

26 [Philp, pp. 250–54. (12 Nov. 1957.)]
27 [Cf. supra, par. 1645.]

get into our heads. The divine paradox is the source of unending suffering to man. Job cannot avoid seeing it and thus he sees more than God himself. This explains why the God-image has to come down "into the flesh." The paradox, expressed of course with many hesitations in the particularities of the myth and in the Catholic dogma, is clearly discernible in the fact that the "Suffering Righteous man" is, historically speaking, an erroneous conception, not identical with the suffering God, because he is Jesus Christ, worshipped as a separate God (he is a mere prefiguration, painfully included in a triunity) and not an ordinary man who is forced to accept the suffering of intolerable opposites he has not invented. They were preordained. He is the victim, because he is capable of three-dimensional consciousness and ethical decision. (This is a bit condensed. Unlike Yahweh, man has self-reflection.)

1681   I don't know what Job is supposed to have seen. But it seems possible that he unconsciously anticipated the historical future, namely the evolution of the God-image. God had to become man. Man's suffering does not derive from his sins but from the maker of his imperfections, the paradoxical God. The righteous man is the instrument into which God enters in order to attain self-reflection and thus consciousness and rebirth as a divine child trusted to the care of adult man.

1682   Now this is not the statement of a truth, but the psychological reading of a mythological text—a model constructed for the purpose of establishing the psychological linking together of its contents. My aim is to show what the results are when you apply modern psychology to such a text. Higher Criticism and Hebrew philology are obviously superfluous, because it is simply a question of the text which the layman has under his eyes. The Christian religion has not been shaped by Higher Criticism.

1683   The trouble I have with my academic reader is that he cannot see a psychic structure as a relatively autonomous entity, because he is under the illusion that he is dealing with a concept. But in reality it is a living thing. The archetypes all have a life of their own which follows a biological pattern. A Church that has evolved a masculine Trinity will follow the old pattern: $3 + 1$, where 1 is a female and, if $3 =$ good, 1 as a woman will mediate between good and evil, the latter being the devil and the shadow of the Trinity. The woman will inevitably be the Mother-Sister of the Son-God, with whom she will be united *in thalamo*, i.e., in the ἱερος γάμος, *quod est demonstratum* by the second Encyclical concerning the Assumption.[28]

1684   A passionate discourse between the man Job and God will logically lead to a mutual rapprochement: God will be humanized, man will be "divinized." Thus Job will be followed by the idea of the Incarnation of God and the redemption and apotheosis of man. This development, however, is seriously impeded by the fact that the "woman," as always, inevitably brings in the problem of the shadow. Therefore *mulier taceat in ecclesia.* The arch-sin the Catholic Church is ever after is sexuality, and the ideal *par excellence* virginity, which puts a definite stop to life. But if life should insist on going on, the shadow steps in and sin becomes a serious problem, because the shadow cannot be left to eternal damnation any more. Consequently, at the end of the first millennium of the Christian aeon, as predicted in the Apocalypse, the world was suspected of being created by the devil.[29] The impressive and still living myth of the Holy Grail came to life with its two significant figures of Parsifal and Merlin. At the same time we observe an extraordinary development of alchemical philosophy with its central figure of the *filius macrocosmi,* a chthonic equivalent of Christ.

1685   This was followed by the great and seemingly incurable schism of the Christian Church, and last but not least by the still greater and more formidable schism of the world towards the end of the second millennium.

1686   A psychological reading of the dominant archetypal images reveals a continuous series of psychological transformations, depicting the autonomous life of archetypes behind the scenes of consciousness. This hypothesis has been worked out to clarify and make comprehensible our religious history. The treatment of psychological troubles and the inability of my patients to understand theological interpretations and terminology have given me my motive. The necessities of psychotherapy have proved to me the immense importance of a religious attitude, which cannot be achieved without a thorough understanding of religious tradition, just as an individual's troubles cannot be understood and cured without a basic knowledge of their biographical antecedents. I have applied to the

---

[28] [*Apostolic Constitution* (*"Munificentissimus Deus"*) *of Pius XII,* sec. 22: "The place of the bride whom the Father had espoused was in the heavenly courts." Sec. 33: ". . . on this day the Virgin Mother was taken up to her heavenly bridal-chamber."]

[29] [*Aion,* pars. 225ff.]

God-image what I have learned from the reconstruction of so many human lives through a knowledge of their unconscious. All this is empirical and may have nothing to do with theology, if theology says so. But if theology should come to the conclusion that its tenets have something to do with the empirical human psyche, I establish a claim. I think that in those circumstances my opinion should be given a hearing. It cannot be argued on the level of metaphysical assertions. It can be criticized only on its own psychological level, regardless of whether it is a psychologically satisfactory interpretation of the facts or not. The "facts" are the documented historical manifestations of the archetype, however "erroneous" they may be.

1687   I have stated my point of view bluntly (for which I must ask your forgiveness!) in order to give you a fair chance to see it as clearly as possible. The end of your letter, where you deal with Christ, leaves me with a doubt. It looks to me as if you were trying to explain the empirical man Jesus, while I am envisaging the archetype of the Anthropos and its very general interpretation as a collective phenomenon and not as the best possible interpretation of an individual and historical person. Christianity as a whole is less concerned with the historical man Jesus and his somewhat doubtful biography than with the mythological Anthropos or God-Son figure. It would be rather hazardous to attempt to analyse the historical Jesus as a human person. "Christ" appears from a much safer (because mythological) background, which invites psychological elucidation. Moreover it is not the Jewish rabbi and reformer Jesus, but the archetypal Christ who touches upon the archetype of the Redeemer in everybody and carries conviction.

1688   My approach is certainly not theological and cannot be treated as a theologoumenon. It is essentially a psychological attempt based upon the archetypal, amoral God-image, which is not a concept but rather an irrational and phenomenal experience, an *Urbild*. But in so far as theologians are also concerned with the adult human psyche (perhaps not as much as medical psychology), I am convinced that it would be of advantage to them to become acquainted with the psychological aspects of the Christian religion. I will not conceal the fact that theological thinking is very difficult for me, from which I conclude that psychological thinking must be an equally laborious undertaking for the theologian. This may explain why I inundate you with such a long letter.

1689   When I see how China (and soon India) will lose her old culture under the impact of materialistic rationalism, I grow afraid that the Christian West will succumb to the same malady, simply because the old symbolic language is no longer understood and people cannot see any more where and how it applies. In Catholic countries anyone leaving the Church becomes frankly atheistic. In Protestant countries a small number become sectarians, and the others avoid the churches for their cruelly boring and empty sermons. Not a few begin to believe in the State—not even knowing that they themselves are the State. The recent broadcasts of the B.B.C.[30] give a good picture of the educated layman's mind with regard to religion. What an understanding! All due to the lack of a psychological standpoint, or so it seems to me.

1690   I am sorry that I am apparently a *petra scandali*. I do not mean to offend. Please accept my apologies for my bluntness. I am sincerely grateful to you for giving me your attention.

Faithfully yours, C. G. JUNG

[30] [Probably a series of five talks on "Religion and Philosophy," by Robert C. Walton, J. D. Mabbott, Alasdair MacIntyre, and the Rev. F. A. Cockin, broadcast in Sept.–Oct. 1957, according to information from the B.B.C.]

XIII

ALCHEMICAL STUDIES

(related to Volumes 12, 13, and 14 of the Collected Works)

FOREWORD TO A CATALOGUE ON ALCHEMY[1]

1691   Alchemy is the forerunner or even the ancestor of chemistry, and is therefore of historical interest to the student of chemistry, in so far as it can be proved to contain recognizable descriptions of chemical substances, reactions, and technical procedures. How much may be gained in this respect from alchemical literature is shown by the comprehensive work of E. O. von Lippmann, *Entstehung und Ausbreitung der Alchemie* (Berlin, 1919). The peculiar character of this literature lies, however, in the fact that there exists a comparatively large number of treatises from which, apart from the most superficial allusions, absolutely nothing of a chemical nature can be extracted. It was therefore supposed—and many of the alchemists themselves wanted us to believe—that their mysterious sign-language was nothing but a skilful way of disguising the chemical procedures which lay behind it. The adept would see through the veil of hieroglyphics and recognize the secret chemical process. Unfortunately, alchemists of repute destroyed this legend by their admission that they were unable to read the riddle of the Sphinx, complaining that the old authors, like Geber and Raymundus Lullius, wrote too obscurely. And indeed, a careful study of such treatises, which perhaps form the majority, will reveal nothing of a chemical nature but something which is purely symbolic, i.e., *psychological.* Alchemical language is not so much *semeiotic* as *symbolic:* it does not disguise a known content but suggests an unknown one, or rather, this unknown content *suggests itself.* This content can only be psychological. If one analyses these symbolic forms of speech, one comes to the conclusion that archetypal contents of the collective unconscious are being projected. Consequently, alchemy acquires a new and interesting aspect as a *projected psychology of the collective unconscious,* and thus ranks in importance with mythology and folklore. Its symbolism has the closest connections with dream symbolism on the one hand, and the symbolism of religion on the other.

[1] [K. A. Ziegler (bookseller): *Alchemie* II, List No. 17 (Bern, May 1946). Foreword published in both German and English (here slightly revised). Reprinted as a prefatory note to Ian MacPhail, comp., *Alchemy and the Occult,* A Catalogue of Books and Manuscripts from the Collection of Paul and Mary Mellon Given to Yale University Library (New Haven, 1968).]

FAUST AND ALCHEMY[1]

1692 The drama of *Faust* has its primary sources in alchemy; these are on the one hand dreams, visions, and parables, on the other, personal and biographical notes regarding the Great Opus. One of the latest and most perfect examples of this sort is the *Chymische Hochzeit* of Christian Rosencreutz (1616), actually written by Johann Valentin Andreae (1586–1634), a theologian of Württemberg who was also the author of *Turbo* (1616), a comedy written in Latin.[2] The hero of this play is a learned know-it-all who, disillusioned with the sciences, finally returns to Christianity. The *Chymische Hochzeit* represents the *opus Alchymicum* under the aspect of the *hierosgamos* of brother and sister (Venus gives birth to a hermaphrodite). But these things are only hinted at in veiled terms. Because the royal children are still too infantile (identification with the parents, incest with the mother), they are slain, purified, and put together again, by being subjected to every alchemical procedure. To be restituted, the bridal pair is taken over the sea, and a kind of Aegean festival is celebrated with nymphs and sea-goddesses and a paean to love is sung. Rosencreutz is revealed as the father of the young king or, respectively, the royal couple.

1693 Alchemy had long known that the mystery of transformation applies not only to chemical materials but to man as well. The central figure is Mercurius, to whom I have devoted a special study.[3] He is a chthonic spirit, related to Wotan and the Devil.

1694 Faust is introduced like Job, but it is not he who suffers; it is others who suffer through him, and even the Devil is not left unscathed. Mercurius enters in the shape of Mephistopheles (Devil and Satan), as a dog to begin with, son of Chaos, and fire (alch. *filius canis*, arises out of chaos, *natura ignea*). He becomes the ser-

[1] [(Translated by H. N.) Author's abstract of a lecture given to the Psychological Club, Zurich, on 8 Oct. 1949; published in the Club's *Jahresbericht*, 1949–50. A typescript (38 pp.) of the entire lecture, made from a stenogram and evidently not corrected by Jung, is in the Jung archives.]

[2] [See "The Psychology of the Transference" (C.W., vol. 16), par. 407 and n. 18.]

[3] ["The Spirit Mercurius" (C.W., vol. 13), orig. 1942.]

vant of Faust (*familaris, servus fugitivus*). Mephisto has two ravens (cf. Wotan). He is the "northern phantom" and has his "pleasure-ground" in the "north-west."

1695   The axiom of Maria (3 + 1) pervades the whole work (4 main phases, 4 thieves, 4 (−1) grey women, 4 elements, Pluto's four-in-hand team of horses, 3 + 1 boys, 1 + 2 + 3 + 4 = 10 in the witches' tables, 3–4, 7–8 Kabiri, "Three and one and one and three," etc.).

1696   Mephisto brings about the projection onto the anima with its tragic end (child murder). There follows the suppression of Eros by the power drive (Walpurgisnacht = overpowering by the shadow). In the fire magic and the gold swindle there appears the Boy Charioteer, a Mercurius *juvenis,* on the one hand hermaphrodite like his preform, the Devil, a *kyllenios,* and on the other an analogy to Christ and the Holy Spirit; at the same time he brings the wild host (Wotan!).

1697   The underworld tripod embodies the feminine chthonic trinity (Diana, Luna, Hecate, and Phorkyads). It corresponds to the *vas hermeticum* (and the early Christian communion table of the catacombs with 3 loaves and 1 fish). The *Tripus Aureus* of alchemy is the one that Hephaestus cast into the sea.

1698   Faust falls into a faint when he tries to possess Helen. This is the beginning of Phase II, and the second upsurge of Eros. Faust is again rejuvenated (as in Phase I) as the Baccalaureus; the Devil, however, is "old." The Homunculus corresponds to the Boy Charioteer. His father is Wagner (Rosencreutz); his cousin is the Devil, hence Mercurius in a younger shape. Faust is taken to the classic "world of fable" (collective unconscious) for "healing." The "water" heals (*aqua permanens, mare nostrum*). From it emerges the mountain (rebirth of the personality, alch. arising of the *terra firma* out of the sea). The Aegean Festival is the *hierosgamos* of Homunculus and Galatea (both are "stones brought to life") in the sea. Touching the tripod with the key and the *hierosgamos* prefigure the "chymical" marriage of Faust to Helen, the sister anima. Their child Euphorion is the third renewal form of Mercurius.

1699   Phase III ends with the death of Euphorion, and once again the next and last phase begins with the power drive. The devout Philemon and Baucis are murdered. After Faust's death the Devil is cheated. The conflict goes on. Faust's place is taken by his "entelechy," the *puer aeternus,* who never can realize his united double nature because Faust is always the victim of whatever his shape may be at the time. He loses himself in smatterings of knowledge, in autoerotic Eros, in magic and deception, in the delusion of being a demigod (Helena), and finally in the inflation of thinking himself the saviour of the whole world. He is always blind about himself, does not know what he is doing, and lacks both responsibility and humour. But the Devil knows who he himself is; he does not lie to himself, he has humour and the small kind of love (insects), all of which Faust lacks. The shadow cannot be redeemed unless consciousness acknowledges it as a part of its own self—that is, understands its compensatory significance. The "blessed boy" is therefore only a representation of a prenatal state that in no way throws light on what the experience of earthly life was really for. Dr. Marianus is the "son of the mother." A possible parallel might be an eighth-century alchemist, Morienes, Morienus, Marianus,[4] who was one of the most spiritual of all alchemists and understood the *opus* as a human transformation system. He says: "Temporum quidem longa mutatio hominem sub tempore constitutum confundit et mutat . . . ultimam autem mutationem mors dira subsequitur."[5]

[4] [In the alchemical literature, usually Morienus Romanus. See *Psychology and Alchemy,* C.W., vol. 12, par. 386 and n. 88, and par. 558.]

[5] ["For the long lapse of time upsets man, who is under the law of time, and transforms him . . . after the final transformation, however, fearful death follows."—Morienus Romanus, "De transmutatione metallorum," *Artis auriferae* (Basel, 1610), II, p. 14.]

ALCHEMY AND PSYCHOLOGY[1]

1700   Throughout the history of alchemy we find—besides a considerable knowledge of substances (minerals and drugs) and a limited
knowledge of the laws of chemical processes—indications of an accompanying "philosophy" which received the name "Hermetic"
in the later Middle Ages. This natural philosophy appears first and
particularly clearly in the Greek alchemists of the first to the sixth
centuries A.D. (Pseudo-Demokritus, Zosimos of Panopolis, and
Olympiodorus). It was also especially evident in the sixteenth and
seventeenth centuries, when it reached its full development. This
development owed a great deal to Paracelsus and his pupils (Gerard
Dorn and Heinrich Khunrath). In the interval between these two
periods, philosophical speculation gave way to a more religious tendency (ideas were produced which ran parallel to the dogmatic
concepts), hand in hand with a "mystical" tendency which gives
alchemy its peculiar character. As the alchemists had no real knowledge of the nature and behaviour of chemical substances, they drew
conscious parallels between the unknown processes and mythological motifs and thus "explained" the former (cf. Dom Pernety, *Dictionnaire mytho-hermétique*, 1756) and they amplified these unknown processes by the projection of unconscious contents. This
explains a peculiarity of the texts: on the one hand, the authors
repeat what was said by their predecessors again and again and,
on the other, they give a free rein to unlimited subjective fantasy
in their symbolism. Comparative research has proved that the alchemical symbols are partly variations of mythological motifs, belonging to the conscious world of the alchemists, and partly spontaneous products of the unconscious. This becomes evident in the
parallel character of the symbolism in modern dreams and that
of alchemy. The alchemical symbols portray partly the substances
or their unknown "mystical" nature and partly the process which

---

[1] [Written in English for *Encyclopedia Hebraica* (Tel Aviv, 1951; Hebrew
year 5711), where it was published in vol. III, in a Hebrew translation. Nearly
all the allusions are explained in *Psychology and Alchemy*, C.W., vol. 12.
The English original is published here with minor stylistic changes.]

leads to the goal of the work. It is the latter aspect that gives rise to the most highly pictorial development. The principal symbol of the substance that is transformed during the process is *Mercurius*. His portrait in the texts agrees in all essentials with the characteristics of the unconscious.

1701   At the beginning of the process, he is in the *massa confusa,* the chaos or *nigredo* (blackness). In this condition, the elements are fighting each other. Here Mercurius plays the role of the *prima materia,* the transforming substance. He corresponds to the Nous or Anthropos, sunk in Physis, of Greek alchemy. In later days he is also called the "world soul in chains," a "system of the higher powers in the lower," etc. This depicts a dark ("unconscious") condition of the adept or of a psychic content. The procedures in the next phase have the purpose of illuminating the darkness by a *union of the opposed elements.* This leads to the *albedo* (whitening), which is compared to the sunrise or to the full moon. The white substance is also conceived as a pure body which has been refined by the fire but which still lacks a soul. It is considered to be feminine and is therefore called *sponsa* (bride), silver, or moon. Whereas the transformation of the darkness into light is symbolized by the theme of the fight with the dragon, it is the motif of the *hierosgamos* (sacred marriage of sister and brother or mother and son) which appears in this phase. The quaternity (*quaternio*) of the elements here becomes a duality (*binarius*). The reddening (*rubedo*) follows the whitening. By means of the *coniunctio* the moon is united with the sun, the silver with the gold, the female with the male.

1702   The development of the *prima materia* up to the *rubedo* (*lapis rubeus, carbunculus, tinctura rubra, sanguis spiritualis s. draconis,* etc.) depicts the conscious realization (*illuminatio*) of an unconscious state of conflict which is henceforth kept in consciousness. During this process, the scum (*terra damnata*) which cannot be improved must be thrown out. The white substance is compared to the *corpus glorificationis,* and another parallel is the *ecclesia.* The feminine character of the *lapis albus* corresponds to that of the unconscious, symbolized by the moon. The sun corresponds to the "light" of consciousness.

1703   Becoming conscious of an unconscious content amounts to its integration in the conscious psyche and is therefore a *coniunctio Solis et Lunae.* This process of integration is one of the most important, helpful factors in modern psychotherapy, which is preeminently concerned with the psychology of the unconscious, for both the nature of consciousness and that of the unconscious are altered by it. As a rule the process is accompanied by the phenomenon of the *transference,* that is, the projection of unconscious contents on to the doctor. We also meet this phenomenon in alchemy, where a woman adept often plays the role of the *soror mystica* (Zosimos and Theosebeia, Nicolas Flamel and Peronelle, John Pordage and Jane Leade, and in the nineteenth century Mr. South and his daughter, Mrs. Atwood).

1704 The *coniunctio* produces the *lapis philosophorum,* the central symbol of alchemy. This lapis has innumerable synonyms. On the one hand, its symbols are quaternary or circular figures and, on the other, the *rebis* or the hermaphroditic Anthropos who is compared to Christ. He has a trichotomus form (*habat corpus, animam et spiritum*) and is also compared to the Trinity (*trinus et unus*). The symbolism of the *lapis* corresponds to the mandala (circle) symbols in dreams, etc., which represent wholeness and order and therefore express the personality that has been altered by the integration of the unconscious. The alchemical *opus* portrays the process of individuation but in a projected form because the alchemists were unconscious of this psychic process.[2]

---

[2] [Jung appended the following bibliography:] Berthelot, *Collection des anciens alchimistes grecs* (1887); *Artis auriferae,* II (1593); *Theatrum chemicum* (1602–61), VI; Manget, *Bibliotheca chemica curiosa* (1702), II; Herbert Silberer, *Problems of Mysticism and Its Symbolism* (New York, 1917); R. Wilhelm and Jung, *The Secret of the Golden Flower* (1931); Jung, *Paracelsica* (1942), *Psychologie und Alchemie* (1944), *Die Psychologie der Uebertragung* (1946), *Symbolik des Geistes* (1948).

XIV

THE SPIRIT IN MAN, ART, AND LITERATURE

(related to Volume 15 of the Collected Works)

MEMORIAL TO J. S.[1]

1705   Death has laid its hand upon our friend. The darkness out of which his soul had risen has come again and has undone the life of his earthly body, and has left us alone in pain and sorrow.

1706   To many death seems to be a brutal and meaningless end to a short and meaningless existence. So it looks, if seen from the surface and from the darkness. But when we penetrate the depths of the soul and when we try to understand its mysterious life, we shall discern that death is not a meaningless end, the mere vanishing into nothingless—it is an accomplishment, a ripe fruit on the tree of life. Nor is death an abrupt extinction, but a goal that has been unconsciously lived and worked for during half a lifetime.

1707   In the youthful expansion of our life we think of it as an ever-increasing river, and this conviction accompanies us often far beyond the noonday of our existence. But if we listen to the quieter voices of our deeper nature we become aware of the fact that soon after the middle of our life the soil begins its secret work, getting ready for the departure. Our of the turmoil and terror of our life the one precious flower of the spirit begins to unfold, the four-petaled flower of the immortal light, and even if our mortal consciousness should not be aware of its secret operation, it nevertheless does its secret work of purification.

1708   When I met J. S. for the first time I found in him a man of rare clarity and purity of character and personality. I was deeply impressed with the honesty and sincerity of his purpose. And when I worked with him, helping him to understand the intricacies of the human psyche, I could not but admire the kindness of his feeling and the absolute truthfulness of his mind. But though it was a privilege to teach a man of such rare human qualities, it was not the thing that touched me most. Yes, I did teach him, but he taught me too. He spoke to me in the eternal language of symbols, which I did not grasp until the awe-inspiring conclusion, the culmination

---

[1] [Published in *Spring*, 1955 (Analytical Psychology Club of New York), with the note: "These words, spoken in 1927, are printed here with . . . permission of Dr. Jung." Evidently written in English. Club records indicate that J. S. was Jerome Schloss, of New York, but no other details have been available.]

in death, became manifest. I shall never forget how he liberated his mind from the turmoil of modern business life, and how, gradually working back, he freed himself from the bonds that held him fast to his earthly parents and to his youth; and how the eternal image of the soul appeared to him, first dimly, then slowly taking shape in the vision of his dreams, and how finally, three weeks before his death, he beheld the vision of his own sarcophagus from which his living soul arose.

1709   Who am I that I should dare say one word beyond this vision? Is there a human word that could stand against the revelation given to the chosen one? There is none.

1710   Let us return, therefore, to the external language and let us hear the words of the sacred text. And as the ancient words will give truth to us, we will give life to them. (I Corinthians 13; 15:37–55.)

FOREWORD TO SCHMID-GUISAN:
"TAG UND NACHT"[1]

1711   The atmosphere of this book is only too familiar to me. On reading the manuscript, I found it difficult at first to extricate myself from the toils of day-to-day psychotherapeutic practice—until I succeeded in viewing the book against its historical background. It is indeed something of a literary orphan, seeming to have no affinities with the present. Its strange form—the adventures of an allegorical hero—reminds one of the eighteenth century. But this is no more than a reminder, for the book is quite alien to the eighteenth century in its feeling. The problem of feeling is altogether modern, and the book opens up a world of experience that seems to have been locked away since the time of René d'Anjou—the whole sensuous world of Eros, which the latest Papal Encyclical on Christian marriage[2] and the penalistic conscience of modern man have conspired to suppress in a quite terrifying manner. Actually it is an esoteric book, a petal fallen from the unfading mystic rose which the troubadours accused the Church of hiding under a veil of secrecy. As though any Church had ever known the secret, or knowing it could have tolerated it! This book is neither for nor of the masses. For the multitude, it had better not been written, or should be read only because of its bad reputation. They will be lucky if they emerge unscathed. Nearly five hundred years ago a similar book was written, again at a cultural turning-point, and again a petal from that mystic rose—a knightly adventure and a stumbling-block to the vulgar, the *Hypnerotomachia*[3] of that celebrated Poliphilo, who for a moment twitched the veil from the psychic background of the Cinquecento. From the preface to that book I would like to set down a classical passage which shows how the Knights of the Rose join hands across the centuries:

[1] [Zurich and Munich, 1931. For Hans Schmid-Guisan (1881–1932), see Jung's letter of 6 Nov. 1915, in *Letters,* ed. G. Adler, vol. 1.]
[2] [*Casti Connubii* of Pius XI, 31 Dec. 1930.]
[3] [By Francesco Colonna, 1499. Cf. infra, pars. 1751ff., "Foreword to Fierz–David: *The Dream of Poliphilo.*"]

From this it is evident that all wise men have practised their sciences beneath the shadow of the fairest, innermost secrets of Love. Love was, and is still, the graceful brush which traces out all that is strange and appointed by Fate, as much among the higher as the lower powers, and all that is subject to them. . . .

Know, see and hear, and you will wisely remark that the most splendid, sublime, and precious mysteries are hidden beneath the beauties of Love, from which they issue anew, for Love is the joyful soul of everything that lives. . . .

Should I discover that some profane person had put forth his odious hand to this book to finger it, or that some unworthy creature should make bold to turn its pages, or that some shameless dissembler, under the cloak of piety, should derive a vulgar pleasure from it, or that some evil-minded spectator of these sovereign gifts should seek, from boredom, the profit that by right belongs only to loving hearts, I would break the pen which has described so many configurations of the great secret, and, utterly forgetful of myself, would expunge all memory of the satisfaction I have found in the narration, delicately veiled in the semblance of pretty fictions, of things most wonderful and rare, which serve but to elevate a man to all that is virtuous, and denying myself the very life of my life, I would abstain from the eager pursuit of those voluptuous charms which draw men towards the sacred delights.[4]

1712 Since witless literal-mindedness has not died out in four hundred years, I would like to impress upon the reader the classical warning which the unconscious gave Poliphilo on his journey into the darkness: "Whoever thou mayest be, take of this treasure as much as thou willst. Yet I warn thee, take from the head and touch not the body."[5]

Hans Schmid-Guisan: In Memoriam[6]

1713 Life is in truth a battle, in which friends and faithful companions-in-arms sink away, struck by the wayward bullet. Sorrowfully I see the passing of a comrade, who for more than twenty

---

[4] [This is from the "Receuil stéganographique," the introduction to Béroalde de Verville's French translation of 1600, and is not represented in the above-cited English version. The trans. here, by A.S.B. Glover, is from the French.]

[5] "Quisquis es quantumque libuerit, huius thesauri sume: at moneo, aufer caput, corpus ne tangiot." [Cf. *The Dream of Poliphilo,* p. 39.]

[6] [*Basler Nachrichten,* 25 Apr. 1932.]

years shared with me the experiment of life and the adventure of the modern spirit.

1714 I first met Hans Schmid-Guisan at a conference of psychiatrists in Lausanne,[6a] where I discussed for the first time the impersonal, collective nature of psychic symbols. He was then assistant physician at the Mahaim Clinic in Cery. Not long afterwards he came to Zurich, in order to study analytical psychology with me. This collaborative effort gradually broadened into a friendly relationship, and the problems of psychological practice frequently brought us together in serious work or round a convivial table. At that time we were especially interested in the question of the relativity of psychological judgments, or, in other words, the influence of temperament on the formation of psychological concepts. As it turned out, he developed instinctively an attitude type which was the direct opposite of my own. This difference led to a long and lively correspondence,[7] thanks to which I was able to clear up a number of fundamental questions. The results are set forth in my book on types.

1715 I remember a highly enjoyable bicycle tour which took us to Ravenna, where we rode along the sand through the waves of the sea. This tour was a continual discussion which lasted from coffee in the morning, all through the dust of the Lombardy roads, to the round-bellied bottle of Chianti in the evening, and continued even in our dreams. He stood the test of this journey: he was a good companion and always remained so. He battled valiantly with the hydra of psychotherapy and did his best to inculcate into his patients the same humanity for which he strove as an ideal. He never actually made a name for himself in the scientific world, but shortly before his death he had the pleasure of finding a publisher for his book *Tag und Nacht*,[8] in which he set down many of his experiences in a form peculiarly his own. Faithful to his convictions, he wrote it as he felt he had to write it, pandering to nobody's prejudices. His humanity and his sensitive psychological understanding were not gifts that dropped down from heaven, but the fruit of unending work on his own soul. Not only relatives and friends stand mourning today by his bier, but countless people for whom he opened the treasure-house of the psyche. They know what this means to them in a time of spiritual drought.

[6a] [Cf. *The Freud/Jung Letters*, 259J, of 12 June 1911.]
[7] [See *Psychological Types*, C.W., vol. 6, p. xii.]   [8] [Cf. supra.]

ON THE TALE OF THE OTTER[1]

1716   In writing a few introductory words to this publication, one of his last, I am discharging a duty to my dead friend, Oskar A. H. Schmitz. I am not a literary man, nor am I competent to pass judgment on aesthetic questions. Moreover, the literary value of "The Tale of the Otter" is of little concern to me. I readily admit that, as a fairytale, it is as good or as bad as any other that a writer has invented. Such tales, as we know, even though invented by a great writer, do not breathe the flowery, woodland magic of the popular fairytale. Usually they can be shown to be products of the author's personal psychology, and they have a problematical air that makes them slightly unnatural. This is true also of "The Tale of the Otter." It is only a literary form for a content that could have been expressed in quite other words and in quite another way. Nevertheless, it was not chosen fortuitously. The content clothed itself in fairytale form not with the secret pretence of being an allegory, but because in this guise it could find the simplest and most direct access to the reader's heart. Childlike simplicity of heart was a basic trait of Schmitz's nature, known to very few people, and one which he himself recognized only late in life. Thanks to this simplicity, he could speak to the hearts of those he wished to touch.

1717   I happen to know how the tale came to be written. It was not born of any conscious intention to reach a particular kind of public; it was never even thought out, but flowed unconsciously from his pen. Schmitz had learnt how to switch off his critical intellect for certain purposes and to place his literary powers at the disposal of the heart's wisdom. In this way he was able to say things that are infinitely far removed from the usual style of his writings. At times, it became a real necessity for him to express himself in this way. For many things which reason wrestles with

---

[1] ["Vorwort zum Märchen vom Fischotter," i.e., foreword to one tale in Oscar A. H. Schmitz, *Märchen aus dem Unbewussten* (Munich, 1932), with drawings by Alfred Kubin. For Schmitz (1873–1931), see Jung's letter of 26 May 1923 in *Letters*, ed. G. Adler, vol. I.]

in vain flow easily and effortlessly into a pen emptied of all critical intentions.

1718   The result may seem very simple, indeed naïve, and anyone who read it as one reads a popular fairytale would be disappointed. It is equally idle to take it as an allegory. Schmitz himself did not really know what his tale meant. He told me so himself, for we often talked about it.

1719   The utterances of the heart—unlike those of the discriminating intellect—always relate to the whole. The heartstrings sing like an Aeolian harp only under the gentle breath of a mood, an intuition, which does not drown the song but listens. What the heart hears are the great, all-embracing things of life, the experiences which we do not arrange ourselves but which happen to us. All the pyrotechnics of reason and literary skill pale beside this, and language returns to the naïve and childlike. Simplicity of style is justified only by significance of content, and the content acquires its significance only from the revelation of experience. The decisive experience of Schmitz's life was his discovery of the reality of the psyche and the overcoming of rationalistic psychologism. He discovered that the psyche is something that really exists. This changed his life and his work outlook.

1720   For those who are vouchsafed such a discovery, the psyche appears as something objective, a psychic non-ego. This experience is very like the discovery of a new world. The supposed vacuum of a merely subjective psychic space becomes filled with objective figures, having wills of their own, and is seen to be a cosmos that conforms to law, and among these figures the ego takes its place in transfigured form. This tremendous experience means a shattering of foundations, an overturning of our arrogant world of consciousness, a cosmic shift of perspective, the true nature of which can never be grasped rationally or understood in its full implications.

1721   An experience of this kind induces an almost frightening need to communicate with sympathetic fellow-beings, to whom one then turns with naïve words. "The Tale of the Otter" describes an experience of the unconscious and the resultant transformation both of the personality and of the figures in the psyche. The King stands for the ruling principle of consciousness, which strays further and further away from the unconscious. (The fish disappear from the waters of the kingdom.) The stagnation of consciousness finally compels the King to make contact with the unconscious again. (The

King's pilgrimage.) The otter, the unconscious partner of the ego, seeks to bring about a reconciliation with consciousness. (Gilgamesh-Eabani motif.) This is successful, and a new world of consciousness arises on an apparently firm foundation. But as the King represents only the best part of the personality, and not the inferior part, the shadow, which should also be included in the transformation, the old King dies and his good-for-nothing nephew succeeds to the throne. The second half of the tale is concerned with the far more difficult task of including the weaknesses of the personality and its useless, adolescent traits in the process of transformation. This is especially difficult because the shadow is burdened with a still more inferior, feminine component, a negative anima figure (Brolante, the harlot). While the masculine components are successfully brought into harmony with the vital instincts (represented by animals), there is a final separation between the spiritual and the physical nature of the anima. The masculine half is rescued from evil, but the feminine half becomes its victim.

1722   "The Tale of the Otter" gives touching and modest expression to an all-embracing and all-transforming initiation. Read it with care and meditate upon it! For when all this has been fulfilled in him, Schmitz died. In this little fairytale he tells posterity how it fared with him and what transformations his soul had to undergo before it was ready to lay aside its garment and end its lifelong experiment.

IS THERE A FREUDIAN TYPE OF POETRY?[1]

1723   Poetry, like every product of the human mind, is naturally dependent on a man's general psychological attitude. If a writer is
sick, psychically sick, it is highly probable that whatever he produces will bear the stamp of his sickness. This is true with reservations, of course; for there actually are cases where the creative
genius so far transcends the sickness of the creator that only a few
traces of human imperfection are to be seen in the work. But these
are exceptions; the general rule is that a neurotic poet will make
neurotic poems. The more neurotic a poem is, the less it is a creative
work of art and the more it is a symptom. It is therefore very
easy to point out infantile symptoms in such cases and to view
the product in the light of a particular theory; indeed, it is sometimes possible to explain a work of art in the same way as one
can explain a nervous illness in terms of Freud's theory or Adler's.
But when it comes to great poetry the pathological explanation,
the attempt to apply Freudian or Adlerian theory, is in effect a
ridiculous belittlement of the work of art. The explanation not only
contributes nothing to an understanding of the poetry, but, on the
contrary, deflects our gaze from that deeper vision which the poet
offers. The Freudian and the Adlerian theory alike formulate nothing but the human-all-too-human aspects of the commonplace neurosis. So when one applies this point of view to great poetry, one
is dragging it down to the level of dull ordinariness, when actually
it towers above it like a high mountain. It is quite obvious that
all human beings have father and mother complexes, and it therefore means nothing if we discern traces of a father or mother complex in a great work of art; just as little as would the discovery
that Goethe had a liver and two kidneys like any other mortal.

1724   If the meaning of a poetic work can be exhausted through the
application of a theory of neurosis, then it was nothing but a patho-

[1] [Written originally in German, in answer to the question "Existe-t'il une
poésie de signe freudien?" and published in a French trans. in the *Journal des
poètes* (Brussels), III:5 (11 Dec. 1932), under the heading "La Psychanalyse
devant la poésie," with answers also from R. Allendy and Louis Charles
Baudouin.]

logical product in the first place, to which I would never concede the dignity of a work of art. Today, it is true, our taste has become so uncertain that often we no longer know whether a thing is art or a disease. I am convinced, however, that if a work of art can be explained in exactly the same way as the clinical history of a neurosis, either it is not a work of art, or the explainer has completely misunderstood its meaning. I am quite convinced that a great deal of modern art, painting as well as poetry, is simply neurotic and that it can, consequently, be reduced like an hysterical symptom to the basic, elementary facts of neurotic psychology. But so far as this is possible, it ceases to be art, because great art is man's creation of something superhuman in defiance of all the ordinary, miserable conditions of his birth and childhood. To apply to this the psychology of neurosis is little short of grotesque.

FOREWORD TO GILBERT:
"THE CURSE OF INTELLECT"[1]

1725   The author has kindly given me a chance of reading his book in manuscript. I must say, I have read it with the greatest interest and pleasure. It is most refreshing, after the whole nineteenth century and a stretch of the twentieth, to see the intellect once more turned loose upon herself, not exactly in the dispassionate form of a "Critique of Pure Reason," but in the rather impassioned way of a most temperamental onslaught on herself. As a matter of fact, it is a wholesome and vitalizing tearing into sorry shreds of what all "healthy-minded" people believed in as their most cherished securities. I am human enough to enjoy a juicy piece of injustice when it comes in the right moment and in the right place. Sure enough, Intellect has done her worst in our "Western Civilization," and she is still at it with undoubted force. Kant could still afford to deal with the contemporaneous intellect in a polite, careful, and gentle way, because she then was but a mere fledgling. But our time is concerned with a monster completely grown up and so fat that it can easily begin to devour itself.

1726   At the funeral somebody will be allowed to say only something nice about the deceased. In anticipation of that future event I will say it now: The chief trouble seems to be that the intellect escaped the control of man and became his obsession, instead of remaining the obedient tool in the hands of a creator, shaping his world, adorning it with the colourful images of his mind.

January 1934

1 [Written in English. The book was never published. For J. Allen Gilbert, M.D. (1867–1948), American psychotherapist, see Jung's letters of 19 June 1927 and 8 Jan. 1934 (relevant to this MS) in *Letters,* ed. G. Adler, vol. 1.]

FOREWORD TO JUNG:
"WIRKLICHKEIT DER SEELE" (1934)[1]

¹⁷²⁷ This, the fourth volume of my "Psychologische Abhandlungen," contains a number of essays that faithfully reflect the manifold facets of the more recent psychology. It is not long since the psychology of the personality broke free from the all too narrow confines of the consulting room on the one hand, and of materialistic and rationalistic assumptions on the other. It is therefore no wonder if much still clings to it that is in need of clarification. Until recently the worst chaos prevailed in the realm of theory, and only now have serious attempts been made to clear away the confusion. Dr. Kranefeldt's contributions[2] are devoted to this task. Dr. Rosenthal's contribution[3] is an application of the typological viewpoint to the scientific study of religion. The archetypical figures of anima and animus form a special department of depth psychology. Emma Jung discusses the phenomenology of the animus complex.[4]

¹⁷²⁸ My own contributions are concerned on the one hand with the philosophical problems of modern psychology, and on the other hand with its applications. Since this time, too, my essays came into being as answers to questions addressed to me by the public,[5] their unusual diversity may be taken as an indication that recent psychological insights have left their mark on as many diverse realms of the mind. Not only doctors and teachers, but writers and educated laymen, and—last but not least—even publishers are now evincing an interest in things psychological.

¹⁷²⁹ These many facets of complex psychology, lighting up the most

---

[1] [("Reality of the Soul"; subtitled "Applications and Advances of the New Psychology.") Besides the four contributions of other writers, there are nine essays by Jung, which were assigned to several vols. of the C.W.]

[2] [W. M. Kranefeldt, "Der Gegensatz von Sinn und Rhythmus im seelischen Geschehen," and " 'Ewige Analyse'. Bemerkung zur Traumdeutung und zum Unbewussten."]

[3] [Hugo Rosenthal, "Der Typengegensatz in der jüdischen Religionsgeschichte."]

[4] [Emma Jung, "Ein Beitrag zum Problem des Animus." Trans. by Cary F. Baynes, "On the Nature of the Animus," in *Animus and Anima* (Analytical Psychology Club of New York, 1957).]

[5] [Cf. "Foreword to *Seelenprobleme der Gegenwart*," supra, par. 1292.]

varied walks of life and domains of the mind, are in turn a much simplified reflection of the measureless diversity and iridescence of the psyche itself. Although one could never dream of exhausting its mysteries and fathoming all its secrets, it nevertheless seems to me one of the foremost tasks of the human mind to labour without cease for an ever deeper knowledge of man's psychic nature. For the greatest enigma in the world, and the one that is closest to us, is man himself.

September 1933

FOREWORD TO MEHLICH: "J. H. FICHTES SEELENLEHRE UND IHRE BEZIEHUNG ZUR GEGENWART"[1]

1730   Although I owe not a little to philosophy, and have benefited by the rigorous discipline of its methods of thought, I nevertheless feel in its presence that holy dread which is inborn in every observer of facts. The unending profusion of concepts spawning yet other concepts, rolling along like a great flood in the history of philosophy, is only too likely to inundate the little experimental gardens of the empiricist, so carefully marked out, swamping his well-ploughed fields, and swallowing up the still unexplored virgin land. Confronting the flux of events with unprejudiced gaze, he must fashion for himself an intellectual tool stripped of all preconceptions, and anxiously eschew as perilous temptations all those modes of thinking which philosophy offers him in such excessive abundance.

1731   Because I am an empiricist first and foremost, and my views are grounded in experience, I had to deny myself the pleasure of reducing them to a well-ordered system and of placing them in their historical and ideological context. From the philosophical standpoint, of whose requirements I am very well aware, this is indeed a painful omission. Even more painful to me, however, is the fact that the empiricist must also forswear an intellectual clarification of his concepts such as is absolutely imperative for the philosopher. His thinking has to mould itself to the facts, and the facts have as a rule a distressingly irrational character which proves refractory to any kind of philosophical systematization. Thus it comes about that empirical concepts are concerned for the most part with the chaos of chance events, because it is their function to produce a provisional order amid the disorder of the phenomenal world. And because they are wholly bent on this urgent task, they neglect—sometimes only too readily—their own philosophical development and inner clarification, for a thinker who performs the first task satisfactorily will seldom be able to complete the second.

[1] [Zurich and Leipzig, 1935. ("Fichte's Psychology and Its Relation to the Present.") The author, Dr. Rose Mehlich, closed her book with a chapter on Fichte and Jung.]

770

1732   These two aspects became overwhelmingly clear to me as I read this admirable study of Fichte's psychology: on the one hand the apparent carelessness and vagueness of my own concepts when it comes to systematic formulation, and on the other the precision and clarity of a philosophical system which is singularly unencumbered by empirical impedimenta. The strange but undeniable analogy between two points of view derived from totally different sources certainly gives one food for thought. I am not aware of having plagiarized Fichte, whom I have not read. Naturally I am familiar with Leibniz, C. G. Carus, and von Hartmann, but I never knew till now that my psychology is "Romantic." Unlike Rickert[2] and many other philosophers and psychologists, I hold that, in spite of all abstraction, objectivity, absence of bias, and empiricism, everyone thinks as *he* thinks and sees as *he* sees. Accordingly, if there is a type of mind, or a disposition, that thinks and interprets "romantically," analogous conclusions will emerge no matter whether they are coloured by the subject or by the object. It would be vain to imagine—gamely competing with Baron Münchhausen—that one could disembarrass oneself of one's own weight and thus get rid of the ultimate and most fundamental of all premises—one's own disposition. Only an isolated and hypertrophied psychic function is capable of cherishing such an illusion. But a function is only a part of the human whole, and its limited character is beyond all doubt. Were it not for these considerations the analogy between Fichte and me would certainly have to be regarded as a minor miracle.

1733   It is a bold undertaking—for which the author deserves all the more credit—to bring Fichte into line with a modern empirical psychology based on facts that were wholly inaccessible to this philosopher—an empiricism, morever, which has unearthed conceptual material that is singularly unsuited to philosophical evaluation. But it seems that this undertaking has been successful, for I learn to my amazement that the Romantic Movement has not been relegated to the age of fossils, but still has living representatives. This is probably no accident, for it appears that besides the self-evident experience of the "objective" world there is an *experience of the psyche,* without which an experience of the world would not be possible at all. It seems to me that the secret of Romanticism is that it confronted the all-too-obvious *object* of experience with a

2 [Heinrich Rickert (1863–1936), German philosopher, taught that an individual's bias influences what he learns.]

subject of experience, which it proceeded to objectify thanks to the infinite refractive powers of consciousness. There is a psychology that always has another person or thing for an object—a fairly well-differentiated kind of behaviourism which might be described as "classical." But besides this there is a psychology which is a knowing of the knower and an experiencing of the experiment.

1734   The indirect influence of the type of mind exemplified by Hume, Berkeley, and Kant can hardly be overestimated. Kant in particular erected a barrier across the mental world which made it impossible for even the boldest flight of speculation to penetrate into the object. Romanticism was the logical counter-movement, expressed most forcefully, and most cunningly disguised, in Hegel, that great psychologist in philosopher's garb. Nowadays it is not Kant but natural science and its de-subjectivized world that have erected the barrier against which the speculative tendency rebounds. Its essentially behaviourist statements about the object end in meaninglessness and nonsense. That is why we seek the meaning in the statements of the subject, believing we are not in error if we assume that the subject will first of all make statements about itself. Is it the empiricist in me, or is it because analogy is not identity, that makes me regard the "Romantic" standpoint simply as a point of departure and its statements as "comparative material"?

1735   I admit that this attitude is disappointingly sober, but the psychic affinity with a romantic philosopher prompts me to a critical utterance which seems to me the more in place as there are only too many people for whom "Romantic" always means something out of a romance.

1736   Apart from this critical proviso, which the author herself stresses, her book is a welcome contribution of the study of a specific attitude of mind which has recurred many times in the course of history and presumably will also recur in the future.

FOREWORD TO VON KOENIG-FACHSENFELD: "WANDLUNGEN DES TRAUMPROBLEMS VON DER ROMANTIK BIS ZUR GEGENWART"[1]

1737   The author has asked me to write a foreword to her dissertation. I am happy to comply with her request because this comprehensive and well-documented work deserves to be known to a wider scientific public. Although we already possess a number of valuable "synoptic" studies which give a fairly complete account of the various doctrines prevalent in modern psychology—I would mention in particular the works of W. Kranefeldt, G. R. Heyer, and Gerhard Adler—there was always a noticeable gap as regards the historical and philosophical side of complex psychology. The more conscious it became of the magnitude of its task—the study of the human psyche in its totality—the more contacts it made with other fields of thought where the psyche has an equal right to speak, above all with philosophy. For whenever a science begins to grow beyond its narrow specialist boundaries, the need for fundamental principles is forced upon it, and with this it moves into the sovereign sphere of philosophy. If the science happens to be psychology, a confrontation with philosophy is unavoidable for the very reason that it had been a philosophic discipline from the beginning, resolutely breaking away from philosophy only in quite recent times, when it established itself within the philosophical and the medical faculties as an independent empirical science with mechanistic techniques. The experimental psychology inaugurated by W. Wundt was succeeded by the psychology of the neuroses, which had been developed almost simultaneously by Freud in Vienna and by Pierre Janet in Paris. My own course of development was influenced primarily by the French school and later by Wundt's psychology. Later, in 1906, I made contact with Freud, only to part company with him in 1913, after seven years of collaboration, owing to differences of scientific opinion. It was chiefly considerations of principle that brought

---

[1] [Stuttgart, 1935. ("Transformations of Dream Problems from Romanticism to the Present.") For Dr. Olga von Koenig-Fachsenfeld, see Jung's letter of 5 May 1941 in *Letters,* ed. G. Adler, vol. 1.]

about the separation, above all the recognition that psychopathology can never be based exclusively on the psychology of psychic disease, which would restrict it to the pathological, but must include normal psychology and the full range of the psyche. Modern medicine quite rightly adheres to the principle that pathology must be based on a thorough knowledge of normal anatomy and physiology. The criterion by which we judge disease does not and cannot lie in the disease itself, as most of the medieval physicians thought, but only in the normal functioning of the body. Disease is a variation of the normal. The same considerations apply to therapy.

1738   For a long time it seemed as though experimental and medical psychologists could get along with purely scientific methods. But the view gradually gained ground that a critique of certain ideals originating in the humanistic disciplines was not out of place, since a careful investigation of the aetiology of pathological states had shown how the general attitude of the patient which led to the morbid variation depended on just these ideal or moral premises, not to mention the interpretation of facts and the theories resulting therefrom. But as soon as medical psychology reached this point, it turned out that the principles which had hitherto held unlimited sway over men's minds were of a purely rationalistc or materialistic nature, and, in spite of their "scientific" pretensions, had to be subjected to philosophical criticism because the object of their judgment was the *psyche itself*. The psyche is an extremely complex factor, so fundamental to all premises that no judgment can be regarded as "purely empirical" but must first indicate the premises by which it judges. Modern psychology can no longer disguise the fact that the object of its investigation is its own essence, so that in certain respects there can be no "principles" or valid judgments at all, but only *phenomenology*—in other words, *sheer experience*. On this level of knowledge, psychology has to abdicate as a science, though only on this very high level. Below that, judgments and hence science are still possible, provided that the premises are always stated, and to that extent the prospects for psychology as a science are by no means hopeless. But once it ceases to be conscious of the factors conditioning its judgments, or if it has never attained to this consciousness, it is like a dog chasing his own tail.

1739   So far, then, as psychology takes its own premises into account, its relevance to philosophy and the history of ideas is self-evident, and this is where the present book comes in. No one can deny that certain of these premises are a restatement of ideas dating back to the time of the Romantics. However, it is not so much the ideal premises that justify the author's historical approach as the supposedly "modern" phenomenological standpoint of "sheer experience," which was not only anticipated by the Romantics but actually pertains to their very nature. It was the essence of Romanticism to "experience" the psyche rather than to "investigate" it. This was once again an age of philosopher-physicians, a phenomenon that was observed for the first time in the post-Paracelsan era, more especially in philosophical alchemy, whose most important practitioners were usually doctors. In keeping with the pre-scientific spirit of the times, the Romantic psychology of the early nineteenth century was a child of Romantic natural philosophy—one thinks of C. G. Carus—although the beginnings of empiricism were already discernible in Justinus Kerner. The psychology of the sixteenth century, on the other hand, still had occult and religious undercurrents, and though it called itself "philosophy" a later, "enlightened" age would hardly have countenanced the name. The psyche as experience is the hallmark of the Romantics who sought the blue flower,[2] as well as of the philosophical alchemists who sought the *lapis noster.*

1740   This book performs the valuable service of unlocking a veritable treasure-house of contemplative Romantic poetry for modern psychology. The parallelism with my psychological conceptions is sufficient justification for calling them "Romantic." A similar inquiry into their philosophical antecedents would also justify such an epithet, for every psychology that takes the psyche as "experience" is from the historical point of view both "Romantic" and "alchemystical." Below this experimental level, however, my psychology is scientific and rationalistic, a fact I would beg the reader not to overlook. The premise underlying my judgments is the *reality of everything psychic,* a concept based on the appreciation of the fact that the psyche can also be pure experience.

1741   The author has carried out her task with great professional expertise, and I warmly recommend her book to everyone who is interested in the problems of modern complex psychology.

[2] [A symbol of the poet's search, in German romantic poetry. Cf. *Psychology and Alchemy,* C.W., vol. 12, pars. 99ff.]

FOREWORD TO GILLI: "DER DUNKLE BRUDER"[1]

1742   By writing a foreword to Gertrud Gilli's drama in verse, I do not wish to evoke the impression that it needs a psychological explanation in order to heighten its effect. Works of art are their own interpretation. *The Dark Brother* does not share the modern obscurantism of certain contemporary paintings, nor is it a direct product of unconscious activity which would require interpretation and transcription into generally intelligible language.

1743   The play is modern, however, in so far as the central process of Christianity, the divine drama, is reflected in the sphere of human motivations. A bold stroke indeed! But has not the personality of Judas always been a problematical figure in the redemption mystery? For certain Protestant theologians and historians, Christ himself has been stripped of his divine incarnation and become simply a founder of religion, a very superior and exemplary one, it is true, and his passion mere human suffering for the sake of an ideal, thus lending considerably more plausibility to the human protagonists and antagonists. Only in the mythological phase of the mind are heroes representatives of light and purity, and their adversaries embodiments of absolute evil. The real man is a mixture of good and bad, of self-determination and supine dependence, and the borderline between genuine ideals and personal striving for power is often very difficult to draw. As for the genius, his role as the mouthpiece and proclaimer of new truths is not always felt as an unmixed blessing by ordinary mortals, especially where religious beliefs are concerned.

1744   In one form or another, the figure of the redeemer is universal because it partakes of our common humanity. It invariably emerges from the unconscious of the individual or the people when an intolerable situation cries out for a solution that cannot be implemented by conscious means alone. Thus the Messianic expectations of the Jews were bound to rise to fever pitch when, as a result of the

[1] [Zurich, 1938. ("The Dark Brother.") Gertrud Gilli was a graphologist. Cf. her article, "C. G. Jung in seiner Handschrift," in *Die kulturelle Bedeutung der komplexen Psychologie* (1935).]

corruption that followed in the wake of Herod the Great, all hope of an independent sacerdotal order or kingdom had vanished, and the country had become a Roman province lacking any form of autonomy. It is therefore readily understandable that these Messianic expectations centred on a political redeemer, and that more than one enthusiastic patriot sought to fulfil this role—above all Judas of Galilee, whose insurrection is reported by Flavius Josephus,[2] and who, boldly but quite logically, entangles the eponymous hero of this drama in a similar task.

1745   But underlying the divine drama there is a different plan, which is not concerned with man's outward, social, or political liberation. It focuses rather on the inner man and his psychic transformation. What is the use of changing the external conditions if man's inner attitude remains the same? It is all the same, psychologically, whether his subjection is the result of external circumstances or of intellectual or moral systems. True "redemption" comes about only when he is led back to that deepest and innermost source of life which is generally called God. Jesus was the channel for a new and direct experience of God, and how little this depends on external conditions is amply demonstrated by the history of Christianity.

1746   Man lives in a state of continual conflict between the truth of the external world in which he has been placed and the inner truth of the psyche that connects him with the source of life. He is pulled now to one side and now to the other until he has learnt to see that he has obligations to both. In this sense Gertrud Gilli's play gives expression to a universal and timeless human fact: beyond our personal and time-bound consciousness, in our interior selves, there is enacted the everlasting drama in which the all-too-human players reach out, yearning and shrinking at once, for the deeper truth, and seek to bend it to their own purposes and their own ruin.

1747   If Judas in Gilli's play is depicted as the dark brother of Jesus, and if his character and fate are reminiscent of Hamlet's, there may well be deeper reasons for this. One could imagine him more active and aggressive, for instance as a fiery patriot who has to get rid of Jesus from inner necessity, because Jesus as the corrupter of the people obstructs his plans for their liberation, or else because Judas sees him as the political Messiah and then betrays him out

[2] [*The Jewish War*, II, 56; A.D. 6 or 7.]

777

of disappointment and rage. In this sense, too, Judas would be his dark brother, since in the story of the Temptation the devil of worldly power stepped up to Jesus in much the same way as Mara tempted the Buddha. Judas might easily have become a hero after the manner of classical drama. But because his dependence catches him on every side and he can scarcely act on his own initiative, he becomes an exponent of the human drama which, though played out within the confines of the earth's shadow, has at all times accompanied the divine drama and often eclipsed it.

GÉRARD DE NERVAL[1]

1748   Gérard de Nerval (pseudonym of Gérard Labrunie, 1808–
1853) was a lyric poet and translator of Goethe and Heine.
He is best known by his posthumously published novel *Aurélia*,
in which he relates the history of his anima and at the same time
of his psychosis. The dream at the beginning, of a vast edifice and
the fatal fall of a winged daemon, deserves special attention. The
dream has no lysis. The daemon represents the self, which no longer
has any room to unfold its wings. The disastrous event preceding
the dream is the projection of the anima upon "une personne ordi-
naire de notre siècle," with whom the poet was unable to work
on the *mysterium* and in consequence jilted Aurélia. Thus he lost
his "pied à terre" and the collective unconscious could break in.
His psychotic experiences are largely descriptions of archetypal
figures. During his psychosis the real Aurélia appears to have died,
so that his last chance of connecting the unconscious with reality,
and of assimilating its archetypal contents, vanished. The poet
ended by suicide. The MS of *Aurélia* was found on his body.

[1] [Author's abstract of a lecture given to the Psychological Club, Zurich,
on 9 June 1945; published in the Club's *Jahresbericht*, 1945–46. A typescript
(24 pp.) of the entire lecture, made from a stenogram and evidently not
corrected by Jung, is in the Jung archives.]

FOREWORD TO FIERZ-DAVID:
"THE DREAM OF POLIPHILO"[1]

1749   It must be twenty-five years since Francesco Colonna's *Hypnerotomachia Poliphili* first came my way in the French translation published by Béroalde de Verville in 1600. Later, in the Morgan Library, New York, I saw and admired the first Italian edition[2] with its superb woodcuts. I set about reading the book, but soon got lost in the mazes of its architectural fantasies, which no human being can enjoy today. Probably the same thing has happened to many a reader, and we can only sympathize with Jacob Burckhardt, who dismissed it with a brief mention while bothering little about its contents. I then turned to the "Recueil Stéganographique," Béroalde's Introduction, and in spite of its turgid and high-flown verbiage I caught fleeting glimpses which aroused my curiosity and encouraged me to continue my labours, for labours they are in a case like this. My efforts found their reward, for plodding on, chapter by chapter, I sensed, rather than recognized, more and more things I was later to encounter in my study of alchemy. Indeed, I cannot even say how far it was this book that put me on the track of the royal art. In any case, not long afterwards I began to collect the old Latin treatises of the alchemists, and in a close study of them lasting many years I did eventually succeed in unearthing those subterranean processes of thought from which sprang not only the world of alchemical imagery but also Poliphilo's dream. What first found expression in the poetry of the minnesingers and troubadours can be heard here as a distant echo of a dreamlike past, but it is also a premonition of the future. Like every proper dream, the *Hypnerotomachia* is Janus-faced: it is a picture of the Middle Ages on the brink of the Renaissance—a transition between two eras, and therefore highly relevant to the world today, which is even more obviously a time of transition and change.

1750   So it was with considerable interest that I read the manuscript

[1] [Linda Fierz-David, *Der Liebestraum des Poliphilo, ein Beitrag zur Pyschologie der Renaissance und der Moderne* (Zurich, 1947); trans. by Mary Hottinger, *The Dream of Poliphilo* (Bollingen Series XXV, New York, 1950). The translation of the foreword is revised here.]

[2] [Venice, 1499.]

sent me by Mrs. Linda Fierz-David, for it is the first serious attempt to unlock Poliphilo's secret and to unravel its crabbed symbolism with the help of modern psychology. In my opinion, her undertaking has been entirely successful. She has pursued the psychological problem which forms the central theme of the book through all the twists and turns of the story, demonstrating its personal and suprapersonal character as well as bringing to light its significance for the world of that time. Many of her interpretations are so astute and illuminating that this seemingly outlandish and baroque tale, eagerly read in the sixteenth and seventeenth centuries, is once more brought within the intellectual orbit of the modern reader. With an intelligence equalled only by her intuition, she has painted a picture of that peculiar Renaissance psychology whose literary monument is the *Hypnerotomachia,* while giving that picture a timeless background. Thus, the tale reappears in all the freshness of its original colours and makes a direct appeal to the man of today by virtue of its imperishable psychological truth.

1751   On its voyage through uncharted seas, the book owes some of its happiest discoveries to the sensitiveness of the feminine mind, which, delicately indiscreet, can take a peep behind Francesco Colonna's richly ornate baroque façade. It was because of this feminine gift that St. Catherine was consulted by the heavenly assembly "in all difficult cases," as we learn from Anatole France's amusing account in *Penguin Island.* "While on earth, St. Catherine had confounded fifty very learned doctors. She was versed in the philosophy of Plato as well as the Scriptures, and possessed rhetoric." Hence, it is no matter for surprise if Mrs. Fierz-David has brought off some dazzling feats of interpretation which throw considerable light on the obscurities of Poliphilo's symbolism. The tortuous ways of the masculine mind, setting traps for itself with its own vanities, are here exposed and illuminated, and modern man would do well to learn from this example.

1752   In her commentary, she takes us deep into psychological problems that remain unfathomable to the modern mind and set it a hard task. The book is not easy reading—indeed, it requires some effort. But it is a rich and stimulating repast, and will amply reward the attentive reader who comes to meet it halfway. For myself, I am grateful to the author for the enriched knowledge and insight her book has brought me.

February 1946

781

FOREWORD TO CROTTET: "MONDWALD"[1]

The author of this book is no ordinary explorer, of whom there
is no lack nowadays, but one who still understands the almost forgotten art of travelling with all his senses open. This art or, as
we might also say, this gift bestowed by the grace of heaven, enables
the traveller to bring back from distant shores more than can ever
be captured by cameras and tape-recorders, to wit, his own experience through which we glimpse the lure of foreign lands and
peoples. This alone makes them come alive for us as we listen to
the tale of the clash of two worlds. The "subjectivity" so rightly
feared by science here becomes a source of illumination, conveying
to us flashes of insight which no description of facts however complete can attain. This is a matter of taking notes with scrupulous
objectivity. Instead, the "sensitive traveller" creates an experience
which does not, like a factual record, consist merely of the data
of the senses and the intellect, but of those countless, indescribable,
subliminal impressions which hold the traveller captive in a foreign
land. Certainly his objective description tells us a great deal, but
his emotion, his being carried away, means far more. It reveals
something that cannot be expressed in words: the wholeness of prehistoric nature and preconscious humanity, which for the civilized
man and inhabitant of a virtually enslaved earth is utterly alien
and unfathomable. All sorts of possibilities hang invisibly in the
air, yet somehow we have always known of them; realities of which
an age-old, nearly forgotten knowledge in us evokes a distant echo;
a longing that looks back to the golden haze of a childhood morning, and forward to fulfilment at the millennium. It is the intimation of a pristine wholeness, lost and now hoped for again, that
hovers over the primeval landscape and its inhabitants, and only
the story-teller's emotion can bring it home to us. We understand
and share his passionate desire to preserve and perpetuate this
fathomless splendour, for which a National Park would be but a
feeble substitute, and we lament with him the devastation that

[1] [Zurich, 1949. By Robert Crottet. ("Moon-Forest," subtitled "Lappish
Stories.")]

threatens it because of our civilizing barbarism. In Kenya an old squatter once said to me: "This ain't man's country, it's God's country." Today it is dotted with goldmines, schools, mission stations—and where are the slow rivers of grazing herds, the human dwellings clustering like wasps' nests on yellow and red cliffs beneath the shade of acacias, the soundless eternity of a life without history?

1754   The author's aim is to preserve the life of a primitive people, the Lappish Skolts in northern Finland, who have been robbed of their reindeer herds, and thus protect at least a little bit of that primeval age from irremediable disaster. May his wish be granted.

March 1949

FOREWORD TO JACOBI:
"PARACELSUS: SELECTED WRITINGS"[1]

1755   The author has asked me for some introductory words to the English edition of her book on Paracelsus. I am more than willing to comply with this request, for Paracelsus, an almost legendary figure in our time, was a preoccupation of mine when I was trying to understand alchemy, especially its connection with natural philosophy. In the sixteenth century, alchemical speculation received a strong impetus from this master, notably from his singular doctrine of "longevity"—a theme ever dear to the alchemist's heart.

1756   In her book, Dr. Jacobi emphasizes the moral aspect of Paracelsus. She wisely lets the master speak for himself on crucial points, so that the reader can gain first-hand information about this strange Renaissance personality, so amply endowed with genius. The liberal use of original texts, with their vivid, imaginative language, helps to develop a striking picture of the man who exerted a powerful influence not only on his own time but on succeeding centuries.

1757   A contradictory and controversial figure, Paracelsus cannot be brought into line with any stereotype—as Sudhoff,[2] for instance, sought to do when, arbitrarily and without a shadow of evidence, he declared that certain aberrant texts were spurious. Paracelsus remains a paradox, like his contemporary, Agrippa von Nettesheim. He is a true mirror of his century, which even at this late date presents many unsolved mysteries.

1758   An excellent feature of Dr. Jacobi's book is her glossary of Paracelsus' concepts, each furnished with a succinct definition. To follow the language of this physician, this natural philosopher and mys-

[1] [Written in German; trans., with the entire book, by Norbert Guterman (Bollingen Series XXVIII, New York, 1951), and slightly revised here. The original book, edited by Jolande Jacobi (see supra, par. 1121, n. 1) was *Theophrastus Paracelsus: Lebendiges Erbe* ("Living Heritage") (Zurich, 1942).]

[2] [Karl Sudhoff, editor of the *Sämmtliche Werke* of Paracelsus, in 14 vols. (1922–1935).]

784

tic—a language freighted with technical terms and neologisms—is not easy for readers unfamiliar with alchemical writings.

1759   The book abounds in pictorial material which, coming for the most part from Paracelsus' time and from the places where he lived, rounds out and sharpens the presentation.

May 1949

1760   Dr. Otto Kankeleit has given me the manuscript of his book
and has asked me to write a foreword. It is not a scientific study
of a theoretical nature, but a descriptive survey of the multitudinous
phenomena and problems which beset the practising psychotherapist in his daily work. It is a kaleidoscopic assortment of images,
visions, flickerings on the edge of the mind—a phantasmagoria of
all the things the doctor wonders about. He finds himself confronted
with a mass of problems stretching into a limitless horizon. That
is the particular value of this book: it opens vistas into reaches
of the psyche extending far beyond the confines of the consulting
room, giving the reader a glimpse into a world hitherto unknown
to him. It does not stop short at the pathological and does not
apply to the sick the psychopathology of the sick. It leads beyond
that to the wide realm of psychic life in general, to an abiding
concern with the sick person, for the principal aim of modern medicine is not so much to eliminate the symptoms of sickness as to
guide the patient back to a normal and balanced life.

1761   Naturally this can be done only if he is given a balanced picture
of the human psyche to offset his morbid and limited experience
of it. For this purpose, as the author very rightly points out, it
is necessary for doctor and patient to come to terms with the nature
of the unconscious, since, for good or ill, they are both involved
in its mysterious reality.

1762   The book is in many respects extremely instructive for the doctor, and a very sympathetic one because of its unbiased standpoint.

Jung's Contribution

Among the "testimonials from scholars, writers, and artists" (subtitle of Dr. Kankeleit's book) are Jung's answers (ibid., pp. 68f.) to
the following questionnaire:

[1] [Munich and Basel, 1959. ("The Unconscious as Seedbed of the Creative,"
subtitled "Testimonials from Scholars, Poets, and Artists.")]

What is the respective share of the conscious and the unconscious in the creative process?

1763   Like all psychic life the creative process stems from the unconscious. If you identify with the creative process you usually end up by imagining that you yourself are the creator.

Have you, at the onset of a new period of creativity, observed in yourself exceptional states of any kind, in which the unconscious took the lead?

1764   Speaking for myself, I must confess that I always notice the strangest things at the onset of a new period of creativity. (I don't doubt that there are people who never notice such things.) The unconscious takes the lead nightly in our dreams, so it is not at all surprising that it should usher in the creative process with all sorts of spontaneous phenomena.

Do you occasionally resort to stimulants of any kind (alcohol, morphine, hashish, etc.)?

1765   Oh no! Never! A new idea is intoxicating enough.

Do you think dreams play a part in the creative process?

1766   For years my dreams used to anticipate my creative activities as well as other things.

Have you ever experienced exceptional states of any kind (precognition, telepathy, etc.) which are not dependent on the creative process?

1767   On closer analysis, I don't think any exceptional states can be separated from the creative process, because life itself is creativity par excellence.

I would like very much to have a detailed description of a creative process.

1768   I could give you a detailed description but will not do so because for me the whole thing is too mysterious. I stand in such awe of the great mysteries that I am unable to talk about them. In any case, a close study of any dream series will provide perfect examples.

FOREWORD TO SERRANO: "THE VISITS OF THE QUEEN OF SHEBA"[1]

1769   This book is an extraordinary piece of work. It is dreams within dreams, highly poetic I should say, and most unlike the spontaneous products of the unconscious I am used to, although well-known archetypal figures are clearly discernible. The poetic genius has transformed this primordial material into almost musical shapes, just as, conversely, Schopenhauer understood music as the movement of archetypical ideas. The principal formative factor seems to be a strong aesthetic tendency. The reader is caught in an endlessly proliferating dream, in ever-expanding space and immeasurable depths of time. On the other hand the cognitive element plays no significant role—it even recedes into a misty background, yet alive with the wealth of colourful images. The unconscious or whatever we designate by this name presents itself to the author under its poetic aspect, while I envisage it chiefly under its scientific and philosophical or, to be more accurate, its religious aspect. The unconscious is surely the *Pammeter,* the Mother of All (i.e., of all psychic life), being the matrix, background, and foundation of all the differentiated phenomena we call psychic—religion, science, philosophy, art. The experience of the unconscious, whatever form it may take, is an approach to wholeness, the one experience lacking in our modern civilization. It is the *via regia* to the *Unus Mundus.*

[1] [Bombay and London (Asia Publishing House), 1960; republished by Routledge & Kegan Paul, London, 1972. For Miguel Serrano, see Jung's letter of 31 Mar. 1960 in *Letters,* ed. G. Adler, vol. 2. The present foreword was originally a letter in English to Serrano, 14 Jan. 1960; here somewhat revised.]

IS THERE A TRUE BILINGUALISM?[1]

1770   You have asked me a question which I cannot answer precisely. I would not be able to define what you understand by "bilingualism."

1771   There are certainly people living abroad who have become so used to a new language that they not only think but even dream in the idiom of the country. I, personally, have experienced this after a rather long stay in England. I suddenly caught myself definitely thinking in English.

1772   This has never happened to me with the French language, but I noticed that after a comparatively short stay in France my vocabulary unexpectedly increased. This was caused not so much by intense reading of French nor by conversation with French people, but was more the influence of the atmosphere—if this expression is permissible. This is a fact that has been observed quite often. But once one returns to one's country these riches generally disappear.

1773   I am absolutely convinced that in many cases a second language can be implanted in this fashion—even at the expense of the original language. But as one's memory is not without limit, a bi- or tri-lingual state ends by damaging the scope of one's vocabulary as well as the greatest potential use of each language.

[1] [Letter in answer to this question published (in French) in the *Flinker Almanac 1961* (Librairie Française et Etrangère, Paris). For another letter to Martin Flinker, 17 Oct. 1957, published in his *Almanac 1958,* see *Letters,* ed. G. Adler, vol. 2.]

XV

THE PRACTICE OF PSYCHOTHERAPY

(related to Volume 16 of the Collected Works)

REVIEWS OF BOOKS BY HEYER

Der Organismus der Seele[1]

1774   The author of this book has performed the grateful service of giving a comprehensive account of the chaos—one can hardly say less—that reigns in the field of psychotherapy. I know of no book that grasps the essential problems of modern therapy and its conflicting views in just this knowledgeable, unprejudiced, and wholly impartial manner. Unfortunately, most other books of the kind are written in the interests of some system and therefore suffer from that distressing theoretical narrow-mindedness which, on occasion, borders on sectarian bigotry. Many of these authors appear to have forgotten that psychology, of all the sciences, demands the most constant self-criticism. Every psychologist should realize first and foremost that his point of view is his own subjective prejudice. This particular prejudice is certainly no worse than any other, moreover it is extremely likely to be a fundamental assumption with many other people as well. Hence it is generally worth while pursuing one's point of view as far as possible. It will doubtless bear fruit that have a certain usefulness. But under no circumstances should one indulge in the unscientific delusion that one's own subjective prejudice represents a universal and fundamental psychological truth. No true science can spring from this, only a faith whose shadow is intolerance and fanaticism. Contradictory views are necessary for the evolution of any science; they must not be set up in opposition to each other, but should seek the earliest possible synthesis. Books like Heyer's have long been wanting. They are absolutely indispensable if we are ever to create an objective psychology, which can never be the work of a single individual but only the result of the concerted labours of many. Heyer's book offers a conspectus of the main contemporary doctrines of Freud, Adler, and myself. Separate accounts of these may be known to the reader, but until

[1] [*Europäische Revue* (Berlin), IX:10 (Oct. 1933), 639. Gustav Richard Heyer, *Der Organismus der Seele* (Munich, 1932); trans. by E. and C. Paul, *The Organism of the Mind* (London, 1933). For Heyer (1890–1967), see Jung's letter of 20 Apr. 1934, in *Letters*, ed. G. Adler, vol. i.]

now they have not, as a rule, been related to one another, so that each formed a closed system. Heyer's book thus fills a long-felt need. It is written in a lively style and is richly interspersed with the author's own practical experiences—perhaps the most commendable book I know on this subject.

Praktische Seelenheilkunde[2]

1775   One is often tempted to think that it was a fatal error of medical psychology in the days of its infancy to suppose that the neuroses were quite simple things which could be explained by a single hypothesis. This optimism was probably inevitable; had it been otherwise, perhaps nobody would have plucked up courage to venture any theory about the psyche at all. The difficulties and complications that beset the psychology of neuroses are nowhere more apparent than in the great variety of possible methods of treatment. There are so many of them that the layman in psychiatry may easily be driven to despair when it comes to choosing the method which suits not only the neurosis to be treated but the doctor treating it. We are familiar enough, nowadays, with the idea that physical illnesses derive from all sorts of causes and are subject to all sorts of conditions and therefore generally need treating from various angles; but it is still taken too much for granted that, among all these physical illnesses, a neurosis is just another illness or, at best, another category of illness. The reason for this prejudice is that modern medicine has only recently discovered the "psychological factor" in illness, and now clings to the idea that this "factor" is a simple quantity, one of the many conditioning factors or causes of physical disease. The psyche is thus vested with the kind of reality we concede to a toxin, a bacillus, or a cancer cell; but we are altogether disinclined to attribute to the psyche anything like the real existence with which we unthinkingly endow the body.

1776   In this book, Heyer again presents us, as he did with such signal success in his earlier work *Organismus der Seele,* with a synoptic view, not of theories this time, but of the practical methods of treatment. He offers a survey, richly documented with case histories, of all the techniques which the psychotherapist requires for his everyday medical work and which are therefore also of great interest

2 [*Zentralblatt für Psychotherapie,* IX:3 (1936), 184–86. Heyer, *Praktische Seelenheilkunde* (Munich, 1935).]

to the general practitioner. The latter regards his neurotic patients as being physically ill, like the other patients who are suffering from predominantly physical disturbances. Illnesses that are psychogenic in origin are naturally, to his way of thinking, physical, and so his first thought will be of a physical cure. The attitude of the orthodox psychotherapist who makes a sharp cut between neurosis and the pathology of the body is foreign to him. But neuroses, too, are unorthodox things and do not always prove resistant to physical treatment. The truth is that some neuroses are predominantly physical and others predominantly psychological. And often it is a diagnostic feat to make out to which category a particular case belongs. Thus psychotherapy is inevitably, at least for the time being, a curious mixture of psychological and physiological therapeutics. On all this Heyer's book provides a wealth of information that should be of the greatest value to the psychotherapist as well as to the general practitioner and the medical student.

1777   It is sometimes said that when many remedies are prescribed for a certain disease, none of them can claim to be particularly efficacious. The multitude of views in psychotherapy does not, however, arise from this source of confusion, but rather from the fact that neurosis is not so much *one* disease as an amalgam of several diseases which require an equal number of remedies. It is exceedingly probable that the psyche is analogous to the body and is capable of having as many diseases. The future has still to discover a pathology of the psyche to match that of the body. That modest "psychological factor" will, in time, broaden out and cover a field of medical experience no whit inferior to that of the body in scope and significance. Hence we would do well to infer, from the diversity of psychotherapeutic methods, a corresponding diversity of psychopathological states. Every one of the types of treatment mentioned corresponds, up to a point, to one aspect of the so-called "neurosis"—in other words, to a genuine form of sickness. But our present knowledge of psychopathology is not yet sufficiently advanced for us to specify without a doubt what particular form of psychic sickness calls for what treatment. We are still in the position of the physicians in the Middle Ages who, lacking the requisite knowledge of anatomy, physiology, and pathological anatomy, were solely dependent on practical experience, intuition, and the *physician's art*. They were not necessarily bad doctors for that, any more than primitive medicine-men are bad doctors. It is precisely through the various kinds of treatment, their successes and failures, that we shall get to know the various kinds of psychic pathology, psychic biology, and psychic structure.

1778   Heyer's book is an important milestone on the road to the discovery of the diseases of the psyche and their specific remedies. It is written from practical experience and will be particularly valuable to the general practitioner. In its arrangement it relies on clinical pictures of illness; thus Chapter II deals with disturbances in the respiratory and circulatory systems, Chapter III with digestive disturbances, Chapter IX with sexual disturbances, and Chaper X with insomnia. Chapters I, IV, and V form an introduction to psychology. Three chapters deal with the various kinds of therapy. The book is equipped with a very readable appendix by Lucy Heyer, giving an account of the physical aids to psychotherapy, such as gymnastics, breathing, massage, etc.

1779   I regret the absence of a similar account dealing with the artistic and spiritual remedies, for in practice these play no small part along with the purely physical ones. Maldevelopment and inhibitedness exist in the psyche as well as in the body and are in just as much need of exercise and reeducation.

ON THE "ROSARIUM PHILOSOPHORUM"[1]

1780   The *Rosarium* is one of the first, if not *the* first, synoptic texts covering the whole field of alchemy. It may have originated about 1350. The author is anonymous. It has been attributed to Peter of Toledo, who is supposed to have been an older brother of the famous Arnaldus de Villanova (1235–1313). Certain parts of it may date back to the former, but not the whole text, which was first printed in 1550 and contains numerous quotations from Arnaldus. The 1550 edition is a compilation consisting of two different parts, each a separate treatise. There are also interpolations of some length from various authors, for instance a letter of Raymundus Lullius to Rupertum Regem Franciae. (This Rupertus may be identical with Robert I, the Wise, 1309–1343.)

1781   The text begins with a kind of preface or introduction in which the author discusses the "art" in general terms. He emphasizes that the art operates only "within Nature." Only *one* thing is needed for the procedure, and not several things. Operating "outside Nature" leads nowhere. The author stresses that the laborant must have a sound mental disposition. The art consists in *uniting the opposites,* which are represented as male and female, form and matter. In addition the *4 roots* (radices, rhizomata, elements) are needed. The *prima materia* (initial material) is found everywhere. It is also called *lapis* = stone, or "salt" or "water." The water (*aqua permaens*) is identical with *argentum vivum* (quicksilver). The elements are likewise represented as pairs of opposites:

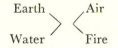

[1] [Author's abstract of two lectures given at the Psychological Club, Zurich, on unknown dates; published in the Club's *Jahresbericht,* 1936–37. The symbolic illustrations of the *Rosarium philosophorum* are used by Jung as a parallel to the modern psychotherapeutic process in "The Psychology of the Transference" (C.W., vol. 16), first published as *Die Psychologie der Übertragung* (Zurich, 1946). The present lectures were an early exercise toward that publication.]

The author warns against taking the terminology *literally;* only fools would do this.

1782   In the preface we find the following verses:

> Hic lapis exilis extat, precio quoque vilis,
> Spernitur a stultis, amatur plus ab edoctis.
> (Here stands the mean, uncomely stone,
> 'Tis very cheap in price!
> The more it is despised by fools,
> The more loved by the wise.) [2]

1783   The "lapis exilis" may correspond to the "lapsit exillis," Wolfram von Eschenbach's name for the Grail. [3]

1784   The text proper opens with a pictorial representation of the alchemical process: [4] a fountain from which the *aqua permanens* flows out of three pipes in the form of *lac virginis* (virgin's milk), *acetum fontis* (vinegar of the fount), and *aqua vitae* (water of life). Above the fountain is a star, with the sun to the left and the moon to the right (as opposites). Surmounting the star is the two-headed Mercurial Serpent, symbolizing the contamination of opposites in the unconscious. The picture is flanked by two columns of cloud or smoke, an indication of the "spiritual" (volatile) nature of the process. In the corners are four stars, alluding to the quaternity of the elements. The three springs form the *material Trinity* (the spirit of God, brooding over the chaos, penetrated into matter and became water). Together with inert matter (earth) they constitute the unity which is indicated by the quaternity of the elements $(3 + 1 = 4)$.

1785   For some alchemists the *prima materia* is something that can be found everywhere, for others it has first to be produced out of the "imperfect body" or substance. The contradiction resolves itself when one takes account of the amply documented theory of the *humidum radicale:* all chemical substances contain, in greater or lesser degree, the moisture, the water of the beginning that was brooded over by the spirit of God. This water was the *prima materia.* The opening words of the first chapter can thus be understood without difficulty:

> The imperfect body has been changed into the *prima materia,* and this water, combined with our water (*aqua permanens*), produces *one*

---

[2] [Jung carved the Latin text on a cube of hewn stone at his "Tower" in Bollingen, in 1950. Cf. *Memories, Dreams, Reflections,* pp. 226f./215f.]
[3] [Cf. *Psychology and Alchemy,* par. 246, n. 125.]
[4] [Cf. "The Psychology of the Transference," Fig. 1.]

pure, clear water (solvent) that purifies everything and contains within itself everything needful (i.e., for the process of self-transformation). . . . Out of this water and with this water our procedure is brought to completion. But it dissolves the bodies not by means of the common solvent (*solutione vulgari*), as transmitted by the ignorant who transform the body into rain-water, but by means of the true philosophical solvent in which the body is transformed into the original water whence it arose in the beginning. This same water reduces the bodies themselves to ashes. You must know that the art of alchemy is a gift of the Holy Spirit.

1786   The dissolution of the imperfect body transforms it back into the watery initial state, i.e., into the *prima materia*. The *aqua nostra* (our water), as is evident from the text and from numerous other sources, is also *fire*, the baptismal water, and at the same time the Holy Spirit this contains. *Aqua nostra* is therefore a "spirit water," which is united with the *prima materia* in the same way as the spirit of God brooded over the water of the beginning and from it created the world.

1787   The process of creation is performed outwardly through a chemical operation and inwardly through *active imagination:* "And imagine this with the true and not with the fantastic imagination," the text enjoins.[5] Matter was thought of as entirely passive; everything creative and active proceeded from the mind. *Aqua nostra* as "spirit water" was a chemical body endowed with spirit, which was produced by the art; it was named the "tincture" or "quintessence." Medieval man thought in terms of spirit, whereas we always start with matter. We can understand how matter alters mind, but cannot see how mind can transform matter, although logically there is a reciprocal relationship between the two processes.

1788   The second chapter is concerned mainly with the secret of the *aqua nostra*. This water, as we have said, is the *humidum radicale*, a *spirituale corpus* also named *sapo sapientum* ("soap of the wise," a play on words). It is so named in *Clavis sapientiae* of Alfonso X, king of Castile, who reigned 1252–1284. His treatise is said to be a translation from the Arabic. The *humidum radicale* is identical with the *serpens mercurialis*, the dragon, hence is also named "dragon's blood." The body to be transformed must be dissolved in its own liquid, its "blood"; this tincture, the elixir or *lapis,* is identical with *aqua nostra*. The texts are very confused on this point. But the confusion is not so bad if one bears in mind that the "water"

[5] [*Psychology and Alchemy,* par. 360.]

799

is either extracted by sublimation from a body that contains a particularly large amount of it, or that the elixir already extracted is used for dissolving the body. The texts deal sometimes with the one and sometimes with the other, or more generally with both at once, as does the *Rosarium*. Other synonyms for the water are *pinguedo* (fat), *unctuositas, vapor unctuosus* (fatty vapour).

1789   These basic ideas are developed and embroidered on in the following chapters, particularly the idea of the *coniunctio*. By this is meant the reunion of the imperfect body with its soul (*anima*), of which it had been deprived.[6] Here the *anima* (= *humidum radicale*) serves as a vehicle for the spirit, which through active imagination permeates the watery solution. Usually the spirit is active and male, the material body passive and female. (Occasionally it is the other way round!) The male is red (red tincture, red slave, sun, red rose), the female white (white tincture, white spouse, moon, lily, white rose). The myth of Gabricus and Beya is the model for the *coniunctio* symbolism,[7] one of the commonest and most impressive motifs in alchemy. It is concerned with the problem of opposites projected into matter, with the union of opposites for the purpose of producing a third thing, the Hermaphroditus or Rebis ("consisting of two"),[8] or the "living" Stone of the Wise. This symbol is something that originates in man, like a child, and continues to exist in him, as an ancient treatise, probably of Arabic origin and attributed to Rosinus (Zosimos), says. ("Rosinus ad Sarratantam," *Artis auriferae,* II, 1593, p. 311.) The stone has the significance of a panacea, of a drink of immortality, of a redeemer in general, and hence is an *allegoria Christi*.

[6] ["The Psychology of the Transference," Fig. 9.]
[7] [Ibid., par. 457.]
[8] [Ibid., Fig. 10.]

PREFACE TO AN INDIAN JOURNAL
OF PSYCHOTHERAPY[1]

1790   Dr. Bannerjee has kindly asked me to write a foreword to the special number of this journal devoted to my psychological work. It is a great pleasure to express my appreciation of the attentive interest given to my modest attempts at furthering the development of psychological understanding in general and the deepening of insight into the workings of the unconscious. India with her highly differentiated spiritual culture enjoys certain advantages over the European mind, inasmuch as the latter, owing to its origin in ancient Greek culture, is more handicapped by its dependence upon the sensory aspects of the external world. We expect of India and her spiritual attitude a unique contribution—an introspection originating in a different point of view which would compensate the one-sidedness of the European outlook. We look forward hopefully to a collaboration with the Indian mind, knowing that the mystery of the psyche can be understood only when approached from opposite sides.

1791   I believe that the coming age will be in desperate need of a common basic understanding of man, which would enable mankind to become a brotherhood rather than a chaos of power-driven usurpers.

[1] [*Psychotherapy,* I:1 (April 1956), organ of the Indian Psychotherapeutical Society, Calcutta. Dr. Samiran Bannerjee was honorary secretary. Jung's typescript, in English, is dated 7 Sept. 1955.]

ON PICTURES IN PSYCHIATRIC DIAGNOSIS[1]

1792   The case that you lay before me presents every ground for thinking of latent schizophrenia. This diagnosis is confirmed by the pictures. There is a distinct tendency to translate living reality into
abstractions in order to cut off the emotional rapport with the object. This forces the ego into an unsuitable power stance with the
sole aim of domination. His (the artist's) commentary is very enlightening in this respect. Under these conditions there naturally
can be no point in looking for symbols of the self,[2] since there
is an overwhelming tendency to push the ego into the foreground
and suppress the self. The ego is an arbitrary fragment, and the
self the unwanted whole. No trace of the latter can be seen in
the pictures.

[1][(Translated by H. N.) Commentary on Walter Pöldinger, "Zur Bedeutung
bildernischen Gestaltens in der psychiatrischen Diagnostik," *Die Therapie des
Monats* (Mannheim), IX:2 (1959), with reproductions of pictures by a
patient. Pöldinger was on the staff of a mental hospital in Lucerne.]
[2] [Refers to a question asked in regard to one picture.]

XVI

THE DEVELOPMENT OF PERSONALITY

(related to Volume 17 of the Collected Works)

FOREWORD TO EVANS: "THE PROBLEM
OF THE NERVOUS CHILD"[1]

1793   I have read the manuscript of Mrs. Evans' book, *The Problem of the Nervous Child,* with great pleasure and interest. Mrs. Evans' knowledge of her subject-matter is based on a solid foundation of practical experience, an experience gained in the difficult and toilsome treatment and education of nervous children. Whoever has had to deal with nervous children knows what an amount of patience, as well as skill, is needed to guide a child out of a wrong pathological attitude into a normal life. This book, as the reader can see on almost every page, is the fruit of extensive work in the field of neuroses and abnormal characters. Despite the fact that there are numerous books on education, there are very few that concern themselves with a child's most intimate problems in such a careful and painstaking way. It is self-evident that this contribution will be of great value to anyone interested in educational questions. The physician should be particularly indebted to the author, as her book will be a valuable ally in the fight against the widespread evil of neuroses in adults. More and more the neurologist of today realizes that the origin of the nervousness of his patients is very rarely of recent date, but goes back to the early impressions and developments in childhood. There lies the source of many later nervous diseases. Most of the neuroses originate from a wrong psychological attitude which hinders adjustment to the environment or to the individual's own requirements. This wrong psychological position which is at the bottom of almost every neurosis has, as a rule, been built up during the course of the years and very often began in early childhood as a consequence of incompatible familial influences. Knowing this, Mrs. Evans lays much stress on the parent's mental attitude and its importance for the child's psychology. One easily overlooks the enormous power of imitation in children. Parents too easily content themselves with the belief that a thing hidden from the child cannot influence it. They forget that infantile

[1] [New York, 1920; London, 1921. By Elida Evans, an American child specialist. The foreword appears to have been written in English.]

805

imitation is less concerned with action than with the parent's state of mind from which the action emanates. I have frequently observed children who were particularly influenced by certain unconscious tendencies of the parents, and, in such cases, I have often advised the treatment of the mother rather than of the child. Through the enlightenment of the parents, their wrong influences can at least be avoided, and thus much can be done for the prevention of later neuroses in the children.

1794   The author particularly insists upon the importance of watching the manifestations of the sexual instinct in childhood. Anyone concerned with the education of abnormal children will confirm the existence and the frequency of sexual symptoms in these children. Despite the fact that sexual activity does not belong to the infantile period, it frequently manifests itself in a symptomatic way, as a symptom of abnormal development. An abnormal development does not provide sufficient opportunity for the normal display of the child's energies. Thus, the normal outlet being blocked, the energy accumulates and forcibly seeks an abnormal outlet in premature and perverted sexual interests and activities. Infantile sexuality is the most frequent symptom of a morbid psychological attitude. In my view, it is wrong to consider sexual phenomena in early childhood as the expression of an organic disposition; most of the cases are due to an environment unsuited to the child's psychological nature. The attitude of the child towards life is certainly determined by the inherited disposition, but only to a certain extent; on the other side it is the result of the immediate parental influences and of education. While the inherited disposition cannot be changed, these latter influences can be improved by suitable methods, and thus the original unfavourable disposition can be overcome. Mrs. Evans' book shows the way, and how to treat even the most intricate cases.

October 1919

FOREWORD TO HARDING:
"THE WAY OF ALL WOMEN"[1]

1795   It is a pleasure to comply with the author's wish that I should write an introduction to her book. I have read her work with the greatest interest, and am gratified to find that it does not come into the category of those sententious books, bristling with prejudices, which expatiate on the psychology of women with gushing eloquence, and finally overflow in a sentimental hymn to "holy motherhood." Such books have another unpleasant characteristic: they never speak of things as they are, but only as they should be, and instead of taking the problem of the feminine psyche seriously, they conveniently gloss over all the dark and disagreeable truths with advice that is as ineffectual as it is patently good. Such books are not always written by men—if they were they might be excusable—but many are written by women who seem to know as little about feminine feelings as men do.

1796   It is a foregone conclusion among the initiated that men understand nothing of women's psychology as it actually is, but it is astonishing to find that women know nothing of themselves either. However, we are only surprised as long as we naïvely and optimistically imagine that mankind understands anything fundamental about the psyche. This is indeed one of the most difficult tasks the investigating mind can set itself. The latest developments in psychology show with ever-increasing clarity not only that there are no simple formulas from which the world of the psyche might be derived, but that we have never yet succeeded in defining the field of psychic experience with sufficient exactitude. Despite the immense surface area, scientific psychology has not even begun to break down the mountain of prejudices that persistently block the way to the psyche as it really is. Psychology is the youngest of the sciences and is suffering from all those childhood ailments which afflicted the adolescence of other sciences in the late Middle Ages. There still exist psychologies which limit the field of psychic experience to the con-

---

[1] [New York and London, 1933. The foreword, written in German, was trans. for the book by Cary F. Baynes. The present version is somewhat revised. For Esther Harding, see supra, par. 1125, n. 1.]

807

sciousness and its contents, or understand the psyche as a purely reactive phenomenon without any trace of autonomy. The fact of an unconscious psyche has not yet gained undisputed acceptance, despite an overwhelming mass of empirical material which proves beyond all doubt that there can be no psychology of consciousness without a recognition of the unconscious. Lacking this foundation, it is impossible to deal with a psychological datum that is in any way complex, and the actual psyche we have to deal with in real life is complexity itself. Consequently, a psychology of woman cannot be written without an adequate knowledge of the unconscious background of the mind.

1797 Drawing on her rich psychotherapeutic experience, Dr. Harding has sketched a picture of the feminine psyche which, in scope and thoroughness, far surpasses previous works in this field. Her presentation is refreshingly free from prejudice and remarkable for the love of truth it displays. Her arguments never lose themselves in dead theories and fanatical fads, which unfortunately are so frequently met with in this field of work, and she has succeeded in penetrating with the light of knowledge into crannies and depths where before darkness prevailed. Only one half of feminine psychology can be grasped with the aid of biological and social concepts, and in this book it becomes clear that woman possesses a peculiar spirituality very strange to man, to which Dr. Harding has devoted a special chapter. Without a knowledge of the unconscious this new aspect, so essential for an understanding of the psychology of woman, could never have been brought out with such clarity and completeness. The fructifying influence of the psychology of the unconscious is also evident in many other places in the book.

1798 At a time when the divorce rate has broken all records, when the relation of the sexes has become a perplexing problem, a book like this seems to me of the greatest help. To be sure, it does not provide the one thing everybody expects—a generally acceptable recipe for solving this dreadful tangle of questions in a simple and practical way, so that we need rack our brains about it no longer. On the other hand, the book contains an ample store of what we actually need very badly, and that is understanding—understanding of psychic facts and conditions with the help of which we can orient ourselves in the complicated situations of life.

1799 Why after all do we have a psychology? Why is it that we are especially interested in psychology just now? The answer is that everyone is in desperate need of it. Humanity seems to have reached a point where the concepts of the past are no longer adequate, and we begin to realize that our nearest and dearest are actually strangers to us, whose language we no longer understand. It is beginning to dawn on us that the people living on the other side of the mountain are not made up exclusively of red-headed devils who are responsible for all the evil on this side of the mountain. A little of this uneasy suspicion has filtered through into the relations between sexes; not everyone is utterly convinced that everything good is in "me" and everything evil in "you." Already we can find super-moderns who ask themselves in all seriousness whether there may not be something wrong with us, whether perhaps we are too unconscious, too antiquated, and whether this may not be the reason why when confronted with difficulties in sexual relationships we still continue to employ with disastrous results the methods of the Middle Ages if not those of the caveman. There are indeed people who have read with horror the Pope's Encyclical on Christian marriage,[2] and yet must admit that for cavemen our so-called "Christian" marriage is a cultural step forward. Although we are still far from having overcome our prehistoric mentality, which enjoys its most signal triumphs just in the sphere of sex, where man is made most vividly aware of his mammalian nature, certain ethical refinements have nevertheless crept in which permit anyone with ten to fifteen centuries of Christian education behind him to progress towards a slightly higher level.

1800   On this level the spirit—from the biological point of view an incomprehensible psychic phenomenon—plays a not unimportant role psychologically. It had a weighty word to say on the subject of Christian marriage, and it still participates vigorously in the discussion whenever marriage is doubted and depreciated. It appears in a negative capacity as counsel for the instincts, and in a positive one as the defender of human dignity. Small wonder, then, that a wild and confusing conflict breaks out between man as an instinctual creature of nature and man as a spiritual and cultural being. The worst thing about it is that the one is forever trying violently to suppress the other in order to bring about a so-called harmonious solution of the conflict. Unfortunately, too many people still believe in this procedure, which is all-powered in politics; there are only a few here and there who condemn it as barbaric and would like to set up in its place a just compromise whereby each side of man's nature is given a hearing.

[2] [*Casti Connubii* of Pius XI, 31 Dec. 1930.]

1801　　But unhappily, in the problem between the sexes, no one can bring about a compromise by himself alone; it can only be achieved in relation to the other sex. Hence the need for psychology! On this level, psychology becomes a kind of special pleading—or rather, a *method of relationship*. It guarantees real knowledge of the other sex instead of arbitrary opinions, which are the source of the incurable misunderstandings now undermining in increasing numbers the marriages of our time.

1802　　As a weighty contribution to this striving for a deeper knowledge of human nature and for a clarification of the confusion in the relations between the sexes, Dr. Harding's book is heartily to be welcomed.

February 1932

DEPTH PSYCHOLOGY AND SELF-KNOWLEDGE[1]

Is depth psychology a new way to self-knowledge?

1803   Yes, depth psychology must be termed a new way, because in all the methods practised up to now no account was taken of the existence of the unconscious. Thus a new factor entered our field of vision, which has seriously complicated and fundamentally altered the situation. Formerly, the fact had not been reckoned with that man is a "twofold" being—a being with a conscious side which he knows, and an unconscious side of which he knows nothing but which need be no secret to his fellows. How often one makes all sorts of mistakes without being conscious of them in the least, while they are borne in upon others all the more painfully! Man lives as a creature whose one hand doesn't know what the other is doing. The recognition that we have to allow for the existence of an unconscious is a fact of revolutionary importance. Conscience as an ethical authority extends only as far as consciousness extends. When a man lacks self-knowledge he can do the most astonishing or terrible things without calling himself to account and without ever suspecting what he is doing. Unconscious actions are always taken for granted and are therefore not critically evaluated. One is then surprised at the incomprehensible reactions of one's neighbours, whom one holds to be responsible; that is, one fails to see what one does oneself and seeks in others the cause of all the consequences that follow from one's own actions.

1804   Marriages furnish an instructive example of how easily one sees the mote in another's eye but not the beam in one's own. Of far greater, indeed truly monstrous, proportions are the projections of war propaganda, when the lamentably bad manners of civil life are exalted into a principle. Our unwillingness to see our own faults and the projection of them on to others is the source of most quar-

[1] [Written in answer to questions from Dr. Jolande Jacobi. Published in *DU: Schweizerische Monatsschrift* (Zurich), III:9 (Sept. 1943), and in an English trans. by an unknown hand in *Horizon* (London), VIII:48 (Dec. 1943). This trans. is reproduced here in revised form. It was previously published in *Spring,* 1969.]

rels, and the strongest guarantee that injustice, animosity, and persecution will not easily die out. When one remains unconscious of
oneself one is frequently unaware of one's own conflicts; indeed
the existence of unconscious conflicts is actually held to be impossible. There are many marriages in which the partners skirt round
every possible conflict with the greatest caution, the one actually
imagining himself to be immune from such things, while the other
is filled to the neck with laboriously repressed complexes and almost
choked by them. Such a situation often has injurious effects on
the children too. We know that children often have dreams dealing
with the unconfessed problems of their parents. These problems
weigh upon the children because the parents, being themselves unconscious of them, have never attempted to come to grips with
their own difficulties, and this creates something like a poisoning
of the atmosphere. For this reason the neuroses of childhood depend
to a considerable degree upon the parents' conflicts.

*How is depth psychology distinguished from the previous methods
of psychological research? Where does it coalesce with other
disciplines?*

1805   Psychology up till now took no account of the motivation of
conscious contents due to the existence of the unconscious. Once
the unconscious is included in the calculation, everything suddenly
gets a double bottom, as it were. We have to look at everything
from two sides, whereas the old psychology was satisfied with the
contents of consciousness. Thus the old method of explaining the
appearance of psychogenic (psychologically caused) symptoms
could rest content with the supposition that they were auto-sug-
gested figments of the imagination. The modern explanation, which
lets the unconscious psyche of the patient have its say, investigates
his dreams, fantasies, and complexes, i.e., that segment of his life-
history which is responsible for the formation of the symptoms.
No one questions today that neurotic symptoms are produced by
processes in the unconscious. The conscious realization of the unconscious causative factors therefore has a definite therapeutic value.
Psychogenic symptoms are products of the unconscious. These symptom also include various opinions and convictions which, though
they may be uttered consciously enough, nevertheless are determined in reality by unconscious motives. Thus a too importunate
and one-sided assertion of principles can often be traced back to
an unconscious failure to live up to them. I knew someone, for
instance, who, on every occasion, suitable or not, paraded his princi-

ple of honesty and truthfulness before the public. As I soon discovered, he suffered from a rather too lively imagination, which
now and then seduced him into gross lies. The whole question of
truth therefore occasioned in him a not undeserved "sentiment d'in-
complétude," which in turn moved him to exceptionally loud ethical protestations, no small part of whose aim was to beget in himself
a conviction of honesty.

1806   With the recognition that every conscious process rests in part
upon an unconscious one and may represent it symbolically, our
previous views of psychic causality are radically called into question.
Direct causal sequences in consciousness appear doubtful, and every
experience of psychic contents urgently requires them to be supplemented by their unconscious aspect. Although depth psychology
is a discipline in itself, it lurks invisibly, thanks to the fact of the
unconscious, in the background of all other disciplines. Just as the
discovery of radioactivity overthrew the old physics and necessitated
a revision of many scientific concepts, so all disciplines that are in
any way concerned with the realm of the psychic are broadened
out and at the same time remoulded by depth psychology. It raises
new problems for philosophy; it greatly enriches pedagogics and
still more the study of human character; it also poses new problems
for criminology, especially as regards criminal motives; for medicine
it opens up an unsuspected store of fresh insights and possibilities
through the discovery of the interdependence of bodily and psychic
processes and the inclusion of the neurotic factor; and it has richly
fecundated, less closely related sciences such as mythology, ethnology, etc.

Are the various schools of depth psychology similar in their aims?

1807   The difference between the principal schools of depth psychology up to date are based upon as many different aspects of the unconscious. The unconscious possesses a biological, a physiological, a
mythical, a religious aspect, and so on. This means that the most
varied conceptions are not only possible but even necessary. Each
has its own justification, though none to the exclusion of others,
for the unconscious is a highly complex phenomenon to which one
single concept can never do justice. One cannot judge a person
from a moral standpoint *only,* for example, but has to regard him
from this standpoint *too!* Certain contents of the unconscious can
be understood as strivings for power, others as the expression of
sexual or other drives, while yet others allow no explanation in
terms of biological drives under any circumstances.

813

Has "analytical psychology," i.e., the Jungian school of depth psychology, definite guiding principles?

1808   I should prefer not to use the term "guiding principles" in this connection. Just because of the extreme variety and complexity of the aspects of the unconscious and its possible meanings, every "guiding principle" works as an arbitrary assumption, as an actual prejudice that tries to anticipate its irrational manifestations, though these cannot be determined in advance, and perhaps force them into an unsuitable mould. One must avoid all assumptions so far as possible in order to grasp the pure manifestation itself. This must carry its own interpretation with it, to such an extent that its significance is immediately evident from the nature of the phenomenon and is not forced upon it by the observer. He must, in fact, accustom himself to be guided more by the material than by his own opinions, however well founded they may appear to him. Every item of psychic experience presents itself in an individual form, even though its deeper content may be collective. One can never determine in advance, however, which of its principal aspects lies concealed behind the individual form. "Guiding principles" are therefore admissible at most as working hypotheses, and this only in the realm of scientific research. The practical material is best accepted *mente vacua* (without any preconceived theories).

What are the principal tools of analytical psychology? Does the interpretation of dreams occupy a central place?

1809   The analytical situation has a fourfold aspect: (*a*) The patient gives me in his own words a picture of the situation as he consciously sees it. (*b*) His dreams give me a compensating picture of the unconscious aspect of it. (*c*) The relational situation in which the patient is placed vis-à-vis the analyst adds an objective side to the two other subjective ones. (*d*) Working through the material collected under *a*, *b*, and *c* fills out the total picture of the psychological situation. The necessity of working through it arises from the fact that the total picture often stands in the liveliest contrast to the views of the ego-personality and therefore leads to all sorts of intellectual and emotional reactions and problems, which in their turn clamour for solution and answer. Since the final goal of the undertaking can only consist in restoring the original wholeness of the personality in a viable form, one cannot dispense with a knowledge of the unconscious. The purest product of the unconscious is the dream. The dream points directly to the unconscious, for it "happens" and we have not invented it. It brings us unfalsified material.

What has passed through consciousness is already sifted and remodelled. As we can deduce from the lava ejected by a volcano the constitution of the strata from which it comes, so we can draw deductions as to the unconscious situation from the contents of dreams. Only dream material plus conscious material reveals the picture of the *whole* man. And only in this way can we find out who our antagonist is.

1810 Although dreams disclose the unconscious to us with perhaps the nearest approach to faithfulness we can attain, we also come upon its traces in every form of creative activity, such as music and poetry, and in all other forms of art. It appears in all manifestations of a spontaneous and creative kind, the further these are removed from everything mechanical, technical, and intellectual. As well as from dreams we can therefore draw conclusions from such things as drawings in which patients are encouraged to reveal their inner images. Although obviously the personality of the patient holds the centre of our attention, and introspection is an indispensable instrument of our work in common, yet this is anything rather than *brooding*. Brooding is a sterile activity which runs round in a circle and never reaches a reasonable goal. It is not *work* but a weakness, even a vice. On the other hand, if you feel out of sorts, you can legitimately make yourself an object of serious investigation, just as you can earnestly search your conscience without lapsing into moral weakness. Anyone who is in bad odour with himself and feels in need of improvement, anyone who in brief wishes to "grow," must take counsel with himself. Unless you change yourself inwardly too, outward changes in the situation are worthless or even harmful. It is not enough to jump up, puff yourself out, and shout: "I take the responsibility!" Not only mankind but fate itself would like to know *who* promises to take this weighty step and whether it is someone who *can* take the responsibility. We all know that anyone can *say* so. It is not the position that makes the man, but the man who does his work. Therefore self-searching, with the help of one or more persons, is—or rather should be—the essential condition for taking on a higher responsibility, even if it is only that of realizing the meaning of individual life in the best possible form and to the fullest possible degree. Nature always does that, but *without responsibility*, for this is the fated and divinely allotted task of man.

Is not an important milestone in the development of self-knowledge, which has increased the difficulties of the "way to onself," to be

815

found in the Reformation and in the loss of confession for Protestants, and so for millions of people? Has not self-searching become keener and deeper because of the loss of the dialogue that the Catholic has with his confessor, and the loss of absolution?

1811   The difficulties have indeed become enormously greater, as evidenced by the increased prevalence of complexes among Protestants, which has been statistically established. But these increased difficulties constitute—if the Protestant will really face and grapple with them—an exceptionally advantageous basis for self-knowledge. They can, however, just as easily lead, precisely because a confessor is lacking, either to sterile brooding or to thoughtless superficiality. Most people need someone to confess to, otherwise the basis of experience is not sufficiently real. They do not "hear" themselves, cannot contrast themselves with something different, and thus they have no outside "control." Everything flows inwards and is answered only by oneself, not by another, someone different. It makes an enormous difference whether I confess my guilt only to myself or to another person. This being thrown back upon themselves often leads Protestants to spiritual arrogance and to isolation in their own ego. Although analytical psychology guards against being considered a substitute for confession, in practice it must often function willy-nilly as such. There are so many Catholics who no longer go to confession, and still more Protestants who do not even know what confession is, that it is not surprising some of them yield to their need of communication and share their burdens with an analyst in a way which could almost be called confession. The difference, however, is considerable, inasmuch as the doctor is no priest, no theological and moral authority, but, at best, a sympathetically listening confidant with some experience of life and knowledge of human nature. There is no admonition to repentance unless the patient does it himself, no penance unless—as is almost the rule—he has got himself in a thorough mess, and no absolution unless God has mercy on him. Psychology is admittedly only a makeshift, but at the present time a necessary one. Were it not a necessity it would have collapsed long ago from inner emptiness. It meets a need that unquestionably exists.

Does a knowledge of the "other side," that is, one's own unconscious side, bring relief, release? Does not self-knowledge rather increase the tension between what one is and what one would like to be?

1812   Being able to talk things over freely can in itself be a great relief. In general, working with the unconscious brings an increase of tension at first, because it activates the opposites in the psyche by making them conscious. This entirely depends, though, on the situation from which one starts. The carefree optimist falls into a depression because he has now become conscious of the situation he is in. On the other hand, the pressure on the inward brooding person is released. The initial situation decides whether a release or increase of pressure will result. Through self-searching in analysis people suddenly become aware of their real limitations. How often a woman has previously felt herself a snow-white dove and had no suspicion of the devil concealed within her! Without this knowledge she can neither be healed nor attain wholeness. For one person deeper knowledge of himself is a punishment, for another a blessing. In general, every act of conscious realization means a tensing of opposites. It is in order to avoid this tension that people repress their conflicts. But if they become conscious of them, they get into a corresponding state of tension. This supplies in turn the driving power for a solution of the problems they are faced with.

Doesn't a systematic preoccupation with oneself lead to egocentricity?

1813　　At first glance, from an external and superficial point of view, it does make one egocentric. But I consider this justifiable up a point. One *must* occupy oneself with oneself; otherwise one does not grow, otherwise one can never develop! One must plant a garden and give it increasing attention and care if one wants vegetables; otherwise only weeds flourish. "Egocentric" has an unpleasant undertone of pathological egoism. But as I have said, occupation with and meditation on one's own being is an absolutely legitimate, even necessary activity if one strives after a real alteration and improvement of the situation. Outwardly changing the situation, doing something else, forgetting what one was, alters nothing essential. Indeed, even when a bad man does good, he is nevertheless not good but suffers from a good symptom without being altered in character. How many drinkers, for example, have turned teetotalers without being freed from their psychic alcoholism! And only too soon they succumbed again to their vice. There are essentially bad natures that actually specialize in being good and, if they chance to become some kind of educator, the results are catastrophic. A *systematic* preoccupation with oneself serves a purpose. It is work and achievement. Often, in fact, it is much better to educate oneself first before one educates others. It is by no means certain that the man with good intentions is under all circumstances a good man. If he is not, then his best intentions will lead to ruin as daily experience proves.

Doesn't an exact knowledge of one's own nature with all its contradictions and absurdities, make one unsure? Doesn't it weaken self-confidence and so lessen the ability to survive in the battle of life?

1814   Much too often people have a pathetic cocksureness which leads them into nothing but foolishness. It is better to be unsure because one then becomes more modest, more humble. It is true that an inferiority complex always harbours within it the danger of outdoing itself and compensating the supposed lack by a flight into the opposite. Wherever an inferiority complex exists, there is good reason for it. There actually is an inferiority of some kind, though not precisely where one is persuaded it is. Modesty and humility are not the signs of an inferiority complex. They are highly estimable, indeed admirable, virtues and not complexes. They prove that their fortunate possessor is not a presumptuous fool, but knows his own limitations, and will therefore never stumble beyond the bounds of humanity, dazzled and intoxicated by his imagined greatness. The people who fancy they are sure of themselves are the ones who are truly unsure. Our life is unsure, and therefore a feeling of unsureness is much nearer to the truth than the illusion and the bluff of sureness. In the long run it is the better-adapted man who triumphs, not the wrongly self-confident, who is at the mercy of dangers from without and within. Measure not by money or power! Peace of soul means more.

Can depth psychology assist social adaptation and increase the capacity for human contacts?

1815   The increased self-knowledge which depth psychology necessitates also creates greater possibilities of communication: you can interpret yourself in the analytical dialogue and learn through self-knowledge to understand others. In that way you become more just and more tolerant. Above all, you can remedy your own mistakes, and this is probably the best chance of making a proper adaptation to society. Naturally you can also make wrong use of self-knowledge, just as any other knowledge.

Has self-knowledge a healing, liberating effect?

1816   Repentance, confession, and purification from sin have always been the conditions of salvation. So far as analysis helps confession, it can be said to bring about a kind of renewal. Again and again we find that patients dream of the analysis as of a refreshing and purifying bath, or their dreams and visions present symbols of re-birth, which show unmistakably that knowledge of their uncon-scious and its meaningful integration in their psychic life give them renewed vitality, and do indeed appear to them as a deliverance from otherwise unavoidable disaster or from entanglement in the skeins of fate.

How does the integration of the unconscious express itself in the actual psychic situation?

1817   This question can be answered only in a very general sense. Individuality is so varied that in each single case the integration of the unconscious takes place in a different and unforeseen way. One could describe this only with the help of concrete examples. The human personality is incomplete so long as we take simply the ego, the conscious, into account. It becomes complete only when supplemented by the unconscious. Therefore knowledge of the un-conscious is indispensable for every true self-investigation. Through its integration, the centre of the personality is displaced from the limited ego into the more comprehensive self, into that centre which embraces both realms, the conscious and the unconscious, and unites them with each other. This self is the mid-point about which the true personality turns. It has therefore been since remotest times the goal of every method of development based upon the principle of self-knowledge, as, for example, Indian yoga proves. From the Indian standpoint our psychology looks like a "dialectical" yoga. I must remark, however, that the yogi has quite definite notions as to the goal to be reached and does everything to attain this postulated goal. With us, intellectualism, rationalism, and volun-tarism are such dangerous psychic forces that psychotherapy must whenever possible avoid setting itself any such goal. If the goal of wholeness and of realizing his originally intended personality should grow naturally in the patient, we may sympathetically assist him towards it. If it does not grow of itself, it cannot be implanted without remaining a permanent foreign body. Therefore we re-nounce such artifices when nature herself is clearly not working to this end. As a medical art, equipped only with human tools, our psychotherapy does not presume to preach salvation or a way thereto, for that does not lie within its power.

FOREWORD TO SPIER: "THE HANDS
OF CHILDREN"[1]

1818 Chirology is an art which dates back to very ancient times. The ancient physicians never hesitated to make use of such auxiliary techniques as chiromancy and astrology for diagnostic purposes, as is shown, for instance, by the little book written by Dr. Goclenius,[2] who lived at the end of the sixteenth century in Würzburg. The rise of the natural sciences and hence of rationalism in the eighteenth century brought these ancient arts, which could look back on a thousand or more years of history, into disrepute, and led to the rejection of everything that, on the one hand, defied rational explanation and verification by experiment or, on the other, made too exclusive a claim on intuition. On account of the uncertainty and paucity of scientific knowledge in the Middle Ages, even the most conscientious thinkers were in danger of applying their intuition more to the promotion of superstition than of science. Thus all early, and particularly medieval, treatises on palmistry are an inextricable tangle of empiricism and fantasy. To establish a scientific method and to obtain reliable results it was necessary, first of all, to make a clean sweep of all these irrational procedures. In the twentieth century, after two hundred years of intensive scientific progress, we can risk resurrecting these almost forgotten arts which have lingered on in semi-obscurity and can test them in the light of modern knowledge for possible truths.

1819 The view of modern biology that man is a totality, supported by a host of observations and researches, does not exclude the possibility that *hands*, those organs so intimately connected with the psyche, might reveal by their shape and functioning the psychic peculiarities of the individual and thus furnish eloquent and intelligible clues to his character. Modern science is steadily abandoning

---

[1] [Translated from a German MS by Victor Grove for the English trans. of Julius Spier, *The Hands of Children: An Introduction to Psycho-chirology* (London, 1944); 2nd edn., 1955, with an appendix, "The Hands of the Mentally Diseased," by Herta Levi. The trans. has been revised.]

[2] [Rodolphus Goclenius, *Uranoscopiae, chiroscopiae, metoposcopiae et opthalmoscopiae contemplatio* (Frankfurt, 1608).]

the medieval conception of the dichotomy of body and mind, and just as the body is now seen to be something neither purely mechanical nor chemical, so the mind seems to be but another aspect of the living body. Conclusions drawn from one as to the nature of the other seem therefore to be within the realm of scientific possibility.

1820   I have had several opportunities of observing Mr. Spier at work, and must admit that the results he has obtained have made a lasting impression on me. His method, though predominantly intuitive, is based on wide practical experience. Experiences of this nature can be rationalized to a large extent, that is to say they admit of a rational explanation once they have happened. Apart from routine, however, the manner in which they are obtained depends at all decisive points on a finely differentiated, creative intuition which is in itself a special talent. Hence persons with nothing but an average intelligence can hardly be expected to master the method. There is, nevertheless, a definite possibility that people who are intuitively gifted will be able to obtain similar results provided they are properly taught and trained. Intuition is not by any means an isolated gift but a regular function which is capable of being developed. Like the functions of seeing and hearing it has a specific field of experience and a specific range of knowledge based upon this.

1821   The findings presented in this book are of fundamental importance for psychologists, doctors, and teachers. Spier's chirology is a valuable contribution to the study of human character in its widest sense.

FOREWORD TO THE HEBREW EDITION OF JUNG: "PSYCHOLOGY AND EDUCATION"[1]

1822   I have before me the Hebrew edition of my essays on psychology and education.[2] Not knowing this language, I am unable to appreciate the merits of the translation, so I can only bid it welcome as a "firstling" that is unique in my experience.

1823   As the study of the child psyche and the question of education may fairly be said to occupy a privileged position today, it does not seem inappropriate that the contributions of analytical psychology should receive some attention. I have never made the child psyche an object of special research, but have merely collected experiences from my psychotherapeutic practice. These do however give rise to a number of interesting observations, firstly in regard to adults who have not yet rid themselves of their disturbing infantilism, secondly in regard to the complex relations between parents and children, and thirdly in regard to the children themselves.

1824   The complex psychology of the child and in particular the psychic disorders of children are more often than not causally connected with the psychology of the parents, and in most cases one would do well to pay more attention to the faulty attitude of parents and educators than to the child's psyche, which in itself would function correctly if it were not disturbed by the harmful influence of the parents. The most important question next to the education of the child is the education of the educator. I hope these essays will prove stimulating in this respect, which is the one I would recommend to the especial consideration of the reader.

[1] [Tel-Aviv, 1958. Trans. here from the original German MS.]
[2] ["Psychic Conflicts in a Child," "Analytical Psychology and Education," and "The Gifted Child" (C.W., vol. 17), the contents of *Psychologie und Erziehung* (1946).]

ADDENDA

FOREWORD TO "PSYCHOLOGISCHE ABHANDLUNGEN," VOLUME I[1]

1825   The *Psychologische Abhandlungen* (Psychological Papers) comprise the works of my friends and pupils as well as other colleagues, and also my own contributions to psychology. In accordance with the character of our psychological interests, this series will include not only works in the area of psychopathology, but also investigations of a general psychological nature. The present state of psychology seems to make it advisable that schools or movements have their own organs of publication; in this way a troublesome scattering of works among many different periodicals can be avoided, and mutuality of outlook can achieve suitable expression through publication in one consistent place.

Küsnacht-Zurich, May 1914   The Editor:
                                                      C. G. JUNG

---

[1] [(Translated by L. R.) Leipzig and Vienna: Deuticke, 1914. The volume contained papers by Josef Lang, J. Vodoz, Hans Schmid, and C. Schneiter. The series was not used again until 1928, when Jung published *Über die Energetik der Seele* as vol. II (Zurich: Rascher, henceforward). This and the succeeding volumes were devoted to Jung's writings, sometimes with contributions by colleagues: III (1931), *Seelenprobleme der Gegenwart,* with a contribution by W. M. Kranefeldt; IV (1934), *Wirklichkeit der Seele,* with contributions by Hugo Rosenthal, Emma Jung, and W. M. Kranefeldt; V (1944), *Psychologie und Alchemie;* VI (1948), *Symbolik des Geistes,* with a contribution by R. Schärf; VII (1950), *Gestaltungen des Unbewussten,* with a contribution by Aniela Jaffé; VIII (1951), *Aion,* with a contribution by M.-L. von Franz; IX (1954), *Von den Wurzeln des Bewusstseins;* X–XII (1955–56), *Mysterium Coniunctionis,* with a contribution by M.-L. von Franz (= an edition of *Aurora Consurgens,* constituting vol. XII).]

ADDRESS AT THE PRESENTATION
OF THE JUNG CODEX[1]

Mr. President, Mr. Minister, viri magnifici, Ladies and Gentlemen!

1826   It gives me much pleasure to accept this precious gift in the name of our Institute. For this I thank you, and also for the surprising and undeserved honour you have done me in baptising the Codex with my name. I would like to express my special thanks both to Mr. Page, who through generous financial assistance made the purchase of the papyrus possible, and to Dr. Meier, who through unflagging efforts has given it a home.

1827   Dr. Meier has asked me to say a few words to you about the psychological significance of Gnostic texts. Of the four tracts con-

1 [(Translation revised and augmented by L. R.) The text of this address given above, pars. 1514–1517 (q.v.), was obtained by the Editors from the Jung archives at Küsnacht in the early 1960's and was assigned to R.F.C. Hull for translation on the assumption that it represented the text that Jung read at the convocation in Zurich, 15 Nov. 1953. In 1975, when the present vol. was in page proof, a considerably augmented version was published (in German) by Professor Gilles Quispel as an appendix to the volume *C. G. Jung: een mens voor deze tijd* (Rotterdam), consisting of essays (in Dutch) on Jung's work by Quispel ("Jung and Gnosis"), C. Aalders, and J. H. Plokker. Quispel had obtained this text of the Address some years earlier from one of the persons who had arranged the convocation. Subsequently, Professor C. A. Meier provided an even fuller version of Jung's actual remarks, and that is translated here (the added material being indicated by a vertical line in the left margin). Jung had first written the shorter version, then had expanded it prior to the occasion, but the shorter version had been circulated.

George H. Page, of Switzerland, donated funds that enabled the Jung Institute to purchase the Codex from the estate of Albert Eid, a Belgian dealer in antiquities who had acquired it in Egypt. Professor Meier, then director of the Institute, had played the leading role in tracing and negotiating for the Codex. In accordance with the original agreement, the Codex was eventually given to the Coptic Museum in Cairo.]

tained in this codex, I should like to single out especially the *Evangelium Veritatis,* an important Valentinian text that affords us some insight into the mentality of the second century A.D. "The Gospel of Truth" is less a gospel than a highly interesting commentary on the Christian message. It belongs therefore to the series of numerous "phenomena of assimilation," its purpose being to assimilate this strange and hardly understandable message to the Hellenistic-Egyptian world of thought. It is evident that the author was appealing to the intellectual understanding of his reader, as if in remembrance of the words: "We preach Christ crucified, unto the Jews a stumbling-block, and unto the Greeks foolishness" (I Cor. 1.23). For him Christ was primarily a metaphysical figure, a light-bringer, who went forth from the Father in order to illuminate the stupidity, darkness, and unconsciousness of mankind and to lead the individual back to his origins through self-knowledge. This deliverance from *agnosia* relates the text to the accounts which Hippolytus, in his *Elenchos,* has left of the Gnostics, and of the Naassenes and Peratics in particular. There we also find most of what I call the "phenomena of assimilation." By this term I mean to delineate those specifically psychic reactions aroused by the impact that the figure and message of Christ had on the pagan world, most prominently those allegories and symbols such as fish, snake, lion, peacock, etc., characteristic of the first Christian centuries, but also those much more extensive amplifications due to Gnosticism, which clearly were meant to illuminate and render more comprehensible the metaphysical role of the Saviour. For the modern mind this accumulation of symbols, parables, and synonyms has just the opposite effect, since it only deepens the darkness and entangles the light-bringer in a network of barely intelligible analogies.

1828   Gnostic amplification, as we encounter it in Hippolytus, has a character in part hymn-like, in part dream-like, which one invariably finds where an aroused imagination is trying to clarify an as yet still unconscious content. These are, on the one hand, intellectual, philosophical—or rather, theosophical—speculations, and, on the other, analogies, synonyms, and symbols whose psychological nature is immediately convincing. The phenomenon of assimilation mainly represents the reaction of the psychic matrix, i.e., the unconscious, which becomes agitated and responds with archetypal images, thereby demonstrating to what degree the message has penetrated into the depths of the psyche and how the unconscious interprets the phenomenon of Christ.

1829   It is not likely that the Gnostic attempts at elucidation met with success in the pagan world, quite aside from the fact that the Church very soon opposed them and whenever possible suppressed them. Luckily during this process some of the best pieces (to judge by their content) were preserved for posterity, so that today we are in a position to see in what way the Christian message was taken up by the unconscious of that age. These assimilation phenomena are naturally of especial significance for psychologists and psychiatrists, who are professionally concerned with the psychic background, and this is the reason why our Institute is so interested in acquiring and translating authentic Gnostic texts.

1830   Although suppressed and forgotten, the process of assimilation that began with Gnosticism continued all through the Middle Ages, and it can still be observed in modern times whenever individual consciousness is confronted with its own shadow, or the inferior part of the personality. This aspect of human personality, which is most often repressed owing to its incompatibility with one's self-image, does not consist only of inferior characteristics but represents the entire unconcious; that is, it is almost always the first form in which unconsciousness brings itself to the attention of consciousness. Freud's psychology occupied itself exclusively, so to speak, with this aspect. Behind the shadow, however, the deeper layers of the unconscious come forward, those which, so far as we are able to ascertain, consist of archetypal, sometimes instinctive, structures, so-called "patterns of behaviour." Under the influence of extraordinary psychic situations, especially life crises, these archetypal forms or images may spontaneously invade consciousness, in the case of sick persons just as in the case of healthy ones. The general rule, however, is that modern man needs expert help to become conscious of his darkness, because in most cases he has long since forgotten this basic problem of Christianity: the moral and intellectual *agnosia* of the merely natural man. Christianity, considered as a psychological phenomenon, contributed a great deal to the development of consciousness, and wherever this dialectical process has not come to a standstill we find new evidence of assimilation. Even in medieval Judaism a parallel process took place over the centuries, independently of the Christian one, in the Kabbala. Its nearest analogy in the Christian sphere was philosophical alchemy, whose psychological affinities with Gnosticism can easily be demonstrated.

1831   The urgent therapeutic necessity of confronting the individual with his own dark side is a secular continuation of the Christian development of consciousness and leads to phenomena of assimilation similar to those found in Gnosticism, the Kabbala, and Hermetic philosophy.

1832 The reactions of the matrix that we observe these days are not only comparable, both in form and in content, with Gnostic and medieval symbols, but presumably are also of the same sort, and have the same purpose as well, in that they make the figure of *Hyios tou anthropou,* Son of Man, the innermost concern of the individual, and also expand it into a magnitude comparable with that of the Indian *purusha-atman,* the *anima mundi.* At this time, however, I would prefer not to go any further into these modern tendencies, which indeed were developing among the Gnostics.

1833 Since comparison with these earlier historical stages is of the greatest importance in interpreting the modern phenomena, the discovery of authentic Gnostic texts is, especially for the direction our research is taking, of the greatest interest, all the more so in that it is not only of a theoretical but also of a practical nature. If we seek genuine psychological understanding of the human being of our own time, we must know his spiritual history absolutely. We cannot reduce him to mere biological data, since he is not by nature merely biological but is a product also of spiritual presuppositions.

1834 I must unfortunately content myself with these bare outlines in attempting to explain our interest in a Gnostic text. Further proof of our interest in Gnosticism and detailed explanations may be found in a number of studies that have already been published.

BIBLIOGRAPHY

BIBLIOGRAPHY

The bibliography does not, as a rule, list works that are the source of contents of this volume. Details of such works are given in the initial footnote of the respective items of contents.

ADAMSKI, GEORGE, with DESMOND LESLIE. *Flying Saucers Have Landed.* London, 1953.

ADLER, GERHARD. *Entdeckung der Seele; Von Sigmund Freud und Alfred Adler zu C. G. Jung.* Zurich, 1934.

——. *Studies in Analytical Psychology.* New edn., London, 1966; New York, 1967. (Original: *Zur analytischen Psychologie.* Zurich, 1952.)

——. See also JUNG, *Letters.*

AKSAKOW, A. N. *Animismus und Spiritismus.* Leipzig, 1894.

Amitāyur Dhyāna Sūtra. Translated by F. Max Müller and Junjiro Takakusu. In: *Buddhist Mahāyāna Sūtras,* Part II. (Sacred Books of the East, 49.) Oxford, 1894.

AMMIANUS MARCELLINUS. *History.* Translated by John C. Rolfe. (Loeb Classical Library.) London and Cambridge, Mass., 1956.

L'Année psychologique (Paris), XIV (1908).

ANONYMOUS. *Die Tyroler ekstatischen Jungfrauen. Leitsterne in die dunklen Gebiete der Mystik.* Regensburg, 1843.

APULEIUS. *The Golden Ass.* Translated by W. Adlington, revised by S. Gaselee. (Loeb Classical Library.) London and Cambridge, Mass., 1915.

AUGUSTINE, SAINT. *Tractatus in Johannis Evangelium.* In MIGNE. *P.L.,* vol. 35.

Avalon, Arthur, pseud. (Sir John Woodroffe), ed. and trans. *The Serpent Power, being the Sat-Cakra-Nirūpana and Pādukā-Pañcaka.* (Tantrik Texts.) London, 1919. 6th edn., Madras, 1958.

Ballet, Gilbert. *Swedenborg: Histoire d'un visionnaire au XVIII siècle.* Paris, 1899.

Baynes, H. G. *Germany Possessed.* London, 1941.

———. *Mythology of the Soul.* London, 1940.

Beit, Hedwig von. *Gegensatz und Erneuerung im Märchen.* (Symbolik des Märchen, 2.) Bern and Munich, 1957; 2nd edn., rev., 1965.

———. *Symbolik des Märchens. Versuch einer Deutung.* Bern, 1952.

Benoît, Pierre. *L'Atlantide.* Paris, 1919. Trans. by M. C. Tongue and M. Ross: *Atlantida.* New York, 1920.

Béroalde de Verville, François (trans.). *Le tableau des riches inventions . . . representées dans le Songe de Poliphile.* Paris, 1600. (Contains the "Recueil Stéganographique.") See also Colonna; Fierz-David.

Berthelot, Marcellin. *Collection des anciens alchimistes grecs.* Paris, 1887–88. 3 vols.

Blanke, Fritz. *Bruder Klaus von Flüe.* Zurich, 1948.

Bleuler, Paul Eugen. *Die Psychoanalyse Freuds.* Leipzig and Vienna, 1911. (Original: *Jahrbuch für psychoanalytische und psychopathologische Forschungen,* II:2 (1910).)

Bourget, Paul. *L'Étape.* Paris, 1902.

Bousset, Wilhelm. "Die Himmelsreise der Seele," *Archiv für Religionswissenschaft* (Tübingen and Leipzig), IV (1901), 136–69.

British Medical Journal (London). Leading article, 9 Feb. 1952.

Buber, Martin. *Eclipse of God: Studies in the Relation Between Religion and Philosophy.* New York, 1952.

———. *Die Erzählungen der Chassidim.* Zurich, 1949. Translated by Olga Marx: *Tales of the Hasidim.* New York, 1947.

———. "Religion und modernes Denken," *Merkur,* VI:2 (Feb. 1952). Translated as "Religion and Modern Thought" in *Eclipse of God,* supra.

834

BÜCHNER, LUDWIG. *Kraft und Stoff.* Leipzig, 1871.

BUDGE, E. A. WALLIS. *Egyptian Literature.* Vol. 1: *Legends of the Gods.* (Books on Egypt and Chaldea, 32.) London, 1912.

CAPRON, E. W. *Modern Spiritualism; Its Facts and Fanaticisms, Its Consistencies and Contradictions.* New York and Boston, 1855.

CASSINI, JACQUES DOMINIQUE, COMTE DE THURY. *Les Tables parlantes au point de vue de la physique générale.* Geneva, 1855.

CODEX:
Oxford. Bodleian Library. MS. Bruce 96. (Codex Brucianus).

COLONNA, FRANCESCO. *Hypnerotomachia Poliphili.* . . . Venice, 1499. For French translation, see BÉROALDE DE VERVILLE; for English paraphrase, see FIERZ-DAVID.

CORBIN, HENRY. *Creative Imagination in the Ṣūfism of Ibn ʿArabī.* Translated by Ralph Manheim. Princeton (Bollingen Series XCI) and London, 1969.

CROOKES, WILLIAM. "Notes of an Enquiry into the Phenomena called Spiritual, during the years 1870–73," *Quarterly Journal of Science* London, XI (n.s., IV) (1874).

CUMONT, FRANZ. *Textes et monuments figurés relatifs aux mystères de Mithra.* Brussels, 1894–99. 2 vols.

CUSTANCE, JOHN. *Wisdom, Madness and Folly.* New York and London, 1951.

DAVIE, T. M. "Comments upon a Case of 'Periventricular Epilepsy,'" *British Medical Journal* (London), 11 (Aug. 17, 1935).

DEMANT, VIGO AUGUSTE. *The Religious Prospect.* London, 1941.

DESSOIR, MAX. *Das Doppel-Ich.* Leipzig, 1890.

DIETERICH, ALBRECHT. *Eine Mithrasliturgie.* Leipzig, 1903; 2nd edn., 1910. Translated by G.S.R. Mead: *A Mithraic Ritual.* London and Benares, 1907.

DORN, GERARD. "Congeries Paracelsicae chemicae de transmutationibus metallorum," in: *Theatrum chemicum,* vol. I. Ursel, 1602.

DUNS SCOTUS, JOANNES. *Quaestiones Scoti super Universalibus Porphyrii.* . . . Venice, 1520.

DUSSAUD, RENÉ. *Notes du mythologie syrienne.* Paris, 1903–5.

[ECKHART, MEISTER.] [*Works of*] *Meister Eckhart*. Translated by C. de B. Evans. London, 1924–52. 2 vols.

ELIADE, MIRCEA. *Shamanism: Archaic Techniques of Ecstasy*. Translated by W. R. Trask. New York (Bollingen Series LXXVI) and London, 1964.

[ELIEZER BEN HYRCANUS.] *Pirkê de Rabbi Eliezer*. Translated and edited by Gerald Friedlander. London and New York, 1916.

ELLENBERGER, HENRI F. *The Discovery of the Unconscious*. New York and London, 1970.

Encyclopedia of Islam. Edited by M. Th. Houtsma et al. Leiden and Leipzig, 1913–34.

Encyclopedia Judaica. Edited by Jacob Klatzkin. Berlin, 1928–34.

EPIPHANIUS. *Panarium, sive Arcula (Contra Octoginta Haereses)*. In MIGNE, *P.G.*, vol. 41, col. 173, to vol. 42, col. 852.

EVANS-WENTZ, W. Y. *The Tibetan Book of the Dead*. London, 1927; 3rd edn., with commentary by C. G. Jung, 1957.

FIERZ-DAVID, LINDA. *The Dream of Poliphilo*. Translated by Mary Hottinger. With a foreword by C. G. Jung. New York (Bollingen Series XXV) and London, 1950.

FLAVIUS JOSEPHUS. *The Jewish War*. Translated by H. St.J. Thackeray. (Loeb Classical Library.) London and Cambridge, Mass., 1956.

FOUCART, P. F. *Les Mystères d'Eleusis*. Paris, 1914.

FRANCE, ANATOLE. *Penguin Island*. Translated by A. W. Evans. New York, 1909.

―――. *The White Stone*. Translated by C. E. Roche. (Works of Anatole France, Autograph Edition, 14.) New York, 1924.

FRAZER, JAMES G. *The Golden Bough*. London, 1911–15. 12 vols.

FREI, GEBHARD. *Probleme der Parapsychologie: Gesammelte Aufsätze*. Edited by A. Resch. Munich, 1969.

FREUD, SIGMUND. *Five Lectures on Psychoanalysis*. In: Standard Edition of the Complete Psychological Works, translated under the editorship of James Strachey, 11. London, 1957. (Original: *Über Psychoanalyse*, 1910.)

————. *The Interpretation of Dreams.* Standard Edition, 4, 5. London, 1953. (Original: *Die Traumdeutung,* 1900.)

————. "Notes upon a Case of Obsessional Neurosis." In: Standard Edition, 10. London, 1955. (Original: "Bemerkungen über einen Fall von Zwangsneurose," 1909.)

————. *An Outline of Psycho-Analysis.* In: Standard Edition, 23. London, 1964. (Original: *Abriss der Psychoanalyse,* 1940.)

———— and C. G. JUNG. *The Freud/Jung Letters.* Edited by William McGuire. Translated by R.F.C. Hull and Ralph Manheim. Princeton (Bollingen Series XCIV) and London, 1974.

FREUNDLICH, JAKOB. Article in *Deutsches Archiv für klinische Medizin* (Berlin), 177:4 (1934).

FROMM, ERICH. *Psychoanalysis and Religion.* (The Terry Lectures.) New Haven, 1950.

GAYOT DE PITAVAL, FRANÇOIS. *Causes célèbres et intéressantes avec les jugements qui les ont décidés (1734–43).* Paris, 1772–88.

GILLI, GERTRUD. "C. G. Jung in seiner Handschrift," in *Die kulturelle Bedeutung der komplexen Psychologie.* (Festschrift for Jung's 60th Birthday.) Berlin, 1935.

GLAUBER, JOHANN RUDOLF. *De Elia Artista.* Amsterdam, 1668.

GLOVER, EDWARD. *Freud or Jung.* London, 1950.

GNOSIUS, DOMINICUS. *Hermetis Trismegisti Tractatus vere Aureus . . . cum scholiis Dominici Gnosii.* Leipzig, 1610.

GOCLENIUS, RODOLPHUS. *Uranoscopiae, chiroscopiae, metoposcopiae et ophthalmoscopiae contemplatio.* Frankfurt a. M., 1608.

GÖRRES, JOHAN JOSEPH VON. *Die christliche Mystik.* Regensburg and Landshut, 1836–42. 4 vols.

————. *Emanuel Swedenborg, seine Visionen und sein Verhaltnis zur Kirche.* Speyer, 1827.

GOETHE, JOHANN WOLFGANG VON. *Egmont.* Leipzig, 1788. For translation see: *Dramatic Works of Goethe.* Translated by Sir Walter Scott and revised by Henry G. Bohn. London, 1872.

————. *Faust, Part Two.* Translated by Philip Wayne. (Penguin Classics.) Harmondsworth, 1959.

GOLDBRUNNER, JOSEF. *Individuation: A Study of the Depth Psychology of Carl Gustav Jung.* Translated by Stanley Godman. London and New York, 1955. (Original: *Individuation: Die Tiefenpsychologie in Carl Gustav Jung.* Munich, 1949.)

GRENFELL, BERNARD P., and ARTHUR S. HUNT (eds. and trans.). *New Sayings of Jesus and Fragment of a Lost Gospel from Oxyrhynchus.* New York and London, 1904.

GUILLAUME DE DIGULLEVILLE. *Le Pèlerinage de la vie humaine. Le Pèlerinage de l'ame. Le Pèlerinage de Jésus Christ.* In: JOSEPH DELACOTTE. *Guillaume de Digulleville . . . Trois romans-poèmes du XIVe siècle.* Paris, 1932.

GURNEY, EDMUND, FREDERIC W. H. MYERS, and FRANK PODMORE. *Phantasms of the Living.* London, 1886. 2 vols.

HAGGARD, HENRY RIDER. *She: A History of Adventure.* London and New York, 1887.

HARDING, M. ESTHER. *The Way of All Women.* With a foreword by C. G. Jung. New York, 1933.

————. *Woman's Mysteries: Ancient and Modern.* New York, 1935. 2nd edn., with foreword by C. G. Jung, New York, 1955.

HARRISON, JANE E. *Prolegomena to the Study of Greek Religion.* 3rd edn., Cambridge, 1922.

HASTINGS, JAMES. *Encyclopedia of Religion and Ethics.* New York, 1908–27. 13 vols.

HELVETIUS, JOHANN FRIEDRICH. "Vitulus aureus," in *Musaeum hermeticum,* pp. 815–63. Amsterdam, 1667.

HERMAS. *The Shepherd.* In: *The Apostolic Fathers.* With an English translation by Kirsopp Lake. (Loeb Classical Library.) London and New York, 1917. 2 vols. (Vol. 2, pp. 6–305.)

HERODOTUS. *The Histories.* Translated by Aubrey de Selincourt. (Penguin Classics.) Harmondsworth, 1954.

HEYER, GUSTAV RICHARD. *The Organism of the Mind.* Translated by E. and C. Paul. London, 1933.

HIPPOLYTUS. *Elenchos (Refutatio omnium haeresium).* (*Werke,* Vols. III and IV.) Edited by Paul Wendland. (Griechische christliche Schriftsteller.) Leipzig, 1916. For translation, see: *Philosophoumena, or The Refutation of All Heresies.* Translated by Francis Legge. London and New York, 1921. 2 vols.

HOCHE, ALFRED E. *Handbuch der gerichtlichen Psychiatrie.* Berlin, 1901; 3rd edn., rev., 1934.

HUBERT, HENRI, and MARCEL MAUSS. *Mélanges d'histoire des religions.* Paris, 1909.

IAMBLICHUS. *Vita Pythagorica.* Edited by L. Deubner. Leipzig, 1937.

IBSEN, HENRIK. *The Lady from the Sea.* In *Plays.* Translated by U. Ellis-Fermor and P. Watts. (Penguin Classics.) Harmondsworth, 1950ff. (Original, 1888.)

IGNATIUS OF LOYOLA, SAINT. *Exercitia Spiritualia.* Translated and edited by Joseph Rickaby, S.J., as *The Spiritual Exercises.* 2nd edn., London, 1923.

Imago: Zeitschrift für Anwendung der Psychoanalyse auf die Geisteswissenschaften. Leipzig and Vienna, 1912–1937.

IRENAEUS, SAINT. *Contra* [or *Adversus*] *haereses libri quinque.* See MIGNE, *P.G.*, vol. 7, cols. 433–1224. For transaltion, see *Five Books of Irenaeus against Heresies.* Translated by John Keble. (Library of Fathers of the Holy Catholic Church.) Oxford, 1872. Also: *The Writings of Irenaeus.* Translated by Alexander Roberts and W. H. Rambaut. Vol. I. (Ante-Nicene Christian Library, 5.) Edinburgh, 1868.

JACOBI, JOLANDE. *Complex/Archetype/Symbol in the Psychology of C. G. Jung.* Translated by Ralph Manheim. With a foreword by C. G. Jung. New York (Bollingen Series LVII) and London, 1959.

————. *The Psychology of C. G. Jung.* Translated by K. W. Bash. London, 1942; New Haven, 1943. Revised edition, translated by Ralph Manheim, 1958. (Several later editions.) (Original: *Die Psychologie von C. G. Jung.* Zurich, 1940.)

JAFFÉ, ANIELA. "Bilder und Symbole aus E. T. A. Hoffmanns Märchen 'Der goldne Topf,'" in: C. G. JUNG. *Gestaltungen des Unbewussten.* Zurich, 1950.

Jahrbuch für psychoanalytische und psychopathologische Forschungen. Edited by C. G. Jung under the direction of Eugen Bleuler and Sigmund Freud. Leipzig and Vienna, 1909–1913.

JAMES, MONTAGUE RHODES, trans. *The Apocryphal New Testament.* Oxford, 1924.

JAMES, WILLIAM. *The Varieties of Religious Experience.* New York and London, 1902.

JOSEPHUS, FLAVIUS. *The Jewish War.* (Loeb Classical Library.) London and Cambridge, Mass., 1927.

Journal für Psychologie und Neurologie. Leipzig, 1903– .

JUNG, CARL GUSTAV. "The Aims of Psychotherapy." In: *The Practice of Psychotherapy.* Coll. Works, 16.

———. *Aion: Researches into the Phenomenology of the Self.* Coll. Works, 9, ii.

———. *Alchemical Studies.* Coll. Works, 13.

———. "Answer to Job." In: *Psychology and Religion: West and East.* Coll. Works, 11.

———. *The Archetypes and the Collective Unconscious.* Coll. Works, 9, i.

———. "Archetypes of the Collective Unconscious." In: *The Archetypes and the Collective Unconscious.* Coll. Works, 9, i.

———. *Aufsätze zur Zeitgeschichte.* Zurich, 1946.

———. "Brother Klaus." In: *Psychology and Religion: West and East.* Coll. Works, 11.

———. "A Case of Hysterical Stupor in a Prisoner in Detention." In: *Psychiatric Studies.* Coll. Works, 1.

———. *Civilization in Transition.* Coll. Works, 10.

———. *Collected Papers on Analytical Psychology.* Edited by Constance E. Long. London and New York, 1916.

———. "Commentary on 'The Secret of the Golden Flower'." In: *Alchemical Studies.* Coll. Works, 13.

———. "The Complications of American Psychology." In: *Civilization in Transition.* Coll. Works, 10.

———. "Concerning Mandala Symbolism." In: *The Archetypes and the Collective Unconscious.* Coll. Works, 9, i.

———. "Concerning Psychoanalysis." In: *Freud and Psychoanalysis.* Coll. Works, 4.

———. "Concerning Rebirth." In: *The Archetypes and the Collective Unconscious.* Coll. Works, 9, i.

———. "The Content of the Psychoses." In: *The Psychogenesis of Mental Disease.* Coll. Works, 3.

———. *Contributions to Analytical Psychology.* Translated by H. G. and C. F. Baynes. London and New York, 1928.

———. *The Development of Personality.* Coll. Works, 17.

———. *Diagnostische Assoziationsstudien.* 2 vols. Leipzig, 1906–9.

———. "Dream Symbols of the Process of Individuation." In: *The Integration of Personality.* Translated by Stanley Dell. New York, 1939; London, 1940. Revised as "Individual Dream Symbolism in Relation to Alchemy," in: *Psychology and Alchemy.* Coll. Works, 12.

———. *Essays on Contemporary Events.* Translated by Barbara Hannah et al. London, 1947.

———. *Experimental Researches.* Coll. Works, 2.

———. "Ein Fall von hysterischem Stupor bei einer Untersuchungsgefangenen," in *Journal für Psychologie und Neurologie,* I:3 (1902).

———. "The Familial Constellations." In: *Experimental Researches.* Coll. Works, 2.

———. "Flying Saucers: A Modern Myth of Things Seen in the Skies." In: *Civilization in Transition,* Coll. Works, 10.

———. Foreword to White's *God and the Unconscious.* In: *Psychology and Religion: West and East.* Coll. Works, 11.

———. *Freud and Psychoanalysis.* Coll. Works, 4.

———. "General Aspects of Dream Psychology." In: *The Structure and Dynamics of the Psyche.* Coll. Works, 8.

———. *Gestaltungen des Unbewussten.* (With a contribution by Aniela Jaffé.) Zurich, 1950.

———. *L'Homme à la découverte de son âme.* Edited by Roland Cahen. Geneva, 1944; 6th edn., Paris, 1962.

———. "Instinct and the Unconscious." In: *The Structure and Dynamics of the Psyche*. Coll. Works, 8.

———. *Letters*. Selected and edited by Gerhard Adler, in collaboration with Aniela Jaffé. Translated by R. F. C. Hull. Princeton (Bollingen Series XCV) and London, 1973, 1975. 2 vols.

———. *Memories, Dreams, Reflections*. Recorded and edited by Aniela Jaffé. New York and London, 1963.

———. "Mind and Earth." In: *Civilization in Transition*. Coll. Works, 10.

———. *Ein Moderner Mythus: Von Dingen, die am Himmel gesehen werden*. Zurich, 1958.

———. *Modern Man in Search of a Soul*. New York and London, 1933.

———. *Mysterium Coniunctionis*. Coll. Works, 14.

———. "New Paths in Psychology." In: *Two Essays on Analytical Psychology*. Coll. Works, 7.

———. "On the Importance of the Unconscious in Psychopathology." In: *The Psychogenesis of Mental Disease*. Coll. Works, 3.

———. "On the Nature of Dreams." In: *The Structure and Dynamics of the Psyche*. Coll. Works, 8.

———. "On the Nature of the Psyche." In: *The Structure and Dynamics of the Psyche*. Coll. Works, 8.

———. "On the Practical Use of Dream Analysis." In: *The Practice of Psychotherapy*. Coll. Works, 16.

———. "On Psychic Energy." In: *The Structure and Dynamics of the Psyche*. Coll. Works, 8.

———. "On the Psychogenesis of Schizophrenia." In: *The Psychogenesis of Mental Disease*. Coll. Works, 3.

———. "On Psychological Understanding." In: *The Psychogenesis of Mental Disease*. Coll. Works, 3.

———. "On the Psychology and Pathology of So-Called Occult Phenomena." In: *Psychiatric Studies*. Coll. Works, 1.

———. *Paracelsica*. Zurich, 1942.

————. "Paracelsus as a Spiritual Phenomenon." In: *Alchemical Studies*. Coll. Works, 13.

————. "The Phenomenology of the Spirit in Fairytales." In: *The Archetypes and the Collective Unconscious*. Coll. Works, 9, i.

————. "The Philosophical Tree." In: *Alchemical Studies*. Coll. Works, 13.

————. *The Practice of Psychotherapy*. Coll. Works, 16.

————. *Psychiatric Studies*. Coll. Works, 1.

————. *The Psychogenesis of Mental Disease*. Coll. Works, 3.

————. "A Psychological Approach to the Dogma of the Trinity." In: *Psychology and Religion: West and East*. Coll. Works, 11.

————. "Psychological Factors Determining Human Behaviour." In: *The Structure and Dynamics of the Psyche*. Coll. Works, 8.

————. "The Psychological Foundations of Belief in Spirits." In: *The Structure and Dynamics of the Psyche*. Coll. Works, 8.

————. *Psychological Types*. Coll. Works, 6.

————. *Die Psychologie der Übertragung*. Zurich, 1946.

————. *Psychologie und Alchemie*. Zurich, 1944.

————. *Psychologie und Erziehung*. Zurich, 1946.

————. *Psychology and Alchemy*. Coll. Works, 12.

————. "Psychology and Literature." In: *The Spirit in Man, Art, and Literature*. Coll. Works, 15.

————. *Psychology and Religion*. (The Terry Lectures.) New Haven and London, 1938. Cf. "Psychology and Religion." In: Coll. Works, 11.

————. *Psychology and Religion: West and East*. Coll. Works, 11.

————. "The Psychology of Dementia Praecox." In: *The Psychogenesis of Mental Disease*. Coll. Works, 3. Cf. *The Psychology of Dementia Praecox*. (Nervous and Mental Diseases Monograph Series No. 3.) Translated by A. A. Brill and F. Peterson. New York, 1909.

————. "The Psychology of Eastern Meditation." In: *Psychology and Religion: West and East*. Coll. Works, 11.

843

————. "The Psychology of the Transference." In: *The Practice of Psychotherapy*. Coll. Works, 16.

————. *Psychology of the Unconscious: A Study of the Transformations and Symbolisms of the Libido. A Contribution to the History of the Evolution of Thought*. Translated by B. M. Hinkle. New York and London, 1916.

————. "Psychotherapy Today." In: *The Practice of Psychotherapy*. Coll. Works, 16.

————. "The Reaction-Time in the Association Experiment." In: *Experimental Researches*. Coll. Works, 2.

————. "Realities of Practical Psychotherapy." In: *The Practice of Psychotherapy*. Coll. Works, 16.

————. "The Relations between the Ego and the Unconscious." In: *Two Essays on Analytical Psychology*. Coll. Works. 7.

————. "A Review of the Complex Theory." In: *The Structure and Dynamics of the Psyche*. Coll. Works, 8.

————. "Richard Wilhelm: In Memoriam." In: *The Spirit in Man, Art, and Literature*. Coll. Works, 15.

————. "The Role of the Unconscious." In: *Civilization in Transition*. Coll. Works, 10.

————. "Septem Sermones ad Mortuos." In: *Memories, Dreams, Reflections*, revised edn., appendix V.

————. "The Significance of the Father in the Destiny of the Individual." In: *Freud and Psychoanalysis*. Coll. Works, 4.

————. "The Soul and Death." In: *The Structure and Dynamics of the Psyche*. Coll. Works, 8.

————. *The Spirit in Man, Art, and Literature*, Coll. Works, 15.

————. "The Spirit Mercurius." In: *Alchemical Studies*. Coll. Works, 13.

————. *The Structure and Dynamics of the Psyche*. Coll. Works, 8.

————. "The Structure of the Unconscious." In: *Two Essays on Analytical Psychology*. Coll. Works, 7.

———— (ed.). *Studies in Word-Association*. Translated by M. D. Eder. London and New York, 1918.

————. "A Study in the Process of Individuation." In: *The Archetypes and the Collective Unconscious*. Coll. Works, 9, i.

————. *Symbolik des Geistes*. Zurich, 1948.

————. *Symbols of Transformation*. Coll. Works, 5.

————. "Synchronicity: An Acausal Connecting Principle." In: *The Structure and Dynamics of the Psyche*. Coll. Works, 8.

————. "The Theory of Psychoanalysis." In: *Freud and Psychoanalysis*. Coll. Works, 4.

————. The Therapeutic Value of Abreaction." In: *The Practice of Psychotherapy*. Coll. Works, 16.

————. "The Transcendent Function." In: *The Structure and Dynamics of the Psyche*. Coll. Works, 8.

————. "Transformation Symbolism in the Mass." In: *Psychology and Religion: West and East*. Coll. Works, 11.

————. "Traumsymbole des Individuationsprozesses," *Eranos Jahrbuch 1935*. Zurich, 1936. For translation, see "Dream Symbols of the Process of Individuation."

————. *Two Essays on Analytical Psychology*. Coll. Works, 7.

————. *Über psychische Energetik und das Wesen der Träume*. Zurich, 1948.

————. *Über die Psychologie des Unbewussten*. Zurich, 1943.

————. "Versuch einer Darstellung der psychoanalytischen Theorie," *Jahrbuch für psychoanalytische und psychopathologische Forschungen* (Leipzig and Vienna), V:1 (1913).

————. *Wandlungen und Symbole der Libido*. Leipzig, 1912.

————. "Wotan." In: *Civilization in Transition*. Coll. Works, 10.

————, and M.-L. VON FRANZ, JOSEPH L. HENDERSON, JOLANDE JACOBI, and ANIELA JAFFÉ. *Man and His Symbols*. London and New York, 1964.

———— and W. PAULI. *The Interpretation of Nature and the Psyche*. Translated by R.F.C. Hull. New York (Bollingen Series LI), 1955. (Original: *Naturerklärung und Psyche*. Zurich, 1952.)

———— and FREDERICK PETERSON. "Psychophysical Investigations

with the Galvanometer and Pneumograph in Normal and Insane Individuals." In: *Experimental Researches*. Coll. Works, 2.

———— and CHARLES RICKSHER. "Further Investigations on the Galvanic Phenomenon and Respiration in Normal and Insane Individuals." In: *Experimental Researches*. Coll. Works, 2.

———— and RICHARD WILHELM. *The Secret of the Golden Flower*. See WILHELM.

JUNG, EMMA. "On the Nature of the Animus." Translated by Cary F. Baynes. In: EMMA JUNG. *Animus and Anima*. New York (The Analytical Psychology Club of New York), 1957. (Original: "Ein Beitrag zum Problem des Animus," in: C. G. JUNG. *Wirklichkeit der Seele*. Zurich, 1934.)

KANT, IMMANUEL. *Anthropologie in pragmatischer Hinsicht*. Königsberg, 1798.

————. *Critique of Pure Reason*. Translated by Norman Kemp Smith. London, 1964.

————. *Dreams of a Spirit-Seer, Illustrated by Dreams of Metaphysics*. Translated by E. F. Goerwitz. New York and London, 1900.

KARDEC, ALLAN. *Buch der Medien*. See translation by Emma A. Wood: *Experimental Spiritism. A Book on Mediums: Or, Guide for Mediums and Invocators*. Boston, 1874.

KERNER, JUSTINUS. *Blätter aus Prevorst; Originalien und Lesefrüchte für Freunde des inneren Lebens* . . . Karlsruhe, 1831–39. 12 vols. in 3.

————. *Die Geschichte des Thomas Ignaz Martin, Landsmanns zu Gallardon, über Frankreich und dessen Zukunft im Jahre 1816 geschaut*. Heilbronn, 1835.

————. *Die somnambulen Tische. Zur Geschichte und Erklärung dieser Erscheinungen*. Stuttgart, 1853.

KEYHOE, DONALD EDWARD. *Flying Saucers from Outer Space*. New York, 1953; London, 1954.

KEYSERLING, COUNT HERMANN. "Begegnungen mit der Psychoanalyse," *Merkur*, IV:11 (Nov. 1950), 1151–68.

KOPP, HERMANN. *Die Alchemie in älterer und neuerer Zeit*. Heidelberg, 1886. 2 vols.

KRAFFT-EBING, RICHARD VON. *Lehrbuch der Psychiatrie auf klinischer Grundlage.* Stuttgart, 1879. Authorized translation by C. G. Chaddock: *Text-book of Insanity based on Clinical Observations.* Philadelphia, 1904.

KRANEFELDT, W. M. " 'Ewige Analyse.' Bemerkungen zur Traumdeutung und zum Unbewussten," in: C. G. JUNG. *Wirklichkeit der Seele.* Zurich, 1934.

———. "Der Gegensatz von Sinn und Rhythmus im seelischen Geschehen," in ibid.

———. " 'Komplex' und Mythos," in: C. G. JUNG. *Seelenprobleme der Gegenwart.* Zurich, 1930.

———. *Secret Ways of the Mind.* With an introduction by C. G. Jung. Translated by Ralph M. Eaton. New York, 1932; London, 1934.

LACHAT, PÈRE WILLIAM. *La Réception et l'action du Saint-Esprit dans la vie personnelle et communautaire.* Neuchâtel, 1953.

LANGE, WILHELM. *Hölderlin: eine Pathographie.* Stuttgart, 1909.

LAO-TZU. *Tae-te-ching.* See: ARTHUR WALEY. *The Way and Its Power.* London, 1934.

LE BON, GUSTAVE. *The Crowd, a Study of the Popular Mind.* New York, 1896; London, 1897. (Original: *Psychologie des foules.* Paris, 1895.)

LEIBNIZ, GOTTFRIED WILHELM. *Nouveaux Essais sur l'entendement humain.* Paris, 1704. Translation by A. G. Langley: *New Essays concerning Human Understanding.* LaSalle, Ill., 1949.

LÉVY-BRUHL, LUCIEN. *How Natives Think.* Translated by Lilian A. Clare. London, 1926. (Original: *Les Fonctions mentales dans les sociétés inférieures.* Paris, 1912.)

LIPPMANN, E. O. VON. *Entstehung und Ausbreitung der Alchemie.* Berlin, 1919.

LÖWENFELD, LEOPOLD. *Der Hypnotismus: Handbuch der Lehre von der Hypnose und der Suggestion.* Wiesbaden, 1901.

MALININE, M., H. C. PUECH, and G. QUISPEL, eds. *Evangelium Veritatis.* Zurich, 1956.

MANGET, JEAN JACQUES, ed. *Bibliotheca chemica curiosa.* Geneva, 1702. 2 vols.

MEAD, G.R.S. *The Gnostic John the Baptizer.* London, 1924.

MICHELSEN, JOHANN. *Ein Wort an geistigen Adel deutscher Nation.* Munich, 1911.

MIEG, JOANNES FRIDERICUS. *De raptu Eliae.* 1660.

MORIENUS ROMANUS. "Sermo de transmutatione metallorum," in: *Artis auriferae,* vol. II. Basel, 1610. 2 vols.

MOSER, FANNY. *Der Okkultismus: Täuschungen und Tatsachen.* Zurich, 1935.

MURRAY, HENRY A., ed. (directing workers at the Harvard Psychological Clinic). *Explorations in Personality: A Clinical and Experimental Study of Fifty Men of College Age.* New York and London, 1938.

NELKEN, JAN. "Analytische Beobachtungen über Phantasien eines Schizophrenen," *Jahrbuch für psychoanalytische und psychopathologische Forschungen,* IV:1 (1912).

NERVAL, GÉRARD DE, pseud. (Gérard Labrunie). *Aurélia.* Paris, 1926.

NEUMANN, ERICH. *Amor and Psyche.* Translated by Ralph Manheim. New York (Bollingen Series LIV) and London, 1952.

————. *The Origins and History of Consciousness.* Translated by R.F.C. Hull. New York (Bollingen Series XLII) and London, 1954. (Original: *Ursprungsgeschichte des Bewusstseins.* Zurich, 1949.)

NIETZSCHE, FRIEDRICH WILHELM. *On the Genealogy of Morals.* Translated by Walter Kaufmann and R. J. Hollingdale. New York, 1967.

————. *Thus Spake Zarathustra.* Translated by Thomas Common and revised by Oscar Levy and J. L. Beevers. 6th edn., London, 1932.

The Observer (London), 11 Oct. 1936.

PARACELSUS (Theophrastus Bombast of Hohenheim). *De vita longa.* Edited by Adam von Bodenstein. Basel, 1562.

————. *Sämmtliche Werke.* Edited by Karl Sudhoff and Wilhelm Matthiessen. Munich and Wiesbaden, 1922–35. 14 vols.

PERNETY, A. J. *Dictionnaire mytho-hermétique.* Paris, 1756.

PHILO JUDAEUS. *Works.* Translated by F. H. Colson. (Loeb Classical Library.) London and Cambridge, Mass., 1956–62.

Pirkê de Rabbi Eliezer. See ELIEZER BEN HYRCANUS.

PIUS XI, POPE. *Casti Connubii.* 31 Dec. 1930.

PIUS XII, POPE. *Apostolic Constitution "Munificentissimus Deus."* Translated into English. Dublin (Irish Messenger Office), 1950.

PRICE, HARRY. *An Account of Some Further Experiments with Willy Schneider.* New York, 1925.

———. *The Phenomena of Rudi Schneider.* New York, 1926.

PRYZWARA, ERICH. *Deus semper maior.* Freiburg im Breisgau, 1938. 3 vols.

RASMUSSEN, KNUD. *Across Arctic America.* New York, 1927.

RHINE, J. B. *New Frontiers of the Mind.* New York, 1937; London, 1938.

———. *The Reach of the Mind.* New York and London, 1948.

ROSENCREUTZ, CHRISTIAN. *Chymische Hochzeit.* (1616.) Edited by Richard van Dülmen. Stuttgart, 1973.

ROSENTHAL, HUGO. "Der Typengegensatz in der jüdischen Religionsgeschichte," in: C. G. JUNG. *Wirklichkeit der Seele.* Zurich, 1934.

"Rosinus ad Sarratantam episcopum," in: *Artis auriferae quam chemiam vocant. . . . ,* vol. I. Basel, [1593]. 2 vols.

Samyutta-Nikaya. See: *The Book of the Kindred Sayings.* (Sangyutta-Nikaya.) Translated by Mrs. C.A.F. Rhys Davids. London and New York, 1917–20.

SCHAER, HANS. *Religion and the Cure of Souls in Jung's Psychology.* Translated by R.F.C. Hull, New York (Bollingen Series XXI) and London, 1950. (Original: *Religion und Seele in der Psychologie C. G. Jungs.* Zurich, 1946.)

———. *Erlösungsvorstellungen und ihre psychologischen Aspekte.* (Studien aus dem C. G. Jung-Institut, II.) Zurich, 1950.

SCHÄRF (-KLUGER), RIWKAH. *Satan in the Old Testament.* Translated by Hildegard Nagel. Evanston, Ill., 1967. (Original: "Die Gestalt Satans im Alten Testament," in: C. G. JUNG. *Symbolik des Geistes.* Zurich, 1948.)

SCHMALTZ, GUSTAV. *Östliche Weisheit und westliche Psychotherapie.* Stuttgart, 1951.

SCHOPENHAUER, ARTHUR. *Parerga und Paralipomena.* Leipzig, 1874; new edn., Oxford, 1974.

————. *The World as Will and Idea.* Translated by R. B. Haldane and J. Kemp. (English and Foreign Philosophical Library, 22–24.) London, 1883–86. 3 vols. London, 6th edn., 1957.

SCHREBER, DANIEL PAUL. *Memoirs of My Nervous Illness.* Translated by Ida Macalpine and Richard A. Hunter. (Psychiatric Monograph Series, 1.) London, 1955. (Original: *Denkwürdigkeiten eines Nervenkranken.* Leipzig, 1903.)

SCHULINUS (Johann Heinrich Schuelin). *Dissertatio philologica de Elia corvorum alumno.* Altorfii Noricorum, 1718.

SCHÜRER, EMIL. "Zur Vorstellung von der Besessenheit im Neuen Testament," *Jahrbuch für protestantische Theologie* (Leipzig), 1892.

SHAW, GEORGE BERNARD. *Man and Superman: A Comedy and A Philosophy.* London, 1903. (Penguin edn., 1952.)

SILBERER, HERBERT. *Problems of Mysticism and Its Symbolism.* Translated by Smith Ely Jelliffe. New York, 1917. (Original: *Probleme der Mystik und ihrer Symbolik.* Leipzig, 1914.)

————. "Über die Symbolbildung," *Jahrbuch für psychoanalytische und psychopathologische Forschungen,* III:1 (1911).

————. "Von den Kategorien der Symbolik," *Zentralblatt für Psychoanalyse und Psychotherapie* (Wiesbaden), II:4 (1912).

[SOPHOCLES.] "Life of Sophocles," in: *Sophoclis Fabulae.* Edited by A. C. Pearson. Oxford, 1924.

SPENCER-BROWN, G. "Statistical Significance in Psychical Research," *Nature,* 175 (25 July 1953).

STOLL, OTTO. *Suggestion und Hypnotismus in der Völkerpsychologie.* 2nd edn., Leipzig, 1904.

STRACK, HERMANN L., and PAUL BILLERBECK. *Kommentar zum Neuen Testament aus Talmud und Midrasch.* Munich, 1922–28. 4 vols.

TACITUS. *Historiae.* Translated by C. H. Moore. (Loeb Classical Library.) London and Cambridge, Mass., 1956.

TERENCE. *Heauton Timorumenos.* Translated by J. Sargeaunt. (Loeb Classical Library.) London and Cambridge, Mass., 1953.

TERTULLIAN. *De praescriptione hereticorum 40.* Edited by T. Herbert Bindley. Oxford, 1893.

Theatrum chemicum, praecipuos selectorum auctorum tractatus . . . continens. Ursel and Strasbourg, 1602–61. 6 vols.

THOMAS AQUINAS, SAINT. *The Summa Theologica.* Literally translated by the Fathers of the English Dominican Province. London, 1911–22. 18 vols.

THOMPSON, R. CAMPBELL (trans.). *The Epic of Gilgamish.* London, 1928.

THURY, PROFESSOR. See CASSINI.

TYRRELL, G.N.M. *The Personality of Man.* London, 1947.

VIRGIL. *Eclogues.* Translated by H. R. Fairclough. (Loeb Classical Library.) London and Cambridge, Mass., 1967.

WAGNER, RICHARD. *The Flying Dutchman.* Original, 1843.

———. *Parsifal.* Original, 1882.

WALSER, HANS H. "An Early Psychoanalytical Tragedy: J. J. Honegger and the Beginnings of Training Analysis" (translated by A. K. Donoghue), *Spring* (Zurich and New York), 1974.

WELLS, HERBERT GEORGE. *The Time Machine.* New York, 1895.

———. *The War of the Worlds.* London, 1898.

WHITE, STEWART EDWARD. *Across the Unknown.* New York, 1939.

———. *The Betty Book.* New York, 1937; London, 1945.

———. *The Road I Know.* New York, 1942; London, 1951.

———. *The Unobstructed Universe.* New York, 1940; London, 1949.

WHITE, VICTOR. *God and the Unconscious.* With a foreword by C. G. Jung. London, 1952; Chicago, 1953.

WHYTE, LANCELOT LAW. *The Unconscious before Freud.* New York, 1960; London, 1962.

WICKES, FRANCES G. *The Inner World of Childhood.* New York and London, 1927.

851

————. *The Inner World of Man*. New York and Toronto, 1938.

WILHELM, RICHARD (trans.). *The I Ching or Book of Changes*. Rendered into English by Cary F. Baynes. With a foreword by C. G. Jung. New York (Bollingen Series XIX) and London, 1950; 3rd edn., Princeton and London, 1967.

———— (trans.). *The Secret of the Golden Flower*. With a Commentary and Memorial by C. G. Jung. Translated by Cary F. Baynes. London and New York, 1931; new edn., 1962. (Original: *Das Geheimnis der goldenen Blüte*. Zurich, 1929.)

WILLCOX, A. R. *The Rock Art of South Africa*. Johannesburg, 1963.

WITCUTT, W. P. *Catholic Thought and Modern Psychology*. London, 1943.

————. *Return to Reality*. London, 1954; New York, [?1956].

WOLFF, TONI. "Einführung in die Grundlagen der komplexen Psychologie." in: *Die kulturelle Bedeutung der Komplexen Psychologie*. Berlin, 1935. Reprinted in *Studien zu C. G. Jungs Psychologie*. Zurich, 1959.

Zentralblatt für Psychoanalyse. Wiesbaden, 1910–1914.

INDEX

INDEX OF TITLES

The titles of articles in this volume are here listed alphabetically, with beginning page number, except for reviews, abstracts, forewords, etc., which are readily located in the main index under the name of the subject author.

INDEX

A

Aalders, C., 826n
abaissement du niveau mental, 67, 74, 79, 222, 335; in schizophrenia, 351
abdomen, crab as representation of, 92
Abegg, Lily: *Ostasien denkt anders,* J.'s foreword, 654–55
Abraham and Isaac, 688
Abraham Ibn Ezra, 675
Abraham, Karl, 398&n, 423&n, 485
absolution, 287; and cure, 273
Abyssinians, 46
active imagination, 6, 169, 170, 172, 530–31, 799, 800; archetypal motifs in, 653; and dream-series, 174, 176
Adam, and Christ, 231, 280
Adam Kadmon, 280
Adamski, George: *Flying Saucers Have Landed,* 627n
adaptation: in analysis, 450, 451; energetics of, 450; psychological, 449–52
Adler, Alfred/Adlerian, 6, 62, 124–26, 128, 423&n, 517, 534; confession, 126; on "guiding fictions," 481; on masculine protest, 481; on power-drive, 480; psychology/ school of psychology, 125, 127, 423n, 480; theory, 61; ed. (with Stekel), *Zentralblatt für Psychoanalyse,* 425&n
Adler, Gerhard, 474, 773; *Entdeckung der Seele,* 127n; J.'s foreword, 517; *Studies in Analytical Psychol-*

ogy, 474n; J.'s foreword, 523, 524
adolescence, 233
adumbratio, 234
advice, idealistic, 634
Aerial Phenomena Research Organization (APRO), 626n, 632; *Bulletin,* 632
aesthetics, 341
affect(s), 23, 43; blocking of, 478; emotion as, 25; infectiousness of, 596; influence of, on psyche, 375; and intellectual feelings, distinguished, 375; and invasions, 32; James-Lange theory of, 25, 27
affectivity, 375
Africa, 46; "going native" in, 148; J.'s journey to, 554–57, 623
Africa, Central, 15
Africa, East, Elgonyi tribe in, *see* Elgonyi
Africa, South, rock-carvings in, 39n
Agadir, Morocco, 566&n
agnosia, 671, 672, 826
agnosticism, 734
agoraphobia, 365
Agrippa von Nettesheim, Cornelius, 784
Aion, god, 121, 122
aischrologia, 121&n
Aksakow, A. N.: *Animismus und Spiritismus,* 293n
Albertus Magnus, 678; *De mirabilis mundi,* 511
alchemist(s)/alchemy, 120, 167, 280, 286, 546; art of, "requires the whole man," 619; Byzantine, 211;

analogy, 576; as symbol, 244–45, 257; tree of, and *arbor philosophica,* 591; as union of opposites, 735; *see also* crucifixion

Crottet, Robert: *Mondwald,* J.'s foreword, 782–83

crowd, emotion in, 138

crucifixion: of thieves, with Christ, 97; on wheel, 38–39; *see also* cross

crypt, 115, 116

cryptomnesia, 15, 200, 201

cul de Paris, 571

culture: contemporary, pathological nature of, 658; essence of, 583; Freud's theory of, 479

Cumont, Franz: *Textes et monuments,* 676

cura animarum/care of souls, 246

curses, Christianity and, 646

Cusanus, Nicholas, 682, 725

Custance, John: *Wisdom, Madness, and Folly,* 667; J.'s foreword, 349–352

Cybele cult, 554

Cyrillic script, 188

D

dagger, in dream of Toledo cathedral, 112–13, 118, 121, 166

daimonia, psychic, 664

damnation, eternity of, 690, 693, 727

Dana, Martha, 692*n*

dances, *yaibichy,* of Navaho, 516

Dante and Beatrice, 545*n*

Darshana, 265

Darwin, Charles, 213

Davenport brothers, mediums, 299

Davie, T. M., 133; "Comments upon a Case of 'Periventricular Epilepsy'," 65*n*

dead, return of, 328

Dead Sea, 108

death: fear of, 107; as goal, 757; philosophy and, 315; preparation for, 234, 315; spectre of, 246;

symbolic, as salvation, 735; unknown approach of, 234

Déesse Raison, 261

deities, *see* god(s)

Delphi, 117; oracle at, 239

delusional ideas: and archetypal motifs, 652; understanding of, 651

delusions, and mythological motifs, 354

Demant, V. A., 704; *The Religious Prospect,* 704*n*

dementia praecox, *see* schizophrenia

Demeter, 120, 121*n*

demiurge, Gnostic, 622

democracy, 572–74, 580, 695

Democritus, pseudo, 270, 751

demon(s): autochthonous, 591; metaphorical, 666; possession by, 593; psychic powers embodied in, 587, 593, 594, 599, 601

demonism, 648; of nature, 593

demotivation, 370

Deo concedente, 722

depression, 32

depth psychology, 616, 811–13, 818; J.'s encyclopedia article on, 477–86

descensus ad inferos, 38

descent, double, 658

Dessoir, Max, 341; *Das Doppel-Ich,* 341*n*

determination, principle of, 430

deus absconditus, 678, 680, 682

"deus ultionum," 684

Devas, angel (Sanskrit)/devil (Persian), 444

devil/Satan, 680; Christ and, *see* Christ *s.v.*; eternity of, 690; as fourth member of quaternity, 712, 732; as left hand of God, 682; as son of God, 687, 689, 690, 709, 710; —, *benê Elohim,* 716

Dharma, 261

diagnosis, and paintings of patients, 181

dialectical discussion with unconscious, 664, 667

diaphragm, seat of psychic activity, 10

function(s) (*cont.*):
scious, subjective components of, 22; in consciousness, 12, 36; cross of, 17; differentiated, 351; ectopsychic, 12; endopsychic, 21, 22, 37; four, 28, 43, 57, 97–98, 122, 483, 712; inferior, 19–21, 98, 732; psychological, 16; rational, 13; of religious symbols, 244–52; subjective components of, 43; thinking, 12–14, 16, 17, 43, 219; -types, four, 219, 471, 534
Fürst, Emma: "Statistische Untersuchungen über Wortassoziationen," J.'s abstract, 410–11
Fürth, first German railway to, 308n
future: historic, 281; unconscious concern with, 236

G

Game, Margaret, 3, 4
Ganser's symptom, 415, 416
gas, poison, 567
Gaul, 108
Gayot de Pitaval, François, 397&n
Geber (Jabir ibn Hayyan) 747
Gemütlichkeit, 48
genitals, suspension by, 445, 446
George, St., 676
Germany/German(s), 48, 161, 164, 569, 573, 574, 596, 597, 600; and collective guilt, 715; France and, *see* France *s.v.*; inferiority complex of, 604, 605, 607; language, 14, 15, 30, 87, 136, 176; national character of, 603; Nazis in, *see* Nazism; philosophy, 62; and prejudice, 241; primitivity of, 254; psychology, *see* psychology *s.v.*; sentimentality of, 47, 152; southern, 121; S.S. in, 580, 601; and triadic mandalas, 715; *see also* National Socialism
Gerry, Peggy, 692n
Gerster, Georg, 626n
ghosts, 319, 328; explanation of, 326; primitive fear of, 318, 319; *sel-*

elteni, Elgonyi and, 318; stories, 318, 319, 326–28; as symbol, 328
Gilbert, J. Allen, 767n; "The Curse of Intellect" (unpublished), J.'s preface, 767
Gilgamesh, *see* Babylon *s.v.* Gilgamesh Epic
Gilli, Gertrud: *Der dunkle Bruder,* J.'s foreword, 776–78; "C. G. Jung in seiner Handschrift," 776n
Glaphyra, 100–101
Glauber, Johann: *De Elia Artista,* 676
Glover, A.S.B., 589n, 673n, 679n
Glover, Edward: *Freud or Jung,* 706
gnosis, 730; of empirical method, 669
Gnosius, Dominicus: *Hermetis Trismegisti Tractatus vere Aureus de Lapide philosophici secreto,* 189n
Gnosticism, 280, 621, 651–53, 663; and assimilation, 672, 827; and collective unconscious, 652, 664; and evil, 727; father in, "devoid of consciousness," 653; and Holy Ghost as feminine, 99; in John's Gospel, 652, 686, 727; Jung considered as, 663, 664, 666, 727, 728, 730; morality, 720; "philosophoumena" of, 668; psychological significance of, 671, 826–28; and shadow (of Christ), cut off, 716, 722
Goclenius, Rodolphus: *Uranoscopiae, chiroscopiae, metoposcopiae,* 820&n
God: as Begetter, 156; belief in, Jung's own, 706; child of, 279; compensating, 678; as *complexio oppositorum,* see *complexio oppositorum;* devil and, *see* devil *s.v.*; evil principle in, 709, 710, 712, 713, 723; fear of, 206, 279; feminine counterpart, 733; and Godhead, 715; help of the lonely, 286; incarnation of, 687; metaphysical, 668; of Old and New Testaments, 679, 680, 729; the one who made the sun (St. Augustine), 10, 288; pneuma of, 689; self as, 621; speaks

H

575; like Mohammed, 281; and *pseudologia phantastica,* 604; psychological effect of, 607

Hitlerism, 164

Hitschmann, Eduard: *Freuds Neurosenlehre,* J.'s review, 422

Hoare, Sir Samuel, *later* Viscount Templewood, 576&*n*

Hoche, Alfred E., 386; *Handbuch der gerichtlichen Psychiatrie,* 386*n*

Hoffman, Michael L., 438&*n*

Hoffmann, Ernst Theodor Wilhelm: "The Golden Pot," 327&*n*, 525&*n*

Holy Communion, 273, 281

Holy Ghost/Spirit, 679–91; as Christ's father, *see* Christ *s.v.*; as *complexio oppositorum,* 689; as feminine, in Gnosticism, 99; identification with, 735; invocation of, 681; as psychic experience, 690; as revolutionary, 685; as transcendental fact, 682; two aspects of, 685; and union of opposites, 689, 691

Holy Roman Empire, 576

Home, Mr., spiritualistic medium, 299, 300

Homeric age, 10

homo interior, Christ as, 695

homo sapiens, 215

homosexuality and law in Germany, 382

Honegger, Johann Jakob, 426&*n*

Hopkins, W., 289, 290

Horst, Georg Conrad, 340&*n*

Horton, —, 680, 685, 686

Horus, 185; four sons of, 717, 732

Hosea, 685, 720, 724

Hottentots, 158

Howe, Eric Graham, 27, 28, 58–60, 62

Hubert, Henri, and M. Mauss: *Mélanges d'histoire des religions,* 38&*n*

Hull, R.F.C., 183, 449*n*

human mind, medical approach to, 354

humanities and psychology of neuroses, 357

Humbaba, *see* Babylon *s.v.* Gilgamesh Epic

Hume, David, 772

Hungarian uprising, 636

Hunt, Arthur S., *see under* Grenfell, B. P.

Huxley, Aldous, 638*n*

hydrogen bomb, *see* bomb(s)

hygiene, psychic, 310

Hyious tou anthropou/Son of Man, 828

Hyliaster, *see* Paracelsus

hypnosis, 295, 303, 379; movement, 377; and rapport, 143, 144; and suggestion method, 699

hypnotic: methods of treatment, 215, 378; sleep, 379

hypnotism, 339, 340, 515; forensic significance of, 378; forms and techniques of, 377; mass, 601

hypothesis, fulfilment/living of, 280, 281

hysteria, 58; aetiology, 374; anaesthesia in, 388; and association tests, 353; in childhood, 374; complex in, 410; differential diagnosis, 374; dissociation in, 100; among mediums, 302; a "metaphysical problem," 465; psychic symptoms in, 374; psychogenesis, 374, 388; psychology of, 369; riddle of, 369; root phenomena of, 372; sexual trauma theory, 478; sociological and historical aspects, 372; theory, 370; treatment for, 375

hysterical: anaesthesia, 187; choreic affections, 374; disturbance of sensation, 371; hyperaesthesias, 371; intellect, 371; pain, 27; pain-apraxia, 371; paralysis, 371, 374; psychogenesis of symptom, 388, 478

hysterics: analysis of, 430, 431; and lies, 197; spontaneous phenomena in, 303

I

male and female: as opposites, 714, 716; principle, 118–20, 122

Malinine, M., with H. C. Puech and G. Quispel, eds., *Evangelium Veritatis*, 671*n*

Malinowski, Bronislaw, 561*n*

man: archaic, 228; dehumanization of, 593; governed by demon, 594; isolated in cosmos, 255; "is what he eats," 598; modern, 205, 256; original, 280; scientific and inventive mind of, 260; as totality, 317

mana, 240, 241, 715

Mandaean(s), 676

mandala(s), 178, 179, 537, 538, 577, 578; healing purpose of, 123; and individuation, 719; Lamaic, *see* Lamaism; Mahāyāna, 717; motif, 67*n*; of Rhodesia, prehistoric, 516; as rotating figure, 578; swastika as, 578; symbolism of, 178, 515; —, and God-image, 659; trinity and triad in, 714, 716

Manget, J. J.: *Bibliotheca chemica curiosa*, 733*n*

manic depression, 31, 351, 375, 385

Manichaean dualism, 726

manipura chakra, 67, 95

mankind, as one individual, 244

Mann, Thomas, 697*n*

Marduk, spring-god in Babylonian myth, 105

Maria, axiom of, and *proportio sesquitertia*, 476

Marie, A.: "Sur quelques troubles fonctionnels de l'audition chez certains débiles mentaux," 421*n*

Mark, St., 247

marriage: Christian, 157, 809; compensatory character of, 476; cross-cousin, 473; heavenly, 299; horoscopes, 495, 502, 503; psychology of, 77; *quaternio*, 473

Marseilles, 113*n*

Marti, Fritz, 429&*n*

Martin, P. W., 606*n*

Martin, Thomas Ignaz, 299; *Die Geschichte des Thomas Ignaz Martin*, by J. Kerner, 299*n*

Mary, Mother of God: Assumption of, 689, 713, 714, 742; *Assumptio Beatae Virginis*, 714, 731; as bride in bridal-chamber, 681&*n*, 742*n*; as Co-Redemptrix, 714, 731; Immaculate Conception/*conceptio immaculata*, 714, 738; and Marianic movement, 714; as *omnium gratiarum mediatrix*, 689; Protestant view of, 687; as *virgo terra*, 689

Mary Magdalene, 692

Mass, the: Host in, and Mithras cult, 270; as living mystery, 270; miracle of, 276

mass(es): conversions, 602; danger of, 590; evil and, 601; hypnotism, 601; individual in, and unconscious compensation, 476; -mindedness, 605; phenomenon, demonic features in, 601; politics and, 564; psychology of, 161, 571, 586, 605; psychosis, 607; suggestion, 595, 596, 601, 602

Mater Magna, 554

materialism, 603*n*, 733, 734; and psychology, 523; scientific, 314, 463, 734; and spiritual devastation, 583

matriarchal symbolism, 521

matter, physical, 255

Matthew, Book of, 231

maturation, analysis as, 172

Matuta, goddess of death, 91

Mauss, M., *see under* Hubert, H.

Maya, 464, 670

Mead, G.R.S.: *The Gnostic John the Baptizer*, 694*n*

mechanization, 370

Mechtild of Magdeburg, 444

medicina catholica, 699; lapis as, 722

medicine: ancient Egyptian, *see* Egypt *s.v.*; ancient Greek, *see* Greek *s.v.*; and borrowing from other sciences, 357, 358; lack of psychological understanding, 355

medicine-man, 285, 286, 570; ability to "smell," 325; on dreams, 557

Moll, Albert (*cont.*):
punkte der Psychotherapie und des Occultismus, J.'s review, 377, 378
monad, Anthropos as, 715
Monakow, Constantin von, 333&*n*
monasteries, 282
money: devaluation of, 576; dilution of, 573; fictitious character of, 567; hollowing out of, 573; the State and, 572–4
Monogenes, 122
moon: conjunction, in marriage horoscopes, 495, 496, 498, 499, 502–7; as symbol of unconscious, 180
Moorish Kingdom, 114
moral law as psychic fact, 619
morality: and greed, 612; in large organizations, 571; relativity of, 713; sexual, and psychoanalysis, 394, 395; social v. individual, 383
Moral Re-Armament movement, Caux centre, 681&*n*, 683
Morgan, D. Glan, 283–85
Morienus Romanus, 750&*n*; "De transmutatione metallorum," in *Artis auriferae,* 750*n*
Moroney, M. J., 507*n*
Moser, Fanny: *Okkultismus: Täuschungen und Tatsache,* 317*n*; *Spuk: Irrlaube oder Wahrglaube?,* 317; –, J.'s foreword, 317–26
Moses, 205; and Elijah, parallels, 674
Moses ben Leon, 675
Moses Cordovero, 675
Mosley, Sir Oswald, 575&*n*
mother-dragon, 91, 105
mother: dual, motif of, 658; earth-, 484; and feeling function, 89; figures, three, 732; fixation, 277; -love, crushing weight of, 338; significance of, in life of K. F. Meyer, 337, 338; terrible, 91
Mother: all-compassionate, 276; Earth, 255; of God, as arch-saint, 99; Great, 239, 255; —, sacrifice to, 446

motif: of hostile brothers, 228; mythological, *see* myth *s.v.*
motivation, and psychotherapy: of patient, 609, 613; of teacher, 610, 611
mountain: climbing, and dream, 207; sickness, 78, 79, 88, 89, 96
movement(s), automatic, 303–5
mulier taceat in ecclesia, 742
Müller, Hermann: "Beiträge zur Kenntnis der Hypermesis Gravidarum," J.'s abstract, 414; "Ein Fall von induzierten Irresein nebst anschliessenden Erörterungen," 414
mulungu, 240
mungu, 240
Murray, Henry A.: "Conclusions" to *Explorations in Personality,* 269*n*
Mürren, advertisement for, 170
Mussolini, Benito/Il Duce, 127, 165, 576, 578, 579
mutilation, numinous, 348
Myers, F.H.W., 477
mysteria of early Christianity, 115
mysterium: iniquitatis, 690; *tremendum,* 270
mystery(-ies): ancient, 120, 122; as expression of psychological condition, 270
mystical experiences, 577
mysticism, 98; medieval, 280
mystics, and experience of archetypes, 98
myth(s), 38; and collective unconscious, 487; as mental therapy, 238; motifs, 38, 39, 228, 515; and mythologizing factor, 592; reinterpretation of, 736; as symbols that happened, 247
mythologem, theological preaching as, 682
mythology, 41, 91, 354; ambivalence in, 443; archetypal motifs in, 658; Greek, *see* Greek *s.v.*; opposites in, 443, 444; a psychic phenomenon of the present, 327; Scandinavian, 92; truth of, 328

N

Naassenes, 671, 827

Näcke, Paul: *Ueber Familienmord durch Geisteskranke,* J.'s review, 386

Nagel, Hildegard, 645n, 654n

Nägeli, —, (Freiburg im Breisgau), 296

Nag Hamadi, Upper Egypt, 671n

Nagy, Peter: trans. into Hungarian of Jung's *On the Psychology of the Unconscious,* J.'s foreword, 455–56

namazu, 33n

Napoleon I, 221, 222

Napoleon III, 299

nation(s): in collective misery, 577; psychology of, 571

National Industrial Recovery Act (U.S.A.), 575n

National Investigations Committee on Aerial Phenomena (NICAP), 626n; J.'s statement to, 631, 632

nationalism, 567

National Recovery Administration (U.S.A.), 575&n

National Socialism/Nazi(sm), 165, 289, 574, 594, 715

Nature, 156; conquest of, 261; de-deification of, 593, 602; demands death, 275; demonism of, 593, 594; de-psychization of, 591, 593–95; man and, 255, 260; populated with monstrous machines, 260; -spirit, 649

Navaho, *see* American Indians: North

Nazi(s), *see* National Socialism

Neanderthalensis, 214

Near East, symbolism of dying god in, 239

Nebuchadnezzar, dream of, 109, 110

negativism, 371

Negro(es), 35, 46, 47, 148; dreams of, 37–40, 552&n; myth, 119; psychoses of, 552; religion of, 552; thoughts "in the belly," 10; and white man, idealization of, 552

Neiditsch, Jeanne, 398n

Nekyia, 38, 107

Nelken, Jan, 433n; "Analytische Beobachtungen über Phantasien eines Schizophrenen," J.'s comment on Tausk's criticism, 433–37

neo-paganism, 569, 576, 647

Nerval, Gérard de (pseudonym of Gérard Labrunie), 545; J.'s lecture on, 779

nervous system, of analyst, 154

Neue Preussische Zeitung, 296

Neue Zürcher Zeitung, J.'s letters in, 427n

Neumann, Erich, 474, 485, 529; *Amor and Psyche,* 668; *Depth Psychology and a New Ethic,* J.'s foreword, 616–20; *The Origins and History of Consciousness,* 474n; J.'s foreword, 474–75

Neumann, Karl Eugen: *Die Reden Gotamo Buddhos,* J.'s comment on, 697&n

Neumann, Therese, *see* Therese of Konnersreuth

neuralgia, 374

neurology(-ists), 341; Freud's theories and, 388

neurosis, 24, 340; adaptation process in, 449; as attempt at self-cure, 168, 169; childhood as origin of, in later life, 420; compulsion, *see* compulsion; definition, 167; as expression of affections of whole man, 357; a moral problem, 617; psychogenic nature of, 380; psychological conception of, 341, 390; psychology and therapy of, 357, 358; reason for, 274; sexual theory of, 388, 402, 438; structure of, 665; symbolic value of, 652; a *terra incognita,* 354; as transitory phase, 284

neurotic(s): behaviour of, 197; complexes in, 353; isolation of, 105; symptoms, 187

New Mexico, J.'s visit to, 123, 554

New York *Times,* 438, 564n

Nicholas of Cusa, 682

O

Tacitus: *Historiae,* 674
Tagus river, 112
Talmud, 83, 248
Tantalus Club, 445
Tantra *chakra,* 578
Tantric(-ism), 95, 120; J.'s seminar on, 707&*n*; mandala in, 578; philosophy, 553; Yoga, 11, 516
Tao, 69, 119, 667, 717; and Christ, contrasted, 737; as dyadic monad, 715; and opposites, cooperation of, 719; as self, 720
Taoist, 68
Tao-te-ching (Lao-tzu), 539*n*
Tarpeian rock, 117
Tausk, Victor, 433–37, 433*n*
Tavistock Clinic, *see* Institute of Medical Psychology
Tavistock Institute of Human Relations, 606*n*
teacher, and shadow, 485
team-spirit, 585–87
technology, effect of, on psyche, 614, 615
telepathic phenomena, 15
temenos, 123, 178, 179
Temple, Frederick, Archbishop, 679
temple: in magic circle, 178; prostitution rite in Babylon, 159
Terence: *Heauton Timorumenos,* 45*n*
tertium comparationis, 364, 653
Tertullian: *De praescriptione hereticorum,* 676
tetrad, God as, 715
Tetrarch of Palestine, 108
Thayer, Ellen, 654*n*
Theatrum chemicum, 753*n*
theologoumenon, 743
theology: and the practical man, 268; and primordial images, 716; and psychology, 354, 716, 742, 743
Theosebeia, 545
theosophy, 554; primitive projection in, 316
Therapeutai, 108
therapist, character of, 439; *see also* analyst; doctor

Therese of Konnersreuth (Therese Neumann), 660&*n*
Thesmophoria, 121*n*
thinking: in the belly, 10; function, 12, 13, 16, 17, 43, 219; in the heart, 10; mechanistic, 316; of primitives, 10; subliminal, 461; type, *see* type *s.v.;* *see also* thought(s)
thirteen, 256
Thomas Aquinas, St., 688; *Summa theologica,* 688*n*
Thomist philosophy, 475
Thompson, R. Campbell: *The Epic of Gilgamish,* 105*n*
thought(s): a late discovery, 241; -patterns, collective, 234; *see also* thinking
three plus one, 713, 732, 741; ratio/ *proportio sesquitertia,* 473, 476
Thury, Professor, *see* Cassini
Tiamat, dragon in Babylonian myth, 105
Tibetan philosophy, 95
Tifereth, 738
time machine, 28
time and space, *see* space and time
timelessness, and realization of self, 694
Tiresias, 38
Toledo, 121, 122; cathedral, 112–15
Toletum, 114
tongue, slips of, 532
totalitarianism, 596, 659
totality: Eastern apperception of, 655; as four, 715; image of, 9; of man, 122; psychic, and quaternity symbol, 473; as three, 715
tractability, 371, 372
trance: and demonism, 648; speaking in, 302, 304
transcendence, prayer and, 681
transcendent function, 690
transference, 134–37, 472, 492, 577; aetiology of, 143; in alchemy, 753; to animals, 141; and archetypes, 164, 486; collapse of, 142; as compensation, 168; counter-, 140, 142,

150; as dialogue between partners, 493; dreams in, *see* dreams *s.v.*; erotic, 141; father, 160, 277; Freud on, 480, 486; heightened, 451, 452; as hindrance, 151; intensity of, 142, 152; mutual unconsciousness in, 149; neurosis, 480; as projection, 136–38, 151, 152, 155; teleological value of, 168; therapy of, 154, 160
transformation, in alchemy, 591
transubstantiation, 591
Transvaal, 39*n*
transvestism, 347–48
trauma theory, 430
treasure, 166; in the depths, 118; integration of, 152; singular feeling as, 329; in transference, 143
treatment, reductive, 224
tree(s): fig-tree, 646; of knowledge, 603; of Life, 675; symbol: and Christ, 239; —, of Great Mother, 239
tremors, intended, 303
triad: and Kepler's astronomy, 473; lower/inferior, 713, 732
Trinity: as archetype, 99; devil/Satan as fourth in, *see* devil *s.v.*; man as part of, 687, 689; and Mary as fourth, 681, 687, 689, 712, 714; masculine, 99, 689, 714, 733, 741; and psychological viewpoint, 649; and quaternity, 688; shadow of, 716, 741; as symbol, 714
Tripitaka, 730
Tripus aureus, 749
truth: eschatological, 618; experience of, 558; how we know it, 288; relative or absolute, 703
Turbo, 748
twilight states, 302; hysterical, 415, 416
Tylor, E. B., 562
type(s): attitude-, 471, 483; classification into, 220; complex-constellation, 407; and dream-analysis, 217, 218; function-, 219, 471, 534; intellectual, 20; predicate, 407; thinking, 17, 43, 56
typology, psychological, 471
typos (imprint), 37
Die Tyroler ekstatischen Jungfrauen (anon.), 295*n*
Tyrrell, G.N.M.: *The Personality of Man,* 313*n*

U

ὕδωρ θεῖον (hudor theion), 591
Ufos/flying saucers, 626–33; and American Air Force, 627, 632, 633; extra-terrestrial origin of, 628, 629, 632; *Flying Saucer Review,* 626*n*; in history, 631; and parapsychological processes, 628, 630; as psychic phenomenon, 626, 630, 631; as symbols, 626
Ulysses, 38
Unamuno, Miguel de, 581&*n*
unconscious (the): ambivalence/two aspects of, 682, 683; apprehension, 305, 306; capriciousness of, 306; and Christ-phenomenon, 828; combination, 305; continuous, 9; as creative matrix of consciousness, 482; deliberations of, 237; depreciation of, 206; different conceptions of, 62, 124; discovery of, 317; as dustbin of the conscious mind, 206; empirical approach to, 477; energic charge of, 353; energy of, compared with consciousness, 314, 315; extent of, unknown, 316; goodwill of, 235; has no known limits, 738; has no time, 287; integration of, 695; interventions of, 249; as land of dreams, 315; language of, 279, 285; localization of, 319; in manic state, 351; meaning of term, 8; message of, 207; neutrality of, 704; physiological aspect of, 607; powers of, 665; powers of perception of, 326; problems, exteriorization of, 322; religious aspect of, 701; Satan as

THE COLLECTED WORKS OF

C. G. JUNG

T HE PUBLICATION of the first complete edition, in English, of the works of C. G. Jung was undertaken by Routledge and Kegan Paul, Ltd., in England and by Bollingen Foundation in the United States. The American edition is number XX in Bollingen Series, which since 1967 has been published by Princeton University Press. The edition contains revised versions of works previously published, such as *Psychology of the Unconscious*, which is now entitled *Symbols of Transformation*; works originally written in English, such as *Psychology and Religion*; works not previously translated, such as *Aion*; and, in general, new translations of virtually all of Professor Jung's writings. Prior to his death, in 1961, the author supervised the textual revision, which in some cases is extensive. Sir Herbert Read (d. 1968), Dr. Michael Fordham, and Dr. Gerhard Adler compose the Editorial Committee; the translator is R. F. C. Hull (except for Volume 2) and William McGuire is executive editor.

The price of the volumes varies according to size; they are sold separately, and may also be obtained on standing order. Several of the volumes are extensively illustrated. Each volume contains an index and in most a bibliography; the final volumes will contain a complete bibliography of Professor Jung's writings and a general index to the entire edition.

In the following list, dates of original publication are given in parentheses (of original composition, in brackets). Multiple dates indicate revisions.

* Published 1957; 2nd edn., 1970.　　　　† Published 1973.

(*continued*)

* Published 1960.   † Published 1961.
‡ Published 1956; 2nd edn., 1967. (65 plates, 43 text figures.)

* Published 1971.   † Published 1953; 2nd edn., 1966.
‡ Published 1960; 2nd edn., 1969.

* Published 1959; 2nd edn., 1968. (Part I: 79 plates, with 29 in colour.)

* Published 1964; 2nd edn., 1970. (8 plates.)
† Published 1958; 2nd edn., 1969.

A Psychological Approach to the Dogma of the Trinity (1942/1948)
Transformation Symbolism in the Mass (1942/1954)
Forewords to White's "God and the Unconscious" and Werblowsky's
   "Lucifer and Prometheus" (1952)
Brother Klaus (1933)
Psychotherapists or the Clergy (1932)
Psychoanalysis and the Cure of Souls (1928)
Answer to Job (1952)
   EASTERN RELIGION
Psychological Commentaries on "The Tibetan Book of the Great
   Liberation" (1939/1954) and "The Tibetan Book of the Dead"
   (1935/1953)
Yoga and the West (1936)
Foreword to Suzuki's "Introduction to Zen Buddhism" (1939)
The Psychology of Eastern Meditation (1943)
The Holy Men of India: Introduction to Zimmer's "Der Weg zum
   Selbst" (1944)
Foreword to the "I Ching" (1950)

*12. PSYCHOLOGY AND ALCHEMY (1944)
Prefatory note to the English Edition ([1951?] added 1967)
Introduction to the Religious and Psychological Problems of Alchemy
Individual Dream Symbolism in Relation to Alchemy (1936)
Religious Ideas in Alchemy (1937)
Epilogue

†13. ALCHEMICAL STUDIES
Commentary on "The Secret of the Golden Flower" (1929)
The Visions of Zosimos (1938/1954)
Paracelsus as a Spiritual Phenomenon (1942)
The Spirit Mercurius (1943/1948)
The Philosophical Tree (1945/1954)

‡14. MYSTERIUM CONIUNCTIONIS (1955-56)
   AN INQUIRY INTO THE SEPARATION AND
   SYNTHESIS OF PSYCHIC OPPOSITES IN ALCHEMY
The Components of the Coniunctio
The Paradoxa
The Personification of the Opposites
Rex and Regina   (continued)

* Published 1953; 2nd edn., completely revised, 1968. (270 illustrations.)
† Published 1968. (50 plates, 4 text figures.)
‡ Published 1963; 2nd edn., 1970. (10 plates.)

* Published 1966.
† Published 1954; 2nd edn., revised and augmented, 1966. (13 illustrations.)
‡ Published 1954.

The Development of Personality (1934)
Marriage as a Psychological Relationship (1925)

18. THE SYMBOLIC LIFE
Miscellaneous Writings

19. BIBLIOGRAPHY OF C. G. JUNG'S WRITINGS

20. GENERAL INDEX TO THE COLLECTED WORKS

See also:

C. G. JUNG: LETTERS

Selected and edited by Gerhard Adler, in collaboration with Aniela Jaffé.
Translations from the German by R.F.C. Hull.

VOL. 1: 1906–1950
VOL. 2: 1951–1961

THE FREUD/JUNG LETTERS
Edited by William McGuire, translated by
Ralph Manheim and R.F.C. Hull